D1531916

LAW IN THE HEALTH
AND HUMAN SERVICES

LAW IN THE HEALTH
AND
HUMAN SERVICES

A Guide for Social Workers, Psychologists, Psychiatrists, and Related Professionals

Donald T. Dickson

THE FREE PRESS

NEW YORK   LONDON   TORONTO   SYDNEY   TOKYO   SINGAPORE

FREE PRESS
A Division of Simon & Schuster, Inc.
1230 Avenue of the Americas
New York, NY 10020

Copyright © 1995 by The Free Press
All rights reserved,
including the right of reproduction
in whole of in part in any form.

FREE PRESS and colophon are trademarks
of Simon & Schuster, Inc.

Designed by
Manufactured in the United States of America

10 9 8 7 6 5 4 3 2 1

Library of Congress Cataloging-In-Publication Data

Dickson, Donald T.
    Law in the health and human services: a guide for social workers,
psychologists, psychiatrists, and related professionals/Donald T. Dickson.
        p.   cm.
    ISBN 0-7432-6743-5
    1. Medical laws and legislation—United States. 2. Medical care—
Law and legislation—United States. 3. Social legislation—United
States. I. Title.
    KF3821.D53   1995
344.73' 041—dc20
[347.3041]   94-23670
                                                              CIP

For information regarding the special discounts for bulk purchases, please contact Simon &
Schuster Special Sales at 1-800-456-6798 or business@simonandschuster.com

To my parents

Alice Dickson Ball
William John Dickson

CONTENTS

Preface   vii

Acknowledgments   ix

Part I. The Legal Context of the Health and Human Services

Chapter 1. Law in the Health and Human Services   3

Chapter 2. Reading and Using Legal Materials   15

Chapter 3. Constitutional Law, Due Process, and Equal Protection   46

Part II. Legal Concepts for the Professional

Chapter 4. Ethics and the Law in the Health and Human Services   81

Chapter 5. Privacy, Personal Autonomy, and Records   95

Chapter 6. Confidential Communications: Principles and Limitations   122

Chapter 7. Informed Consent   156

Chapter 8. Incompetence and Guardianship   208

Part III. Social Problems and Vulnerable Populations

Chapter 9. Families and Children I: Family Composition, Marriage,
   Divorce, Children, and the Law   247

Chapter 10. Families and Children II: Child Abuse, Termination
   of Parental Rights, Foster Care, and Domestic Violence   314

Chapter 11. Law and the Mentally Ill   375

Chapter 12: Legal Issues for Individuals with Disabilities   407

Chapter 13: AIDS and the Law   444

Part IV. Law in Professional Practice: Workplace and Courtroom Issues, Malpractice and Administrative Liability

Chapter 14. Law in the Workplace: Sexual Harassment, Drug Testing, and Employee Assistance Programs   483

Chapter 15. Malpractice and Administrative Liability   520

Chapter 16. Courtroom Testimony: Fact and Expert Witnesses   573

Notes   595

Index of Cases   623

General Index   629

PREFACE

The health and human services field is wide-ranging and rapidly changing. It now comprises a major portion of federal funding and a major part of state budgetary expenditures. Employment in this field is growing dramatically, and a vast number of individuals are now directly affected by or participate in health and human services programs. At the same time, the legal aspects of this field have grown in coverage and complexity, ranging from child abuse to elder abuse, from the rights of the unborn to the rights of the terminally ill.

This book attempts to address the law as it applies to the broad health and human services field, rather than to approach it from the perspective of a particular profession as is often the case. The reasoning behind this is that health and human services students and professionals—social workers, psychologists, psychiatrists, mental health workers, child welfare workers, administrators, and so forth—often work in the same settings, face the same or similar challenges, and must deal with the same or similar laws, whether they be the laws of malpractice, sexual harassment, or informed consent.

The book is designed for two types of audiences, students in upperclass college or graduate courses, and professionals in the health and human services field. For the former, the text and case materials will hopefully provide a sound foundation in the legal aspects of the health and human services; for the latter, it is intended as a reference book to guide practice, raise questions, and provide some answers.

The intent is to give a picture of a range of important legal issues in the health and human services field across the country. In this, and in sixteen chapters, obviously not all issues can be explored, nor can all of federal or state law be included. Given the distinct differences which are often present among the states—as well as variations in local practice—the reader must also consult his or her own state law. Those teaching from this text are urged to add statutory and case material from their own state where appropriate as well as to consult the most recent statutes and cases for changes in the law.

Following the typical pattern, cases have been edited and most case citations have been omitted. Case footnotes have been renumbered.

Finally, one must always remember that the law in the books does not necessarily reflect what actually happens in the professions and the fields of practice. Students and professionals both must be alert to practices, procedures, and policies which are inconsistent with, or in some cases, are violations of the law, both for their own professional protection and the protection of their patients and clients.

ACKNOWLEDGMENTS

Many thanks are owed. A number of friends and colleagues have provided assistance. In particular I want to acknowledge support, assistance, and helpful comments from colleagues at Rutgers, particularly Paul Lerman, Ursula Gerhart, and Alexander Brooks; the secretarial and administrative services of Betty McCoy and Gloria Johnson; and the support of Deans Mary Davidson and Harold Demone, who are particularly aware of the importance of law in the health and human services field. Several anonymous reviewers have provided very useful comments and suggestions. Much is also owed to Susan Arellano and Jennifer Shulman, my editors at The Free Press, and Linnea Johnson, the copy editor who endured what must have seemed endless pages of cases and citations, raising many questions and making many helpful comments. Also I must credit David Dickson, my son, for his forbearance and understanding, putting up with the unavailability of his father at times and with delayed dinners more often.

A great debt is owed to the numerous students in my classes at Rutgers who have used previous drafts of these cases and materials, raised questions, and made comments, and who have provided in class and in their term papers a real picture of the impact of law on the health and human services.

In conducting the research for this text I have been able to draw upon the resources of a number of libraries, including those at Rutgers and Princeton Universities; the University of California, Berkeley; and the New Jersey and California State Libraries.

For graciously providing copies of their Codes of Ethics, a debt is owed to the following professional associations: American Association for Marriage and Family Therapy; American Counseling Association; American Psychiatric Association; American Psychological Association; American School Counselor Associations; and National Association of Social Workers. This text has been greatly enhanced by the contributions of all of the above; any errors and omissions are, of course, mine alone.

PART I

THE LEGAL CONTEXT OF THE HEALTH AND HUMAN SERVICES

The first three chapters address the context and role of law in the health and human services. While all health and human services professionals have encountered specific legal provisions and requirements in their work, Chapter 1 examines the broader meaning of law and advances and discusses some relevant definitions. Different types of law, their sources, and interrelationships are reviewed. Finally, the American legal system is discussed, particularly in light of the concept of federalism.

Chapter 2 provides an introduction to using legal materials. While some of this material may be familiar, it is likely that much of the information is new to many in the health and human services. First some key legal concepts and terms are presented, then a case is briefly traced from its beginnings through a court hearing. Much of the chapter is devoted to how to read legal materials—cases, statutes, and regulations. Those who have worked with legal materials know that reading and understanding them is a skill in itself, one that improves with experience. Along with gaining familiarity with the materials, there are several other purposes to this section. First, the court decisions have been selected to introduce a fundamental legal concept, due process—which is explored further in the following chapter. Two different types of cases, criminal and civil, both address the same concept, the constitutional right to counsel, and result in very different outcomes. Second, the statutory and regulatory materials selected—

family planning programs and abortion—illustrate the interplay between statutes and regulations (and Congress and the executive branch) and the role of the courts. In the last section, two important topics—locating legal materials and using legal citations—are discussed.

Chapter 3 deals with constitutional law. While entire books have been devoted to the U.S. Constitution, this chapter presents an overview of the main constitutional provisions and amendments, and discusses in greater detail the Fourteenth Amendment, which has particular significance for the health and human services. Due process, both procedural and substantive, is examined in light of some major Supreme Court cases, and then the concept of equal protection is analyzed. Together, the Due Process and the Equal Protection clauses form a base for much of the material that follows in the text.

CHAPTER 1

LAW IN THE HEALTH AND HUMAN SERVICES

THE ROLE OF LAW

The importance of law in the health and human services has grown dramatically in recent years. Paralleling the rapid expansion of the health and human services fields—in terms of populations served, problems addressed, and funds allocated—has been a virtual explosion in both the range of legal issues addressed and the volume of litigation in these areas.[1]

Law, including legislation, court decisions, and administrative regulations, now permeates almost every aspect of the health and human services:

1. The entrance into and exit from health and human services delivery systems

2. The criteria used to determine eligibility for treatment, benefits, or services

3. The rights to which patients and clients are entitled

4. The rights to which professionals and staff are entitled

5. The way in which health and human services programs are administered and regulated

6. The relationship between the professional and the patient or client

7. The practice of the health and human services professional

Entrance into some human service systems, such as those health and welfare programs where the individual desires assistance and benefits, is voluntary. In other systems—such as juvenile justice, corrections, and sometimes mental health and child welfare—the entrance is based on judicial or administrative action and is often involuntary. Entrance into correctional or juvenile justice systems usually requires court action and a determination that the individual committed a criminal or delinquent act. Most regular involuntary civil commitments to mental hospitals require a judicial determination that the individual is mentally ill and dangerous before a commitment can be made. Many times before a child enters the child welfare system a court or a child welfare agency will have to decide that the child is dependent, neglected, or abused as defined by statutory law. In sum, the actual entrance determination is often made on the basis of legal criteria.

Even where the entrance is not governed by legal criteria, legal rules often have an impact. For example, entrance into a hospital is a medical decision, but requirements that hospital emergency rooms treat all patients who appear and that hospitals must provide uncompensated care to a proportion of indigent patients are legal requirements.[2]

Eligibility to receive treatment, benefits, or services may be governed by legal criteria incorporating income level or need, such as public welfare and Medicaid, or by the legal definition of a condition or ability, such as the statutory definition of developmental disabilities.

Due process and equal protection are two of the most important constitutional rights afforded to all persons. Within the concept of due process, the courts have found a right to privacy, which broadly means, within certain limits, the right of the individual to be let alone or to make decisions without interference by the state. These decisions may extend to a woman's right to make a decision with her physician whether or not to abort a fetus before it becomes viable, to an individual's right to receive or reject treatment, and in some instances an individual's right to choose life or death.

The rights of health and human services patients and clients may be found in constitutional law, judicial decisions, statutes, and regulations. They may include a presumption of competence, the retention of civil rights, a right to privacy, a right to informed consent before treatment, and the use of least intrusive interventions or least restrictive living arrangements.

The rights of health and human services staff in the workplace have a similar legal basis, and include the rights to privacy, free speech, and assembly, and protection against illegal searches, polygraph tests, and sexual harassment.

While the administration of health and human services programs rests with the policies, plans, and decisions made by program directors and administrators, it takes place within a legal context and includes administrative rules and regulations covering many aspects of the life and work of health and human service patients, clients, and professionals within the agency. For example, legal decisions and rules affect personnel policies, staff hiring and firing, and the testing for drug and alcohol abuse. Agency, executive, and worker liability is determined by law. The law may even specify the steps involved in the evaluation, treatment, and review of clients, such as in the case of individualized educational plans for disabled students or individualized habilitation plans for those developmentally disabled individuals receiving services.

The context and the content of the relationship between health and human services professionals and patients or clients is substantially shaped by the law. The concepts of informed consent, knowing waiver, confidential communications, privacy, and competence have a great impact on the professional relationship, as do legal limitations such as mandates to report child abuse or to take steps to protect an individual from harm to self, others, or property.

Finally, regulatory and ethical standards for health and human services professionals may be used in a court of law to determine whether the professional has performed according to the standards of the profession or is liable for negligence or malpractice, or they may be used by a licensing board to determine suspensions or the withdrawal of a professional license.

WHAT IS LAW?

Before examining the range of laws which impact on the health and human services, we should be clear what is meant by "law." Many definitions have been advanced ranging from philosophical and sociological to economic, political, and psychological. Lawrence Friedman describes law as "slippery as glass, as elusive as a soap bubble"(Friedman, 1984: 2). Donald Black succinctly defines law as "governmental social control"(Black, 1976: 2).

A famous jurist, Benjamin Cardozo, wrote that law is "a principle or rule of conduct so established as to justify a prediction with reasonable certainty that it will be enforced by the courts if its authority is challenged"(Cardozo, 1924: 52).

This definition has four main elements:

1. A rule of conduct, or law as reflecting a normative order

2. Enforcement of law, or law as coercive

3. A reasonable certainty, or law as usually predictable

4. Enforcement through the courts, thus insuring the enforcement is legitimate and public

Law and the Normative Order

Law broadly reflects the will of the people as expressed through elected or appointed representatives and officials: the legislatures, which have the role of making law; and the courts, which have the role of interpreting the law. When states adopt policies that penalize murder and rape, prohibit the sale of illegal drugs, penalize domestic violence, place a priority on keeping families intact, and refuse to legitimate the marriage of individuals of the same sex, these policies are generally seen as reflecting the existing normative order and desires of the people or at least important interest groups within the populace.

Law and Enforcement

Laws without enforcement often have little effect. Behind most effective laws are the enforcement powers of the state. This is most clear in the area of criminal law, where violations result in fines, imprisonment, or even death, but it is also true in civil law, where damage awards must be paid, provisions of wills carried out, and eviction orders enforced.

Law and Predictability

For law to be predictable, similar legal disputes must usually be resolved in the same way. If as part of a lease the landlord agrees to repair a substandard apartment and then refuses to do so, the tenant can go to court and if the lease is legal, the court will enforce the agreement and order the work done, rent returned, or terminate the lease. If the same situation occurs the following week with another apartment, there is reasonable certainty that the court will give the same order. Without this element of certainty there would be legal chaos and individuals would not know whether, which, or when laws would be enforced.

An extension of predictability is the concept of *precedent*. Precedent, sometimes called *stare decisis*, means that prior decisions of a court will generally be followed in future decisions, or the decisions of a higher court will be followed by a lower court within the same judicial system. In this way, individuals can generally predict what a court will do and what rule of law lower courts will follow. Of course, a court may sometimes decide to overrule its precedents, ignore them, or distinguish them in fact or law from the case at hand. This results in some uncertainty and is an important source of change in the law.

Enforcement by the Courts

The fourth of Cardozo's elements is that the enforcement is through the courts and is therefore legitimated and public. While courts enforce laws, they rely heavily on public law enforcement agencies to actually carry out the enforcement duties. Being agents of the state, the law enforcement officials are responsible to the public for their actions, and the enforcement is generally viewed as legitimate by society.[3]

CLASSIFICATIONS OF LAW

Laws can be classified in a number of ways. One very broad distinction is between *civil* and *criminal* laws. *Civil law* in this context refers to that great body of law ranging from the law of contracts and property to the law of torts and wills. Most of the laws that the health and human services professional will come in contact with are civil laws, that is, laws that do not involve criminal penalties. *Criminal law* identifies offenses against the state that can result in a fine or a loss of liberty in jail or prison. This civil–criminal law distinction is important, for as we shall see, courts traditionally have provided far more protection for those facing criminal charges than those who appear in civil cases. Since criminal acts are offenses against the state, the prosecution of these violations is conducted by the state. In contrast, civil actions are usually brought by private parties although in some instances such as in determinations of delinquency or child abuse they may be brought by the state.

Some laws have both criminal and civil aspects. Child abuse can be a civil proceeding where the issues are whether the child is abused and, if so, how to protect the child. States also have criminal child abuse statutes ranging from prohibitions against child endangerment to criminal sexual assault. In these the focus is whether the individual—for example, a parent or guardian—committed the criminal act against the child as charged.

In addition, the individual harmed by a criminal act also can bring a civil action against the accused—for example, for damages sustained because of the criminal act. Someone representing the interests of an abused child could bring a civil damages action against someone, for example the operator of a day care center, who was also the alleged perpetrator charged in a criminal case.

Some areas of law although technically civil are similar to criminal law in their outcomes. For many years, juvenile delinquency proceedings have been considered a civil proceeding, with the intent to protect and rehabilitate the child and keep the child from carrying a criminal record through life. A criminal penalty can only attach if the juvenile is waived to an adult criminal court for trial on the same basis as an adult. However, juveniles adjudicated delinquent in juvenile or family courts can be committed to a state training school for an extended period ranging up to their age of majority. Similarly, commitment to a state mental hospital is a civil proceeding but the confinement is involuntary, indeterminate, and could last for years or a lifetime.

Civil law also refers to a whole legal approach found in many continental European countries, as contrasted to *common law* found in the United States and many English-speaking countries. Civil law countries rely heavily on written or codified laws such as the Napoleonic Code, while in common law countries much of the law was originally customary and unwritten. Within the United States, Louisiana retains its civil law heritage.

Another distinction is between *substantive* and *procedural* law. Substantive law includes that body of law which defines the rights, duties, and obligations of the citizens and of the state, while procedural law has to do with the procedures by which the substantive law is applied.

As a general rule, laws which fix the duties, establish rights and responsibilities among and for persons, natural or otherwise are "substantive laws" in character, while those which merely prescribe the manner in which such rights and responsibilities may be exercised and enforced in a court are "procedural laws." (*Black's Law Dictionary*, 1991)

For example, various substantive laws specify what criminal acts consist of: what is murder, what is rape, what is armed robbery. Procedural law deals with how those laws are applied: laws about arrest, interrogation, arraignment, juries, and so forth. Similarly, substantive laws define civil child abuse, and procedural laws deal with child protective services investigations, removals, and court hearings.

Finally, one can make a distinction between *public* law and *private* law. Public law has to do with laws that affect the state and its actions toward its citizens.[4] Criminal proceedings are always brought by the state against the person accused of committing a crime; child abuse proceedings are brought by the child welfare agency against the alleged abuser. In contrast, private law is concerned with issues solely between private citizens or entities.[5] Public law includes areas such as taxation, zoning, and all criminal law. Private law includes such areas as contracts between private citizens, private landlord and tenant law, and malpractice and negligence law where the parties are private citizens.

TYPES OF LAW

The American legal system consists of four basic types of law: constitutional law, statutory law, case law, and administrative law.

Constitutional law is the overarching law and in the federal system is that which establishes the other types of law. The three other distinct types of law have their sources in the three branches of government established by the Constitution: *statutory law* is enacted by the legislative branch; *case law* consists of decisions made by the judicial branch; and *administrative law* consists of rules and regulations promulgated by the executive branch.

Constitutional Law

The federal government has a constitution, as does every state. The federal constitution contains the enabling laws for establishing the government and the legal system, and providing for basic rights of the people. Articles I, II, and III of the United States Constitution establish the executive, legislative, and judiciary branches, list qualifications and terms of office, and enumerate powers. The first eight amendments to the U.S. Constitution establish basic rights of all citizens, such as the right to free speech and assembly and the right to counsel in criminal cases.

Statutory Law

Statutory law or legislation is what many people think of as the "law." This law is enacted by federal and state legislative bodies. In the health and human services it covers a broad range of areas, from abuse of children to zoning. At the local level, such laws are commonly called ordinances. Since statutory law is enacted by elected representatives, this law in a broad sense reflects the wishes of society or the electorate.

Case Law

The role of the judge is to apply existing law to a set of facts in a dispute brought before the court and decide which party should prevail. However, by interpreting laws or by filling gaps in the existing law, judges may make law as well. The disputes that come before the court may be as narrow as whether an individual child has been neglected or whether a particular zoning ordinance should apply to a group home for disabled citizens or as broad as whether all institutionalized developmentally disabled individuals throughout the country have a constitutional right to habilitation or whether the death penalty can be applied to juveniles convicted of certain crimes.

Administrative Law

This large, complex, detailed, and very important body of law includes both federal and state administrative codes, state agency policies and procedures, and local government regulations. Sometimes the legislative branch will delegate broad rule-making powers to the executive branch; other times the delegation is not clear or not stated. Administrative regulations have the force of law. Correctional administrators are delegated the power to make regulations for operating prisons, school officials are delegated the power to make regulations for running the schools, and Medicaid administrators have the power to make regulations for medical assistance programs.

Executive orders are another example of administrative rule making, where the chief executive issues an order about a particular subject. Examples are President Reagan's executive orders mandating a drug free workplace or requiring care for newborn children with disabilities.[6]

WHO MAKES LAW?

Law is made by legislators, judges, and administrators. The first two types of lawmakers are the most obvious, the third less so. Legislators pass statutes; courts decide cases and issue judicial opinions. In both of these, the lawmaking is public. Legislative hearings are usually open to the public and statutes are enacted through public votes. Most court hearings are open to the public and many appellate and supreme court decisions are published.

Administrative law, the law made by the executive branch, has a significant but less obvious impact on the patients or clients within the health and human services systems. Professor Kenneth Davis has analyzed administrative law in depth, and has identified its key elements. Unlike legislation and court decisions, most administrative law is adopted with minimal public involvement, and much administrative law is not reviewed, questioned, or challenged. For example, in the area of federal administrative law, after first publishing a proposed regulation in the *Federal Register*, the executive branch must wait a statutory period for public comment, and then can publish the final regulation. Whether there is comment or not and whether it is favorable or not need not be decisive, for in drafting its final regulations, the administration must consider but need not be governed by those comments. The final draft of the proposed regulation then becomes law.[7]

This lack of public involvement and review led Davis to analyze the concept of *administrative discretion*, that is, the power legally delegated to administrators to act or not to act in a given situation, what rules to make, and how to enforce them. Discretionary decision making is not in itself bad; indeed it is often necessary. Using their discretion, administrators establish rules for the enforcement of child abuse statutes and determining removals of children from the home, for the provision of patient rights and release of institutionalized mental patients, or for running a correctional facility, a hospital, or a school.[8]

LEGAL SYSTEMS

The legal picture in America is far more complex because state and national governments and their corresponding state and national laws coexist. This is the principle of *federalism*: Power is shared by state and federal governments, and the states, although part of the national system, remain in many ways separate. Under the Supremacy Clause of Article VI of the Constitution, the U.S. Constitution and federal laws are the "supreme law of the land." However, the Tenth Amendment provides that "[t]he powers not delegated to the United States by the Constitution nor prohibited by it to the states are reserved to the states respectively, or to the people."

While federalism implies a shared power, the term "federal" is distinct, often referring to the national government. As illustrated below, the American legal system combines parallel federal (national) and state legal systems which include their own constitutional, statutory, judicial, and administrative law.

THE AMERICAN LEGAL SYSTEM

Federal System	State Systems
(U.S. Constitution)	(State constitutions)
Federal statutes	State statutes
Federal court decisions	State court decisions
Federal regulations	State regulations

Because each state government with its legal system is essentially independent from the others, the American legal system consists of fifty state systems and one federal system, each with its own laws which may be similar or very different. The result is fifty-one legislative bodies enacting statutory law; fifty-one court systems producing judicial opinions; and fifty-one executive branches producing administrative regulations.

While the federal system overarches the state systems and federal constitutional law takes precedence over state laws, in many areas the states remain independent. For example, the federal government cannot easily require states to post a particular speed limit, define developmentally disabled individuals in a particular way, or initiate twenty-four-hour hot lines for receiving child abuse reports. Nor can the federal government easily require that states adopt one specific legal definition of child abuse, mental illness, or juvenile delinquency. However, the federal government can substantially influence legislation by providing federal funds if certain legal steps are taken or withholding funds if they are not. Thus the Child Abuse Prevention and Treatment Act of 1974, 42 U.S.C. §§5101–5107, provides funding to states that have statutes prohibiting child abuse and include in their statutes specific reporting requirements. The Developmentally Disabled Assistance and Bill of Rights Act, 42 U.S.C. §6000 *et seq*, specifies a functional rather than categorical definition of developmental disabilities and states adopting this definition are eligible to receive federal monies.

Another example of state independence is that each state has its own criminal code, specifying which acts are criminal and how they are to be punished. Although there are a number of federal crimes, these are more limited in scope. Similarly, each state has its own procedures specifying how to apply criminal law, and these may differ from procedures of other states and from the federal rules of criminal procedure.

Some of the complexities inherent in federalism can be seen in "federal enclaves"—federal territory that has been carved out of the states. Military bases are one example, Veterans Administration (VA) hospitals another. As part of the federal government they are governed by federal law, which is sometimes different from state laws. For example, federal law specifies that if a VA patient is infected with HIV, physicians and counselors may disclose this to spouses or sexual partners if they reasonably believe that the patient will not make the disclosure and it is necessary to protect the health of the spouse or partner. In many states, such a warning would be regarded as an invasion of privacy and could be actionable under state law.[9]

THE FEDERAL AND STATE COURT SYSTEMS

Federalism also means that there are separate federal and state court systems, with each state having its own hierarchy of courts independent from the other states. The federal system and most states follow a similar three-tiered pattern as illustrated below.[10]

FEDERAL AND STATE COURT STRUCTURE

Federal System	State System
U.S. Supreme Court	State supreme court
U.S. courts of appeals	State appellate courts
U.S. district courts	State trial courts

Most cases originate at the trial court level, and if the result there is appealed, the appeals are heard first at the appellate level, and then sometimes at the highest level, called the supreme court in the federal and in most state systems.

In the federal system, the U.S. District Court is usually the trial court, the U.S. Court of Appeals, sometimes known as the Circuit Court, is the intermediate appellate court, and the highest court is the U.S. Supreme Court.[11] The same pattern generally exists within the states, although the names will vary, and some court systems have only two levels. The trial court may be a county court, a family court, a criminal court, or any number of other courts of original jurisdiction where cases are first heard. Most states have an intermediate appellate court, and all states have a highest court which is the final decision maker for the cases in that state unless an appeal is allowed into the federal system. Names can be confusing: In most states the highest court is the supreme court, but in New York, the N.Y. Supreme Court is the trial court for many cases, while the N.Y. Court of Appeals is the highest court in the state. The health and human services professional should become familiar with local terminology to avoid confusion.

Most federal courts are organized geographically. One or more U.S. district courts are located within a state and hear cases within a geographic region—all or part of the state. A U.S. court of appeals will hear cases from district courts in a number of neighboring states in one region, known as a circuit. However, a single U.S. district court's jurisdiction generally does not extend beyond one state's boundaries, and the jurisdiction of a U.S. court of appeals generally does not extend beyond the boundaries of the circuit. In some states, such as New Jersey and Wyoming, one U.S. district court covers the entire state, while others such as New York and Texas have multiple district courts. The U.S. Supreme Court will hear appeals from all the U.S. courts of appeal.[12]

The legal concept of *jurisdiction* pertains to which cases or disputes may be heard by a specific court.[13] Federal jurisdiction, or the range of cases which can be heard in the federal system, is specified in Article III, Section 2 of the U.S. Constitution and in federal statutory law.[14]

Article III, Section 2 of the Constitution provides:

> The judicial power shall extend to all cases, in law and equity, arising under this Constitution, the laws of the United States, and treaties made, or which shall be made, under their authority; to all cases affecting ambassadors, other public ministers, and consuls; to all cases of admiralty and maritime jurisdiction; to controversies to which the United States shall be a party; to controversies between two or more States; between a State and citizens of another State; between citizens of different States; between citizens of the same State claiming lands under grants of different States, and between a State, or the citizens thereof, and foreign states, citizens, or subjects.

Within the health and human services, most federal cases will involve a federal statute, a federal regulation, a U.S. Constitutional question or will result from what is called diversity jurisdiction, where the parties in the dispute or the issue being disputed are located in different states. Federal statutory law currently limits diversity cases to those disputes where at least $50,000 is involved. (See 28 U.S.C. §1332.)

Generally either or both parties may appeal a decision by a trial court to an intermediate appellate court. Usually the appeal must be based on legal, not factual issues. That is, a party can appeal on the basis that laws or procedures were misstated, misapplied, or violated in the lower court proceeding, but generally a party cannot appeal solely on the factual determinations of the case. Appeals beyond the intermediate appellate court to the highest court are usually not automatic or by right but are discretionary and require permission of the higher court. In the federal system, an appeal to the Supreme Court is by *writ of certiorari*, which essentially means that the Court has agreed to have the case argued before it. Of the thousands of cases appealed to the U.S. Supreme Court each year, the court grants only about 100 to 130 writs of certiorari. In deciding not to hear a case, the Court need not give any reason or justification.[15] In addition, the Supreme Court has original jurisdiction—that is, acts as the trial court—in a limited range of cases. (See 28 U.S.C. §1251.)

If a case is not appealed from a U.S. court of appeals or if the U.S. Supreme Court refuses to hear the case, then the decision is binding (precedent) within that circuit, and may or may not be followed in other circuits.

Appeals within state systems are similar. Either or both parties have the right to appeal most decisions to the next higher court level on the basis of legal not factual issues. Appeals beyond that level are usually discretionary, with the highest court having the ability to choose which cases it wishes to hear.

SELECTED REFERENCES

Black, D. J. *The Behavior of Law* (1976).
Cardozo, B. N. *The Growth of the Law* (1924).
Curie, D. *Federal Court—Cases and Materials* (1982).
Davis, K. C. *Discretionary Justice: A Preliminary Inquiry* (1969).
Davis, K. C., and Pierce, R. J. *Administrative Law Treatise* (1994).
Friedman, L. M. *American Law: An Introduction* (1984).
Llewellyn, K.N. *The Bramble Bush: On Our Law and Its Study* (1960).
Wright, C. A. *Federal Courts* (3rd ed, 1976).

CHAPTER 2

READING AND USING LEGAL MATERIALS

For many, professionals and nonprofessionals alike, law is a separate, sometimes mysterious and incomprehensible field. This chapter will provide some of the basic legal terminology used in this text, some guidance to reading legal materials, and some suggestions for conducting legal research.

The language of law is in many ways distinct from everyday discourse. Legal terms often have their own meanings. Even if the basic legal terminology is understood, using legal materials requires practice and skill. We will look now at some common legal terms, then carefully read examples of the three basic types of law: case decisions, statutes, and administrative regulations. Finally, since many health and human services professionals will find that they need to update their knowledge periodically, we will discuss how to locate and research legal materials.

BASIC CONCEPTS AND TERMINOLOGY

Many legal terms have come from other earlier societies and foreign languages including Latin, Old English, and French.[1] Some words have solely legal meanings, such as tort (a civil wrong) or malpractice; others may be used very differently in law and everyday conversation. Words such as action, case, class, motion, pardon, party, plead, prayer, standing, and suit all have legal meanings that are very different from their common meanings. A few of the important terms and concepts are explained below.

Adversary System

A defining concept of the American legal system is that it is based on an adversarial model in which most courts only deal with legal matters where there is a dispute or controversy. Occasionally a state court may have the power to issue advisory opinions, indicating what that court would do if the issue were brought to it or how it would interpret a statute if asked, but usually courts hear only cases with two opposing sides and a real dispute. If the sides reach an agreement prior to the court's decision or if the issue ceases to exist then the case usually will be dismissed as "moot."

The philosophy behind the adversarial system is that the only way to resolve a conflict is to have the disputing parties—with their legal representatives when present—argue before an impartial tribunal. Each side has the opportunity to present its case and to challenge and question the other so that all relevant material will be learned; an impartial decision maker will then decide on the basis of what has been presented which side shall prevail. Thus a key element of the system is conflict, which is indicated in the names of the disputes: *State v. Smith* or *Roe v. Wade*, where one side is against or *versus* the other. Some juvenile, mental health, and family law issues are titled "in the matter of," "in the interest of" or "in re," indicating that the proceeding is at least technically nonadversarial.

In an adversarial proceeding, each side is expected to present the strongest possible case and to challenge, dispute, and raise doubts about the other side. Some have questioned whether this system of structured conflict is the most appropriate, particularly for disputes such as divorce and child custody, and alternate mechanisms such as arbitration and mediation are being used in some dispute settlements.

Parties

Those who are directly affected by and are a part of a lawsuit are the *parties* to the legal action.[2] Usually their names will appear in the case name. A party may be an individual, such as a patient in a mental hospital, or a number of individuals, such as all the physicians, psychologists, nurses, and social workers who had contact with a patient, or it may be an agency, such as the hospital where the patient resided. A party may also include larger groups such as all state welfare recipients or all state mental hospital patients. These latter groups are sometimes considered legally as a *class*, because they have a common characteristic—recipients of welfare or patients in mental hospitals—and the lawsuit is called a *class action*.

The party bringing a lawsuit in a civil case is usually called the *plaintiff*, but depending upon usage in a particular jurisdiction that party may also be termed the *complainant* or the *petitioner*. The party being sued is usually termed the *defendant*, but may also be called the *respondent*. And the party being sued may file a *counterclaim* and sue the plaintiff. In a criminal case, the State or the People bring the action against the person accused of committing the criminal act, who is usually termed the *defendant*. If a case is being appealed, the party bringing the appeal is often called the *petitioner* or *appellant*;

the other party may be termed the *respondent* or the *appellee*. Jurisdictions differ in which terminology is used.

Only those directly affected by the lawsuit may participate in it, and they are said to have *standing* in the suit.[3] Courts may differ as to how directly affected the party must be. For example, there is probably no question that a parent of a child currently in a public grade school class where time is set aside for prayer has standing to challenge that period of prayer under the First Amendment separation of church and state. Less clear is whether a childless individual living in the community has standing to challenge the prayer session, and it is even less clear whether an individual residing in a different community or state has standing. Sometimes individuals or groups who have an interest in the result but who are not directly involved in the dispute may participate in a limited way. If the court agrees, an interested party may be allowed to participate as *amicus curiae*, or friend of the court, and file a legal brief in support of that position.

Individuals who are without funds to hire an attorney are not prohibited from appearing in court. Legally they are termed *indigents*. As we will see, indigent criminal defendants now are provided with a number of procedural protections, including the right to counsel supplied by the state. Depending on the type of lawsuit, legal services or legal aid programs may provide counsel for indigents in civil law suits.

Burden of Proof, Standard of Proof

The burden of proving a case, sometimes called the burden of persuasion, usually falls upon the plaintiff. In some actions, for example civil child abuse cases in some states, when the plaintiff establishes a *prima facie* case—one sufficient to prove the assertion unless rebutted—the burden then shifts to the defendant to prove there was no abuse.

The standard of proof, sometimes also known as the burden of proof, is the amount or degree of proof required to prevail. In most civil cases, the standard of proof is a *preponderance of the evidence*, where the party with the burden of proof must establish its case by showing that it was more likely than not. In criminal cases, a far more demanding standard must be met, proof *beyond a reasonable doubt*, requiring a great degree of certainty. This standard is also required in juvenile delinquency commitments and for the termination of parental rights of Native Americans. Between these two is an intermediate standard, *clear and convincing evidence*, requiring more proof than a preponderance of the evidence but less than beyond a reasonable doubt. In the health and human services, the clear and convincing standard is found in mental hospital civil commitment proceedings and termination of parental rights proceedings, among others.

Jurisdiction

Jurisdiction is an important legal concept, referring to a court's legal authority to hear a case.[4] There are two main types of jurisdiction, *subject matter jurisdiction* and *personal jurisdiction*. Subject matter jurisdiction is jurisdiction over the type of dispute; personal jurisdiction is jurisdiction over persons or things residing or located within the court's geographic boundaries. Subject matter jurisdiction might include a family court's jurisdiction over divorce, custody, and child abuse; a tax court's jurisdiction over tax issues; a probate court's jurisdiction over wills and estates, incompetence and guardianship; an appellate court's jurisdiction over appeals from lower courts, and so forth. In personal jurisdiction, a court must have jurisdiction either over the parties or the items in dispute.

Decisions and Judgments

The court's *decision*, or what is sometimes called its *holding*, is what the court has determined in a specific case. The *judgment* of a court usually is which party has won the dispute. A key point in the American legal system is that courts are only supposed to decide issues that properly come before them. Thus much of case law is a function of the types of disputes that reach the courts, especially the appellate courts.[5] As part of its decision, an appellate court may *affirm* or *reverse* a lower court—that is, uphold or reject the lower court decision—or may order a *remand*, returning the case to the lower court to be reheard following certain guidelines or requirements. Occasionally a court will reverse itself and reject its previous ruling on the same issue. When the court does this, it *overrules* a prior decision.

Precedent and *Res Judicata*

A decision by a court or a higher court in the same system is *precedent* or legal authority for similar cases that follow in that particular court or the courts under it. This means that those courts are usually bound to follow this ruling if the same or a similar issue is presented. A final decision by a court is *res judicata* for the parties in the case, which means that it cannot be reopened and relitigated without an appeal.

HOW A CASE PROCEEDS THROUGH THE LEGAL SYSTEM

While terminology will differ across states, in civil actions the plaintiff files a *complaint* (sometimes called a petition) with the court which sets forth the nature of the legal action and its legal basis. The complaint is accompanied by an *affidavit* which certifies that the material in the complaint is true. The defendant is then notified of the legal action through *service of process*: The individual either receives notification through delivery in person, *personal service,* or depending upon the jurisdiction, by *constructive service,* perhaps by mail or by publication of a legal notice in an appropriate newspaper. The party receiving the summons should have *adequate and timely notice* of the proceedings, that is, should be given sufficient information to understand what is at issue and sufficient time to prepare. The individual receiving service then files a response with the court. This may take the form of an *answer* to the complaint, a *motion to dismiss,* or a *cross-motion* and *counterclaim.* If the individual receiving legal service does not respond within a specified time limit, the party is said to be in *default* and faces the possibility of losing the case. When all the filings, motions, and appearances have been made, the case may proceed to *discovery,* where each party submits *interrogatories*—written questions—to the other. These may be short or may cover hundreds of pages. Sometimes pretrial personal testimony—oral or written—called *depositions* are taken. The individuals being deposed are sworn, the testimony is recorded, and it may be used later in court.

At this point, a party may file a motion with the court for a *summary judgment,* which essentially concedes the factual points and argues that when the law is applied to these facts, the party is entitled to prevail. If this motion is denied, the case is set down for a full *hearing* or *trial.* However, a considerable period of time may elapse before the hearing or trial occurs, and at any point before a judgment is rendered the parties may *settle* the dispute. In fact, most lawsuits are settled prior to going to court and only a small proportion actually reach a decision by judge or jury.

If the case goes to trial, depending on the subject matter of the action and the law of the state, the defendant may request a *jury trial.* In suits alleging malpractice or monetary damages stemming from a breach of contract, jury trials are usually possible; in child abuse, other family matters, or civil commitment to mental hospitals, jury trials are not allowed in many states. If the defendant could have a jury trial and decides for a trial before the judge alone, the defendant is said to have *waived* the right to a jury trial and the trial is sometimes called a *bench trial.*

Some possible outcomes of a civil trial that results in a verdict or decision in favor of one party are a *judgment* awarding *monetary damages,* which may include *compensatory damages* (to compensate the injured party for the harm done) and perhaps *punitive damages* (to penalize the defendant), an order to do a certain thing that was agreed to (*specific performance*), and *temporary or permanent injunctions* or *restraining orders* requiring a party to do something or refrain from certain activities.[6]

READING LEGAL MATERIALS

Some examples of case decisions, statutes, and administrative regulations are presented here to illustrate their differences and to provide some guidance in reading and understanding them.

Different types of legal materials require very different reading styles. Case decisions—or judicial opinions, as they are sometimes called—are written by the judges and may be short or lengthy; clear, murky, or ambiguous; in a writing style that may be lucid or turgid, concise or repetitive. There are few rules for writing decisions, and cases are written by many judges, who, with varying amounts of assistance from their law clerks, write in many styles.

One cautionary note. The cases used here and throughout the text have been edited for conciseness. When editing has taken place, a series of asterisks (***) indicates that text has been deleted, but the reader will be unable to tell how much material—a word, a paragraph, or entire pages—has been deleted without researching the original. Also, for brevity, references to other cases often have been omitted.

Statutes and regulations must be read very carefully. Every word takes on importance. Even the choice of a particular punctuation mark such as a comma or a semicolon may make a dramatic difference in the meaning of the law.

Reading Court Decisions

Judges' written opinions serve a number of purposes. Among these are: (1) to present a decision to a dispute; (2) to explain how that decision was reached, how it fits within existing law, and why alternative resolutions were rejected; (3) to provide guidance to lower courts, lawyers, and litigants; and (4) to explain and justify the decision to the legal community and to the public at large. Most important for the health and human services professional is to understand what the decision is and what it means, where it applies, and what the ramifications are for future cases. The following is one guide to reading and understanding a case decision.

Guide to Reading Cases

1. *Who* are the parties, *what* court is deciding the case, and *when* was the case decided? Answers to these questions will tell the reader who is involved in the case, where the decision applies, and whether the decision is recent or happened some time ago. Key parties are usually found in the case name. The court deciding the case and often the date are found in the case citation, discussed below.

Knowing what court decided the case is important because the decision is binding precedent on the court deciding the case and usually on lower courts in the same legal system. A lower court decision has less value as precedent, and there remains the possibility of an appeal and a different outcome at a higher judicial level. A decision by the highest court in the state is usually final unless an appeal is made into the federal system. A decision by the U.S. Supreme Court is final, unless that court reviews the issue at a later time. When a case was decided puts the issue into an historical context. A case decided some time ago may still be good law, but it may have been overruled. Only further legal research will tell.

2. What are the *facts* of the case? Cases are generally based on facts— something that happened or didn't happen, although these facts may be contested or given different interpretations. Courts often recite what they consider to be key facts in a case. Sometimes the court will state "The facts of the case are . . . " At other times it will take some work to identify the important facts, and sometimes the court will not include facts at all. The facts that are presented in a case are not necessarily all the facts, but only those that the court believes to be relevant to the decision.

3. What is the *legal issue* in the case? This is the focal point of the case— the issue to be decided. Sometimes the court will clearly state "The question is . . .", or "The issue to be decided is . . ." but other times this will not be so clear and it will take some work to extract the information.

4. If the case being decided is on appeal, what is the *judicial* or *procedural history*—what happened in the lower court or courts? Most of the cases in this text, and most published cases, are from appellate courts where a previous court's decision has been appealed. To clarify the issues and what has happened in the appellate process, it is useful to learn what the lower court or courts did. However, this information is not always included in a decision, and in this text it may have been edited out.

5. What was the *decision* or *holding* in the case? What was the judgment of the court? Here again, the court may state "We decide that . . ." or "We hold that . . ." or "judgment for the plaintiff," and the result of the case will be clear. At other times, the court's decision will be less clear. Sometimes all that the reader is told is that the judgment of the lower court is affirmed or reversed (or sometimes affirmed in part and reversed in part), or that the case is remanded for a new hearing in light of the court's opinion. It may take more work to clarify what the case really decided or which party prevailed.

6. Why was the decision reached—what was the *legal reasoning* behind

the decision? Knowing how the court reached its conclusion is very useful in predicting what the court will do in a similar situation at a later time.[7]

7. If there are *concurring* or *dissenting* opinions, what do they say? Sometimes a judge will file a separate opinion, agreeing or disagreeing with the majority. A judge who concurs basically agrees with the outcome, but may wish to express differences with it or with the legal reasoning used by the majority. A judge who disagrees with a decision may file a dissent. Dissenting opinions are useful for several reasons. The dissenting judge may point out errors, present other pertinent facts, and make it easier to understand the majority opinion. Concurring or dissenting opinions may forecast future directions of the court.[8]

Following are two U.S. Supreme Court decisions. The first addresses an indigent's right to counsel in criminal court, the second an indigent's right to counsel in a civil proceeding, the termination of parental rights. Both rely on the U.S. Constitution and the Due Process Clause, but the results are quite different. *Gideon v. Wainwright* overrules a prior decision, *Betts v. Brady*, 316 U.S. 455 (1942), and in a major decision of the time, the Court holds that accused felons appearing in state criminal court trials who cannot afford an attorney must be provided one by the state. In *Lassiter v. Department of Social Services*, the Court rules that under the Constitution, indigent defendants in termination of parental rights hearings need not be provided counsel automatically.

THE RIGHT TO COUNSEL IN CRIMINAL CASES

The Sixth Amendment of the U.S. Constitution provides "In all criminal prosecutions, the accused shall enjoy the right ... to have the assistance of counsel for his defense." Originally meaning the right to be accompanied by counsel, the provision was extended to the right to appointed counsel for indigents tried for capital offenses in *Powell v. Alabama*, 287 U.S. 45 (1932), and indigents' right to appointed counsel in federal criminal cases in *Johnson v. Zerbst*, 304 U.S. 458 (1938). The question in *Betts v. Brady* was whether this right was constitutionally required in state criminal cases. The problem was that the Supreme Court in *Baron v. Mayor of Baltimore*, 32 U.S. (7 Pet.) 243 (1833), had held that the first eight amendments, the Bill of Rights, were ratified as limitations on the federal government, and did not automatically apply to the states. Over time, many of these provisions were applied to the states through the Fourteenth Amendment Due Process Clause as essential to "fundamental fairness." *Betts* held that an indigent's right to an appointed counsel in a criminal court was not essential but could be left to the discretion of the trial court. Twenty years later, the Court reversed itself in *Gideon v.*

Wainwright, holding that the assistance of counsel is fundamental and essential to a fair trial.

GIDEON v. WAINWRIGHT, CORRECTIONS DIRECTOR
372 U.S. 335 (1963)
U.S. SUPREME COURT

MR. JUSTICE BLACK delivered the opinion of the court.

Petitioner was charged in a Florida state court with having broken and entered a poolroom with intent to commit a misdemeanor. This offense is a felony under Florida law. Appearing in court without funds and without a lawyer, petitioner asked the court to appoint counsel for him, whereupon the following colloquy took place:

> "THE COURT: Mr. Gideon, I am sorry, but I cannot appoint Counsel to represent you in this case. Under the laws of the State of Florida, the only time the Court can appoint Counsel to represent a Defendant is when that person is charged with a capital offense. I am sorry, but I will have to deny your request to appoint Counsel to defend you in this case.
>
> "THE DEFENDANT: The United States Supreme Court says I am entitled to be represented by Counsel."

Put to trial before a jury, Gideon conducted his defense about as well as could be expected from a layman. He made an opening statement to the jury, cross-examined the State's witnesses, presented witnesses in his own defense, declined to testify himself, and made a short argument "emphasizing his innocence to the charge contained in the Information filed in this case." The jury returned a verdict of guilty, and petitioner was sentenced to serve five years in the state prison. Later, petitioner filed in the Florida Supreme Court this habeas corpus petition attacking his conviction and sentence on the ground that the trial court's refusal to appoint counsel for him denied him rights "guaranteed by the Constitution and the Bill of Rights by the United States Government." Treating the petition for habeas corpus as properly before it, the State Supreme Court, "upon consideration thereof" but without an opinion, denied all relief. Since 1942, when *Betts v. Brady,* 316 U.S. 455, was decided by a divided Court, the problem of a defendant's federal constitutional right to counsel in a state court has been a continuing source of controversy and litigation in both state and federal courts. To give this problem another review here, we granted certiorari. 370 U.S. 908. Since Gideon was proceeding *in forma pauperis,* we appointed counsel to represent him and requested both sides to discuss in their briefs and oral arguments the following: "Should this Court's holding in *Betts v. Brady,* 316 U.S. 455, be reconsidered?"

The facts upon which Betts claimed that he had been unconstitutionally denied the right to have counsel appointed to assist him are strikingly like the facts upon which Gideon here bases his federal constitutional claim. Betts was indicted for robbery in a Maryland state court. On arraignment, he told the trial judge of his lack of funds to hire a lawyer and asked the court to appoint one for him. Betts was advised that it was not the practice in that county to appoint counsel for indigent defendants except in murder and rape cases. He then pleaded not guilty, had witnesses summoned, cross-examined the State's witnesses, examined his own, and chose not to testify himself. He was found guilty by the judge, sitting without a jury, and sentenced to eight years in prison. Like Gideon, Betts sought release by habeas corpus, alleging that he had been denied the right to assistance of counsel in violation of the Fourteenth Amendment. Betts was denied any relief, and on review this Court affirmed. It was held that a refusal to appoint counsel for an indigent defendant charged with a felony did not necessarily violate the Due Process Clause of the Fourteenth Amendment, . . .***

Treating due process as "a concept less rigid and more fluid than those envisaged in other specific and particular provisions of the Bill of Rights," the Court held that refusal to appoint counsel under the particular facts and circumstances in the *Betts* case was not so "offensive to the common and fundamental ideas of fairness" as to amount to a denial of due process. Since the facts and circumstances of the two cases are so nearly indistinguishable, we think the *Betts* v. *Brady* holding if left standing would require us to reject Gideon's claim that the Constitution guarantees him the assistance of counsel. Upon full reconsideration we conclude that *Betts* v. *Brady* should be overruled.

The Sixth Amendment provides, "In all criminal prosecutions, the accused shall enjoy the right . . . to have the Assistance of Counsel for his defence." We have construed this to mean that in federal courts counsel must be provided for defendants unable to employ counsel unless the right is competently and intelligently waived.[3] Betts argued that this right is extended to indigent defendants in state courts by the Fourteenth Amendment.*** In order to decide whether the Sixth Amendment's guarantee of counsel is of this fundamental nature, the Court in Betts set out and considered "[r]elevant data on the subject . . . afforded by constitutional and statutory provisions subsisting in the colonies and the States prior to the inclusion of the Bill of Rights in the national Constitution, and in the constitutional, legislative, and judicial history of the States to the present date." 316 U.S., at 465. On the basis of this historical data the Court concluded that "appointment of counsel is not a fundamental right, essential to a fair trial."***

We accept *Betts* v. *Brady's* assumption, based as it was on our prior cases, that a provision of the Bill of Rights which is "fundamental and essential to a fair trial" is made obligatory upon the States by the Fourteenth Amendment. We think the Court in *Betts* was wrong, however, in concluding that the Sixth Amendment's guarantee of counsel is not one of these fundamental rights.

[In] 1938 this Court said:

"[The assistance of counsel] is one of the safeguards of the Sixth Amendment deemed necessary to insure fundamental human rights of life and liberty. . . . The Sixth Amendment stands as a constant admonition that if the constitutional safeguards it provides be lost, justice will not 'still be done.'" *Johnson* v. *Zerbst*, 304 U.S. 458, 462 (1938).

The fact is that in deciding as it did—that "appointment of counsel is not a fundamental right, essential to a fair trial"—the Court in *Betts* v. *Brady* made an abrupt break with its own well-considered precedents. In returning to these old precedents, sounder we believe than the new, we but restore constitutional principles established to achieve a fair system of justice. Not only these precedents but also reason and reflection require us to recognize that in our adversary system of criminal justice, any person haled into court, who is too poor to hire a lawyer, cannot be assured a fair trial unless counsel is provided for him. This seems to us to be an obvious truth. Governments, both state and federal, quite properly spend vast sums of money to establish machinery to try defendants accused of crime. Lawyers to prosecute are everywhere deemed essential to protect the public's interest in an orderly society. Similarly, there are few defendants charged with crime, few indeed, who fail to hire the best lawyers they can get to prepare and present their defenses. That government hires lawyers to prosecute and defendants who have the money hire lawyers to defend are the strongest indications of the widespread belief that lawyers in criminal courts are necessities, not luxuries. The right of one charged with crime to counsel may not be deemed fundamental and essential to fair trials in some countries, but it is in ours. From the very beginning, our state and national constitutions and laws have laid great emphasis on procedural and substantive safeguards designed to assure fair trials before impartial tribunals in which every defendant stands equal before the law. This noble ideal cannot be realized if the poor man charged with crime has to face his accusers without a lawyer to assist him. The Court in *Betts* v. *Brady* departed from the sound wisdom upon which the Court's holding in *Powell* v. *Alabama* rested. Florida, supported by two other States, has asked that *Betts* v. *Brady* be left intact. Twenty-two States, as friends of the Court, argue that *Betts* was "an anachronism when handed down" and that it should now be overruled. We agree.

The judgment is reversed and the cause is remanded to the Supreme Court of Florida for further action not inconsistent with this opinion.

Reversed.

Questions About *Gideon*

(To give the reader some guidance, we will pose and then answer the seven questions in the previous guide to reading a court decision.)

1. The parties in the case name are Gideon and Wainwright. We know from the case itself Gideon was the petitioner, charged with committing a felony. We know from the case name Wainwright was the corrections director. Why a corrections director is the other party, the respondent, is not easy to answer. It has to do with some technical legal issues discussed in Question 4. From the case citation we know that this is a U.S. Supreme Court case and that it was decided in 1963. (Case citations are discussed at p. 41*ff.*)

2. Important facts are: Gideon had no money, asked the court to appoint counsel, and was denied. He was tried before a jury and defended himself. He "conducted his defense about as well as could be expected from a layman." He cross-examined the state's witnesses, presented his own, chose not to testify, and made a brief closing argument. He was found guilty and sentenced to five years. He appealed this decision.

3. Although not stated precisely, the legal issue has to do with "the problem of a defendant's federal constitutional right to counsel in a state court," and "should *Betts v. Brady* be reconsidered."
4. The procedural history includes: Gideon was found guilty at the trial court level, and filed a *habeas corpus* petition with the Florida Supreme Court on the grounds that his Constitutional rights had been violated. His appeal was denied without an opinion. A writ of *habeas corpus*—technically *habeas corpus ad subjiciendum*—is a legal writ challenging the state's right to incarcerate the defendant and requires that the person detaining the defendant produce the defendant in court so that the court can decide if the detention is legal. In bringing this writ, Gideon is suing the person responsible for his confinement, Wainwright, the corrections director.
5. In its decision, the Supreme Court held that "one charged with crime" has a fundamental right to counsel under the Constitution and if a person is too poor to hire a lawyer, one must be provided in a criminal case. The Court says *Betts* was wrongly decided and is overruled. The judgment against Gideon is reversed and the case is remanded to the Florida courts.
6. In its reasoning, the Court relied on precedents and on "reason and reflection." Under the Sixth Amendment, the accused in criminal prosecutions has the right to the assistance of counsel. In *Johnson v. Zerbst*, 304 U.S. 458 (1938), the Court held this provision meant that unless waived, counsel must be provided in federal court if the defendant could not afford one. In *Betts*, the Court held that the appointment of counsel was not "a fundamental right, essential to a fair trial," and so the Sixth Amendment right was not automatically imposed upon the states by the Fourteenth Amendment. However, in *Gideon* the Court examines other precedents and concludes that the provision of counsel is fundamental to a fair trial. The Court also compares the amount of money the state spends to try defendants and points out that those who are accused of crimes and have sufficient funds hire the best possible attorneys.

Notes and Issues for Discussion

1. Was the issue before the Supreme Court whether Gideon was guilty of a felony? What was the issue to be decided?
2. What is due process? Note how difficult the concept is to articulate: Quoting from *Betts v. Brady*, the Court suggests that violations of due process involve "a denial of fundamental fairness" and are "shocking to the universal sense of justice," although whether there is a violation may depend upon "other considerations." The Court calls due process "a concept less rigid and more fluid" than other parts of the Bill of Rights. It has to do with those "fundamental principles of liberty and justice which lie at the base of all our civil and political institutions."
3. In *Betts*, the Court suggested that the defendant was of average intelligence, had been in criminal court before, and the issue was a simple one— whether the victim who identified Betts should be believed or whether

Betts and his alibi witnesses should be believed. Also the court noted that in Maryland, counsel would be provided at the discretion of the trial judge if circumstances dictated and this was an adequate protection. Does Betts need a lawyer?

While not stated in the facts of the case, Gideon's situation was similar. He was seen at the scene of the crime about the time it was committed, he was found carrying a sum of money after the crime and although he had no alibi witnesses, argued he was elsewhere at the time. Does Gideon need a lawyer? Why? What could a lawyer do for Gideon?

4. For those who would argue that a lawyer is unnecessary, consider the following information from Betts's trial:

   "The robbery victim testified: The robber 'had on a dark overcoat and a handkerchief around his chin and a pair of dark amber glasses. . . . I told the police that I wasn't sure I could identify him without the glasses and the handkerchief, after seeing him when it was almost dark that evening.' The *only* man in the lineup the day the victim came to the jail to identify the robber was Betts. And he could only be identified when he put on the dark coat, the smoked glasses and the handkerchief." Kamisar, "The Right to Counsel and the Fourteenth Amendment: A Dialogue on 'The Most Pervasive Right' of the Accused," 30 *U. Chicago L. Rev.* 1, 42–56 (1962).

5. How did Gideon's case get to the U.S. Supreme Court? Gideon appearing *in forma pauperis* filed a handwritten appeal to the Supreme Court in which he argued that he had a right to an attorney and was refused. The Court decided to explore the issue. The State of Florida was asked to respond and filed a lengthy document citing various reasons why there was no need for counsel, relying heavily on *Betts*. This was sent by the Court to Gideon, who wrote that he couldn't make a legal response since he had no access to legal materials in the Florida prison, but concluded quite eloquently, "It makes no difference how old I am or what color I am or what church I belong to if any. The question is I did not get a fair trial. The question is very simple. I requested the court to appoint me a attorney and the court refused. . . ."[9] The U.S. Supreme Court then decided that the issue should be heard and appointed counsel for Gideon for that purpose. The *Gideon* case was the subject of a book by Anthony Lewis, *Gideon's Trumpet*, and a movie by the same name.

6. Although *Gideon* did decide that there was a right to counsel under the Due Process Clause for indigent criminal defendants in state trials, many questions were left undecided, including: Who is indigent? Must a person have no money, a little money, or not enough money to pay for counsel? Who supplies and pays for the appointed counsel? What kinds of criminal cases does *Gideon* apply to? And, finally, what happens to Gideon?

   Briefly, the court left to the states the determination of standards of indigence and how to provide—and pay for—legal representation. Gideon was charged with a felony, and although not decided in this case, the court later limited the decision to felonies. Somewhat later, in *Argersinger v. Hamlin*, 407 U.S. 25 (1972), the court extended the right to counsel to lesser offenses, holding "no person may be imprisoned for any offense, whether classified as petty, misdemeanor or felony unless he was represented by counsel." According to Anthony Lewis, the State of Florida decided to retry Gideon. He maintained his innocence and was dissatisfied with his appointed counsel who wanted him to plead guilty. Gideon demanded and got another lawyer, and in the subsequent trial, his lawyer was able to create substantial doubt about the veracity of the state's eyewitnesses. The jury found Gideon not guilty.

THE RIGHT TO COUNSEL IN CIVIL CASES

If counsel is supplied to indigents in criminal cases, is it constitutionally required in civil cases? Contrast the following civil case with *Gideon*.

LASSITER v. DEPARTMENT OF SOCIAL SERVICES
452 U.S. 18 (1981)
U.S. SUPREME COURT

Justice Stewart delivered the opinion of the Court.

In the late spring of 1975, after hearing evidence that the petitioner, Abby Gail Lassiter, had not provided her infant son William with proper medical care, the District Court of Durham County, N.C., adjudicated him a neglected child and transferred him to the custody of the Durham County Department of Social Services, the respondent here. A year later, Ms. Lassiter was charged with first-degree murder, was convicted of second-degree murder, and began a sentence of 25 to 40 years of imprisonment.[1] In 1978 the Department petitioned the court to terminate Ms. Lassiter's parental rights because, the Department alleged, she "has not had any contact with the child since December of 1975" and "has willfully left the child in foster care for more than two consecutive years without showing that substantial progress has been made in correcting the conditions which led to the removal of the child, or without showing a positive response to the diligent efforts of the Department of Social Services to strengthen her relationship to the child, or to make and follow through with constructive planning for the future of the child."****

A social worker from the respondent Department was the first witness. She testified that in 1975 the Department "received a complaint from Duke Pediatrics that William had not been followed in the pediatric clinic for medical problems

[1] The North Carolina Court of Appeals, in reviewing the petitioner's conviction, indicated that the murder occurred during an altercation between Ms. Lassiter, her mother, and the deceased: "Defendant's mother told [the deceased] to 'come on.' They began to struggle and deceased fell or was knocked to the floor. Defendant's mother was beating deceased with a broom. While deceased was still on the floor and being beaten with the broom, defendant entered the apartment. She went into the kitchen and got a butcher knife. She took the knife and began stabbing the deceased who was still prostrate. The body of deceased had seven stab wounds. . ." *State v. Lassiter*, No. 7614SC1054 (June 1, 1977).***

and that they were having difficulty in locating Ms. Lassiter. . . ." She said that in May 1975 a social worker had taken William to the hospital, where doctors asked that he stay "because of breathing difficulties [and] malnutrition and [because] there was a great deal of scarring that indicated that he had a severe infection that had gone untreated." The witness further testified that, except for one "pre-arranged" visit and a chance meeting on the street, Ms. Lassiter had not seen William after he had come into the State's custody, and that neither Ms. Lassiter nor her mother had "made any contact with the Department of Social Services regarding that child." When asked whether William should be placed in his grandmother's custody, the social worker said he should not, since the grandmother "has indicated to me on a number of occasions that she was not able to take responsibility for the child" and since "I have checked with people in the community and from Ms. Lassiter's church who also feel that this additional responsibility would be more than she can handle." The social worker added that William "has not seen his grandmother since the chance meeting in July of '76 and that was the only time."***

Ms. Lassiter conducted a cross-examination of the social worker, who firmly reiterated her earlier testimony. The judge explained several times, with varying degrees of clarity, that Ms. Lassiter should only ask questions at this stage; many of her questions were disallowed because they were not really questions, but arguments.

Ms. Lassiter herself then testified, under the judge's questioning, that she had properly cared for William. Under cross-examination, she said that she had seen William more than five or six times after he had been taken from her custody and that, if William could not be with her, she wanted him to be with her mother since, "He knows us. Children know they family. . . . They know they people, they know they family and that child knows us anywhere. . . . I got four more other children. Three girls and a boy and they know they little brother when they see him."

Ms. Lassiter's mother was then called as a witness. She denied, under the questioning of the judge, that she had filed the complaint against Ms. Lassiter, and on cross-examination she denied both having failed to visit William when he was in the State's custody and having said that she could not care for him.

The court found that Ms. Lassiter "has not contacted the Department of Social Services about her child since December, 1975, has not expressed any concern for his care and welfare, and has made no efforts to plan for his future." Because Ms. Lassiter thus had "wilfully failed to maintain concern or responsibility for the welfare of the minor," and because it was "in the best interests of the minor," the court terminated Ms. Lassiter's status as William's parent.

On appeal, Ms. Lassiter argued only that, because she was indigent, the Due Process Clause of the Fourteenth Amendment entitled her to the assistance of counsel, and that the trial court had therefore erred in not requiring the State to provide counsel for her.***

For all its consequences, "due process" has never been, and perhaps can never be, precisely defined. "[U]nlike some legal rules," this Court has said, due process "is not a technical conception with a fixed content unrelated to time, place and circumstances." *Cafeteria Workers* v. *McElroy*, 367 U.S. 886, 895. Rather, the phrase expresses the requirement of "fundamental fairness," a requirement whose meaning can be as opaque as its importance is lofty. Applying the Due Process Clause is therefore an uncertain enterprise which must discover what "fundamental fairness" consists of in a particular situation by first considering any relevant precedents and then by assessing the several interests that are at stake.

The pre-eminent generalization that emerges from this Court's precedents on an indigent's right to appointed counsel is that such a right has been recognized to exist only where the litigant may lose his physical liberty if he loses the litigation. Thus, when the Court overruled the principle of *Betts* v. *Brady*, 316 U.S. 455, that counsel in criminal trials need be appointed only where the circumstances in a given case demand it, the Court did so in the case of a man sentenced to prison for five years. *Gideon* v. *Wainwright*, 372 U.S. 335.***

Significantly, as a litigant's interest in personal liberty diminishes, so does his right to appointed counsel. In *Gagnon* v. *Scarpelli*, 411 U.S. 778, the Court gauged the due process rights of a previously sentenced probationer at a probation-revocation hearing.*** [T]he Court in *Scarpelli* declined to hold that indigent probationers have, *per se*, a right to counsel at revocation hearings, and instead left the decision whether counsel should be appointed to be made on a case-by-case basis.

Finally, the Court has refused to extend the right to appointed counsel to include prosecutions which, though criminal, do not result in the defendant's loss of personal liberty.***

In sum, the Court's precedents speak with one voice about what "fundamental fairness" has meant when the Court has considered the right to appointed counsel, and we thus draw from them the presumption that an indigent litigant has a right to appointed counsel only when, if he loses, he may be deprived of his physical liberty. It is against this presumption that all the other elements in the due process decision must be measured.

The case of *Mathews* v. *Eldridge*, 424 U.S. 319, 335, propounds three elements to be evaluated in deciding what due process requires, viz., the private interests at stake, the government's interest, and the risk that the procedures used will lead to erroneous decisions. We must balance these elements against each other, and then set their net weight in the scales against the presumption that there is a right to appointed counsel only where the indigent, if he is unsuccessful, may lose his personal freedom.

This Court's decisions have by now made plain beyond the need for multiple citation that a parent's desire for and right to "the companionship, care, custody, and management of his or her children" is an important interest that "undeniably warrants deference and, absent a powerful countervailing interest, protection." Here the State has sought not simply to infringe upon that interest, but to end it. If the State prevails, it will have worked a unique kind of deprivation. A parent's interest in the accuracy and justice of the decision to terminate his or her parental status is, therefore, a commanding one.

Since the State has an urgent interest in the welfare of the child, it shares the parent's interest in an accurate and just decision.***

The State's interests, however, clearly diverge from the parent's insofar as the State wishes the termination decision to be made as economically as possible and thus wants to avoid both the expense of appointed counsel and the cost of the lengthened proceedings his presence may cause. But though the State's pecuniary interest is legitimate, it is hardly significant enough to overcome private interests as important as those here, particularly in light of the concession in the respondent's brief that the "potential costs of appointed counsel in termination proceedings . . . is [sic] admittedly *de minimis* compared to the costs in all criminal actions."

Finally, consideration must be given to the risk that a parent will be erroneously deprived of his or her child because the parent is not represented by counsel.***

The respondent argues that the subject of a termination hearing—the parent's relationship with her child—far from being abstruse, technical, or unfamiliar, is one as to which the parent must be uniquely well informed and to which the parent must have given prolonged thought. The respondent also contends that a termination hearing is not likely to produce difficult points of evidentiary law, or even of substantive law, since the evidentiary problems peculiar to criminal trials are not present and since the standards for termination are not complicated.***

Yet the ultimate issues with which a termination hearing deals are not always simple, however commonplace they may be. Expert medical and psychiatric testimony, which few parents are equipped to understand and fewer still to confute, is sometimes presented. The parents are likely to be people with little education, who have had uncommon difficulty in dealing with life, and who are, at the hearing, thrust into a distressing and disorienting situation. That these factors may combine to overwhelm an uncounseled parent is evident from the findings some courts have made.***

***To summarize the above discussion of the *Eldridge* factors: the parent's interest is an extremely important one (and may be supplemented by the dangers of criminal liability inherent in some termination proceedings); the State shares with the parent an interest in a correct decision, has a relatively weak pecuniary interest, and, in some but not all cases, has a possibly stronger interest in informal procedures; and the complexity of the proceeding and the incapacity of the uncounseled parent could be, but would not always be, great enough to make the risk of an erroneous deprivation of the parent's rights insupportably high.

If, in a given case, the parent's interests were at their strongest, the State's interests were at their weakest, and the risks of error were at their peak, it could not be said that the *Eldridge* factors did not overcome the presumption against the right to appointed counsel, and that due process did not therefore require the appointment of counsel. But since the *Eldridge* factors will not always be so distributed, and since "due process is not so rigid as to require that the significant interests in informality, flexibility and economy must always be sacrificed," neither can we say that the Constitution requires the appointment of counsel in every parental termination proceeding. We therefore adopt the standard found appropriate in *Gagnon* v. *Scarpelli*, and leave the decision whether due process calls for the appointment of counsel for indigent parents in termination proceedings to be answered in the first instance by the trial court, subject, of course, to appellate review.***

***In view of all these circumstances, we hold that the trial court did not err in failing to appoint counsel for Ms. Lassiter.

JUSTICE BLACKMUN, with whom JUSTICE BRENNAN and JUSTICE MARSHALL join, dissenting.

***

In this case, the State's aim is not simply to influence the parent-child relationship but to *extinguish* it. A termination of parental rights is both total and irrevocable. Unlike other custody proceedings, it leaves the parent with no right to visit or communicate with the child, to participate in, or even to know about, any important decision affecting the child's religious, educational, emotional, or physical development.***

The magnitude of this deprivation is of critical significance in the due process calculus, for the process to which an individual is entitled is in part determined "by the extent to which he may be 'condemned to suffer grievous loss.'" Surely there can be few losses more grievous than the abrogation of parental rights. Yet the Court today asserts that this deprivation somehow is less serious than threatened losses deemed to require appointed counsel, because in this instance the parent's own "personal liberty" is not at stake.***

The problem of inadequate representation is painfully apparent in the present case. Petitioner, Abby Gail Lassiter, is the mother of five children. The State moved to remove the fifth child, William, from petitioner's care on the grounds of parental neglect. Although petitioner received notice of the removal proceeding, she did not appear at the hearing and was not represented. In May 1975, the State's District Court adjudicated William to be neglected under North Carolina law and placed him in the custody of the Durham County Department of Social Services. At some point, petitioner evidently arranged for the other four children to reside with and be cared for by her mother, Mrs. Lucille Lassiter. They remain under their grandmother's care at the present time.

As the Court notes, petitioner did not visit William after July 1976. She was unable to do so, for she was imprisoned as a result of her conviction for second-degree murder. In December 1977, she was visited in prison by a Durham County social worker who advised her that the Department planned to terminate her parental rights with respect to William. Petitioner immediately expressed strong opposition to that plan and indicated a desire to place the child with his grandmother.***

At the termination hearing, the State's sole witness was the county worker who had met petitioner on the one occasion at the prison. This worker had been assigned to William's case in August 1977, yet much of her testimony concerned events prior to that date; she represented these events as contained in the agency record. Petitioner failed to uncover this weakness in the worker's testimony. That is hardly surprising, for there is no indication that an agency record was introduced into evidence or was present in court, or that petitioner or the grandmother ever had an opportunity to review any such record. The social worker also testified about her conversations with members of the community. In this hearsay testimony, the witness reported the opinion of others that the grandmother could not handle the additional responsibility of caring for the fifth child. There is no indication that these community members were unavailable to testify, and the County Attorney did not justify the admission of the hearsay. Petitioner made no objection to its admission.

The court gave petitioner an opportunity to cross-examine the social worker, but she apparently did not understand that cross-examination required questioning rather than declarative statements. At this point, the judge became noticeably impatient with petitioner. Petitioner then took the stand, and testified that she wanted William to live with his grandmother and his siblings. The judge questioned her for a brief period, and expressed open disbelief at one of her answers. The final witness was the grandmother. Both the judge and the County Attorney questioned her. She denied having expressed unwillingness to take William into her home, and vehemently contradicted the social worker's statement that she had complained to the Department about her daughter's neglect of the child. Petitioner was not told that she could question her mother, and did not do so.***

Petitioner plainly has not led the life of the exemplary citizen or model parent. It may well be that if she were accorded competent legal representation, the ultimate result in this particular case would be the same. But the issue before the Court is not petitioner's character; it is whether she was given a meaningful opportunity to be heard when the State moved to terminate absolutely her parental rights. In light of the unpursued avenues of defense, and of the experience petitioner underwent at the hearing, I find virtually incredible the Court's conclusion today that her termination proceeding was fundamentally fair. To reach that conclusion, the Court simply ignores the defendant's obvious inability to speak effectively for herself, a factor the Court has found to be highly significant in past cases.***

Notes and Issues for Discussion

1. Is the issue in the Supreme Court's decision whether the parental rights of Abby Gail Lassiter should be terminated? If not, what is the issue?
2. Dissenting judges attacked the majority's footnote 1 as being irrelevant and prejudicial. What is the relevance of the murder to Lassiter's request for counsel? Should she have less of a right to counsel in the termination proceeding because she was found guilty of murder?
3. Under *Gideon,* counsel is supplied for indigents unless competently waived. Under *Argersinger v. Hamlin,* counsel is supplied for indigents facing any incarceration, even one night in a county jail. Yet in *Lassiter* counsel is not necessarily provided to indigents facing termination of parental rights where they can lose contact with their child forever. What is the logic behind this result? Is it persuasive?
4. Does Lassiter need a lawyer? What points might a lawyer make in her behalf? Consider the following excerpts from the transcript of Lassiter's termination hearing:
   "THE COURT: All right. Do you want to ask her any questions?
   "(PETITIONER): About what? About what she—
   "THE COURT: About this child.
   "(PETITIONER): Oh, yes.
   "THE COURT: All right. Go ahead.

"(PETITIONER): The only thing I know is that when you say—
"THE COURT: I don't want you to testify.
"(PETITIONER): Okay.
"THE COURT: I want to know whether you want to cross-examine her or ask any questions.
"(PETITIONER): Yes, I want to. Well, you know, the only thing I know about is my part that I know about it. I know—
"THE COURT: I am not talking about what you know. I want to know if you want to ask her any questions or not.
"(PETITIONER): About that?
"THE COURT: Yes. Do you understand the nature of this proceeding?
"(PETITIONER): Yes.
"THE COURT: And that is to terminate any rights you have to the child and place it for adoption, if necessary.
"(PETITIONER): Yes, I know.
"THE COURT: Are there any questions you want to ask her about what she has testified to?
"(PETITIONER): Yes.
"THE COURT: All right. Go ahead.
"(PETITIONER): I want to know why you think you are going to turn my child over to a foster home? He knows my mother and he knows all of us. He knows her and he knows all of us." 452 U.S. 18, footnote 22.

5. The interests to be balanced in the test from *Mathews v. Eldridge* 424 U.S. 319 (1976), are those of the parent and the state combined with the risk of an error in this proceeding. Is the risk of error as small as the majority suggests? Can you argue the loss is so significant that counsel should be automatically provided to minimize the error?

6. The court did not say that counsel was always unnecessary in termination proceedings, but that leaving the decision to the discretion of the trial judge subject to appellate review was constitutionally sufficient. Unlike criminal trials, the provision of counsel to those without funds is not *constitutionally* mandated in most civil cases. States may provide counsel and many do in some civil proceedings, such as involuntary commitment to mental hospitals, child abuse determinations, and termination of parental rights, or counsel may be provided through legal services or legal aid.

Reading Statutes and Regulations

The other two major types of law are statutes and regulations. Both are often very technical. As was discussed in Chapter 1, statutory law expresses the intent of Congress or the legislature in various areas and is broadly reflective of the electorate and society at large. The role of the administrative regulation is to implement this intent through detailed and specific rules.

The purpose of reading the following excerpts is twofold: First, it gives the reader experience in using these quite different types of law. The second purpose is a little more complex but is a crucial point for the health and human services professional, to illustrate the power and reach of administrative law. In the example below, by proposing and making final several sets of regulations, the executive branch attempted to substantially alter and limit the existing statutory law. (Note that the symbol used to indicate a statute section is §, or §§ for multiple sections.)

FAMILY PLANNING STATUTES AND REGULATIONS

In the area of family planning, Congress enacted statutes for grants and contracts to programs. The executive branch then promulgated regulations. At a later point, a new administration amended these regulations. In this section, we will present the statutes, the regulations, and then the amended regulations, illustrating the amending process.

Title 42 §300 of the U.S. Code addresses voluntary family planning programs.

§300. Project grants and contracts for family planning services
(a) Authority of Secretary
The Secretary is authorized to make grants to and enter into contracts with public or nonprofit private entities to assist in the establishment and operation of voluntary family planning projects which shall offer a broad range of acceptable and effective family planning methods and services (including natural family planning methods, infertility services, and services for adolescents). To the extent practical, entities which receive grants or contracts under this subsection shall encourage family participation in projects assisted under this subsection.***

§300a-4. Grants and Contracts
(a) Promulgation of regulations governing execution; amount of grants
Grants and contracts made under this subchapter shall be made in accordance with such regulations as the Secretary may promulgate.***
(c) Prerequisites; "low-income family" defined
A grant may be made or contract entered into under section 300 or 300a of this title for a family planning service project or program only upon assurances satisfactory to the Secretary that—
(1) priority will be given in such project or program to the furnishing of such services to persons from low-income families; and
(2) no charge will be made in such project or program for services provided to any person from a low-income family except to the extent that payment will be made by a third party (including a government agency) which is authorized or is under legal obligation to pay such charge.
For purposes of this subsection, the term "low-income family" shall be defined by the Secretary in accordance with such criteria as he may prescribe so as to insure that economic status shall not be a deterrent to participation in the programs assisted under this subchapter.

Notes and Issues for Discussion

1. What powers are delegated to the Secretary in §300?
2. What kinds of family planning methods and services are to be offered?
3. What does the statute say about family participation?
4. What authority is delegated to the Secretary in §300a-4?
5. What assurances are required before entering into grants and contracts?
6. How and by whom is "low income family" defined?

Now consider some administrative regulations promulgated by the executive branch. They are first published in the *Federal Register* as proposed regulations. There follows a statutory thirty-day waiting period during which comments are accepted, and then they may (or may not) be revised and are published in the *Federal Register* in final form. The final regulations are subsequently published in the *Code of Federal Regulations* (abbreviated C.F.R.), a topical compilation of all federal regulations.[10]

42 CFR PART 59—GRANTS FOR FAMILY PLANNING SERVICES

Subpart A— Project Grants for Family Planning Services
***

§59.2 Definitions.
As used in this subpart:

Act means the Public Health Service Act, as amended.

Family means a social unit composed of one person, or two or more persons living together, as a household.

Family planning means the process of establishing objectives for the number and spacing of one's children and selecting the means by which those objectives may be achieved. These means include a broad range of acceptable and effective methods and services to limit or enhance fertility, including contraceptive methods (including natural family planning and abstinence) and the management of infertility (including adoption). Family planning services includes preconceptional counseling, education, and general reproductive health care (including diagnosis and treatment of infections which threaten reproductive capability). Family planning does not include pregnancy care (including obstetric or prenatal care). As required by section 1008 of the Act, abortion may not be included as a method of family planning in the title X project. Family planning, as supported under this subpart, should reduce the incidence of abortion.

Grantee means the organization to which a grant is awarded under section 1001 of the Act.

Low income family means a family whose total annual income does not exceed 100 percent of the most recent Community Services Administration Income Poverty Guidelines (45 CFR 1060.2). *Low-income family* also includes members of families whose annual family income exceeds this amount, but who, as determined by the Title X project director, are unable, for good reasons, to pay for family planning services. For example, unemancipated minors who wish to receive services on a confidential basis must be considered on the basis of their own resources.

Nonprofit, as applied to any private agency, institution, or organization, means that no part of the entity's net earnings benefit, or may lawfully benefit, any private shareholder or individual.

Prenatal care means medical services provided to a pregnant woman to promote maternal and fetal health.

Program and *project* are used interchangeably and mean a coherent assembly of plans, activities and supporting resources contained within an administrative framework.

Secretary means the Secretary of Health and Human Services and any other officer or employee of the Department of Health and Human Services to whom the authority involved has been delegated.***

§59.5 What requirement must be met by a family planning project?

(a) Each project supported under this part must:

(1) provide a broad range of acceptable and effective medically approved family planning methods (including natural family planning methods) and services (including infertility services and services for adolescents). If an organization offers only a single method of family planning, such as natural family planning, it may participate as part of the title X project as long as the entire title X project offers a broad range of family planning services.

(2) Provide services without subjecting individuals to any coercion to accept services or to employ or not to employ any particular methods of family planning. Acceptance of services must be solely on a voluntary basis and may not be made a prerequisite to eligibility for, or receipt of, any other service, assistance from or participation in any other program of the applicant.

(3) Provide services in a manner which protects the dignity of the individual.

(4) Provide services without regard to religion, race, color, national origin, handicapping condition, age, sex, number of pregnancies, or marital status.

(5) Provide that priority in the provision of services will be given to persons from low-income families.***

Notes and Issues for Discussion

1. Section 59.2 presents some basic definitions to be used in the family planning regulations; §59.5 presents some of the requirements for funding. First, note the specificity of the definitions of family, family planning, low-income family, and the Secretary. This is typical of administrative regulations.
2. The last sentence of the low-income family definition is: "For example, unemancipated minors who wish to receive services on a confidential basis

must be considered on the basis of their own resources." Consider two examples: (1) a minor from a low-income family as defined applies for family planning services. The minor is eligible under the low-income family definition; (2) a minor from a family which is not low income applies for services. Is the minor eligible? Yes, provided the minor's *own* resources meet the low-income requirement.

In early 1983, the Reagan administration published proposed amendments to these regulations in the *Federal Register*, and after the statutory waiting period, published them in their final form. These are presented below.

FEDERAL REGISTER / VOL. 40, NO. 18
WEDNESDAY, JANUARY 28, 1983

PART 59—[AMENDED]
§59.2 [Amended]
  1. The last sentence of the definition of "low income family" in 42 CFR 59.2 is revoked and removed.
  2. 42 CFR 59.5 is amended by adding thereto the following paragraph (a)(12), to read as follows:
§59.5 What requirements must be met by a family planning project?
  (a) ***
  (12) Encourage, to the extent practical, family participation in the provision of the project's services to unemancipated minors. Notwithstanding any other requirement of this subpart, a project shall,
  (i)(A) When prescription drugs or prescription devices are initially provided by the project to an unemancipated minor, notify a parent or guardian that they were provided, within 10 working days following their provision. The project must tell the minor prior to the provision of services about this notification requirement. As used in this subsection, the phrase "parent or guardian" shall refer to a parent or guardian residing with the minor or otherwise exercising ordinary parental functions with respect to the minor. The project shall verify by certified mail (with restricted delivery and return receipt requested), or other similar form of documentation, that the notification has been received. Where the project is unable to verify that notification was received, the project shall not provide additional prescription drugs or devices to the minor.
  (B) A project is not required to comply with paragraph (a)(12)(i)(A) of this section where the project director or clinic head (when specifically so designated by the project director) determines that notification will result in physical harm to the minor by a parent or guardian.
  (C) For the purposes of this paragraph (a)(12)(i), an "unemancipated minor" is an individual who is age 17 or under and is not, with respect to factors other than age, emancipated under State law.
  (D) The project must keep records of notifications provided pursuant to

the first sentence of paragraph (a)(12)(i)(A), and of verification that those notifications were received. The project must also keep records of the number of determinations made under paragraph (a)(12)(i)(B) and the factual basis for such determinations. The project must make records required by this subparagraph available to the Secretary on request.

(E) This paragraph (a)(12)(i) does not apply where prescription drugs are provided for the treatment of sexually transmitted diseases.

(ii) Where State law requires the notification or consent of a parent or guardian to the provision of family planning services to an individual who is an unemancipated minor under State law, provide such services only in the compliance with such law.

Notes and Issues for Discussion

1. There are two amendments, one altering the definition of "low-income family" in §59.2, the other adding a lengthy section a(12) to §59.5. What is the effect of deleting the last sentence from the low-income minor definition? What is the effect of adding section a(12) to the requirements?

2. Several lawsuits followed the final publication of these regulations, and they were enjoined from becoming effective. In *Planned Parenthood of America, Inc. v. Heckler*, 719 F. 2d 650 (1983), the court upheld Planned Parenthood's argument that the proposed amendments went beyond the Secretary's authority and did not follow the intent of Congress, which was to provide services to adolescents and to the extent practical encourage family participation. The court rejected the administration's interpretation that Congress intended the sentence "To the extent practical . . . shall encourage family participation" to mean that family participation *must* be encouraged, with the logical consequence that the parental notification amendment was merely a way to insure that family participation took place.

In September 1984, the Administration published the following notice in the *Federal Register* withdrawing the amendments:

FEDERAL REGISTER / VOL. 49, NO. 189
THURSDAY, SEPTEMBER 27, 1984

---

42 CFR Part 59
Grants for Family Planning Projects; Parental Notification Requirement
AGENCY: Public Health Service, DHHS
ACTION: Final rule.
SUMMARY: In 1983, the Department of Health and Human Services published regulations requiring, among other things, parental notification for the provision of prescription contraceptives to minors seeking services from family planning providers funded under Title X of the Public Health Service Act. The implementation of those regulations was subsequently enjoined by Federal District Courts. This rule removes those regulations from the Code of Federal Regulations.
EFFECTIVE DATE: This rule is effective on September 27, 1984.
SUPPLEMENTARY INFORMATION: On January 26, 1983, the Secretary of Health and Human Services published regulations amending the regulations applicable to the program for family planning services, Title X of the Public Health Services Act, 42 U.S.C. 300, *et seq.* 48 FR 3600. The regulations, codified at 42 CFR 59.5(a)(12), required parental notification for the provision of prescription contraceptives to minors. They also amended 42 CFR 59.2 by revoking the last sentence of the definition of "low income family."
The rules were scheduled to become effective on February 25, 1983. However, in mid-February, they were enjoined by two Federal District Courts, and both District Court decisions were upheld on appeal. See *State of New York* v. *Schweiker*, Civil No. 83 CIV 0726 (S.D.N.Y., 1983), *aff'd*, *State of New York* v. *Heckler*, 719 F.2d 1191 (2nd Cir., 1983): *Planned Parenthood Federation of America, Inc.* v. *Schweiker*, 559 F. Supp. 658 (D.D.C., 1983), *aff'd*, *Planned Parenthood Federation of America, Inc.* v. *Heckler*, 712 F.2d 650 (D.C. Cir., 1983). The decisions of the Courts of Appeal were not appealed further. Consequently, the parental notification regulations never went into effect.
In order to remove the parental notification regulations from Part 59 of 42 Code of Federal Regulations, it is necessary to issue a rule removing them. Accordingly, the rule below removes 42 CFR 59.5(a)(12). Furthermore, the revocation of the last sentence of the definition of "low income family" in 42 CFR 59.2 effected by the January 26, 1983 amendment was likewise ineffective, for the reasons set out above. Thus, the rule below restores the definition of that term, as it will appear in the Code of Federal Regulations, to the one in effect prior to January 26, 1983:
PART 59—[AMENDED]
Accordingly, 42 CFR Part 59 Subpart A is hereby amended as set forth below.***

§59.5 [Amended]
    2. 42 CFR 59.5(a)(12) is removed.
§59.2 [Amended]
    3. The definition of "low income family" at 42 CFR 59.2 is amended by adding at the end thereof the following words: "For example, unemancipated minors who wish to receive services on a confidential basis must be considered on the basis of their own resources."

ABORTION COUNSELING STATUTES AND REGULATIONS

Section 300a-6 of the same statute provides: "None of the funds appropriated under this subchapter shall be used in programs where abortion is a method of family planning" (42 U.S.C. 300a-6). In 1988, the administration published a set of regulations interpreting "method of family planning" as used in this statute to include prohibiting abortion counseling and referrals for abortion services in family planning agencies and prohibiting activities that encourage, promote, or advocate abortion, with the penalty for violating these regulations a loss of funding.[11] (See 42 C.F.R. §§59.7, 59.8., 59.10.) In *Rust v. Sullivan*, 500 U.S.___ , 114 L. Ed.2d 233 (1991), a five–four decision, the Supreme Court upheld these regulations. The dissenting judges argued that the regulations exceeded the statutory authority and imposed restrictions on free speech.

The abortion counseling regulations had a complex subsequent history. Although they were upheld by the Supreme Court, in response to protests from the medical establishment they were amended to avoid imposing limits on patient-physician consultation. Following this, in a challenge to the amending process, they were enjoined from becoming effective. Before this could be rectified, the Bush administration lost the presidential election and no further steps were taken. As one of his first actions upon taking office, President Clinton issued an executive order rescinding the regulations.

FINDING LEGAL MATERIALS

Many of the statutes, court decisions, and regulations cited in this text are available in law school libraries, state and county law libraries, and to a lesser extent in public, college, or university libraries. Most federal statutes, case decisions, and regulations are published and are available in many of these locations. State statutes, state supreme court decisions, and—depending on the state—some appellate and trial court decisions and some regulations are published.

The combination of one federal and fifty state constitutions, statutory laws, court decisions, and administrative regulations—all of them constantly updated, amended and expanded—results in an overwhelming and complex collection of primary legal materials.

One fairly simple way for the health and human services professional to begin to manage this material is through the use of *legal citations*. A citation will quickly indicate to the professional whether the material is part of a state or the federal legal system; whether the material is statutory, a court decision, or administrative regulation; and—if it is a court decision—what level court decided the case. Every published case, statute, and regulation should be accompanied by a citation that provides this information. Following is a brief overview of legal citations:[12]

Federal Statutes

Federal statutes may have several citations, one referring to *Session Laws*, chronological compilations of laws enacted by each session of Congress and another to the *United States Code* (or its annotated form, the *U.S. Code Annotated*), which is a compilation of all federal statutory law organized by subject matter (annotated indicating the inclusion of references to pertinent case decisions and other material). Session law citations contain both a public law number, for example *Pub. L. No.* 96-142, and a reference to the *Statutes at Large*, where the laws are published chronologically—for example 96 Stat. 1400. Laws published in the U.S. Code are organized topically into titles: broad subjects such as education or public health. Citations of the U.S. Code include the title number, the abbreviation for the U.S. Code (U.S.C., or U.S.C.A. if the annotated version is used), and the specific section where the material is located: 42 U.S.C. §1983 refers to section 1983 of Title 42 of the U.S. Code. In this text, the U.S.C. citations will usually be used. In addition statutes are often given popular names, which may or may not follow their official designations. For example, the Americans with Disabilities Act is cited as Pub. L. No. 101-336, 104 Stat. 328, and also as 42 U.S.C. §12101 *et seq.*, where the abbreviation for *et sequentia*, "and the following," indicates there are multiple sections of the statute. Recently enacted statutes may be found in paperbound supplements to the U.S. Code, sometimes known as "pocket parts" and included at the end of a particular volume. *Always* look at the supplements to find recent changes and new law.

State Statutes

State statutes can be organized chronologically into session laws or codified by subject matter. Each state is different, and the health and human services professional should become familiar with relevant state patterns. Recent state statutes also may be found in "pocket parts," located at the end of the codified statute volume, or in a loose-leaf form. Again, to keep current, *these must be consulted.*

Federal Court Decisions

Citations to court decisions include the case name, followed by the volume number of the series of legal reports where the decision is printed, the name of the series, the page where the case is found, and often the date when the case was decided. This is an easy way to tell which level of court decided the case, since most reports include only one court level. For example the citation in *Gideon*, 372 U.S. 335 (1963), tells us that the case appears in volume 372 of the *U.S. Reports* beginning at page 335. Since only U.S. Supreme Court cases are printed in the *U.S. Reports*, *Gideon* is a U.S. Supreme Court decision.

U.S. Supreme Court decisions are compiled in three collections of reports, one official and two unofficial, and may have as many as three citations. The *U.S. Reports* is the official version and is abbreviated U.S. The other two are the *Supreme Court Reporter*, abbreviated S.Ct., and the *Supreme Court Reports, Lawyers Edition*, abbreviated L.Ed. (or L.Ed.2d. for the second series). Of the three, the official citation is preferred. The multiple citations are called parallel citations. An example of a complete U. S. Supreme Court citation is *Roe v. Wade*, 410 U.S. 113, 93 S.Ct. 705, 35 L.Ed.2d 147 (1973). Another source of U.S. Supreme Court decisions is the *U.S. Law Weekly*, (abbreviated U.S.L.W.), which prints recent Supreme Court cases and some lower court cases in a weekly updated loose-leaf format.

The official citation will be used when available. However, the official *U. S. Reports* version is the last to be published and the *Lawyers Edition* is the first, so the reader will occasionally find a citation with partial information such as *Rust v. Sullivan*, 500 U.S.___ , 111 S.Ct.___ , 114 L.Ed.2d 233 (1991), indicating the case has not yet been published in all three reports.

U.S. Court of Appeals decisions are published in the *Federal Reporter*, abbreviated simply F. An example of a court of appeals citation is *Rennie v. Klein*, 653 F.2d 836 (1981), indicating that the case appears in volume 653 of the *Federal Reporter* (where 2d refers to the second series of the *Reporter*), beginning at page 836. A *Federal Reporter* citation indicates that the case is being decided in the U.S. Court of Appeals, the intermediate court in the federal system.

U.S. district court case decisions are published in the *Federal Supplement*, abbreviated F.Supp. An example of a Federal District Court citation is *Halderman v. Pennhurst State School* 446 F.Supp 1295 (1977), with F.Supp. indicating a federal trial court level.

State Court Decisions

A similar pattern exists for cases decided within the state courts. The case name is followed by a volume number, the name of the state reporter, the page number, and the date of the decision. Cases decided by the state's highest court often will have the initials of that state as the name of the reports, such as *Tarasoff v. Regents of University of California*, 17 Cal.3d 425 (1976). Some state appellate decisions and occasional state trial court decisions are published, usually with their own unique citations.

Many state supreme and appellate court cases are also compiled in the *National Reporter System*, an unofficial collection of cases organized into *Regional Reporters*. Each *Regional Reporter* includes state court cases from a somewhat arbitrarily designated geographic region. For example, state court cases from southeastern states appear in the *Southeast Reporter*, state court cases from the West will appear in the *Pacific Reporter*, and so forth. The same pattern for citation is followed: *Smith v. Smith*, 123 S.E.2d 456 (1955), *Jones v. Jones*, 321 P.2d. 654 (1992). *Regional Reporters* include Atlantic (A.), Southeast (S.E.), Northeast (N.E.), Northwest (N.W.), Southwest (S.W.), and Pacific (P.), as well as separate compilations for New York (N.Y.S.) and California (Cal.Rptr.) decisions. Some states do not publish their own reports and designate the regional reporter as their official source.[13]

Federal Regulations

Federal regulations first appear as proposed regulations in the *Federal Register*, abbreviated Fed. Reg. Once the regulations have been adopted, they are printed in final form in the *Federal Register* and are organized by subject matter in the *Code of Federal Regulations*, abbreviated C.F.R. A reference to a federal regulation would be 42 C.F.R. §2001(d).

State Regulations

States vary in the manner in which state regulatory law is compiled and published, but published regulations will have a similar pattern of citation.

Secondary Legal Materials

Federal and state statutes, case decisions, and regulations are called primary legal sources, that is, they are the law. For those trying to understand the law better or conduct legal research there are a wide range of secondary legal sources and commentaries available. Among these are legal periodicals, loose-leaf services, legal treatises, legal encyclopedias, restatements, and commentaries.

Law reviews, or legal periodicals published by law schools and other organizations, contain numerous articles and notes on current legal topics. Often the articles include detailed footnotes and cross references to additional cases, statutes, regulations, or secondary sources, making them a very useful research source. Although sometimes quite technical, the topics are often relevant to the health and human services. The law reviews will be found in law school libraries and in other libraries with legal materials. The law journal articles are indexed in the *Index of Legal Periodicals, The Current Law Index,* and the *Legal Resource Index.*

Loose-leaf services are usually topical compilations of legal materials, such as the *Family Law Reporter.*

Legal treatises, restatements, and commentaries cover a wide range of topics and may be highly technical, but also very comprehensive and detailed. Some, known as "hornbooks," often present a lucid summary of the law in a specific area.

Legal encyclopedias include *American Law Reports* (A.L.R.), now in its fifth series, *Corpus Juris Secundum,* and *American Jurisprudence,* both in their second series. The A.L.R. presents detailed summaries about points of law or discusses important cases in both federal and state systems.

Digests are topical compilations of cases that contain brief summaries or excerpts from cases, and may be indexed for one particular court or region or more broadly, for all published case decisions.

Two major computerized systems for retrieving legal materials are *Lexus* and *WestLaw.* These may be available to the health and human services professional and with some practice can be very useful. Both operate on the principle of searching by key words or fields. Each has its own particular advantages and limitations.

SELECTED REFERENCES

James, F., and Hazard, G. *Civil Procedure* (1985).

Llewellyn, K.N., *The Common Law Tradition* (1970).

Lewis, A., *Gideon's Trumpet* (1966).

Statsky, W.P., and Wernet, R. J. *Case Analysis and Fundamentals of Legal Writing* (1989).

CHAPTER 3

CONSTITUTIONAL LAW, DUE PROCESS, AND EQUAL PROTECTION

The federal government and all states have constitutions which establish governmental structure and specify basic rights of their citizens. Here we will deal only with the Federal Constitution, and because of its impact on the health and human services primarily with the Fourteenth Amendment.[1]

THE UNITED STATES CONSTITUTION

The United States Constitution establishes the three branches of government: legislative, executive, and judiciary, and enumerates the powers of each. As we saw in the last chapter, each branch of government provides a source of law. The U.S. Constitution overarches these and provides the framework in which they operate.

Article I establishes Congress, the legislative branch of government. Rules for election to the House and Senate, qualifications of their members, and the powers of Congress are enumerated. Some limitations on state and federal government are set forth in sections 9 and 10.

Article II vests executive power in the President, and prescribes term of office, election procedures, qualifications of the individual, and enumerates the powers and some limitations of that office.

Article III establishes the judicial branch including a Supreme Court and "such inferior courts as Congress may from time to time ordain and establish." (Note that the Constitution only mandates a Supreme Court, the remaining federal courts are created by Congress.) Section 2 presents in broad terms the range of federal jurisdiction, which is further elaborated by statute.

Article IV discusses the privileges and immunities of citizens and provides that full faith and credit of the legal proceedings in any state be given in all other states.

Article V details the process for amending the Constitution.

Article VI contains the Supremacy Clause which makes the Constitution and the laws of the United States the "supreme law of the land," and provides that "the judges in every State shall be bound thereby."

Article VII sets forth procedures for ratification.

Constitutional Amendments

The Constitution was signed in 1787. In 1789, a Bill of Rights specifying rights of individuals and limitations to the power of the federal government was proposed as a series of Constitutional amendments. The first ten amendments to the Constitution were ratified in 1791. Over the next two centuries, a number of amendments have been proposed but as of 1994, only sixteen have been ratified.

The Bill of Rights

The ten amendments to the Constitution that constitute the Bill of Rights are:

Amendment I—free exercise of religion; freedom of speech, the press, and assembly

Amendment II—the right to bear arms

Amendment III—forbidding in peacetime the quartering of soldiers in private homes without consent

Amendment IV—protection against unreasonable searches and seizures, and the requirements for search warrants

Amendment V—requirement of a grand jury indictment for major crimes, protection against double jeopardy, protection against self-incrimination, provision of due process, and the protection of property

Amendment VI—the right to a speedy and public trial in criminal cases, as well as the right to an impartial jury, the right to know of what one is accused, to confront witnesses against oneself, and to the assistance of counsel

Amendment VII—the right to a jury trial in common law cases

Amendment VIII—prohibition against excessive bail and cruel and unusual punishment

Amendment IX—retention of rights not enumerated in the Constitution to the people

Amendment X—retention by the states or the people of those powers not specifically delegated to the United States or prohibited by the Constitution from the states

Debate continues whether the original intent of those who drew up and ratified the Bill of Rights was to apply these rights to the states as well as the federal government. With the passage of the Fourteenth Amendment, which among other provisions prohibits the states from depriving any person of due process of law, there has been a gradual acceptance by the Supreme Court that most if not all of the provisions enumerated in the Bill of Rights should be applied to state governments through the Due Process Clause. As we have seen this was one of the issues raised in both the *Betts* and *Gideon* decisions—whether the Due Process Clause of the Fourteenth Amendment applied the Sixth Amendment right to counsel in criminal proceedings to state courts.

Subsequent Amendments

As of 1994, the Constitution has been amended a total of twenty-six times including the Bill of Rights. The most recent amendment, extending the vote to eighteen-year-olds, was ratified in 1971. Perhaps the best known recently proposed amendment which has not been ratified to date is the Equal Rights Amendment, which would provide that "equality of rights under the law shall not be denied or abridged by the United States or by any state on account of sex."

THE FOURTEENTH AMENDMENT—DUE PROCESS AND EQUAL PROTECTION

One of the three post–Civil War amendments,[2] the Fourteenth Amendment during the twentieth century has become a major vehicle for social change. The ramifications of this amendment—and in particular its Due Process and Equal Protection clauses—for the health and human services are very significant. In part, the Fourteenth Amendment provides:

No State shall make or enforce any law which shall abridge the privileges or immunities of citizens of the United States; nor shall any State
deprive any person of life, liberty, or property without due process of
law; nor deny to any person within its jurisdiction the equal protection
of the laws.

While the protection of a citizen's "privileges or immunities" could have
been the primary vehicle for protecting individual rights, courts instead have
relied most heavily on the concepts of due process and equal protection. The
following sections will examine those concepts: first the requirement that
there be some action by the state before constitutional due process or equal
protection applies, then procedural due process—those procedures necessary to a fundamentally fair resolution of disputes—and finally substantive
due process—certain basic rights that are protected by the Constitution. The
chapter will conclude with an analysis of the constitutional concept of equal
protection.

State Action

A key threshold element of the Fourteenth Amendment is that it only applies
where there has been some action by the state. Here, the concept of state action has been extended to include not only actions by state governments, but
by any government—state, county or local. However, if the action in question is not related to the state broadly defined, then the protections found in
the Fourteenth Amendment are usually not available.
    Yet the lines are not always clear: Actions by the State of California, Los
Angeles County, or the City of San Francisco would be covered by the Fourteenth Amendment. A private citizen in California acting in a private capacity normally would not. Actions by a state-funded and state-operated shelter
for homeless children would be covered by the Fourteenth Amendment; actions by a privately funded shelter would not. Less clear is whether actions
by a privately run program that accepts a substantial proportion of its clients
paid for by public agencies would be covered.[3]
    Two Supreme Court cases identify some of the boundaries of state action.
In *Burton v. Wilmington Parking Authority*, 365 U.S. 715 (1961), the court held
that a privately run restaurant which operated in a city-owned and -operated
parking structure could not under the Equal Protection Clause refuse to
serve minorities. The Supreme Court said:

Addition of all these activities, obligations and responsibilities of the
Authority, the benefits mutually conferred, together with the obvious
fact that the restaurant is operated as an integral part of a public build-

ing devoted to a public parking service, indicates that degree of state participation and involvement in discriminatory action which it was the design of the Fourteenth Amendment to condemn. 365 U.S. at 724.

On the other hand, in *Jackson v. Metropolitan Edison Co.*, 419 U.S. 345 (1974), the Court held that an electric utility which was privately owned but subjected to extensive state regulation did not meet the test of state participation and did not have to provide due process protections—notice and a hearing—prior to disconnecting customers.

Procedural Due Process

As we have seen, one division of law is between procedural and substantive law. The same is true of the concept of due process. Procedural due process deals with the procedural rights and protections that must be provided prior to any deprivation of "life, liberty, or property" by the state. As we saw in *Gideon* and *Betts*, the concept of due process is "less rigid and more fluid" than other parts of the Bill of Rights but is "implicit in the concept of ordered liberty," and "fundamental and essential to a fair trial."

Once state action has been established, there must be some deprivation to trigger due process, and more specifically a deprivation of "life, liberty, or property." First, the deprivation must be real and not insignificant or "*de minimus.*" Then, the deprivation must fall within the protected categories of life, liberty, and property. Here the professional should be aware that these categories have been expanded over time and now take on complex legal meanings. A deprivation of "life" certainly means the actual taking of a life by the state, as in capital punishment. See *Furman v. Georgia*, 408 U.S. 238 (1972). But life has been extended to include welfare benefits (see *Goldberg v. Kelley*, p. 51), and it could be argued that the taking of one's children is also a deprivation of part of one's life (*Lassiter*, p. 28). Deprivation of "liberty" and "property" are sometimes viewed as separate and sometimes overlapping categories by the courts. Property extends beyond real property and liberty extends beyond confinement by the state. Among those interests protected under liberty or property are a high school education (*Goss v. Lopez*, p. 54), one's children (*Lassiter*, above), the accumulation of "good time" reducing one's time in a correctional institution (*Wolff v. McDonnell*, 418 U.S. 539 [1974]), welfare benefits (*Goldberg v. Kelley*, above), and one's reputation (*Wisconsin v. Constantineau*, 400 U.S. 433, [1971]).[4]

Models of Procedural Due Process

Due process is a changing, evolving concept, depending on societal notions of "fundamental fairness," and the interests at stake. As *Gideon* and *Lassiter* illustrate, due process protections are greater in criminal trials, with a potential loss of liberty, than in civil proceedings where loss of liberty, at least in an adult correctional institution, is not a possible outcome. The amount of due process—the extent of procedural protection—also varies in civil cases with the court's perception of the severity of loss faced by the individual and, in some cases, the possibility for an erroneous deprivation.

The question remains: How much due process is required? Following are two models of procedural due process, the fair hearing and the rudimentary due process required for high school suspensions.

WELFARE FAIR HEARINGS

GOLDBERG v. KELLEY
397 U.S. 254 (1970)
U.S. SUPREME COURT

Mr. Justice Brennan delivered the opinion of the Court.

The question for decision is whether a State that terminates public assistance payments to a particular recipient without affording him the opportunity for an evidentiary hearing prior to termination denies the recipient procedural due process in violation of the Due Process Clause of the Fourteenth Amendment.

This action was brought in the District Court for the Southern District of New York by residents of New York City receiving financial aid under the federally assisted program of Aid to Families with Dependent Children (AFDC) or under New York State's general Home Relief program. Their complaint alleged that the New York State and New York City officials administering these programs terminated, or were about to terminate, such aid without prior notice and hearing, thereby denying them due process of law. At the time the suits were filed there was no requirement of prior notice or hearing of any kind before termination of financial aid. However, the State and city adopted procedures for notice and hearing after the suits were brought, and the plaintiffs, appellees here, then challenged the constitutional adequacy of those procedures.***

The constitutional issue to be decided, therefore, is the narrow one whether the Due Process Clause requires that the recipient be afforded an evidentiary hearing *before* the termination of benefits. The District Court held that only a pretermination evidentiary hearing would satisfy the constitutional command, and rejected the argument of the state and city officials that the combination of the post-termination "fair hearing" with the informal pre-termination review disposed of all due process claims.***We affirm.

Appellant does not contend that procedural due process is not applicable to the termination of welfare benefits. Such benefits are a matter of statutory entitlement for persons qualified to receive them. Their termination involves state action that adjudicates important rights. The constitutional challenge cannot be answered by an argument that public assistance benefits are "a 'privilege' and not a 'right.'"*** The extent to which procedural due process must be afforded the recipient is influenced by the extent to which he may be "condemned to suffer grievous loss," and depends upon whether the recipient's interest in avoiding that loss outweighs the governmental interest in summary adjudication. Accordingly, as we said in *Cafeteria & Restaurant Workers Union v. McElroy*, 367 U.S. 886, 895 (1961), "consideration of what procedures due process may require under any given set of circumstances must begin with a determination of the precise nature of the government function involved as well as of the private interest that has been affected by governmental action."

But we agree with the District Court that when welfare is discontinued, only a pre-termination evidentiary hearing provides the recipient with procedural due process. For qualified recipients, welfare provides the means to obtain essential food, clothing, housing, and medical care. Thus the crucial factor in this context is that termination of aid pending resolution of a controversy over eligibility may deprive an *eligible* recipient of the very means by which to live while he waits. Since he lacks independent resources, his situation becomes immediately desperate. His need to concentrate upon finding the means for daily subsistence, in turn, adversely affects his ability to seek redress from the welfare bureaucracy.

We also agree with the District Court, however, that the pre-termination hearing need not take the form of a judicial or quasi-judicial trial. *** [T]he statutory "fair hearing" will provide *** a full administrative review. *** [A] complete record and a comprehensive opinion, which would serve primarily to facilitate judicial review and to guide future decisions, need not be provided at the pre-termination stage. We recognize, too, that both welfare authorities and recipients have an interest in relatively speedy resolution of questions of eligibility, that they are used to dealing with one another informally, and that some welfare departments have very burdensome caseloads. These considerations justify the limitation of the pre-termination hearing to minimum procedural safeguards, adapted to the particular characteristics of welfare recipients, and to the limited nature of the controversies to be resolved.***

"The fundamental requisite of due process of law is the opportunity to be heard." The hearing must be "at a meaningful time and in a meaningful manner." In the present context these principles require that a recipient have timely and adequate notice detailing the reasons for a proposed termination, and an effective opportunity to defend by confronting any adverse witnesses and by presenting his own arguments and evidence orally.***

We are not prepared to say that the seven-day notice currently provided by New York City is constitutionally insufficient *per se*, although there may be cases where fairness would require that a longer time be given. Nor do we see any constitutional deficiency in the content or form of the notice. New York employs both a letter and a personal conference with a caseworker to inform a recipient of the precise questions raised about his continued eligibility. Evidently the recipient is told the legal and factual bases for the Department's doubts. This combination is probably the most effective method of communicating with recipients.

The city's procedures presently do not permit recipients to appear personally with or without counsel before the official who finally determines continued eligibility. Thus a recipient is not permitted to present evidence to that official orally, or to confront or cross-examine adverse witnesses. These omissions are fatal to the constitutional adequacy of the procedures.

The opportunity to be heard must be tailored to the capacities and circumstances of those who are to be heard. It is not enough that a welfare recipient may present his position to the decision maker in writing or secondhand through his caseworker. Written submissions are an unrealistic option for most recipients, who lack the educational attainment necessary to write effectively and who cannot obtain professional assistance. Moreover, written submissions do not afford the flexibility of oral presentations; they do not permit the recipient to mold his argument to the issues the decision maker appears to regard as important. Particularly where credibility and veracity are at issue, as they must be in many termination proceedings, written submissions are a wholly unsatisfactory basis for decision. The secondhand presentation to the decision maker by the caseworker has its own deficiencies; since the caseworker usually gathers the facts upon which the charge of ineligibility rests, the presentation of the recipient's side of the controversy cannot safely be left to him. Therefore a recipient must be allowed to state his position orally. Informal procedures will suffice; in this context due process does not require a particular order of proof or mode of offering evidence.

In almost every setting where important decisions turn on questions of fact, due process requires an opportunity to confront and cross-examine adverse witnesses.*** Welfare recipients must therefore be given an opportunity to confront and cross-examine the witnesses relied on by the department.

"The right to be heard would be, in many cases, of little avail if it did not comprehend the right to be heard by counsel." We do not say that counsel must be provided at the pre-termination hearing, but only that the recipient must be allowed to retain an attorney if he so desires. Counsel can help delineate the issues, present the factual contentions in an orderly manner, conduct cross-examination, and generally safeguard the interests of the recipient. We do not anticipate that this assistance will unduly prolong or otherwise encumber the hearing.

Finally, the decisionmaker's conclusion as to a recipient's eligibility must rest solely on the legal rules and evidence adduced at the hearing. To demonstrate compliance with this elementary requirement, the decision maker should state the reasons for his determination and indicate the evidence he relied on, though his statement need not amount to a full opinion or even formal findings of fact and conclusions of law. And, of course, an impartial decision maker is essential. We agree with the District Court that prior involvement in some aspects of a case will not necessarily bar a welfare official from acting as a decision maker. He should not, however, have participated in making the determination under review. *Affirmed.*

Notes and Issues for Discussion

1. What is the state action in *Goldberg*? What is the deprivation? What does the Court say is the constitutional issue in the case?
2. What does the Court see wrong with relying on a post-termination hearing? With forbidding personal appearances and relying only on the recipient's written statements or a presentation by the caseworker?
3. How does the *Goldberg* court decide how much process is due—that is, how much procedural protection should be provided to welfare recipients?
4. *Goldberg* establishes the elements of a *fair hearing*, a relatively informal, speedy mechanism for resolving disputes. Among the elements identified by the Court are (1) adequate and timely notice; (2) an opportunity to be heard in person; (3) informal procedures; (4) an opportunity to confront and cross-examine adverse witnesses; (5) representation by counsel if desired, but no mandate that the state supply counsel; (6) an impartial decision maker, who need not be a judge and could be an official not involved in the original dispute; and (7) a decision based solely on legal rules and evidence presented at the hearing and which includes the reasons and the evidence relied upon.

    This basic model is used widely in the health and human services, including hearings for denials of food stamps, Supplemental Social Insurance benefits, and Social Security Disability Insurance, eviction from public housing, revocation of parole or probation, and prison disciplinary hearings among others.
5. An important point is that fair hearings are not automatic but place the burden on the claimant to request the hearing and follow through. What are the consequences of this? Why might a recipient with a valid claim *not* request a hearing?

HIGH SCHOOL SUSPENSIONS

GOSS v. LOPEZ
419 U.S. 565 (1975)
U.S. SUPREME COURT

Mr. Justice White delivered the opinion of the Court.

This appeal by various administrators of the Columbus, Ohio, Public School System (CPSS) challenges the judgment of a three-judge federal court, declaring that appelles—various high school students in the CPSS—were denied the due process of law contrary to the command of the Fourteenth Amendment in that they were temporarily suspended from their high schools without a hearing either prior to suspension or within a reasonable time thereafter, and enjoining the administrators to remove all references to such suspensions from the students' records.

Ohio law, Rev. Code Ann. §3313.64 (1972), provides for free education to all children between the ages of six and 21. Section 3313.66 of the Code empowers the principal of an Ohio public school to suspend a pupil for misconduct for up to 10 days or to expel him. In either case, he must notify the student's parents within 24 hours and state the reasons for his action. A pupil who is expelled, or his parents, may appeal the decision to the Board of Education and in connection therewith shall be permitted to be heard at the board meeting. The Board may reinstate the pupil following the hearing. No similar procedure is provided in §3313.66 or any other provision of state law for a suspended student. Aside from a regulation tracking the statute, at the time of the imposition of the suspensions in this case the CPSS itself had not issued any written procedure applicable to suspensions. Nor, so far as the record reflects, had any of the individual high schools involved in this case.[1] Each, however, had formally or informally described the conduct for which suspension could be imposed.

The nine named appellees, each of whom alleged that he or she had been suspended from public high school in Columbus for up to 10 days without a hearing pursuant to §3313.66, filed an action under 42 U.S.C. §1983 against the Columbus Board of Education and various administrators of the CPSS. The complaint sought a declaration that §3313.66 was unconstitutional in that it permitted public school administrators to deprive plaintiffs of their rights to an education without a hearing of any kind, in violation of the procedural due process component of the Fourteenth Amendment. It also sought to enjoin the public school officials from issuing future suspensions pursuant to §3313.66 and to require them to remove references to the past suspensions from the records of the students in question.

The proof below established that the suspensions arose out of a period of widespread student unrest in the CPSS during February and March 1971. Six of the named plaintiffs, Rudolph Sutton, Tyrone Washington, Susan Cooper, Deborah Fox, Clarence Byars, and Bruce Harris, were students at the Marion-Franklin High School and were each suspended for 10 days on account of disruptive or disobedient conduct committed in the presence of the school administrator who ordered the suspension. One of these, Tyrone Washington, was among a group of students demonstrating in the school auditorium while a class was being conducted there. He was ordered by the school principal to leave, refused to do so, and was suspended. Rudolph Sutton, in the presence of the principal, physi-

---

[1] According to the testimony of Phillip Fulton, the principal of one of the high schools involved in this case, there was an informal procedure applicable at the Marion-Franklin High School. It provided that in the routine case of misconduct, occurring in the presence of a teacher, the teacher would describe the misconduct on a form provided for that purpose and would send the student, with the form, to the principal's office. There, the principal would obtain the student's version of the story, and, if it conflicted with the teacher's written version, would send for the teacher to obtain the teacher's oral version—apparently in the presence of the student. Mr. Fulton testified that, if a discrepancy still existed, the teacher's version would be believed and the principal would arrive at a disciplinary decision based on it.

cally attacked a police officer who was attempting to remove Tyrone Washington from the auditorium. He was immediately suspended. The other four Marion-Franklin students were suspended for similar conduct. None was given a hearing to determine the operative facts underlying the suspension, but each, together with his or her parents, was offered the opportunity to attend a conference, subsequent to the effective date of the suspension, to discuss the student's future.

Two named plaintiffs, Dwight Lopez and Betty Crome, were students at the Central High School and McGuffey Junior High School, respectively. The former was suspended in connection with a disturbance in the lunchroom which involved some physical damage to school property. Lopez testified that at least 75 other students were suspended from his school on the same day. He also testified below that he was not a party to the destructive conduct but was instead an innocent bystander. Because no one from the school testified with regard to this incident, there is no evidence in the record indicating the official basis for concluding otherwise. Lopez never had a hearing.

Betty Crome was present at a demonstration at a high school other than the one she was attending. There she was arrested together with others, taken to the police station, and released without being formally charged. Before she went to school on the following day, she was notified that she had been suspended for a 10-day period. Because no one from the school testified with respect to this incident, the record does not disclose how the McGuffey Junior High School principal went about making the decision to suspend Crome, nor does it disclose on what information the decision was based. It is clear from the record that no hearing was ever held.

On the basis of this evidence, the three-judge court declared that plaintiffs were denied due process of law because they were "suspended without hearing prior to suspension or within a reasonable time thereafter," and that Ohio Rev. Code Ann. §3313.66 (1972) and regulations issued pursuant thereto were unconstitutional in permitting such suspensions. It was ordered that all references to plaintiffs' suspensions be removed from school files.***

The defendant school administrators have appealed the three-judge court's decision.***We affirm.***

The Due Process Clause also forbids arbitrary deprivation of liberty. "Where a person's good name, reputation, honor, or integrity is at stake because of what the government is doing to him," the minimal requirements of the Clause must be satisfied. School authorities here suspended appellees from school for periods of up to 10 days based on charges of misconduct. If sustained and recorded, those charges could seriously damage the students' standing with their fellow pupils and their teachers as well as interfere with later opportunities for higher education and employment. It is apparent that the claimed right of the State to determine unilaterally and without process whether that misconduct has occurred immediately collides with the requirements of the Constitution.

Appellants proceed to argue that even if there is a right to a public education protected by the Due Process Clause generally, the Clause comes into play only when the State subjects a student to a "severe detriment or grievous loss." The loss of 10 days, it is said, is neither severe nor grievous and the Due Process Clause is therefore of no relevance. Appellants' argument is again refuted by our prior decisions; for in determining "whether due process requirements apply in the first place, we must look not to the 'weight' but to the *nature* of the interest at stake." Appellees were excluded from school only temporarily, it is true, but the length and consequent severity of a deprivation, while another factor to weigh in determining the appropriate form of hearing, "is not decisive of the basic right" to a hearing of some kind.***A 10-day suspension from school is not *de minimis* in our view and may not be imposed in complete disregard of the Due Process Clause.

A short suspension is, of course, a far milder deprivation than expulsion. But, "education is perhaps the most important function of state and local governments" and the total exclusion from the educational process for more than a trivial period, and certainly if the suspension is for 10 days, is a serious event in the life of the suspended child. Neither the property interest in educational benefits temporarily denied nor the liberty interest in reputation, which is also implicated, is so insubstantial that suspensions may constitutionally be imposed by any procedure the school chooses, no matter how arbitrary.

"Once it is determined that due process applies, the question remains what process is due." We turn to that question, fully realizing as our cases regularly do that the interpretation and application of the Due Process Clause are intensely practical matters and that "[t]he very nature of due process negates any concept of inflexible procedures universally applicable to every imaginable situation." ***"The fundamental requisite of due process of law is the opportunity to be head," a right that "has little reality or worth unless one is informed that the matter is pending and can choose for himself whether to . . . contest." At the very minimum, therefore, students facing suspension and the consequent interference with a protected property interest must be given *some* kind of notice and afforded *some* kind of hearing.***

It also appears from our cases that the timing and content of the notice and the nature of the hearing will depend on appropriate accommodation of the competing interests involved. The student's interest is to avoid unfair or mistaken exclusion from the educational process, with all of its unfortunate consequences. The Due Process Clause will not shield him from suspensions properly imposed, but it disserves both his interest and the interest of the State if his suspension is in fact unwarranted. The concern would be mostly academic if the disciplinary process were a totally accurate, unerring process, never mistaken and never unfair. Unfortunately, that is not the case, and no one suggests that it is. Disciplinarians, although proceeding in utmost good faith, frequently act on the reports and advice of others; and the controlling facts and the nature of the conduct under challenge are often disputed. The risk of error is not at all trivial, and it should be guarded against if that may be done without prohibitive cost or interference with the educational process.

The difficulty is that our schools are vast and complex. Some modicum of discipline and order is essential if the educational function is to be performed. Events calling for discipline are frequent occurrences and sometimes require immediate, effective action. Suspension is considered not only to be a necessary tool to maintain order but a valuable educational device. The prospect of imposing elaborate hearing requirements in every suspension case is viewed with great concern, and many school authorities may well prefer the untrammeled power to act unilaterally, unhampered by rules about notice and hearing. But it would be a strange disciplinary system in an educational institution if no communication was sought by the disciplinarian with the student in an effort to inform him of his dereliction and to let him tell his side of the story in order to make sure that an injustice is not done.***

We do not believe that school authorities must be totally free from notice and hearing requirements if their schools are to operate with acceptable efficiency. Students facing temporary suspension have interests qualifying for protection of the Due Process Clause, and due process requires, in connection with a suspension of 10 days or less, that the student be given oral or written notice of the charges against him and, if he denies them, an explanation of the evidence the authorities have and an opportunity to present his side of the story. The Clause requires at least these rudimentary precautions against unfair or mistaken findings of misconduct and arbitrary exclusion from school.

There need be no delay between the time "notice" is given and the time of the hearing. In the great majority of cases the disciplinarian may informally discuss the alleged misconduct with the student minutes after it has occurred. We hold only that, in being given an opportunity to explain his version of the facts at this discussion, the student first be told what he is accused of doing and what the basis of the accusation is.***Since the hearing may occur almost immediately following the misconduct, it follows that as a general rule notice and hearing should precede removal of the student from school. We agree with the District Court, however, that there are recurring situations in which prior notice and hearing cannot be insisted upon. Students whose presence poses a continuing danger to persons or property or an ongoing threat of disrupting the academic process may be immediately removed from school. In such cases, the necessary notice and rudimentary hearing should follow as soon as practicable, as the District Court indicated.***

The District Court found each of the suspensions involved here to have occurred without a hearing, either before or after the suspension, and that each suspension was therefore invalid and the statute unconstitutional insofar as it permits such suspensions without notice or hearing. Accordingly, the judgment is *Affirmed.*

Notes and Issues for Discussion

1. What is the state action in *Goss*? What is the deprivation—is it a deprivation of life, of liberty, or of property?
2. Consider the procedures used for student misconduct in the Marion-Franklin High School described in footnote 1. Is there a hearing? Is it fair?
3. "At the very minimum, therefore, students facing suspension and the consequent interference with a protected property interest must be given *some* kind of notice and afforded *some* kind of hearing." What kind of notice?

What kind of hearing?

4. For suspensions of up to ten days, do students have less due process than that afforded to welfare recipients in fair hearings? Why?

5. The Court does not make clear who will give notice, explain charges, hear the student, and decide whether to impose suspension. A "disciplinarian" is mentioned. Who might this be?

6. Consider again the procedures in use at Marion-Franklin (footnote 1). How different are these from those required by the Court in *Goss*?

Substantive Due Process

Substantive due process applies concepts of fairness and reasonableness to the content of the law.[5] Once discredited due to its use by a conservative Supreme Court to void federal and state legislation promoting progressive economic and social reform,[6] the concept has reemerged as an important vehicle for protecting basic rights and liberties of individuals.

Two early formulations give an idea of the range of substantive due process. In *Meyer v. Nebraska*, 262 U.S. 390 (1923), the Court struck down a state statute designed to promote "civic development" by forbidding the teaching of foreign languages to children before completion of eighth grade. Holding that this was a violation of a due process liberty interest, the court said:

While this court has not attempted to define with exactness the liberty thus guaranteed, the term has received much consideration and some of the included things have been definitely stated. Without doubt, it denotes not merely freedom from bodily restraint but also the right of the individual to contract, to engage in any of the common occupations of life, to acquire useful knowledge, to marry, establish a home and bring up children, to worship God according to the dictates of his own conscience, and generally to enjoy those privileges long recognized at common law as essential to the orderly pursuit of happiness by free men. 262 U.S. at 399.[7]

In *Poe v. Ullman*, 367 U.S. 497 (1961), Justice Harlan wrote:

. . . [T]he full scope of the liberty guaranteed by the Due Process Clause cannot be found in or limited by the precise terms of the specific guarantees elsewhere provided in the Constitution. This "liberty" is not a series of isolated points pricked out in terms of the taking of property; the freedom of speech, press and religion; the right to keep and bear arms; the freedom from unreasonable searches and seizures; and so on. It is a rational continuum which, broadly speaking, includes a freedom from all substantial arbitrary impositions and purposeless restraints, . . .

and which also recognizes, what a reasonable and sensitive judgement must, that certain interests require particularly careful scrutiny of the state needs asserted to justify their abridgement. 367 U.S. at 543 (dissenting opinion).

Among the personal interests that have been protected by substantive due process are decisions about marriage, sterilization, contraception, abortion, raising and educating children, family relationships, and some decisions to end life.[8]

THE RIGHT OF PRIVACY

One of the most widely known and controversial areas of substantive due process is the right of privacy. The Constitution does not specifically guarantee a right of privacy, or indeed mention the word, although courts have found this right implicit in various amendments, particularly the Fourteenth Amendment due process concept of liberty. The boundaries of this substantive due process concept still lack a clear definition but a significant body of law has developed.[9] In a frequently quoted dissenting opinion in *Olmstead v. United States*, 277 U.S. 438 (1928), Justice Brandeis described this right:

The makers of our Constitution . . . sought to protect Americans in their beliefs, their thoughts, their emotions, and their sensations. They conferred, as against the government, the right to be let alone—the most comprehensive of rights and the right most valued by civilized men. 277 U.S. at 478.

In striking down a statute making the provision of contraceptive devices or counseling a criminal offense, the Court found the right of privacy inherent in several provisions of the Bill of Rights. (See *Griswold v. Connecticut*, p. 96). In voiding a statute making the performing of or having an abortion a crime, the Court was more clear that the privacy right is implicit in the Fourteenth Amendment protection of liberty. (See *Roe v. Wade*, p. 98.)

EQUAL PROTECTION

Key to understanding equal protection in Constitutional law is that the concept does not in general forbid the state from making classifications and treating individuals in different classes differently, as long as individuals within the same class are treated similarly and the classifications are not invidious.[10] For example those under eighteen may not vote, and in many states those under twenty-one may not purchase alcoholic beverages. Senior citizens over a certain age may receive benefits not available to those below that age. For most classifications, the courts have held that as long as there is a "rational basis" for the economic or social legislation that establishes the classification, it is constitutionally permissible:

> The general rule is that legislation is presumed to be valid and will be sustained if the classification drawn by the statute is rationally related to a legitimate state interest. . . . When social or economic legislation is at issue, the Equal Protection Clause allows the states wide latitude and the Constitution presumes that even improvident decisions will eventually be rectified by the democratic processes. (*Cleburne v. Cleburne Living Center*, 473 U.S. at 440).

Early equal protection cases upheld most state legislation by finding some "rational basis." Later the Supreme Court adopted a "two-tiered" approach and held that some classifications—those "that disadvantage a 'suspect class' or that impinge upon the exercise of a 'fundamental right'" are "presumptively invidious." (*Plyler v. Doe*, 457 U.S. 202 [1982]). Classifications generally found unacceptable include those based on race, alienage, or national origin. The Court said that these classifications are "highly suspect," will be subjected to "strict scrutiny," and will be sustained only if they serve a "compelling state interest."

More recently, the Court has fashioned an "intermediate level" between these two where certain classifications are subjected to a "heightened level of scrutiny." That is, certain legislative classifications are not impermissible on their face, but require greater justification than a rationale basis. Among these are classifications based on gender and illegitimacy.

Thus there are at present three levels used in equal protection analysis, one where classifications are almost always impermissible, another where classifications are permitted as long as there is some rational basis, and between them an intermediate level requiring more justification than a rational basis but which is not automatically impermissible. Most classifications will be constitutionally acceptable under the rational basis standard. A few are highly suspect and usually will be found constitutionally unacceptable, and several more lie between and may be invalidated unless there are very good reasons justifying the classification.[11]

To give a better idea of the meaning and content of these concepts, we will examine the three levels.

Rational Basis Classifications

Most legislative classifications in the areas of economics and social welfare are constitutionally acceptable if there is "some rational relationship to legitimate state purposes." In the following case, however, the court found no rational basis for the zoning classification which excluded housing for mentally retarded citizens.

CLEBURNE v. CLEBURNE LIVING CENTER
473 U.S. 432 (1985)
U.S. SUPREME COURT

JUSTICE WHITE delivered the opinion of the Court.

A Texas city denied a special use permit for the operation of a group home for the mentally retarded, acting pursuant to a municipal zoning ordinance requiring permits for such homes. The Court of Appeals for the Fifth Circuit held that mental retardation is a "quasi-suspect" classification and that the ordinance violated the Equal Protection Clause because it did not substantially further an important governmental purpose. We hold that a lesser standard of scrutiny is appropriate, but conclude that under that standard the ordinance is invalid as applied in this case.

In July 1980, respondent Jan Hannah purchased a building at 201 Featherston Street in the city of Cleburne, Texas, with the intention of leasing it to Cleburne Living Center, Inc. (CLC), for the operation of a group home for the mentally retarded. It was anticipated that the home would house 13 retarded men and women, who would be under the constant supervision of CLC staff members. The house had four bedrooms and two baths, with a half bath to be added. CLC planned to comply with all applicable state and federal regulations.

The city informed CLC that a special use permit would be required for the operation of a group home at the site, and CLC accordingly submitted a permit application. In response to a subsequent inquiry from CLC, the city explained that under the zoning regulations applicable to the site, a special use permit, renewable annually, was required for the construction of "[h]ospitals for the insane or feeble-minded, or alcoholic [sic] or drug addicts, or penal or correctional institutions." The city had determined that the proposed group home should be classified as a "hospital for the feeble-minded." After holding a public hearing on CLC's application, the City Council voted 3 to 1 to deny a special use permit.

CLC then filed suit in Federal District Court against the city and a number of its officials, alleging, *inter alia*, that the zoning ordinance was invalid on its face and as applied because it discriminated against the mentally retarded in violation of the equal protection rights of CLC and its potential residents. The District Court found that "[i]f the potential residents of the Featherston Street home were not mentally retarded, but the home was the same in all other respects, its use would be permitted under the city's zoning ordinance," and that the City Council's decision "was motivated primarily by the fact that the residents of the home would be persons who are mentally retarded." Even so, the District Court held the ordinance and its application constitutional. Concluding that no fundamental right was implicated and that mental retardation was neither a suspect nor a quasi-suspect classification, the court employed the minimum level of judicial scrutiny applicable to equal protection claims. The court deemed the ordinance, as written and applied, to be rationally related to the city's legitimate interests in "the legal responsibility of CLC and its residents, . . . the safety and fears of residents in the adjoining neighborhood," and the number of people to be housed in the home.

The Court of Appeals for the Fifth Circuit reversed, determining that mental retardation was a quasi-suspect classification and that it should assess the validity of the ordinance under intermediate-level scrutiny.***

The Equal Protection Clause of the Fourteenth Amendment commands that no State shall "deny to any person within its jurisdiction the equal protection of the laws," which is essentially a direction that all persons similarly situated should be treated alike.*** The general rule is that legislation is presumed to be valid and will be sustained if the classification drawn by the statute is rationally related to a legitimate state interest. When social or economic legislation is at issue, the Equal Protection Clause allows the States wide latitude, and the Constitution presumes that even improvident decisions will eventually be rectified by the democratic processes.

The general rule gives way, however, when a statute classifies by race, alienage, or national origin. These factors are so seldom relevant to the achievement of any legitimate state interest that laws grounded in such considerations are deemed to reflect prejudice and antipathy—a view that those in the burdened class are not as worthy or deserving as others. For these reasons and because such discrimination is unlikely to be soon rectified by legislative means, these laws are subjected to strict scrutiny and will be sustained only if they are suitably tailored to serve a compelling state interest.***

Legislative classifications based on gender also call for a heightened standard of review. That factor generally provides no sensible ground for differential treatment. "[W]hat differentiates sex from such nonsuspect statuses as intelligence or physical disability . . . is that sex characteristic frequently bears no relation to ability to perform or contribute to society." *Frontiero v. Richardson*, 411 U.S. 677, 686 (1973) (plurality opinion). Rather than resting on meaningful considerations, statutes distributing benefits and burdens between the sexes in different ways very likely reflect outmoded notions of the relative capabilities of men and women. A gender classification fails unless if is substantially related to a sufficiently important governmental interest. *Mississippi University for Women v. Hogan*, 458 U.S. 718 (1982). Because illegitimacy is beyond the individual's control and bears "no relation to the individual's ability to participate in and contribute to society," official discriminations resting on that characteristic are also subject to somewhat heightened review. Those restrictions "will survive equal protection scrutiny to the extent they are substantially related to a legitimate state interest."

We have declined, however, to extend heightened review to differential treatment based on age:

"While the treatment of the aged in this Nation has not been wholly free of discrimination, such persons, unlike, say, those who have been discriminated against on the basis of race or national origin, have not experienced a 'history of purposeful unequal treatment' or been subjected to unique disabilities on the basis of stereotyped characteristics not truly indicative of their abilities." *Massachusetts Board of Retirement v. Murgia*, 427 U.S. 307, 313 (1976).

***In such cases, the Equal Protection Clause requires only a rational means to serve a legitimate end.

Against this background, we conclude for several reasons that the Court of Appeals erred in holding mental retardation as a quasi-suspect classification calling for a more exacting standard of judicial review than is normally accorded economic and social legislation. First, it is undeniable, and it is not argued otherwise here, that those who are mentally retarded have a reduced ability to cope with and function in the everyday world. Nor are they all cut from the same pattern: as the testimony in this record indicates, they range from those whose disability is not immediately evident to those who must be constantly cared for. They are thus different, immutably so, in relevant respects, and the States' interest in dealing with and providing for them is plainly a legitimate one. How this large and diversified group is to be treated under the law is a difficult and often a technical matter, very much a task for legislators guided by qualified professionals and not by the perhaps ill-informed opinions of the judiciary. Heightened scrutiny inevitably involves substantive judgments about legislative decisions, and we doubt that the predicate for such judicial oversight is present where the classification deals with mental retardation.

Second, the distinctive legislative response, both national and state, to the plight of those who are mentally retarded demonstrates not only that they have unique problems, but also that the lawmakers have been addressing their difficulties in a manner that belies a continuing antipathy or prejudice and a corresponding need for more intrusive oversight by the judiciary. Thus, the Federal Government has not only outlawed discrimination against the mentally retarded in federally funded programs, see §504 of the Rehabilitation Act of 1973, 29 U.S.C. §794, but it has also provided the retarded with the right to receive "appropriate treatment, services, and habilitation" in a setting that is "least restrictive of [their] personal liberty." Developmental Disabilities Assistance and Bill of Rights Act, 42 U.S.C. §§6010(1), (2). In addition, the Government has conditioned federal education funds on a State's assurance that retarded children will enjoy an education that, "to the maximum extent appropriate," is integrated with that of nonmentally retarded children. Education of the Handicapped Act, 20 U.S.C. §1412(5)(B).***

Such legislation thus singling out the retarded for special treatment reflects the real and undeniable differences between the retarded and others. That a civilized and decent society expects and approves such legislation indicates that governmental consideration of those differences in the vast majority of situations is not only legitimate but also desirable.***

Fourth, if the large and amorphous class of the mentally retarded were deemed quasi-suspect for the reasons given by the Court of Appeals, it would be difficult to find a principled way to distinguish a variety of other groups who have perhaps immutable disabilities setting them off from others, who cannot themselves mandate the desired legislative responses, and who can claim some degree of prejudice from at least part of the public at large. One need mention in this respect only the aging, the disabled, the mentally ill, and the infirm. We are reluctant to set out on that course, and we decline to do so.***

Our refusal to recognize the retarded as a quasi-suspect class does not leave them entirely unprotected from invidious discrimination. To withstand equal protection review, legislation that distinguishes between the mentally retarded and others must be rationally related to a legitimate governmental purpose. This standard, we believe, affords government the latitude necessary both to pursue policies designed to assist the retarded in realizing their full potential, and to freely and efficiently engage in activities that burden the retarded in what is essentially an incidental manner.***

We turn to the issue of the validity of the zoning ordinance insofar as it requires a special use permit for homes for the mentally retarded.***

The constitutional issue is clearly posed. The city does not require a special use permit in an R–3 zone for apartment houses, multiple dwellings, boarding and lodging houses, fraternity or sorority houses, dormitories, apartment hotels, hospitals, sanitariums, nursing homes for convalescents or the aged (other than for the insane or feebleminded or alcoholics or drug addicts), private clubs or fraternal orders, and other specified uses. It does, however, insist on a special permit for the Featherston home, and it does so, as the District Court found, because it would be a facility for the mentally retarded. May the city require the permit for this facility when other care and multiple-dwelling facilities are freely permitted?

Because in our view the record does not reveal any rational basis for believing that the Featherston home would pose any special threat to the city's legitimate interests, we affirm the judgment below insofar as it holds the ordinance invalid as applied in this case.

The short of it is that requiring the permit in this case appears to us to rest on an irrational prejudice against the mentally retarded, including those who would occupy the Featherston facility and who would live under the closely supervised and highly regulated conditions expressly provided for by state and federal law.

The judgment of the Court of Appeals is affirmed insofar as it invalidates the zoning ordinance as applied to the Featherston home. The judgment is otherwise vacated, and the case is remanded.

JUSTICE MARSHALL, with whom JUSTICE BRENNAN and JUSTICE BLACKMUN join, concurring in the judgment in part and dissenting in part.

The Court holds that all retarded individuals cannot be grouped together as the "feebleminded" and deemed presumptively unfit to live in a community. Underlying this holding is the principle that mental retardation per se cannot be a proxy for depriving retarded people of their rights and interests without regard to variations in individual ability. With this holding and principle I agree. The equal protection clause requires attention to the capacities and needs of retarded people as individuals.

I cannot agree, however, with the way in which the Court reaches its result or with the narrow, as-applied remedy it provides for the City of Cleburne's equal protection violation. The Court holds the ordinance invalid on rational basis grounds and disclaims that anything special, in the form of heightened scrutiny, is taking place. Yet Cleburne's ordinance surely would be valid under the traditional rational basis test applicable to economic and commercial regulation. In my view, it is important to articulate, as the Court does not, the facts and principles that justify subjecting this zoning ordinance to the searching review—the heightened scrutiny—that actually leads to its invalidation.***

First, the interest of the retarded in establishing group homes is substantial. The right to "establish a home" has long been cherished as one of the fundamental liberties embraced by the Due Process Clause. For retarded adults, this right means living together in group homes, for as deinstitutionalization has progressed, group homes have become the primary means by which retarded adults may enter life in the community.***Excluding group homes deprives the retarded of much of what makes for human freedom and fulfillment—the ability to form bonds and take part in the life of a community.

Second, the mentally retarded have been subject to a "lengthy and tragic history," University of California Regents v Bakke, 438 US 265 (1978), of segregation and discrimination that can only be called grotesque. During much of the nineteenth century, mental retardation was viewed as neither curable nor dangerous and the retarded were largely left to their own devices. By the latter part of the century and during the first decades of the new one, however, social views of the retarded underwent a radical transformation. Fueled by the rising tide of Social Darwinism, the "science" of eugenics, and the extreme xenophobia of those years, leading medical authorities and others began to portray the "feeble minded" as a "menace to society and civilization . . . responsible in large degree for many, if not all, of our social problems." A regime of state-mandated segregation and degradation soon emerged that in its virulence and bigotry rivaled, and indeed paralleled, the worst excesses of Jim Crow. Massive custodial institutions were built to warehouse the retarded for life; the aim was to halt reproduction of the retarded and "nearly extinguish their race." Retarded children were categorically excluded from public schools, based on the false stereotype that all were ineducable and on the purported need to protect nonretarded children from them. State laws deemed the retarded "unfit for citizenship."

Segregation was accompanied by eugenic marriage and sterilization laws that extinguished for the retarded one of the "basic civil rights of man"—the right to marry and procreate. Skinner v Oklahoma, 316 US 535, 541 (1942). Marriages of the retarded were made, and in some states continue to be, not only voidable but also often a criminal offense. The purpose of such limitations, which frequently applied only to women of childbearing age, was unabashedly eugenic: to prevent the retarded from propagating. To assure this end, 29 states enacted compulsory eugenic sterilization laws between 1907 and 1931.***But most important, lengthy and continuing isolation of the retarded has perpetuated the ignorance, irrational fears, and stereotyping that long have plagued them.

In light of the importance of the interest at stake and the history of discrimination the retarded have suffered, the Equal Protection Clause requires us to do more than review the distinctions drawn by Cleburne's zoning ordinance as if they appeared in a taxing statute or in economic or commercial legislation. The searching scrutiny I would give to restrictions on the ability of the retarded to establish community group homes leads me to conclude that Cleburne's vague generalizations for classifying the "feeble minded" with drug addicts, alcoholics, and the insane, and excluding them where the elderly, the ill, the boarder, and the transient are allowed, are not substantial or important enough to overcome the suspicion that the ordinance rests on impermissible assumptions or outmoded and perhaps invidious stereotypes.***

Notes and Issues for Discussion

1. Legislation is generally presumed valid if there is a rational basis for the classification. Can you argue a rational basis for Cleburne's exclusion of "hospitals for the insane or feeble-minded, or alcoholic or drug addicts, or penal or correctional institutions" from an apartment house district as provided by the ordinance? Can you argue no rational basis?
2. Cleburne Living Center argued that mentally retarded citizens should be extended a heightened scrutiny. What are the arguments for extending "heightened scrutiny" and regarding the mentally retarded as a "quasi-suspect classification"? What are the arguments for not doing this? Which are more persuasive?
3. The concepts of least restrictive alternative, deinstitutionalization, and normalization argue for integrating group homes for retarded citizens within the community. Does the *Cleburne* decision further this integration? How might it deter it?
4. Classifications based on age have been upheld if there is a rational basis. In *Massachusetts Bd. of Retirement v. Murgia*, 427 U.S. 307 (1976), the court upheld a mandatory retirement statute at age fifty for uniformed state police officers, finding a rational basis in the testimony linking the increase in various physical disabilities with advancing age.

Intermediate Level or Quasi-Suspect Classifications

The intermediate or quasi-suspect classifications are only upheld if they further substantial state interests. In the following case, the Court held that the admissions policy of the Mississippi school, which excluded males, did not further such an interest.

MISSISSIPPI COLLEGE FOR WOMEN v. HOGAN
458 U.S. 718 (1982)
U.S. SUPREME COURT

JUSTICE O'CONNOR delivered the opinion of the Court.

This case presents the narrow issue of whether a state statute that excludes males from enrolling in a state-supported professional nursing school violates the Equal Protection Clause of the Fourteenth Amendment.

The facts are not in dispute. In 1884, the Mississippi Legislature created the Mississippi Industrial Institute and College for the Education of White Girls of the State of Mississippi, now the oldest state-supported all-female college in the United States. The school, known today as Mississippi University for Women (MUW), has from its inception limited its enrollment to women.

In 1971, MUW established a School of Nursing, initially offering a 2-year associate degree. Three years later, the school instituted a 4-year baccalaureate program in nursing and today also offers a graduate program. The School of Nursing has its own faculty and administrative officers and establishes its own criteria for admission.

Respondent, Joe Hogan, is a registered nurse but does not hold a baccalaureate degree in nursing. Since 1974, he has worked as a nursing supervisor in a medical center in Columbus, the city in which MUW is located. In 1979, Hogan applied for admission to the MUW School of Nursing's baccalaureate program. Although he was otherwise qualified, he was denied admission to the School of Nursing solely because of his sex. School officials informed him that he could audit the courses in which he was interested, but could not enroll for credit.

Hogan filed an action in the United States District Court for the Northern District of Mississippi, claiming the single-sex admission policy of MUW's School of Nursing violated the Equal Protection Clause of the Fourteenth Amendment. Hogan sought injunctive and declaratory relief, as well as compensatory damages. Following a hearing, the District Court denied preliminary injunctive relief.***

The Court of Appeals for the Fifth Circuit reversed, holding that, because the admissions policy discriminates on the basis of gender, the District Court improperly used a "rational relationship" test to judge the constitutionality of the policy. Instead, the Court of Appeals stated, the proper test is whether the State has carried the heavier burden of showing that the gender-based classification is substantially related to an important governmental objective. Recognizing that the State has a significant interest in providing educational opportunities for all its citizens, the court then found that the State had failed to show that providing a unique educational opportunity for females, but not for males, bears a substantial relationship to that interest. Holding that the policy excluding Hogan because of his sex denies him equal protection of the laws, the court vacated the summary judgment entered against Hogan as to his claim for monetary damages, and remanded for entry of a declaratory judgment in conformity with its opinion and for further appropriate proceedings.***

We begin our analysis aided by several firmly established principles. Because the challenged policy expressly discriminates among applicants on the basis of gender, it is subject to scrutiny under the Equal Protection Clause of the Fourteenth Amendment. That this statutory policy discriminates against males rather than against females does not exempt it from scrutiny or reduce the standard of review. Our decisions also establish that the party seeking to uphold a statute that classifies individuals on the basis of their gender must carry the burden of showing an "exceedingly persuasive justification" for the classification. The burden is met only by showing at least that the classification serves "important governmental objectives and that the discriminatory means employed" are "substantially related to the achievement of those objectives."

Although the test for determining the validity of a gender-based classification is straightforward, it must be applied free of fixed notions concerning the roles and abilities of males and females. Care must be taken in ascertaining whether the statutory objective itself reflects archaic and stereotypic notions. Thus, if the statutory objective is to exclude or "protect" members of one gender because they are presumed to suffer from an inherent handicap or to be innately inferior, the objective itself is illegitimate.

If the State's objective is legitimate and important, we next determine whether the requisite direct, substantial relationship between objective and means is present. The purpose of requiring that close relationship is to assure that the validity of a classification is determined through reasoned analysis rather than through the mechanical application of traditional, often inaccurate, assumptions about the proper roles of men and women. The need for the requirement is amply revealed by reference to the broad range of statutes already invalidated by this Court, statutes that relied upon the simplistic, outdated assumption that gender could be used as a "proxy for other, more germane bases of classification," to establish a link between objective and classification.

Applying this framework, we now analyze the arguments advanced by the State to justify its refusal to allow males to enroll for credit in MUW's School of Nursing.

The State's primary justification for maintaining the single-sex admission policy of MUW's School of Nursing is that it compensates for discrimination against women and, therefore, constitutes educational affirmative action. As applied to the School of Nursing, we find the State's argument unpersuasive.

In limited circumstances, a gender-based classification favoring one sex can be justified if it intentionally and directly assists members of the sex that is disproportionately burdened. However, we consistently have emphasized that "the mere recitation of a benign, compensatory purpose is not an automatic shield which protects against any inquiry into the actual purposes underlying a statutory scheme."***

It is readily apparent that a State can evoke a compensatory purpose to justify an otherwise discriminatory classification only if members of the gender benefited by the classification actually suffer a disadvantage related to the classification.

***Mississippi has made no showing that women lacked opportunities to obtain training in the field of nursing or to attain positions of leadership in that field when the MUW School of Nursing opened its doors or that women currently are deprived of such opportunities. In fact, in 1970, the year before the School of

Nursing's first class enrolled, women earned 94 percent of the nursing baccalaureate degrees conferred in Mississippi and 98.6 percent of the degrees earned nationwide.***

Rather than compensate for discriminatory barriers faced by women, MUW's policy of excluding males from admission to the School of Nursing tends to perpetuate the stereotyped view of nursing as an exclusively woman's job. By assuring that Mississippi allots more openings in its state-supported nursing schools to women than it does to men, MUW's admissions policy lends credibility to the old view that women, not men, should become nurses, and makes the assumption that nursing is a field for women a self-fulfilling prophecy. Thus, we conclude that, although the State recited a "benign, compensatory purpose," it failed to establish that the alleged objective is the actual purpose underlying the discriminatory classification.

The policy is invalid also because it fails the second part of the equal protection test, for the State has made no showing that the gender-based classification is substantially and directly related to its proposed compensatory objective. To the contrary, MUW's policy of permitting men to attend classes as auditors fatally undermines its claim that women, at least those in the School of Nursing, are adversely affected by the presence of men.***

Thus, considering both the asserted interest and the relationship between the interest and the methods used by the State, we conclude that the State has fallen far short of establishing the "exceedingly persuasive justification" needed to sustain the gender-based classification. Accordingly, we hold that MUW's policy of denying males the right to enroll for credit in its School of Nursing violates the Equal Protection Clause of the Fourteenth Amendment.***

Notes and Issues for Discussion

1. To be a "quasi-suspect" class the group must "(1) have suffered a history of discrimination; (2) exhibit obvious, immutable, or distinguishing characteristics that define them as a discrete group; and (3) show that they are a minority or politically powerless, or alternatively show that the statutory classification at issue burdens a fundamental right." *High Tech Gays v. Defense Industry Security Clearance Office*, 895 F 2d 563 (1990). Do the criteria apply to gender-based classifications? Can you make an argument that they apply to the mentally retarded?

2. In *Craig v. Boren*, 429 U.S. 190 (1976), the Court held that an Oklahoma statute which allowed the purchase of 3.2% beer by eighteen- to twenty-year-old females but not by males of the same age, constituted "invidious discrimination" under the Equal Protection Clause and was unconstitutional.

3. In *Fronterio v. Richardson*, 411 U.S. 677 (1972), the issue was the constitutionality of a federal statute that allowed a serviceman to claim his wife as a dependent automatically, but required a servicewoman to show that her husband was dependent upon her for over one-half of his support. The statute was held unconstitutional on equal protection grounds. While four

judges held that "classifications based upon sex, like classifications based upon race, alienage, or national origin, are inherently suspect, and must therefore be subjected to strict judicial scrutiny," four other judges found the statute impermissible only because there was no rational basis, and a ninth judge voted to uphold the statute. Thus there was no majority holding gender-based distinctions inherently suspect.

4. Are homosexuals as a class entitled to increased constitutional protection under the Equal Protection Clause? In the *High Tech Gays* case (above) the court reversed a lower court decision extending heightened scrutiny to homosexuals. In that case, the plaintiffs challenged a Department of Defense policy which required that known homosexual applicants for Secret or Top Secret classifications be subjected to extensive investigation and in effect excluded homosexuals along with others who participate "in deviant sexual activities" from those classifications. See also *Ben-Shalom v. March*, 881 F.2d 454 (1989) (military could refuse to let lesbians re-enlist); compare *Watkins v. U.S. Army*, 847 F.2d 1329 (1989) (homosexuals are held to be a suspect class, voiding Army discharge on the grounds of homosexuality). (For a Supreme Court decision on homosexual sodomy, *Bowers v. Hardwick*, which was relied on heavily by the courts in *High Tech Gays* and *Ben-Shalom*, see p. 105.)

5. In *Plyler v. Doe*, 457 U.S. 202 (1982), the Court invalidated Texas statutes providing education funds only for children who were U.S. citizens or legal aliens, applying a higher standard than rational basis. "If the State is to deny a discrete group of innocent children the free public education that it offers to other children residing within its borders, that denial must be justified by a showing that it furthers some substantial state interest. No such showing was made here." (457 U.S. at 230).

Highly Suspect Classifications

The most stringent standard in equal protection analysis applies to classifications based on race, alienage, or national origin.

PALMORE v. SIDOTI
466 U.S. 429 (1984)
U.S. SUPREME COURT

CHIEF JUSTICE BURGER delivered the opinion of the Court.

We granted certiorari to review a judgment of a state court divesting a natural mother of the custody of her infant child because of her remarriage to a person of a different race.

When petitioner Linda Sidoti Palmore and respondent Anthony J. Sidoti, both Caucasians, were divorced in May 1980 in Florida, the mother was awarded custody of their 3-year-old daughter.

In September 1981 the father sought custody of the child by filing a petition to modify the prior judgment because of changed conditions. The change was that the child's mother was then cohabiting with a Negro, Clarence Palmore, Jr., whom she married two months later. Additionally, the father made several allegations of instances in which the mother had not properly cared for the child.

After hearing testimony from both parties and considering a court counselor's investigative report, the court noted that the father had made allegations about the child's care, but the court made no findings with respect to these allegations. On the contrary, the court made a finding that "there is no issue as to either party's devotion to the child, adequacy of housing facilities, or respectability of the new spouse of either parent."

The court then addressed the recommendations of the court counselor, who had made an earlier report "in [another] case coming out of this circuit also involving the social consequences of an interracial marriage. From this vague reference to that earlier case, the court turned to the present case and noted the counselor's recommendation for a change in custody because "[t]he wife [petitioner] has chosen for herself and for her child, a life-style unacceptable to the father *and to society.* . . . The child . . . is, or at school age will be, subject to environmental pressures not of choice." (emphasis added).

The court then concluded that the best interests of the child would be served by awarding custody to the father. The court's rationale is contained in the following:

"The father's evident resentment of the mother's choice of a black partner is not sufficient to wrest custody from the mother. It is of some significance, however, that the mother did see fit to bring a man into her home and carry on a sexual relationship with him without being married to him. Such action tended to place gratification of her own desires ahead of her concern for the child's future welfare. *This Court feels that despite the strides that have been made in bettering relations between the races in this country, it is inevitable that Melanie will, if allowed to remain in her present situation and attains school age and thus more vulnerable to peer pressures, suffer from the social stigmatization that is sure to come.*" (emphasis added).

The Second District Court of Appeal affirmed without opinion.***

The judgment of a state court determining or reviewing a child custody decision is not ordinarily a likely candidate for review by this Court. However, the court's opinion, after stating that the "father's evident resentment of the mother's choice of a black partner is not sufficient" to deprive her of custody, then turns to what it regarded as the damaging impact on the child from remaining in a racially mixed household. This raises important federal concerns arising from the Constitution's commitment to eradicating discrimination based on race.

The Florida court did not focus directly on the parental qualifications of the natural mother or her present husband, or indeed on the father's qualifications to have custody of the child. The court found that "there is no issue as to either party's devotion to the child, adequacy of housing facilities, or respectability of the new spouse of either parent." This, taken with the absence of any negative finding as to the quality of the care provided by the mother, constitutes a rejection of any claim of petitioner's unfitness to continue the custody of her child.

The court correctly stated that the child's welfare was the controlling factor. But that court was entirely candid and made no effort to place its holding on any ground other than race. Taking the court's findings and rationale at face value, it is clear that the outcome would have been different had petitioner married a Caucasian male of similar respectability.

A core purpose of the Fourteenth Amendment was to do away with all governmentally imposed discrimination based on race. Classifying persons according to their race is more likely to reflect racial prejudice than legitimate public concerns; the race, not the person, dictates the category. Such classifications are subject to the most exacting scrutiny; to pass constitutional muster, they must be justified by a compelling governmental interest and must be "necessary... to the accomplishment" of their legitimate purposes, *McLaughlin v. Florida*, 379 U.S. 184, 196 (1964). See *Loving v. Virginia*, 388 U.S. 1, 11 (1967).

The State, of course, has a duty of the highest order to protect the interests of minor children, particularly those of tender years. In common with most states, Florida law mandates that custody determinations be made in the best interests of the children involved. Fla. Stat. §61.13(2)(b)(1) (1983). The goal of granting custody based on the best interests of the child is indisputably a substantial governmental interest for purposes of the Equal Protection Clause.

It would ignore reality to suggest that racial and ethnic prejudices do not exist or that all manifestations of those prejudices have been eliminated. There is a risk that a child living with a stepparent of a different race may be subject to a variety of pressures and stresses not present if the child were living with parents of the same racial or ethnic origin.

The question, however, is whether the reality of private biases and the possible injury they might inflict are permissible considerations for removal of an infant child from the custody of its natural mother. We have little difficulty concluding that they are not. The Constitution cannot control such prejudices but neither can it tolerate them. Private biases may be outside the reach of the law, but the law cannot, directly or indirectly, give them effect.

***The effects of racial prejudice, however real, cannot justify a racial classification removing an infant child from the custody of its natural mother found to be an appropriate person to have such custody.

The judgment of the District Court is reversed.

Notes and Issues for Discussion

1. The trial court decided that "the best interests of the child would be served by awarding custody to the father." What harm did the court find in the living arrangement?
2. Among the early cases holding that racial classifications are inherently suspect are *Loving v. Virginia*, 388 U.S. 1 (1967), and *McLaughlin v. Florida*, 379 U.S. 184 (1964). *Loving* struck down a state statute making interracial

marriage a crime, *McLaughlin* held unconstitutional a state statute making it a crime for unmarried white and black Americans habitually to live in the same room at night.

3. Perhaps the most far-reaching decision striking down racial classifications was *Brown v. Board of Education,* 347 U.S. 483 (1954). In *Brown,* the Court said: "We conclude that in the field of public education the doctrine of 'separate but equal' has no place. Separate educational facilities are inherently unequal. Therefore we hold that the plaintiffs and others similarly situated for whom the actions have been brought are, by reason of the segregation complained of, deprived of the equal protection of the laws guaranteed by the Fourteenth Amendment." 347 U.S. at 495. In a second hearing to address implementation issues, *Brown v. Board of Education* (II), 349 U.S. 294 (1955), the Court ordered the lower federal courts to "take such proceedings and enter such orders and decrees consistent with this opinion as are necessary and proper to admit to public schools on a racially nondiscriminatory basis with all deliberate speed the parties to these cases." 349 U.S. at 301.

4. In *University of California Regents v. Bakke,* 438 U.S. 265 (1978), the Court held that a special admissions program to the U.C. Davis Medical School designed to insure admission of a specific number of students from certain minority groups was unconstitutional. "We have held that in 'order to justify the use of a suspect classification, a State must show that its purpose of interest is both constitutionall permissible and substantial, and that its use of the classification is necessary to the accomplishment of its purpose or safeguarding of its interests.'. . . [I]t is evident that the Davis special admissions program involves the use of an explicit racial classification never before countenanced by this Court. It tells applicants who are not Negro, Asian, or Chicano that they are totally excluded from a specific percentage of the seats in an entering class. . . . The fatal flaw in petitioner's preferential program is its disregard of individual rights as guaranteed by the Fourteenth Amendment. . . . such rights are not absolute. But when a State's distribution of benefits or imposition of burdens hinges on ancestry or color of a person's skin, that individual is entitled to a demonstration that the challenged classification is necessary to promote a substantial state interest. Petitioner has failed to carry this burden." 438 U.S. at 305 *ff.* The Court did cite with approval several admissions programs which considered race or ethnic background as a "plus" but did not impose racial or ethnic quotas.

5. In *Washington v. Davis,* 426 U.S. 229 (1976), the Court upheld the use of standardized tests and a requirement for a high school diploma for police applicants, despite proof that this discriminated against black applicants. The Court said "our cases have not embraced the proposition that a law or other official act, without regard to whether it reflects a racially discriminatory purpose, is unconstitutional *solely* because it has a racially disproportionate impact." 426 U.S. at 239. However, the Court did note that disproportionate impact might be sufficient to bring an action under Title VII of the Civil Rights Act, 42 U.S.C. §2000e. In *City of Richmond v. J. A. Cro-*

son Company, 488 U.S. 469 (1989), the Court invalidated an ordinance requiring contractors dealing with the city to subcontract 30 percent or more of their business to Minority Business Enterprises, defined as those businesses "at least 51 percent of which is owned or controlled . . . by minority group members," with minority groups defined as Black, Spanish-speaking, Oriental, Indian, Eskimo, or Aleut. The Court said: "In sum, none of the evidence presented by the city points to any identified discrimination in the Richmond construction industry. We, therefore, hold that the city has failed to demonstrate a compelling interest in apportioning public contracting opportunities on the basis of race. To accept Richmond's claim that past social discrimination alone can serve as the basis for rigid racial preferences would be to open the door to competing claims for 'remedial relief' for every disadvantaged group." 488 U.S. at 505.

6. Classifications based on alienage and national origin are also inherently suspect. See *Graham v. Richardson*, 304 U.S. 365 (1971), and *Korematsu v. U.S.*, 323 U.S. 214 (1944).

OTHER CONSTITUTIONAL PROVISIONS

While the Fourteenth Amendment due process and equal protection provisions are perhaps most significant for the health and human services professions, many other constitutional amendments have relevance. Several are discussed below.

Cruel and Unusual Punishment

The Eighth Amendment provides: "Excessive bail shall not be required, nor excessive fines imposed, nor cruel and unusual punishments inflicted." In general these provisions are applied to the states through the Fourteenth Amendment. In *Robinson v. California*, 379 U.S. 660 (1961), the Supreme Court invalidated a California statute which made the addiction to narcotics a misdemeanor as a violation of the Eighth and Fourteenth Amendments. The court wrote:

This statute, therefore, is not one which punishes a person for the use of narcotics, for their purchase, sale or possession, or for antisocial or disorderly behavior resulting from their administration. It is not a law which even purports to provide or require medical treatment. Rather, we deal with a statute which makes the "status" of narcotic addiction a criminal offense, for which the offender may be prosecuted "at any time before he reforms." . . . We hold that a state law which imprisons a person thus afflicted as a criminal, even though he has never touched

any narcotic drug within the State or been guilty of any irregular behavior there, inflicts a cruel and unusual punishment in violation of the
Fourteenth Amendment. 379 U.S. at 666–667.

However, in *Powell v. Texas*, 392 U.S. 514 (1967), the Court refused to extend *Robinson* to alcoholism. Leroy Powell, a chronic alcoholic, was convicted
of public intoxication and fined. In his appeal he argued that this was cruel
and unusual punishment in violation of the Eighth and Fourteenth Amendments. The court disagreed, finding that there was insufficient knowledge
about alcoholism and whether or not it is a disease. The court said:

> On its face the present case does not fall within that holding [*Robinson*],
> since appellant was convicted, not for being a chronic alcoholic, but for
> being in public while drunk on a particular occasion. The State of Texas
> thus has not sought to punish a mere status, as California did in *Robinson*;
> nor has it attempted to regulate appellant's behavior which may create
> substantial health and safety hazards, both for appellant and for mem-
> bers of the general public, and which offends the moral and the esthetic
> sensibilities of a large segment of the community.... 392 U.S. at 532.

The dissent argued that *Robinson* was far broader in scope and stood for
the principle that "criminal penalties may not be inflicted upon a person for
being in a condition he is powerless to change." 392 U.S. at 567.

In *Ingraham v. Wright*, 430 U.S. 651 (1976), the Court refused to extend cruel
and unusual punishment to corporal punishment in public schools, holding that the constitutional provision is only applicable to criminal punishments. The Court went on to hold that there were adequate procedural safeguards in the Florida statute to satisfy Fourteenth Amendment procedural
due process. See p. 302.

Search and Seizure

Under the Fourth Amendment, "[t]he right of the people to be secure in their
persons, houses, papers, and effects, against unreasonable searches and seizures, shall not be violated, and no warrants shall issue, but upon probable
cause...."

Although usually thought of as a protection from unreasonable searches
of the person or a dwelling place, the amendment has recently been applied
by the Connecticut Supreme Court to certain personal property of a homeless person living under a bridge abutment. See *State v. Mooney*, 588 A.2d 145
(Conn. 1991). Warrantless searches in the schools based on "reasonable
cause," have been held constitutionally adequate. See *New Jersey v. T.L.O.*,
469 U.S. 325 (1984). (See also p. 306).

Free Speech

The First Amendment provides in part that "Congress shall make no law . . . abridging the freedom of speech. . . ." Noting "[i]t can hardly be argued that either students or teachers shed their constitutional rights to freedom of speech or expression at the school house gate," the Supreme Court held a public school policy forbidding students to wear armbands protesting the Vietnam war violated the Free Speech Clause of the First Amendment. *Tinker v. Des Moines Indep. Comm. School Dist.*, 393 U.S. 503 (1969). However there remain some restrictions on free speech in the schools. In *Bethel School District v. Fraser*, 478 U.S. 675 (1986), the Court upheld a suspension of a high school student for making sexually suggestive remarks in a school nominating speech. In *Hazelwood School District v. Kuhlmeier*, 484 U.S. 260 (1987), the Court upheld a school official's right to censor a school newspaper. (See p. 307*ff.*)

More recently, in *R.A.V. v. St. Paul,* ——U.S. ——, 120 L. Ed. 2d 305 (1992), the court found a "St. Paul Bias-Motivated Crime Ordinance" to be an unconstitutional violation of free speech. The ordinance provided:

> Whoever places on public or private property a symbol, object, appellation, characterization or graffiti, including, but not limited to, a burning cross or Nazi swastika, which one knows or has reasonable grounds to know arouses anger, alarm or resentment in others on the basis of race, creed, religion or gender commits disorderly conduct and shall be guilty of a misdemeanor. 120 L. Ed. 2d. at 315.

The Court held that penalizing certain speech or "fighting words" while permitting other "fighting words" was a violation of the First Amendment:

> . . . the ordinance applies only to "fighting words" that insult, or provoke violence, "on the basis of race, color, creed, religion or gender." Displays containing abusive invective, no matter how vicious or severe, are permissible unless they are addressed to one of the specified disfavored topics. Those who wish to use "fighting words" in connection with other ideas—to express hostility, for example, on the basis of political affiliation, union membership or homosexuality—are not covered. The First Amendment does not permit St. Paul to impose special prohibitions on those speakers who express views on disfavored subjects. 120 L. Ed. 2d at 323.

SELECTED REFERENCES

Carroll, W. A., and Smith, N. B. *American Constitutional Rights* (1991).

Gunther, G. *Constitutional Law* (1989 Supplement by F. Schauer) (11th ed., 1989).

————. *Individual Rights and Constitutional Law* (5th ed., 1991).

Lockhart, W., *et al. Constitutional Rights and Liberties* (7th ed., 1991).

Mashaw, J. *Due Process in the Administrative State* (1985).

Murphy, W., Fleming, J., and Harris, W. *American Constitutional Interpretation* (1986).

Tribe, L. H. *American Constitutional Law* (1st ed., 1978; 2nd ed. 1988).

PART II

LEGAL CONCEPTS FOR THE PROFESSIONAL

In Part II, some basic legal concepts used by health and human services professionals in their work are examined in depth.

Chapter 4 analyzes some of the codes of ethics under which many professionals operate, pointing out differences and similarities. These are not law, strictly speaking, but are professional codes of conduct. They incorporate many of the legal concepts in the chapters that follow in this text. They may be used to determine unethical conduct and impose professional sanctions, and they may be used in courts of law to establish standards of performance.

In Chapter 5, the meanings of privacy are explored. Privacy is first of all a substantive due process concept which has to do with an individual's right to make decisions in a number of areas without state interference. The Supreme Court has held that an individual has a privacy right that extends to a number of personal areas from raising children to abortion. Although the Court has held that the privacy right extends generally to one's own home, in a recent decision the Court held that a state criminal statute prohibiting sodomy was constitutional as applied to homosexual behavior in a private bedroom. A second type of privacy is the protection against state disclosure about an individual without that person's consent and includes the provisions of the Federal Privacy Act which prohibits federal disclosure of many records without consent. A third type of privacy is the privacy of the individual to be free from governmental search and intrusion.

In Chapter 6, patient and client confidentiality are explored. The narrower concept of privilege is examined, which further protects certain discussions and disclosures between the patient and client and specific professionals. Important limitations to confidential and privileged communications are then addressed—limitations that may allow or mandate disclosure of confidential communications when there is a reasonable belief that child abuse has occurred or when the professional reasonably believes that the patient or client may harm another or self.

The topic of informed consent is addressed in Chapter 7. Once primarily limited to the medical field, the legal concept has developed substantially and is a key part of decision making in the health and human services. First, elements of adequate disclosure, competence to understand, and absence of coercion are examined. Then the related areas of therapeutic privilege—where the professional may legitimately withhold information, waivers, withdrawals, and refusals of consent—are discussed. Finally, problems involving the thorny issues of consent for minors and withholding or withdrawing life-supporting treatment are addressed.

Chapter 8 discusses the legal concepts of incompetence and guardianship. Legally there is a presumption of competence for most adults and usually a person cannot be found incompetent without a court determination. The competent person retains civil rights and rights to make personal and financial decisions. However, if someone is found incompetent, all or most of these decision-making powers are lost and become vested in a guardian. Difficult questions arise for the professional when a specific decision must be made for an incompetent individual, such as the decision to perform a medical procedure or to terminate life support systems. In addition, there are a host of issues surrounding children who for many purposes are not legally competent until they reach the age of eighteen.

CHAPTER 4

ETHICS AND LAW IN THE HEALTH AND HUMAN SERVICES

Ethics is generally defined as a philosophical discipline concerned with human conduct and moral decision making. . . . Unlike a discipline such as mathematics, ethics is normative rather than factual. It is concerned with principles that ought to govern human conduct rather than those that do govern it. (Van Hoose and Kottler, 1985: 3)

CODES OF ETHICS

Codes of ethics establish broad rules of conduct for a profession and its members, and thus can be differentiated from an individual moral code which governs particular decisions in both private and professional life. Codes of ethical conduct for the professional and moral decisions for the individual overlap with legal requirements but are distinct from them. While codes of ethics in the health and human services provide the professional with rules and guidance, they are not legally binding as such unless they are otherwise codified or incorporated into law. Unethical conduct may be sanctioned by a professional association, resulting in an admonishment, suspension from practice or expulsion from the profession.[1] However, whether the unethical conduct is legally actionable remains a different question and will depend on applicable legal provisions.

Van Hoose and Kottler have identified several purposes served by codes of ethics. One main function is to provide guidance for professional conduct and decision making. A second function is to legitimate the profession in the eyes of the public, and a third is to preempt governmental regulation and the imposition of external standards. A fourth function is to establish rules of conduct with which a professional's conduct can be compared, either to protect the professional who operates within that code or to discipline the professional who violates its provisions (Van Hoose and Kottler, 1985).

Codes of Ethics and Law

Legal provisions and professional codes of ethics are often in agreement—
that is, professional conduct is usually both legal and ethical, or occasionally
both illegal and unethical. Sometimes, however, the two may not clearly co-
incide and the resulting conflict may pose some real dilemmas for the health
and human services professional.[2] Professional conduct may be unethical
and yet remain legal; in some instances conduct may be illegal and yet still be
ethical. A simple topology will illustrate the relation between law and ethics.

	ETHICS	
	Ethical Conduct	Unethical Conduct
Legal Conduct	I	II
LAW		
Illegal Conduct	III	IV

CELL I. ETHICAL AND LEGAL CONDUCT

Examples abound. Preserving client confidentiality, not exploiting or harming a patient, making an appropriate diagnosis, providing adequate care, appropriately terminating treatment, or making an appropriate referral all meet
legal and ethical requirements.

CELL IV. UNETHICAL AND ILLEGAL CONDUCT

The issues are usually clear. Forcible rape of a client, defrauding a patient,
and certain violations of patient confidentiality are illegal and unethical.[3]

CELL II. LEGAL BUT UNETHICAL CONDUCT

With a few exceptions, in most states it is not illegal to engage in voluntary
sexual intercourse with competent, adult, present or former patients or
clients (although such conduct if harmful may give rise to later malpractice
or liability actions). Yet most health and human services professional codes
of ethics make it clear that sexual relations with current patients is unethical
conduct and a few codes state that sexual intercourse with former patients or
clients is unethical.[4] In a few states, specific health and human services professionals have no legal obligation to report knowledge that child abuse has

occurred, although most codes of ethics would obligate the professional to prevent harm. Most states do not legally require that a professional inform a patient or client of the limitations of confidentiality or how confidential information may be used, but many professional codes of ethics require that this be provided.[5]

CELL III. ILLEGAL BUT ETHICAL CONDUCT

While such conduct may at first appear highly unlikely, there are situations where it may occur.[6] Ethical commitments to social justice or against discrimination, found in many professional codes of ethics, may result in illegal conduct such as sit-ins, disruptions, or demonstrations.[7] Informing a sexual partner that the patient or client has AIDS or is HIV positive without that individual's knowledge and consent is illegal in many states. However, where it is reasonably clear that the patient will not inform or take measures to protect the third party, such conduct appears to be ethical for psychiatrists providing outpatient psychiatric services, and may be ethical for a number of other health and human services professionals under a broad ethical duty to protect third parties from harm.[8] Assisting or advising a competent terminally ill patient who wants to commit suicide is illegal in many states, but may be ethical under professional guidelines which call for promoting patient or client self-determination.[9]

SPECIFIC ETHICAL PROVISIONS

In this section, a number of health and human services professional codes of ethics will be considered in relation to specific legal topics. The treatment is not intended to be complete or exhaustive; not all codes and not all topics are included. The intent is to illustrate by selected topics and provisions the ethical necessity for the health and human services professional to be aware of the law in general and in specific areas. We have drawn upon the codes of ethics of the following professional groups: American Association for Marriage and Family Therapy (AAMFT), American Counseling Association (ACA), American School Counselor Association (ASCA), American Psychiatric Association (APA-AMA), American Psychological Association (APA), and National Association of Social Workers (NASW). The American Psychiatric Association's ethics are based on the American Medical Association's (AMA) "Principles of Medical Ethics," with annotations applicable for psychiatry. The American School Counselor Association's ethics incorporate those of the American Counseling Association as well. Most of the ethical codes have been revised recently. Those of the American Psychological Association, the American Psychiatric Association, and the American School Counselor Association were revised in 1992. The Code of Ethics of the American Association for Marriage and Family Therapy was revised in 1991,[10] the National Association of Social Workers Code was revised in 1990.

Awareness and Knowledge of the Law

In all codes there is a professional responsibility to be aware of and follow the law. For example, the physician (and therefore the psychiatrist) "shall respect the law..." (APA-AMA Section 3); the social worker "should not engage in any action that violates or diminishes the civil or legal rights of clients" (NASW G-1); a school counselor "adheres to ... relevant statutes established by federal, state and local government" (ASCA B-6); and psychologists "plan and conduct research in a manner consistent with federal and state law..." (APA 6.08). Psychiatrists ordered by a court to reveal confidential material "may comply or ... may ethically hold the right to dissent within the framework of the law" (APA-AMA 4-9). Several codes reflect an obligation to bring about legal change: "Marriage and family therapists are concerned with developing laws and regulations pertaining to marriage and family therapy that serve the public interest, and with altering such laws and regulations that are not in the public interest" (AAMFT 6-1); the social worker "should advocate changes in policy and legislation to improve the social conditions and to promote social justice" (NASW P-1).

Privacy and Records

All six professional codes contain provisions relating to privacy, records, and/or storage and retrieval of information. The American Psychological Association's Ethical Principles are particularly detailed about maintaining records and access to databases:

> Psychologists maintain appropriate confidentiality in creating, storing, accessing, transferring, and disposing of records under their control, whether these are written, automated, or in any other medium. Psychologists maintain and dispose of records in accordance with law... (APA 5.04).
>
> If confidential information concerning recipients of psychological services is to be entered into databases or systems of records available to persons whose access has not been consented to by the recipient, then psychologists use coding or other techniques to avoid the inclusion of personal identifiers. (APA 5.07)

The American Counseling Association maintains that records of a counseling relationship are professional information and not part of the agency where the counselor is employed unless so provided by state law (ACA B-5), and further:

In view of the extensive data storage and processing capacities of the computer, the member must ensure that data maintained on a computer is (a) limited to information that is appropriate and necessary for the services being provided; (b) destroyed after it is determined that the information is no longer of any value in providing services; and (c) restricted in terms of access to appropriate staff members involved in the provision of services by using the best computer security methods available. (ACA B-6)

Confidentiality and Limitations

All codes contain numerous provisions concerning confidentiality and the limitations of that confidentiality.

MAINTAINING CONFIDENTIALITY

Every code mandates that professional members maintain patient or client confidentiality. The American Psychological Association code provides:

Psychologists have a primary obligation and take reasonable precautions to respect the confidentiality rights of those with whom they work or consult, recognizing that confidentiality may be established by law, institutional rules, or professional or scientific relationships. (APA 5.02)

The American Psychiatric Association's code states:

A physician shall respect the rights of patients, of colleagues, and of other health professionals, and shall safeguard patient confidences within the constraints of the law. . . . (APA-AMA Section 4).
   Confidentiality is essential to psychiatric treatment. (APA-AMA 4-1)

For social workers:

The social worker should . . . hold in confidence all information obtained in the course of professional service. (NASW Section H)

The American Counseling Association provides:

The counseling relationship and information resulting therefrom must be kept confidential, consistent with the obligations of the member as a professional person. In a group counseling setting, the counselor must set a norm of confidentiality regarding all group participants' disclosures. (ACA B-2)

In addition, confidentiality in the workplace is addressed:

Members must establish interpersonal relations and working agreements with supervisors and subordinates regarding counseling or clinical relationships, confidentiality, distinctions between public and private material, maintenance and dissemination of recorded information. . . . Working agreements in each instance must be specified and made known to those concerned. (ACA G-2)

The AAMFT code provides:

Marriage and family therapists have unique confidentiality concerns because the client in a therapeutic relationship may be more than one person. Therapists respect and guard the confidences of each individual client. (AAMFT Section 2)

School counselors have responsibilities to both students and parents. The school counselor "protects the confidentiality of student records and releases personal data only according to prescribed laws and school policies . . ." (ASCA A-8).

"Protects the confidentiality of information received in the counseling relationship as specified by law and ethical standards. . . . In a group setting, the counselor sets a norm of confidentiality and stresses its importance, yet clearly states that confidentiality in a group setting cannot be guaranteed" (ASCA A-9).

The counselor "treats information received from parents in a confidential and appropriate manner" (ASCA B-4).

In addition, psychologists should include in written and oral reports "only information germane to the purpose for which the communication is made," and should discuss confidential information "only for appropriate scientific or professional purposes, and only with persons clearly concerned with such matters." (APA 5.03). In consulting with colleagues, psychologists should not include confidential information which "reasonably could lead to the identification" of the person or client without prior consent or unless the disclosure "cannot be avoided," and psychologists "share information only to the extent necessary to achieve the purposes of consultation" (APA 5.06).

Psychiatric records shall be protected "with extreme care" (APA-AMA 4-1). Materials used in writing or teaching have to be "adequately disguised to preserve anonymity..." (APA-AMA 4-3). Confidentiality is to be preserved in any consultation, and a psychiatrist can disclose only information "relevant to a given situation" (APA-AMA 4-4, 4-5).

Social workers are to allow clients "reasonable access" to their official social work records although confidences of others in those records should be protected (NASW H-4). Social workers evaluating services or cases should "discuss them only for professional purposes" and "only with persons directly or professionally concerned" (NASW E-4).

LIMITATIONS TO CONFIDENTIALITY

All codes address limitations to confidentiality but vary in detail and specificity.

> Psychologists disclose confidential information without the consent of the individual only as mandated by law, or where permitted by law for a valid purpose, such as (1) to provide needed professional services to the patient or the individual or organizational client, (2) to obtain appropriate professional consultations, (3) to protect the patient or client or others from harm, or (4) to obtain payment for services, in which instance disclosure is limited to the minimum that is necessary to achieve that purpose. (APA 5.05)

> A psychiatrist may release confidential information only with the authorization of the patient or under proper legal compulsion ... (APA-AMA 4-2). Psychiatrists at times may find it necessary, in order to protect the patient or the community from imminent danger, to reveal confidential information disclosed by the patient. (APA-AMA 4-8)

> The social worker should share with others confidences revealed by clients, without their consent, only for compelling professional reasons. (NASW H-1)

> When the client's condition indicates that there is clear and imminent danger to the client or others, the member must take reasonable personal action or inform responsible authorities. Consultation with other professionals must be used where possible. (ACA B-4)

Responsibilities of the school counselor include taking steps to protect the individual, consulting with others, and informing the individual what has been done. The school counselor

informs the appropriate authorities when the counselee's condition indicates a clear and imminent danger to the counselee or others. This is to be done after careful deliberation and, where possible, after consultation with other professionals. The counselor informs the counselee of actions to be taken so as to minimize confusion and clarify expectations. (ASCA A-10)

NOTICE OF LIMITS OF CONFIDENTIALITY

Most codes require that the professional inform the patient or client of the limits of confidentiality and some specify that this discussion should, if possible, take place at the outset:

Psychologists discuss with persons and organizations with whom they establish a scientific or professional relationship . . . (1) the relevant limitations on confidentiality, including limitations where applicable in group, marital, and family therapy or in organizational consulting, and (2) the foreseeable uses of the information generated through their services. Unless it is not feasible or is contraindicated, the discussion of confidentiality occurs at the outset of the relationship and thereafter as new circumstances may warrant. (APA 5.01)

The continuing duty of the psychiatrist to protect the patient includes fully apprising him/her of the connotations of waiving the privilege of privacy. This may become an issue when the patient is being investigated by a government agency, is applying for a position, or is involved in legal action. (APA-AMA 4-2)

The social worker should inform clients fully about the limits of confidentiality in a given situation, the purposes for which information is obtained, and how it may be used. (NASW H-2)

A counselor "must inform the client of the purposes, goals, techniques, rules of procedure and limitations that may affect that relationship at or before the time that the counseling relationship is entered" (ACA B-8).
The school counselor, as follows,

informs the counselee of the purposes, goals, techniques and rules of procedure under which she/he may receive counseling assistance at or before the time when the counseling relationship is entered. Prior notice includes confidentiality issues such as the possible necessity for consulting with other professionals, privileged communication, and legal or authoritative restraints. The meaning and limits of confidentiality are clearly defined to the counselee. (ASCA A-3)

Informed Consent

Psychologists must obtain informed consent to "therapy or related procedures" in understandable language. The principles make clear that the patient or client must have the capacity to consent, the consent must be voluntary, and the patient or client "has been informed of significant information concerning the procedure." Such consent shall be documented[11] (APA 4.02).

When providing services to couples or families, the psychologist is to clarify at the outset who is the patient or client, the role of the psychologist, and the "probable uses of services provided or the information obtained" (APA 4.03).

Informed consent shall be obtained for research using "reasonably understandable language." Participants are to be told "the nature of the research," and that "they are free to participate or to withdraw." They should be given an explanation of "foreseeable consequences of declining or withdrawing," and should be told of "significant factors that may be expected to influence their willingness to participate" and "other aspects about which the prospective participants inquire" (APA 6.11).

Before deciding that certain types of research ("anonymous questionnaires, naturalistic observations, or certain kinds of archival research") do not require informed consent, the psychologist is to "consider applicable regulations and institutional review board requirements" and "consult with colleagues as appropriate" (APA 6.12).

Informed consent is to be obtained from research participants prior to filming or recording "unless the research involves simply naturalistic observations in public places and it is not anticipated that the recording will be used in a manner that could cause personal identification or harm" (APA 6.13).

Deception, which is an exception to informed consent, should not be used unless "the use of deceptive techniques is justified by the study's prospective scientific, educational, or applied value and . . . equally effective alternative procedures that do not use deception are not feasible" (APA 6.15a). Psychologists are not to deceive participants about "significant aspects that would affect their willingness to participate, such as physical risks, discomfort, or unpleasant emotional experiences" (APA 6.15c).

Psychiatrists can release confidential material "only with the authorization of the patient" or by force of law (APA-AMA 4-2). Informed consent is required before presenting a patient to a scientific gathering or to a public gathering or news media (APA-AMA 4-10, 4-11).

Social workers who are conducting research should "ascertain that the consent of participants in the research is voluntary and informed..." (NASW E-2). Social workers are to provide clients with "accurate and complete information" relating to services available, and should "apprise clients of their risks, rights, opportunities, and obligations" in connection with services (NASW F-6, F-7). Social workers are to obtain informed consent before "taping, recording or permitting third-party observations" (NASW H-5).

Incompetence and Guardianship

If a patient or client is "legally incapable of giving informed consent," the psychologist is to obtain informed consent from "a legally authorized person, if such substitute consent is permitted by law" (APA 4.02b). The psychologist should inform the legally incapable person "about the proposed interventions in a manner commensurate with the person's psychological capacities," "seek their assent," and "consider such person's preferences and best interest" (APA 4.02c).

Social workers acting for clients who are legally incompetent "should safeguard the interests and rights of the client" (NASW G-1). When another is legally authorized to act for a client, the social worker should "deal with that person always with the client's best interests in mind" (NASW G-2).

Discrimination

Virtually all codes forbid discrimination. Psychologists are prohibited in their "work-related activities" from engaging in "unfair discrimination based on age, gender, race, ethnicity, national origin, religion, sexual orientation, disability, socioeconomic status, or any basis proscribed by law" (APA 1.10). They also "do not knowingly" engage in "harassing or demeaning" behavior at work "based on factors such as those persons' age, gender, race, ethnicity, national origin, religion, sexual orientation, disability, language, or socioeconomic status" (APA 1.12).

Psychiatrists should not be part of any policy that "excludes, segregates, or demeans the dignity of any patient because of ethnic origin, race, sex, creed, age, socioeconomic status, or sexual orientation." (APA-AMA 1-2).

Social workers should not "practice, condone, facilitate, or collaborate with any form of discrimination on the basis of race, color, sex, sexual orientation, age, religion, national origin, marital status, political belief, mental or physical handicap, or any other preference or personal characteristic, condition, or status" (NASW F-3). They are expected to try to prevent "practices that are inhumane or discriminatory" (NASW C-2). Social workers are expected to try to "prevent and eliminate discrimination" in employer's work assignments, employment policies and practices, and should "act to prevent and eliminate discrimination against any person . . ." (NASW L-3, P-1).

Family therapists "do not discriminate against or refuse professional service . . . on the basis of race, sex, religion or national origin" (AAMFT 1.1).

Sexual Harassment

Several of the recently revised codes directly address sexual harassment.

Psychologists do not engage in sexual harassment. Sexual harassment is sexual solicitation, physical advances, or verbal or nonverbal conduct that is sexual in nature, that occurs in connection with the psychologist's activities or roles as a psychologist, and that either: (1) is unwelcome, is offensive, or creates a hostile workplace environment, and the psychologist knows or is told this; or (2) is sufficiently severe or intense to be abusive to a reasonable person in the context. Sexual harassment can consist of a single intense or severe act or of multiple persistent or pervasive acts. Psychologists accord sexual-harassment complainants and respondents dignity and respect. (APA 1.11)

For counselors:

Members to not condone or engage in sexual harassment which is defined as deliberate or repeated comments, gestures, or physical contacts of a sexual nature. (ACA A-9)

Marriage and family therapists do not engage in sexual or other harassment or exploitation of clients, students, trainees, supervisees, employees, colleagues, research subjects, or actual or potential witnesses or complainants in investigations and ethical proceedings. (AAMFT 3.5)

Malpractice Issues

PROFESSIONAL COMPETENCE

All codes require professional competence and have prohibitions pertaining to practice outside one's area of competence.

"Psychologists provide services, teach and conduct research only within the boundaries of their competence . . ."; they must "undertake appropriate study, training, supervision, and/or consultation from persons who are competent in new areas or new techniques before providing services, teaching or conducting research in those areas" and, in "emerging areas" where there are no standards for preparation, psychologists take "reasonable steps to ensure the competence of their work and protect patients, clients, students, research participants and others from harm" (APA 1.04).

To maintain expertise, psychologists must "maintain a reasonable level of awareness of current scientific and professional information in their fields of activity" and "undertake ongoing efforts to maintain competence in the skills they use." (APA 1.05).

Psychiatrists are to continue "to study, apply and advance scientific knowledge . . ." (APA-AMA Section 5). A psychiatrist who "regularly practices outside his/her area of professional competence" is considered unethical (APA-AMA 2-3).

Social workers should base their practice "upon recognized knowledge relevant to social work," and they should "critically examine, and keep current with, emerging knowledge relevant to social work" (NASW O-1).

For counselors, "[d]ifferent tests demand different levels of competence for administration, scoring and interpretation. Members must recognize the limits of their competence and perform only those functions for which they are prepared" (ACA C-4).

Family therapists do not "diagnose, treat, or advise" in areas "outside the recognized boundaries of their competence," and in teaching supervising and conducting research, are "dedicated to high standards of scholarship" and presenting "accurate information" (AAMFT 3.6, 3.3). Family therapists "remain abreast of new developments" (AAMFT 3.4).

Most codes address terminations and referrals, and most have general admonitions to avoid harm.[12]

EXPLOITATION

All codes prohibit exploitation of others, including patients, clients, students, or research subjects, and many address the problems of dual or multiple relationships and conflicts of interest. For example:

The patient may place his/her trust in his/her psychiatrist knowing that the psychiatrist's ethics and professional responsibilities preclude him/her gratifying his/her own needs by exploiting the patient. . . . (APA-AMA 1-1). The psychiatrist should diligently guard against exploiting information furnished by the patient and should not use the unique position of power afforded him/her by the psychotherapeutic situation to influence the patient in any way not directly relevant to the treatment goals. (APA-AMA 2-2)

Social workers "should not exploit professional relationships for personal gain," and should not "exploit relationships with clients for personal advantage" (NASW D-2, F-2).

Counselors avoid "engaging in activities that seek to meet the counselor's personal needs at the expense of the client" (ACA A-8).

Marriage and family therapists "do not exploit the trust and dependency of students, employees and supervisees" (AAMFT Section 4).

SEXUAL INTIMACIES

All codes hold that sexual relations with patients or clients are unethical:

"Psychologists do not engage in sexual intimacies with current patients or clients" (APA 4.05).

"Sexual activity with a patient is unethical" (Psychiatrists; APA-AMA 2-1).

"The social worker should under no circumstances engage in sexual activities with a client." (NASW F-5).

"The member will avoid any type of sexual intimacies with clients. Sexual relationships with clients are unethical. (Counselors; ACA B-14).

"Sexual intimacy with clients is prohibited." (Marriage and family therapists; AAMFT 1.2).

Many codes also specify that sexual relations with students or supervisees are unethical conduct.[13]

The American Psychological Association states that therapy with former sexual partners is unethical (APA 4.06), and sexual intimacies with former therapy patients within two years of the termination of professional services is also unethical (APA 4.07). The psychologist who engages in sexual intimacies after two years bears the burden of demonstrating that there has been no exploitation, in light of all relevant factors, including (1) the amount of time that has passed since therapy terminated, (2) the nature and duration of the therapy, (3) the circumstances of termination, (4) the patient's or client's personal history, (5) the patient's or client's current mental status, (6) the likelihood of adverse impact on the patient or client and others, and (7) any statements or actions made by the therapist during the course of therapy suggesting or inviting the possibility of a posttermination sexual or romantic relationship with the patient or client. (APA 4.07)

The AAMFT also prohibits sexual intimacies with former clients within two years of termination (AAMFT 1.2).

SELECTED REFERENCES

American Counseling Association. *Ethical Standards* (1988).

American Medical Association. *The Principles of Medical Ethics* (1992).

American Psychiatric Association. *Principles of Medical Ethics With Annotations Especially Applicable to Psychiatry* (1992).

American Psychological Association. *Ethical Principles of Psychologists and Code of Conduct* (1992).

American School Counselor Association. *Ethical Standards for School Counselors* (1992).

Hofling, C. K. (Ed.) *Law and Ethics in the Practice of Psychiatry* (1981).

National Association of Social Workers. *Code of Ethics of the National Association of Social Workers* (1990).

Reamer, F. G. *Ethical Dilemmas in Social Service* (2nd ed., 1991).

Rhodes, M. L. *Ethical Dilemmas in Social Work Practice* (1986).

Van Hoose, W. H., and Kottler, J. A. *Ethical and Legal Issues in Counseling and Psychotherapy* (1985).

CHAPTER 5

PRIVACY, PERSONAL AUTONOMY, AND RECORDS

Privacy is a key legal concept in the health and human services. Although there is no mention of privacy in the U.S. Constitution, courts have found this right to be implicit in various amendments, particularly in the Fourteenth Amendment due process concept of liberty. The boundaries of this substantive due process concept still lack a clear definition but a significant body of law has developed.[1]

There are at least three types of privacy:

1. A privacy right that protects the individual's personal autonomy to make decisions without governmental interference or compulsion

2. A privacy right that protects the individual from the government's unauthorized disclosure of personal information, records or files

3. A privacy right that protects the individual from governmental surveillance and intrusion, perhaps clearest in the protection from unauthorized and illegal searches.[2]

However, as with many legal concepts the right of privacy is not absolute. Personal autonomy and decision making have limits: the state may forbid or regulate various kinds of conduct ranging from child abuse to third-trimester abortions. The disclosure of some personal material is permissible in emergencies or under other conditions. A search that would be illegal on the street may be permitted in the school. The materials that follow develop the concept of privacy and indicate some of the limitations.

PRIVACY AS PERSONAL AUTONOMY

Of the three types of privacy, the broadest is the individual's freedom to live and make decisions without governmental regulation and intrusion. This type of privacy was forecast in the Supreme Court decisions that invalidated state attempts to limit education (*Meyer v. Nebraska*, 320 U.S. 390 [1923]), child rearing *Pierce v. Society of Sisters*, 268 U.S. 510 (1925)), and to mandate involuntary sterilizations (*Skinner v. Oklahoma*, 316 U.S. 535 [1942]). In *Skinner*, the Court invalidated Oklahoma's involuntary sterilization law for certain habitual offenders, and observed: "We are dealing here with [a decision] which involves one of the basic civil rights of man" (316 U.S. at 541).

While there are numerous court decisions in the area of personal autonomy, ranging from child rearing and education to permissible hair length and speech in public schools, we will focus on the line of cases that involve abortion decisions and sexual freedom to illustrate the concepts and problems.

Privacy in Contraception and Abortion

Privacy as personal autonomy was found to have an explicit Constitutional basis in *Griswold v. Connecticut* and this was more clearly developed in subsequent cases dealing with contraception and a woman's right to an abortion.

GRISWOLD v. CONNECTICUT
381 U.S. 479 (1965)
U.S. SUPREME COURT

MR. JUSTICE DOUGLAS delivered the opinion of the court.

Appellant Griswold is Executive Director of the Planned Parenthood League of Connecticut. Appellant Buxton is a licensed physician and a professor at the Yale Medical School who served as Medical Director for the League at its Center in New Haven—a center open and operating from November 1 to November 10, 1961, when appellants were arrested.

They gave information, instruction, and medical advice to *married persons* as to the means of preventing conception. They examined the wife and prescribed the best contraceptive device or material for her use. Fees were usually charged, although some couples were serviced free.

The statutes whose constitutionality is involved in this appeal are §§ 53-32 and 54-196 of the General Statutes of Connecticut (1958 rev). The former provides:

"Any person who uses any drug, medicinal article or instrument for the purpose of preventing contraception shall be fined not less than fifty dollars or imprisoned not less than sixty days nor more than one year or be both fined and imprisoned."

Section 54-196 provides:

"Any person who assists abets counsels, causes, hires or commands another to commit any offense may be prosecuted and punished as if he were the principal offender."

The appellants were found guilty as accessories and fined $100 each, against the claim that the accessory statute as so applied violated the Fourteenth Amendment. The Appellate Division of the Circuit Court affirmed. The Supreme Court of Errors affirmed that judgment.***

Coming to the merits, we are met with a wide range of questions that implicate the Due Process Clause of the Fourteenth Amendment.***

The association of people is not mentioned in the Constitution nor in the Bill of Rights. The right to educate a child in a school of parents' choice—whether public or private or parochial—is also not mentioned. Nor is the right to study any particular subject or any foreign language. Yet the First Amendment has been construed to include certain of those rights.

By Pierce v Society of Sisters, the right to educate one's children as one chooses is made applicable to the States by the force of the First and Fourteenth Amendments. By Meyer v. Nebraska, the same dignity is given the right to study the German language.***

The Fourth and Fifth Amendments were described in Boyd v. United States, as protection against all governmental invasions "of the sanctity of a man's home and the privacies of life." We recently referred in Mapp v. Ohio. to the Fourth Amendment as creating a "right to privacy, no less important than any other right carefully and particularly reserved to the people."***

The present case, then, concerns a relationship lying within the zone of privacy created by several fundamental constitutional guarantees. And it concerns a law which, in forbidding the *use* of contraceptives rather than regulating their manufacture or sale, seeks to achieve its goals by means having a maximum destructive impact upon that relationship. Such a law cannot stand in light of the familiar principle, so often applied by this Court, that a "governmental purpose to control or prevent activities constitutionally subject to state regulation may not be achieved by means which sweep unnecessarily broadly and thereby invade the area of protected freedoms." Would we allow the police to search the sacred precincts of marital bedrooms for telltale signs of the use of contraceptives? The very idea is repulsive to the notions of privacy surrounding the marriage relationship.

We deal with a right of privacy older than the Bill of Rights—older than our political parties, older than our school system. Marriage is a coming together for better or for worse, hopefully enduring, and intimate to the degree of being sacred. It is an association that promotes a way of life, not causes; a harmony in living, not political faiths; a bilateral loyalty, not commercial or social projects. Yet it is an association for as noble a purpose as any involved in our prior decisions.

Reversed.

Notes and Issues for Discussion

1. What law did Griswold and Buxton violate? What are their privacy interests? Are these reasonable?
2. Where in the Constitution does Justice Douglas find a right of privacy? Where outside of the Constitution does he find one?
3. While the scope of privacy is not clear, *Griswold* suggests that there are "notions of privacy surrounding the marriage relationship." Following *Griswold*, the Court expanded these "notions of privacy" in *Eisenstadt v. Baird*, 405 U.S. 438 (1972). There the Court held unconstitutional a Connecticut law which made the distribution of contraceptives to unmarried individuals a criminal offense. While the case was not clearly based on privacy rights, Justice Brennen wrote in his opinion, "If the right of privacy means anything, it is the right of the *individual*, married or single, to be free from unwarranted governmental intrusion into matters so fundamentally affecting a person as the decision whether to bear or beget a child." 405 U.S. at 453.
4. In *Carey v. Population Services International*, 431 U.S. 678 (1975), the Supreme Court held unconstitutional a New York law making it a crime for anyone to sell or distribute any contraceptive to minors under age sixteen; for anyone but a licensed pharmacist to distribute contraceptives to anyone over sixteen and for anyone to advertise or display contraceptives.

Perhaps no decision has engendered as much controversy as has *Roe v. Wade*. *Roe* establishes a woman's right to make an abortion decision in consultation with her doctor. It also places the right to privacy squarely within the Fourteenth Amendment.

ROE v. WADE
410 U.S. 113 (1973)
U.S. SUPREME COURT

MR. JUSTICE BLACKMUN delivered the opinion of the Court.

This Texas federal appeal and its Georgia companion, *Doe* v. *Bolton*, present constitutional challenges to state criminal abortion legislation. The Texas statutes under attack here are typical of those that have been in effect in many States for approximately a century.***

The Texas statutes that concern us here are Arts. 1191–1194 and 1196 of the State's Penal Code. These make it a crime to "procure an abortion," as therein defined, or to attempt one, except with respect to "an abortion procured or attempted by medical advice for the purpose of saving the life of the mother." Similar statutes are in existence in a majority of the States.***

Jane Roe, a single woman who was residing in Dallas County, Texas, instituted this federal action in March 1970 against the District Attorney of the county. She sought a declaratory judgment that the Texas criminal abortion statutes were unconstitutional on their face, and an injunction restraining the defendant from enforcing the statutes.

Roe alleged that she was unmarried and pregnant; that she wished to terminate her pregnancy by an abortion "performed by a competent, licensed physician, under safe, clinical conditions"; that she was unable to get a "legal" abortion in Texas because her life did not appear to be threatened by the continuation of her pregnancy; and that she could not afford to travel to another jurisdiction in order to secure a legal abortion under safe conditions. She claimed that the Texas statutes were unconstitutionally vague and that they abridged her right of personal privacy, protected by the First, Fourth, Fifth, Ninth, and Fourteenth Amendments. By an amendment to her complaint Roe purported to sue "on behalf of herself and all other women" similarly situated.***

The Constitution does not explicitly mention any right of privacy. In a line of decisions, however, going back perhaps as far as *Union Pacific R. Co. v. Botsford*, 141 U.S. 250, 251 (1891), the Court has recognized that a right of personal privacy, or a guarantee of certain areas or zones of privacy, does exist under the Constitution.***

This right of privacy, whether it be founded in the Fourteenth Amendment's concept of personal liberty and restrictions upon state action, as we feel it is, or, as the District Court determined, in the Ninth Amendment's reservation of rights to the people, is broad enough to encompass a woman's decision whether or not to terminate her pregnancy. The detriment that the State would impose upon the pregnant woman by denying this choice altogether is apparent. Specific and direct harm medically diagnosable even in early pregnancy may be involved. Maternity, or additional offspring, may force upon the woman a distressful life and future. Psychological harm may be imminent. Mental and physical health may be taxed by child care. There is also the distress, for all concerned, associated with the unwanted child, and there is the problem of bringing a child into a family already unable, psychologically and otherwise, to care for it. In other cases, as in this one, the additional difficulties and continuing stigma of unwed motherhood may be involved. All these are factors the woman and her responsible physician necessarily will consider in consultation.

On the basis of elements such as these, appellant and some *amici* argue that the woman's right is absolute and that she is entitled to terminate her pregnancy at whatever time, in whatever way, and for whatever reason she alone chooses. With this we do not agree. Appellant's arguments that Texas either has no valid interest at all in regulating the abortion decision, or no interest strong enough to support any limitation upon the woman's sole determination, are unpersuasive. The Court's decisions recognizing a right of privacy also acknowledge that some state regulation in areas protected by that right is appropriate. As noted above, a State may properly assert important interests in safeguarding health, in maintaining medical standards, and in protecting potential life. At some point in pregnancy, these respective interests become sufficiently compelling to sustain regulation of the factors that govern the abortion decision. The privacy right involved, therefore, cannot be said to be absolute.***

We, therefore, conclude that the right of personal privacy includes the abortion decision, but that this right is not unqualified and must be considered against important state interests in regulation.***

The Constitution does not define "person" in so many words. Section 1 of the Fourteenth Amendment contains three references to "person." The first, in defining "citizens," speaks of "persons born or naturalized in the United States." The word also appears both in the Due Process Clause and in the Equal Protection Clause. "Person" is used in other places in the Constitution.***But in nearly all these instances, the use of the word is such that it has application only postnatally. None indicates, with any assurance, that it has any possible pre-natal application.

All this, together with our observation, that throughout the major portion of the 19th century prevailing legal abortion practices were far freer than they are today, persuades us that the word "person," as used in the Fourteenth Amendment, does not include the unborn.***

The pregnant woman cannot be isolated in her privacy. She carries an embryo and, later, a fetus, if one accepts the medical definitions of the developing young in the human uterus.***As we have intimated above, it is reasonable and appropriate for a State to decide that at some point in time another interest, that of health of the mother or that of potential human life, becomes significantly involved. The woman's privacy is no longer sole and any right of privacy she possesses must be measured accordingly.

Texas urges that, apart from the Fourteenth Amendment, life begins at conception and is present throughout pregnancy, and that, therefore, the State has a compelling interest in protecting that life from and after conception. We need not resolve the difficult question of when life begins. When those trained in the respective disciplines of medicine, philosophy, and theology are unable to arrive at any consensus, the judiciary, at this point in the development of man's knowledge, is not in a position to speculate as to the answer.

It should be sufficient to note briefly the wide divergence of thinking on this most sensitive and difficult question. There has always been strong support for the view that life does not begin until live birth. This was the belief of the Stoics. It appears to be the predominant, though not the unanimous, attitude of the Jewish faith. It may be taken to represent also the position of a large segment of the Protestant community, insofar as that can be ascertained; organized groups that have taken a formal position on the abortion issue have generally regarded abortion as a matter for the conscience of the individual and her family. As we have noted, the common law found greater significance in quickening. Physicians and their scientific colleagues have regarded that event with less interest and have tended to focus either upon conception, upon live birth, or upon the interim point at which the fetus becomes "viable," that is, potentially able to live outside the mother's womb, albeit with artificial aid. Viability is usually placed at about seven months (28 weeks) but may occur earlier, even at 24 weeks. The Aristotelian theory of "mediate animation," that held sway throughout the Middle Ages and the Renaissance in Europe, continued to be official Roman Catholic dogma until the 19th century, despite opposition to this "ensoulment" theory from those in the Church who would recognize the existence of life from the moment of conception. The latter is now, of course, the official belief of the Catholic Church. As one brief *amicus* discloses, this is a view strongly held by many non-Catholics as well, and by many physicians. Substantial problems for precise definition of this view are posed, however, by new embryological data that purport to indicate that conception is a "process" over time, rather than an event, and by new medical techniques such as menstrual extraction, the "morning-after" pill, implantation of embryos, artificial insemination, and even artificial wombs.

In areas other than criminal abortion, the law has been reluctant to endorse any theory that life, as we recognize it, begins before live birth or to accord legal rights to the unborn except in narrowly defined situations and except when the rights are contingent upon live birth. For example, the traditional rule of tort law denied recovery for prenatal injuries even though the child was born alive. That rule has been changed in almost every jurisdiction. In most States, recovery is said to be permitted only if the fetus was viable, or at least quick, when the injuries were sustained, though few courts have squarely so held. In a recent development, generally opposed by the commentators, some States permit the parents of a stillborn child to maintain an action for wrongful death because of prenatal injuries. Such an action, however, would appear to be one to vindicate the parents' interest and is thus consistent with the view that the fetus, at most, represents only the potentiality of life. Similarly, unborn children have been recognized as acquiring rights or interests by way of inheritance or other devolution of property, and have been represented by guardians *ad litem*. Perfection of the interests involved, again, has generally been contingent upon live birth. In short, the unborn have never been recognized in the law as persons in the whole sense.

In view of all this, we do not agree that, by adopting one theory of life, Texas may override the rights of the pregnant woman that are at stake. We repeat, however, that the State does have an important and legitimate interest in preserving and protecting the health of the pregnant woman, whether she be a resident of the State or a nonresident who seeks medical consultation and treatment there, and that it has still *another* important and legitimate interest in protecting the potentiality of human life. These interests are separate and distinct. Each grows in substantiality as the woman approaches term and, at a point during pregnancy, each becomes "compelling."

With respect to the State's important and legitimate interest in the health of the mother, the "compelling" point, in the light of present medical knowledge, is at approximately the end of the first trimester. This is so because of the now-established medical fact, that until the end of the first trimester mortality in abortion may be less than mortality in normal childbirth. It follows that, from and after this point, a State may regulate the abortion procedure to the extent that the regulation reasonably relates to the preservation and protection of maternal health. Examples of permissible state regulation in this area are requirements as to the qualifications of the person who is to perform the abortion; as to the licensure of that person; as to the facility in which the procedure is to be performed, that is, whether it must be a hospital or may be a clinic or some other place of less-than-hospital status; as to the licensing of the facility; and the like.

This means, on the other hand, that, for the period of pregnancy prior to this "compelling" point, the attending physician, in consultation with his patient, is free to determine, without regulation by the State, that, in his medical judgment, the patient's pregnancy should be terminated. If that decision is reached, the judgment may be effectuated by an abortion free of interference by the State.

With respect to the State's important and legitimate interest in potential life, the "compelling" point is at viability. This is so because the fetus then presumably has the capability of meaningful life outside the mother's womb. State regulation protective of fetal life after viability thus has both logical and biological justifications. If the State is interested in protecting fetal life after viability, it may go so far as to proscribe abortion during that period, except when it is necessary to preserve the life or health of the mother.

Measured against these standards, Art. 1196 of the Texas Penal Code, in restricting legal abortions to those "procured or attempted by medical advice for the purpose of saving the life of the mother," sweeps too broadly. The statute makes no distinction between abortions performed early in pregnancy and those performed later, and it limits to a single reason, "saving" the mother's life, the legal justification for the procedure. The statute, therefore, cannot survive the constitutional attack made upon it here.***

To summarize and to repeat:

1. A state criminal abortion statute of the current Texas type, that excepts from criminality only a *life-saving* procedure on behalf of the mother, without regard to pregnancy stage and without recognition of the other interests involved, is violative of the Due Process Clause of the Fourteenth Amendment.

(a) For the stage prior to approximately the end of the first trimester, the abortion decision and its effectuation must be left to the medical judgment of the pregnant woman's attending physician.

(b) For the stage subsequent to approximately the end of the first trimester, the State, in promoting its interest in the health of the mother, may, if it chooses, regulate the abortion procedure in ways that are reasonably related to maternal health.

(c) For the stage subsequent to viability, the State in promoting its interest in the potentiality of human life may, if it chooses, regulate, and even proscribe, abortion except where it is necessary, in appropriate medical judgment, for the preservation of the life or health of the mother.

2. The State may define the term "physician," as it has been employed in the preceding paragraphs to mean only a physician currently licensed by the State, and may proscribe any abortion by a person who is not a physician as so defined.***

This holding, we feel, is consistent with the relative weights of the respective interests involved, with the lessons and examples of medical and legal history, with the lenity of the common law, and with the demands of the profound problems of the present day. The decision leaves the State free to place increasing restrictions on abortion as the period of pregnancy lengthens, so long as those restrictions are tailored to the recognized state interests.

Notes and Issues for Discussion

1. *Roe* struck down a Texas statute making it a crime to have an abortion or to perform an abortion. The Court states ". . . the right of personal privacy includes the abortion decision, but this right is not unqualified and must be considered against important state interests." What are these interests? When do they come into play? When and how can the state restrict abortions?

2. The Court indicates that "person" as used in the Fourteenth Amendment does not include the unborn. What arguments can be made that it does? That it doesn't? The Court avoids the issue of when life begins: "We need not resolve the difficult question of when life begins" and later indicates that ". . . we do not agree that, by adopting one theory of life, Texas may override the rights of the pregnant woman that are at stake."

3. *Roe* balances state and maternal interests depending upon the stage of the pregnancy. Much of the approach is based on then existing medical knowledge about the stages of pregnancy and fetal development. What if this changes?

4. Note that *Roe* doesn't mention a spouse or potential father of the unborn. Does he have rights? Do they have rights if they are not the same persons? In *Planned Parenthood of Missouri v. Danforth*, 428 U.S. 52 (1976), the Court struck down a Missouri statute which required prior written spousal consent for an abortion during the first twelve weeks of pregnancy stating "that the State cannot 'delegate to a spouse a veto power which the state itself is absolutely and totally prohibited from exercising during the first trimester of pregnancy.'" (See p. 192).

5. *Roe* does not reach the question of abortion funding, but two later court decisions, *Maher v. Roe*, 432 U.S. 464 (1977), and *Harris v. McRae*, 448 U.S. 297 (1980), make it clear that the states are not constitutionally obligated to pay for abortions. *Maher* upheld a Connecticut law that did not include nontherapeutic, medically unnecessary abortions within a Medicaid funded program. Although the case was based on equal protection, not privacy, the reasons in the majority and dissenting opinions are of interest. In *Maher*, Justice Powell wrote:

   "The Connecticut regulation places no obstacles—absolute or otherwise—in the pregnant woman's path to an abortion. An indigent woman who desires an abortion suffers no disadvantage as a consequence of Connecticut's decision to fund childbirth; she continues as before to be dependent on private sources for the service she desires. The State may have made childbirth a more attractive alternative, thereby influencing the woman's decision, but it has imposed no restriction on access to abortions that was not already there. The indigency that may make it difficult—and in some cases, perhaps, impossible—for some women to have abortions is neither created nor in any way affected by the Connecticut regulation. We conclude that the Connecticut regulation does not impinge upon the fundamental right recognized in *Roe*." 432 U.S. at 474.

In his dissent, Justice Brennen argued there was a "distressing insensitivity to the plight of impoverished pregnant women" inherent in the majority opinion. "The stark reality for too many, not just 'some' indigent pregnant women is that indigency makes access to competent licensed physicians not merely 'difficult' but 'impossible.' As a practical matter many indigent women will feel they have no choice but to carry their pregnancies to term because the State will pay for the associated medical services, even though they would have chosen to have abortions if the State had also provided funds for that procedure.... This disparity in funding by the State clearly operates to coerce indigent pregnant women to bear children they would not otherwise choose to have, and just as clearly, this coercion can only operate upon the poor, who are uniquely the victims of this form of financial pressure." 432 U.S. at 482-483.

6. In *Harris v. McRae*, the Court rejected a substantive due process challenge and upheld the Hyde Amendment which with few exceptions prohibited the use of federal funds in Medicaid for reimbursement of abortion costs. There the court observed:

"... [I]t simply does not follow that a woman's freedom of choice carries with it a constitutional entitlement to the financial resources to avail herself of the full range of protected choices.... Although government may not place obstacles in the path of a woman's exercise of her freedom of choice, it need not remove those not of its own creation. Indigency falls in the latter category...." 448 U.S. at 316.

Justice Brennen in his dissent took issue with this:

"*Roe* and its progeny established that the pregnant woman has a right to be free from state interference with her choice to have an abortion—a right which, at least prior to the end of the first trimester, absolutely prohibits any governmental regulation of that highly personal decision. The proposition for which these cases stand thus is not that the State is under an affirmative obligation to ensure access to abortions for all who may desire them; it is that the State must refrain from wielding its enormous power and influence in a manner that might burden the pregnant woman's freedom to choose whether to have an abortion. The Hyde Amendment's denial of public funds for medically necessary abortions plainly intrudes upon this constitutionally protected decision, for both by design and in effect it serves to coerce indigent pregnant women to bear children that they would otherwise elect not to have." 448 U.S. at 330.

7. Do minors have a right to an abortion? Can parental consent be required? Parental notification? At this time a minor does have a right to an abortion, parental consent may be required as long as the minor is provided an alternate route such as a "judicial bypass" where a judge provides the consent, and parental notification statutes for unemancipated minors under sixteen years of age living at home and dependent upon their parents for their support are constitutionally acceptable. (See, generally, p. 195*ff*.)

8. In a recent abortion decision, *Planned Parenthood v. Casey*, 505 U.S.——, 120 L.Ed. 2d 674 (1992), a majority of the Court upheld the *Roe v. Wade*

woman's constitutional liberty right to an abortion, although with limitations including providing abortion information to the woman twenty-four hours prior to the abortion, informed consent, and some reporting and recordkeeping requirements. Three of the majority justices rejected the trimester framework of *Roe*, instead advancing an "undue burden" standard which would permit state regulation of abortion unless it imposes an undue burden on the woman. 120 L. Ed. 2d at 714.

The Right of Privacy and Sexual Conduct

Griswold and *Eisenstadt* develop the concept of a privacy right to make decisions about birth control; *Roe* develops more broadly the right to make decisions about one's body in the area of abortion. In *Stanley v. Georgia*, 394 U.S. 557 (1967), the Court invalidated a state statute that made it a criminal offense to possess or read obscene material in a private home, noting: "If the First Amendment means anything, it means that a State has no business telling a man, sitting alone in his house, what books he may read or what films he may watch." 394 U.S. at 565. The following case which challenges a Georgia statute making sodomy a criminal offense suggests some limits to this privacy.

BOWERS v. HARDWICK
478 U.S. 186 (1986)
U.S. SUPREME COURT

JUSTICE WHITE delivered the opinion of the Court.

In August 1982, respondent Hardwick (hereafter respondent) was charged with violating the Georgia statute criminalizing sodomy[1] by committing that act with another adult male in the bedroom of respondent's home. After a preliminary hearing, the District Attorney decided not to present the matter to the grand jury unless further evidence developed.

Respondent then brought suit in the Federal District Court, challenging the constitutionality of the statute insofar as it criminalized consensual sodomy. He asserted that he was a practicing homosexual, that the Georgia sodomy statute, as administered by the defendants, placed him in imminent danger of arrest, and that the statute for several reasons violates the Federal Constitution. The District Court granted the defendants' motion to dismiss for failure to state a claim.***

A divided panel of the Court of Appeals for the Eleventh Circuit reversed.***

This case does not require a judgment on whether laws against sodomy be-

---

[1] Georgia Code Ann § 16-6-2 (1984) provides, in pertinent part, as follows:

"(a) A person commits the offense of sodomy when he performs or submits to any sexual act involving the sex organs of one person and the mouth or anus of another. . . .

"(b) A person convicted of the offense of sodomy shall be punished by imprisonment for not less than one nor more than 20 years. . . ."

tween consenting adults in general, or between homosexuals in particular, are wise or desirable. It raises no question about the right or propriety of state legislative decisions to repeal their laws that criminalize homosexual sodomy, or of state-court decisions invalidating those laws on state constitutional grounds. The issue presented is whether the Federal Constitution confers a fundamental right upon homosexuals to engage in sodomy and hence invalidates the laws of the many States that still make such conduct illegal and have done so for a very long time. The case also calls for some judgment about the limits of the Court's role in carrying out its constitutional mandate.

We first register our disagreement with the Court of Appeals and with respondent that the Court's prior cases have construed the Constitution to confer a right of privacy that extends to homosexual sodomy and for all intents and purposes have decided this case. The reach of this line of cases was sketched in Carey v Population Services International, 431 US 678 (1977). Pierce v Society of Sisters, 268 US 510 (1925), were described as dealing with child rearing and education; Prince v Massachusetts, 321 US 158 (1944), with family relationships; Skinner v Oklahoma ex rel. Williamson, 316 US 535 (1942), with procreation; Loving v Virginia, 388 US 1 (1967), with marriage; Griswold v Connecticut, and Eisenstadt v Baird, with contraception; and Roe v Wade, 410 US 113 (1973), with abortion. The latter three cases were interpreted as construing the Due Process Clause of the Fourteenth Amendment to confer a fundamental individual right to decide whether or not to beget or bear a child.

Accepting the decisions in these cases and the above description of them, we think it evident that none of the rights announced in those cases bears any resemblance to the claimed constitutional right of homosexuals to engage in acts of sodomy that is asserted in this case. No connection between family, marriage, or procreation on the one hand and homosexual activity on the other has been demonstrated, either by the Court of Appeals or by respondent. Moreover, any claim that these cases nevertheless stand for the proposition that any kind of private sexual conduct between consenting adults is constitutionally insulated from state proscription is unsupportable.***

Precedent aside, however, respondent would have us announce, as the Court of Appeals did, a fundamental right to engage in homosexual sodomy. This we are quite unwilling to do. It is true that despite the language of the Due Process Clauses of the Fifth and Fourteenth Amendments, which appears to focus only on the processes by which life, liberty, or property is taken, the cases are legion in which those Clauses have been interpreted to have substantive content, subsuming rights that to a great extent are immune from federal or state regulation or proscription. Among such cases are those recognizing rights that have little or no textual support in the constitutional language. Meyer, Prince, and Pierce fall in this category, as do the privacy cases from Griswold to Carey.

Striving to assure itself and the public that announcing rights not readily identifiable in the Constitution's text involves much more than the imposition of the Justices' own choice of values on the States and the Federal Government, the Court has sought to identify the nature of the rights qualifying for heightened judicial protection. In Palko v Connecticut, 302 US 319 (1937), it was said that this category includes those fundamental liberties that are "implicit in the concept of ordered liberty," such that "neither liberty nor justice would exist if [they] were sacrificed." A different description of fundamental liberties appeared in Moore v East Cleveland, 431 US 494 (1977), where they are characterized as those liberties that are "deeply rooted in this Nation's history and tradition."

It is obvious to us that neither of those formulations would extend a fundamental right to homosexuals to engage in acts of consensual sodomy. Proscriptions against that conduct have ancient roots. Sodomy was a criminal offense at common law and was forbidden by the laws of the original 13 States when they ratified the Bill of Rights. In 1868, when the Fourteenth Amendment was ratified, all but 5 of the 37 States in the Union had criminal sodomy laws. In fact, until 1961, all 50 States outlawed sodomy, and today, 25 States and the District of Columbia continue to provide criminal penalties for sodomy performed in private and between consenting adults. Against this background, to claim that a right to engage in such conduct is "deeply rooted in this Nation's history and tradition" or "implicit in the concept of ordered liberty" is, at best, facetious.***

Respondent, however, asserts that the result should be different where the homosexual conduct occurs in the privacy of the home. He relies on Stanley v Georgia, 394 US 557 (1969), where the Court held that the First Amendment prevents conviction for possessing and reading obscene material in the privacy of one's home: "If the First Amendment means anything, it means that a State has no business telling a man, sitting alone in his house, what books he may read or what films he may watch."

Stanley did protect conduct that would not have been protected outside the home, and it partially prevented the enforcement of state obscenity laws; but the decision was firmly grounded in the First Amendment. The right pressed upon us here has no similar support in the text of the Constitution, and it does not qualify for recognition under the prevailing principles for construing the Fourteenth Amendment. Its limits are also difficult to discern. Plainly enough, otherwise illegal conduct is not always immunized whenever it occurs in the home. Victimless crimes, such as the possession and use of illegal drugs, do no escape the law where they are committed at home.***And if respondent's submission is limited to the voluntary sexual conduct between consenting adults, it would be difficult, except by fiat, to limit the claimed right to homosexual conduct while leaving exposed to prosecution adultery, incest, and other sexual crimes even though they are committed in the home. We are unwilling to start down that road.

Even if the conduct at issue here is not a fundamental right, respondent asserts that there must be a rational basis for the law and that there is none in this case other than the presumed belief of a majority of the electorate in Georgia that homosexual sodomy is immoral and unacceptable. This is said to be an inadequate rationale to support the law. The law, however, is constantly based on notions of morality, and if all laws representing essentially moral choices are to be invalidated under the Due Process Clause, the courts will be very busy indeed. Even respondent makes no such claim, but insists that majority sentiments about the morality of homosexuality should be declared inadequate. We do not agree, and are unpersuaded that the sodomy laws of some 25 States should be invalidated on this basis.

Accordingly, the judgment of the Court of Appeals is reversed.

JUSTICE BLACKMUN, with whom JUSTICE BRENNAN, JUSTICE MARSHALL, and JUS-
TICE STEVENS join, dissenting.

This case is no more about "a fundamental right to engage in homosexual
sodomy," as the Court purports to declare, ante, than Stanley v Georgia was
about a fundamental right to watch obscene movies, or Katz v United States, 389
US 347 (1967), was about a fundamental right to place interstate bets from a telephone booth. Rather, this case is about "the most comprehensive of rights and the
right most valued by civilized men," namely, "the right to be let alone." Olmstead v United States, 277 US 438, 478 (1928) (Brandeis, J., dissenting).

The statute at issue, Ga Code Ann §16-6-2 (1984), denies individuals the right
to decide for themselves whether to engage in particular forms of private, consensual sexual activity. The Court concludes that §16-6-2 is valid essentially because "the laws of . . . many States . . . still make such conduct illegal and have
done so for a very long time." Like Justice Holmes, I believe that "[i]t is revolting
to have no better reason for a rule of law than that so it was laid down in the time
of Henry IV. It is still more revolting if the grounds upon which it was laid down
have vanished long since, and the rule simply persists from blind imitation of the
past." Holmes, The Path of the Law, 10 Harv L Rev 457, 469 (1897).***

In its haste to reverse the Court of Appeals and hold that the Constitution does
not "confe[r] a fundamental right upon homosexuals to engage in sodomy," ante,
the Court relegates the actual statute being challenged to a footnote and ignores
the procedural posture of the case before it. A fair reading of the statute and of the
complaint clearly reveals that the majority has distorted the question this case
presents.

First, the Court's almost obsessive focus on homosexual activity is particularly had to justify in light of the broad language Georgia has used. Unlike the
Court, the Georgia Legislature has not proceeded on the assumption that homosexuals are so different from other citizens that their lives may be controlled in a
way that would not be tolerated if it limited the choices of those other citizens.
Rather, Georgia has provided that "[a] person commits the offense of sodomy
when he performs or submits to any sexual act involving the sex organs of one
person and the mouth or anus of another." Ga Code Ann §16-6-2(a) (1984). The
sex or status of the persons who engage in the act is irrelevant as a matter of state
law.***Michael Hardwick's standing may rest in significant part on Georgia's apparent willingness to enforce against homosexuals a law it seems not to have any
desire to enforce against heterosexuals. But his claim that §16-6-2 involves an unconstitutional intrusion into his privacy and his right of intimate association does
not depend in any way on his sexual orientation.

***I believe we must analyze respondent Hardwick's claim in the light of the
values that underlie the constitutional right to privacy. If that right means anything, it means that, before Georgia can prosecute its citizens for making choices
about the most intimate aspects of their lives, it must do more than assert that the
choice they have made is an "'abominable crime not fit to be named among
Christians.'"***

***We protect those rights not because they contribute, in some direct and ma-
terial way, to the general public welfare, but because they form so central a part
of an individual's life.***

Only the most willful blindness could obscure the fact that sexual intimacy is "a sensitive, key relationship of human existence, central to family life, community welfare, and the development of human personality."***The fact that individuals define themselves in a significant way through their intimate sexual relationships with others suggests, in a nation as diverse as ours, that there may be many "right" ways of conducting those relationships, and that much of the richness of a relationship will come from the freedom an individual has to *choose* the form and nature of these intensely personal bonds.

In a variety of circumstances we have recognized that a necessary corollary of giving individuals freedom to choose how to conduct their lives is acceptance of the fact that different individuals will make different choices.

***The Court claims that its decision today merely refuses to recognize a fundamental right to engage in homosexual sodomy; what the Court really has refused to recognize is the fundamental interest all individuals have in controlling the nature of their intimate associations with others.

Notes and Issues for Discussion

1. Justice White characterizes the issue as simply ". . . whether the Federal Constitution confers a fundamental right upon homosexuals to engage in sodomy and hence invalidates the laws of the many States that still make such conduct illegal. . . ." Is this the issue? Does the Georgia statute prohibit only homosexual sodomy?
2. The arrest took place in Hardwick's home, in his bedroom. What privacy rights are involved here? How different are they from those involved in prohibiting the use of contraceptives by married couples in their bedroom, the conduct proscribed by Connecticut in *Griswold?* How different is it from that involved in *Stanley v. Georgia?*
3. The court makes a distinction between the substantive privacy protections described in *Palko v. Connecticut:* "fundamental liberties such that neither liberty or justice would exist if [they] were sacrificed" and the issue presented in *Hardwick.* If the *Hardwick* case is about the state proscribing private conduct in one's own bedroom between consenting adults is this a real distinction?
4. Georgia concedes that it has not enforced the statute against heterosexuals. Should this make a difference? Why?
5. What is sodomy in Georgia? If one means of spreading AIDS is through sodomy, does this give a rational basis for the statute?
6. The decision in *Hardwick* has been relied upon to deny a quasi-suspect classification and heightened protection to homosexuals. See *High Tech Gays v. Defense Industry Security Clearance Office,* 895 F.2d 563 (1990) and the discussion on pp. 70–71.

PRIVACY AS PROTECTION FROM GOVERNMENTAL DISCLOSURE

Federal, state, and local governments are gathering and storing more and more information about individuals. At the same time, maintaining the privacy of this information and protecting the individual is becoming increasingly difficult. Federal and some state statutes forbid disclosure of large amounts of information without an individual's consent and waiver. The problem remains where there is an unauthorized disclosure of private information made through carelessness or ignorance.

DOE v. BOROUGH OF BARRINGTON
729 F. Supp. 376 (1990)
U.S. DISTRICT COURT

BROTMAN, District Judge.

Presently before the court is the motion of plaintiffs Jane Doe and her children for partial summary judgment against defendants Borough of Runnemede ("Runnemede") and Officer Smith.***This case presents novel issues concerning the privacy rights of individuals who have contracted Acquired Immune Deficiency Syndrome ("AIDS") and the privacy rights of their family members. For the reasons stated in this opinion, plaintiffs' motion for summary judgment against defendants Runnemede and Smith will be granted.***

The facts are largely undisputed. On March 25, 1987, Jane Doe, her husband, and their friend James Tarvis were traveling in the Doe's pickup truck through the Borough of Barrington ("Barrington"). At approximately 9:00 a.m., a Barrington police officer stopped the truck and questioned the occupants. As a result of the vehicle stop, Barrington officers arrested Jane Doe's husband and impounded the pickup truck. Barrington officers escorted Jane Doe, her husband, and James Tarvis to the Barrington Police Station.

When he was initially arrested, Jane Doe's husband told the police officers that he had tested HIV positive and that the officers should be careful in searching him because he had "weeping lesions."***

Sometime in the late afternoon of the same day, Jane Doe and James Tarvis drove Tarvis's car to the Doe residence in the Borough of Runnemede ("Runnemede"). The car engine was left running, and the car apparently slipped into gear, rolling down the driveway into a neighbor's fence. The neighbors owning the fence are Michael DiAngelo and defendant Rita DiAngelo. Rita DiAngelo is an employee in the school district in Runnemede.

Two Runnemede police officers, Steven Van Camp and defendant Russell Smith, responded to the radio call about the incident. While they were at the scene, Detective Preen of the Barrington police arrived and, in a private conversation with Van Camp, revealed that Jane Doe's husband had been arrested earlier in the day and had told Barrington police officers that he had AIDS. Van Camp then told defendant Smith.

After Jane Doe and Tarvis left the immediate vicinity, defendant Smith told the DiAngelos that Jane Doe's husband had AIDS and that, to protect herself, Rita DiAngelo should wash with disinfectant.*** Defendant Rita DiAngelo became upset upon hearing this information. Knowing that the four Doe children attended the Downing School in Runnemede, the school that her own daughter attended, DiAngelo contacted other parents with children in the school. She also contacted the media. The next day, eleven parents removed nineteen children from the Downing School due to a panic over the Doe children's attending the school. The media was present, and the story was covered in the local newspapers and on television. At least one of the reports mentioned the name of the Doe family. Plaintiffs allege that as a result of the disclosure, they have suffered harassment, discrimination, and humiliation. They allege they have been shunned by the community.

Plaintiffs brought this civil rights action against the police officer Smith and the municipalities of Barrington and Runnemede for violations of their federal constitutional rights pursuant to 42 U.S.C. § 1983 (1982). The federal constitutional right is their right to privacy under the fourteenth amendment.***

Defendants assert that there are no conclusive facts about AIDS, therefore, a material issue of fact exists whether warning the DiAngelos was justified. Defendants cite one article to demonstrate that, although no case of AIDS has yet been attributed to casual contact with an infected person, so much is unknown about the disease that infection through casual contact cannot be ruled out.***Defendants ignore the multitude of information, available in 1987, that flatly rejects their argument that AIDS may be spread through casual contact.

This court must take medical science as it finds it; its decision may not be based on speculation of what the state of medical science may be in the future.***'AIDS is *not* spread by casual contact and this fact was established before March 25, 1987.***

The linchpin here is whether the Constitution protects plaintiffs' confidentiality with respect to Jane Doe's husband's AIDS. If the Constitution does not protect the Does from disclosure of Jane Doe's husband's condition, there is no constitutional violation to support a section 1983 claim against the officer or the municipality. There is no case directly on point. Plaintiffs assert that this privacy right was recognized in *Roe v. Wade.****

This court finds that the Constitution protects plaintiffs from governmental disclosure of their husband's and father's infection with the AIDS virus. The United States Supreme Court has recognized that the fourteenth amendment protects two types of privacy interests. "One is the individual interest in avoiding disclosure of personal matters, and another is the interest in independence in making certain kinds of important decisions." *Whalen v. Roe.* Disclosure of a family member's medical condition, especially exposure to or infection with the AIDS virus, is a disclosure of a "personal matter."***

The United States Supreme Court has indicated that the government's duty to avoid unwarranted disclosures arguably has its roots in the federal Constitution.***

Lower courts have held that, once the government has confidential information, it has the obligation to avoid disclosure of the information. In *Carter v. Broadlawns Medical Center*, 667 F.Supp. 1269, the court held that a public hospital had violated plaintiffs' constitutional rights by giving chaplains open access to patient medical records without patient authorization. The court noted that, in permitting free access to medical records, the hospital did not properly respect a patient's confidentiality and privacy as recognized in *Whalen v. Roe*. The court concluded that a chaplain could review patient medical records only upon prior express approval of the individual patient or his or her guardian.

At least one court has addressed disclosure of a patient's condition with AIDS. In *Woods v. White*, 689 F.Supp. 874 (W.D. Wis. 1988), the court held that prison officials who discussed the fact that plaintiff had tested positive for AIDS with nonmedical prison personnel and with other inmates violated the inmate's constitutional rights and could be held liable under section 1983. The court recognized plaintiff's privacy interest in the information. The court stated that, to define the scope of the right to privacy in personal information, it must balance the individual's right to confidentiality against the governmental interest in disclosure. The court noted that information about one's body and state of health is particularly sensitive, and that such information has traditionally been treated differently from other types of personal information. Noting the most publicized aspect of the disease, that it is related more closely than other diseases to sexual activity and intravenous drug use, the court stated that "it is difficult to argue that information about this disease is not information of the most personal kind, or that an individual would not have an interest in protecting against the dissemination of such information." The court held that plaintiff had a constitutional right to privacy in his medical records.***

This court finds the reasoning employed by the *Carter* and *Woods* courts persuasive. The sensitive nature of medical information about AIDS makes a compelling argument for keeping this information confidential. Society's moral judgments about the high-risk activities associated with the disease, including sexual relations and drug use, make the information of the most personal kind. Also, the privacy interest in one's exposure to the AIDS virus is even greater than one's privacy interest in ordinary medical records because of the stigma that attaches with the disease. The potential for harm in the event of a nonconsensual disclosure is substantial; plaintiff's brief details the stigma and harassment that comes with public knowledge of one's affliction with AIDS.

The hysteria surrounding AIDS extends beyond those who have the disease. The stigma attaches not only to the AIDS victim, but to those in contact with AIDS patients, *see* N.Y. Times, Sept. 8, 1985, at A1, col 1 (doctor of gay patients threatened with eviction), and to those in high risk groups who do not have the disease. *See Poff v. Caro*, 549 A.2d 900, 903 (N.J.Super.Law Div.1987) (landlord refused to rent to three gay men for fear of AIDS); Newsweek, July 1, 1985, at 61 (healthy gay men fired because of AIDS phobia); Nat'l L.J., July 25, 1983, at 3, 11 (California police demand masks and rubber gloves be used when dealing with gays); N.Y. Times, June 28, 1983, at A18, col. 1, 4 (Haitians denied employment because of fear of AIDS). Revealing that one's family or household member has AIDS causes the entire family to be ostracized. The right to privacy in this information extends to members of the AIDS patient's immediate family. Those sharing a household with an infected person suffer from disclosure just as the victim does. Family members, therefore, have a substantial interest in keeping this information confidential. Disclosures about AIDS cause a violation of the family's privacy much greater than simply revealing any other aspect of their family medical history.

An individual's privacy interest in medical information and records is not absolute. The court must determine whether the societal interest in disclosure outweighs the privacy interest involved.***

The government's interest in disclosure here does not outweigh the substantial privacy interest involved. The government has not shown a compelling state interest in breaching the Does' privacy. The government contends that Officer Smith advised the DiAngelos to wash with disinfectant because of his concern for the prevention and avoidance of AIDS, an incurable and contagious disease. While prevention of this deadly disease is clearly an appropriate state objective, this objective was not served by Smith's statement that the DiAngelos should wash with disinfectant. Disclosures of the Does' confidential information did not advance a compelling governmental interest.***

This court concludes that the Does have a constitutional right of privacy in the information disclosed by Smith and the state had no compelling interest in revealing that information. As such, the disclosure violated the Does' constitutional rights.***

Notes and Issues for Discussion

1. Does the Doe family have a constitutional right to privacy? Where in the constitution does the court find that right?
2. What kinds of harm have the Doe family suffered?
3. Note that the Doe family may also bring an action in state court for invasion of privacy and emotional distress.

   The portion of the decision dealing with liability has been deleted. Generally it is not easy to successfully sue municipal governments. Later in the decision the court stated: "To maintain an action under section 1983 against Runnemede [the borough], plaintiffs must show that the unconstitutional actions of a municipal employee were taken pursuant to a municipal policy or custom. Plaintiffs must also establish a 'direct causal link' between the unconstitutional municipal policy or custom and the actions of the municipal employee to establish liability." 729 F. Supp. at 387.

   In *Doe* the court found the municipality liable because of its failure to train its officers. "In light of the duties assigned to police officers, the need for police training about AIDS is obvious. Officers frequently come into contact with members of high risk populations, such as intravenous drug users, therefore, police must understand the disease and its transmission to protect themselves and the public. . . . The absence of training here is a deliberate and conscious choice by the municipality. . . . Runnemede's failure to train its officers about AIDS and the need to keep confidential the identity of those known to police to have the disease falls within the Supreme Court's definition of 'deliberate indifference' that caused the violation of Does' constitutional rights." 729 F. Supp. at 389.

4. If the police force had specific AIDS training, it seems unlikely that the municipality would be liable. Does your agency have AIDS training? Training about AIDS confidentiality and privacy?

5. What are some examples of invasions of privacy that you have encountered in the work situation? Did any of these result in actual harm to the patient or client? Did the patient or client seek legal redress? If not, why not?

6. What steps has your agency taken to limit invasions of privacy? Are there specific policies and procedures?

The Federal Privacy Act

Protecting the confidentiality of records and information is becoming more difficult within the health and human services as both the volume and type of information gathered about clients increases dramatically and the technology for receiving, storing, compiling, and transmitting information has expanded exponentially. Client records have become more voluminous as more information is gathered, and more information is seen as important in decision making or as necessary to provide protection from potential legal action.

A "record," which once may have consisted of a single file card containing very basic information, now may include hundreds of pages of written and photographic material as well as audio and video tape recordings. Computerized technology for reading, recording, storing, sorting, compiling, retrieving and transmitting material has allowed for expanding the amount of material kept on file and has simplified and broadened access to that material. Along with these issues, the emergence of federal, state, and private third-party payors has greatly increased the potential for broad dispersion of the information.

Privacy is protected by statutory law as well as constitutional law. The Federal Privacy Act of 1974 as amended by the Computer Matching and Privacy Protection Act of 1988, 5 U.S.C. §552a, comprises the major federal statutory law protecting the privacy of an individual's records maintained by federal agencies. Coupled with the Freedom of Information Act (FOIA), 5 U.S.C. §552b, the statute limits access to or transmission of an individual's records without notice and consent, allows the individual to access and correct the records, and permits free public access to other governmental information. Some states have similar statutory provisions as well. Here we will deal only with the Federal Privacy Act, which is quite technical and complex.

COVERAGE

The act covers an "individual" defined as "a citizen of the United States or an alien lawfully admitted for permanent residence." §552a(a)(2). Given this definition, a business, a non-citizen and an unlawful alien are excluded. The act applies to a "record" and a "systems of records". Records are defined as "any item, collection or grouping of information" and include identifiable educational, financial, employment, medical and criminal information. §552a(d)(4).[3] Systems of records are defined as a group of records which the agency controls and from which information is retrieved by identifying name or number. §552a(a)(5). Thus the records must be under control of the agency to be covered and must contain identifiable information. Agencies primarily are limited to federal agencies within the executive branch and independent regulatory agencies. Congressional and judiciary agencies are excluded. §552a(e).

DISCLOSURE

The general privacy rule is:

> No agency shall disclose any record which is contained in a system of records by any means of communication to any person, or to another agency, except pursuant to a written request by, or with the prior written consent of, the individual to whom the record pertains . . . §552a(b).

With the general disclosure rule, there are a series of twelve exceptions. The most relevant for our purposes are:

> (1) to those officers and employees of the agency which maintains the record who have a need for the record in the performance of their duties;
> (2) required under section 552 of this title;[4]
> (3) for a routine use as defined in subsection (a)(7) of this section and described under section (e)(4)(D) of this section;[5] . . .
> (7) to another agency or to an instrumentality of any governmental jurisdiction with or under the control of the United States for a civil or criminal law enforcement activity if the activity is authorized by law, and if the head of the agency or instrumentality has made a written request to the agency which maintains the record specifying the particular portion desired and the law enforcement activity for which the record is sought;

(8) to a person pursuant to a showing of compelling circumstances affecting the health or safety of an individual if upon such disclosure notification is transmitted to the last known address to such individual; . . .

(11) pursuant to the order of a court of competent jurisdiction; . . ." §552a(b).

Other provisions (1) require an accurate accounting of disclosures (except for within agency or FOIA disclosures) and making the accounting of disclosures available to the individual (except for law enforcement disclosures), 5 U.S.C. §552a(c); (2) allow access by the individual, and either permit an amendment by the individual or, if the agency refuses to permit the change, provide for a procedure for the individual to challenge that refusal, §552a(d); (3) limit the information kept, require that it be collected directly from the individual if it may have an adverse impact, and specify that when collecting information from an individual, the individual is to be informed of the authority, purpose, routine use, and adverse effects of refusing to supply the information, §552a(e)(1)–(3); (4) require that each agency publish annually in the *Federal Register* a notice of the existence of its records, including the name and location of the system, the categories of individuals and records covered, the routine use of the information, policies, and practices around storage, access, retention, and disposal, and procedures whereby the individual can be notified how to gain access or contest the information kept, §552a(e)(4); and (5) require that the information kept by the agency in making any determination about the individual be accurate, relevant, timely, and complete "as is reasonably necessary" to assure a fair determination, §552a(e)(5).

The act provides for civil action where there is a refusal to amend a record or a failure to follow amendment procedures, a failure to maintain accurate, relevant, timely, and complete information under §552a(e)(5), or any other failure under the act that results in an adverse effect, and it permits the court to amend the record, and assess reasonable attorney fees and costs. If there has been an adverse effect and the court determines that the agency acted in an intentional or willful manner, actual damages (with a minimum of $1,000) plus costs and attorney's fees can be assessed. §552a(g)(1). The act specifies that it is a misdemeanor with a $5,000 maximum fine when any officer or employee of the agency knowingly discloses prohibited information to any person or agency not entitled to receive it or willfully maintains a system of records without meeting the annual notice requirements. §552a(i)(1). Finally, some records such as law enforcement are generally exempt from the act, and others may be specifically exempted. §552a(j),(k).

Under the Computer Matching and Privacy Protection Act of 1988, the Privacy Act was amended to include "matching programs," defined as computerized comparisons of "two or more automated systems of records or a system of records with non-Federal records" if the purpose was "establishing or verifying the eligibility or continuing compliance with" requirements by applicants, recipients, beneficiaries, participants, or providers of federal benefits programs or recouping payments or delinquencies in federal benefit programs, as long as the matches are not for statistical, law enforcement, or tax purposes or used for routine administrative purposes. The act requires a prior written agreement before a computer match can be made, including procedures for initial and periodic notice to individuals within the computer programs, procedures to verify, retain, and destroy records, and prohibits taking any action against an individual until there is some independent verification of the material and the individual affected has an opportunity to challenge to material. 5 U.S.C. §552a(f)(p). The act also calls for the creation of a data integrity board to oversee and review the systems and agreements. §552a(f)(u).

PRIVACY AS PROTECTION FROM GOVERNMENTAL INTRUSION

A third and somewhat different kind of privacy is "the right of the individual to be free in his private affairs from governmental surveillance and intrusion." *Whalen v. Roe*, 429 U.S. at 599. The right may be implicit in a due process "liberty" interest, but this protection also has been found directly in the Fourth Amendment's prohibition on unreasonable searches and seizures.

GILLARD v. SCHMIDT
579 F. 2d 825 (1978)
U.S. COURT OF APPEALS

ROSENN, Circuit Judge.

On February 4, 1976, a political cartoon, drawn over the signature "Ed Ucation," appeared in a local newspaper of Fair Lawn, New Jersey, the "Fair Lawn Shopper." The cartoon ridiculed the financial and personnel policies of the Fair Lawn, New Jersey, Board of Education by depicting the Board members as poker players, apparently gambling away employees' salaries and jobs. At the first meeting of the Board following publication of the cartoon, defendant-appellee Harold Schmidt, an elected member of the Board, directed the Board's attention to the cartoon, which he characterized as a "total disgrace to the elected body," and urged the Board to find the artist and punish him. The Board never took any action on the matter.

Schmidt subsequently received information indicating that Francis Gillard, plaintiff-appellant, a guidance counselor employed by the Fair Lawn School System, was the offending cartoonist. On the evening of February 10, 1976, Schmidt went to Gillard's school, the Thomas Jefferson Junior High School, which was open that evening for participants in the Adult Education Program. After entering the building, Schmidt found a janitor with a pass key, and directed him to unlock the door to the guidance counselor's suite—one large room partitioned into five smaller offices. In the janitor's presence, Schmidt reconnoitered the offices to ascertain which one was Gillard's. When he had located it, he entered it to search for clues linking Gillard to the cartoon. Observing a slightly open drawer in Gillard's desk, Schmidt pulled it completely open, revealing copies of the cartoon. Having confirmed his expectations, Schmidt left the office without further rummaging through Gillard's desk, and the janitor followed him out, locking the office behind him.

Gillard brought suit in the United States District Court for the District of New Jersey, alleging a violation of his fourth amendment rights to be free from unreasonable government intrusion, and asserting a cause of action under 42 U.S.C. §1983. The district court, trying the case without a jury, found that Schmidt had surreptitiously searched Gillard's office as part of a campaign to retaliate against Gillard's unflattering cartoon. Accepting, *arguendo*, plaintiff's contention that he had a reasonable expectation of privacy from his employer's investigatory desk search, the district court nevertheless dismissed the complaint, reasoning that the injury alleged fell outside the protection of the fourth amendment. We disagree and we reverse.

42 U.S.C. §1983 reads, in pertinent part:
Every person who, under color of any statute, ordinance, regulation, custom, or usage, of any State or Territory, subjects or causes to be subjected, any citizen of the United States ... to the deprivation of any rights, privileges, or immunities secured by the Constitution and laws, shall be liable to the party injured in an action at law, suit in equity ...

Recovery in a section 1983 action requires the presence of two elements: deprivation of a right secured by the "Constitution and laws" of the United States, and a showing that such deprivation occurred under color of state law.***
The fourth amendment to the Constitution reads:

The right of the people to be secure in their persons, houses, papers, and effects, against unreasonable searches and seizures, shall not be violated, and no Warrants shall issue, but upon probable cause, supported by Oath or affirmation, and particularly describing the place to be searched, and the person or things to be seized.

A primary object of this amendment is to "safeguard the privacy and security of individuals against arbitrary invasions by governmental officials." Thus, the Supreme Court has extended fourth amendment protection beyond the "paradigmatic entry" into a house by police officers in search of criminal evidence to civil investigations of business premises. The Court has reasoned that "[i]f the government intrudes on a person's property, the privacy interest suffers whether the government's motivation is to investigate violations of criminal law or breaches of other statutory or regulatory standards." The Supreme Court has stated explicitly that this "privacy interest," the right of a citizen to be free in his private affairs from government intrusion, *Whalen v. Roe*, as one facet of a broad constitutional right to privacy, "is directly protected by the Fourth Amendment."

These cases demonstrate that the fourth amendment embraces privacy rights asserted in the context of an unreasonable government search, as alleged here. Therefore, we hold that the plaintiff has properly alleged a violation of a fourth amendment right cognizable in the federal courts.

Having decided only that the fourth amendment protects against the type of privacy invasion alleged here, our analysis is not yet complete. We must now determine whether the warrantless search in this case compels application of the fourth amendment, for Gillard may claim its protection only if the area searched was one in which he had "a reasonable expectation of freedom from governmental intrusion."

As a guidance counselor, Gillard dealt daily with students' private, personal problems. Working in an office secured by a locked door at a desk containing psychological profiles and other confidential student records, Gillard had a reasonable expectation that papers in his desk would remain safe from prying eyes. Gillard's privacy expectation was by no means atypical, for as the Fair Lawn Superintendent of Schools testified at trial:

> Speaking not only as superintendent of schools, but as a former teacher, my desk as a teacher was probably the only place within the classroom or within a department that you could keep private. . . . I think it is reasonable for any teacher or any administrator to assume that if they would put something in their desk, that it would be for their eyes only and not accessible to anyone else.

Furthermore, the Fair Lawn School Board impliedly approved this expectation of privacy by issuing a statement shortly after Schmidt's search disapproving it:

> By virtue of his position as trustee, the Board president, vice-president, and committee chairman or member has no right to enter the closed school building unless he or she is in the company of the proper school administrator, does so at the specific direction of the Board, does so solely for a purpose directly related to his or her duty as Board officer, committee chairman or member. The Board does not and cannot authorize, approve or condone the entry into a closed school building by one or more of its members under any other circumstances.

We therefore hold that a guidance counselor, charged with maintaining sensitive student records, in the absence of an accepted practice or regulation to the contrary, enjoys a reasonable expectation of privacy in his school desk.

Defendant's contention that Gillard cannot claim a fourth amendment violation because the desk belonged to the school system is unsupported by the case law. Applicability of the fourth amendment does not turn on the nature of the property interest in the searched premises, but on the reasonableness of the person's privacy expectation. Furthermore, defendant's assertion that a public employer is free to search the premises of an employee is a broad overstatement of the relevant law. The cases indicate that an employer may conduct a search in accordance with a regulation or practice that would dispel in advance any expectations of privacy.***Our reading of the record, however, reveals no regulation or practice which would act to negative Gillard's reasonable expectation of privacy in his desk. We conclude, therefore, that Gillard has proven the first element of a section 1983 action, deprivation of a right secured by the Constitution and laws of the United States.***

Notes and Issues for Discussion

1. The Fourth Amendment usually applies to unlawful searches related to criminal evidence. How does the court expand this to Schmidt's search?
2. Fourth Amendment prohibitions apply to governmental searches. Why is the search in *Gillard* a governmental search?
3. Gillard would certainly have a "reasonable expectation of freedom from governmental intrusion" if the search was conducted in his home. Does it make any difference that Gillard's desk belonged to the school system?
4. What elements of a guidance counselor's work lead to an expectation of privacy?
5. Is your office desk private? May your employer have access to it without permission? If you are an administrator, what are your policies for accessing employee desks?

RECORDS AND RECORD KEEPING

Along with access to records, a crucial issue for the health and human services professional is what and when to record.

Documentation in the health and human services is crucial, not only for dealing professionally with a patient or client, but for recording a decision or course of action which may be later called into question, or which may require testimony in court.

Whether a health and human services patient or client will have complete access to a record will depend upon state and federal law, as well as agency policy. As a general rule, patients and clients have access to their records unless they contain confidential information or information that may be damaging to the client. Moreover, records can be subpoenaed and may have to be produced. Therefore, the professional should carefully record only necessary information and should avoid recording that which does not belong, such as unsubstantiated rumors and personal observations that have no bearing on a course of treatment.

SELECTED REFERENCE

Franklin, J. D., and Bouchard, R. F., *Guidebook to the Freedom of Information and Privacy Act of 1974* (1986).

CHAPTER 6

CONFIDENTIAL COMMUNICATIONS

Principles and Limitations

What is confidentiality? What are privileged communications? How do they differ? What are their limitations? What should a patient or client be told about them? When? These and many other questions about confidentiality and privilege frequently arise throughout the health and human services. Unlike privacy—a broader concept having to do with keeping an individual's personal life from public scrutiny and protecting individual autonomy—confidentiality and privilege have to do with the protection of client information and the purposes and conditions under which it may be released. Confidentiality and privilege are sometimes used interchangeably. Here, however, *confidentiality* will refer to the general protection afforded to client communications, information, and records received and kept by the health and human services professional and agency; *privilege* will refer to a narrow range of protected communications between patients or clients and certain health and human services professionals.

BASIC CONCEPTS

Confidential means "intrusted with the confidence of another or with his secret affairs or purposes; intended to be held in confidence or kept secret." Confidence means "reliance on discretion of another" (Black's *Law Dictionary*, 1991). Privileged communications are "those statements made by a certain person within a protected relationship . . . which the law protects from forced disclosure on the witness stand . . ." (Black's *Law Dictionary*, 1991).

Confidentiality is the broader concept that includes an expectation that confidential material will not be divulged or shared with others, while privileged communications carry with them a requirement that they may not be divulged even in court. Confidential material covers much of the patient- or client-related information, data, records, and files in the health and human services. Privileged communications are limited to communications and information occurring in specific "protected relationships"—such as physician and patient—which are usually specified by statute. For example, a health and human services worker not covered by privilege might learn about a hit-and-run accident, illegal drug sales, or welfare fraud from a client. While these disclosures cannot generally be made public, the worker might feel the need—or under agency regulations be required—to report any of these to the appropriate agency and could be called to testify in court. If the same disclosures were made to a health and human services professional covered by privilege, such as a psychiatrist, psychologist, or social worker, these would be considered privileged communications in many jurisdictions, and the professional could not divulge them even in court without the permission of the client, the holder of the privilege.

However, for most health and human services professionals, confidentiality and privilege are not absolute but have limitations. Depending upon the jurisdiction, the recipient of confidential or privileged communications may be legally required to disclose certain types of information, such as suspected child abuse, elder abuse, criminal acts, or threats to one's self or others. The area is complex and will be dealt with later in this chapter.

CONFIDENTIALITY

The confidentiality of patient or client communications, information, or records in the health and human services may be based on statutes, court decisions, or professional codes of ethics. Violations of confidentiality may be actionable in criminal or civil actions or as professional misconduct under state licensing laws. Depending on the state law, type of violation, and degree of resulting harm, criminal fines, damage awards, or suspension from practice could result. Even if none of these occur, the patient or client whose confidences are revealed may suffer emotional distress and the professional making the unauthorized disclosure may suffer professional harm.

Most violations of confidentiality by health and human services professionals probably stem from carelessness or even ignorance. Chance comments about a client or patient may be made and overheard in offices, halls, elevators, homes, or at social events. Telephone conversations in which clients are identified and cases discussed may be overheard by visitors. Confidential reports and files may be left in typewriters, on computer screens, on desks and tables, in cars, or—in violation of many agencies' regulations—

may be taken home. Many of these infractions can be avoided with adequate care, policies, and supervision.

Confidential material may appropriately be seen by others. For example, information provided by a client usually may be discussed with colleagues and supervisors for professional purposes in case conferences and consultations. The client may be referred by a court which requires reporting information back to the court. Depending on the law, others within the same agency (or sometimes related agencies) may have access to the information if they are providing services to the same client or the client's family. (However, for transmittal of information outside an agency, a release should regularly be obtained from the client.)

Confidentiality in Specific Settings

FEDERAL DRUG AND ALCOHOL PROGRAMS

Federally funded drug and alcohol treatment programs are bound by particularly restrictive confidentiality laws:

> Records of the identity, diagnosis, prognosis or treatment of any patient which are maintained in connection with the performance of any drug abuse prevention function conducted, regulated or directly or indirectly assisted by any department or agency of the United States shall . . . be confidential and be disclosed only for the purpose and circumstances expressly authorized. . . . 42 U.S.C. §290ee-3.

The same restrictions for "any program or activity relating to alcoholism, alcohol abuse education, training, treatment, rehabilitation, or research" are provided in 42 U.S.C. §290dd-3. Fines for improper release under either section are up to $500 for the first offense and up to $5,000 for succeeding offenses. Exceptions include releases with prior written consent by the patient, to medical personnel in medical emergencies or for research and audit purposes, in cases of child abuse, or by court order upon a showing of good cause.[1]

HEALTH, MENTAL HEALTH, AND DEVELOPMENTAL DISABILITIES AGENCIES

Records in health agencies, mental health agencies, and agencies for the developmentally disabled are generally protected by specific statutes mandating confidentiality of client information and records. Access may be permitted under certain conditions including *bona fide* research, external audits, or by a court order. Myers (1992: 28 ff.) discusses a number of cases permitting access to privileged mental health records in child abuse, termination of parental rights, child custody, and visitation litigation.

JUVENILE COURTS, CHILD PROTECTIVE SERVICES AGENCIES

Records of the juvenile courts are generally confidential. In many jurisdictions, when the juvenile attains majority (usually eighteen years) the records are sealed or destroyed. However, some states are currently considering legislation allowing access to these records, particularly in the case of serious offenses, by police, school personnel, and others.

Records pertaining to child abuse are confidential and in most jurisdictions information may not be released. However, depending upon state statutes, it may be possible for defendants in child abuse proceedings to access confidential or privileged records. In *Pennsylvania v. Ritchie*, 480 U.S. 39 (1987), the Court refused to permit full disclosure of child protective service records, but allowed access through an *in camera* review by the trial judge, with disclosure of any material information, and permitted the defendant to request specific information.[2]

ADOPTION RECORDS

Adoption records are sealed and in most jurisdictions cannot be accessed to release the identity of biological parents without showing good cause. Some states provide for access by adult adoptees if they can show a psychological need to know who their biological parents are or if the biological parents have registered with a statewide adoption registry, indicating their desire to contact their adopted child.[3]

EDUCATIONAL RECORDS

Confidentiality of educational records is protected under federal law, 20 U.S.C. §1232g, sometimes known as the Buckley Amendment. This statute applies to any public or private educational agency or institution that receives federal funds, and prohibits federal funding for programs that either deny parental access to a student's educational records or that permit the release of educational records without written consent of the parents or students over eighteen. Without consent, only "directory information" may be released by the educational program, which is limited to the student's name, address, telephone number, date and place of birth, major, dates of attendance and a few other items of information. 20 U.S.C. §1232g(a)(5)(A). Among the records excluded from parental access are

> records of instructional, supervisory and administrative personnel and educational personnel ancillary thereto which are in the sole possession of the maker thereof and which are not accessible or revealed to any other person except a substitute;

and

> records on a student who is eighteen years of age or older, or is attending an institution of post secondary education, which are made or maintained by a physician, psychiatrist, psychologist, or other recognized professional or paraprofessional acting in his professional or paraprofessional capacity and which are made, maintained or used only in connection with the provision of treatment to the student and are not available to anyone other than persons providing such treatment. . . . 20 U.S.C. §1232(a)(4)(B).

Exceptions to the provision requiring written consent prior to release of educational records are limited to other school officials including teachers who have legitimate educational interests, and for other limited purposes such as receipt of financial aid, audits, research and in emergencies "if the knowledge of such information is necessary to protect the health or safety of the student or other persons." 20 U.S.C. §1232(g)(b)(1).

PERSONS WITH AIDS

A critical issue is the confidential treatment of information about persons who have been diagnosed as HIV positive or who have AIDS. While there may be a conflict between the interests of the HIV positive or AIDS carrying individual and those who may believe they have a right to know of this condition, the law in most jurisdictions presently protects the confidentiality of the person with AIDS. However, increasingly there are exceptions to this rule, including public health reporting and in some cases disclosure to a spouse or sexual partner. The topic is discussed more fully in Chapter 13, but the health and human services professional should keep abreast of current laws and regulations and proceed carefully in this area.[4]

PRIVILEGED COMMUNICATIONS

Privilege has a very technical legal meaning. Privileged communications are

> those statements made by a certain person within a protected relation-
> ship . . . which the law protects from forced disclosure on the witness
> stand at the option of [the holder of the privilege] which the law will
> not permit to be divulged, or allow them to be inquired into in a court
> of justice. . . . (Black's *Law Dictionary*, 1991)

While privilege extends to a range of relationships including spouses, lawyers and clients, and reporters and sources, here the focus will be limited to communications between patients or clients and the health and human services professional.

The rationale for privilege is that certain types of relationships need to be protected to insure open communication and a free flow of information. Privilege extends to testimony in court and is an exception to the general rule that all relevant information should be available in the courtroom.[5]

Dean Wigmore, in his classic treatise on evidence, identifies four conditions necessary for privilege:

1. The communication must originate in a confidence that it will not be disclosed.

2. This element of confidentiality must be essential to the full and satisfactory maintenance of the relationship between the parties.

3. The relation must be one which in the opinion of the community ought to be sedulously fostered.

4. The injury that would inure to the relation by the disclosure of the communication must be greater than the benefit thereby gained for the correct disposal of litigation. (Wigmore, 1961: 52)

At common law only attorney-client communications had the status of privileged communications (Wilson, 1978: 100). Depending on the jurisdictions, privilege now has been extended to communications between patients or clients and a wide range of health and human services professionals, including physicians, dentists, chiropractors, nurses, psychiatrists, psychologists, marriage counselors, social workers, sexual assault counselors, and domestic violence counselors.

A number of issues must be considered in privileged communications in the human services:

1. Who can claim the privilege; who is a patient or client?

2. What types of communications are privileged?

3. Which of the health and human services professions have privilege?

4. What constitutes a waiver of the privilege?

5. What are the limitations to the privilege?

Who Can Claim Privilege, What Communications Are Privileged?

The patient or client as "holder" of the privilege makes the decision whether or not the information may be disclosed. A guardian is the holder of privilege for an incompetent ward. Unless it has been waived, the health and human services professional may assert the privilege on behalf of the patient or client. Generally a parent can assert privilege for a child, or with sufficient maturity, a child may be allowed to assert the privilege him or herself.[6]

States vary extensively in what constitutes a patient or client and what communications are covered by privilege. Within a single state, there may be substantial differences across the professions so that client or patient is defined broadly in some professions and narrowly in others, and what is privileged may similarly be broadly or narrowly defined. For some professions only certain communications or information are privileged; for others, the privilege extends to all communications between the patient or client and the professional. Therefore, it is important for the health and human services professional to ascertain the relevant state privilege provisions. The following examples do not cover the range of privilege in all states or within any one state, rather they are drawn to show the range of some statutes.

In Wisconsin, patients of physicians, registered nurses, chiropractors, or psychologists are included. The privilege is extended to "confidential communications made or information obtained or disseminated for purposes of diagnosis or treatment of the patient's physical, mental or emotional condition. . . ." Wis. Stat. Ann. §905.04.

In New Jersey, a patient of a physician, and presumably a psychiatrist, is "a person who, for the sole purpose of securing preventative, palliative or curative treatment, or a diagnosis preliminary to such treatment, of his physical or mental condition, consults a physician, or submits to an examination by a physician. . . ." Privileged communications are "such information transmitted between physician and patient, including information obtained by examination of the patient, as is transmitted in confidence . . ." where "the patient or the physician reasonably believed the communication to be necessary or helpful to enable the physician to make a diagnosis of the condition of the patient or to prescribe or render treatment therefore. . . ." N.J. Stats. Ann. 2A:84A-22.1, 22.2.

In the same state, patients of licensed practicing psychologists include "individuals, couples, families or groups" and confidential communications are put on the same basis as lawyer-client privilege, N.J.S.A.45:14B-28, while marriage counselor privilege covers "Any communication between a marriage counselor and the person or persons counseled. . . ." N.J.S.A. 45:8B-29.

In Washington, patient-physician privilege extends to "any information acquired from persons consulting the individual in professional capacity when that information was necessary to enable the individual to render professional services. . . ." Wash. Rev. Code §18.19.180.

In New York, the patient-physician privilege includes physicians, dentists, chiropractors, and nurses and extends to "any information which he [the professional] acquired in attending a patient in a professional capacity, and which was necessary to enable him to act in that capacity." N.Y. Civ. Prac. Law §4504.

In Massachusetts, the patient of a psychotherapist is "a person who during the course of diagnosis or treatment, communicates with a psychotherapist," and the communication includes ". . . conversations, correspondence, actions and occurrences relating to diagnosis or treatment before, during or after institutionalization, regardless of the patient's awareness of such conversations, correspondence, actions and occurrences, and any records, memoranda or notes of the foregoing." Mass. Gen. Laws Ann. ch. 233 §20B.

If the individual believes him or herself to be a patient or client and this is not the case, or considers the professional receiving the communication to be within a protected category when the professional is not, states differ in whether there is privilege.

STATE v. MILLER
300 Ore. 203, 709 P.2d 225 (1985)
OREGON SUPREME COURT

CARSON, Justice.

This case involves the scope of the psychotherapist-patient privilege in Oregon, under OEC 504.***

Just before midnight on August 6, 1982, defendant telephoned his brother in California and told him that he had just "strangled a kid." Defendant's brother advised him to call a mental hospital or talk to someone who could help him with his problem. Minutes later, defendant telephoned Dammasch State Hospital and asked to speak to a doctor, giving a false name to the secretary-receptionist, Ms. Smith. When Ms. Smith asked him "what the problem [was]," he replied, "Murder. I just killed a man." Ms. Smith then said she would let him speak to a psychiatrist. She asked defendant for the telephone number from which he was calling; he told her the number, stating it was in a public telephone booth.

Ms. Smith telephoned the Clackamas County Sheriff's office, explained the situation, and gave them defendant's telephone number. Then Ms. Smith called Dr. Wendy Saville, the psychiatrist on duty that night at the hospital and asked her to keep defendant on the line so that the Sheriff's office could "trace the call."

Dr. Saville talked to defendant for 10 or 15 minutes, asking him for background information, similar to what she usually obtained from a patient in a psychiatric interview. At trial, however, she testified that she was only talking to defendant so that the police could find him and that she only asked him about his background because it seemed the "safest" thing to talk about. When she questioned defendant about his name, he asked whether their conversation was confidential. Dr. Saville assured defendant that she would not disclose his confidences; only then did he give her his true name. During the conversation, defendant made a number of incriminating statements about his homosexual encounter with the victim, his fantasies and his role in the victim's death.

While defendant conversed with Dr. Saville, the Sheriff's office contacted the Portland Police Bureau, which located the telephone booth and sent a uniformed officer to investigate. When the officer arrived at the telephone booth and determined that defendant was the person talking to the state hospital, he physically removed defendant from the telephone booth, patted him down for weapons, found none, removed defendant's wallet and placed him in the locked rear passenger area of his patrol car.

The officer returned to the telephone booth to talk to Dr. Saville. She initially declined to give him any information about what defendant had told her because she believed it was a confidential communication protected by the psychotherapist-patient privilege. When the officer became "angry" and "pushed" her to tell him what happened, she told him that defendant told her he murdered someone.

The officer returned to the patrol car and questioned defendant, without advising him of his *Miranda* rights. Defendant responded that he wanted to speak to a lawyer, but the officer continued to ask him several times whether he had hurt someone and where the person was. During this questioning, defendant admitted that he had "hurt someone," that he "couldn't wake him up," and indicated that the person was in defendant's room in a residential hotel. Defendant then pulled his room keys out of his pocket and the officer took them.

The officer called for an ambulance, drove to the hotel one block away, entered the locked room using defendant's keys, and discovered the deceased victim's body. The officer returned to the car and for the first time advised defendant of his *Miranda* rights. Defendant did not respond to further police questioning.

Defendant's room was searched, and the victim's body and other evidence was removed. The next day, a search warrant was sought and issued, authorizing a search of defendant's room, from which other evidence was removed.

Defendant was charged with murder. ORS 163.115. He moved to suppress (1) his statements to Ms. Smith; (2) his statements to Dr. Saville; (3) his statements to the police officer; (4) evidence seized from his person; (5) evidence obtained during the warrantless entry and search of his room; and (6) all derivative evidence from the alleged illegalities. The trial court suppressed only his statements to the police officer, made during custodial interrogation without advice of *Miranda* rights and after he asserted his right to counsel. After a trial to the court, defendant was convicted of first degree manslaughter.***

The psychotherapist-patient privilege in Oregon is governed by OEC 504. The purpose of this privilege is to foster a relationship that is deemed important to society and one whose success is dependent upon full and free communication.***

OEC 504(2) provides:

> "A patient has a privilege to refuse to disclose and to prevent any other person from disclosing confidential communications made for the purposes of diagnosis or treatment of the patient's mental or emotional condition among the patient, the patient's psychotherapist, or persons who are participating in the diagnosis or treatment under the direction of the psychotherapist, including members of the patient's family."

"Patient" is defined as "a person who consults or is examined or interviewed by a psychotherapist." OEC 504(1)(b).

"Psychotherapist" is defined as:

> "***a person who is licensed, registered, certified or otherwise authorized under the laws of any state to engage in the diagnosis or treatment of a mental or emotional condition, or reasonably believed by the patient so to be, while so engaged." OEC 504(1)(c).

"Confidential communication" is defined as:

> "***a communication not intended to be disclosed to third persons except: Persons present to further the interest of the patient in the consultation, examination or interview; persons reasonably necessary for the transmission of the communication; or persons who are participating in the diagnosis and treatment under the direction of the psychotherapist, including members of the patient's family." OEC 504(1)(a).

The rule only protects from disclosure a "confidential communication," defined as "a communication not intended to be disclosed to third persons." OEC 504(1)(a).***

The communication must also be "made for the purposes of diagnosis or treatment." OEC 504(2). The purpose of the communication may be inferred from the surrounding circumstances. A patient's reasonable belief that the communication is being made for the purposes of diagnosis or treatment will suffice.***

The trial court and four judges on the Court of Appeals seem to have concluded that defendant could not be a "patient" and invoke the privilege until a psychotherapist-patient relationship had been established that had been "agreed upon by both sides." They considered controlling the fact that defendant had not previously been a patient at the hospital, that the psychiatrist did not anticipate an ongoing psychotherapist-patient relationship to develop, and that she testified she was not actually diagnosing or treating defendant, but only keeping him on the telephone line until the police arrived.

A previously established psychotherapist-patient relationship is not required before the privilege can be invoked.***

In light of the policy behind the rule and its similarity to the attorney-client privilege, we conclude that the psychotherapist-patient privilege protects communications made in an initial conference for the purpose of establishing a psychotherapist-patient relationship, even if such a relationship is never actually formed. The psychotherapist-patient privilege "necessarily includes communications made in the course of diagnostic interviews and examinations which might reasonably lead to psychotherapy." *Allred v. State,* 554 P.2d 411, 420 (Alaska 1976). This is required to encourage patients to discuss frankly and freely their mental or emotional problems so that the professional can accurately determine whether he or she is qualified to treat them. If information revealed during the initial conference indicates to either party that an ongoing professional relationship should not be formed, the confidences revealed in the initial consultation are protected nevertheless.

This is not to say, however, that a prospective patient who meets a person known to be a psychotherapist in a supermarket and immediately makes an unsolicited confession can claim the privilege solely because the patient intends the communication to be confidential and hopes to receive diagnosis or treatment. In order for statements made in an initial encounter to be covered by the privilege, the psychotherapist and patient must agree, or at least reasonably appear to agree, that they intend to establish a psychotherapist-patient relationship. There must be some indication from the psychotherapist that he or she is willing to embark upon such a relationship. An indication of this intent may be inferred from the circumstances. It might come from the setting alone. For example, if a prospective patient talks to a licensed psychotherapist in a professional practice setting, such as a mental health clinic or a private practice office, the patient could fairly infer that the psychotherapist has indicated a willingness to enter into a confidential relationship. The requisite willingness could also be shown by the psychotherapist's behavior, apart from the setting. If the prospective client in the above-stated supermarket example is assured by the psychotherapist that his statements will be kept confidential and is questioned about his problem, then the therapist has reasonably indicated a willingness to enter into a psychotherapist-patient relationship, and the privilege attaches when the first words are spoken.

Where a psychotherapist has given reasonable assurances to the patient that they are embarking upon a privileged relationship, an ulterior motive or purpose on the part of the psychotherapist will not prevent the patient from claiming the privilege.***

Thus, where a patient consults a psychotherapist for professional assistance for a mental or emotional problem and reasonably believes that the psychotherapist is willing to embark upon a professional relationship, the fact that the psychotherapist has a secret ulterior purpose for the interview or examination will not prevent the patient from claiming the privilege as to confidential communications. To hold otherwise would effectively transfer the privilege from the patient (who holds it under OEC 504(3)) to the psychotherapist. Such a shift is not supported by the language of the rule, its underlying policy, or caselaw.

Turning to the facts of this case, defendant herein specifically requested, and was assured of, confidentiality. Only then did he divulge his true name. This is a clear indication that defendant intended his conversation with the psychiatrist to be confidential.

At his brother's suggestion, defendant telephoned Dammasch State Hospital and asked to speak to a doctor. He was described as distraught and depressed. No one has disputed that he was seeking professional assistance for his emotional condition. He talked to a psychiatrist for 10 or 15 minutes, until the conversation was interrupted by the police officer removing him from the telephone booth. During this conversation the psychiatrist did not engage in "small talk" or idle chatter. She testified that she spoke to the defendant and questioned him in much the same way she would have in a psychiatric interview. Based upon these facts, the only reasonable conclusion is that defendant reasonably believed that the communication was made "for the purposes of diagnosis or treatment."

We thus hold that defendant's statements to Dr. Saville were covered by the psychotherapist-patient privilege and should not have been admitted into evidence.

Notes and Issues for Discussion

1. According to the Oregon court, the purpose of privilege is to protect and foster an important relationship with full and free communication. Is a communication about murder one that should be protected? Why?
2. A key element in the *Miller* case seems to be that the psychotherapist promised confidentiality and then engaged in a professional interview, despite the fact that she did not intend to establish a professional relationship. The court says that if the therapist acts in this way and the client reasonably believes that a patient-psychotherapist relationship has been established, then it has. Is Miller's belief in confidentiality reasonable?
3. The Oregon court held that the communication with the receptionist was also privileged. However, the court upheld Miller's conviction on the grounds that there was other evidence sufficient for a conviction.
4. In *State v. Martin*, 274 N.W. 2d 893 (1979), the defendant made an early morning call to a licensed certified psychiatric social worker with whom he had talked before and told him "I just killed somebody." The social worker told Martin that he would have to notify the police and did so. The police investigated and found the murder victim at Martin's house. One of the issues on appeal was whether the conversation between Martin and the social worker was privileged under South Dakota law. The South Dakota statute, states: "No licensed certified social worker, social worker, or social work associate or his employee may disclose any information he may have acquired from persons consulting him in his professional capacity that was necessary to enable him to render services in his profes-

sional capacity to those persons...." SDCL 36-26-30. The court held the conversation was not privileged because there was no indication that it was made in confidence or with the expectation that it would be confidential. Martin had been a patient of the social worker for six to eight months "and apparently had faith in him." Should this make a difference? Is the case different from *Miller?*

Professionals with Privilege

Communications between patients or clients and a variety of professions are covered by privilege statutes, depending on state law. Most communications between physicians and their patients are covered by privilege statutes. Professionals such as nurses or social workers who collect information from patients for the purpose of diagnosis or treatment by the physician are also usually covered by the same privilege. In many jurisdictions, communications with psychiatrists, who must also be medical doctors, will have the same privilege. In others, there are separate statutes governing psychiatrists' privilege or they may be included with other human services professionals. Communications with priests and clergy are usually privileged, although there may be limitations on who qualifies as a clergyperson and the communications may be restricted to confessions. Licensed professionals such as psychologists, social workers, psychotherapists, and marriage counselors often have separate and quite different privilege provisions. In recent years, privilege has been extended to counselors of rape victims, sexual assault counselors, and domestic violence counselors, among others.

Waiver of Privilege

The patient or client as holder of the privilege can waive it. Waiver may take a number of forms, although a clearly written, signed, and dated release is preferable. Most states specify that there must be a "knowing" waiver, that is, that the individual must wish to end the privilege and be aware of the consequences. If the patient or client communicates the privileged information to a third party, this may in itself constitute a waiver, although some states also require that the individual understand that such communication will terminate it. If a third party not an employee of the professional or agent or parent of the patient hears or intercepts the communication, it may no longer be privileged. California has removed this exception, called the "eavesdropper rule." See *Menendez v. Superior Court,* 834 P 2d 786 (1992).

LIMITATIONS ON CONFIDENTIALITY AND PRIVILEGE

For most health and human services professionals, neither confidentiality nor privilege is absolute. In many jurisdictions communications that indicate that serious physical harm to oneself or to an identifiable third party will probably occur are not protected. In most states communications that lead one to suspect, or in some states to reasonably suspect, child abuse or neglect has occurred must be disclosed and the abuse reported. Commission of a crime and abuse of an elderly, handicapped, or institutionalized individual are reportable in some jurisdictions. In addition, a court may order the disclosure of privileged information in a range of actions, including child custody, child visitation, termination of parental rights, and child abuse.

INFORMING ABOUT CONFIDENTIALITY AND ITS LIMITS

If confidentiality and privilege are not absolute, how and when to inform patients or clients of the limitations is a difficult issue for many in the health and human services. Some professional codes of ethics call for providing this information at the beginning of the professional relationship, and by statute some states require that such information be provided.[7] In many states, however, the law is silent on the subject. The following case shows some of the problems that can occur.

STATE IN THE INTEREST OF J.P.B.
143 N.J. Super. 96 (1976)
NEW JERSEY APPELLATE COURT

The opinion of the court was delivered by HANDLER, J. A. D.

J.B. and A.T., juveniles, were adjudged delinquent upon a finding that they robbed and murdered one Malcolm Tyler. The central issue on these consolidated appeals is whether particular confessions, the only evidence linking them with the crime, were improperly admitted at their trial.***

In November 1973 J.B., then 16 years old, was committed to the Highfields Residential Group Center.*** As part of the Highfields program residents are required to participate in what is called "guided group instruction." Residents are assigned to a group as they enter Highfields and thereafter meet regularly with them. Generally, each 90-minute session focuses exclusively on one "student's" problems.

Albert Axelrod, the Superintendent of Highfields, testified that the premise of the group sessions is that only by dealing honestly with themselves and their past anti-social behavior can the residents begin to be rehabilitated. It is part of the rehabilitation process, Axelrod stated, to draw things out which are locked in a resident's mind so that troubling or terrifying thoughts may be looked at and dealt with. Participants are therefore encouraged (in Axelrod's phrase) to "bare their souls." Although no formal regulations are issued, it is understood by all involved that "What you say in the group will stay in the group." It is also understood that failure to participate fully can result in being returned to court as unsuitable for the Highfields program, which in turn is understood to mean revocation of probation and confinement at Yardville.

The first session to focus on J.B. was that of December 18, 1974. It is traditional at Highfields that at his first meeting a resident gives his life history, including "all problems with the law." During the early part of the evening, J.B. informed the group that he had just finished "doing time" at Stokes. ("Stokes" is the Stokes Forest unit of the Youth Correctional Institution at Annandale.) Axelrod stated that he knew—based on J.B.'s records and history and Highfield's entrance requirements—that this could not be so and confronted J.B. with his lie, telling him that he'd be hurting himself in the program if he lied. Later in the evening J.B. stated that he had been involved in a mugging and that at some subsequent date he learned that the victim might have died. Axelrod's best recollection of J.B.'s admissions is as follows:

> He and his accomplice followed the individual, I believe, down a road. He struck this individual with a pipe, the individual fell, and his accomplice then struck the man rather forcefully in the head with his pipe at least once. Then I think he took the man's wallet and fled, and then he added that some time later, several months later, they heard that a body had been found in this area and that they felt that this was the individual that they had assaulted.

Axelrod testified that on previous occasions he had been privy to revelations of criminal activity during group meetings but that he had never taken any action concerning that information. Following the December 18 meeting, however, he called J.B.'s probation officer and related the incident. Shortly thereafter Axelrod was visited by two State Troopers who convinced him to question J.B. further about the killing, and particularly the identity of his accomplice. Axelrod complied with their request and at a group meeting held on January 3, 1974 directed questions at J.B. for the specific purpose of determining who his accomplice was. The name was revealed by J.B. and, following the meeting, Axelrod gave it to the State Police. Axelrod had not told J.B. prior to the January 3 meeting that he had made any mention of J.B.'s confession to the police; neither did he give J.B. the *Miranda* warnings nor make any attempt to contact J.B.'s parents with regard to his further questioning of J.B.

On February 14 two State Troopers, Detective Sergeant Hunter and Detective Graham, went to Highfields to interview J.B., arriving between 1 and 2 P.M. Although J.B. was apparently given *Miranda* warnings at the outset of the interview, no attempt was made to contact his parents at that time. At approximately 3 P.M., the troopers advised Axelrod that they wished to take J.B. to Trenton for a polygraph examination. Axelrod gave his permission.

Hunter testified that J.B. initially denied any involvement in the Tyler death after being told by Hunter that information "from the street" linked him to the incident. Hunter pushed the point that his information seemed reliable, but that J.B. could clear himself by a polygraph examination. J.B., who is classified by his I.Q. as "dull normal," agreed to the test. When Hunter contacted the polygraph unit, someone there raised the question of parental permission and Hunter responded that Axelrod could give such permission.

The polygraph test was administered by State Police Detective Vona, and lasted from about 3:15 P.M. until after 5:00. Prior to the test Detective Vona was told of J.B.'s admissions in the group meetings.

Following the examination Detectives Vona, Hunter and Graham met with J.B. to discuss the test. Vona told the other troopers in J.B.'s presence that the test showed that he had lied and that he "was guilty of the crime but would not admit it." J.B. denied that he had lied, but Vona pointed out specific lies revealed by the examination. Finally, confronted with the test result, J.B. agreed to give a statement and admitted to being involved in the Tyler killing. The formal statement was taken after J.B., Hunter and Graham had supper and returned to Highfield. Although J.B. was again read the *Miranda* warnings, his parents had still not been contacted and he was not told that he could call them. The statement was begun at 7:55 P.M. and completed at 9:25 P.M. Approximately half-way through the statement, when J.B. had not yet named his accomplice, Axelrod interrupted and took him into the hall. During their private conversation Axelrod, for the first time, informed J.B. that the confidentiality of the therapy group had been breached and that the information he related in the group had been delivered to the State Police. J.B. then continued his statement and named his accomplice. At no time were J.B.'s parents called, and at no time during the entire eight hours of custody was he advised that a parent or other relative could be with him during questioning.

The trial judge ruled that all of J.B.'s statements were inadmissible except that made at the first group meeting on December 18, 1974. Statements made at subsequent group meetings were properly excluded.***

The juvenile maintains on this appeal that the initial statement made on December 18 should also have been excluded. We agree.

The context in which that statement was elicited constituted custodial interrogation. Axelrod was employed by the State as a supervisor of a state institution directly involved in dealing with juvenile offenders. The questioning conducted by him was by virtue of his authority as an agent of the State. The group session at which the incriminating statement was given focused upon J.B. as the primary subject. While the session's concentration on J.B. was not literally an investigation of J.B. as a criminal suspect or an interrogation directed to any particular crime, it was nevertheless aimed at uncovering personal anti-social behavior and its thrust was the revelation of the individual's past history, including criminal acts. Moreover, the questioning had coercive aspects. In addition to the custodial setting, each boy participating in the group therapy sessions was instructed to give a full statement of his personal problems, including criminal behavior when he was the subject or focus of the particular meeting. Also, it was generally understood among the "students" at Highfield that failure to cooperate fully in the group sessions would entail sanctions and that unresponsive person would be considered "unsuitable" for the Highfield program and be remanded to the court for sentencing to Yardville.

This congerie of factors constituted the essential ingredients which trigger *Miranda* protections—custodial interrogation under state authority directed against one believed to have been involved in crime. In these circumstances the *Miranda* warnings were required to be given in order that incriminating statements obtained could be admitted into evidence at a criminal trial or juvenile hearing.***

When, as here, the State exacts information under a promise or assurance of confidentiality, it cannot, consistent with due process and fundamental fairness, violate that confidentiality and defeat the expectations raised by its promise by using the information in a criminal trial as incriminating evidence against the one who offered it.***

We are satisfied that the use of the statement given by J.B. on December 18, 1973 in the trial against him for juvenile delinquency was contrary to basic standards of due process and fundamental fairness, and, as previously stated, reliance upon it as inculpatory proof at the trial did not comport with the constitutional privilege against self-incrimination. It should not therefore have been received in evidence. Since J.B.'s adjudication of delinquency was based entirely in his inadmissible statement, it is reversed.

Notes and Issues for Discussion

1. J.P.B.'s statements were made while on probation and undergoing interrogation in a custodial setting. This is the basis for the court requiring a *Miranda* warning. See *Miranda v. Arizona*, 384 U.S. 436 (1967);). In *Estelle v. Smith*, 451 U.S. 454 (1981), the Supreme Court overturned a death sentence based on psychiatric testimony gathered during a "mental status examination," that is, a competence to stand trial determination. The psychiatrist testified at the sentencing hearing that Smith "is going to go ahead and commit other similar or same criminal acts if given the opportunity to do so" and that he "has no remorse or sorrow for what he has done," although the psychiatrist never told Smith or his attorney that he was gathering information for use by the State. The Court held that this was a violation of Smith's Fifth Amendment protection and he should have received a *Miranda* warning prior to the examination:

   "The considerations calling for the accused to be warned prior to custodial interrogation apply with no less force to the pretrial psychiatric examination at issue here. Respondent was in custody at the Dallas county jail where the examination was ordered and where it was conducted. That the respondent was questioned by a psychiatrist designated by the trial lawyer to conduct a neutral competency examination, rather than by a police officer, governmental informant, or prosecuting attorney, is immaterial. When Dr. Grigson went beyond simply reporting to the court on the issue of competence and testified for the prosecution at the penalty phase on the crucial issue of respondent's future dangerousness, his role changes and became essentially like that of an agent of the State recounting unwarned statement made in a postarrest custodial setting." 384 U.S. at 467.

2. Several California cases have held that a protective services worker is not required to give a suspected child abuser a *Miranda* warning prior to eliciting information even though it may be incriminating, although in one case the court indicated an expectation that the worker will inform the person of the limits of confidentiality at the outset. *People v. Younghauz*, 202 Cal. Rptr. 907 (1984); *People V. Battaglia*, 203 Cal. Rptr. 370 (1984).

3. "What you say in the group will stay in the group." "Tell it like it is." What are the problems with these statements? Confidentiality and privilege in group settings or with multiple clients presents particular problems. Some states have a general rule that the presence of a third person, unless necessary for the transmission of the information, ends the privilege. In some jurisdictions there are exceptions for marriage counseling, which may involve multiple clients and communications are confidential or privileged unless there is an action against the marriage counselor. Some self-help groups such as Alcoholics Anonymous promise confidentiality in their meetings, but in the absence of a state statute or perhaps the presence of a professional covered by privilege, there is none and members can probably be compelled to disclose information received by the group.

4. In the State of Washington the following disclosure requirement applies to a range of human services professions: "Persons registered or certified under this chapter shall provide clients at the commencement of any program of treatment with accurate disclosure of information concerning their practice ... that will inform clients of the purpose of and resources available under this chapter including ... the extent of confidentiality provided by this chapter..." Wash. Bus. and Prof. Code §18.19.060. The regulations applying to federally funded drug and alcohol abuse programs require oral and written summaries of the applicable federal confidentiality provisions and exceptions. 42 C.F.R. Part 2, §2.22.

5. What is your agency's policy for informing patients or clients about confidentiality and its legal and ethical limitations? Is the information provided at the outset? What form should it take? Does it make a difference if that client is a child? Mentally ill? Retarded or developmentally disabled? Should the information be in writing? Should it be provided only once? At every meeting? Is it documented? What do you yourself tell your clients about confidentiality?

6. What is the impact of telling the patient or client that some communications may not be confidential? Will it harm the relationship? Can it improve the relationship? A concern frequently expressed is that if the professional informs the patient or client about the limits of confidentiality, this will have a chilling effect and the client may not divulge important information. However, reporting disclosures that were believed to be confidential could have a damaging effect on the professional relationship and could affect relationships with other clients. How do you resolve this dilemma?

7. If you are a health and human services administrator, how can you insure

that your workers are informing clients about agency policy on confidentiality?

DUTY TO PROTECT THIRD PARTIES

Many states now require that health and human services professionals take steps to protect third parties from harm if there is a reasonable belief the individuals are in danger, even if this results in a breach of confidentiality. However, there are many complexities to this general rule. In some states third parties must be identifiable, in others this is not required. Some have no requirement for protecting a third party in danger. Some have apparently rejected the duty to protect doctrine.[8]

In 1976, the California Supreme Court found a duty to warn and more broadly a duty to protect an identifiable foreseeable victim in the *Tarasoff* cases. *Tarasoff* was widely discussed in the legal and health and human service literature, and the ruling has been adopted in a number of jurisdictions by case and statutory law.

TARASOFF v. REGENTS OF UNIVERSITY OF CALIFORNIA
17 Cal.3d 425, 551 P. 2d 334 (1976)
CALIFORNIA SUPREME COURT

TOBRINER, Justice.

On October 27, 1969, Prosenjit Poddar killed Tatiana Tarasoff. Plaintiffs, Tatiana's parents, allege that two months earlier Poddar confided his intention to kill Tatiana to Dr. Lawrence Moore, a psychologist employed by the Cowell Memorial Hospital at the University of California at Berkeley. They allege that on Moore's request, the campus police briefly detained Poddar, but released him when he appeared rational. They further claim that Dr. Harvey Powelson, Moore's superior, then directed that no further action be taken to detain Poddar. No one warned plaintiffs of Tatiana's peril.

Concluding that these facts set forth causes of action against neither therapists and policemen involved, nor against the Regents of the University of California as their employer, the superior court sustained defendants' demurrers to plaintiffs' second amended complaints without leave to amend. This appeal ensued.

Plaintiffs' complaints predicate liability on two grounds: defendants' failure to warn plaintiffs of the impending danger and their failure to bring about Poddar's confinement pursuant to the Lanterman-Petris-Short Act (Welf. & Inst. Code, §5000ff.) Defendants, in turn, assert that they owed no duty of reasonable care to Tatiana and that they are immune from suit under the California Tort Claims Act of 1963 (Gov.Code, §810ff.).

We shall explain that defendant therapists cannot escape liability merely because Tatiana herself was not their patient. When a therapist determines, or pursuant to the standards of his profession should determine, that his patient presents a serious danger of violence to another, he incurs an obligation to use reasonable care to protect the intended victim against such danger. The discharge of this duty may require the therapist to take one or more of various steps, depending upon the nature of the case. Thus it may call for him to warn the intended victim or others likely to apprise the victim of the danger, to notify the police, or to take whatever other steps are reasonably necessary under the circumstances.***

In the case at bar, plaintiffs admit that defendant therapists notified the police, but argue on appeal that the therapists failed to exercise reasonable care to protect Tatiana in that they did not confine Poddar and did not warn Tatiana or others likely to apprise her of the danger. Defendant therapists, however, are public employees. Consequently, to the extent that plaintiffs seek to predicate liability upon the therapists' failure to bring about Poddar's confinement, the therapists can claim immunity under government Code section 856. No specific statutory provision, however, shields them from liability based upon failure to warn Tatiana or others likely to apprise her of the danger, and Government Code section 820.2 does not protect such failure as an exercise of discretion.

Plaintiffs therefore can amend their complaints to allege that, regardless of the therapists' unsuccessful attempt to confine Poddar, since they knew that Poddar was at large and dangerous, their failure to warn Tatiana or others likely to apprise her of the danger constituted a breach of the therapists' duty to exercise reasonable care to protect Tatiana.***

The second cause of action can be amended to allege that Tatiana's death proximately resulted from defendants' negligent failure to warn Tatiana or others likely to apprise her of her danger. Plaintiffs contend that as amended, such allegations of negligence and proximate causation, with resulting damages, establish a cause of action. Defendants, however, contend that in the circumstances of the present case they owed no duty of care to Tatiana or her parents and that, in the absence of such duty, they were free to act in careless disregard of Tatiana's life and safety.

In analyzing this issue, we bear in mind that legal duties are not discoverable facts of nature, but merely conclusory expressions that, in cases of a particular type, liability should be imposed for damage done. As stated in *Dillon v. Legg* (1968) 68 Cal.2d 728: "The assertion that liability must . . . be denied because defendant bears no 'duty' to plaintiff 'begs the essential question—whether the plaintiff's interests are entitled to legal protection against the defendant's conduct. . . . [Duty] is not sacrosanct in itself, but only an expression of the sum total of those considerations of policy which lead the law to say that the particular plaintiff is entitled to protection.' (Prosser, Law of Torts [3d ed. 1964] at pp. 332–333.)"

In the landmark case of *Rowland v. Christian* (1968) 69 Cal.2d 108, Justice Peters recognized that liability should be imposed "for an injury occasioned to another by his want of ordinary care or skill" as expressed in section 1714 of the Civil Code. Thus, Justice Peters , quoting from *Heaven v. Pender* (1883) 11 Q.B.D. 503, 509 stated: "'whenever one person is by circumstances placed in such a position with regard to another . . . that if he did not use ordinary care and skill in his own conduct . . . he would cause danger of injury to the person or property of the other, a duty arises to use ordinary care and skill to avoid such danger.'"

We depart from "this fundamental principle" only upon the "balancing of a number of considerations"; major ones "are the foreseeability of harm to the plaintiff, the degree of certainty that the plaintiff suffered injury, the closeness of the connection between the defendant's conduct and the injury suffered, the moral blame attached to the defendant's conduct, the policy of preventing future harm, the extent of the burden to the defendant and consequences to the community of imposing a duty to exercise care with resulting liability for breach, and the availability, cost and prevalence of insurance for the risk involved."

The most important of these considerations in establishing duty is foreseeablity. As a general principle, a "defendant owes a duty of care to all persons who are foreseeably endangered by his conduct, with respect to all risks which make the conduct unreasonably dangerous." As we shall explain, however, when the avoidance of foreseeable harm requires a defendant to control the conduct of another person, or to warn of such conduct, the common law has traditionally imposed liability only if the defendant bears some special relationship to the dangerous person or to the potential victim. Since the relationship between a therapist and his patient satisfies this requirement, we need not here decide whether foreseeability alone is sufficient to create a duty to exercise reasonably care to protect a potential victim of another's conduct.

Although, as we have stated above, under the common law, as a general rule, one person owed no duty to control the conduct of another nor to warn those endangered by such conduct, the courts have carved out an exception to this rule in cases in which the defendant stands in some special relationship to either the person whose conduct needs to be controlled or in a relationship to the foreseeable victim of that conduct. Applying this exception to the present case, we note that a relationship of defendant therapists to either Tatiana or Poddar will suffice to establish a duty of care; as explained in section 315 of the Restatement Second of Torts, a duty of care may arise from either "(a) a special relation . . . between the actor and the third person which imposes a duty upon the actor to control the third person's conduct, or (b) a special relation . . . between the actor and the other which gives to the other a right of protection."

Although plaintiffs' pleadings assert no special relation between Tatiana and defendant therapists, they establish as between Poddar and defendant therapists the special relation that arises between a patient and his doctor or psychotherapist. Such a relationship may support affirmative duties for the benefit of third persons. Thus, for example, a hospital must exercise reasonable care to control the behavior of a patient which may endanger other persons. A doctor must also warn a patient if the patient's condition or medication renders certain conduct, such as driving a car, dangerous to others.***

Defendants contend, however, that imposition of a duty to exercise reasonable care to protect third persons is unworkable because therapists cannot accurately predict whether or not a patient will resort to violence. In support of this argument amicus representing the American Psychiatric Association and other professional societies cites numerous articles which indicate that therapists, in the present state of the art, are unable reliably to predict violent acts; their forecasts, amicus claims, tend consistently to overpredict violence, and indeed are more often wrong than right. Since predictions of violence are often erroneous, amicus concludes, the courts should not render rulings that predicate the liability of therapists upon the validity of such predictions.

The role of the psychiatrist, who is indeed a practitioner of medicine, and that of the psychologist who performs an allied function, are like that of the physician who must conform to the standards of the profession and who must often make diagnoses and predictions based upon such evaluations. Thus the judgment of the therapist in diagnosing emotional disorders and in predicting whether a patient presents a serious danger of violence is comparable to the judgment which doctors and professionals must regularly render under accepted rules of responsibility.

We recognize the difficulty that a therapist encounters in attempting to forecast whether a patient presents a serious danger of violence. Obviously we do not require that the therapist, in making that determination, render a perfect performance; the therapist need only exercise "that reasonable degree of skill, knowledge, and care ordinarily possessed and exercised by members of [that professional specialty] under similar circumstances." Within the broad range of reasonable practice and treatment in which professional opinion and judgment may differ, the therapist is free to exercise his or her own best judgment without liability; proof, aided by hindsight, that he or she judged wrongly is insufficient to establish negligence.

In the instant case, however, the pleadings do not raise any question as to failure of defendant therapists to predict that Poddar presented a serious danger of violence. On the contrary, the present complaints allege that defendant therapists did in fact predict that Poddar would kill, but were negligent in failing to warn.

Amicus contends, however, that even when a therapist does in fact predict that a patient poses a serious danger of violence to others, the therapist should be absolved of any responsibility for failing to act to protect the potential victim. In our view, however, once a therapist does in fact determine, or under applicable professional standards reasonably should have determined, that a patient poses a serious danger of violence to others, he bears a duty to exercise reasonable care to protect the foreseeable victim of that danger. While the discharge of this duty of due care will necessarily vary with the facts of each case,[1] in each instance the adequacy of the therapist's conduct must be measured against the traditional negligence standard of the rendition of reasonable care under the circumstances.***

The risk that unnecessary warnings may be given is a reasonable price to pay for the lives of possible victims that may be saved. We would hesitate to hold that the therapist who is aware that his patient expects to attempt to assassinate the

---

[1] Defendant therapists and amicus also argue that warnings must be given only in those cases in which the therapist knows the identity of the victim. We recognize that in some cases it would be unreasonable to require the therapist to interrogate his patient to discover the victim's identity, or to conduct an independent investigation. But there may also be cases in which a moment's reflection will reveal the victim's identity. The matter thus is one which depends upon the circumstances of each case, and should not be governed by any hard and fast rule.

President of the United States would not be obligated to warn the authorities because the therapist cannot predict with accuracy that his patient will commit the crime.

Defendants further argue that free and open communication is essential to psychotherapy; that "Unless a patient . . . is assured that . . . information [revealed by him] can and will be held in utmost confidence, he will be reluctant to make the full disclosure upon which diagnosis and treatment . . . depends." (Sen.Com. on Judiciary, comment on Evid.Code, §1014.) The giving of a warning, defendants contend, constitutes a breach of trust which entails the revelation of confidential communications.[2]

We recognize the public interest in supporting effective treatment of mental illness and in protecting the rights of patients to privacy, and the consequent public importance of safeguarding the confidential character of psychotherapeutic communication. Against this interest, however, we must weigh the public interest in safety from violent assault.***

We realize that the open and confidential character of psychotherapeutic dialogue encourages patients to express threats of violence, few of which are ever executed. Certainly a therapist should not be encouraged routinely to reveal such threats; such disclosures could seriously disrupt the patient's relationship with his therapist and with the persons threatened. To the contrary, the therapist's obligations to his patient require that he not disclose a confidence unless such disclosure is necessary to avert danger to others, and even then that he do so discreetly, and in a fashion that would preserve the privacy of his patient to the fullest extent compatible with the prevention of the threatened danger.***

The revelation of a communication under the above circumstances is not a breach of trust or a violation of professional ethics; as stated in the Principles of Medical Ethics of the American Medical Association (1957), section 9: "A physician may not reveal the confidence entrusted to him in the course of medical attendance . . . *unless he is required to do so by law or unless it becomes necessary in order to protect the welfare of the individual or of the community.*" (Emphasis added.) We conclude that the public policy favoring protection of the confidential character of patient-psychotherapist communications must yield to the extent to which disclosure is essential to avert danger to others. The protective privilege ends where the public peril begins.

Our current crowded and computerized society compels the interdependence of its members. In this risk-infested society we can hardly tolerate the further exposure to danger that would result from a concealed knowledge of the therapist that his patient was lethal. If the exercise of reasonable care to protect the threatened victim requires the therapist to warn the endangered party or those who can reasonably be expected to notify him, we see no sufficient societal interest

[2] Counsel for defendant Regents and amicus American Psychiatric Association predict that a decision of this court holding that a therapist may bear a duty to warn a potential victim will deter violence-prone persons from seeking therapy, and hamper the treatment of other patients. This contention was examined in Fleming and Maximov, The Patient or His Victim: The Therapist's Dilemma (1974) 62 Cal.L.Rev. 1025, 1038-1044; they conclude that such predictions are entirely speculative.

that would protect and justify concealment. The containment of such risks lies in the public interest. For the foregoing reasons, we find that plaintiffs' complaints can be amended to state a cause of action against defendants Moore, Powelson, Gold, and Yandell and against the Regents as their employer, for breach of a duty to exercise reasonable care to protect Tatiana.***

Notes and Issues for Discussion

1. "When a therapist determines or pursuant to the standards of his profession should determine, that his patient presents a serious danger of violence to another, he incurs an obligation to use reasonable care to protect the intended victim against such danger." What is a "therapist?" What is a "serious danger of violence?" When is "another" identifiable? What is "reasonable care to protect?" For the most part these questions have no easy answers. They will be discussed in following sections.
2. In *Tarasoff*, the therapists are a psychologist and his supervisor, a psychiatrist. Read narrowly, the case would apply to these fields. Read more broadly, it might apply to any health and human services professional engaging in therapy.
3. A serious danger of violence would seem to be a clinical determination, and if made pursuant to the standards of the profession, would be a determination corresponding to what other professionals would make in a similar situation. In *Tarasoff*, although Poddar did not identify Tarasoff by name, as his girl friend she was easily identifiable. The California court gives some examples of steps to protect, including warning the victim or others in a position to apprise the victim of danger or notifying the police.
4. The reader must keep in mind that *Tarasoff* directly applies *only* to the State of California, although many other jurisdictions have accepted its logic in their own decisions or statutes. California has codified the *Tarasoff* duty. Cal. Civ. Code §43.92.
5. Over a decade later, *Tarasoff* continues to be widely discussed and debated. See for example, Applebaum, 1985; 1988; Kermani and Dorb, 1987; Note: "Psychiatric Duty to Warn," 1987. For a study of the impact of *Tarasoff* on practice, see Weil and Sanchez, 1983.

Duty to protect or duty to warn cases continue to be the subject of litigation in many states, and many of the *Tarasoff* issues are still being debated today.

Who Must Take Steps to Protect?

As noted, the case applies to the attending psychologist and his psychiatrist supervisor. There is an assumption in the literature that a similar duty applies to other health and human services professionals, such as social workers, counselors, and clergy, but it is not clear from this case. Recall in *State v.*

Miller (p. 129), the court found a privileged relationship even when the psychiatrist did not intend one, focusing on the patient's reasonable expectations. Some jurisdictions that have followed the *Tarasoff* duty have not clarified which health and human services professionals have a duty to protect.

When Is There a Foreseeable Danger?

The debate continues regarding how accurately psychiatrists and other health and human services professionals can predict dangerousness. The American Psychiatric Association has filed *amicus curiae* (friend of court) briefs in which they argue that it is impossible to predict dangerous behavior with any certainty. (See p. 381*ff*.). Nonetheless, courts have generally held, as in *Tarasoff*, that predictions of dangerousness can be made pursuant to professional standards.

Where death threats are made, a weapon is at hand, and the individual has a clear plan of action, there is a strong case for taking steps to protect a readily identifiable victim. When the patient or client may be potentially dangerous, the decision is more difficult. To err on the side of caution may protect the victim, but could lead to an action for breach of confidentiality.

Danger to Whom?

In many jurisdictions following *Tarasoff*, the victim must be readily identifiable before there is a duty to protect; in some others, the fact that the patient or client presents a foreseeable probable danger to anyone is sufficient. Some states have enacted statutes limiting the duty to identifiable individuals.

Brady v. Hopper, 570 F.Supp. 1313 (1983), involved an action for damages by Brady, injured in an attempt to assassinate President Reagan, against Hopper, the therapist of the perpetrator, John Hinckley. The court held that even if Hinckley was dangerous, there was no duty to protect unidentifiable potential victims. Similarly, in *Thompson v. County of Alameda*, 614 P.2d 728 (1980), the California court held that there was no duty to protect in a case where a delinquent child with a prior history of violence was released, although he had said he would kill a child in his neighborhood, and upon release did kill a young child. The court stated "for policy reasons the duty to warn depends upon and arises from the existence of a prior threat to a specific identifiable victim."

However, courts in some other states have taken a different view. In *Milano v. McIntosh*, 403 A.2d 500 (1979), a New Jersey court found the duty to protect both in the therapist-patient relationship, as in *Tarasoff*, and "in an obligation a practitioner may have to protect the welfare of the community, which is analogous to the obligation a physician has to warn third persons of infectious or contagious disease." Under this logic, if there is a probable danger to *anyone*, there would seem to be an obligation to take steps to protect. Similarly, in *Lipari v. Sears Roebuck & Co.*, 497 F. Supp. 185 (1980), an individual who did not appear dangerous was released from a VA hospital and subsequently fired a gun into a crowded nightclub, blinding Lipari and killing her husband. The court found liability "when in accordance with the standards of his profession, the therapist knows or should know that the patient's dangerous propensities present an unreasonable risk of harm to others." Here, the decision extends *Tarasoff* to situations where the victim is unidentifiable but the dangerousness is foreseeable.[9]

In *Menendez v. Superior Court*, 834 P.2d 786 (1992), two brothers, Lyle and Erik Menendez, were charged with the murder of their parents. The police, with a search warrant, seized audiotapes of notes and actual counseling sessions between the brothers and Dr. Oziel, a clinical psychologist. Dr. Oziel asserted psychotherapist-patient privilege on the part of the brothers and the tapes were sealed. The State argued that there was no privilege, and if there was one, exceptions applied which terminated privilege to patients dangerous to self or others (Cal. Evidence Code §1024) or seeking advice to plan or commit a crime or escape detection (Cal. Evidence Code §1018). The California court held there was no privilege for two of the conversations during which the brothers threatened the psychotherapist, his wife, and his lover, and when Dr. Oziel disclosed the conversations to both wife and lover in separate warnings. The court held that if there was reasonable cause to believe the patients were dangerous, and whether or not a warning was given, the communications were not privileged. The other two counseling sessions were privileged in that the two exceptions did not apply, and although there was disclosure to a third party or a third party obtained copies of the tapes, the communications remained privileged.

What Steps Must Be Taken?

Although *Tarasoff* and related decisions are often called "duty to warn" cases, the duty is usually broader. The court in *Tarasoff* said that the therapist had an obligation "to use reasonable care to protect. . . " and included taking steps to warn the potential victim, to warn others who would warn the potential victim, to notify the police, and to "take other steps reasonably necessary," which later in the decision included confining the potentially dangerous individual. Another court has added reassessment, changes in medication, and hospitalization. (*Schuster v. Altenberg*, 424 N.W.2d 159 (1988). In *Jablonski by Pahls v. U.S.*, 712 F.2d 391 (1983), the patient had threatened his girlfriend's mother with a sharp object, attempted to rape her, had a past history of violence toward women he had lived with, and had made obscene phone calls. Although diagnosed as an "antisocial personality" and "potentially dangerous" he was treated on an outpatient basis. The girlfriend told the therapist that she felt insecure around him and was concerned about his unusual behavior. The therapist recommended that she leave him at least while he was undergoing evaluation, and another doctor told her "if she was afraid of her husband and that he didn't fit the criteria to be held in the hospital, that she could consider staying away from him." The patient attacked and killed his girlfriend. In upholding a wrongful death action on behalf of the decedent's daughter, the court sustained a trial court finding that the warnings were "totally unspecific and inadequate under the circumstances."

DUTY TO PROTECT FROM SELF-HARM

The *Tarasoff* decision did not deal with the individual who may constitute a danger to him or herself. How do you determine whether there is such a danger? If you believe there is a danger, what steps must be taken to protect the individual? Does it make a difference if the individual is a child or an adult, an inpatient or an outpatient? In the following case, school counselors were told by the friends of a thirteen year old student that she intended suicide. When asked directly, the girl denied it.

EISEL v. BOARD OF EDUCATION
324 Md. 376, 597 A.2d 447 (1991)
MARYLAND COURT OF APPEALS

RODOWSKY, Judge.
    The legal theory advanced by the plaintiff in this wrongful death and survival action is that school counselors have a duty to intervene to attempt to prevent a student's threatened suicide. The specific question presented is whether the duty contended for may be breached by junior high school counselors who fail to inform a parent of suicidal statements attributed to the parent's child by fellow students where, when the counselors sought to discuss the subject, the adolescent denied ever making the statements. The circuit court granted summary judgment for the defendants, premised on the absence of any duty. As explained below, we shall hold that summary judgment was erroneously entered.
    The decedent, Nicole Eisel (Nicole), was a thirteen year old student at Sligo Middle School in Montgomery County. She and another thirteen year old girl consummated an apparent murder-suicide pact on November 8, 1988. Nicole's father, Stephen Eisel (Eisel), brought the instant action. His amended complaint alleges negligence on the part of two counselors at Nicole's school, among others.***

The amended complaint avers that Nicole became involved in satanism, causing her to have an "obsessive interest in death and self-destruction." During the week prior to the suicide, Nicole told several friends and fellow students that she intended to kill herself. Some of these friends reported Nicole's intentions to their school counselor, Morgan, who relayed the information to Nicole's school counselor, Jones. Morgan and Jones then questioned Nicole about the statements, but Nicole denied making them. Neither Morgan nor Jones notified Nicole's parents or the school administration about Nicole's alleged statements of intent. Information in the record suggests that the other party to the suicide pact shot Nicole before shooting herself. The murder-suicide took place on a school holiday in a public park at some distance from Sligo Middle School. The other party of the pact attended another school.***

On the issue of duty Eisel argued that, by the School Board's own policy, counselors were required to contact the parents of any child who had expressed suicidal thoughts. Eisel pointed to deposition testimony on that subject by the principal, who said: "If the student is in danger, of course, you take care of that first. Then the next thing you do would be to notify a parent. If the student is in no apparent danger, you will notify the parent."***

At least one case has concluded that a professional therapist may be held liable when a patient commits suicide, even if the therapist or the therapist's hospital does not have custody over the patient. *Bellah v. Greenson,* 81 Cal.App.3d 614 (1978).***

Recent attempts to extend the duty to prevent suicide beyond custodial or therapist-patient relationships have failed. For instance, the Supreme Court of California refused to impose a duty on a church pastor to refer a twenty-four year old suicidal counselee to a mental health professional. *Nally,* 47 Cal.3d at 299–300. Although on its facts *Nally* dealt only with religious counselors, the court appeared to extend its no-duty rule to all "nontherapist counselors," who were defined as "persons other than licensed psychotherapists, who counsel others concerning their emotional and spiritual problems." *Id.* at 283.***

A number of factors distinguish the instant matter from those cases finding an absence of any duty, reviewed above, in which the custodial relationship between the suicide victim and the defendant was other than that of hospital and patient or jailer and prisoner. Eisel's claim involves suicide by an adolescent. The negligence relied on is a failure to communicate to the parent the information allegedly possessed by the defendants concerning the child's contemplated suicide, not a failure by the school authorities physically to prevent the suicide by exercising custody and control over Nicole. The theory of Eisel's case is that he could have exercised his custody and control, as parent, over Nicole, had he been warned, and inferentially, that there was nothing known to the counselors about Eisel's relationship with Nicole that would make such a warning unreasonable.***

Further, we have recognized

> "the doctrine that the relation of a school vis á vis a pupil is analogous to one who stands in loco parentis, with the result that a school is under a special duty to exercise reasonable care to protect a pupil from harm."

Finally, the relationship of school counselor and pupil is not devoid of therapeutic overtones. The "Counselor Job Description," published by the Department of Professional Personnel of the Board lists the first two "[p]riorities of the counseling profession" to be:

"1. Counseling with individuals and groups concerning school adjustment, physical and emotional development, educational planning, and career awareness. . . .
"2. Identifying students with significant problems and taking steps to provide help for these students."***

Foreseeability is the most important variable in the duty calculus, *Ashburn,* 306 Md. at 628, 510 A.2d at 1083, and without it there can be no duty to prevent suicide. Comment, *Civil Liability for Suicide,* 12 Loy.L.A.L.Rev. at 991. Here Nicole's suicide was foreseeable because the defendants allegedly had direct evidence of Nicole's intent to commit suicide.***

Nor would reasonable persons necessarily conclude that the harm ceased to be foreseeable because Nicole denied any intent to commit suicide when the counselors undertook to draw out her feelings, particularly in light of the alleged declarations of intent to commit suicide made by Nicole to her classmates. "An adolescent who is thinking of suicide is more likely to share these feelings with a friend than with a teacher or parent or school guidance counselor. But, we all—parents, teachers, administrators, service providers and friends—can learn what the warning signs are and what to do." 3 Maryland Office for Children and Youth, *Monthly Memo,* at 3 (Apr.1986).***

The General Assembly has made it quite clear that prevention of youth suicide is an important public policy, and that local schools should be at the forefront of the prevention effort. A Youth Suicide Prevention School Programs Act (the Act) was enacted as Md.Code (1978, 1989 Repl.Vol.), §§ 7-4A-01 through 7-4A-06 of the Education Article (EA). The uncodified preamble to the Act states that "[t]he rate of youth suicide has increased more than threefold in the last two decades," and that "[o]ver 5,000 young Americans took their lives [in 1985], including over 100 young people in Maryland. . . . "

In 1987 the Maryland State Department of Education (the Department) published its "YOUTH SUICIDE PREVENTION SCHOOL PROGRAM for the Public Schools of Maryland." It presented goals, objectives and strategies for youth suicide prevention, intervention and "postvention," *i.e.,* coping with the aftermath of a student's attempted suicide, or completed suicide." *Id.* at 2.

Nicole's school had a suicide prevention program prior to her death. Eisel requested that the Superintendent of Schools for Montgomery County produce "all published rules. . . or other written directives available as of November 1, 1988, to . . . counselors . . . or other school system staff relating to staff responses to alleged student intent to commit suicide." In response, the superintendent produced, *inter alia*, a memorandum dated February 18, 1987, from the office of the principal to the staff of Sligo Middle School on the subject of "Suicide Prevention." It consists of a top sheet setting forth the "steps [that] must be followed."[1] The top sheet is supplemented by materials on other pages reproduced from various sources. These materials include lists of the methods of, and motives for, suicide and important warning signs ("[A]lmost all who have committed suicide *have* communicated their intent beforehand."). Part IX lists ten answers to the question, *"How Can You Help In A Suicidal Crisis?"* Answer D is:

"Tell others—As quickly as possible, share your knowledge with parents, friends, teachers or other people who might be able to help. Don't worry about breaking a confidence if someone reveals suicidal plans to you. You may have to betray a secret to save a life."

There is no indication in the Act that the Legislature intended to create a statutorily based cause of action against school counselors who negligently fail to intervene in a potential suicide. Nevertheless, holding counselors to a common law duty of reasonable care to prevent suicides when they have evidence of a suicidal intent comports with the policy underlying this Act.***

The harm that may result from a school counselor's failure to intervene appropriately when a child threatens suicide is total and irreversible for the child, and severe for the child's family. It may be that the risk of any particular suicide is remote if statistically quantified in relation to all of the reports of suicidal talk that are received by school counselors. We do not know. But the consequence of the risk is so great that even a relatively remote possibility of a suicide may be enough to establish duty.***

Moreover, when the risk of death to a child is balanced against the burden sought to be imposed on the counselors, the scales tip overwhelmingly in favor of duty. Certainly the physical component of the burden on the counselors was slight. Eisel claims only that a telephone call, communicating information known to the counselors, would have discharged that duty here. We agree.

The counselors argue that there are elements of confidentiality with discretion in their relationships with students that would be destroyed by the imposition of a duty to notify parents of all reports of suicidal statements.

[1] The description of the steps, in relevant part, reads:
"1. Notify the appropriate grade level counselor and administrator immediately.
"2. It will be the grade level administrator's responsibility to call a team meeting. . . .
"3. The committee will decide jointly as to the next steps—i.e., contacting parents, outside agencies, etc.
"4. Reminders:
(a) Our counselors are trained to counsel with a youngster who is contemplating suicide; there are also full-time professionals who are available.

Confidentiality does not bar the duty, given that the school policy explicitly disavows confidentiality when suicide is the concern.

The defendants further point out that counselors are required to exercise discretion when dealing with students. Their discretion, however, cannot be boundless when determining whether to treat a student as a potential suicide. Discretion is relevant to whether the standard of conduct has been breached under the circumstances of a given case. Discretion does not create an absolute immunity, which would be the effect of denying any duty.***

The Centers for Disease Control (CDC) in Atlanta has reported on a new survey of high school students, which revealed that twenty-seven percent "thought seriously" about suicide in the preceding year, and "one in 12 said they had actually tried." *The Sun* (Baltimore), Sept. 20, 1991, at 3A, col. 3. The CDC report noted that suicide rates among teenagers between fifteen and nineteen years old had quadrupled between 1950 and 1988. The General Assembly had similar numbers before it when it adopted the Act. "Changing social conditions lead constantly to the recognition of new duties." *Prosser & Keeton on The Law of Torts* §53, at 359 (5th ed. 1984) (footnote omitted); *see, e.g., B.N. v. K.K.*, 312 Md. 135, 538 A.2d 1175 (1988) (transmission of herpes).

Considering the growth of this tragic social problem in the light of the factors discussed above, we hold that school counselors have a duty to use reasonable means to attempt to prevent a suicide when they are on notice of a child or adolescent student's suicidal intent. On the facts of this case as developed to date, a trier of fact could conclude that that duty included warning Eisel of the danger.

Notes and Issues for Discussion

1. If under a promise of confidentiality Nicole had told her counselor directly of the suicide pact, the school's suicide prevention policies are quite clear that confidentiality should be breached. More complicated is the issue of predictability, given that she denied suicidal intent. Given the age of the student and the state's and school's obvious concern for youth suicides, should any suicide threat be reported to the administration and parents?

2. In *Bellah v. Greenson*, 146 Cal. Rptr. 535 (1978), a California appellate court did not seem to extend *Tarasoff* to a danger of self-inflicted harm, although the case was determined by the expiration of the one-year statute of limitations. In *Bellah*, parents of an adult daughter who had committed suicide brought a wrongful death action against the psychiatrist who was treating her on an outpatient basis for a failure to protect when he knew or should have known she was suicidal. While the court said there could be a traditional medical malpractice action, the court distinguished the case from inpatient situations where there was a clear duty to protect: "Obviously, the duty imposed upon those responsible for the care of a patient in an in-

stitutional setting differs from that which may be involved in the case of a psychiatrist treating patients on an out-patient basis," and observed there was no duty to warn third parties of "vague or even specific manifestations of suicidal tendencies on the part of the patient who is being treated in an out-patient setting." 146 Cal. Rptr. at 535.

3. In *Nally v. Grace Community Church of the Valley*, 763 P.2d 948 (1988), Nally became severely depressed and potentially suicidal. He was seen by various professionals and received religious counseling from several pastoral counselors from the church. There is some disagreement whether he indicated suicide to them. Shortly thereafter, he attempted suicide. When visited by the church pastors the next day, he told them he was sorry he didn't succeed in his suicide attempt. Thereafter Nally resided with one of the pastors for a few days and discussed suicide with another. They referred him to several church physicians for physical examinations but not to a psychiatrist. Several days later, Nally committed suicide. In a lengthy opinion, the California Supreme Court distinguished between a psychiatrist's or professional therapist's duty to protect a suicidal patient and the responsibility of a lay or pastoral counselor. The court reasoned:

"Imposition of a duty to refer Nally necessarily would imply a general duty on all nontherapists to refer all potentially suicidal persons to licensed medical practitioners. . . . While under some circumstances counselors may conclude that referring a client to a psychiatrist is prudent and necessary, our past decisions teach that it is inappropriate to impose a duty to refer—which may stifle all gratuitous or religious counseling—based on foreseeability alone. Mere foreseeability of the harm or knowledge of the danger is insufficient to create a legally cognizable special relationship giving rise to a legal duty to prevent harm. . . . " 763 P.2d at 959.

IMMUNITY FROM LIABILITY

At least a dozen states now address the duty to protect by statute and provide civil and criminal immunity from liability if certain steps are followed.[10] (Applebaum et al., 1989). Ohio has gone so far as to provide by statute that there is no duty to protect, and Florida has apparently taken the same position with case law.[11] The California statute requires a "serious threat of physical violence," the New Jersey statute a "threat of imminent serious physical violence," and Indiana requires statements indicating an imminent danger to others. Most states limit the duty to readily identifiable potential victims; some include self-inflicted harm. Steps taken which will discharge the duty to protect vary among the states, but include one or more of the following: warning the victim; notifying the police; attempting a civil commitment; and voluntary hospitalization. Immunity from civil liability includes both immunity for disclosure of privileged communications and immunity from harm following from the violent act.

REPORTING CHILD ABUSE

All states now require that suspected child abuse be reported. Some states require that any person suspecting child abuse must make a report, others require reports only from named professionals. Some statutes clearly state that the reporting obligation supersedes confidentiality or privilege. In other states this is not so clear. In these jurisdictions there is both an obligation to report suspected child abuse and an obligation on the part of the health and human services professional to maintain confidentiality or treat communications as privileged. Here it is vital for the professional to determine the applicable state law. (See, generally, Chapter 10.)[12]

Where the law is unsettled, the health and human services worker must decide which course of action to take. Many states have criminal penalties for failure to report child abuse, and tort actions have been brought for negligent failure to report. Refusal to testify in court about communications related to child abuse could result in a contempt citation with a fine or imprisonment until the contempt is purged.[13]

REPORTING ELDER ABUSE

A 1981 report by the House Select Committee on Aging estimated that up to one million elderly persons may be subjected to some form of abuse, although the problem tended to be underreported, and recommended state legislation.[14] Ten years later, the Committee released a report titled "Elder Abuse: A Decade of Shame and Inaction." That report estimated abuse of the elderly had grown to about 1.5 million a year. At the time of the latter report, some forty-three states had enacted some form of elder abuse legislation, and at present, virtually every state has some form of legislation. Some of these laws refer specifically to the elderly, others include elder abuse in broader adult protective services statutes or domestic violence statutes.

Abuse of the elderly ranges from physical abuse to financial to emotional and psychological. Statutes vary in their coverage, with the willful or negligent infliction of physical abuse or neglect more common, infliction of emotional or psychological abuse less common.

Reporting provisions in most states either mandate that specific health and human services professionals must report or that anyone must report if there is reasonable cause to believe elder abuse has taken place. As with child abuse, there is immunity for reporting, or in some states, immunity for good faith reporting.

SELECTED REFERENCES

Applebaum, P. S., Zonana, H., and Bonnie, R. "Statutory approaches to limiting psychiatrists' liability for their patient's violent acts." 146 *Am. J. Psychiatry* 821 (1989).

———. "The new preventive detention: Psychiatry's problematic response for the control of violence," 144 *Am. J. Psychiatry* 197 (1988).

———. "*Tarasoff* and the clinician: Problems in fulfilling the duty to protect," 142 *Am. J. Psychiatry* 425 (1985).

Bruce, J. A. C. *Privacy and Confidentiality of Health Care Information* (1984).

House Select Committee on Aging, 97th Cong., 1st Sess., *Elder Abuse: An Examination of a Hidden Problem* (1981).

Kermani, E. J., and Dorb, S. L. "*Tarasoff* decision: A decade later dilemma still faces psychotherapists," 41 *Am. J. Psychotherapy* 271 (1987).

Knapp, S., and VandeCreek, L. *Privileged Communications in the Mental Health Professions* (1987).

McCormick, C. *McCormick on Evidence.* (E. Cleary, Ed., 3rd ed., 1984).

Mills, M. J., Sullivan, G., and Eth, S. "Protecting third parties: A decade after *Tarasoff*," 144 *Am. J. Psychiatry* 68 (1987).

Myers, J. E. B. *Evidence in Child Abuse and Neglect Cases* (2nd ed., 1992).

Note, "Developments in the law—privileged communications," 98 *Harvard L. Rev.* 1450 (1985).

Note, "Elder abuse and the states' protective response," 42 *Hastings L. J.* 859 (1991).

Note, "The psychiatric duty to warn: Walking a tightrope of uncertainty," 56 *Cincinnati L. R.* 269 (1987).

Stromberg, C., Schneider, J., and Joondeph, B. "Dealing with potentially dangerous patients," in National Register of Health Service Providers in Psychology, *The Psychologist's Legal Update* (August 1993).

VandeCreek, L., Knapp, S., and Herzog, C. "Privileged communications for social workers," 69 *Social Casework* 28 (1988).

Weil, M., and Sanchez, E. "The impact of *Tarasoff* on clinical social work practice," 57 *Social Service Rev.* 112 (1983).

Wilson, S. J. *Confidentiality in Social Work* (1978).

CHAPTER 7

INFORMED CONSENT

Traditionally informed consent has been an issue in making medical decisions, but the concept is now recognized as having broader implications for the health and human services (Reamer, 1987). Consent for treatment or therapy, voluntary admission to mental hospitals, voluntary out-of-home placement of children, consent for medical and psychological research, and making an informed decision about life or death are only some of the types of decisions a patient or client might be called upon to make. At its broadest, informed consent can occur in any area of the health and human services where patients or clients are asked to make a major decision or where another makes the decision due to the patient's or client's inability or incapacity to make it.

BASIC PRINCIPLES

Informed consent has both ethical and legal foundations. Ethically, it has been traced to certain principles:

1. Autonomy and self-determination: that the individual has the right to accept or reject treatment;

2. Patient welfare: that the individual should benefit from and not be harmed by the treatment

3. Justice and fairness: that it is unfair to withhold necessary information from the individual.[1]

Legally, the concept has its roots in tort actions for battery—the intentional and unlawful touching of another; and in negligence—the unintentional harm to another resulting from an action that a reasonable person in the same situation would not have taken or from the failure to take the action that a reasonable person would have taken.[2]

156

At law, informed consent originated in the physician-patient relationship, and developed from the basic principle that a physician should obtain some sort of agreement from a patient prior to treatment. For example, in an early English case, *Slater v. Baker and Stapleton*, recovery was allowed for a patient when his physician injured him by doing more than he was hired to do, including refracturing and straightening the patient's crooked leg and detaching some bony material. At trial, the patient testified that he would not have consented to the procedures if he had known about them. The court stated:

> [I]t appears from the evidence of the surgeons that it was improper to [perform the surgery] without consent; this is the usage and law of surgeons . . . it is reasonable that a patient should be told what is about to be done to him, that he may take courage and put himself in such a situation as to enable him to undergo the operation. *Slater v. Baker and Stapleton* 2 Wils K.B. 362 (1767).[3]

However, that case did not turn on the issue of *informed* consent, but whether there was any agreement at all. This pattern was followed in American case law throughout the nineteenth and the first half of the twentieth century, where the issues were the absence of any consent or the physician going beyond the procedures that had been consented to. In 1914 Judge Cardozo wrote:

> Every human being of adult years and sound mind has a right to determine what shall be done with his own body; and a surgeon who performs an operation without his patient's consent commits an assault, for which he is liable in damages. *Schloendorff v. Society of New York Hospitals*, 211 N.Y. 125 at 128, 105 N.E. 92 at 93 (1914).

Not until recently, however, has informed consent been extended from a simple agreement to a course of action to making an informed choice based on adequate information. Apparently the term "informed consent" did not appear in an American court decision until *Salgo v. Leland Stanford Jr. Board of Trustees*, 317 P.2d 170 (1957), a 1957 California case where the court found the physician had a duty (although limited) to disclose the facts necessary for the patient to make an intelligent choice.[4] Similarly, in a 1960 Kansas decision, *Natanson v. Kline*, 350 P.2d 1093 (1960), the court found that the physician had the obligation

> to disclose and explain to the patient in language as simple as necessary the nature of the ailment, the nature of the proposed treatment, the probability of success or of alternatives, and perhaps the risks of unfortunate results and unforeseen conditions within the body. 350 P.2d at 1106.

Key elements of informed consent include:

1. Adequate disclosure of information
2. Capacity of the patient or client to understand the information and make an informed decision
3. A voluntary choice made without coercion[5]

Seemingly straightforward, these issues become complex and clouded by questions such as whether the disclosure is adequate from the professional or patient perspective, how much information must be disclosed, when can information be withheld, how does one determine capacity, and when is consent truly voluntary.

ADEQUATE DISCLOSURE

Standards for Disclosure

An informed choice requires that the individual has the information necessary to make the choice. In determining the standard to be used in deciding how much information is necessary, states generally have taken two different approaches. The more common is often called the "professional standard," and is typically based on how much information a reasonable physician or health and human services professional would believe to be adequate. However, a growing number of states have adopted the "reasonable patient" or "prudent patient" standard, where the amount of information necessary to be disclosed is what a reasonable patient or client would need to make an informed choice. The issue, then, is one of perspective: Is the disclosure determined to be necessary by the professional or by the patient?

LARGEY v. ROTHMAN
110 N.J. 204, 540 A.2d 504 (1988)
NEW JERSEY SUPREME COURT

PER CURIAM

This medical malpractice case raises an issue of a patient's informed consent to treatment. The jury found that plaintiff Janice Largey had consented to an operative procedure performed by the defendant physician. The single question presented goes to the correctness of the standard by which the jury was instructed to determine whether the defendant, Dr. Rothman, had adequately informed his patient of the risks of that operation.***

Plaintiffs argued below, and repeat the contention here, that the proper standard is one that focuses not on what information a reasonable doctor should impart to the patient (the "professional" standard) but rather on what the physician should disclose to a reasonable patient in order that the patient might make an informed decision (the "prudent patient" or "materiality of risk" standard). The latter is the standard announced in *Canterbury v. Spence*, 464 F.2d 772 (D.C.Cir.).***

On plaintiffs' petition we granted certification, to address the correct standard for informed consent. We now discard *Kaplan's* "reasonable physician" standard and adopt instead the *Canterbury* "reasonable patient" rule. Hence, we reverse and remand for a new trial.

The narrow issue before us can be placed in satisfactory context by our adopting in pertinent part the Appellate Division's recitation of the facts.

> In the course of a routine physical examination plaintiff's gynecologist, Dr. Glassman, detected a "vague mass" in her right breast. The doctor arranged for mammograms to be taken. The radiologist reported two anomalies to the doctor: an "ill-defined density" in the subareola region and an enlarged lymph node or nodes, measuring four-by-two centimeters, in the right axilla (armpit). The doctor referred plaintiff to defendant, a surgeon. Defendant expressed concern that the anomalies on the mammograms might be cancer and recommended a biopsy. There was a sharp dispute at trial over whether he stated that the biopsy would include the lymph nodes as well as the breast tissue. Plaintiff claims that defendant never mentioned the nodes.
>
> Plaintiff submitted to the biopsy procedure after receiving a confirmatory second opinion from a Dr. Slattery. During the procedure defendant removed a piece of the suspect mass from plaintiff's breast and excised the nodes. The biopsies showed that both specimens were benign. About six weeks after the operation, plaintiff developed a right arm and hand lymphedema, a swelling caused by inadequate drainage in the lymphatic system. The condition resulted from the excision of the lymph nodes. Defendant did not advise plaintiff of this risk. Plaintiff's experts testified that defendant should have informed plaintiff that lymphedema was a risk of the operation. Defendant's experts testified that it was too rare to be discussed with a patient.***

Although the requirement that a patient give consent before the physician can operate is of long standing, the doctrine of *informed* consent is one of relatively recent development in our jurisprudence. It is essentially a negligence concept, predicated on the duty of a physician to disclose to a patient such information as will enable the patient to make an evaluation of the nature of the treatment and of any attendant substantial risks, as well as of available options in the form of alternative therapies.

An early statement of the "informed consent" rule is found in *Salgo v. Leland Stanford, Jr. Univ. Bd. of Trustees*, 154 Cal.App.2d 560, 317 P.2d 170, in which the court declared that "[a] physician violates his duty to his patient and subjects himself to liability if he withholds any facts which are necessary to form the basis of an intelligent consent by the patient to the proposed treatment." *Salgo* recognized that because each patient presents a "special problem," the physician has a certain amount of discretion in dismissing the element of risk, "consistent, of course, with the full disclosure of facts necessary to an informed consent."

Further development of the doctrine came shortly thereafter, in *Natanson v. Kline*, 186 *Kan.* 393, 350 *P.*2d 1093, which represented one of the leading cases on informed consent at that time. In *Natanson* a patient sustained injuries from excessive doses of radioactive cobalt during radiation therapy. Even though the patient had consented to the radiation treatment, she alleged that the physician had not informed her of the nature and consequences of the risks posed by the therapy.***The court concluded that when a physician either affirmatively misrepresents the nature of an operation or fails to disclose the probable consequences of the treatment, he may be subjected to a claim of unauthorized treatment. The *Natanson* court established the standard of care to be exercised by a physician in an informed consent case as "limited to those disclosures which a reasonable medical practitioner would make under the same or similar circumstances." At bottom the decision turned on the principle of a patient's right of self-determination:

> Anglo-American law starts with the premise of thorough self-determination. It follows that each man is considered to be master of his own body, and he may, if he be of sound mind, expressly prohibit the performance of life-saving surgery, or other medical treatment. A doctor might well believe that an operation or form of treatment is desirable or necessary but the law does not permit him to substitute his own judgment for that of the patient by any form of artifice or deception. [*Id.* at 406-07, 350 *P.*2d at 1104.]

After *Salgo* and *Natanson* the doctrine of informed consent came to be adopted and developed in other jurisdictions, which, until 1972, followed the "traditional" or "professional" standard formulation of the rule. Under that standard, as applied by the majority of the jurisdictions that adopted it, a physician is required to make such disclosure as comports with the prevailing medical standard in the community—that is, the disclosure of those risks that a reasonable physician in the community, of like training, would customarily make in similar circumstances. A minority of the jurisdictions that adhere to the "professional" standard do not relate the test to any kind of community standard but require only such disclosures as would be made by a reasonable medical practitioner under similar circumstances. In order to prevail in a case applying the "traditional" or "professional" standard a plaintiff would have to present expert testimony of the community's medical standard for disclosure in respect of the procedure in question and of the defendant physician's failure to have met that standard.

In both the majority and minority formulations the "professional" standard rests on the belief that a physician, and *only* a physician, can effectively estimate both the psychological and physical consequences that a risk inherent in a medical procedure might produce in a patient. The burden imposed on the physician under this standard is to "consider the state of the patient's health, and whether the risks involved are mere remote possibilities or real hazards which occur with appreciable regularity***." A second basic justification offered in support of the "professional" standard is that "a general standard of care, as required under the prudent patient rule, would require a physician to waste unnecessary time in reviewing with the patient *every* possible risk, thereby interfering with the flexibility a physician needs in deciding what form of treatment is best for the patient."***

In 1972 a new standard of disclosure for "informed consent" was established in *Canterbury v. Spence.* The case raised a question of the defendant physician's duty to warn the patient beforehand of the risk involved in a laminectomy, a surgical procedure the purpose of which was to relieve pain in plaintiff's lower back, and particularly the risk attendant on a myelogram, the diagnostic procedure preceding the surgery. After several surgical interventions and hospitalizations, plaintiff was still, at the time of trial, using crutches to walk, suffering from urinary incontinence and paralysis of the bowels, and wearing a penile clamp.

The *Canterbury* court announced a duty on the part of a physician to "warn of the dangers lurking in the proposed treatment" and to "impart information [that] the patient has every right to expect," as well as a duty of "reasonable disclosure of the choices with respect to proposed therapy and the dangers inherently and potentially involved." *Id.* at 782. The court held that the scope of the duty to disclose

> must be measured by the patient's need, and that need is the information material to the decision. Thus the test for determining whether a particular peril must be divulged is its materiality to the patient's decision: all risks potentially affecting the decision must be unmasked. And to safeguard the patient's interest in achieving his own determination on treatment, the law must itself set the standard for adequate disclosure. [*Id.* at 786–87.]

The breadth of the disclosure of the risks legally to be required is measured, under *Canterbury,* by a standard whose scope is "not subjective as to either the physician or the patient," *id.* at 787; rather, "it remains *objective* with due regard for the patient's informational needs and with suitable leeway for the physician's situation." A risk would be deemed "material" when a reasonable patient, in what the physician knows or should know to be the patient's position, would be "likely to attach significance to the risk or cluster of risks" in deciding whether to forego the proposed therapy or to submit to it.

The foregoing standard for adequate disclosure, known as the "prudent patient" or "materiality of risk" standard, has been adopted in a number of jurisdictions.***

The jurisdictions that have rejected the "professional" standard in favor of the "prudent patient" rule have given a number of reasons in support of their preference. Those include:

> (1) The existence of a discernible custom reflecting a medical consensus is open to serious doubt. The desirable scope of disclosure depends on the given fact situation, which varies from patient to patient, and should not be subject to the whim of the medical community in setting the standard.

(2) since a physician in obtaining a patient's informed consent to proposed treatment is often obligated to consider non-medical factors, such as
a patient's emotional condition, professional custom should not furnish the
legal criterion for measuring the physician's obligation to disclose.
Whether a physician has conformed to a professional standard should***be
important [only] where a pure medical judgment is involved, e.g. in ordinary malpractice actions, where the issue generally concerns the quality of
treatment provided to the patient.

(3) Closely related to both (1) and (2) is the notion that a professional
standard is *totally* subject to the whim of the physicians in the particular
community. Under this view a physician is vested with virtually unlimited
discretion in establishing the proper scope of disclosure; this is inconsistent with the patient's right of self-determination. As observed by the
court in *Canterbury v. Spence:* "Respect for the patient's right of self-
determination***demands a standard set by law for physicians rather than
one which physicians may or may not impose upon themselves."

(4) The requirement that the patient present expert testimony to establish the professional standard has created problems for patients trying to
find physicians willing to breach the "community of silence" by testifying
against fellow colleagues. [Louisell and Williams, *supra*, §22.12 at 22-45 to
-47 (footnotes omitted).]

Taken together, the reasons supporting adoption of the "prudent patient"
standard persuade us that the time has come for us to abandon so much of the
decision by which this Court embraced the doctrine of informed consent as accepts the "professional" standard.

***At the outset we are entirely unimpressed with the argument, made by
those favoring the "professional" standard, *supra* at 210-11 that the "prudent patient" rule would compel disclosure of *every* risk (not just *material* risks) to *any* patient (rather than the *reasonable* patient). As *Canterbury* makes clear,

[t]he topics importantly demanding a communication of information
are the inherent and potential hazards of the proposed treatment, the alternatives to that treatment, if any, and the results likely if the patient remains
untreated. The factors contributing significance to the dangerousness of a
medical technique are, of course, the incidence of injury and the degree of
harm threatened. [464 *F*.2d at 787-88.]

The court in *Canterbury* did not presume to draw a "bright line separating the
significant [risks] from the insignificant"; rather, it resorted to a "rule of reason,"
id. at 788, concluding that "[w]henever non-disclosure of particular risk information is open to debate by reasonable-minded men, the issue is one for the finder
of facts." The point assumes significance in this case because defendant argues
that the risk of lymphedema from an axillary node biopsy is remote, not material.
Plaintiff's experts disagree, contending that she should have been informed of

that risk. Thus there will be presented on the retrial a factual issue for the jury's resolution: would the risk of lymphedema influence a prudent patient in reaching a decision on whether to submit to the surgery?

Perhaps the strongest consideration that influences our decision in favor of the "prudent patient" standard lies in the notion that the physician's duty of disclosure "arises from phenomena apart from medical custom and practice": the patient's right of self-determination. The foundation for the physician's duty to disclose in the first place is found in the idea that "it is the prerogative of the patient, not the physician, to determine for himself the direction in which his interests seem to lie." In contrast the arguments for the "professional" standard smack of an anachronistic paternalism that is at odds with any strong conception of a patient's right of self-determination.

***We therefore align ourselves with those jurisdictions that have adopted *Canterbury*'s "prudent patient" standard.

Notes and Issues for Discussion

1. If the reasonable professional standard is used, what is "reasonable" would have to be established by expert testimony as to what a similar professional in similar circumstances would reasonably disclose. What are the advantages of the "reasonable professional" standard for the professional? What are the disadvantages for the patient or client?
2. Most states using the reasonable professional standard adhere to a national standard—that followed by the profession across the country. Some follow a community standard, based on local practice. There may be more variation in local practice as compared to a national standard. Also, a national standard may be more rigorous. What are the advantages and disadvantages of each for the professional? For the patient or client?
3. Is it possible to describe a "reasonable" patient or client? The reasonable patient standard has been described as objective, in that it reflects an external standard for comparison. Proof would go toward showing what information a reasonable or prudent person in the patient's position would need to make an informed choice.
4. A subjective standard would be what the particular patient or client in the particular situation would need know to make an informed choice. This standard has been criticized as leading to perfect hindsight on the part of the patient or client and producing self-serving testimony, but has been defended as acceptable in other legal disputes. (See Katz, 1984: 71–80.)
5. In order to justify the adequacy of the information the professional would need to document what information was provided and why it was believed to be adequate. If certain information was withheld, the professional would need to document what was withheld and why this was done.
6. What policies does your agency have for obtaining informed consent? What form does it take? What situations are covered? What situations are

not covered? Are there specific requirements for record keeping? Should there be?

Content of Disclosure

With either approach, the question remains how much and what information should be disclosed to the patient or client.

SARD v. HARDY
379 A.2d 1014 (1977)
MARYLAND COURT OF APPEALS

LEVINE, Judge.

The central issue on this appeal is whether appellants, Katie Sue Sard and David Penn Sard, Jr., presented legally sufficient evidence to permit a jury to decide whether appellee, Dr. Erving D. Hardy, a physician specializing in obstetrics and gynecology, was negligent in failing to advise the Sards that a tubal ligation, the sterilization operation which he performed on Mrs. Sard, might not succeed in preventing future pregnancies and in failing to disclose alternative means of achieving the desired result. Resolution of this question requires that we address for the first time the so-called doctrine of informed consent.***

Evidence at trial revealed that there were essentially six methods in common use in the United States employed to effectuate female sterilization by tubal ligation: Madlener technique; Pomery technique; Irving method; Uchida method; Aldridge method; and Erlich method. Evidence adduced through Dr. Hardy, who was called as an adverse witness by appellants, indicated that the Madlener technique used by appellee on Mrs. Sard, while the simplest to accomplish, had a 2% risk of failure when performed at the time of Caesarean section delivery. The Uchida and Irving methods, on the other hand, showed fail-rates of less than 1/10 of 1% under similar circumstances. Dr. Hardy acknowledged that he had never discussed the various methods with appellants prior to the operation. Nor did he explain to Mrs. Sard that the fail-rates for all of the procedures diminished dramatically when performed at some time other than Caesarean birth, thereby effectively denying her the option of undergoing sterilization at a later date with a correspondingly greater likelihood of success. Mrs. Sard testified that appellee never informed her that the operation might fail to eliminate completely the possibility of future pregnancy. Moreover, she testified, appellee had affirmatively assured her before the operation that she would not be having any more children. Despite this assurance and the performance of the tubal ligation, Mrs. Sard became pregnant for the fourth time, and in January 1971, delivered her third healthy child by an uneventful Caesarean section.

Some 10 to 15 minutes before being wheeled into the delivery room for the Caesarean delivery and tubal ligation, Mrs. Sard had been handed a standard hospital consent form, which she signed without reading. In part, it provided:

"I/We understand what is meant by sterilization and I/We understand that if this operation is successful, the above named patient will be unable in the future to produce children, but I/We understand that an operation intended to effect sterilization is not effective in all cases."

Previously, Mr. Sard, whose testimony revealed that he was functionally illiterate, had signed the same form. In directing a verdict for appellee on the informed consent count, the trial court ruled that the issue was conclusively settled against appellants, since, by signing the consent form, they had acknowledged their understanding that the sterilization procedure was not effective in all cases.***

The doctrine of informed consent, which we shall apply here, follows logically from the universally recognized rule that a physician, treating a mentally competent adult under non-emergency circumstances, cannot properly undertake to perform surgery or administer other therapy without the prior consent of his patient. In order for the patient's consent to be effective, it must have been an "informed" consent, one that is given after the patient has received a fair and reasonable explanation of the contemplated treatment or procedure.

The fountainhead of the doctrine of informed consent is the patient's right to exercise control over his own body, at least when undergoing elective surgery, by deciding for himself whether or not to submit to the particular therapy.*** Whatever its source, the doctrine of informed consent takes full account of the probability that unlike the physician, the patient is untrained in medical science, and therefore depends completely on the trust and skill of his physician for the information on which he makes his decision.

Simply stated, the doctrine of informed consent imposes on a physician, before he subjects his patient to medical treatment, the duty to explain the procedure to the patient and to warn him of any material risks or dangers inherent in or collateral to the therapy, so as to enable the patient to make an intelligent and informed choice about whether or not to undergo such treatment.

This duty to disclose is said to require a physician to reveal to his patient the nature of the ailment, the nature of the proposed treatment, the probability of success of the contemplated therapy and its alternatives, and the risk of unfortunate consequences associated with such treatment.***

We think, then, that the proper test for measuring the physician's duty to disclose risk information is whether such data will be material to the patient's decision:

"The scope of the physician's communications to the patient, then, must be measured by the patient's need, and that need is whatever is material to the decision. Thus, the test for determining whether a potential peril must be divulged is its materiality to the patient's decision." *Cobbs v. Grant*, 104 Cal.Rptr. at 515.

By focusing on the patient's need to obtain information pertinent to the proposed surgery or therapy, the materiality test promotes the paramount purpose of the informed consent doctrine—to vindicate the patient's right to determine what shall be done with his own body and when.

We hold, therefore, that the scope of the physician's duty to inform is to be measured by the materiality of the information to the decision of the patient. A material risk is one which a physician knows or ought to know would be significant to a reasonable person in the patient's position in deciding whether or not to submit to a particular medical treatment or procedure.***

Although the scope of disclosure is keyed to the patient's need to know facts that might influence his decision to undergo therapy, there are definite limits on what a physician must communicate to his patient. The physician need not deliver a "lengthy polysyllabic discourse on all possible complications. A mini-course in medical science is not required[.]" *Cobbs v. Grant*, 104 Cal.Rptr. at 515.

We stress that a physician is not burdened with the duty of divulging *all* risks, but only those which are material to the intelligent decision of a reasonably prudent patient. Even then, the physician retains a qualified privilege to withhold information on therapeutic grounds, as in those cases where a complete and candid disclosure of possible alternatives and consequences might have a detrimental effect on the physical or psychological well-being of the patient, or where the patient is incapable of giving his consent by reason of mental disability or infancy, or has specifically requested that he not be told. Likewise, the physician's duty to disclose is suspended where an emergency of such gravity and urgency exists that it is impractical to obtain the patient's consent. Finally, disclosure is not required where the risk is either known to the patient or is so obvious as to justify presumption of such knowledge, nor is the physician under a duty to discuss the relatively remote risks inherent in common procedures, when it is common knowledge that such risks inherent in the procedure are of very low incidence. Conversely, where the physician does not know of a risk and should not have been aware of it in the exercise of ordinary care, he is under no obligation to make disclosure.***

The Court of Special Appeals, following the modern trend, adopted the materiality test to define the scope of disclosure. We disagree with its holding, however, that the information withheld here by appellee would not, as a matter of law, have been material to the decision of a reasonable person in the position of Mrs. Sard.

First, there is evidence that appellee never directly disclosed to Mrs. Sard that the operation might not be 100% successful regardless of what technique he employed; nor that other surgical methods would have been significantly more effective. What is more, Mrs. Sard testified that appellee had affirmatively assured her before the operation that she would not bear any more children after the sterilization. Evidence was also produced to the effect that Mrs. Sard elected to undergo sterilization because she was concerned about the possibility of damage to her physical well-being and the financial burden of raising a third child. Given these facts, a jury could have found that a reasonable person in Mrs. Sard's position would have attached considerable significance to the projected risk of failure for the tubal ligation, and therefore should have been informed of the risk of fertility.***

Moreover, it is undisputed that appellee chose not to inform Mrs. Sard about the increased risk of failure inherent in sterilizations performed at the time of Caesarean delivery. She was therefore denied the opportunity of deciding whether to undergo sterilization at delivery or at a later time when the risk of failure would have been drastically reduced. The jury could reasonably have concluded that this information would have been of material significance to a woman desirous of permanently preventing childbirth in the most effective manner. Finally, there was evidence permitting the jury to find that Dr. Hardy did not discuss the possibility of vasectomy with either appellant, even though, as appellee himself acknowledged, it was customary for physicians to discuss this subject when consulted by patients about sterilization.

We hold only that all of this evidence, taken together, was sufficient in this sterilization case to warrant submission to the jury the question whether the information withheld in this case was material to the patient's decision.***

Notes and Issues for Discussion

1. Rozovsky (1990) has identified the following areas which many states by statute or case law require be disclosed to obtain informed consent in medical treatment:
    Probable benefits
    Probable risks
    Reasonable alternatives
    Diagnostic tests which may affect the decision (Rozovsky, 1990: 44-58).
    Regarding risks and benefits, the author suggests disclosure of the following:
    "1. the likely outcome of diagnostic tests;
    2. the likely benefits of diagnostic workups . . .
    3. the probable outcome of . . . [the] interventions
    4. the likely benefits . . .
    5. an explanation of what . . . [the] procedure will involve including any probable complications and any temporary discomfort, disability, or disfigurement;
    6. an explanation of any permanent results . . . , and
    7. a disclosure of risks that are reasonably foreseeable at the time that consent is obtained" (Rozovsky, 1990: 46–47).

2. Note that there is no general obligation to disclose *all* information:
    "A mini-course in medical science is not required; the patient is concerned with the risk of death or bodily harm, and problems of recuperation. Second, there is no physician's duty to discuss the relatively minor risks inherent in common procedures, when it is common knowledge that such risks inherent in the procedure are of very low incidence." *Cobbs v. Grant*, 502 P.2d 1 at 11.

3. Items of information which need not be disclosed, even using the reasonable patient standard, include:
    "1. risks that are known to the patient;
    2. risks that are so obvious that it may be presumed that the patient has knowledge of them;

3. relatively remote risks inherent in a procedure, when it is commonly known that such risks are present but are of very low incidence [unless they are more probably due to a particular condition]; and

4. risks the professional did not know about at the time or in the exercise of ordinary care could not ascertain" (Rozovsky, 1990: 61).

These guidelines are specifically applicable to medical treatment. Can they be applied more broadly across the health and human services?

Limits to Disclosure

There may be times when the health and human services professional believes that the disclosure of information would be harmful to the individual. Some states have recognized the principal of *therapeutic privilege*, which permits the professional not to disclose otherwise necessary information. In *Canterbury v. Spence*, 464 F.2d 772 (1972), the court observed:

It is recognized that patients occasionally become so ill or emotionally distraught on disclosure as to foreclose a rational decision, or complicate or hinder the treatment, or perhaps even pose psychological damage to the patient. When this is so, the cases have generally held that the physician is armed with a privilege to keep the information from the patient. . . . The physician's privilege to withhold information for therapeutic reasons must be carefully circumscribed, however, for otherwise it might devour the disclosure rule itself. The privilege does not accept the paternalistic notion that the physician may remain silent simply because divulgence might prompt the patient to forego therapy the physician feels the patient really needs. . . . Nor does the privilege contemplate operation save where the patient's reaction to risk information, as reasonably foreseen by the physician, is menacing. And even in a situation of that kind, disclosure to a close relative with a view to securing consent to the proposed treatment may be the only alternative open to the physician. 464 F.2d at 789.[6]

Notes and Issues for Discussion

1. Therapeutic privilege has been criticized because it is paternalistic and subject to abuse. On the other hand, it has been defended as a legitimate means to protect the patient or client in certain situations. Does your agency have any policies pertaining to its use? How would you permit the privilege yet limit the potential for abuse?

2. What if the patient or client requests that no information be given: "Don't tell me. I don't want to know about it. Do what you have to." The indi-

vidual is unwilling to hear the information but still gives consent. Case and statutory law generally support these decisions made with inadequate information as an exception to the general informed consent rule.[7]

3. Documentation may be critical in defending the decision not to disclose information. Rozovsky suggests that the following be recorded at the time of the decision:

> "1. The practitioner's observations of the patient;
> 2. The reasons why he or she believes certain details should be withheld;
> 3. The information that was not disclosed;
> 4. A summary of the . . . findings that the practitioner has used to justify the use of therapeutic privilege; and
> 5. The details that were disclosed to the patient" (Rozovsky, 1990: 86–7).

CAPACITY TO CONSENT

In most jurisdictions, the adult client or patient is presumed to have the capacity to consent unless there has been a judicial decision that the individual lacks that capacity. The presumption of capacity generally continues when the individual has been institutionalized. The individual generally retains decision-making powers, including granting or withholding consent for treatment. (See, generally, Chapter 8).

Serious problems may occur when patients or clients retain their legal capacity to make informed decisions but functionally lack that capacity. If the professional reasonably believes that the individual patient or client actually lacks the capacity to make an informed choice, steps should be taken to obtain additional consent from a family member where this is legally sufficient, or to apply for a court order for a determination of capacity.

In the following case, the plaintiff was found wandering along a Florida highway injured and disoriented, was brought to a mental health screening facility where he was "hallucinating, confused, psychotic, and believed he was in heaven." He signed himself into the hospital on a voluntary basis. Was there informed consent?

ZINERMON v. BURCH
494 U.S. 113 (1990)
U.S. SUPREME COURT

JUSTICE BLACKMUN delivered the opinion of the Court.

Respondent Darrell Burch brought this suit under 42 U.S.C. §1983 against the 11 petitioners, who are physicians, administrators, and staff members at Florida State Hospital (FSH) in Chattahoochee, and others. Respondent alleges that petitioners deprived him of his liberty, without due process of law, by admitting him to FSH as a "voluntary" mental patient when he was incompetent to give informed consent to his admission. Burch contends that in his case petitioners should have afforded him procedural safeguards required by the Constitution before involuntary commitment of a mentally ill person, and that petitioners' failure to do so violated his due process rights.

Petitioners argue that Burch's complaint failed to state a claim under §1983 because, in their view, it alleged only a random, unauthorized violation of the Florida statutes governing admission of mental patients.***

On December 7, 1981, Burch was found wandering along a Florida highway, appearing to be hurt and disoriented. He was taken to Apalachee Community Mental Health Services (ACMHS) in Tallahassee. ACMHS is a private mental health care facility designated by the State to receive patients suffering from mental illness. Its staff in their evaluation forms stated that, upon his arrival at ACMHS, Burch was hallucinating, confused, and psychotic and believed he was "in heaven." His face and chest were bruised and bloodied, suggesting that he had fallen or had been attacked. Burch was asked to sign forms giving his consent to admission and treatment. He did so. He remained at ACMHS for three days, during which time the facility's staff diagnosed his condition as paranoid schizophrenia and gave him psychotropic medication. On December 10, the staff found that Burch was "in need of long-term stabilization," and referred him to FSH, a public hospital owned and operated by the State as a mental health treatment facility. Later that day, Burch signed forms requesting admission and authorizing treatment at FSH. He was then taken to FSH by a county sheriff.

Upon his arrival at FSH, Burch signed other forms for voluntary admission and treatment. One form, entitled "Request for Voluntary Admission," recited that the patient requests admission for "observation, diagnosis, care and treatment of [my] mental condition," and that the patient, if admitted, agrees "to accept such treatment as may be prescribed by members of the medical and psychiatric staff in accordance with the provisions of expressed and informed consent." Two of the petitioners, Janet V. Potter and Marjorie R. Parker, signed this form as witnesses. Potter is an accredited records technician; Parker's job title does not appear on the form.

On December 23, Burch signed a form entitled "Authorization for Treatment." This form stated that he authorized "the professional staff of [FSH] to administer treatment, except electroconvulsive treatment"; that he had been informed of "the purpose of treatment; common side effects thereof; alternative treatment modalities; approximate length of care"; and of his power to revoke consent to treatment; and that he had read and fully understood the Authorization. Petitioner Zinermon, a staff physician at FSH, signed the form as the witness.

On December 10, Doctor Zinermon wrote a "progress note" indicating that Burch was "refusing to cooperate," would not answer questions, "appears distressed and confused," and "related that medication has been helpful." A nursing assessment form dated December 11 stated that Burch was confused and unable to state the reason for his hospitalization and still believed that "[t]his is heaven." Petitioner Zinermon on December 29 made a further report on Burch's condition, stating that, on admission, Burch had been "disoriented, semi-mute, confused and bizarre in appearance and thought," "not cooperative to the initial interview," and "extremely psychotic, appeared to be paranoid and hallucinating." The doctor's report also stated that Burch remained disoriented, delusional, and psychotic.

Burch remained at FSH until May 7, 1982, five months after his initial admission to ACMHS. During that time, no hearing was held regarding his hospitalization and treatment.

After his release, Burch complained that he had been admitted inappropriately to FSH and did not remember signing a voluntary admission form.***

In February 1985, Burch filed a complaint in the United States District Court for the Northern District of Florida. He alleged, among other things, that ACMHS and the 11 individual petitioners, acting under color of Florida law, and "by and through the authority of their respective positions as employees at FSH . . . as part of their regular and official employment at FSH, took part in admitting Plaintiff to FSH as a 'voluntary' patient." Specifically, he alleged:

> "Defendants, and each of them, knew or should have known that Plaintiff was incapable of voluntary, knowing, understanding and informed consent to admission and treatment at FSH. Nonetheless, Defendants, and each of them, seized Plaintiff and against Plaintiff's will confined and imprisoned him and subjected him to involuntary commitment and treatment for the period from December 10, 1981, to May 7, 1982. For said period of 149 days, Plaintiff was without the benefit of counsel and no hearing of any sort was held at which he could have challenged his involuntary admission and treatment at FSH."

Burch's complaint thus alleges that he was admitted to and detained at FSH for five months under Florida's statutory provision for "voluntary" admission. These provisions are part of a comprehensive statutory scheme under which a person may be admitted to a mental hospital in several different ways.***

Finally, a person may be admitted as a voluntary patient. Mental hospitals may admit for treatment any adult "making application by express and informed consent," if he is "found to show evidence of mental illness and to be suitable for treatment." §394.465(1)(a). "Express and informed consent" is defined as "consent voluntarily given in writing after sufficient explanation and disclosure . . . to enable the person . . . to make a knowing and willful decision without any element of force, fraud, deceit, duress, or other form of constraint or coercion." §394.455(22). A voluntary patient may request discharge at any time. If he does, the facility administrator must either release him within three days or initiate the involuntary placement process. §394.465(2)(a).***

Burch, in apparent compliance with §394.465(1), was admitted by signing forms applying for voluntary admission. He alleges, however, that petitioners violated this statute in admitting him as a voluntary patient, because they knew or should have known that he was incapable of making an informed decision as to his admission. He claims that he was entitled to receive the procedural safeguards provided by Florida's involuntary placement procedure, and that petitioners violated his due process rights by failing to initiate this procedure. The question presented is whether these allegations suffice to state a claim under §1983.***

Due process, as this Court often has said, is a flexible concept that varies with the particular situation. To determine what procedural protections the Constitution requires in a particular case, we weigh several factors:

> First, the private interest that will be affected by the official action; second, the risk of an erroneous deprivation of such interest through the procedures used, and the probable value, if any, of additional or substitute procedural safeguards; and finally, the Government's interest, including the function involved and the fiscal and administrative burdens that the additional or substitute procedural requirement would entail." *Mathews* v. *Eldridge*, 424 U.S. 319, 335 (1976).

Applying this test, the Court usually has held that the Constitution requires some kind of a hearing *before* the State deprives a person of liberty or property.***

[W]e must ask whether the predeprivation procedural safeguards could address the risk of deprivations of the kind Burch alleges. To do this, we examine the risk involved. The risk is that some persons who come into Florida's mental health facilities will apparently be willing to sign forms authorizing admission and treatment, but will be incompetent to give the "express and informed consent" required for voluntary placement under §394.465(1)(a). Indeed, the very nature of mental illness makes it foreseeable that a person needing mental health care will be unable to understand any proffered "explanation and disclosure of the subject matter" of the forms that person is asked to sign, and will be unable "to make a knowing and willful decision" whether to consent to admission. §394.455(22) (definition of informed consent). A person who is willing to sign forms but is incapable of making an informed decision is, by the same token, unlikely to benefit from the voluntary patient's statutory right to request discharge. See §394.465(2)(a). Such a person thus is in danger of being confined indefinitely without benefit of the procedural safeguards of the involuntary placement process, a process specifically designed to protect persons incapable of looking after their own interests. See §§394.467(2).***

Persons who are mentally ill and incapable of giving informed consent to admission would not necessarily meet the statutory standard for involuntary placement, which requires either that they are likely to injure themselves or others, or that their neglect or refusal to care for themselves threatens their well-being. See §394.467(1)(b). The involuntary placement process serves to guard against the confinement of a person who, though mentally ill, is harmless and can live safely outside an institution. Confinement of such a person not only violates Florida law, but also is unconstitutional.***

The very risks created by the application of the informed-consent requirement to the special context of mental health care are borne out by the facts alleged in this case. It appears from the exhibits accompanying Burch's complaint that he was simply given admission forms to sign by clerical workers, and, after he signed, was considered a voluntary patient. Burch alleges that petitioners knew or should have known that he was incapable of informed consent. This allegation is supported, at least as to petitioner Zinermon, by the psychiatrist's admission notes, described above, on Burch's mental state. Thus, the way in which Burch allegedly was admitted to FSH certainly did not ensure compliance with the statutory standard for voluntary admission.

We now consider whether predeprivation safeguards would have any value in guarding against the kind of deprivation Burch allegedly suffered.***

The Florida statutes, of course, do not allow incompetent persons to be admitted as "voluntary" patients. But the statutes do not direct any member of the facility staff to determine whether a person is competent to give consent, nor to initiate the involuntary placement procedure for every incompetent patient. A patient who is willing to sign forms but incapable of informed consent certainly cannot be relied on to protest his "voluntary" admission and demand that the involuntary placement procedure be followed. The staff are the *only* persons in a position to take notice of any misuse of the voluntary admission process and to ensure that the proper procedure is followed.

Florida chose to delegate to petitioners a broad power to admit patients to FSH, *i.e.*, to effect what, in the absence of informed consent, is a substantial deprivation of liberty. Because petitioners had state authority to deprive persons of liberty, the Constitution imposed on them the State's concomitant duty to see that no deprivation occurs without adequate procedural protections.

It may be permissible constitutionally for a State to have a statutory scheme like Florida's, which gives state officials broad power and little guidance in admitting mental patients. But when those officials fail to provide constitutionally required procedural safeguards to a person whom they deprive of liberty, the state officials cannot then escape liability.***It is immaterial whether the due process violation Burch alleges is best described as arising from petitioners' failure to comply with state procedures for admitting involuntary patients, or from the absence of a specific requirement that petitioners determine whether a patient is competent to consent to voluntary admission. Burch's suit is neither an action challenging the facial adequacy of a State's statutory procedures, nor an action based only on state officials' random and unauthorized violation of state laws. Burch is not simply attempting to blame the State for misconduct by its employees. He seeks to hold state officials accountable for their abuse of their broadly delegated, uncircumscribed power to effect the deprivation at issue.***

We conclude that petitioners cannot escape §1983 liability by characterizing their conduct as a "random, unauthorized" violation of Florida law which the State was not in a position to predict or avert, so that all the process Burch could possibly be due is a postdeprivation damages remedy. Burch, according to the allegations of his complaint, was deprived of a substantial liberty interest without either valid consent or an involuntary placement hearing, by the very state officials charged with the power to deprive mental patients of their liberty and the duty to implement procedural safeguards. Such a deprivation is foreseeable, due to the nature of mental illness, and will occur, if at all, at a predictable point in the admission process.***

We express no view on the ultimate merits of Burch's claim; we hold only that his complaint was sufficient to state a claim under §1983 for violation of his procedural due process rights.

The judgment of the Court of Appeals is affirmed.

Notes and Issues for Discussion

1. Burch contends that the hospital staff knew or should have known that he was incapable of informed consent. How should they have known, and what steps might they have taken?
2. How would you ensure that your patient or client was capable of giving informed consent? What steps would you take if you believed the individual lacked the capacity for informed consent?
3. What are your agency's policies to ensure that those who enter programs on a voluntary basis have the capacity to give informed consent? What are the policies when staff is unsure if the individual has the capacity for informed consent?
4. The voluntary admission aspects of this case are discussed at p. 377

VOLUNTARY CHOICE

Along with adequate disclosure and the capacity to make a decision, a valid consent needs also be voluntary—freely given and without coercion. If the patient or client is incompetent, that voluntary choice rests with the guardian.

By their nature, health and human services settings—agencies, facilities, institutions or hospitals—may be intimidating and coercive and the health and human services professional may, unintentionally or intentionally, attempt to promote one particular course of action or otherwise influence the choice. A subtle form of coercion occurs when the receipt of one benefit or service is conditioned on the consent to another.

RELF v. WEINBERGER
372 F. Supp. 1196 (1974)
U.S. DISTRICT COURT

GESELL, District Judge.

These two related cases, which have been consolidated with the consent of all parties, challenge the statutory authorization and constitutionality of regulations of the Department of Health, Education and Welfare (HEW) governing human sterilizations under programs and projects funded by the Department's Public Health Service and its Social and Rehabilitation Service. 39 Fed.Reg. 4730–34 (1974). Plaintiffs are the National Welfare Rights Organization (NWRO), suing on behalf of its 125,000 members, and five individual women, proceeding by class action on behalf of all poor persons subject to involuntary sterilization under the challenged regulations. Defendants are the Secretary of HEW, under whose authority the regulations were issued, 42 U.S.C. §216, and two high-level HEW officials charged with the administration of federal family planning funds.

The issues have been fully briefed and argued, and are now before the Court on separate motion for summary judgment by the respective plaintiffs and on the Secretary's motion for dismissal or summary judgment. Declaratory and injunctive relief is sought in both cases. The effective date of the regulations has been voluntarily deferred by the Secretary at the Court's request until March 18, 1974, to facilitate resolution of these issues.

Congress has authorized the funding of a full range of family planning services under two basic procedures. The Public Health Service administers federal grants to state health agencies and to public and private projects for the provision of family planning services to the poor, 42 U.S.C. §§300 et seq., 708(a), and the Social and Rehabilitation Service provides funds for such services under the Medicaid and Aid to Families of Dependent Children programs, 42 U.S.C. §§601 et seq., 1396 et seq.

Although there is no specific reference to sterilization in any of the family planning statutes nor in the legislative history surrounding their passage, the Secretary has considered sterilization to fall within the general statutory scheme and Congress has been made aware of this position. But until recently, there were no particular rules or regulations governing the circumstances under which sterilizations could be funded under these statutes.

Sterilization of females or males is irreversible. The total number of these sterilizations is clearly of national significance. Few realize that over 16 percent of the married couples in this country between the ages of 20 and 39 have had a sterilization operation. Over the last few years, an estimated 100,000 to 150,000 low-income persons have been sterilized annually under federally funded programs. Virtually all of these people have been adults: only about 2,000 to 3,000 per year have been under 21 years of age and fewer than 300 have been under 18. There are no statistics in the record indicating what percentage of these patients were mentally incompetent.

Although Congress has been insistent that all family planning programs function on a purely voluntary basis, there is uncontroverted evidence in the record that minors and other incompetents have been sterilized with federal funds and that an indefinite number of poor people have been improperly coerced into accepting a sterilization operation under the threat that various federally supported welfare benefits would be withdrawn unless they submitted to irreversible sterilization. Patients receiving Medicaid assistance at childbirth are evidently the most frequent targets of this pressure, as the experiences of plaintiffs Waters and Walker illustrate. Mrs. Waters was actually refused medical assistance by her attending physician unless she submitted to a tubal ligation after the birth. Other examples were documented.

When such deplorable incidents began to receive nationwide public attention due to the experience of the Relf sisters in Alabama, the Secretary took steps to restrict the circumstances under which recipients of federal family planning funds could conduct sterilization operations. On August 3, 1973, the Department published in the Federal Register a notice of Guidelines for Sterilization Procedures under HEW Supported Programs. 38 Fed.Reg. 20930 (1973). The notice directed that the policies set forth in the guidelines be implemented through regulations to be issued by the departmental agencies administering programs which provide federal financial assistance for family planning services. Notices of proposed rule making were duly published in the Federal Register on September 21, 1973. 38 Fed. Reg. 26459 (1973). Interested persons were given an opportunity to participate in the rule making by submitting comments on the proposed regulations. Approximately 300 comments, including those of plaintiff NWRO, were received and reviewed by the Department. The final regulations here under attack were issued on February 6, 1974.

These regulations provide that projects and programs receiving PHS or SRS funds, whether for family planning or purely medical services, shall neither perform nor arrange for the performance of a nontherapeutic sterilization unless certain procedures are carried out. These vary depending upon whether the patient is, under state law, a legally competent adult, a legally competent person under the age of 18, a legally incompetent minor, or a mental incompetent. Briefly, they are as follows:

(1) Legally competent adults must give their "informed consent" to sterilization. Such consent must be evidenced by a written and signed document indicating, *inter alia*, that the patient is aware of the benefits and costs of sterilization and of the fact that he may withdraw from the operation without losing federal benefits. 42 CFR §50.-202(f); 45 CFR §205.35(a)(2)(ii).

(2) Legally competent persons under the age of 18 must also give such written consent. In these situations, a special Review Committee of independent persons from the community must also have determined that the proposed sterilization is in the best interest of the patient, taking into consideration (a) the expected mental and physical impact of pregnancy and motherhood on the patient, if female, or the expected mental impact of fatherhood, if male, and (b) the expected immediate and long-term mental and physical impact of sterilization on the patient. 42 CFR §50.-206(a); 45 CFR §205.35(a)(4)(i). The Review Committee must also (a) review appropriate medical, social and psychological information concerning the patient, including the age of the patient, alternative family planning methods, and the adequacy of consent, and (b) interview the patient, both parents of the patient (if available), and such other persons as in its judgment will contribute pertinent information. 42 CFR §50.206(b)(1, 2); 45 CFR §205.35 (a)(4)(i)(A,B). However, parental consent is not required. 42 CFR §50.-203(c); 45 CFR §205.35(a)(5)(ii).

(3) Legally incompetent minors must be afforded the above safeguards, and, in addition, a state court of competent jurisdiction must determine that the proposed sterilization is in the best interest of the patient. 42 CFR §50.203(c); 45 CFR §205.35(a)(1)(iv)(A,B).

(4) The sterilization of mental incompetents of all ages must also be sanctioned by a Review Committee and a court. However, personal consent is not required—it is enough that the patient's "representative" requests sterilization. 42 CFR §50.203(a); 45 CFR §205.-35(a)(1). Although

defendants interpret the term "representative" to mean a person empowered under state law to consent to the sterilization on behalf of the patient, no such definition appears in the regulations themselves.

Plaintiffs do not oppose the voluntary sterilization of poor persons under federally funded programs. However, they contend that these regulations are both illegal and arbitrary because they authorize *involuntary* sterilizations, without statutory or constitutional justification. They argue forcefully that sterilization of minors or mental incompetents is necessarily involuntary in the nature of things. Further, they claim that sterilization of competent adults under these regulations can be undertaken without insuring that the request for sterilization is in actuality voluntary. The Secretary defends the regulations and insists that only "voluntary" sterilization is permitted under their terms.***

For the reasons developed below, the Court finds that the Secretary has no statutory authority under the family planning sections of the Social Security or Public Health Services Acts to fund the sterilization of any person incompetent under state law to consent to such an operation, whether because of minority or of mental deficiency. It also finds that the challenged regulations are arbitrary and unreasonable in that they fail to implement the congressional command that federal family planning funds not be used to coerce indigent patients into submitting to sterilization. In short, federally assisted family planning sterilizations are permissible only with the voluntary, knowing and uncoerced consent of individuals competent to give such consent. This result requires an injunction against substantial portions of the proposed regulations and their revision to insure that all sterilizations funded under the family planning sections are voluntary in the full sense of that term and that sterilization of incompetent minors and adults is prevented.

The dispute with regard to minors and mental incompetents centers around two aspects of the statutory language. On the one hand, Congress included in every section mentioning family planning a requirement that such services be voluntarily requested. On the other hand, these sections purport to offer family planning services to all poor people and two of them specifically include minors. The Secretary argues that this juxtaposition indicates that Congress intended that minors personally and incompetents through their representatives would be able to consent to sterilization under these sections. That conclusion is unwarranted.

Although the term "voluntary" is nowhere defined in the statutes under consideration, it is frequently encountered in the law. Even its dictionary definition assumes an exercise of free will and clearly precludes the existence of coercion or force. And its use in the statutory and decisional law, at least when important human rights are at stake, entails a requirement that the individual have at his disposal the information necessary to make his decision and the mental competence to appreciate the significance of that information.

No person who is mentally incompetent can meet these standards, nor can the consent of a representative, however sufficient under state law, impute voluntariness to the individual actually undergoing irreversible sterilization. Minors would also appear to lack the knowledge, maturity and judgment to satisfy these standards with regard to such an important issue, whatever may be their competence to rely on devices or medication that temporarily frustrates procreation. This is the reasoning that provides the basis for the nearly universal common law and statutory rule that minors and mental incompetents cannot consent to medical operations.

The statutory references to minors and mental incompetents do not contradict this conclusion, for they appear only in the context of family planning services in general. Minors, for example, are not legally incompetent for all purposes, and many girls of child-bearing age are undoubtedly sufficiently aware of the relevant considerations to use temporary contraceptives that intrude far less on fundamental rights. However, the Secretary has not demonstrated and the Court cannot find that Congress deemed such children capable of voluntarily consenting to an irreversible operation involving the basic human right to procreate. Nor can the Court find, in the face of repeated warnings concerning voluntariness, that Congress authorized the imposition of such a serious deprivation upon mental incompetents at the will of an unspecified "representative."

The regulations also fail to provide the procedural safeguards necessary to insure that even competent adults voluntarily request sterilization.***In one respect, however, the consent procedure must be improved. Even a fully informed individual cannot make a "voluntary" decision concerning sterilization if he has been subjected to coercion from doctors or project officers. Despite specific statutory language forbidding the recipients of federal family planning funds to threaten a cutoff of program benefits unless the individual submits to sterilization and despite clear evidence that such coercion is actually being applied, the challenged regulations contain no clear safeguard against this abuse. Although the required consent document must state that the patient can *withdraw* his consent to sterilization without losing other program benefits, there is nothing to prohibit the use of such coercion to extract the initial consent.

In order to prevent express or implied threats, which would obviate the Secretary's entire framework of procedural safeguards, and to insure compliance with the statutory language, the Court concludes that the regulations must also be amended to require that individuals seeking sterilization be orally informed at the very outset that no federal benefits can be withdrawn because of a failure to accept sterilization. This guarantee must also appear prominently at the top of the consent document already required by the regulations. To permit sterilization without this essential safeguard is an unreasonable and arbitrary interpretation of the congressional mandate.***

Notes and Issues for Discussion

1. Were the sterilization decisions voluntary? How were they influenced? The impetus for the case was the discovery of the sterilization of two young black girls, Minnie Relf, twelve, and Mary Alice Relf, fourteen, by an Alabama family planning clinic to prevent them from getting pregnant. Their illiterate mother put her X on a paper she thought gave permission for vaccinations. In their million dollar damage suit, the plaintiffs alleged that as many as nine other girls were sterilized by the same agency. See

New York Times, June 27, 28; July 2–4, 6, 1973.)
2. What are the procedures for informed consent by competent adults? Mentally incompetent individuals? Legally incompetent minors? Are they adequate?
3. Following the *Relf* decision, the government revised the regulations to permit sterilization of legally competent adults with informed consent, and to exclude children or those mentally incompetent under state law. These regulations were upheld on appeal in *Relf v. Weinberger*, 565 F.2d 722 (1977).
4. For further material on sterilization, see p. 277 and p. 423.

APPLICATIONS AND PROBLEM AREAS

Informed consent is complex area, with difficult issues particularly important to the health and human services. Here we will deal with (1) withdrawals and refusals of consent; (2) medical emergencies; (3) informed consent for minors; and (4) informed consent in decisions to terminate life support systems.

If the patient or client has the right to give informed consent to an intervention or treatment, then is there is a corresponding right to refuse the same intervention or treatment? Treatment refusals may run counter to those professional ethical principles which call for helping and healing, but are supported by principles which call for self-determination and autonomy. A refusal or withdrawal of consent should be equally informed.

Withdrawal of Consent

The following, although specific to nurses is sound advice for health and human services professionals in general:

> Once given, consent may be withdrawn at any time. . . . What should nurses do when patients change their minds and no longer wish to permit a particular procedure? First, nurses must be extremely careful not to put pressure on the patient so that the patient may later claim that consent was withdrawn but that the nursing staff resisted and refused to honor the patient's wishes. All the nurse has to do is acknowledge that she understands the patient's wishes and will communicate them to all personnel including physicians. . . . The nurse must immediately document in the patient's chart what happened. Her notes should include the date and time of withdrawal, a description of what the patient said or did to withdraw consent, the patient's emotional state, whether the patient appeared to be lucid and free from the influence of drugs,

etc., as well as the names of any witnesses to the patient's withdrawal. She should then notify all the appropriate personnel of the patient's decision and document that she has done so. Finally, a written document evidencing the patient's withdrawal of consent should be prepared and signed by the patient. (Hogue, 1985: 115)

Refusals of Consent

A competent individual may refuse to give consent, and a guardian can refuse for an incompetent person. If there is a refusal of consent for treatment and if the individual is competent, may the individual still be treated against her or his will? The answer varies, depending on the jurisdiction, the situation, the reasons for refusal, and the consequences for the individual and others dependent upon him or her.

REFUSALS OF CONSENT AND THE STATE'S INTERESTS

NORWOOD HOSPITAL v. MUNOZ
409 Mass. 116, 564 N.E.2d 1017 (1991)
MASSACHUSETTS SUPREME COURT

LIACOS, Chief Justice.

In this case, a competent adult, who is a Jehovah's Witness and a mother of a minor child, appeals from a judgment of the Probate and Family Court authorizing Norwood Hospital to administer blood or blood products without her consent.

We state the facts. Yolanda Munoz, a thirty-eight year old woman, lives in Dedham with her husband, Ernesto Munoz, and their minor son, Ernesto, Jr. Ernesto's father, who is over seventy-five years old, also lives in the same household.

Ms. Munoz has a history of stomach ulcers. Approximately ten years ago, she underwent surgery for a bleeding ulcer. On April 11, 1989, Ms. Munoz vomited blood and collapsed in her home. During the week before she collapsed, Ms. Munoz had taken two aspirin every four hours to alleviate a pain in her arm. The aspirin apparently made her ulcer bleed. Ernesto took his wife to the Norwood Hospital emergency room. Physicians at Norwood Hospital gave Ms. Munoz medication which stopped the bleeding. Ms. Munoz was then admitted to the hospital as an inpatient. During the evening, her hematocrit (the percentage of red blood cells to whole blood) was 17%. A normal hematocrit level for an adult woman is approximately 42%. Ms. Munoz was placed under the care of Dr. Joseph L. Perrotto. It was his medical opinion that the patient had a 50% probability of hemorrhaging again. If Ms. Munoz started to bleed, Dr. Perrotto believed that she would in all probability die unless she received a blood transfusion. Ms. Munoz, however, refused to consent to a blood transfusion in the event of a new hemorrhage.

Ms. Munoz and her husband were baptized as Jehovah's Witnesses over sixteen years ago. They are both members of the Jamaica Plain Kingdom Hall of Jehovah's Witnesses. Ms. Munoz attends three religious meetings every week. A principal tenet of the Jehovah's Witnesses religion is a belief, based on interpretations of the Bible, that the act of receiving blood or blood products precludes an individual resurrection and everlasting life after death.

Norwood Hospital has a written policy regarding patients who refuse to consent to the administration of blood or blood products. According to this policy, if the patient arrives at the hospital in need of emergency medical treatment and there is no time to investigate the patient's circumstances or competence to make decisions regarding treatment, the blood transfusion will be performed if necessary to save the patient's life. If the patient, in a nonemergency situation, refuses to consent to a blood transfusion, and the patient is a competent adult, not pregnant, and does not have minor children, the hospital will accede to the patient's refusal. If the patient, in a non-emergency situation, refuses to consent to a blood transfusion, and the patient is a minor, an incompetent adult, pregnant, or a competent adult with minor children, the hospital's policy is to seek judicial determination of the rights and responsibilities of the parties.

The patient in this case, while no longer in an emergency situation once her ulcer stopped bleeding, has a minor child. The hospital sought a court order; on April 12, the hospital filed a complaint for a declaratory judgment in the Norfolk Division of the Probate and Family Court pursuant to G.L. c. 231A (1988 ed.). The hospital requested that Ms. Munoz be required to accept blood transfusions which her attending physician believed to be reasonably necessary to save her life. On that same day, the judge granted a temporary restraining order authorizing the hospital to "administer transfusions of blood or blood products in the event that [the patient] hemorrhages to the extent that her life is severely threatened by loss of blood in the opinion of her attending physicians." The court also appointed Mr. Jonathan Brant to serve as guardian ad litem for five year old Ernesto, Jr.

On April 13, the judge held a full evidentiary hearing. Dr. Perrotto stated in an unchallenged affidavit that, if Ms. Munoz were to begin bleeding again, she would have an excellent chance of recovering if she received a blood transfusion. If she started to bleed, however, and did not receive a blood transfusion, she would probably die. In addition, Dr. Perrotto stated that there was no alternative course of medical treatment capable of saving the patient's life. Ernesto Munoz and James Joslin, Ms. Munoz's brother-in-law, testified at the hearing in favor of allowing Ms. Munoz to refuse the blood transfusion. The guardian ad litem's report, which recommended that the hospital's request for a declaratory judgment be denied, was admitted in evidence.

On April 14, the judge granted the declaratory judgment authorizing blood transfusions which were "reasonably necessary to save [the patient's] life." The judgment also absolved the hospital and its agents from any civil or criminal liability, except for negligence or malpractice, which might arise from a blood transfusion. On May 11, 1989, the judge issued a detailed opinion explaining his reasons for granting the declaratory judgment. The judge found the patient competent; she understood the nature of her illness, and the potential serious consequences of her decision, including the risk of imminent death if her bleeding resumed and blood transfusions were not administered. While recognizing that a competent adult may usually refuse medical treatment, the judge stated that the hospital could administer the blood transfusions because, if they did not and Ms. Munoz subsequently died, Ernesto, Jr., would be "abandoned." The judge concluded that the State's interest in protecting the well-being of Ernesto, Jr., outweighed Ms. Munoz's right to refuse the medical treatment.

In order further to understand the judge's reasoning, we need to discuss his factual findings in more detail. Ernesto works sixteen hours a day Monday through Friday and seven hours on Saturday driving his own commercial truck. Ms. Munoz works at a beauty salon from 9 A.M. TO 3 P.M. three days a week. Ernesto, Jr., is enrolled in a day-care center Monday through Friday from 9 A.M. until 4 P.M. The judge found that Ms. Munoz was the "principal homemaker and principal caretaker of Ernesto, Jr." The judge also found that, while Ernesto's father was available to assist in caring for Ernesto, Jr., his assistance would be inadequate because of his advanced age, his inability to speak English, his unemployment, his lack of a driver's license, and because he had not, in the past, played a significant role in caring for his grandson. In addition, the judge found, that while Sonia and James Joslin, Ernesto's sister and brother-in-law, expressed a willingness to help Ernest take care of the child in the event that Ms. Munoz died, the family had not formulated a concrete plan for the care and support of Ernesto, Jr. The judge concluded that Ms. Munoz's death "would be likely to cause an emotional abandonment of Ernesto, Jr., which would more probably than not be detrimental to his best interests." The judge ruled that "[t]he State, as parens patriae, will not allow a parent to abandon a child, and so it should not allow this most ultimate of voluntary abandonments."

Ms. Munoz argues that the judge erred because she has a right, as a competent adult, to refuse life-saving medical treatment, and the State's interests do not override that right. We agree.***

We are asked to decide when a competent individual may refuse medical treatment which is necessary to save that individual's life. In *Brophy v. New England Sinai Hosp., Inc.*, 398 Mass. 417 (1986), and in *Superintendent of Belchertown State School v. Saikewicz*, 373 Mass. 728 (1977), we were asked to decide the rights of incompetent patients to refuse medical treatment. In both cases we found it necessary to determine the rights of competent individuals to refuse medical treatment before we discussed the rights of incompetent patients. In both cases we balanced an individual's right to refuse medical treatment against the State's interests in having the medical treatment imposed on the individual.

This court has recognized the right of a competent individual to refuse medical treatment. We have declared that individuals have a common law right to determine for themselves whether to allow a physical invasion of their bodies. We have stated that "a person has a strong interest in being free from nonconsensual invasion of his bodily integrity." *Saikewicz, supra* at 739. Individuals also have a penumbral constitutional right of privacy to reject medical treatment.***

The right to bodily integrity has been developed further through the doctrine of informed consent, which this court recognized in *Harnish v. Children's Hosp. Medical Center.* Under the doctrine, a physician has the duty to disclose to a competent adult "sufficient information to enable the patient to make an informed judgment whether to give or withhold consent to a medical or surgical procedure." It is for the individual to decide whether a particular medical treatment is in the individual's best interests. As a result, "[t]he law protects [a person's] right to make her own decision to accept or reject treatment, whether that decision is wise or unwise." *Lane v. Candura,* 6 Mass.App.Ct. 377, 383 (1978).

There is no doubt, therefore, that Ms. Munoz has a right to refuse the blood transfusion. Initially, it is for her to decide, after having been informed by the medical personnel of the risks involved in not accepting the blood transfusion, whether to consent to the medical treatment. The fact that the treatment involves life-saving procedures does not undermine Ms. Munoz's rights to bodily integrity and privacy, except to the extent that the right must then be balanced against the State's interests.***

The right to refuse medical treatment in life-threatening situations is not absolute. We have recognized four countervailing interests: (1) the preservation of life; (2) the prevention of suicide; (3) the maintenance of the ethical integrity of the medical profession; and (4) the protection of innocent third parties.***

The judge determined that the patient did not want to die. Declining potentially life-saving treatment may not be viewed properly as an attempt to commit suicide. Therefore, it is clear that the second interest listed above does not apply in this case. We proceed to discuss the other three interests.

The State's interest in preserving life has "two separate but related concerns: an interest in preserving the life of the particular patient, and an interest in preserving the sanctity of all life." As to the former, the State's concern is weakened when the decision maker (the individual who refuses to consent to the treatment) is also the patient "because the life that the state is seeking to protect in such a situation is the life of the same person who has competently decided to forgo the medical intervention; it is not some other actual or potential life that cannot adequately protect itself." *Id.* In cases where a competent adult refuses medical treatment for herself, the State's interest in preserving the particular patient's life will not override the individual's decision.

The second concept within the State's interest in the preservation of life is the more abstract notion of protecting the sanctity of life. In determining whether this concept applies, we must keep in mind that the right to privacy is an "expression of the sanctity of individual free choice and self-determination as fundamental constituents of life. The value of life as so perceived is lessened not by a decision to refuse treatment, but by the failure to allow a competent human being the right of choice." "The duty of the State to preserve life must encompass a recognition of an individual's right to avoid circumstances in which the individual [herself] would feel that efforts to sustain life demean or degrade [her] humanity."

In this case, the patient, a fully competent adult, determined for herself that she could not consent to the administration of blood or blood products because to do so would violate a sacred religious belief. The patient decided that she would rather risk death than accept the blood transfusion. We can assume that, for this patient, death without receiving a blood transfusion is preferable to life after receiving the transfusion. The quality and integrity of this patient's life after a blood transfusion would be diminished in her view. Therefore, we conclude that the State's interest in protecting the sanctity of life must give way to the patient's decision to forgo treatment.***

The final, and in this case the most compelling, State interest is the protection of the patient's minor child. The State as parens patriae has an interest in protecting the well-being of children. The issue is whether a competent adult can be prevented from exercising her right to refuse life-saving medical treatment because of the individual's duties to her child.***

***We hold that, in the absence of any compelling evidence that the child will be abandoned, the State's interest in protecting the well-being of children does not outweigh the right of a fully competent adult to refuse medical treatment. Our review of the record in this case reveals no such compelling evidence. The evidence shows that Ernesto Munoz supported his wife's decision not to consent to the blood transfusion. There is no evidence in the record that Ernesto was unwilling to take care of the child in the event that Ms. Munoz died. We note that the father has the financial resources to take care of the child and to make sure that the child's material needs are satisfied. We also note that Ernesto's sister and brother-in-law supported Ms. Munoz's decision, and were willing to assist Ernesto in taking care of the child.

There can also be no doubt that, if Ms. Munoz had died, the entire family, including the young child, would have suffered a great loss. However, the State does not have an interest in maintaining a two-parent household in the absence of compelling evidence that the child will be abandoned if he is left under the care of a one-parent household.***

The patient had the right to refuse to consent to the blood transfusion even though she would have in all probability died if she had started to hemorrhage. The State's interests in preserving the patient's life, in maintaining the ethical integrity of the profession, and in protecting the well-being of the patient's child, did not override the patient's right to refuse life-saving medical treatment. Accordingly, the judgment is reversed and a new judgment declaring the rights of the parties, consistent with this opinion, is to be entered in the Probate Court.

Notes and Issues for Discussion

1. What are Yolanda Munoz's reasons for refusing treatment? Are they persuasive? What are the State's interests in overriding that refusal? Why does the court not find them persuasive?
2. In this case, there is a dependent child, but the court finds that in the event of the mother's death, the father and other relatives are able to provide care. What if Yolanda Munoz were a single parent? Should the state intervene? Would it make a difference if the child were fifteen days old or fifteen years old?

REFUSALS BASED ON RELIGIOUS BELIEFS

The *Munoz* court does not reach the issue of a First Amendment treatment refusal based on religious grounds. Courts have generally upheld refusals if the individual's life is not in danger, but have permitted treatment to save the individual's life.

IN RE MILTON
29 Ohio St. 3d 20, 505 N.E. 2d 255 (1987)
OHIO SUPREME COURT

***

This case arises from an application filed with the Court of Common Pleas of Franklin County, Probate Division, requesting authorization to perform medical treatment on appellant, Nancy Milton. The application, which was filed by Dr. Lewis A. Lindner, the Chief Medical Officer of the Central Ohio Psychiatric Hospital (hereinafter "hospital"), alleged that appellant was unable to give informed, intelligent, and knowing consent for surgery. Dr. Lindner petitioned for an order requiring appellant to submit to radiation treatments, transfusions and possible surgery, stating that without these treatments, the patient would suffer an early death.[1]

A hearing on the application was conducted in the probate court. The hospital called two witnesses at this hearing, Dr. Lewis Lindner and Dr. Eugene Green, a psychiatrist. Dr. Green testified that appellant was alert, responsive, did not appear confused, and could function in many areas of everyday life. Dr. Lindner stated that she was of normal intelligence.

Appellant, a fifty-three-year-old patient of the hospital, refused to consent to this medical treatment primarily because it conflicted with her belief in faith healing. Dr. Lindner claimed that appellant's stated reasons for refusing consent constituted a psychotic delusion and that she was unable to understand and appreciate the information necessary to either provide informed consent or to refuse such consent. Dr. Lindner asserted that appellant's entire belief system was delusional because she had a fixed long-standing delusion that she was the spouse of Rev. LeRoy Jenkins, a faith healer and evangelist who is well known in the central Ohio area.

Dr. Lindner conceded that appellant has never been adjudicated incompetent and that the hospital had accepted, without question as to her competency, her

---

[1] Dr. Lindner testified that apellant had cancer of the uterus which was in "a relatively advanced stage," and that there was a possibility she might be cured by medical treatment. Nevertheless, he estimated that even if she did receive the prescribed medical treatment, there was less than a fifty percent chance that she would be free of cancer for five years or more. At a minimum, he believed the treatment would arrest the tumor and considerably prolong appellant's life. Dr. Lindner further testified that appellant's death from the cancer was almost inevitable if she did not receive this medical treatment.

informed consent for all prior treatments at the hospital, including the biopsy through which the malignant tumor was diagnosed.

The trial court found that appellant had the mental capability to understand the nature of her illness and the contemplated treatment, but held that since appellant was not receiving spiritual treatment from Rev. Jenkins, the court could intervene. Therefore, the trial court authorized the requested medical treatment. The court of appeals affirmed, holding that appellant's beliefs in faith healing "****by all rational evaluation, constitute a delusion."

WRIGHT, JUSTICE.

This is a case of first impression in Ohio. Several difficult and delicate questions are before us, including whether a state acting through its courts may compel an individual to submit to medical treatment which is arguably life-extending in derogation of that individual's religious beliefs. We must also decide whether the court below infringed upon appellant's constitutional right of religious freedom in citing the essence of her belief in faith healing as evidence of her lack of capacity to provide informed consent to medical treatment. We believe these questions should be resolved in favor of appellant and, thus, we reverse the holding of the appellate court.

At the outset, we emphasize that at no time has any court found appellant to be incompetent under state law. Appellant is a voluntary patient of the hospital. However, even if she were to be involuntarily committed, that commitment would not be tantamount to a finding of incompetency. Commitments to a mental institution and adjudications of incompetency are distinct legal proceedings which determine separate issues and often lead to different results. Commitment proceedings focus on proof of dangerousness as the primary determinant of the need for commitment, while incompetency adjudications evaluate a person's cognitive ability to make decisions. "[A] finding of 'mental illness'***and commitment to a hospital, does [sic] not raise even a presumption that the patient is 'incompetent' or unable adequately to manage his own affairs." *Winters v. Miller* (1971), 446 F.2d 65, 68. Thus, a person who is not in a mental institution may be found to be incompetent, and a person properly committed to a mental institution may be legally competent.

Persons admitted to mental hospitals retain all civil rights not specifically denied by statutes or removed by separate adjudications of incompetency. These civil rights include the right to sue or defend in one's own name, sell or dispose of property, marry, draft a will, freely practice one's religion, and refuse medical treatment for religious reasons. In *Winters*, a case factually similar to our own, a Christian Scientist, who was committed to a mental hospital, but who had not been adjudicated incompetent, refused to consent to medical treatment on the basis of her religious beliefs. The court discussed the requirement that only a "[']grave and immediate danger to interests which the state may lawfully protect[']" (*id.* at 69) can justify a state's interference with the freedom of religion and held that "there is no evidence in the record that would indicate that in forcing the unwanted medication on Miss Winters the state was in any way protecting the interest of society or even any third party." *Id.* at 70. Thus, it is apparent that the state may not act in a *parens patriae* relationship to a mental hospital patient unless the patient has been adjudicated incompetent.

The fact that appellant has a long-standing delusion that she is Rev. Jenkins' wife and that he will perchance heal her infirmities simply does not strip appellant of her constitutional rights to freely select and adhere to the religion of her choice. The testimony of Dr. Green, the hospital's own witness, supports a conclusion that appellant's belief in spiritual healing stands on its own, without regard to her delusion. Dr. Green explained that appellant's psychosis was "pretty much limited to delusional imaginations" and that "[c]ertain other parts of her seem pretty much intact."

The First Amendment to the United States Constitution and Section 7, Article I of the Ohio Constitution safeguard an individual's freedom to both choose and employ religious beliefs and practices. A person's religious beliefs are protected absolutely. The state may not interfere with the expression of belief, nor may it "compel behavior offensive to religious principles."

While religiously inspired *acts* do not receive absolute protection, "***[o]nly the gravest abuses, endangering paramount interests, give occasion for permissible limitation.***

Appellee does not suggest any state interest sufficient to justify interfering with appellant's religiously inspired refusal to consent to medical treatment. Appellee argues that appellant's delusion that she was Rev. Jenkins' spouse negated her religious views and made her entire belief in faith healing a delusion. The court of appeals looked to the content of appellant's religious beliefs and found that her belief in faith healing constituted a delusion. We do not accept this contention.

There is a dichotomy between modern medicine which is scientific and based upon provable theories and religion which is *inherently* mystical, intangible and a matter of individual faith. Yet, the Ohio and United States Constitutions mandate that when the dictates of modern medicine and religious beliefs collide, the conflict be resolved by leaving the medical treatment decision to the individual.***

While there may be a variety of opinions as to the efficacy of spiritual healing through faith, the courts below acknowledged that it is a form of religious belief and practice. We recognize that extending constitutional protection to a belief in spiritual healing and other religiously motivated refusals to accept medical treatment can be very troubling to those who do not share these beliefs, since, in cases such as this one, the patient may die as a result of refusing the recommended treatment. "***But freedom to differ is not limited to things that do not matter much. That would be a mere shadow of freedom. The test of its substance is the right to differ as to things that touch the heart of the existing order. If there is any fixed star in our constitutional constellation, it is that no official, high or petty, can prescribe what shall be orthodox in***religion***or force citizens to confess by word or act their faith therein." *West Virginia Bd. of Edn. v. Barnette*, 319 U.S. at 642.***

Appellee also suggests that appellant's beliefs are not entitled to protection because she is not a member of any specific religious denomination or sect and is not being treated in accordance with a recognized method of healing. The trial court noted that if appellant were receiving spiritual treatment from Jenkins the court would have been precluded from ordering the medical treatment. However, since she was not actively receiving such spiritual treatment, the court reasoned that it was under no compulsion to recognize appellant's wishes in this matter. Such a distinction is patently in conflict with appellant's constitutional rights. Religious freedom is one of "'absolute equality before the law, of all religious opinions and sects***. The government is neutral, and, while protecting all, it prefers none, and it disparages none.'"

Appellant has expressed a long-standing belief in spiritual healing, and great weight must be given to her statement of her personal beliefs. We cannot evaluate the "correctness" or propriety of appellant's belief. Absent the most exigent circumstances, courts should never be a party to branding a citizen's religious views as baseless on the grounds that they are non-traditional, unorthodox or at war with what the state or others perceive as reality.

The testimony of Dr. Green supports our conclusion that appellant's belief in spiritual healing stands on its own, without regard to any delusion. We can probe no further. Appellant's religious freedom to believe and act according to the dictates of her belief in spiritual healing prevents a court from ordering treatment against her will that would violate her religious beliefs. Thus, we hold that the state may not compel a legally competent adult to submit to medical treatment which would violate that individual's religious beliefs even though the treatment is arguably life-extending. Therefore, the probate court's determination was erroneous and the judgment of the court of appeals upholding it is reversed.

HOLMES, JUSTICE, dissenting.

While I am in complete agreement with the law and the discussion of such law as contained in the majority opinion, I must dissent therefrom in that I feel the majority has completely misconstrued the facts of this matter and the holding of the lower courts in applying such law.

I am in agreement that the state may not compel the medical treatment of a person who is capable of making the determination of granting or denying the consent for a surgical activity where such determination is based upon a religious belief, even though such belief is strange or incomprehensible to others. However, where the facts show that an individual is so confused in the thinking process that such belief is not rationally formulated and is an outworking of a psychosis, as held by the trial court and the court of appeals here, then the question is not one of a religious infringement but is instead one of the degree of mental instability.

Both of the testifying psychiatrists agreed that her refusal of medical treatment sprang from her belief that she was the wife of LeRoy Jenkins. While her thinking remained undisturbed in other areas, this fixed delusion had already placed her in one life-threatening situation, i.e., police had discovered her living unsheltered in the open fields. It is the very nature of a psychosis that an ordinary part of the personality becomes the medium of expression for the illness. When a belief becomes fixed as part of such illness, then the patient becomes incapable of rationally assessing danger relative to the fixation. This would be true whether the belief occurred as the more typical paranoid delusion manifesting itself in intense fear and/or violence or, as here, in a delusion based upon ordinarily held religious beliefs. Just as the illness has nothing to do with appellant's beliefs, so also the diagnosis of illness is not a value judgment of her beliefs.

Here the probate court and trial court reasonably found that Nancy Milton was unable because of her confused mental condition to give an informed, intelligent and knowing consent for her surgery. Such a finding should be appealed to this court without the esoteric, constitutional free-exercise-of-religion discussion. Appellant has expressed quite enough to demonstrate to the lower courts, and certainly to this court, that she is *incapable* of making her own medical determination. She has asserted that she is married to LeRoy Jenkins, and that this member of the T.V. and now radio clergy would heal her maladies. However, Jenkins has, by way of press announcement in The Columbus Dispatch, publicly removed himself from this appellant and stated that she needs help from others.

It is my view that Nancy Milton does need help from others, and that the probate court of appeals properly recognized that such help should be forthcoming from the medical profession as appropriately prescribed. Accordingly, I would affirm the probate court and the court of appeals.

LOCHER, JUSTICE, dissenting.

I agree with the dissent of Justice Holmes and wish to add a few observations of my own.

Nancy Milton was mentally incapable of receiving information concerning her condition and of consenting to surgery. Dr. Lewis A. Lindner testified at the hearing that the patient had totally denied having a tumor to begin with, and that later she refused to accept that she had it—in spite of her being able to feel it growing in her pelvic area. Dr. Lindner added that her stated reason for refusal was that she was the wife of Rev. LeRoy Jenkins, and that she believed he "would come to the hospital and take her away and heal her supernaturally." It is evident that these psychotic delusions have created an impenetrable "wall" which prevents her from admitting she has the tumor and from consenting to the surgery. For her to consent to surgery would be to deny her belief that LeRoy Jenkins would come and take her away to be healed. Nancy Milton is incapable of surmounting this mental wall created by her own delusions. In conclusion, I am convinced that her refusal to consent to surgery is the result of her delusions concerning LeRoy Jenkins rather than her belief in faith healing.

Notes and Issues for Discussion

1. What are the reasons for the treatment refusal? Are they persuasive?
2. The patient is legally competent. Is she functionally competent?
3. Two dissenting justices agreed with the majority's religious freedom position, but disagreed this was the issue. Justice Holmes wrote:

    "I am in agreement that the state may not compel the medical treatment of a person who is capable of making the determination of granting or denying the consent for a surgical activity where such determination is based upon a religious belief, even though such belief is strange or incomprehensible to others. However, where the facts show that an individual is

so confused in the thinking process that such belief is not rationally formulated and is an outworking of a psychosis ... then the question is not
one of a religious infringement but is instead one of the degree of mental
instability." 505 N.E.2d at 260.

Justice Locher added:

"For her to consent to surgery would be to deny her belief that LeRoy
Jenkins would come and take her away to be healed. Nancy is incapable
of surmounting this mental wall created by her own delusions. In conclusion I am convinced that her refusal to consent to surgery is the result of
her delusions concerning LeRoy Jenkins rather than her belief in faith
healing." (505 N.E.2d at 261).

Medical Emergencies

Treatment may be necessary when it is not possible to obtain consent because
of the individual's condition—for example, unconsciousness or shock. Generally, the professional should contact a family member or other person capable of giving consent. If there is no family or no time to contact a relative or
other person who could give consent and immediate treatment is required,
many states through case decisions or statutes dispense with the consent requirement. In *Canterbury v. Spence*, the court noted:

> The first [exception] comes in to play when the patient is unconscious
> or otherwise incapable of consenting, and harm from a failure to treat is
> imminent and outweighs any harm threatened by the proposed treat-
> ment. When a genuine emergency of that sort arises, it is settled that the
> impracticality of conferring with the patient dispenses with need for it.
> Even in situations of that character the physician should, as current law
> requires, attempt to secure a relative's consent if possible, but if time is
> too short to accommodate discussion, obviously the physician should
> proceed with the treatment." 464 F.2d at 788-789.[8]

Informed Consent and Abortion

Roe v. Wade (p. 98) voided a state statute criminalizing abortions and held that
a woman and her physician had a constitutional right to make an abortion decision. The right is not absolute but can be subjected to state regulation after
the first trimester. In a subsequent case, *Planned Parenthood of Missouri v. Danforth*, 428 U.S. 52 (1975), the Court ruled on the constitutionality of a Missouri
statute which imposed a number of restrictions on a woman's abortion decision. The sections of the court's decision on consent by the pregnant woman
and her spouse are presented below; the part of the court's holding on
parental consent for a minor's abortion is presented at Chapter 7, p.195.

THE PREGNANT WOMAN'S INFORMED CONSENT

A portion of the decision dealt with the requirement that a woman give written consent prior to an abortion:

PLANNED PARENTHOOD OF MISSOURI v. DANFORTH
428 U.S. 52 (1976)
U.S. SUPREME COURT

***

The woman's consent. Under §3(2) of the Act, a woman, prior to submitting to an abortion during the first 12 weeks of pregnancy, must certify in writing her consent to the procedure and "that her consent is informed and freely given and is not the result of coercion." Appellants argue that this requirement is violative of *Roe v. Wade*, 410 U.S. at 164-165, by imposing an extra layer and burden of regulation on the abortion decision.

The District Court's majority relied on the propositions that the decision to terminate a pregnancy, of course, "is often a stressful one," and that the consent requirement of §3(2) "insures that the pregnant woman retains control over the discretions of her consulting physician." 392 F. Supp., at 1368, 1369. The majority also felt that the consent requirement "does not single out the abortion procedure, but merely includes it within the category of medical operations for which consent is required." The third judge joined the majority in upholding §3(2), but added that the written consent requirement was "not burdensome or chilling" and manifested "a legitimate interest of the state that this important decision has in fact been made by the person constitutionally empowered to do so." He went on to observe that the requirement "in no way interposes the state or third parties in the decision-making process."

We do not disagree with the result reached by the District Court as to §3(2). It is true that *Doe* and *Roe* clearly establish that the State may not restrict the decision of the patient and her physician regarding abortion during the first stage of pregnancy. Despite the fact that apparently no other Missouri statute, with the exceptions referred to in n. 6, requires a patient's prior written consent to a surgical procedure, the imposition by §3(2) of such a requirement for termination of pregnancy even during the first stage, in our view, is not in itself an unconstitutional requirement. The decision to abort, indeed, is an important, and often a stressful one, and it is desirable and imperative that it be made with full knowledge of its nature and consequences. The woman is the one primarily concerned, and her awareness of the decision and its significance may be assured, constitutionally, by the State to the extent of requiring her prior written consent.

We could not say that a requirement imposed by the State that a prior written consent for any surgery would be unconstitutional. As a consequence, we see no constitutional defect in requiring it only for some types of surgery as, for example, an intracardiac procedure, or where the surgical risk is elevated above a specific mortality level, or, for that matter, for abortions.***

SPOUSAL CONSENT

Another part of the decision dealt with the requirement that a spouse give prior written consent prior to his wife's abortion:

***

The spouse's consent. Section 3(3) requires the prior written consent of the spouse of the woman seeking an abortion during the first 12 weeks of pregnancy, unless "the abortion is certified by a licensed physician to be necessary in order to preserve the life of the mother."***

In *Roe* and *Doe* we specifically reserved decision on the question whether a requirement for consent by the father of the fetus, by the spouse, or by the parents, or a parent, of an unmarried minor, may be constitutionally imposed. We now hold that the State may not constitutionally require the consent of the spouse, as is specified under §3(3) of the Missouri Act, as a condition for abortion during the first 12 weeks of pregnancy. We thus agree with the dissenting judge in the present case, and with the courts whose decisions are cited above, that the State cannot "delegate to a spouse a veto power which the state itself is absolutely and totally prohibited from exercising during the first trimester of pregnancy."*** Clearly, since the State cannot regulate or proscribe abortion during the first stage, when the physician and his patient make that decision, the State cannot delegate authority to any particular person, even the spouse, to prevent abortion during that same period.

We are not unaware of the deep and proper concern and interest that a devoted and protective husband has in his wife's pregnancy and in the growth and development of the fetus she is carrying. Neither has this Court failed to appreciate the importance of the marital relationship in our society. Moreover, we recognize that the decision whether to undergo or to forgo an abortion may have profound effects on the future of any marriage, effects that are both physical and mental, and possibly deleterious. Notwithstanding these factors, we cannot hold that the State has the constitutional authority to give the spouse unilaterally the ability to prohibit the wife from terminating her pregnancy, when the State itself lacks that right.***

It seems manifest that, ideally, the decision to terminate a pregnancy should be one concurred in by both the wife and her husband. No marriage may be viewed as harmonious or successful if the marriage partners are fundamentally divided on so important and vital an issue. But it is difficult to believe that the goal of fostering mutuality and trust in a marriage, and of strengthening the marital relationship and the marriage institution, will be achieved by giving the husband a veto power exercisable for any reason whatsoever or for no reason at all. Even if the State had the ability to delegate to the husband a power it itself could not exercise, it is not at all likely that such action would further, as the District Court majority phrased it, the "interest of the state in protecting the mutuality of decisions vital to the marriage relationship."***

We recognize, of course, that when a woman, with the approval of her physician but without the approval of her husband, decides to terminate her pregnancy, it could be said that she is acting unilaterally. The obvious fact is that when the wife and the husband disagree on this decision, the view of only one of the two marriage partners can prevail. Inasmuch as it is the woman who physically bears the child and who is the more directly and immediately affected by the pregnancy, as between the two, the balance weighs in her favor. Cf. *Roe* v. *Wade*, 410 U.S. at 153.

We conclude that §3(3) of the Missouri Act is inconsistent with the standards enunciated in *Roe* v. *Wade*, 410 U.S., at 164–165, and is unconstitutional.***

Notes and Issues for Discussion

1. In *Planned Parenthood v. Casey*,—U.S.—, 120 L.Ed.2d 674 (1992), the Supreme Court upheld a Pennsylvania informed consent requirement, including a twenty-four hour waiting period before the abortion and the providing of certain information by the physician, and found no First Amendment free speech violation in specifying the information the physician must provide. (120 L. Ed. 2d 717–721).

2. In the same case, the court struck down a spousal notification requirement:

   "In well-functioning marriages, spouses discuss important intimate decisions such as whether to bear a child. But there are millions of women in this country who are the victims of regular physical and psychological abuse at the hands of their husbands. Should these women become pregnant, they may have very good reasons for not wishing to inform their husbands of their decision for obtaining an abortion. . . . The spousal notification requirement is thus likely to prevent a significant number of women from obtaining an abortion. . . . Section 3209 embodies a view of marriage consonant with the common-law status of married women but repugnant to our present understanding of marriage and of the nature of the rights secured by the Constitution. Women do not lose their constitutionally protected liberty rights when they marry. . . . These considerations confirm our conclusion that §3209 is invalid. 120 L. Ed. 2d at 727–728).

Minors and Capacity to Consent

Minors are generally presumed to lack the capacity to give informed consent, with several significant exceptions. Some states recognize "emancipated minors" or "mature minors," who have the capacity to make a number of decisions, including consent to medical treatment. Others allow a minor to consent to specific types of care or treatment, for example consent to an abortion or treatment for sexual assault, drug abuse, or venereal disease. Where minors lack the capacity for informed consent, parents or guardians are vested with the authority to consent for the minor.

EMANCIPATED MINORS

Many states by statute or court decision recognize the status of emancipated minor. While requirements will vary, among the elements that may produce emancipation for a minor are marriage, being a member of the armed forces, having children, supporting oneself, and living independently. Some states specify that the emancipated minor may give consent for health care treatment. Some states have a minimum age requirement as well. Some states specifically provide good faith immunity for health care workers who provide treatment and reasonably believe the minor meets the emancipation requirement. A typical court decision finding emancipation is *Smith v. Seibly*, 72 Wash. 2d 16 (1967), where the patient was eighteen years old (the age of majority was twenty-one), married, self-supporting, and living with his wife and their child. He requested that a vasectomy be performed because he was afflicted with an incurable progressive disease which he felt would inhibit his ability to work and support a larger family. The physician explained the procedure and its consequences, gave the patient and his wife a consent form and requested they consider the decision. After twelve days, the patient returned with the consent form signed by both him and his wife and the operation was performed. In rejecting a suit brought three years later by the patient, the Washington court noted:

> . . . A married minor, 18 years of age, who has successfully completed high school and is the head of his own family, who earns his own living and maintains his own home, is emancipated for the purpose of giving a valid consent to surgery if a full disclosure of the ramifications, implications and probable consequences of the surgery has been made by the doctor in terms which are fully comprehensible to the minor. Thus, age, intelligence, maturity, training, experience, economic independence or lack thereof, general conduct as an adult and freedom from the control of parents are all factors to be considered in such a case. 431 P.2d 719.

Among the states that recognize emancipated minors by statute are Alaska, Alabama, Colorado, Massachusetts, Montana, Nevada, Illinois, Louisiana, Maryland, Missouri, New York, Oklahoma, Pennsylvania, and Utah. A number of other states recognize emancipated minors by case decisions. Among those where an emancipated minor may consent to treatment are Arizona, Kentucky, New Mexico, West Virginia, and Wyoming (Rosovsky, 1990: 266).

MATURE MINORS

Some minors are recognized by the court as mature enough to have the capacity to understand the treatment decision and the consequences of accepting or rejecting the treatment. Examples of such mature minors include:

A seventeen-year-old's decision (where twenty-one was majority) to have a tumor removed from his ear, where he had been previously treated for the condition and his father was aware of it but not present at the operation. *Bakker v. Welsh*, 108 N.W. 94 (Mich. 1906).

A minor's decision to have a vaccination required by his employer. *Gulf & Ship Island R.R. Co. v. Sullivan*, 119 So. 501 (Miss. 1928).

A seventeen-year-old's decision to have minor surgery to her fingertip. *Younts v. St. Francis Hosp. & School of Nursing*, 469 P. 2d 330 (Kan. 1970).

THE MINOR'S CONSENT TO ABORTION

Roe v. Wade establishes a woman's constitutional privacy right to make an abortion decision with her physician prior to fetal viability. In that case, Jane Roe was an adult woman. Subsequent decisions have addressed a minor's right to an abortion, and requirements of parental consent or notification. In *Planned Parenthood v. Danforth*, the Court struck down a parental consent requirement:

PLANNED PARENTHOOD *of MISSOURI v. DANFORTH*
428 U.S. 52 (1976)
U.S. SUPREME COURT

***

Parental Consent. Section 3(4) requires, with respect to the first 12 weeks of pregnancy, where the woman is unmarried and under the age of 18 years, the written consent of a parent or person *in loco parentis* unless, again, "the abortion is certified by a licensed physician as necessary in order to preserve the life of the mother." It is to be observed that only one parent need consent.

The appellees defend the statute in several ways. They point out that the law properly may subject minors to more stringent limitations than are permissible with respect to adults, and they cite, among other cases, *Prince v. Massachusetts*, 321 U.S. 158 (1944), and *McKeiver v. Pennsylvania*, 403 U.S. 528 (1971). Missouri law, it is said, "is replete with provisions reflecting the interest of the state in assuring the welfare of minors," citing statutes relating to a guardian *ad litem* for a court proceeding, to the care of delinquent and neglected children, to child labor, and to compulsory education. Certain decisions are considered by the State to be outside the scope of a minor's ability to act in his own best interest or in the interest of the public, citing statutes proscribing the sale of firearms and deadly weapons to minors without parental consent, and other statutes relating to minors' exposure to certain types of literature, the purchase by pawnbrokers of property from minors, and the sale of cigarettes and alcoholic beverages to minors. It is pointed out that the record contains testimony to the effect that children of tender years (even ages 10 and 11) have sought abortions. Thus, a State's permitting a child to obtain an abortion without the counsel of an adult "who has responsibility or concern for the child would constitute an irresponsible abdication of the State's duty to protect the welfare of minors." *Id., at 44.* Parental discretion, too, has been protected from unwarranted or unreasonable interference from the State, citing *Meyer* v. *Nebraska,* 262 U.S. 390 (1923); *Pierce* v. *Society of Sisters,* 268 U.S. 510 (1925); *Wisconsin* v. *Yoder,* 406 U.S. 205 (1972). Finally, it is said that §3(4) imposes no additional burden on the physician because even prior to the passage of the Act the physician would require parental consent before performing an abortion on a minor.

The appellants, in their turn, emphasize that no other Missouri statute specifically requires the additional consent of a minor's parent for medical or surgical treatment, and that in Missouri a minor legally may consent to medical services for pregnancy (excluding abortion), venereal disease, and drug abuse. Mo. Rev. Stat. §§431.061–431.063 (Supp. 1975). The result of §3(4), it is said, "is the ultimate supremacy of the parents' desires over those of the minor child, the pregnant patient." It is noted that in Missouri a woman under the age of 18 who marries with parental consent does not require parental consent to abort, and yet her contemporary who has chosen not to marry must obtain parental approval.

The District Court majority recognized that, in contrast to §3(3), the State's interest in protecting the mutuality of a marriage relationship is not present with respect to §3(4). It found "a compelling basis," however, in the State's interest "in safeguarding the authority of the family relationship." The dissenting judge observed that one could not seriously argue that a minor must submit to an abortion if her parents insist, and he could not see "why she would not be entitled to the same right of self-determination now explicitly accorded to adult women, provided she is sufficiently mature to understand the procedure and to make an intelligent assessment of her circumstances with the advice of her physician."

Of course, much of what has been said above, with respect to §3(3), applies with equal force to §3(4). Other courts that have considered the parental-consent issue in the light of *Roe* and *Doe,* have concluded that a statute like §3(4) does not withstand constitutional scrutiny.

We agree with appellants and with the courts whose decisions have just been cited that the State may not impose a blanket provision, such as §3(4), requiring the consent of a parent or person *in loc. parentis* as a condition for abortion of an unmarried minor during the first 12 weeks of her pregnancy. Just as with the requirement of consent from the spouse, so here, the State does not have the constitutional authority to give a third party an absolute, and possibly arbitrary, veto over the decision of the physician and his patient to terminate the patient's pregnancy, regardless of the reason for withholding the consent.

Constitutional rights do not mature and come into being magically only when one attains the state-defined age of majority. Minors, as well as adults, are protected by the Constitution and possess constitutional rights. The Court indeed, however, long has recognized that the State has somewhat broader authority to regulate the activities of children than of adults. It remains, then, to examine whether there is any significant state interest in conditioning an abortion on the consent of a parent or person *in loco parentis* that is not present in the case of an adult.

One suggested interest is the safeguarding of the family unit and of parental authority. It is difficult, however, to conclude that providing a parent with absolute power to overrule a determination, made by the physician and his minor patient, to terminate the patient's pregnancy will serve to strengthen the family unit. Neither is it likely that such veto power will enhance parental authority or control where the minor and the nonconsenting parent are so fundamentally in conflict and the very existence of the pregnancy already has fractured the family structure. Any independent interest the parent may have in the termination of the minor daughter's pregnancy is no more weighty than the right of privacy of the competent minor mature enough to have become pregnant.

We emphasize that our holding that §3(4) is invalid does not suggest that every minor, regardless of age or maturity, may give effective consent for termination of her pregnancy. The fault with §3(4) is that it imposes a special-consent provision, exercisable by a person other than the woman and her physician, as a prerequisite to a minor's termination of her pregnancy and does so without a sufficient justification for the restriction. It violates the strictures of *Roe* and *Doe*.***

Notes and Issues for Discussion

1. Who is a competent minor? When is a minor mature enough to have become pregnant? When she is physically mature? Emotionally mature? When she is capable of making a conscious, mature decision to become pregnant? In any of these situations, who decides maturity? What if the minor is immature? The court doesn't address these questions and some remain unanswered today.

2. In *Bellotti v. Baird* 443 U.S. 622 (1979), the Court rejected a Massachusetts statute requiring that an unmarried minor less than eighteen years old have consent of both parents prior to an abortion or consult with her parents before appearing in court to request a judicial determination of abortion. In its opinion, the Court held that a procedure in which a minor wishing an abortion could utilize a "judicial bypass" was constitutionally acceptable. The minor could appear in court and argue that she was a mature minor who was informed and understood the consequences of her decision. If the court agreed that she was mature, she could proceed with an abortion without further consent. If the court found she was not mature, the court could still approve the requested abortion if it was in the minor's best interests. This approach is now statutory law Massachusetts. Mass Gen. Laws §112-12s. See also *Hodgson v. Minnesota*, 497 U.S. 417 (1990).

3. In *Matter of Mary Moe*, 423 N.E. 2d 1038 (1981), the trial court found that the fourteen-year-old unmarried minor was not mature and that an abortion was not in her best interests, requiring parental consent prior to the abortion. The Massachusetts appellate court reversed and presented some criteria for determining whether the abortion would be in the best interests of the minor found to be not mature. These included any ambivalence about the abortion decision; any evidence of pressure to undergo the abortion; any previous professional counseling; an understanding of the nature and risk of the procedure; and the existence of arrangements made by the minor with a reputable facility to perform the abortion. 423 N.E.2d at 1043.
4. A Utah statute requiring parental notification when the child is not a mature minor was upheld in *H.L. v. Matheson*, 450 U.S. 398 (1981). In that case, the minor who was under sixteen, living at home, and dependent on her parents for support was found not to be mature.

THE MINOR'S CONSENT TO TREATMENT FOR SEXUALLY TRANSMITTED DISEASES, ABUSE OF DRUGS AND ALCOHOL

Many states permit the treatment of a minor for sexually transmitted diseases without parental consent and grant immunity from liability for not obtaining parental or guardian consent. States vary in their provisions, and some have set lower age limits for the minor's consent, such as twelve or fourteen years old.[9] Where parental consent is not required some states permit or mandate parental notification after treatment. Similarly, many states permit treatment of minors for alcoholism or drug abuse without parental consent, some with and some without a minimum age for consent. Parental notification is often permissible. Several states require parental consent prior to methadone treatment. (See, generally, Rozovsky, 1990: 275 *ff.*)

Informed Consent for Termination of Life Support Systems

Almost every state has now codified some form of a "living will." While not a will in the traditional sense of disposing of property after death, a living will generally provides instructions about the use of life-support systems in the eventuality that the individual is incapable of making his or her wishes known.[10] Under certain conditions specified in statutes or court decisions, a guardian or surrogate decision maker may make this decision for an individual unable to make it.[11] Some court cases in this area have been decided on the basis of a right to informed consent, others on the theory that an individual has a privacy right to make decisions about one's own body. Here discussion is primarily directed toward the patient's or client's right of informed consent to make these decisions; in Chapter 8, the role of the guardian in these decisions will be discussed.

LIVING WILLS, ADVANCED DIRECTIVES, AND HEALTH CARE PROXIES

Legal expressions of an individual's intent about medical treatment in the event of incapacity take many forms, including living wills, advanced directives, health care proxies, durable powers of attorney, and do not resuscitate (DNR) orders. While states vary in their living will provisions, there are many commonalities:

> ... similar provisions include: 1) who may make a declaration; 2) the manner of execution of the document; 3) definition sections; 4) revocation procedures; 5) declarations that the current wishes of the patient will supercede any previous declaration; 6) declarations for the transfer of the patient if the attending physician will not comply; and 7) declarations stating that complying physicians will be provided with immunity from civil and criminal penalties. ("Comparisons of living will statutes," 1988:107).

While adults of sound mind are capable of voluntarily making a living will, declarations by minors or those who are incompetent may be excluded. Usually before the intent can become effective, the individual must be terminally ill, although states vary in definitions of "terminal." Many states prohibit the declaration from becoming effective during a woman's pregnancy or if the child can be delivered while the mother is on life-support systems ("Comparisons of living will statutes," 1988:108–112).

> Each of the states' laws establishes that a living will should be executed willfully and voluntarily, written, signed, dated and witnessed. Only four states ... provide specifically for oral declarations. ... All the states require at least two adult witnesses to attest to the signing of the declaration ("Comparisons of living will statutes," 1988:113)

A number of states include actual model living wills in their statutes. California, for example, provides:

(b) A declaration shall substantially contain the following provisions:

DECLARATION

If I should have an incurable and irreversible condition that has been diagnosed by two physicians and that will result in my death within a relatively short time without the administration of life-sustaining treatment or has produced an irreversible coma or persistent vegetative state, and I am no longer able to make decisions regarding my medical treatment, I direct my attending physician, pursuant to the Natural Death Act of California, to withhold or withdraw treatment, including artificially administered nutrition and hydration, that only prolongs the process of dying or the irreversible coma or persistent vegetative state and is not necessary for my comfort or to alleviate pain.

If I have been diagnosed as pregnant, and that diagnosis is known to my physician, this declaration shall have no force or effect during my pregnancy.

Signed this _____ day of _____, _____.

Signature_____

Address_____

The declarant voluntarily signed this writing in my presence. I am not entitled to any portion of the estate of the declarant upon his or her death under any will or codicil thereto of the declarant now existing or by operation of law. I am not a health care provider, an employee of a health care provider, the operator of a community care facility, an employee of an operator of a community care facility, the operator of a residential care facility for the elderly, or an employee of an operator of a residential care facility for the elderly.

Witness_____

Address_____.

(Cal. Health and Safety Code §7186.5)

A more complex living will may combine an *advanced directive* with a *durable health care proxy*. The advanced directive specifies under what conditions the individual wishes life sustaining medical treatment to be withheld or withdrawn and the health care proxy specifies who should make the decision to withhold or withdraw the life support system if the individual is unable to make that decision. The health care proxy is termed "durable" because unlike many proxies or powers of attorney, it continues to be in effect during the individual's incapacity. Generally both can be written without the help of an attorney, and become effective when properly signed and witnessed as required by state law.

Since living will statutes take many forms, do not uniformly apply to the same situations, and require varying degrees of proof, it is vital for the health and human services professional to ascertain the applicable provisions. Some statutes are broadly drawn, some are more narrow and restrictive. Some courts seem more willing to fashion approaches allowing for the removal of life support systems, others less so.[12]

STATE RESTRICTIONS ON THE WITHDRAWAL OF LIFE -SUPPORT SYSTEMS

The right of competent individuals to refuse treatment, even if it results in the loss of their life has been recognized in a number of courts. Opposing this right is the state's right to protect its citizens and promote life. While a number of courts have indicated that at some point the individual's personal right to end his or her life will outweigh the state's interest in preservation of life, there is no uniform pattern. Important in these decisions are (1) the prognosis of the individual, including whether that individual is terminally ill or comatose; (2) the types of life-support systems involved and whether they are intrusive, extraordinary, or simply the provision of liquids and nutrition; (3) the amount of discomfort or pain the individual is experiencing and whether that pain will continue, increase, or abate; and (4) the individual's prior expressed intent regarding life-support systems, including clarity, specificity, recentness, and the form and context in which it was expressed.

CRUZAN v. DIRECTOR, MISSOURI HEALTH DEPARTMENT
497 U.S. 261 (1990)
U.S. SUPREME COURT

CHIEF JUSTICE REHNQUIST delivered the opinion of the Court.

Petitioner Nancy Beth Cruzan was rendered incompetent as a result of severe injuries sustained during an automobile accident. Co-petitioners Lester and Joyce Cruzan, Nancy's parents and co-guardians, sought a court order directing the withdrawal of their daughter's artificial feeding and hydration equipment after it became apparent that she had virtually no chance of recovering her cognitive faculties. The Supreme Court of Missouri held that because there was no clear and convincing evidence of Nancy's desire to have life-sustaining treatment withdrawn under such circumstances, her parents lacked authority to effectuate such a request. We granted certiorari and now affirm.

On the night of January 11, 1983, Nancy Cruzan lost control of her car as she traveled down Elm Road in Jasper County, Missouri. The vehicle overturned, and Cruzan was discovered lying face down in a ditch without detectable respiratory or cardiac function. Paramedics were able to restore her breathing and heartbeat at the accident site, and she was transported to a hospital in an unconscious state. An attending neurosurgeon diagnosed her as having sustained probable cerebral contusions compounded by significant anoxia (lack of oxygen). The Missouri trial court in this case found that permanent brain damage generally results after 6 minutes in an anoxic state; it was estimated that Cruzan was deprived of oxygen from 12 to 14 minutes. She remained in a coma for approximately three weeks and then progressed to an unconscious state in which she was able to orally ingest some nutrition. In order to ease feeding and further the recovery, surgeons implanted a gastrostomy feeding and hydration tube in Cruzan with the consent of her then husband. Subsequent rehabilitative efforts proved unavailing. She now lies in a Missouri state hospital in what is commonly referred to as a persistent vegetative state: generally, a condition in which a person exhibits motor reflexes but evinces no indications of significant cognitive function. The State of Missouri is bearing the cost of her care.

After it had become apparent that Nancy Cruzan had virtually no chance of regaining her mental faculties her parents asked hospital employees to terminate the artificial nutrition and hydration procedures. All agree that such a removal would cause her death. The employees refused to honor the request without court approval. The parents then sought and received authorization from the state trial court for a termination. The court found that a person in Nancy's condition had a fundamental right under the State and Federal Constitutions to refuse or direct the withdrawal of "death prolonging procedures." The court also found that Nancy's "expressed thoughts at age twenty-five in somewhat serious conversation with a housemate friend that if sick or injured she would not wish to continue her life unless she could live at least halfway normally suggests that given her present condition she would not wish to continue on with her nutrition and hydration."

The Supreme Court of Missouri reversed by a divided vote. The court recognized a right to refuse treatment embodied in the common-law doctrine of informed consent, but expressed skepticism about the application of that doctrine in the circumstances of this case. The court also declined to read a broad right of privacy into the State Constitution which would "support the right of a person to refuse medical treatment in every circumstance," and expressed doubt as to whether such a right existed under the United States Constitution. It then decided that the Missouri Living Will statute, Mo Rev Stat §459.010 et seq. (1986), embodied a state policy strongly favoring the preservation of life. The court found that Cruzan's statements to her roommate regarding her desire to live or die under certain conditions were "unreliable for the purpose of determining her intent," "and thus insufficient to support the co-guardians claim to exercise substituted judgment on Nancy's behalf." It rejected the argument that Cruzan's parents were entitled to order the termination of her medical treatment, concluding that "no person can assume that choice for an incompetent in the absence of the formalities required under Missouri's Living Will statutes or the clear and convincing, inherently reliable evidence absent here." The court also expressed its view that "[b]road policy questions bearing on life and death are more properly addressed by representative assemblies" than judicial bodies.

We granted certiorari to consider the question of whether Cruzan has a right under the United States Constitution which would require the hospital to withdraw life-sustaining treatment from her under these circumstances. At common law, even the touching of one person by another without consent and without legal justification was a battery. Before the turn of the century, this Court observed that "[n]o right is held more sacred, or is more carefully guarded, by the common law, than the right of every individual to the possession and control of his own person, free from all restraint or interference of others, unless by clear and unquestionable authority of law."

This notion of bodily integrity has been embodied in the requirement that informed consent is generally required for medical treatment. Justice Cardozo, while on the Court of Appeals of New York, aptly described this doctrine: "Every human being of adult years and sound mind has a right to determine what shall be done with his own body; and a surgeon who performs an operation without his patient's consent commits an assault, for which he is liable in damages." Schloendorff v Society of New York Hospital, 211 NY 125, 129–30 (1914).***

The logical corollary of the doctrine of informed consent is that the patient generally possesses the right not to consent, that is, to refuse treatment. Until about 15 years ago and the seminal decision in In re Quinlan, 70 NJ 10, 355 A2d 647, the number of right-to-refuse-treatment decisions were relatively few. Most of the earlier cases involved patients who refused medical treatment forbidden by their religious beliefs, thus implicating First Amendment rights as well as common law rights of self-determination. More recently, however, with the advance of medical technology capable of sustaining life well past the point where natural forces would have brought certain death in earlier times, cases involving the right to refuse life-sustaining treatment have burgeoned.

In this Court, the question is simply and starkly whether the United States Constitution prohibits Missouri from choosing the rule of decision which it did. This is the first case in which we have been squarely presented with the issue of whether the United States Constitution grants what is in common parlance referred to as a "right to die."

The Fourteenth Amendment provides that no State shall "deprive any person of life, liberty, or property, without due process of law." The principle that a competent person has a constitutionally protected liberty interest in refusing unwanted medical treatment may be inferred from our prior decisions.***

Whether or not Missouri's clear and convincing evidence requirement comports with the United States Constitution depends in part on what interests the State may properly seek to protect in this situation. Missouri relies on its interest in the protection and preservation of human life, and there can be no gainsaying this interest.***

But in the context presented here, a State has more particular interests at stake. The choice between life and death is a deeply personal decision of obvious and overwhelming finality. We believe Missouri may legitimately seek to safeguard the personal element of this choice through the imposition of heightened evidentiary requirements. It cannot be disputed that the Due Process Clause protects an interest in life as well as an interest in refusing life-sustaining medical treatment. Not all incompetent patients will have loved ones available to serve as surrogate decisionmakers. And even where family member are present, "[t]here will, of course, be some unfortunate situations in which family members will not act to protect a patient."***Finally, we think a State may properly decline to make judgments about the "quality" of life that a particular individual may enjoy, and simply assert an unqualified interest in the preservation of human life to be weighed against the constitutionally protected interests of the individual.

In our view, Missouri has permissibly sought to advance these interests through the adoption of a "clear and convincing" standard of proof to govern such proceedings. "The function of a standard of proof, as that concept is embodied in the Due Process Clause and in the realm of factfinding, is to 'instruct the fact-finder concerning the degree of confidence our society thinks he should have in the correctness of factual conclusions for a particular type of adjudication.'" Addington v Texas, 441 US 418, 423. "This Court has mandated an intermediate standard of proof—'clear and convincing evidence'—when the individual interests at stake in a state proceeding are both 'particularly important' and 'more substantial than mere loss of money.'" Santosky v Kramer, 455 US 745, 756 (1982).***

We think it self-evident that the interests at stake in the instant proceedings are more substantial, both on an individual and societal level, than those involved in a run-of-the-mine civil dispute. But not only does the standard of proof reflect the importance of a particular adjudication, it also serves as "a societal judgment about how the risk of error should be distributed between the litigants." The more stringent the burden of proof a party must bear, the more that party bears the risk of an erroneous decision. We believe that Missouri may permissibly place an increased risk of an erroneous decision on those seeking to terminate an incompetent individual's life-sustaining treatment. An erroneous decision not to terminate results in a maintenance of the status quo; the possibility of subsequent developments such as advancements in medical science, the discovery of new evidence regarding the patient's intent, changes in the law, or simply the unexpected death of the patient despite the administration of life-sustaining treatment, at least create the potential that a wrong decision will eventually be corrected or its impact mitigated. An erroneous decision to withdraw life-sustaining treatment, however, is not susceptible of correction.***

No doubt is engendered by anything in this record but that Nancy Cruzan's mother and father are loving and caring parents. If the State were required by the United States Constitution to repose a right of "substituted judgment" with anyone, the Cruzans would surely qualify. But we do not think the Due Process Clause requires the State to repose judgment on these matters with anyone but the patient herself. Close family members may have a strong feeling—a feeling not at all ignoble or unworthy, but not entirely disinterested, either—that they do not wish to witness the continuation of the life of a loved one which they regard as hopeless, meaningless, and even degrading. But there is no automatic assurance that the view of close family members will necessarily be the same as the patient's would have been had she been confronted with the prospect of her situation while competent. All of the reasons previously discussed for allowing Missouri to require clear and convincing evidence of the patient's wishes lead us to conclude that the State may choose to defer only to those wishes, rather than confide the decision to close family members.

The judgment of the Supreme Court of Missouri is affirmed.

Notes and Issues for Discussion

1. Courts have frequently based the right to refuse life-supporting treatment on either a right of informed consent as in *Cruzan* or in an individual's right to privacy under either a state or the federal Constitution. Note that in *Cruzan*, the Court appears to find a right to refuse treatment within the

doctrine of informed consent leaving undecided the issue under what conditions it may be exercised.

2. The Court finds Missouri's "clear and convincing" standard of proof to be constitutionally acceptable. What are the arguments for this more restrictive standard? For the less demanding preponderance of the evidence standard used in most civil cases?

3. The *Cruzan* case was reheard in the lower court and, based on additional evidence of intent, the clear and convincing standard was found to have been met. Nancy Beth Cruzan was disconnected from the life support system and died soon after.

THE PATIENT SELF-DETERMINATION ACT (PSDA) OF 1990

As part of the Omnibus Budget Reconciliation Act of 1990, Congress enacted the Patient Self-Determination Act which mandates certain health care agencies receiving Medicaid or Medicare funding to comply with a series of requirements for developing written policies and procedures to inform patients or clients of their state's living will laws and not to condition an individual's care or treatment on the basis of whether or not a living will has been executed. Under the act, Medicare or Medicaid payments may be withheld from an organization not in compliance. See generally 42 U.S.C. §1395cc (Medicare) and 42 U.S.C. §1396a (Medicaid).

Agencies included in the coverage of the act are hospitals, skilled nursing facilities, home health agencies, and hospice programs. Under the provisions of the act, these agencies must provide written information to each patient or resident concerning

(A)(i) an individual's rights under State law (whether statutory or as recognized by the courts of the State) to make decisions concerning such medical care, including the right to accept or refuse medical or surgical treatment and the right to formulate advance directives (as defined in paragraph (3)), and (ii) written policies of the provider or organization respecting the implementation of such rights;

(B) to document in the individual's medical record whether or not the individual has executed an advance directive;

(C) not to condition the provision of care or otherwise discriminate against an individual based on whether or not the individual has executed an advance directive;

(D) to ensure compliance with requirements of state law (whether statutory or as recognized by the courts of the State) respecting advance directives at facilities of the provider or organization; and

(E) to provide (individually or with others) for education for staff and the community on issues concerning advanced directives. 42 U.S.C. 1395cc(f).

Advanced directive is defined as "a written instruction, such as a living will or durable power of attorney for health care, recognized under State law ... and relating to the provision of such care when the individual is incapacitated."

The information is to be provided to the patient or client upon admission, enrollment, or initial receipt of care, depending upon the organization.

Under the act, "The Secretary may not provide for payment ... with respect to an organization unless the organization provides assurances satisfactory to the Secretary that the organization meets the requirement of [the section relating to maintaining written policies and procedures respecting advance directives]."[13] 42 U.S.C. §1395l(r).

Notes and Issues for Discussion

1. Among the questions raised about the PSDA are whether it is possible in many states to provide advanced directive information that is accurate and that a patient will be able to understand, and whether these health care providers are the appropriate agencies to provide this information. See, generally, Note, "Patient Self-Determination Act of 1990," 8 *J. of Contemp. Health Law and Policy* 455 (1992).
2. How will agencies be monitored to ensure that the Act is followed? How likely is it that federal moneys actually will be withheld if it is not?
3. Assuming compliance, it becomes all the more necessary for many health and human services professionals to become knowledgeable about their state's advance directive provisions and requirements since they will often have to provide the requisite information or training.

Research and Human Subject Experimentation

Informed consent in research and human experimentation is an important area for health and human services professionals engaged in some types of research. Many states in statutory bills of rights for institutionalized patients and clients prohibit research and experimentation without informed consent, and if they lack the capacity to give such consent, then require informed consent by the individual's guardian. A major federal policy, Basic HHS Policy for Protection of Human Research Subjects, 45 C.F.R. §46.101 ff., applies to "all research involving human subjects conducted, supported or otherwise subject to regulation by any federal department or agency which takes appropriate administrative action to make the policy applicable to such research." The policy establishes an Institutional Review Board (IRB) to review all research covered by the policy (45 C.F.R. §46.109) and establishes criteria for review (45 C.F.R. §46.111) and record keeping (45 C.F.R. §46.115). Requirements for informed consent are established in 45 C.F.R. §46.116. Additional protections apply to research involving fetuses, pregnant women, and human *in vitro* fertilization (45 C.F.R. §46.201 *et seq.*); prisoners (45 C.F.R. §46.301 *et seq.*); and children (45 C.F.R. §46.401). Any health and human services professional conducting research or experiments in these areas should read these policies carefully.

SELECTED REFERENCES

Applebaum, P. S., Lidz, C. W., and Meisel, A. *Informed Consent: Legal Theory and Clinical Practice* (1987).

Faden, R. R., and Beauchamp, T. L. *A History and Theory of Informed Consent* (1986).

Hogue, E. *Nursing and Informed Consent* (1985).

Katz, J. *The Silent World of Doctor and Patient* (1984).

Meisel, A., Roth, L. H., and Lidz, C. W. "Toward a model of the legal doctrine of informed consent," 134 *Am. J. Psychiatry* 285 (1977).

Meisel, A., and Roth, L. H. "Toward an informed discussion of informed consent: A review and critique of empirical studies," 25 *Arizona L.R.* 263 (1983).

Melton, G. B., Koocher, G. P., and Saks, M. J. *Children's Competence to Consent* (1983).

Merz, J. F., and Fischoff, B. "Informed consent does not mean rational consent," 11 *J. Legal Medicine* 321 (1990).

Morrissey, J. M., Hofman, A. D., and Thorpe, J. C. *Consent and Confidentiality in Health Care of Children and Adolescents.* (1986).

Note, "Comparisons of living will statutes of the 50 states," 14 *J. Contemporary Law* 135 (1988).

Reamer, F. "Informed consent in social work," 32 *Social Work* 425 (1987).

Roth, L. H. *Informed Consent: A Study of Decisionmaking in Psychiatry* (1984).

———, Applebaum, P. S., Lidz, C. W. et al., "Informed consent in psychiatric research," 39 *Rutgers L.R.* 425 (1987).

Rozovsky, F. A. *Consent to Treatment: A Practical Guide.* (1990).

CHAPTER 8

INCOMPETENCE AND GUARDIANSHIP

Determinations of incompetence, appointment of guardians, and making decisions for incompetent individuals have become increasingly complex and problematic. Historically, competency proceedings usually were instituted to protect property. In medieval England and colonial America, incompetency and guardianship were used as a means to prevent the wasting of assets and to safeguard property for the benefit of the incompetent and the incompetent's family. This economic orientation remained primary until recently, while making personal decisions for the incompetent individual remained far less important (Parry, 1985: 369).

In the last two decades there have been dramatic changes. First, a growing legal acceptance of medical and psychological evidence indicates that incompetence is neither total nor static for many individuals. Moreover, there has been a recognition that removing one's decision-making powers creates a sense of helplessness and reinforces limited functioning. One result has been a move away from a simple all-or-nothing approach and toward a recognition of limited incompetence coupled with limited guardianship in some jurisdictions. Second, there has been a growing recognition that legal protections for incompetent citizens have been inadequate and may lead to abuse. More attention has been paid to due process protections and judicial review. Finally, legal guardians are increasingly faced with making a range of complex and serious personal decisions for incompetent persons, including decisions about medical and surgical interventions, living arrangements, and the use of medications. Medical decisions include using intrusive or high-risk medical procedures, sterilization, and the introduction or withdrawal of life support systems. Decisions about living arrangements range from residence in a community to residence in a nursing home or an institution. Decisions about medications include the use of very potent medications such as psychotropic drugs with potentially serious side effects.

This chapter will first discuss some definitions of competence and incompetence. Then incompetency proceedings, appointment and powers of guardians, and decision-making criteria will be addressed. Following this, three types of particularly problematic decisions for health and human services professionals will be examined: treatment decisions for incompetent adults; medical decisions for minors; and decisions to remove life support systems from comatose or severely impaired incompetent individuals.

A word of warning: Standards and determinations of competence and incompetence vary across states as do the powers and decision-making criteria of guardians. This discussion will not provide an inclusive survey of all states, but rather will address some key issues and examine some representative laws and case decisions. The health and human services professional will need to consult individual state law for relevant legal requirements.[1]

DETERMINATIONS OF INCOMPETENCE

Legal and Clinical Definitions

Competence and incompetence have many meanings. In everyday use, a competent person is capable; an incompetent person is inept. Technical definitions are more complex.

Clinical definitions generally address the cognitive ability to make decisions or the behavioral ability to perform tasks.[2] Faden and Beauchamp present a behavioral definition of competence, "the ability to perform a task," and argue that while this is basic, there will be a range of criteria of competence depending on the context and the specific task (Faden and Beauchamp, 1986: 288). Roth et al. have identified five types of clinical criteria which are used individually or in combination in determining competence:

1. evidencing a choice, where the individual is viewed as competent if any choice can be made

2. reasonable outcome, where competence depends on how reasonable others view the outcome selected

3. choice based on rational reasons, where competence depends on how rational the basis is for the choice

4. ability to understand, where competence is based on how well the individual comprehends in general

5. actual understanding, where competence is based on the individual's actual understanding of the specific issue (Roth *et al.*, 1977: 280).

Applebaum and Roth (1981) have proposed four standards for determining competency:

1. evidencing a choice
2. factual understanding of the issues
3. rational manipulation of information
4. appreciation of the nature of the situation[3]

Legally, a competent person is

[d]uly qualified; answering all requirements; having sufficient capacity, ability or authority; possessing the requisite physical, mental, natural or legal qualifications. . . . (Black's *Law Dictionary*, 1991).

The concepts are complex. If competence generally has to do with the ability to understand choices and outcomes and to make decisions, then, as a number of authors have noted, competency is more a continuum than a specific condition and will vary with the individual and the situation. Some individuals have a greater capacity to make complex decisions than others. Some decisions are more complex or serious and require a higher degree of decision-making ability. Deciding whether or not to remove a life-support system or whether to undergo chemotherapy are very different decisions from deciding what to wear to school, which dress to buy, or whether to have a tooth filled. Moreover, an individual who alone is incapable of making some decisions may nonetheless have the ability to make them with assistance or at least participate in them. Finally, some individuals who lack the capacity to make decisions may at a later time regain that capacity.

In the face of this complex reality the law has drawn some arbitrary lines. Most adults are presumed competent to make decisions and exercise their civil rights. Most minors—usually under 18 years—are presumed to be incompetent. If the individual is mentally ill and civilly committed, mentally retarded, elderly, alcoholic, or a drug addict, then competence may vary according to state law.

It should be emphasized that in a very real sense, the issue of clinical or legal incompetence may never arise for functionally incompetent individuals unless they are unable to make choices when necessary, make choices not acceptable to others, or have no third party such as a spouse or relative available to make decisions for them. (Roth, *et al.*, 1977).

STATUTORY DEFINITIONS

Statutory definitions of incompetence primarily fall within three general groups. Most states have moved away from automatic presumptions of incompetence in cases of civil commitment or disability and toward determinations based on actual behavior. (Parry, 1985). By the mid-1980s, about one-third of the states had adopted the Uniform Probate Code definition of an incapacitated person as one who "lacks sufficient understanding or capacity to make or communicate responsible decisions concerning his person" (Parry, 1985: 371).[4]

For a number of other states, the criteria of inability to care for one's self or to manage one's affairs remain the standard:

The New York statute specifies:

> incompetent to manage himself or his affairs by reason of age, alcohol abuse, mental illness or other cause. . . . N.Y. Mental Hyg. Law, 78.01 (1988).

Maryland is typical of states that specify characteristics of incompetence:

> A guardian shall be appointed if the court determines that . . . the person is unable to manage his property and affairs effectively because of physical or mental disability, senility, or other mental weakness, disease, habitual drunkenness, addiction to drugs, imprisonment, compulsory hospitalization, confinement, detention by a foreign power, or disappearance." Md. Ann. Code, Estates and Trusts, 13-201(c) (1974).[5]

Finally, in a few states, incompetence is still presumed when specific disabilities exist. For example, the Louisiana Code specifies:

> No person . . . who is subject to an habitual state of imbecility, insanity or madness, shall be allowed to take care of his own person and administer his estate, although such person shall, at all times, appear to have the possession of his reason. La. Rev. Stat. Ann. 389.

For the health and human services professional, none of these formulations may be satisfactory since they oversimplify a complex set of phenomena. An American Bar Association Commission has proposed that any formulation of incompetence or incapacity include the following:

1. a recognition that the incapacity may be partial or complete

2. incapacity is a legal not a medical term, and thus there cannot be sole reliance on a medical diagnosis

3. incapacity should be combined with evidence of a continuing functional impairment

4. incapacity should include the likelihood of suffering substantial harm

5. simple categories or labels should be insufficient for a finding of incapacity (Parry, 1988: 404)

Incompetency Proceedings

Legal incompetence requires some type of hearing before a judge who makes the final determination based on the testimony and evidence presented in court. Important issues include who can institute the proceeding, the notice required, representation for the alleged incompetent individual, the physical presence of the alleged incompetent at the hearing, how incompetence is established, and the degree of proof required.

INITIATING THE PROCEEDING

A wide range of individuals or entities may initiate the legal proceeding to establish incompetence. Among those specified in state statutes are interested persons, spouses, other relatives, friends, courts, state agencies, and in some states the allegedly incompetent individual (Parry, 1985).

NOTICE

Some kind of notice must be provided to the alleged incompetent prior to a hearing in virtually all states. However, states vary in their requirements for personal service of the notice (notice by publication or posting may be adequate), the content of the notice, and the amount of time allowed for preparation. Most states require additional notification to the nearest relative and a number specify that the individual with care and custody of the alleged incompetent receive notice (Parry, 1985: 381).

Effective notice should be both adequate and timely. Thus the notice should contain sufficient information so that the recipient knows what is at issue and has sufficient time for preparation. Each state has its own regulations governing the content of notice and the amount of time between notice and hearing. However, the health and human services professional should be aware that depending on the jurisdiction, the alleged incompetent may not understand the language or the content of the notice, may not receive adequate information, and may not have sufficient time for preparation.[6]

LEGAL REPRESENTATION

Almost all states have some provision permitting legal representation, and many require representation by counsel at incompetency hearings (Parry, 1985: 400). A strong argument can be made that any person facing an incompetency proceeding needs an advocate, either an attorney, a health and human services professional, or both. Individuals facing incompetency proceedings may require very specialized assistance, including someone who understands that individual's limitations and has the ability to communicate information about the hearing and the potential outcomes.[7]

PERSONAL PRESENCE

Some states require that the alleged incompetent be present at the hearing—subject to court discretion—and most others specify that the individual has a right to attend. In about one-half of the states, there is a right to close the hearing to the public. A few states mandate jury trials in competency proceedings and in about one-half of the states a jury trial will be provided if requested (Parry, 1985: 382).

STANDARD OF PROOF

The standard of proof necessary for a finding of incompetence varies among the states—from proof beyond a reasonable doubt, as in criminal trials, to clear and convincing evidence, as in mental hospital civil commitments, to the preponderance of evidence standard used in most civil cases. In addition, many states do not specify a particular standard. Parry's 1985 survey indicates that of those states that do specify a standard, clear and convincing evidence is the most common (Parry, 1985: Table 7).

PROVING INCOMPETENCE

Evidence of incompetence is generally provided by a physician or psychiatrist, based on either a court-ordered examination or a certification. The court-ordered examination provides detailed information and supporting documents, while the certification need only state that the individual meets the legal requirements of incompetence (Parry, 1985: 383). Some states include psychologists among those who may provide evidence and several states allow testimony from any mental health professional. Since many health and human services professionals who are not physicians may be highly qualified to give evidence based on their training, experience, knowledge, and in some cases, greater contact with the individual, it can be argued that the categories of professionals who are called upon to give such testimony should be broadened.[8]

PROBLEMS WITH INCOMPETENCE DETERMINATIONS

While most procedural protections are present in many states, in others some or many may be absent. Hommel and Lisi observe:

> Since guardianship proceedings have traditionally been regarded as informal and non-adversarial, due process safeguards to protect the alleged incapacitated person have been seriously lacking. Proceedings have been typically accompanied by one or more of the following: 1) inadequate notice to the proposed ward; 2) absence of the proposed ward at a hearing; 3) use of relaxed rules of evidence; 4) absence of legal counsel to represent the proposed ward; 5) no right to a jury trial; and 6) a finding of incapacity predicated only upon a physician letter. (Hommel and Lisi, 1989: 433)

Similar criticisms have been raised in an Associated Press study of guardianship for the elderly, which cites "a dangerously burdened and troubled system that regularly puts elderly lives in the hands of others with little or no evidence of necessity, then fails to guard against abuse, theft and neglect." (Associated Press, 1987: 1).[9]

In light of these criticisms, the role of the health and human services professional becomes even more important. One cannot assume that due process protections will be routinely provided or that the allegedly incompetent individual will necessarily be protected.

GUARDIANSHIP: APPOINTMENT, POWERS, AND LIMITATIONS

Usually coupled with a determination of incompetence is the court appointment of a guardian to make decisions for the incompetent person, sometimes officially termed the ward.

Criteria for Appointment

Most competent adults can be appointed as guardian. Some states impose limitations, excluding ex-felons, individuals with a monetary interest in the ward, and institutions that are providing services to the individual. Many states establish priorities, particularly for personal guardians. Often a spouse or adult child is preferred as guardian. (See generally, Parry, 1985: Table 7.4).

Powers of Guardians

Guardians may have total decision-making power for the incompetent individual or only partial power. Guardianship of person and property may be vested in one individual or the roles may be separate. Frequently the guardian of the property—an individual, bank, or financial manager—will make decisions such as buying, selling, or investing assets and paying bills, while the guardian of the person—a family member or other relative—will make personal decisions such as medical care, residence, and travel. In addition, someone may be appointed as guardian *ad litem* (guardian at law) for a limited purpose such as consent for a specific medical procedure or for removal from a respirator.

Limitations on Guardianship

Along with potentially broad decision-making powers, guardians may be subjected to some limitations. Being court appointed, the guardian can be made responsible to the court and can be removed by the court. Many states provide for annual or periodic reporting or accounting. Guardians, particularly those handling financial transactions, may have to post bond and their compensation may be supervised by the court. As before, patterns will vary across states.

GUARDIAN DECISION MAKING

The primary role of the guardian is to make decisions the incompetent person is incapable of making. If a competent person has the right to choose among various options, then a difficult issue is how to provide the same right to the incompetent one. Courts have identified at least two approaches to making decisions for incompetent individuals, the *best interests* standard and the *substitute judgment* standard.

Best Interests Standard

In the best interests approach, the decision maker must decide what is best for the incompetent individual. Decision making guided by this standard requires that a surrogate do what, from an objective standpoint, is best for the individual, even if this is in conflict with the incompetent individual's or the surrogate's actual preferences.

Where there are several acceptable courses of action—for example, more than one therapy available—a choice of any of those that are appropriate is probably acceptable under the best interests standard. However, a best interests standard would preclude the choice of a therapy that is totally unacceptable by professional standards, even if the surrogate might choose that treatment for him or herself. Among the considerations in deciding whether a course of treatment would be in the individual's best interests are factors such as relief of suffering, preservation or restoration of functioning, and quality as well as extent of life sustained (President's Commission, 1982: 179–180).

Substitute Judgment Standard

The substitute judgment approach differs from best interests in that the decision maker bases the decision on the incompetent individual's previously expressed preferences regardless of what would be "best" for that individual. In the face of no prior expressed preference, the decision maker bases the decision on a judgment of what course of action the individual would have wanted if the individual was able to make a choice.

> The substituted judgment standard requires that the surrogate attempt to replicate faithfully the decision that the incapacitated person would make if he or she were able to make a choice. In so doing, the patient's interest in achieving well-being as he or she defines it in accordance with personal values and goals, as well as the individual's interest in self-determination, are both honored to the maximum extent possible, given the fundamental reality that the patient literally cannot make a contemporaneous choice. The surrogate's decision is limited, however, by two general external constraints. First, the surrogate is circumscribed by the same limitations that society legitimately imposes on patients who are capable of decisions for themselves, such as not compromising public health (e.g. by refusing mandatory vaccination) or not taking steps contrary to the criminal law (e.g. intentional maiming). Second, there are certain decisions that a patient might be permitted to make but that are outside the discretion of substitute decisionmaking

and must therefore be decided by the standards of "reasonableness." This is especially true for cases in which the decision risks imposing substantial harm on patients or depriving them of substantial benefit; people may volunteer for risky research with no direct therapeutic benefits for themselves but guardians may not enroll people in such research merely because it is known that, when they were competent, they believed that such research was very important. (President's Commission, 1982: 178–179)

HEALTH CARE DECISIONS FOR THE INCOMPETENT INDIVIDUAL

Choosing appropriate health care options for the incompetent individual is a critical area for the health and human services professional. Although relatively few in number compared to all decisions made for incompetent persons, these choices are particularly important because of their complexity, increasing frequency, and serious consequences. Among the difficult issues are how the incompetent individual's right of choice can be preserved, and— within the context of choice—on what basis decisions are made.

Treatment Refusals and Termination of Life Support Systems

Competent individuals generally have the right to an informed choice among treatments or to refuse treatment. (See, generally, Chapter 7). For the incompetent person unable to make this decision, the problem is how to provide the same options, and what decision-making criteria to use. *Quinlan* involves the decision to remove life support systems, the *Saikewicz* case involves the decision to refuse potentially life-prolonging treatment. In each the individual is not competent to make the decision and a guardian is given decision-making powers.

IN RE QUINLAN
70 N.J. 10, 355A.2d 687 (1976)
NEW JERSEY SUPREME COURT

HUGHES, C.J.
   The central figure in this tragic case is Karen Ann Quinlan, a New Jersey resident. At the age of 22, she lies in a debilitated and allegedly moribund state at Saint Clare's Hospital in Denville, New Jersey. The litigation has to do, in final analysis, with her life,—its continuance or cessation,—and the responsibilities, rights and duties, with regard to any fateful decision concerning it, of her family,

her guardian, her doctors, the hospital, the State through its law enforcement authorities, and finally the courts of justice.***Joseph Quinlan, Karen's father, had appealed the adverse judgment of the Chancery Division.

Due to extensive physical damage fully described in the able opinion of the trial judge, Judge Muir, supporting that judgment, Karen allegedly was incompetent. Joseph Quinlan sought the adjudication of that incompetency. He wished to be appointed guardian of the person and property of his daughter. It was proposed by him that such letters of guardianship, if granted, should contain an express power to him as guardian to authorize the discontinuance of all extraordinary medical procedures now allegedly sustaining Karen's vital processes and hence her life, since these measures, he asserted, present no hope of her eventual recovery. A guardian *ad litem* was appointed by Judge Muir to represent the interest of the alleged incompetent.***

On the night of April 15, 1975, for reasons still unclear, Karen Quinlan ceased breathing for at least two 15 minute periods. She received some ineffectual mouth-to-mouth resuscitation from friends. She was taken by ambulance to Newton Memorial Hospital. There she had a temperature of 100 degrees, her pupils were unreactive and she was unresponsive even to deep pain. The history at the time of her admission to that hospital was essentially incomplete and uninformative.

Three days later, Dr. Morse examined Karen at the request of the Newton admitting physician, Dr. McGee. He found her comatose with evidence of decortication, a condition relating to derangement of the cortex of the brain causing a physical posture in which the upper extremities are flexed and the lower extremities are extended. She required a respirator to assist her breathing. Dr. Morse was unable to obtain an adequate account of the circumstances and events leading up to Karen's admission to the Newton Hospital. Such initial history or etiology is crucial in neurological diagnosis. Relying as he did upon the Newton Memorial records and his own examination, he concluded that prolonged lack of oxygen in the bloodstream, anoxia, was identified with her condition as he saw it upon first observation. When she was later transferred to Saint Clare's Hospital she was still unconscious, still on a respirator and a tracheotomy had been performed. On her arrival Dr. Morse conducted extensive and detailed examinations. An electroencephalogram (EEG) measuring electrical rhythm of the brain was performed and Dr. Morse characterized the result as "abnormal but it showed some activity and was consistent with her clinical state." Other significant neurological tests, including a brain scan, an angiogram, and a lumbar puncture were normal in result. Dr. Morse testified that Karen has been in a state of coma, lack of consciousness, since he began treating her.***

Dr. Morse and other expert physicians who examined her characterized Karen as being in a "chronic persistent vegetative state." Dr. Fred Plum, one of such expert witnesses, defined this as a "subject who remains with the capacity to maintain the vegetative parts of neurological function but who***no longer has any cognitive function."

Dr. Morse, as well as the several other medical and neurological experts who testified in this case, believed with certainty that Karen Quinlan is not "brain dead." They identified the Ad Hoc Committee of Harvard Medical School report (*infra*) as the ordinary medical standard for determining brain death, and all of them were satisfied that Karen met none of the criteria specified in that report and was therefore not "brain dead" within its contemplation.***

The experts believe that Karen cannot now survive without the assistance of the respirator; that exactly how long she would live without it is unknown; that the strong likelihood is that death would follow soon after its removal, and that removal would also risk further brain damage and would curtail the assistance the respirator presently provides in warding off infection.

It seemed to be the consensus not only of the treating physicians but also of the several qualified experts who testified in the case, that removal from the respirator would not conform to medical practices, standards and traditions.***

It is the issue of the constitutional right of privacy that has given us most concern, in the exceptional circumstances of this case. Here a loving parent, *qua* parent and raising the rights of his incompetent and profoundly damaged daughter, probably irreversibly doomed to no more than a biologically vegetative remnant of life, is before the court. He seeks authorization to abandon specialized technological procedures which can only maintain for a time a body having no potential for resumption or continuance of other than a "vegetative" existence.***

Although the Constitution does not explicitly mention a right of privacy, Supreme Court decisions have recognized that a right of personal privacy exists and that certain areas of privacy are guaranteed under the Constitution.***

Nor is such right of privacy forgotten in the New Jersey Constitution. *N.J. Const.* (1947), Art. I, par. 1.

The claimed interests of the State in this case are essentially the preservation and sanctity of human life and defense of the right of the physician to administer medical treatment according to his best judgment. In this case the doctors say that removing Karen from the respirator will conflict with their professional judgment. The plaintiff answers that Karen's present treatment serves only a maintenance function; that the respirator cannot cure or improve her condition but at best can only prolong her inevitable slow deterioration and death;***We think that the State's interest *contra* weakens and the individual's right to privacy grows as the degree of bodily invasion increases and the prognosis dims. Ultimately there comes a point at which the individual's rights overcome the State interest. It is for that reason that we believe Karen's choice, if she were competent to make it, would be vindicated by the law. Her prognosis is extremely poor,— she will never resume cognitive life. And the bodily invasion is very great,—she requires 24 hour intensive nursing care, antibiotics, the assistance of a respirator, a catheter and feeding tube.

Our affirmation of Karen's independent right of choice, however, would ordinarily be based upon her competency to assert it. The sad truth, however, is that she is grossly incompetent and we cannot discern her supposed choice based on the testimony of her previous conversations with friends, where such testimony is without sufficient probative weight. 137 *N.J. Super.* at 260. Nevertheless we have concluded that Karen's right of privacy may be asserted on her behalf by her guardian under the peculiar circumstances here present.

If a putative decision by Karen to permit this non-cognitive, vegetative existence to terminate by natural forces is regarded as a valuable incident of her right of privacy, as we believe it to be, then it should not be discarded solely on the basis that her condition prevents her conscious exercise of the choice. The only practical way to prevent destruction of the right is to permit the guardian and family of Karen to render their best judgment, subject to the qualifications hereinafter stated, as to whether she would exercise it in these circumstances. If their conclusion is in the affirmative this decision should be accepted by a society the overwhelming majority of whose members would, we think, in similar circumstances, exercise such a choice in the same way for themselves or for those closest to them. It is for this reason that we determine that Karen's right of privacy may be asserted in her behalf, in this respect, by her guardian and family under the particular circumstances presented by this record.***

We thus arrive at the formulation of the declaratory relief which we have concluded is appropriate to this case.***Upon the concurrence of the guardian and family of Karen, should the responsible attending physicians conclude that there is no reasonable possibility of Karen's ever emerging from her present comatose condition to a cognitive, sapient state and that the life-support apparatus now being administered to Karen should be discontinued, they shall consult with the hospital "Ethics Committee" or like body of the institution in which Karen is then hospitalized. If that consultative body agrees that there is no reasonable possibility of Karen's ever emerging from her present comatose condition to a cognitive, sapient state, the present life-support system may be withdrawn and said action shall be without any civil or criminal liability therefor on the part of any participant, whether guardian, physician, hospital or others. We herewith specifically so hold.

Notes and Issues for Discussion

1. *Quinlan* has been cited as one of the earliest cases where a court has found an individual's privacy right includes a right to discontinue treatment. Where does the *Quinlan* court find the privacy right?
2. The court also acknowledges the state's interest in preserving life. In that the two may be in conflict, according to the court, at what point does the state's interest prevail? The patient's right to discontinue treatment?
3. The court in the *Quinlan* case is not clear on the basis for the guardian's decision. Both a best interests standard and a substituted judgement standard can be read into the case.
4. The final decision to remove the life-support apparatus is to be made "upon the concurrence of the guardian, and family of Karen, should the responsible attending physician conclude that there is no reasonable possibility of Karen's ever emerging from her present comatose condition. . . ." Additionally the hospital ethics committee must concur that there is no reasonable possibility of the individual emerging from the comatose state. What happens if the physician refuses to withdraw treatment even if there is no reasonable possibility of emerging from the coma? What if some of the family disagree or the ethics committee does not concur?

5. In *Matter of Conroy,* 98 N.J. 321 (1985), the New Jersey Supreme Court held that for an elderly, incompetent nursing home patient who was not expected to live a year, the goal was "to determine and effectuate, insofar as possible, the decision that the patient would have made if competent." The primary means to determine this is a *subjective* standard—"not what a reasonable or average person would have chosen to do under the circumstances but what the particular patient would have done if able to choose." How is this determined? The court's preference is for a written document, although an oral directive may be acceptable. Other types of appropriate evidence include a patient's reactions or a consistent pattern of conduct. Thus, accurate documentation is crucial. What is the role of the health and human services professional?

6. Later in the *Conroy* decision, the court outlines two other tests for withholding or withdrawing life-sustaining treatment, a *"limited objective test"* where "there is some trustworthy evidence that the patient would have refused the treatment, and the decision-maker is satisfied that it is clear that the burdens of the patient's continued life with the treatment outweigh the benefits of that life . . ." and a *"pure-objective test"* where not only must the burdens of life with treatment outweigh the benefits, but "the recurring, unavoidable and severe pain of the patient's life with the treatment would be such that the effect of administering life-sustaining treatment would be inhumane." As before, the limited objective test will require evidence of intent, which may have been gathered by the professional. The pure objective test would probably call for testimony about the pain the individual is experiencing. How would you determine pain? How would you document it. See also *Matter of Jobes,* 108 N.J. 394 (1987), *Matter of Peters by Johanning,* 108 N.J. 365 (1987), and *Matter of Farrell,* 109 N.J. 335 (1987), where the court deals with termination of life support in a range of different situations.

7. The New York Court of Appeals has applied a more stringent standard in *In re Westchester County Medical Center on Behalf of O'Connor,* 534 N.Y.S.2d 886 (1988).

SUPERINTENDENT OF BELCHERTOWN v. SAIKEWICZ
373 Mass. 728, 370 N.E.2d 417 (1977)
MASSACHUSETTS SUPREME COURT

LIACOS, JUSTICE.

On April 26, 1976, William E. Jones, superintendent of the Belchertown State School (a facility of the Massachusetts Department of Mental Health), and Paul R. Rogers, a staff attorney at the school, petitioned the Probate Court for Hampshire County for the appointment of a guardian of Joseph Saikewicz, a resident of the State school. Simultaneously they filed a motion for the immediate appointment of a guardian ad litem, with authority to make the necessary decisions concerning the care and treatment of Saikewicz, who was suffering with acute myeloblastic monocytic leukemia. The petition alleged that Saikewicz was a mentally retarded person in urgent need of medical treatment and that he was a person with disability incapable of giving informed consent for such treatment.

On May 5, 1976, the probate judge appointed a guardian ad litem. On May 6, 1976, the guardian ad litem filed a report with the court. The guardian ad litem's report indicated that Saikewicz's illness was an incurable one, and that although chemotherapy was the medically indicated course of treatment it would cause Saikewicz significant adverse side effects and discomfort. The guardian ad litem concluded that these factors, as well as the inability of the ward to understand the treatment to which he would be subjected and the fear and pain he would suffer as a result, outweighed the limited prospect of any benefit from such treatment, namely, the possibility of some uncertain but limited extension of life. He therefore recommended "that not treating Mr. Saikewicz would be in his best interests."

After hearing the evidence, the judge entered findings of fact and an order that in essence agreed with the recommendation of the guardian ad litem.

The judge below found that Joseph Saikewicz, at the time the matter arose, was sixty-seven years old, with an I.Q. of ten and a mental age of approximately two years and eight months. He was profoundly mentally retarded. The record discloses that, apart from his leukemic condition, Saikewicz enjoyed generally good health. He was physically strong and well built, nutritionally nourished, and ambulatory. He was not, however, able to communicate verbally—resorting to gestures and grunts to make his wishes known to others and responding only to gestures or physical contacts. In the course of treatment for various medical conditions arising during Saikewicz's residency at the school, he had been unable to respond intelligibly to inquiries such as whether he was experiencing pain. It was the opinion of a consulting psychologist, not contested by the other experts relied on by the judge below, that Saikewicz was not aware of dangers and was disoriented outside his immediate environment. As a result of his condition, Saikewicz had lived in State institutions since 1923 and had resided at the Belchertown State School since 1928. Two of his sisters, the only members of his family who could be located, were notified of his condition and of the hearing, but they preferred not to attend or otherwise become involved.

On April 19, 1976, Saikewicz was diagnosed as suffering from acute myeloblastic monocytic leukemia.***The disease is invariably fatal.

Chemotherapy, as was testified to at the hearing in the Probate Court, involves the administration of drugs over several weeks, the purpose of which is to kill the leukemia cells. This treatment unfortunately affects normal cells as well. One expert testified that the end result, in effect, is to destroy the living vitality of the bone marrow. Because of this effect, the patient becomes very anemic and may bleed or suffer infections—a condition which requires a number of blood transfusions. In this sense, the patient immediately becomes much "sicker" with the commencement of chemotherapy, and there is the possibility that infections during the initial period of severe anemia will prove fatal. Moreover, while most patients survive chemotherapy, remission of the leukemia is achieved in only thirty to fifty per cent of the cases. Remission is meant here as a temporary return to normal as measured by clinical and laboratory means. If remission does occur, it typically lasts for between two and thirteen months although longer periods of remission are possible. Estimates of the effectiveness of chemotherapy are complicated in cases, such as the one presented here, in which the patient's age becomes a factor. According to the medical testimony before the court below, persons over age sixty have more difficulty tolerating chemotherapy and the treatment is likely to be less successful than in younger patients. This prognosis may be compared with the doctors' estimates that, left untreated, a patient in Saikewicz's condition would live for a matter of weeks or, perhaps, several months. According to the testimony, a decision to allow the disease to run its natural course would not result in pain for the patient, and death would probably come without discomfort.

An important facet of the chemotherapy process, to which the judge below directed careful attention, is the problem of serious adverse side effects caused by the treating drugs. Among these side effects are severe nausea, bladder irritation, numbness and tingling of the extremities, and loss of hair. The bladder irritation can be avoided, however, if the patient drinks fluids, and the nausea can be treated by drugs. It was the opinion of the guardian ad litem, as well as the doctors who testified before the probate judge, that most people elect to suffer the side effects of chemotherapy rather than to allow their leukemia to run its natural course.

***[T]he judge concluded that the following considerations weighed *against* administering chemotherapy to Saikewicz: "(1) his age, (2) his inability to cooperate with the treatment, (3) probable adverse side effects of treatment, (4) low chance of producing remission, (5) the certainty that treatment will cause immediate suffering, and (6) the quality of life possible for him even if the treatment does bring about remission."

The following considerations were determined to weigh in *favor* of chemotherapy: "(1) the chance that his life may be lengthened thereby, and (2) the fact that most people in his situation when given a chance to do so elect to take the gamble of treatment."

Concluding that, in this case, the negative factors of treatment exceeded the benefits, the probate judge ordered on May 13, 1976, that no treatment be administered to Saikewicz for his condition of acute myeloblastic monocytic leukemia except by further order of the court. The judge further ordered that all reasonable and necessary supportive measures be taken, medical or otherwise, to safeguard the well-being of Saikewicz in all other respects and to reduce as far as possible any suffering or discomfort which he might experience.

Saikewicz died on September 4, 1976, at the Belchertown State School hospital. Death was due to bronchial pneumonia, a complication of the leukemia. Saikewicz died without pain or discomfort.***

The question what legal standards govern the decision whether to administer potentially life-prolonging treatment to an incompetent person encompasses two distinct and important subissues. First, does a choice exist? That is, is it the unvarying responsibility of the State to order medical treatment in all circumstances involving the care of an incompetent person? Second, if a choice does exist under certain conditions, what considerations enter into the decision-making process?

We think that principles of equality and respect for all individuals require the conclusion that a choice exists.***[W]e recognize a general right in all persons to refuse medical treatment in appropriate circumstances. The recognition of that right must extend to the case of an incompetent, as well as a competent, patient because the value of human dignity extends to both.***

The "best interests" of an incompetent person are not necessarily served by imposing on such persons results not mandated as to competent persons similarly situated. It does not advance the interest of the State or the ward to treat the ward as a person of lesser status or dignity than others. To protect the incompetent person within its power, the State must recognize the dignity and worth of such a person and afford to that person the same panoply of rights and choices it recognizes in competent persons. If a competent person faced with death may choose to decline treatment which not only will not cure the person but which substantially may increase suffering in exchange for a possible yet brief prolongation of life, then it cannot be said that it is always in the "best interests" of the ward to require submission to such treatment. Nor do statistical factors indicating that a majority of competent persons similarly situated choose treatment resolve the issue. The significant decisions of life are more complex than statistical determinations. Individual choice is determined not by the vote of the majority but by the complexities of the singular situation viewed from the unique perspective of the person called on to make the decision. To presume that the incompetent person must always be subjected to what many rational and intelligent persons may decline is to downgrade the status of the incompetent person by placing a lesser value on his intrinsic human worth and vitality.

This leads us to the question of how the right of an incompetent person to decline treatment might best be exercised so as to give the fullest possible expression to the character and circumstances of that individual.

Saikewicz was profoundly mentally retarded. His mental state was a cognitive one but limited in his capacity to comprehend and communicate. Evidence that most people choose to accept the rigors of chemotherapy has no direct bearing on the likely choice that Joseph Saikewicz would have made. Unlike most people, Saikewicz had no capacity to understand his present situation or his prognosis. The guardian ad litem gave expression to this important distinction in coming to grips with this "most troubling aspect" of withholding treatment from Saikewicz: "If he is treated with toxic drugs he will be involuntarily immersed in a state of painful suffering, the reason for which he will never understand. Patients who request treatment know the risks involved and can appreciate the painful side-effects when they arrive. They know the reason for the pain and their hope makes it tolerable." To make a worthwhile comparison, one would have to ask whether a majority of people would choose chemotherapy if they were told merely that something outside of their previous experience was going to be done to them, that this something would cause them pain and discomfort, that they would be removed to strange surroundings and possibly restrained for extended periods of time, and that the advantages of this course of action were measured by concepts of time and mortality beyond their ability to comprehend.

To put the above discussion in proper perspective, we realize that an inquiry into what a majority of people would do in circumstances that truly were similar assumes an objective viewpoint not far removed from a "reasonable person" inquiry. While we recognize the value of this kind of indirect evidence, we should make it plain that the primary test is subjective in nature—that is, the goal is to determine with as much accuracy as possible the wants and needs of the individual involved. This may or may not conform to what is thought wise or prudent by most people. The problems of arriving at an accurate substituted judgment in matters of life and death vary greatly in degree, if not in kind, in different circumstances.***Joseph Saikewicz was profoundly retarded and noncommunicative his entire life, which was spent largely in the highly restrictive atmosphere of an institution. While it may thus be necessary to rely to a greater degree on objective criteria, such as the supposed inability of profoundly retarded persons to conceptualize or fear death, the effort to bring the substituted judgment into step with the values and desires of the affected individual must not, and need not, be abandoned.

***[W]e now reiterate the substituted judgment doctrine as we apply it in the instant case. We believe that both the guardian ad litem in his recommendation and the judge in his decision should have attempted (as they did) to ascertain the incompetent person's actual interests and preferences. In short, the decision in cases such as this should be that which would be made by the incompetent person, if that person were competent, but taking into account the present and future incompetency of the individual as one of the factors which would necessarily enter into the decision-making process of the competent person. Having recognized the right of a competent person to make for himself the same decision as the court made in this case, the question is, do the facts on the record support the proposition that Saikewicz himself would have made the decision under the standard set forth. We believe they do.

The two factors considered by the probate judge to weigh in favor of administering chemotherapy were: (1) the fact that most people elect chemotherapy and (2) the chance of a longer life. Both are appropriate indicators of what Saikewicz himself would have wanted, provided that due allowance is taken for this individual's present and future incompetency. We have already discussed the perspective this brings to the fact that most people choose to undergo chemotherapy. With regard to the second factor, the chance of a longer life carries the same weight for Saikewicz as for any other person, the value of life under the law having no relation to intelligence or social position. Intertwined with this consideration is the hope that a cure, temporary or permanent, will be discovered during the period of extra weeks or months potentially made available by chemotherapy. The guardian ad litem investigated this possibility and found no reason to hope for a dramatic breakthrough in the time frame relevant to the decision.

The probate judge identified six factors weighing against administration of chemotherapy. Four of these—Saikewicz's age, the probable side effects of treatment, the low chance of producing remission, and the certainty that treatment will cause immediate suffering—were clearly established by the medical testimony to be considerations that any individual would weigh carefully. A fifth factor—Saikewicz's inability to cooperate with the treatment—introduces those considerations that are unique to this individual and which therefore are essential to the proper exercise of substituted judgment. The judge heard testimony that Saikewicz would have no comprehension of the reasons for the severe disruption of his formerly secure and stable environment occasioned by the chemotherapy. He therefore would experience fear without the understanding from which other patients draw strength. The inability to anticipate and prepare for the severe side effects of the drugs leaves room only for confusion and disorientation. The possibility that such a naturally uncooperative patient would have to be physically restrained to allow the slow intravenous administration of drugs could only compound his pain and fear, as well as possibly jeopardize the ability of his body to withstand the toxic effects of the drugs.

The sixth factor identified by the judge as weighing against chemotherapy was "the quality of life possible for him even if the treatment does bring about remission." To the extent that this formulation equates the value of life with any measure of the quality of life, we firmly reject it. A reading of the entire record clearly reveals, however, the judge's concern that special care be taken to respect the dignity and worth of Saikewicz's life precisely because of his vulnerable position. The judge, as well as all the parties, were keenly aware that the supposed ability of Saikewicz, by virtue of his mental retardation, to appreciate or experience life had no place in the decision before them. Rather than reading the judge's formulation in a manner that demeans the value of the life of one who is mentally retarded, the vague, and perhaps ill-chosen, term "quality of life" should be understood as a reference to the continuing state of pain and disorientation precipitated by the chemotherapy treatment. Viewing the term in this manner, together with the other factors properly considered by the judge, we are satisfied that the decision to withhold treatment from Saikewicz was based on a regard for his actual interests and preferences and that the facts supported this decision.

We turn now to a consideration of the procedures appropriate for reaching a decision where a person allegedly incompetent is in a position in which a decision as to the giving or withholding of life-prolonging treatment must be made.***

Commensurate with the powers of the Probate Court already described, the probate judge may, at any step in these proceedings, avail himself or herself of the additional advice or knowledge of any person or group. We note here that many health care institutions have developed medical ethics committees or panels to consider many of the issues touched on here. Consideration of the findings and advice of such groups as well as the testimony of the attending physicians and other medical experts ordinarily would be of great assistance to a probate judge faced with such a difficult decision. We believe it desirable for a judge to consider such views wherever available and useful to the court. We do not believe, however, that this option should be transformed by us into a required procedure. We take a dim view of any attempt to shift the ultimate decision-making responsibility away from the duly established courts of proper jurisdiction to any committee, panel or group, ad hoc or permanent. Thus, we reject the approach adopted by the New Jersey Supreme Court in the *Quinlan* case of entrusting the decision whether to continue artificial life support to the patient's guardian, family, attending doctors, and hospital "ethics committee."***

Notes and Issues for Discussion

1. Saikewicz has an I.Q. of 10, a mental age of under three years, is nonverbal and has been institutionalized for fifty-four years. Is it realistic to make a substituted judgment for him, deciding what he would choose when he never did or could express a preference?
2. Many people faced with the choice of probable death in the near future without treatment or probable extended life with radiation, chemotherapy, and their side effects, would elect prolonged life. Some would not. If most individuals would choose a longer life with treatment, should this be a factor in the Saikewicz decision?
3. Would a best interests standard result in different factors being considered for Saikewicz? A different outcome?
4. Given the facts of the case, if the court asked you to recommend a decision for Saikewicz based on its criteria, what would you recommend? Why? Would it make a difference if Saikewicz was forty years old? Twenty-five?

Sterilization Decisions for Incompetent Individuals

Competent adults may choose to be sterilized, and this decision is part of a constitutional privacy right to make decisions about one's body. To deny that choice to incompetent adults is to deny them a basic privacy right. But to permit that decision requires a choice which the incompetent individual may be incapable of making, which is often irreversible, and which in *In re Grady*, 85 N.J. 235 (1981), p. 423, the court says will "destroy an important part of a person's social and biological identity."

The issue is further clouded by what that court has termed the "sordid past" of compulsory sterilizations. As part of the eugenics movement in the early nineteenth century, a number of states passed statutes permitting compulsory sterilization of various individuals including those who were retarded, mentally ill, disabled, or criminal, among others. The constitutionality of compulsory sterilization statutes was upheld by the U.S. Supreme Court in *Buck v. Bell*, 274 U.S. 200 (1927). There Justice Holmes endorsed a Virginia compulsory sterilization law for retarded individuals, noting: "Three generations of imbeciles are enough," where "imbecile" was a technical term applied to a level of intelligence.

By statute, California permitted sterilizations of inmates in state hospitals, state homes or prisons for their physical, mental or moral benefit beginning in 1909, and at later points added minors, other developmentally disabled persons, and "those suffering from perversion or marked departures from normal mentality" to the list. By 1921, 2,558 individuals had been sterilized in California. Statutory authority for compulsory sterilizations was repealed in

1979. See *Conservatorship of Valerie N.*, 707 P.2d 760 (1985) at 764-766. (For cases dealing with the sterilization of the developmentally disabled, see p. 423).

Health Care Decisions for Minors

Unlike adults, minors are generally presumed legally incompetent, and parents, guardians or others acting in *loco parentis* have the right to make most decisions for them. The Supreme Court stated the basis for parental decision making:

> The law's concept of the family rests on a presumption that parents possess what a child lacks in maturity, experience and capacity for judgment required for making life's difficult decisions. More importantly, historically it has recognized that natural bonds of affection lead parents to act in the best interests of their children. . . . Most children, even in adolescence, simply are not able to make sound judgments concerning many decisions, including their need for medical care or treatment. Parents can and must make those judgments." *Parham v. J.R. and J.L.*, 442 U.S. 584 at 602 (See p. 387.)

A number of authors have observed that the minor's actual decision-making capacity will vary with age, ability, and the complexity and seriousness of the decision, and vesting legal rights at age eighteen is as arbitrary as vesting legal rights at age twenty-one was a few years ago. (Gaylin and Macklin, 1982; Morrissey et al., 1986; Melton et al., 1983).

Yet there are limits to parental decision making. A parent cannot consent to the sterilization of a minor or the abortion of a minor against the minor's wishes. Refusal to supply needed medical treatment although financially able to do so constitutes child abuse or neglect in virtually all states. If a parent refuses to allow lifesaving medical treatment, the state will petition to assume temporary guardianship to allow the procedure. More complicated are situations where the choice is between alternative medical treatments, or decisions to forego all but minimal care for severely handicapped infants.

WEBER v. STONY BROOK HOSPITAL
60 NY.2d 208, 456 N.E.2d 1186 (N.Y. 1983)
NEW YORK COURT OF APPEALS

PER CURIAM
    This case involves a situation in which the parents of a newborn infant, in consultation with others, had responsibly decided upon a course of medical treat-

ment. An application challenging this choice was made by a person not related or known to the family and its situation and, in the absence of any further investigation pursuant to section 1034 of the Family Court Act, the hearing court abused its discretion as a matter of law by permitting this proceeding to go forward. Although we affirm the Appellate Division's ultimate dismissal of the petition, we do so for a different reason.

The parents of Baby Jane Doe, who was born on October 11, 1983 with spina bifida and serious complicating disorders, after consultation with neurological experts, nurses, their religious counselors and a social worker, elected to adopt a conservative course for her medical treatment. A resident of the State of Vermont, with no disclosed connection with Baby Jane Doe or her family, set in motion the judicial proceeding which has now reached our court. Rather than pursuing the procedures prescribed in the Family Court Act, he applied directly to a Justice of the Supreme Court. At the outset it was recognized by the court that the petitioner himself had no direct interest in or relationship to any party. An attempt was then made to remedy the perceived procedural deficiency by the appointment of a guardian ad litem for the baby. That guardian has pressed an application for a judicial authorization for surgery to override the judgment of the parents. To facilitate a quick disposition of the proceeding, the parties consented to the court's jurisdiction of their persons. A broadly grounded motion to dismiss the proceeding was made by the Attorney-General on behalf of the hospital, the initially named respondent. This motion should have been granted.

It would serve no useful purpose at this stage to recite the unusual, and sometimes offensive, activities and proceedings of those who have sought at various stages, in the interests of Baby Jane Doe, to displace parental responsibility for and management of her medical care. It is enough now to identify the fundamental legal principles which are determinative.

The Legislature, recognizing the primary responsibility of parents concerning the choice of medical care for their child, has made explicit provision for those instances calling for governmental intervention. Article 10 of the Family Court Act is expressly "designed to establish procedures to help protect children from injury or mistreatment and to help safeguard their physical, mental, and emotional well-being. It is designed to provide a due process of law for determining when the state, through its family court, may intervene against the wishes of a parent on behalf of a child so that his needs are properly met" (Family Ct Act, §1011). The article contains detailed provisions for child protective proceedings.

Therefore, contrary to the petitioner's contention, there is legislation covering this type of proceeding. Section 1032 of the Family Court Act provides that a child neglect proceeding may be originated by a child protective agency or "a person on the court's direction." Thus primary responsibility for initiating such proceedings has been assigned by the Legislature to child protective agencies which may file a petition whenever in their view court proceedings are warranted. All other persons and entities may only file a petition if directed to do so by the court. The Legislature has further provided that the court may direct a child protective agency to conduct an investigation and report to the court "in order to determine whether a proceeding under this article should be initiated" (Family Ct Act, §1034).

The requirement for court approval or authorization for proceedings prompted by those other than child protective agencies indicates the Legislature's concern that judicial proceedings touching the family relationship should not be casually initiated and imposes upon the courts the obligation to exercise sound discretion before permitting such petitions to be filed. It is evident that the Legislature contemplated that the child protective agencies should play a significant role in making that determination, although that may not always be necessary or appropriate.

In this case the Supreme Court initiated the proceeding at the behest of a person who had no disclosed relationship with the child, her parents, her family, or those treating her illnesses. Indeed it does not appear that the petitioner had any direct or personal knowledge of the facts relating to the child's condition, the treatment she is presently receiving or the factors which prompted her parents to adopt the course they have. There is also no showing that the petitioner communicated his concerns to the Department of Social Services having primary responsibility with these matters. Neither apparently did the court seek the department's investigative assistance, advice or expertise before signing an order initiating this proceeding thus requiring the child's parents, treating physicians, and others involved with her care to appear in court to justify their actions.

There was a failure in this instance to follow the statutory scheme contemplated by the Legislature for the protection of children. To accept the position of the guardian would have far-reaching implications. As the guardian conceded on oral argument, acceptance of the proposition he espouses would be to recognize the right of any person, without recourse to the strictures of the Family Court Act, to institute judicial proceedings which would catapult him into the very heart of a family circle, there to challenge the most private and most precious responsibility vested in the parents for the care and nurture of their children—and at the very least to force the parents to incur the not inconsiderable expenses of extended litigation.

We do not attempt to anticipate or set forth all the circumstances in which a court may be called upon to protect a child's interests. Nor do we mean to define the extent of the court's obligation to conduct an independent investigation or to consult with a child protective agency. There may be occasions when it is appropriate for the court to act without making further inquiry of this nature. On this record, however, no such circumstances are evident.

There are overtones to this proceeding which we find distressing. Confronted with the anguish of the birth of a child with severe physical disorders, these parents, in consequence of judicial procedures for which there is no precedent or authority, have been subjected in the last two weeks to litigation through all three levels of our State's court system. We find no justification for resort to or entertainment of these proceedings.

The order of the Appellate Division dismissing the proceeding should be affirmed, without costs.

Notes and Issues for Discussion

1. If the state child welfare agency had brought the action instead of a stranger, would this make a difference? Compare *Matter of Hofbauer*, 47 N.Y.2d 648 (1979) (p. 322), where the N.Y. Court of Appeals found no neglect when the parents chose medically approved nontraditional treatment for their seven-year-old child suffering from Hodgkin's disease.
2. As a health and human services professional, you have been asked by the parents in the *Weber* case to give advice. Is your responsibility to the parent or the child?
3. As a human service administrator, if the parents in the *Weber* case choose the conservative course of action, what do you do? Would you file a petition of neglect and abuse? Convene a hospital ethics committee? Leave the decision to the parents and their physician?
4. The Child Abuse Prevention and Treatment Act, 42 U.S.C. 5101 *et seq.*, includes regulations pertaining to the withholding of medical treatment from disabled infants. 50 Fed. Reg. 14878.
5. In *U.S. v. University Hospital*, 729 F.2d 144 (1984), the court refused to allow the U.S. government access to hospital records of Baby Jane Doe. The government argued that under §504 of the Rehabilitation Act of 1973 (which prohibits discrimination against handicapped individuals in federally funded programs) it had the right to ascertain if the treatment was a legitimate medical judgment or was based on the child's handicapping condition, and therefore discrimination. The court found no discrimination on the part of the hospital: "In the present case, Baby Jane Doe has been treated in an evenhanded manner at least to the extent that the hospital has always been and remains willing to perform the dual, corrective surgeries if her parents would consent. Requiring the hospital either to undertake the surgery notwithstanding the parents' decision or alternatively, to petition the state court to overturn the parents' decision, would impose a particularly onerous affirmative action burden upon the hospital." 729 F.2d at 160.
6. In *Bowen v. American Hospital Association*, 476 U.S. 610 (1986), the government appealed the *University Hospital* decision to the U.S. Supreme Court. In a narrow decision the court limited the scope to whether the regulations were authorized under §504, and not whether §504 could ever apply to handicapped infants. The Court noted that "handicapped infants are entitled to 'meaningful access' to medical services provided by hospitals, and that a hospital rule or state policy denying or limiting such access would be subject to challenge under §504." However, the Court made it clear that this was not the issue in the case. The Court observed that in its revised regulations the government now conceded that when "a nontreatment decision, no matter how discriminatory, is made by parents, rather than by the hospital, §504 does not mandate that the hospital unilaterally overrule the parental decision and provide treatment. . . ." (476 U.S. at 630) and for the hospital to treat in that situation could involve a

tort for treating without parental consent. Finding no evidence of the hospital's refusal to treat newborns when so requested by parents, and no indication that §504 was enacted to mandate the reporting of medical neglect, the Court invalidated the regulations, observing "Section 504 does not authorize the Secretary to give unsolicited advice either to parents, to hospitals, or to state official who are faced with difficult treatment decisions concerning handicapped children." 476 U.S. at 647.

On what basis and under what circumstances may a parent or guardian permit an invasive procedure to be performed on a minor for the benefit of another? Consider the following decision.

CURRAN v. BOSZE
141 Ill.2d 473, 566 N.E.2d 1319 (1990)
ILLINOIS SUPREME COURT

JUSTICE CALVO delivered the opinion of the court:
Allison and James Curran are 3-1/2-year-old twins. Their mother is Nancy Curran. The twins have lived with Ms. Curran and their maternal grandmother since their birth on January 27, 1987.

The twins' father is Tamas Bosze. Ms. Curran and Mr. Bosze have never been married. As a result of an action brought by Ms. Curran against Mr. Bosze concerning the paternity of the twins, both Mr. Bosze and the twins underwent a blood test in November of 1987. The blood test confirmed that Mr. Bosze is the father of the twins. On February 16, 1989, Mr. Bosze and Ms. Curran entered into an agreed order (parentage order) establishing a parent-child relationship. The parentage order states that Ms. Curran "shall have the sole care, custody, control and educational responsibility of the minor children." Section B, paragraph 4, of the order provides:

"In all matters of importance relating to the health, welfare and education of the children, Mother shall consult and confer with Father, with a view toward adopting and following a harmonious policy. Mother shall advise Father of which school the children will attend and both parents shall be given full access to the school records of the children."***

Mr. Bosze is the father of three other children: a son, age 23; Jean Pierre Bosze, age 12; and a one-year-old daughter. Ms. Curran is not the mother of any of these children. Each of these children has a different mother. Jean Pierre and the twins are half-siblings. The twins have met Jean Pierre on two occasions. Each meeting lasted approximately two hours.

Jean Pierre is suffering from acute undifferentiated leukemia (AUL), also known as mixed lineage leukemia. Mixed lineage leukemia is a rare form of leukemia which is difficult to treat.***Jean Pierre was brought to America in August 1988, and has been treated by Dr. Jong Kwon since that time. Jean Pierre was treated with chemotherapy and went into remission. Jean Pierre experienced a testicular relapse in January 1990, and a bone marrow relapse in mid-June 1990. Dr. Kwon has recommended a bone marrow transplant for Jean Pierre.

Mr. Bosze asked Ms. Curran to consent to a blood test for the twins in order to determine whether the twins were compatible to serve as bone marrow donors for a transplant to Jean Pierre. Mr. Bosze asked Ms. Curran to consent to the twins' undergoing a bone marrow harvesting procedure if the twins were found to be compatible. After consulting with the twins' pediatrician, family members, parents of bone marrow donors and bone marrow donors, Ms. Curran refused to give consent to the twins' undergoing either the blood test or the bone marrow harvesting procedure.

On June 28, 1990, Mr. Bosze filed an emergency petition in the circuit court of Cook County. The petition informed the court that Jean Pierre "suffers from leukemia and urgently requires a [bone] marrow transplant from a compatible donor. Without the transplant he will die in a short period of time, thereby creating an emergency involving life and death." The petition stated that persons usually compatible for serving as donors are parents or siblings of the recipient, and Jean Pierre's father, mother, and older brother had been tested and rejected as compatible donors.

According to the petition, "[t]he only siblings who have potential to be donors and who have not been tested are the children, James and Allison." The petition stated Ms. Curran refused to discuss with Mr. Bosze the matter of submitting the twins to a blood test to determine their compatibility as potential bone marrow donors for Jean Pierre. The petition stated the blood test "is minimally invasive and harmless, and no more difficult than the paternity blood testing which the children have already undergone." According to the petition, there would be no expense involved to Ms. Curran.

In the petition, Mr. Bosze requested the court find a medical emergency to exist and order and direct Ms. Curran to "forthwith produce the parties' minor children***at Lutheran General Hospital***for the purpose of compatibility blood testing." Further, Mr. Bosze requested in the petition that "if the children or either of them, are compatible as donors, that the Court order and direct that [Ms. Curran] produce the children, or whichever one may be compatible, for the purpose of donating bone marrow to their sibling."***

After hearing the testimony of the witnesses, the arguments of counsel, and the arguments of the guardians *ad litem*, the circuit court denied Mr. Bosze's petition for emergency relief. All parties have filed briefs before this court.

Mr. Bosze and the guardian *ad litem* for Jean Pierre strenuously argue that the doctrine of substituted judgment, recognized by this court in *In re Estate of Longeway* (1989), 133 Ill.2d 33, and *In re Estate of Greenspan* (1990), 137 Ill.2d 1, should be applied in this case to determine whether or not the twins would consent, if they were competent to do so, to the bone marrow donation if they, or either of them, were compatible with Jean Pierre. The doctrine of substituted judgment requires a surrogate decision-maker to "attempt[] to establish, with as much accuracy as possible, what decision the patient would make if [the patient] were competent to do so." (*Longeway*, 133 Ill.2d at 49.) Mr. Bosze and the guardian *ad litem* for Jean Pierre contend the evidence clearly and convincingly establishes that the twins, if competent, would consent to the bone marrow harvesting procedure.

Ms. Curran and the guardian ad litem for the twins vigorously object to the application of the doctrine of substituted judgment in this case. It is the position of Ms. Curran and the guardian *ad litem* for the twins that it is not possible to establish by clear and convincing evidence whether the 3-1/2-year-old twins, if they were competent—that is, if they were not minors but were adults with the legal capacity to consent—would consent or refuse to consent to the proposed bone marrow harvesting procedure. According to Ms. Curran and the guardian *ad litem* for the twins, the decision whether or not to give or withhold consent to the procedure must be determined by the best-interests-of-the-child standard. Ms. Curran and the guardian *ad litem* for the twins argue that the evidence reveals it is not in the best interests of the children to require them to submit to the bone marrow harvesting procedure.

This court recognized the doctrine of substituted judgment in *Longeway*. The issue addressed by this court in *Longeway* was whether the guardian of a formerly competent, now incompetent, seriously ill adult patient may exercise a right to refuse artificial nutrition and hydration on behalf of his or her ward and, if so, how this right may be exercised.***

This court recognized two sources of appropriate evidence by which a guardian may be guided in determining whether a formerly competent, now incompetent, patient would choose to refuse artificial nutrition and hydration. The first source requires the surrogate to "determine if the patient had expressed explicit intent regarding this type of medical treatment prior to becoming incompetent." If there is no clear evidence of such intent, then the patient's personal value system must guide the surrogate:

> " ' "[E]ven if no prior specific statements were made, in the context of the individual's entire prior mental life, including his or her philosophical, religious and moral views, life goals, values about the purpose of life and the way it should be lived, and attitudes toward sickness, medical procedures, suffering and death, that individual's likely treatment/nontreatment preferences can be discovered. Family members are most familiar with this entire life context. Articulating such knowledge is a formidable task, requiring a literary skill beyond the capacity of many, perhaps most, families. But the family's knowledge exists nevertheless, intuitively felt by them and available as an important decisionmaking tool." ' "***

The best-interests standard, by which a guardian, in the exercise of his or her judgment, determines what is best for the ward, was rejected by this court in Longeway as an inappropriate vehicle by which a guardian may be guided in determining whether an incompetent patient, in either an irreversible coma or a persistent vegetative state, should have artificial nutrition and hydration withdrawn. This court rejected the best-interests standard because "it lets another make a determination of a patient's quality of life, thereby undermining the foundation of self-determination and inviolability of the person upon which the right to refuse medical treatment stands." (*Longeway*, 133 Ill.2d at 49.) By requiring a guardian to proceed under the doctrine of substituted judgment instead of the best-interests standard, the inquiry is necessarily focused on whether the formerly competent, now incompetent, patient had ever manifested an intent as to whether he or she would consent or refuse to consent to artificial nutrition and hydration.***

Mr. Bosze argues that the twins, if they had the legal capacity, would have the right to consent or refuse to consent to the proposed bone marrow harvesting procedure. Mr. Bosze argues that if the doctrine of substituted judgment is not applied in this case, the twins' right to consent or refuse to consent to medical treatment, which they would have if they were competent, would be violated. Since the twins are without legal capacity to consent or refuse to consent to the proposed bone marrow harvesting procedure, and since the parents do not agree, Mr. Bosze argues that both his and Ms. Curran's opinions regarding whether the twins should serve as bone marrow donors should be read out of the equation, and the court, applying the doctrine of substituted judgment, should look solely to what the twins would decide to do if they were competent. Mr. Bosze argues that the standard of the best interests of the child, traditionally the standard in cases involving minors, may not be used because this court rejected the best-interests standard in *Longeway* and *Greenspan*.

Concerning the use of the doctrine of substituted judgment, this court in *Longeway* recognized that "[a] dilemma [exists]when the patient is an infant or life-long incompetent who never could have made a reasoned judgment about his [or her] quality of life." Mr. Bosze argues that this dilemma was resolved by this court in *Longeway* when it stated that "although actual, specific express intent would be helpful and compelling, the same is not necessary for the exercise of substituted judgment by a surrogate."

Immediately following this statement in *Longeway*, however, this court stated: "In this case, Mrs. Longeway's guardian must substitute her judgment for that of Longeway's, based upon *other* clear and convincing evidence of Longeway's intent." This language addressed the instance where a formerly competent, now incompetent, patient had never "expressed explicit intent regarding [the] type of medical treatment prior to becoming incompetent." This language did not address the dilemma of a guardian substituting the judgment of one who never has been able to make "a reasoned judgment about his [or her] quality of life."***

Under the doctrine of substituted judgment, a guardian of a formerly competent, now incompetent, person may look to the person's life history, in all of its diverse complexity, to ascertain the intentions and attitudes which the incompetent person once held. There must be clear and convincing evidence that the formerly competent, now incompetent, person had expressed his or her intentions and attitudes with regard to the termination of artificial nutrition and hydration before a guardian may be authorized to exercise, on behalf of the incompetent person, the right of the incompetent person to terminate artificial sustenance.

If the doctrine of substituted judgment were to be applied in this case, the guardian of the 3-1/2-year-old twins would have to substitute his or her judgment for that of the twins, based upon clear and convincing evidence of the twins' intent. Because each twin is only 3-1/2 years of age, neither has yet had the opportunity to develop "actual, specific express intent," or any other form of intent, with regard to serving as a bone marrow donor. We agree with Ms. Curran and the guardian ad litem for the twins that it is not possible to determine the intent of a 3-1/2-year-old child with regard to consenting to a bone marrow harvesting procedure by examining the child's personal value system. It is not possible to discover the child's "'likely treatment/nontreatment preferences'" by examining the child's "'philosophical, religious and moral views, life goals, values about the purpose of life and the way it should be lived, and attitudes toward sickness, medical procedures, suffering and death.'" The twins have not yet developed the power of self-determination and are not yet capable of making an informed, rational decision based upon all the available information concerning the risks and benefits associated with serving as bone marrow donors. There is no evidence by which a guardian may be guided in ascertaining whether these 3-1/2-year-old children, if they were adults, would or would not consent to a bone marrow harvesting procedure for another child, their half-brother whom they have met only twice.

The doctrine of substituted judgment requires clear and convincing proof of the incompetent person's intent before a court may authorize a surrogate to substitute his or her judgment for that of the incompetent. Any lesser standard would "undermin[e] the foundation of self-determination and inviolability of the person upon which the right to refuse medical treatment stands." A guardian attempting to prove what a 3-1/2-year-old child would or would not do in a given set of circumstances at a given time in the distant future would have to rely on speculation and conjecture.

Neither justice nor reality is served by ordering a 3-1/2-year-old child to submit to a bone marrow harvesting procedure for the benefit of another by a purported application of the doctrine of substituted judgment. Since it is not possible to discover that which does not exist, specifically, whether the 3-1/2-year-old twins would consent or refuse to consent to the proposed bone marrow harvesting procedure if they were competent, the doctrine of substituted judgment is not relevant and may not be applied in this case.***

We hold that a parent or guardian may give consent on behalf of a minor daughter or son for the child to donate bone marrow to a sibling, only when to do so would be in the minor's best interest.

As sole custodian of the twins, Ms. Curran "may determine the child[ren]'s upbringing, including but not limited to, [the] education, health care and religious training, unless the court, after hearing, finds, upon motion by the noncustodial parent, that the absence of a specific limitation of the custodian's authority would clearly be contrary to the best interests of the child[ren]." Ill.Rev.Stat.1987, ch. 40, par. 608(a).***

Notes and Issues for Discussion

1. The court in *Bosze* discards the substitute judgment standard for the three-and-a-half-year-old twins as involving "speculation and conjecture," and holds that only a best interest standard may apply. What if the bone marrow transplant involves few risks and the half-brother's life might be saved? Is there any situation where it is in the child's best interest to allow a bone marrow harvesting procedure?
2. What if the issue was only a blood transfusion involving minimal risks? Should a best interests standard require that any bodily invasion of the twins which is not for their direct benefit be prohibited if their guardian so decides?
3. What if relations between the parents were acrimonious and the custodial parent's decision was probably based on ill-will, not the best interests?
4. What if both parents agree to the blood test and a transplant? Should the court or a child welfare agency intervene? On what grounds? In *Hart v. Brown*, 29 Conn. Sup. 368, 289 A.2d 386 (1972), a Connecticut Superior Court permitted a kidney transplant from one seven-year-old identical twin to another based on the necessity of the procedure and the "negligible risks involved to both donor and donee." What do you think? See also *Strunk v. Strunk*, 445 S.W.2d 145 (1969), where the court authorized a kidney transplant from an incompetent, retarded, institutionalized, twenty-seven-year-old man who was a ward of the state to his older brother. The court based the decision on substituted judgment, that the incompetent was emotionally and psychologically dependent upon his brother and therefore would want to help him.

Health Care Decisions and the Unborn

Another complex area is making health care decisions for an incompetent adult which may benefit an unborn child. On what basis should the decision be made? Whose interests should prevail?

IN RE A.C.
573 A.2d 1235 (1990)
DISTRICT OF COLUMBIA COURT OF APPEALS

TERRY, ASSOCIATE JUDGE.

We are confronted here with two profoundly difficult and complex issues. First, we must determine who has the right to decide the course of medical treatment for a patient who, although near death, is pregnant with a viable fetus. Second, we must establish how that decision should be made if the patient cannot make it for herself—more specifically, how a court should proceed when faced with a pregnant patient, *in extremis,* who is apparently incapable of making an informed decision regarding medical care for herself and her fetus. We hold that in virtually all cases the question of what is to be done is to be decided by the patient—the pregnant woman—on behalf of herself and the fetus. If the patient is incompetent or otherwise unable to give an informed consent to a proposed course of medical treatment, then her decision must be ascertained through the procedure known as substituted judgment. Because the trial court did not follow that procedure, we vacate its order and remand the case for further proceedings.

This case came before the trial court when George Washington University Hospital petitioned the emergency judge in chambers for declaratory relief as to how it should treat its patient, A.C., who was close to death from cancer and was twenty-six and one-half weeks pregnant with a viable fetus. After a hearing lasting approximately three hours, which was held at the hospital (though not in A.C.'s room), the court ordered that a caesarean section be performed on A.C. to deliver the fetus. Counsel for A.C. immediately sought a stay in this court, which was unanimously denied by a hastily assembled division of three judges. The caesarean was performed, and a baby girl. L.M.C., was delivered. Tragically, the child died within two and one-half hours, and the mother died two days later.***

A.C. was first diagnosed as suffering from cancer at the age of thirteen. In the ensuing years she underwent major surgery several times, together with multiple radiation treatments and chemotherapy. A.C. married when she was twenty-seven, during a period of remission, and soon thereafter she became pregnant. She was excited about her pregnancy and very much wanted the child. Because of her medical history, she was referred in her fifteenth week of pregnancy to the high-risk pregnancy clinic at George Washington University Hospital.

On Tuesday, June 9, 1987, when A.C. was approximately twenty-five weeks pregnant, she went to the hospital for a scheduled check-up. Because she was experiencing pain in her back and shortness of breath, an x-ray was taken, revealing an apparently inoperable tumor which nearly filled her right lung. On Thursday, June 11, A.C. was admitted to the hospital as a patient. By Friday her condition had temporarily improved, and when asked if she really wanted to have her baby, she replied that she did.

Over the weekend, A.C.'s condition worsened considerably. Accordingly, on Monday, June 15, members of the medical staff treating A.C. assembled, along with her family, in A.C.'s room. The doctors then informed her that her illness was terminal, and A.C. agreed to palliative treatment designed to extend her life until at least her twenty-eighth week of pregnancy. The "potential outcome [for] the fetus," according to the doctors, would be much better at twenty-eight weeks than at twenty-six weeks if it were necessary to "intervene." A.C. knew that the palliative treatment she had chosen presented some increased risk to the fetus, but she opted for this course both to prolong her life for at least another two weeks and to maintain her own comfort. When asked if she still wanted to have the baby, A.C. was somewhat equivocal, saying "something to the effect of 'I don't know, I think so.'" As the day moved toward evening, A.C.'s condition grew still worse, and at about 7:00 or 8:00 p.m. she consented to intubation to facilitate her breathing.

The next morning, June 16, the trial court convened a hearing at the hospital in response to the hospital's request for a declaratory judgment. The court appointed counsel for both A.C. and the fetus, and the District of Columbia was permitted to intervene for the fetus as *parens patriae*. The court heard testimony on the facts as we have summarized them, and further testimony that at twenty-six and a half weeks the fetus was viable. *i.e.*, capable of sustained life outside of the mother, given artificial aid. A neonatologist, Dr. Maureen Edwards, testified that the chances of survival for a twenty-six-week fetus delivered at the hospital might be as high as eighty percent, but that this particular fetus, because of the mother's medical history, had only a fifty to sixty percent chance of survival. Dr. Edwards estimated that the risk of substantial impairment for the fetus, if it were delivered promptly, would be less than twenty percent. However, she noted that the fetus' condition was worsening appreciably at a rapid rate, and another doctor—Dr. Alan Weingold, an obstetrician who was one of A.C.'s treating physicians—stated that any delay in delivering the child by caesarean section lessened its chances of survival.

Regarding A.C.'s ability to respond to questioning and her prognosis, Dr. Louis Hamner, another treating obstetrician, testified that A.C. would probably die within twenty-four hours "if absolutely nothing else is done. . . . As far as her ability to interact, she has been heavily sedated in order to maintain her ventilatory function. She will open her eyes sometimes when you are in the room, but as far as her being able to . . . carry on a meaningful-type conversation . . . at this point, I don't think that is reasonable."***

There was no evidence before the court showing that A.C. consented to, or even contemplated, a caesarean section before her twenty-eighth week of pregnancy. There was, in fact, considerable dispute as to whether she would have consented to an immediate caesarean delivery at the time the hearing was held. A.C.'s mother opposed surgical intervention, testifying that A.C. wanted "to live long enough to hold that baby" and that she expected to do so, "even though she knew she was terminal." Dr. Hamner testified that, given A.C.'s medical problems, he did not think she would have chosen to deliver a child with a substantial degree of impairment. Asked whether A.C. had been "confronted with the question of what to do if there were a choice that ultimately had to be made between her own life expectancy and that of her fetus," he replied that the question "was addressed [but] at a later gestational age. We had talked about the possibility at twenty-eight weeks, if she had to be intubated, if this was a terminal event, would we intervene, and the expression was yes, that we would, because we felt at twenty-eight weeks we had much more to offer as far as taking care of the child."***

After hearing this testimony and the arguments of counsel, the trial court made oral findings of fact. It found, first, that A.C. would probably die, according to uncontroverted medical testimony, "within the next twenty-four to forty-eight hours"; second, that A.C. was "pregnant with a twenty-six and a half week viable fetus who, based upon uncontroverted medical testimony, has approximately a fifty to sixty percent chance to survive if a caesarean section is performed as soon as possible"; third, that because the fetus was viable, "the state has [an] important and legitimate interest in protecting the potentiality of human life"; and fourth, that there had been some testimony that the operation "may very well hasten the death of [A.C.]," but that there had also been testimony that delay would greatly increase the risk to the fetus and that "the prognosis is not great for the fetus to be delivered post-mortem. . . ." Most significantly, the court found:

> The court is of the view that it does not clearly know what [A.C.'s] present views are with respect to the issue of whether or not the child should live or die. She's presently unconscious. As late as Friday of last week, she wanted the baby to live. As late as yesterday, she did not know for sure.

Having made these findings the court ordered that a caesarean section be performed to deliver A.C.'s child.

The court's decision was then relayed to A.C., who had regained consciousness. When the hearing reconvened later in the day, Dr. Hamner told the court:

> I explained to her essentially what was going on. . . . I said it's been deemed we should intervene on behalf of the baby by caesarean section and it would give it the only possible chance of it living. Would you agree to this procedure? *She said yes.* I said, do you realize that you may not survive the surgical procedure? *She said yes.* And I repeated the two questions to her again [and] asked her did she understand? *She said yes.* [Emphasis added.]

When the court suggested moving the hearing to A.C.'s bedside, Dr. Hamner discouraged the court from doing so, but he and Dr. Weingold, together with A.C.'s mother and husband, went to A.C.'s room to confirm her consent to the procedure. What happened then was recounted to the court a few minutes later:***

> "DR. WEINGOLD: She does not make sound because of the tube in her windpipe. She nods and she mouths words. One can see what she's saying rather readily. She asked whether she would survive the operation. She asked [Dr.] Hamner if he would perform the operation. He told her he would only perform it if she authorized it but it would be done in any case. She understood that. She then seemed to pause for a few moments and then very clearly mouthed words several times, *I don't want it done. I don't want it done.* Quit clear to me.
>
> I would obviously state the obvious and that is this is an environment in which, from my perspective as a physician, this would not be an informed consent one way or the other. She's under tremendous stress with the family on both sides, but I'm satisfied that I heard clearly what she said.***

After hearing this new evidence, the court found that it was "still not clear what her intent is" and again ordered that a caesarean section be performed. A.C.'s counsel sought a stay in this court, which was denied. *In re A.C.*, 533 A.2d 611, 613 (D.C.1987). The operation took place, but the baby lived for only a few hours, and A.C. succumbed to cancer two days later.***

The personal representative of A.C.'s estate has filed an action separate from this appeal against the hospital, based on the events leading to the trial court's order in this case. In these circumstances we adhere to our prior decisions refusing to dismiss an appeal as moot when resolution of the legal issues might affect a separate action, actual or prospective, between the parties.***

Thus our analysis of this case begins with the tenet common to all medical treatment cases: that any person has the right to make an informed choice, if competent to do so, to accept or forego medical treatment. The doctrine of informed consent, based on this principle and rooted in the concept of bodily integrity, is ingrained in our common law.***

What we distill from the cases discussed in this section is that every person has the right, under the common law and the Constitution, to accept or refuse medical treatment. This right of bodily integrity belongs equally to persons who are competent and persons who are not. Further, it matters not what the quality of a patient's life may be; the right of bodily integrity is not extinguished simply because someone is ill, or even at death's door. To protect that right against intrusion by others—family members, doctors, hospitals, or anyone else, however well-intentioned—we hold that a court must determine the patient's wishes by any means available, and must abide by those wishes unless there are truly extraordinary or compelling reasons to override them. *In re Osborne, supra.* When the patient is incompetent, or when the court is unable to determine competency, the substituted judgment procedure must be followed.

From the record before us, we simply cannot tell whether A.C. was ever competent, after being sedated, to make an informed decision one way or the other regarding the proposed caesarean section. The trial court never made any finding about A.C.'s competency to decide. Undoubtedly, during most of the proceedings below, A.C. was incompetent to make a treatment decision; that is, she was unable to give an informed consent based on her assessment of the risks and benefits of the contemplated surgery.***

We think it is incumbent on any trial judge in a case like this, unless it is impossible to do so, to ascertain whether a patient is competent to make her own medical decisions. Whenever possible, the judge should personally attempt to speak with the patient and ascertain her wishes directly, rather than relying exclusively on hearsay evidence, even from doctors.***

In the previous section we discussed the right of an individual to accept or reject medical treatment. We concluded that if a patient is competent and has made an informed decision regarding the course of her medical treatment, that decision will control in virtually all cases. Sometimes, however, as our analysis presupposes here, a once competent patient will be unable to render an informed decision. In such a case, we hold that the court must make a substituted judgment on behalf of the patient, based on all the evidence. This means that the duty of the court, "as surrogate for the incompetent, is to determine as best it can what choice that individual, if competent, would make with respect to medical procedures." *In re Boyd,* 403 A.2d at 750.

Under the substituted judgment procedure, the court as decision-maker must "substitute itself as nearly as may be for the incompetent, and . . . act upon the same motives and considerations as would have moved her. . . ."***

We have found no reported opinion applying the substituted judgment procedure to the case of an incompetent pregnant patient whose own life may be shortened by a caesarean section, and whose unborn child's chances of survival may hang on the court's decision. Despite this precedential void, we conclude that substituted judgment is the best procedure to follow in such a case because it most clearly respects the right of the patient to bodily integrity.

We begin with the proposition that the substituted judgment inquiry is primarily a subjective one: as nearly as possible, the court must ascertain what the patient would do if competent. Due process strongly suggests (and may even require) that counsel or a guardian ad litem should be appointed for the patient unless the situation is so urgent that there is no time to do so.

Because it is the patient's decisional rights which the substituted judgment inquiry seeks to protect, courts are in accord that the greatest weight should be given to the previously expressed wishes of the patient. This includes prior statements, either written or oral, even though the treatment alternatives at hand may not have been addressed. The court should also consider previous decisions of the patient concerning medical treatment, especially when there may be a discernibly consistent pattern of conduct or of thought. Thus in a case such as this it would be highly relevant that A.C. had consented to intrusive and dangerous surgeries in the past, and that she chose to become pregnant and to protect her pregnancy by seeking treatment at the hospital's high-risk pregnancy clinic. It would also be relevant that she accepted a plan of treatment which contemplated caesarean intervention at the twenty-eighth week of pregnancy, even though the possibility of a caesarean during the twenty-sixth week was apparently unforeseen. On the other hand, A.C. agreed to a plan of palliative treatment which posed a greater danger to the fetus than would have been necessary if she were unconcerned about her own continuing care. Further, when A.C. was informed of the fatal nature of her illness, she was equivocal about her desire to have the baby.

Courts in substituted judgment cases have also acknowledged the importance of probing the patient's value system as an aid in discerning what the patient would choose. We agree with this approach.***

Although treating physicians may be an invaluable source of such information about a patient, the family will often be the best source. Family members or other loved ones will usually be in the best position to say what the patient would do if competent. The court should be mindful, however, that while in the majority of cases family members will have the best interests of the patient in mind, sometimes family members will rely on their own judgments or predilections rather than serving as conduits for expressing the patient's wishes. This is why the court should endeavor, whenever possible, to make an in-person appraisal "of the patient's personal desires and ability for rational choice. In this way the court can always know, to the extent possible, that the judgment is that of the individual concerned and not that of those who believe, however well-intentioned, that they speak for the person whose life is in the balance."****

In short, to determine the subjective desires of the patient, the court must consider the totality of the evidence, focusing particularly on written or oral directions concerning treatment to family, friends, and health-care professionals. The court should also take into account the patient's past decisions regarding medical treatment, and attempt to ascertain from what is known about the patient's value system, goals, and desires what the patient would decide if competent.

After considering the patient's prior statements, if any, the previous medical decisions of the patient, and the values held by the patient, the court may still be unsure what course the patient would choose. In such circumstances the court may supplement its knowledge about the patient by determining what most persons would likely do in a similar situation. When the patient is pregnant, however, she may not be concerned exclusively with her own welfare. Thus it is proper for the court, in a case such as this, to weigh (along with all the other factors) the mother's prognosis, the viability of the fetus, the probable result of treatment or non-treatment for both mother and fetus, and the mother's likely interest in avoiding impairment for her child together with her own instincts for survival.

Additionally, the court should consider the context in which prior declarations, treatment decisions, and expressions of personal values were made, including whether statements were made casually or after contemplation, or in accordance with deeply held beliefs. Finally, in making a substituted judgment, the court should become as informed about the patient's condition, prognosis, and treatment options as one would expect any patient to become before making a treatment decision. Obviously, the weight accorded all of these factors will vary from case to case.***

Notes and Issues for Discussion

1. What statements and actions by A. C. would lead you to believe that she wanted the surgery? What statements and actions would lead you to believe that she did not?
2. The court reaffirms a competent patient's right to accept or reject treatment, but notes that this right is not absolute and discusses a number of cases where state intervention to protect third parties has been allowed. The court does not decide if state intervention is justified here to protect the unborn. What do you think?
3. The court decides that a substitute judgment standard should apply. Note the elements that the court says should be considered. What is the role of the health and human services professional in determining these elements?

SELECTED REFERENCES

American Bar Association. *Recommendations of the National Guardianship Symposium* (1988).

Alderson, P. *Choosing for Children: Parent's Consent to Surgery* (1990).

Applebaum, P. S., and Roth, L. H. "Clinical issues in the assessment of competency," 138 *Am. J. Psychiatry* 1462 (1981).

Applebaum, P. S., Lidz, C. W., and Meisel, A. *Informed Consent: Legal and Clinical Practice* (1987).
Associated Press. *Guardians of the Elderly: An Ailing System* (1987).
Brakel, S. J., Parry, J., and Weiner, B. A. *The Mentally Disabled and the Law* (3rd ed., 1985).
Cantor, N. L. *Legal Frontiers of Death and Dying* (1987).
Drane, J. F. "The many faces of competency," 15 *Hastings Center Rept.* 17 (1985).
Gaylin, W., and Macklin, R. (eds.) *Who Speaks for the Child* (1982).
Hommel, P. A., and Lisi, L. B. "Model standards for guardianship: Ensuring quality surrogate decision making services," *Clearinghouse Rev.* 433 (Summer 1989).
Lidz, C. W., and Arnold, R. M. *The Erosion of Autonomy in Long Term Care* (1992).
Melton, G. B., Koocher, G. P., and Sacks, M. J. *Children's Competence to Consent* (1983).
Morrissey, J. M., Hofman, A. D., and Thorpe, J. C. *Consent and Confidentiality in Health Care of Children and Adolescents* (1986).
Parry, J. "Selected recommendations from the National Guardianship Symposium at Wingspread," 12 *Mental and Physical Disabilities L. Rep.* 398 (1988).
———. "Incompetence, guardianship and restoration," in Brakel, et al. (Eds.). *The Mentally Disabled and the Law* (1985).
President's Commission for the Study of Ethical Problems in Medicine and Biomedical and Behavioral Research. *Making Health Care Decisions: The Ethical and Legal Implications of Informed Consent in the Patient-Practitioner Relationship*, Vol. I (1982).
Roth, L. H., Meisel, A., and Lidz, C. W. "Tests of competency to consent to treatment," 134 *Am. J. Psychiatry* 279 (1977).
Society for the Right to Die. *The Physician and the Hopelessly Ill Patient: Legal, Medical and Ethical Guidelines* (1985).
Subcommittee on Health and Long-term Care, House Select Committee on Aging, 100th Cong., 1st Sess. *Abuses in Guardianship of the Elderly and Infirm: A National Disgrace* (H.R. No. 639, 1987).
Subcommittee on Housing and Consumer Interests, House Select Committee on Aging, 100th Cong., 2nd Sess. *Surrogate Decision Making for Adults: Model Standards to Ensure Quality Guardianship and Representative Payeeship Services* (Comm. Print. 100-705, 1988).

SOCIAL PROBLEMS AND VULNERABLE POPULATIONS

Part III presents legal issues associated with a range of social problems and vulnerable populations. The problems and populations comprise some of the most critical for the health and human services professional today. The listing is necessarily incomplete. Among the key populations and problems addressed are families and children, the mentally ill, the developmentally disabled, child abuse, divorce, termination of parental rights, foster care, domestic violence, and AIDS.

Chapter 9 addresses families, marriage, divorce, and children. Topics include what constitutes a family, marriage and domestic partnerships, divorce and its aftermath. Then the focus shifts to children, examining law related to children in juvenile court and in the public schools. Finally the rights of children, both in consonance with parental wishes and independent of parents are discussed.

In Chapter 10 two major social problem areas, child abuse and domestic violence, are examined in detail. Included here are legal definitions of child abuse, mandatory reporting requirements, child abuse hearings and testimony, and civil liability for failure to report and for committing or allowing child abuse. Along with domestic violence statutes and the battered spouse syndrome, civil liability for failure to enforce domestic violence statutes is addressed. Some of the possible consequences of child abuse, termination of parental rights, and foster care are also examined.

Elements of mental health law are examined in Chapter 11. Included are discussions of voluntary admissions, involuntary civil commitment, and civil commitment of children; the mentally ill criminal offender; and important patient rights for the institutionalized mentally ill, including the right to liberty, the right to treatment, and the right to refuse treatment.

Chapter 12 discusses the law relating to the developmentally disabled and handicapped. Some of the key statutory provisions relating to this large and diverse population are examined, with particular emphasis on Section 504 of the Handicapped Act of 1973 and the Americans with Disabilities Act of 1991. Then some of the Constitutional rights of those in institutions are discussed, including rights to habilitation and safety. Finally very important legal issues concerning medical care and sterilization of disabled individuals, and health care and education of disabled children are examined.

Chapter 13 addresses AIDS, a major social problem of the day. Included here are privacy and confidentiality provisions for persons with AIDS, mandatory blood testing, disclosure of AIDS, and discrimination against persons with AIDS in the workplace, schools, and health care facilities.

CHAPTER 9

FAMILIES AND CHILDREN I

Family Composition, Marriage, Divorce, Children, and the Law

Within broad constitutional mandates and some federal standards often tied to funding initiatives, the law of families and children is primarily state law, with significant differences between jurisdictions. At an earlier time, family law was mostly the law of marriage and divorce. Currently, an expanding family law area goes beyond traditional marriage and divorce issues to include social problems such as child abuse and domestic violence; medical and biological advances such as artificial insemination and surrogate parenting; life-style issues such as unmarried cohabitation and same-sex relationships; state involvement in the family through removal of children, termination of parental rights, and the establishment of foster care; and more generally, the rights of parents and children within the family.

In this chapter, the law concerning marriage and cohabitation, divorce and its aftermath, and selected aspects of children and the law will be addressed. The following chapter will include a survey of legal issues in child abuse, domestic violence, termination of parental rights, foster care, and adoption.

Census data indicate the traditional nuclear family with two parents and their biological offspring is becoming less typical and alternative family arrangements, including unmarried heads of households, same sex parents, adoptive and foster families, and blended families involving remarriages with children of current and prior marriages are becoming more common.

In 1991, a total of almost 2.4 million marriages and almost 1.2 million divorces took place in the United States (U.S. Census Bureau, 1993). In the same year, out of 64.2 million children, 46.6 million lived with two parents, 15.5 million lived only with their mothers and 2.2 million lived only with their fathers. Between 1970 and 1990, the percentage of children living in two-parent homes declined from 85 percent to 73 percent. Looking at the data another way, female-headed households with children grew from 10 percent to 20 percent over the same period, male-headed households with children grew from 1 percent to 4 percent, and two-parent households with children decreased from 89 percent to 76 percent.[1]

Along with the growth of single-parent families, the complexity of families has changed. In 1990, almost one quarter of all married-couple families with children were nontraditional. Seventy-seven percent of 25.3 million married-couple families consisted of parents and their biological or adoptive children; 10 percent consisted of mothers, their children, and a stepfather; less than 1 percent consisted of fathers, their children, and a stepmother; and 11 percent consisted of parents and stepparents, with biological and adoptive children of both parents (U.S. Census Bureau, 1993). Thus over one quarter of all households with children were headed by a single parent, and of the married two-parent households, almost one quarter were nontraditional combinations. At the same time, the number of unmarried couples has grown from .5 million in 1970 to 2.8 million in 1990 (U.S. Census Bureau, 1993).

Several themes run through this chapter: What is a family? How does the state regulate the creation and dissolution of families? When may the state intrude on the family relationship, or alternatively to what extent is there a constitutional privacy right that protects parents from state intrusion? What rights do children have either in conjunction with or independent of their parents? In these areas a knowledge of local state law is important: There are few general constitutional guidelines and great variations across the states. For the health and human services professional the issues are important and the roles of the professional in this area are numerous, ranging from divorce counseling and mediation to juvenile court worker, expert witness, school counselor, and child advocate.

FAMILY PRIVACY

Since *Meyer v. Nebraska*, 262 U.S. 390 (1923), and *Pierce v. Society of Sisters*, 268 U.S. 510 (1925), the Supreme Court has upheld the privacy of families to make decisions and conduct their affairs without state interference. As the Court said, there exists "a private realm of family life which the state cannot enter." *Prince v. Massachusetts*, 321 U.S. 158 at 166 (1944). (These cases and the more recent privacy cases dealing with abortion and sexual freedom are discussed on p. 96*ff*.). Yet this privacy is not unlimited. The state may impose regulations to protect children from abuse and neglect, intervene to require life-preserving medical treatment, and remove children from the home for their protection or because their parents are incapable of exercising parental control, among other actions.

FAMILY COMPOSITION

"Family: The word is used to designate many relationships . . ." (Black's *Law Dictionary*, 1991).

What is a family? Who are parents? These seemingly simple questions have complex legal answers. Often the legal requirements of a family will vary with the circumstances. What is a legal family for some purposes may not be for others. Clearly two adults legally married to each other and living with their unmarried biological or legally adopted offspring constitute a family. But, what if the individuals are not married or are married to others? What if they are of the same sex? What if a number of adults or unrelated children live together? What if some of the children were conceived through artificial insemination with donated sperm or eggs?

The Extended Family

In *Moore v. East Cleveland*, 431 U.S. 494 (1977), the Supreme Court invalidated a city ordinance that limited families living in a geographical area to husbands, wives, their unmarried children and their parents. Inez Moore, who lived with her son and two grandsons who were cousins, not brothers, was fined $25 and sentenced to five days in jail for violating the ordinance. The Court observed that: "freedom of personal choice in matters of marriage and family life is one of the liberties protected by the Due Process Clause of the Fourteenth Amendment," and cited "a host of cases . . . [which] have consistently acknowledged a 'private realm of family life' which the state cannot enter." 431 U.S. at 499.

MOORE v. EAST CLEVELAND
431 U.S. 494 (1977)
U.S. SUPREME COURT

MR. JUSTICE POWELL announced the judgment of the Court.

East Cleveland's housing ordinance, like many throughout the country, limits occupancy of a dwelling unit to members of a single family. § 1351.02. But the ordinance contains an unusual and complicated definitional section that recognizes as a "family" only a few categories of related individuals. § 1341.08.[1] Because her family, living together in her home, fits none of those categories, ap-

---

[1] Section 1341.08 provides:

"'Family' means a number of individuals related to the nominal head of the household or to the spouse of the nominal head of the household living as a single housekeeping unit in a single dwelling unit, but limited to the following:

pellant stands convicted of a criminal offense. The question in this case is whether the ordinance violates the Due Process Clause of the Fourteenth Amendment.

Appellant, Mrs. Inez Moore, lives in her East Cleveland home together with her son, Dale Moore, Sr., and her two grandsons, Dale, Jr., and John Moore, Jr. The two boys are first cousins rather than brothers; we are told that John came to live with his grandmother and with the elder and younger Dale Moores after his mother's death.

In early 1973, Mrs. Moore received a notice of violation from the city, stating that John was an "illegal occupant" and directing her to comply with the ordinance. When she failed to remove him from her home, the city filed a criminal charge. Mrs. Moore moved to dismiss, claiming that the ordinance was constitutionally invalid on its face. Her motion was overruled, and upon conviction she was sentenced to five days in jail and a $25 fine. The Ohio Court of Appeals affirmed after giving full consideration to her constitutional claims, and the Ohio Supreme Court denied review.***

***"This Court has long recognized that freedom of personal choice in matters of marriage and family life is one of the liberties protected by the Due Process Clause of the Fourteenth Amendment." Of course, the family is not beyond regulation. But when the government intrudes on choices concerning family living arrangements, this Court must examine carefully the importance of the governmental interests advanced and the extent to which they are served by the challenged regulation.

When thus examined, this ordinance cannot survive. The city seeks to justify it as a means of preventing overcrowding, minimizing traffic and parking congestion, and avoiding an undue financial burden on East Cleveland's school system. Although these are legitimate goals, the ordinance before us serves them marginally, at best. For example, the ordinance permits any family consisting only of husband, wife, and unmarried children to live together, even if the family contains a half dozen licensed drivers, each with his or her own car. At the same time it forbids an adult brother and sister to share a household, even if both faithfully use public transportation. The ordinance would permit a grandmother to live with a single dependent son and children, even if his school-age children number a dozen, yet it forces Mrs. Moore to find another dwelling for her grand-

---

"(a) Husband or wife of the nominal head of the household.

"(b) Unmarried children of the nominal head of the household or of the spouse of the nominal head of the household, provided, however, that such unmarried children have no children residing with them.

"(c) Father or mother of the nominal head of the household or of the spouse of the nominal head of the household.

"(d) Notwithstanding the provision of subsection (b) hereof, a family may include not more than one dependent married or unmarried child of the nominal head of the household or of the spouse of the nominal head of the household and the spouse and dependent children of such dependent child. For the purpose of this subsection, a dependent person is one who has more than fifty percent of his total support furnished for him by the nominal head of the household and the spouse of the nominal head of the household.

"(e) A family may consist of one individual."

son John, simply because of the presence of his uncle and cousin in the same household. We need not labor the point. Section 1341.08 has but a tenuous relation to alleviation of the conditions mentioned by the city.

The city would distinguish the cases based on Meyer and Pierce. It points out that none of them "gives grandmothers any fundamental rights with respect to grandsons," and suggests that any constitutional right to live together as a family extends only to the nuclear family—essentially a couple and its dependent children.

To be sure, these cases did not expressly consider the family relationship presented here. They were immediately concerned with freedom of choice with respect to childbearing, e.g., LaFleur, Roe v Wade, Griswold, supra, or with the rights of parents to the custody and companionship of their own children, Stanley v Illinois, supra, or with traditional parental authority in matters of child rearing and education. Yoder, Ginsberg, Pierce, Meyer, supra. But unless we close our eyes to the basic reasons why certain rights associated with the family have been accorded shelter under the Fourteenth Amendment's Due Process Clause, we cannot avoid applying the force and rationale of these precedents to the family choice involved in this case.

***Our decisions establish that the Constitution protects the sanctity of the family precisely because the institution of the family is deeply rooted in this Nation's history and tradition. It is through the family that we inculcate and pass down many of our most cherished values, moral and cultural.

Ours is by no means a tradition limited to respect for the bonds uniting the members of the nuclear family. The tradition of uncles, aunts, cousins, and especially grandparents sharing a household along with parents and children has roots equally venerable and equally deserving of constitutional recognition. Over the years millions of our citizens have grown up in just such an environment, and most, surely, have profited from it. Even if conditions of modern society have brought about a decline in extended family households, they have not erased the accumulated wisdom of civilization, gained over the centuries and honored throughout our history, that supports a larger conception of the family. Out of choice, necessity, or a sense of family responsibility, it has been common for close relatives to draw together and participate in the duties and the satisfactions of a common home. Decisions concerning child rearing, which Yoder, Meyer, Pierce and other cases have recognized as entitled to constitutional protection, long have been shared with grandparents or other relatives who occupy the same household—indeed who may take on major responsibility for the rearing of the children. Especially in times of adversity, such as the death of a spouse or economic need, the broader family has tended to come together for mutual sustenance and to maintain or rebuild a secure home life. This is apparently what happened here.

Whether or not such a household is established because of personal tragedy, the choice of relatives in this degree of kinship to live together may not lightly be denied by the State. Pierce struck down an Oregon law requiring all children to attend the State's public schools, holding that the Constitution "excludes any general power of the State to standardize its children by forcing them to accept instruction from public teachers only." By the same token the Constitution prevents East Cleveland from standardizing its children—and its adults—by forcing all to live in certain narrowly defined family patterns.

Reversed.

MR. JUSTICE BRENNAN, with whom MR. JUSTICE MARSHALL joins, concurring.

I join the plurality opinion. I agree that the Constitution is not powerless to prevent East Cleveland from prosecuting as a criminal and jailing[1] a 63-year-old grandmother for refusing to expel from her home her now 10-year-old grandson who has lived with her and been brought up by her since his mother's death when he was less than a year old.[2] I do not question that a municipality may constitutionally zone to alleviate noise and traffic congestion and to prevent overcrowded and unsafe living conditions, in short to enact reasonable land-use restrictions in furtherance of the legitimate objectives East Cleveland claims for its ordinance. But the zoning power is not a license for local communities to enact senseless and arbitrary restrictions which cut deeply into private areas of protected family life. East Cleveland may not constitutionally define "family" as essentially confined to parents and the parents' own children.[3] The plurality's opinion conclusively demonstrates that classifying family patterns in this eccentric way is not a rational means of achieving the ends East Cleveland claims for its ordinance, and further that the ordinance unconstitutionally abridges the "freedom of personal choice in matters of family . . . life [that] is one of the liberties protected by the Due Process Clause of the Fourteenth Amendment." I write only to underscore the cultural myopia of the arbitrary boundary drawn by the East Cleveland ordinance in the light of the tradition of the American home that has been a feature of our society since our beginning as a Nation—the "tradition" in the plurality's words, "of uncles, aunts, cousins, and especially grandparents

[1] This is a criminal prosecution which resulted in the grandmother's conviction and sentence to prison and a fine. Section 1345.99 permits imprisonment of up to six months, and a fine of up to $1,000, for violation of any provision of the Housing Code. Each day such violation continues may, by the terms of this section, consititute a separate offense.

[2] Brief for Appellant 4. In addition, we were informed by appellant's counsel at oral argument that

"application of this ordinance here would not only sever and disrupt the relationship between Mrs. Moore and her own son, but it would disrupt the relationship that is established between young John and young Dale, which is in essence a sibling type relationship, and it would most importantly disrupt the relationship between young John and his grandmother, which is the only maternal influence that he has had during his entire life." Tr of Oral Arg 16. The city did not dispute these representations, and it is clear that this case was argued from the outset as requiring decision in this context.

[3] The East Cleveland ordinance defines "family" to include, in addition to the spouse of the "nominal head of the household," the couple's childless unmarried children, but only one dependent child (married or unmarried) having dependent children, and one parent of the nominal head of the household or of his or her spouse. Thus an "extended family" is authorized in only the most limited sense, and "family" is essentially confined to parents and their own children. Appellant grandmother was charged with violating the ordinance because John, Jr., lived with her at the same time her other grandson, Dale, Jr., was also living in the home; the latter is classified as an "unlicensed roomer" authorized by the ordinance to live in the house.

sharing a household along with parents and children. . . ." The line drawn by this ordinance displays a depressing insensitivity toward the economic and emotional needs of a very large part of our society.

In today's America, the "nuclear family" is the pattern so often found in much of white suburbia. The Constitution cannot be interpreted, however, to tolerate the imposition by government upon the rest of us of white suburbia's preference in patterns of family living. The "extended family" that provided generations of early Americans with social services and economic and emotional support in times of hardship, and was the beachhead for successive waves of immigrants who populated our cities, remains not merely still a pervasive living pattern, but under the goad of brutal economic necessity, a prominent pattern—virtually a means of survival—for large numbers of the poor and deprived minorities of our society. For them compelled pooling of scant resources requires compelled sharing of a household.

The "extended" form is especially familiar among black families. We may suppose that this reflects the truism that black citizens, like generations of white immigrants before them, have been victims of economic and other disadvantages that would worsen if they were compelled to abandon extended for nuclear living patterns. Even in husband and wife households, 13% of black families compared with 3% of white families include relatives under 18 years old, in addition to the couple's own children.[4] In black households whose head is an elderly woman, as in this case, the contrast is even more striking: 48% of such black households, compared with 10% of counterpart white households, include related minor children not offspring of the head of the household.[5]

Notes and Issues for Discussion

1. In *Village of Belle Terre v. Boraas*, 416 U.S. 1 (1974), the Court upheld a zoning ordinance forbidding occupancy by more than two unrelated persons in single-family dwellings as a legitimate exercise of police power. How does this differ from Moore?

2. What are the purposes of the East Cleveland ordinance? Does it achieve them? What are the consequences for the Moores if it is enforced?

3. "Our decisions establish that the Constitution protects the sanctity of the family. . . ." In *Moore*, what is a "family"?

4. The Borough of Glassboro, New Jersey, redefined family as "one or more persons occupying a dwelling unit as a single non-profit housekeeping unit, who are living together as a stable and permanent living unit, being a traditional family unit or the functional equivalency thereof . . ." and limited occupancy or residence with one or two dwelling units to families

---

[4] R. Hill, The Strengths of Black Families 5(1972).

[5] Id., at 5–6. It is estimated that at least 26% of black children live in other than husband-wife families, "including foster parents, the presence of other male or female relatives (grandfather or grandmother, older brother or sister, uncle or aunt), male or female nonrelatives, [or with] only *one* adult (usually mother) present. . . ." Scanzoni, supra, n 6, at 44.

only. In *Borough of Glassboro v. Vallorosi*, 568 A.2d 888 (1990), the New Jersey Supreme Court upheld a lower court decision that ten unrelated college students living in a home purchased by one of them and planning to reside there from sophomore through senior years "shows stability, permanency and can be described as a functional equivalent of a family." What do you think?

Cohabitation and Domestic Partnerships

Do two adults of the same or opposite sex living together in a long-term relationship constitute a family? For some purposes they do. In the *Braschi* case, the question is whether the surviving domestic partner comes under the New York City rent control ordinance so that he cannot be evicted from their apartment.

BRASCHI v. STAHL ASSOCIATES COMPANY
74 N.Y.2d 201, 543 N.E.2d 49 (1989)
NEW YORK COURT OF APPEALS

TITONE, JUDGE.

In this dispute over occupancy rights to a rent-controlled apartment, the central question to be resolved on this request for preliminary injunctive relief (*see,* CPLR 6301) is whether appellant has demonstrated a likelihood of success on the merits by showing that, as a matter of law, he is entitled to seek protection from eviction under New York City Rent and Eviction Regulations 9 NYCRR 2204.6(d). That regulation provides that upon the death of a rent-control tenant, the landlord may not dispossess "either the surviving spouse of the deceased tenant or some other member of the deceased tenant's *family* who has been living with the tenant" (emphasis supplied). Resolution of this question requires this court to determine the meaning of the term "family" as it is used in this context.

Appellant, Miguel Braschi, was living with Leslie Blanchard in a rent-controlled apartment located at 405 East 54th Street from the summer of 1975 until Blanchard's death in September of 1986. In November of 1986, respondent, Stahl Associates Company, the owner of the apartment building, served a notice to cure an appellant contending that he was a mere licensee with no right to occupy the apartment since only Blanchard was the tenant of record. In December of 1986 respondent served appellant with a notice to terminate informing appellant that he had one month to vacate the apartment and that, if the apartment was not vacated, respondent would commence summary proceedings to evict him.

[A]ppellant then moved for a preliminary injunction, pendente lite, enjoining respondent from evicting him until a court could determine whether he was a member of Blanchard's family within the meaning of 9 NYCRR 2204.6(d). After examining the nature of the relationship between the two men, Supreme Court concluded that appellant was a "family member" within the meaning of the regulation.The court based this decision on its finding that the long-term interdependent nature of the 10-year relationship between appellant and Blanchard "fulfills any definitional criteria of the term 'family.'"

The Appellate Division reversed, concluding that section 2204.6(d) provides noneviction protection only to "family members within traditional, legally recognized familial relationships." Since appellant's and Blanchard's relationship was not one given formal recognition by the law, the court held that appellant could not seek the protection of the noneviction ordinance.***We now reverse.***

The present dispute arises because the term "family" is not defined in the rent-control code and the legislative history is devoid of any specific reference to the noneviction provision.

[W]e conclude that the term family, as used in 9 NYCRR 2204.6(d) should not be rigidly restricted to those people who have formalized their relationship by obtaining, for instance, a marriage certificate or an adoption order. The intended protection against sudden eviction should not rest on fictitious legal distinctions or genetic history, but instead should find its foundation in the reality of family life. In the context of eviction, a more realistic, and certainly equally valid, view of a family includes two adult lifetime partners whose relationship is long term and characterized by an emotional and financial commitment and interdependence. This view comports both with our society's traditional concept of "family" and with the expectations of individuals who live in such nuclear units (*see, also, 829 Seventh Ave. Co. v. Reider,* 67 N.Y.2d 930, 931–932 [interpreting 9 NYCRR 2204.6(d)'s additional "living with" requirement to mean living with the named tenant "in a *family unit,* which in turn connotes an arrangement, whatever its duration, bearing some indicia of permanence or continuity" (emphasis supplied)]). In fact, Webster's Dictionary defines "family" *first* as " a group of people united by certain convictions or common affiliation" (Webster's Ninth New Collegiate Dictionary; *see,* Ballantine's Law Dictionary "family" defined as "(p)rimarily, the collective body of persons who live in one house and under one head or management"). Hence, it is reasonable to conclude that, in using the term "family," the Legislature intended to extend protection to those who reside in households having all of the normal familial characteristics. Appellant Braschi should therefore be afforded the opportunity to prove that he and Blanchard had such a household.

The determination as to whether an individual is entitled to noneviction protection should be based upon an objective examination of the relationship of the parties. In making this assessment, the lower courts of this State have looked to a number of factors, including the exclusivity and longevity of the relationship, the level of emotional and financial commitment, the manner in which the parties have conducted their everyday lives and held themselves out to society, and the reliance placed upon one another for daily family services. These factors are most helpful, although it should be emphasized that the presence or absence of one or more of them is not dispositive since it is the totality of the relationship as evidenced by the dedication, caring and self-sacrifice of the parties which should, in the final analysis, control. Appellant's situation provides an example of how the rule should be applied.

Appellant and Blanchard lived together as permanent life partners for more than 10 years. They regarded one another, and were regarded by friends and family, as spouses. The two men's families were aware of the nature of the relationship, and they regularly visited each other's families and attended family functions together, as a couple. Even today, appellant continues to maintain a relationship with Blanchard's niece, who considers him an uncle.

In addition to their interwoven social lives, appellant clearly considered the apartment his home. He lists the apartment as his address on his driver's license and passport, and receives all his mail at the apartment address. Moreover, appellant's tenancy was known to the building's superintendent and doormen, who viewed the two men as a couple.

Financially, the two men shared all obligations including a household budget. The two were authorized signatories of three safe-deposit boxes, they maintained joint checking and savings accounts, and joint credit cards. In fact, rent was often paid with a check from their joint checking account. Additionally, Blanchard executed a power of attorney in appellant's favor so that appellant could make necessary decisions—financial, medical and personal—for him during his illness. Finally, appellant was the named beneficiary of Blanchard's life insurance policy, as well as the primary legatee and coexecutor of Blanchard's estate. Hence, a court examining these facts could reasonably conclude that these men were much more than mere roommates.***

Accordingly, the order of the Appellate Division should be reversed and the case remitted to that court for a consideration of undetermined questions. The certified question should be answered in the negative.

Notes and Issues for Discussion

1. How does the court in *Braschi* define "family" for rent control?
2. Does this definition result in a higher standard than that applied to those with marriage certificates? Should it?
3. Compare the *Braschi* approach with that used in *829 Seventh Ave. v. Reider*, 493 N.E.2d 939, where the court says a family unit "connotes an arrangement, whatever its duration, bearing some indicia of permanence or continuity." If duration is not an indicator, what would be indicators of permanence or continuity?
4. Some cities have enacted domestic partnership ordinances providing for registration of unmarried same- or opposite-sex couples as domestic partners. Among these are Berkeley, Santa Cruz, and Los Angeles in California; Seattle, Washington; and Madison, Wisconsin (Lambda Legal Defense, 1992).
5. In *Marvin v. Marvin*, 134 Cal. Rptr. 815, (1976), the couple lived together for seven years without marrying. According to the plaintiff, they agreed orally that while they lived together, "they would combine their efforts and earnings, and would share equally any and all property accumulated," and that the plaintiff "would further render her services as a companion, homemaker, housekeeper and cook" and the defendant agreed to "provide for all of plaintiff's financial support and needs for the rest of her

life." The court held there could be recovery if there was such an expressed contract and further indicated that implied contracts would be upheld. "The mores of society have indeed changed so radically in regard to cohabitation that we cannot impose a standard based on alleged moral considerations that have apparently been so widely abandoned by so many. . . . We conclude that the judicial barriers that may stand in the way of a policy based upon the fulfillment of the reasonable expectation of the parties to a nonmarital relationship should be removed. As we have explained, the courts now hold that express agreements will be enforced unless they rest on an unlawful meretricious consideration. We add that in the absence of an express agreement, the courts may look to a variety of other remedies in order to protect the parties' lawful expectations." 134 Cal. Rptr. at 831. On the rehearing, the appellate court reversed a trial court award for the plaintiff on the grounds there was no contract.

For the opposite position, see *Hewitt v. Hewitt*, 394 N.E. 2d 1204, where the Illinois Supreme Court refused to uphold an agreement by cohabitants, finding it a violation of public policy and in conflict with the Illinois Marriage Act: "In thus potentially enhancing the attractiveness of a private arrangement over marriage, we believe that the appellate court decision in this case contravenes the Act's policy of strengthening and preserving the integrity of marriage." 394 N.E.2d at 1209.

Who Is a Parent?

Although not married, Peter and Joan Stanley lived together intermittently for eighteen years and had three children. Upon Joan's death, Illinois took the two minor children as wards of the state, under an Illinois dependency statute defining parent as "the father and mother of a legitimate child, or the survivor of them, or the natural mother of an illegitimate child, and includes any adoptive parent." Under the statute Peter was not a parent. The U.S. Supreme Court voided the statute on due process and equal protection grounds, making important statements about families and the rights of unwed fathers.

STANLEY v. ILLINOIS
405 U.S. 645 (1972)
U.S. SUPREME COURT

MR. JUSTICE WHITE delivered the opinion of the Court.

Joan Stanley lived with Peter Stanley intermittently for 18 years, during which time they had three children. When Joan Stanley died, Peter Stanley lost not only her but also his children. Under Illinois law, the children of unwed fathers become wards of the State upon the death of the mother. Accordingly, upon Joan

Stanley's death, in a dependency proceeding instituted by the State of Illinois, Stanley's children were declared wards of the State and placed with court-appointed guardians. Stanley appealed, claiming that he had never been shown to be an unfit parent and that since married fathers and unwed mothers could not be deprived of their children without such a showing, he had been deprived of the equal protection of the laws guaranteed him by the Fourteenth Amendment. The Illinois Supreme Court accepted the fact that Stanley's own unfitness had not been established but rejected the equal protection claim, holding that Stanley could properly be separated from his children upon proof of the single fact that he and the dead mother had not been married. Stanley's actual fitness as a father was irrelevant.

Stanley presses his equal protection claim here. The State continues to respond that unwed fathers are presumed unfit to raise their children and that it is unnecessary to hold individualized hearings to determine whether particular fathers are in fact unfit parents before they are separated from their children. We granted certiorari, to determine whether this method of procedure by presumption could be allowed to stand in light of the fact that Illinois allows married fathers—whether divorced, widowed, or separated—and mothers—even if unwed—the benefit of the presumption that they are fit to raise their children.***

Illinois has two principal methods of removing nondelinquent children from the homes of their parents. In a dependency proceeding it may demonstrate that the children are wards of the State because they have no surviving parent or guardian. Ill.Rev.Stat., c. 37, §§ 702–1, 702–5. In a neglect proceeding it may show that children should be wards of the State because the present parent(s) or guardian does not provide suitable care. Ill.Rev.Stat., c. 37, §§ 702–1, 702–4.

The State's right—indeed, duty—to protect minor children through a judicial determination of their interests in a neglect proceeding is not challenged here. Rather, we are faced with a dependency statute that empowers state officials to circumvent neglect proceedings on the theory that an unwed father is not a "parent" whose existing relationship with his children must be considered. "Parents," says the State, "means the father and mother of a legitimate child, or the survivor of them, or the natural mother of an illegitimate child, and includes any adoptive parent," Ill.Rev.Stat., c. 37, § 701–14, but the term does not include unwed fathers.

Under Illinois law, therefore, while the children of all parents can be taken from them in neglect proceedings, that is only after notice, hearing, and proof of such unfitness as a parent as amounts to neglect, an unwed father is uniquely subject to the more simplistic dependency proceeding. By use of this proceeding, the State, on showing that the father was not married to the mother, need not prove unfitness in fact, because it is presumed at law. Thus, the unwed father's claim of parental qualification is avoided as "irrelevant."

In considering this procedure under the Due Process Clause, we recognize, as we have in other cases, that due process of law does not require a hearing "in every conceivable case of government impairment of private interest." Cafeteria and Restaurant Workers Union etc. v. McElroy, 367 U.S. 886, 894.***

The private interest here, that of a man in the children he has sired and raised, undeniably warrants deference and, absent a powerful countervailing interest, protection. It is plain that the interest of a parent in the companionship, care, custody, and management of his or her children "come[s] to this Court with a momentum for respect lacking when appeal is made to liberties which derive merely from shifting economic arrangements."

The Court has frequently emphasized the importance of the family. The rights to conceive and to raise one's children have been deemed "essential," Meyer v. Nebraska, 262 U.S. 390, 399 (1923), "basic civil rights of man," Skinner v. Oklahoma, 316 U.S. 535, 541 (1942), and "[r]ights far more precious . . . than property rights," May v. Anderson, 345 U.S. 528, 533 (1953). "It is cardinal with us that the custody, care and nurture of the child reside first in the parents, whose primary function and freedom include preparation for obligations the state can neither supply nor hinder." Prince v. Massachusetts, 321 U.S. 158, 166 (1944). The integrity of the family unit has found protection in the Due Process Clause of the Fourteenth Amendment, the Equal Protection Clause of the Fourteenth Amendment, and the Ninth Amendment.

Nor has the law refused to recognize those family relationships unlegitimized by a marriage ceremony. The Court has declared unconstitutional a state statute denying natural, but illegitimate, children a wrongful-death action for the death of their mother, emphasizing that such children cannot be denied the right of other children because familial bonds in such cases were often as warm, enduring, and important as those arising within a more formally organized family unit. Levy v. Louisiana, 391 U.S. 68 (1968).

These authorities make it clear that, at the least, Stanley's interest in retaining custody of his children is cognizable and substantial.

For its part, the State has made its interest quite plain: Illinois has declared that the aim of the Juvenile Court Act is to protect "the moral, emotional, mental, and physical welfare of the minor and the best interests of the community" and to "strengthen the minor's family ties whenever possible, removing him from the custody of his parents only when his welfare or safety or the protection of the public interest cannot be adequately safeguarded without removal..." Ill.Rev.Stat., c. 37, § 701–2. These are legitimate interests, well within the power of the State to implement. We do not question the assertion that neglectful parents may be separated from their children.

But we are here not asked to evaluate the legitimacy of the state ends, rather, to determine whether the means used to achieve these ends are constitutionally defensible. What is the state interest in separating children from fathers without a hearing designed to determine whether the father is unfit in a particular disputed case? We observe that the State registers no gain towards its declared goals when it separates children from the custody of fit parents. Indeed, if Stanley is a fit father, the State spites its own articulated goals when it needlessly separates him from his family.***

It may be, as the State insists, that most unmarried fathers are unsuitable and neglectful parents. It may also be that Stanley is such a parent and that his children should be placed in other hands. But all unmarried fathers are not in this category; some are wholly suited to have custody of their children. This much the State readily concedes, and nothing in this record indicates that Stanley is or has been a neglectful father who has not cared for his children. Given the opportunity to make his case, Stanley may have been seen to be deserving of custody of his offspring. Had this been so, the State's statutory policy would have been furthered by leaving custody in him.***

[I]t may be argued that unmarried fathers are so seldom fit that Illinois need not undergo the administrative inconvenience of inquiry in any case, including Stanley's. The establishment of prompt efficacious procedures to achieve legitimate state ends is a proper state interest worthy of cognizance in constitutional adjudication. But the Constitution recognizes higher values than speed and efficiency. Indeed, one might fairly say of the Bill of Rights in general, and the Due Process Clause in particular, that they were designed to protect the fragile values of a vulnerable citizenry from the overbearing concern for efficiency and efficacy that may characterize praiseworthy government officials no less, and perhaps more, than mediocre ones.

Procedure by presumption is always cheaper and easier than individualized determination. But when, as here, the procedure forecloses the determinative issues of competence and care, when it explicitly disdains present realities in deference to past formalities, it needlessly risks running roughshod over the important interests of both parent and child. It therefore cannot stand.[1]***

We think the Due Process Clause mandates a similar result here. The State's interest in caring for Stanley's children is *de minimis* if Stanley is shown to be a fit father. It insists on presuming rather than proving Stanley's unfitness solely because it is more convenient to presume than to prove. Under the Due Process Clause that advantage is insufficient to justify refusing a father a hearing when the issue at stake is the dismemberment of his family.

The State of Illinois assumes custody of the children of married parents, divorced parents, and unmarried mothers only after a hearing and proof of neglect. The children of unmarried fathers, however, are declared dependent children without a hearing on parental fitness and without proof of neglect. Stanley's claim in the state courts and here is that failure to afford him a hearing on his parental qualifications while extending it to other parents denied him equal protection of the laws. We have concluded that all Illinois parents are constitutionally entitled to a hearing on their fitness before their children are removed from their custody. It follows that denying such a hearing to Stanley and those like him while granting it to other Illinois parents is inescapably contrary to the Equal Protection Clause.

The judgment of the Supreme Court of Illinois is reversed and the case is remanded to that court.***

[1] We note in passing that the incremental cost of offering unwed fathers an opportunity for individualized hearings on fitness appears to be minimal. If unwed fathers, in the main, do not care about the disposition of their children, they will not appear to demand hearings. If they do care, under the scheme here held invalid, Illinois would admittedly at some later time have to afford them a properly focused hearing in a custody or adoption proceeding.***

Notes and Issues for Discussion

1. If Peter had died and Joan lived, would she automatically lose the children? Why is Peter treated differently?
2. What do you think is the purpose of the statute? Without the statute, Illinois would have to find Peter if he were not living at home and then prove by the preponderance of the evidence that he was unfit. With the statute, loss of the children is automatic, and Peter could only regain them in an adoption proceeding proving that he is a fit parent.
3. In *Lehr v. Robertson*, 463 U.S. 248 (1983), the Court held that an unwed biological father who had not formally acknowledged paternity had no constitutional right to notice prior to the adoption of his child by the husband of the child's mother after she had later married. The court distinguished the case from *Stanley* in that there the father had helped to raise the children while in *Lehr* the father had not supported the child and had little contact. The Court noted: "The difference between the developed parent-child relationship that was implicated in *Stanley* . . . and the potential relationship involved . . . in this case is both clear and significant. When an unwed father demonstrates a full commitment to the responsibilities of parenthood by 'com[ing] forward to participate in the rearing of his child,' his interest in personal contact with his child acquires substantial protection under the due process clause. At that point it may be said that he 'act(s) as a father toward his children.' But the mere existence of a biological link does not merit equivalent constitutional protection. . . . The significance of the biological connection is that it offers the natural father an opportunity that no other male possesses to develop a relationship with his offspring. . . . If he fails to do so, the Federal Constitution will not automatically compel a state to listen to his opinion of where the child's best interests lie." 460 U.S. 262.

    Should the unwed father who had not provided support or rarely seen his child have a role? Consider, as the dissent pointed out, that Jonathan Lehr had offered support on several occasions only to have it rejected by the mother; the mother left the hospital with the child without telling Jonathan where they were going to live, and continued to refuse to have contact with him. He briefly saw his child after his detectives located the mother. Should this make a difference?
4. In *Michael H. v. Gerald D.*, 491 U.S. 110 (1989), Carole D. and Gerald D. were married and had a child, Victoria. However, Victoria was very likely the child of Michael H. Thereafter, Carole and Victoria lived with Gerald, then Michael, and then Scott, repeating this sequence and finally returning to Gerald. Rejecting Michael's claim to visitation based on a due process liberty interest, the Court in a plurality opinion noted "the legal issue in the present case reduces to whether the relationship between persons in the situation of Michael and Victoria has been treated as a protected family unit under historic practices of our society, or whether on any other basis it has been accorded special protection. We think it impossible to find that

it has. In fact, quite to the contrary, our traditions have protected the marital family (Gerald, Carole, and the child they acknowledge to be theirs) against the sort of claim Michael asserts." 491 U.S. at 124.

In a sharp dissent rejecting the Court's historical analysis, Justice Brennan observed: "to describe the issue in this case as whether the relationship existing between Michael and Victoria 'has been treated as a protected family unit under the historic practices of our society, or whether on any other basis it has been accorded special protection,' is to reinvent the wheel. The better approach—indeed, the one commanded by our prior cases and by common sense—is to ask whether the specific parent-child relationship under consideration is close enough to the interests that we already have protected to be deemed an aspect of 'liberty' as well. . . . The evidence is undisputed that Michael, Victoria, and Carole did live together as a family; that is, they shared the same household, Victoria called Michael 'Daddy,' Michael contributed to Victoria's support and he is eager to continue his relationship with her. Yet they are not, in the plurality's view, a 'unitary family,' whereas Gerald, Carole, and Victoria do compose such a family. The only difference between these two sets of relationships, however, is the fact of marriage. . . . However, the very premise of *Stanley* and the cases following it is that marriage is not decisive in answering the question whether the constitution protects the parental relationship under consideration. These cases are, after all, important precisely because they involve the rights of *unwed* fathers." 491 U.S. 142–144.

5. In *Karin T. v. Michael T.*, 484 N.Y.S.2d 780 (1985), the N.Y. Department of Social Services brought a support action against Michael T., alleging he was the father of two children. Michael T. argued that he was actually a woman, Marleen A. T., who, unhappy with her female identity had decided to live like a man, changing her name, clothing, and way of life. She lived with Karin T., and went through a marriage ceremony. Two children were born by means of artificial insemination. Prior to their birth, Michael T. signed a document stating that he was the husband and that the children were his. Michael T. argued that she could not be a parent and had no obligation to support. The court held: "The term 'parent' is not defined in said statute except in biological terms and the Court has found no authority to the contrary. . . . In Black's Law Dictionary . . . 'parent' is defined as "one who procreates, begets or brings forth offspring." The actions of this respondent in executing the agreement above referred to certainly brought forth these offspring as if done biologically. The contract and the equitable estoppel which prevail in the case prevent the respondent from asserting her lack of responsibility by reasons of lack of parenthood. . . ." 484 N.Y.S.2d at 784.

CREATING THE FAMILY: MARRIAGE AND COHABITATION

Marriage

"Legal union of one man and one woman as husband and wife" (Black's *Law Dictionary*, 1991).

> Contemporary marriage cannot be legally defined any more precisely than as some sort of relationship between two individuals, of indeterminate duration, involving some kind of sexual conduct, entailing vague mutual property and support obligations, a relationship which may be formed by the consent of both parties and dissolved at the will of either. (Clark, 1987: 81)

The U.S. Supreme Court has held that marriage is part of a fundamental privacy right. In striking down Virginia's ban on interracial marriages, the Court noted: "The freedom to marry has long been recognized as one of the vital personal rights essential to the orderly pursuit of happiness by free men. Marriage is one of the 'basic civil rights of man,' fundamental to our very existence and survival." *Loving v. Virginia*, 388 U.S. 1 at 12.

REGULATION OF MARRIAGE

In spite of this fundamental right, every state imposes some regulations on marriages taking place within its borders. All states forbid marriages between individuals closely related (parent and child, brother and sister, etc.) and many forbid marriage between first cousins. All states have minimum ages, usually eighteen years, for marriage without parental or judicial consent, and most have limitations on marriage of those who lack mental capacity to consent.[2]

No state at this time permits marriage between individuals of the same sex. See, for example, *Baker v. Nelson*, 191 N.W.2d 185 (Minn. 1971).[3] Denial of marriage places these individuals at a disadvantage in terms of support obligations, taxes, social security benefits, workman's compensation, unemployment benefits, inheritance and spousal privilege, among others. (See Note, "A More Perfect Union," 1992.)

In *In re Robert Paul P.*, 471 N.E.2d 424 (1984), the New York Court of Appeals upheld the denial of a petition to allow a fifty-seven-year-old male to adopt his fifty-year-old male companion, stating "If the adoption laws are to be changed so as to permit sexual lovers, homosexual or heterosexual, to adopt one another for the purpose of giving a nonmatrimonial legal status to their relationship, or if a separate institution is to be established for such purpose, it is for the Legislature, as a matter of State public policy, to do so." California permits adult adoptions; see Cal. Civ. Code § 230.10.

COMMON LAW MARRIAGE

Areen notes that by 1985, only thirteen states and the District of Columbia recognized common law marriage by statute or court decision.[4] In these states, without going through a legal marriage, a couple legally capable of marriage, who agree to marry and then live together as husband and wife, create a common law marriage.[5] The children of the marriage are legitimate and the couple has the same rights, responsibilities, and benefits of legal marriage. The legal termination of a common law marriage is a legal divorce. If one common law partner dies, the survivor then has a claim for those benefits a legal spouse would be entitled to.

An important legal issue is the impact of common law marriage on benefits to the surviving spouse. In *Orr v. Bowen*, 648 F.Supp. 1510 (1986), Louisa Orr filed a claim for lump-sum survivor's benefits on the grounds that she was the surviving widow of a common law marriage. Louisa lived with Julian Orr in Texas from 1961 to 1963 and in California and then Nevada from 1963 to 1983, when Julian died. While Texas recognized common law marriages, California and Nevada did not. From 1943 until his divorce in 1981, Julian was legally married to Bernice Orr. After the 1981 divorce, Louisa and Julian made two or three trips to Texas for up to two weeks at a time to visit her daughters. There they told others they were married. The District Court held that the couple had satisfied the Texas common law marriage statutes to which Nevada was bound by statute to give full faith and credit and that Louisa Orr could collect benefits as a surviving widow. Under 42 U.S.C. 416 (h)(1)(A), social security benefits are payable to surviving spouses as defined by state law.

DOMESTIC PARTNERSHIPS

A number of cities now have or are considering domestic partnership registration. The registration may be restricted to city employees, city residents, or it may include nonresident employees. In Seattle, for example, registration of city employees is limited to two competent, unmarried, unrelated adults of the same or opposite sex living together in a close personal relationship, jointly responsible for basic living expenses and not a domestic partner of another. As of 1991, about 5 percent of almost 10,000 Seattle city employees had registered a domestic partnership, of which 30 percent were of the same sex and 70 percent were of opposite sexes. Registration extended medical and dental insurance and sick leave to domestic partners. A few private corporations also recognize domestic partners (Lambda Legal Defense, 1992).

FAMILY DISSOLUTION: DIVORCE AND ITS AFTERMATH

Divorce is the legal severing of the marital bond. Divorce requires making significant decisions under particularly stressful circumstances. These decisions include future care, custody, support, education, and general raising of children; the division of assets and property, perhaps including the family home; and the need for alimony or support on a temporary or long-term basis. With the advent of no-fault divorce, divorce mediation, and divorce with divorce kits and without legal representation (*pro se* divorces), it is possible for more divorces to be less bitter, contentious, and acrimonious. With a prepackaged divorce kit, available in some jurisdictions, the parties can file for and get a divorce without legal advice and the accompanying legal expense. Typically such kits might cost several hundred dollars, while an uncontested divorce might cost several thousand. These *pro se* divorces are particularly useful where both parties understand the issues and consequences, can work cooperatively together, and have no major disagreements or disputes. However, those with limited resources may be tempted to use such kits despite the presence of real issues.[6] Another alternative is a divorce mediator, a professional trained in mediation who can help parties work out their differences. If courts and attorneys are skilled in adversary proceedings and structured conflict, the logic of mediation is to work out differences through compromise and conciliation away from those trained in legal combat. However, some lawyers and legal commentators have criticized mediation for just that reason: that through compromise one party may give up important rights and benefits that he or she might have won through legal combat.

No-Fault and Fault Divorces

Every state now provides for no-fault divorces, either in conjunction with traditional fault grounds for divorce or as the exclusive basis.

Traditional fault grounds (such as extreme cruelty, desertion, and adultery) were once the sole basis for divorce and could be contested as untrue or defended against on the grounds of recrimination (the divorcing party is also at fault), condonation (the divorcing party condoned the fault), and collusion (the parties together colluded in developing the grounds).

With the increasing prevalence of no-fault divorces, the frequency and importance of fault grounds has diminished and become virtually irrelevant in some states that retain them. However, in some states, fault grounds may be considered in related determinations such as alimony, property distribution, and child custody.

The California no-fault statute provides:

A court may decree a dissolution of the marriage or legal separation on either of the following grounds, which shall be pleaded generally:

(1) Irreconcilable differences, which have caused the irremediable breakdown of the marriage.

(2) Incurable insanity.

Irreconcilable differences are those grounds which are determined by the court to be substantial reasons for not continuing the marriage and which make it appear that the marriage should be dissolved.

In any pleadings or proceedings for legal separation or dissolution of marriage ... evidence of specific acts of misconduct shall be improper and inadmissible, except where child custody is in issue and such evidence is relevant to that issue. Cal. Civ. Code § 4506, § 4507, § 4509.

Annulment

After a legal annulment, the parties are viewed as never having had a valid marriage, as opposed to a divorce, which terminates an existing valid marriage. However, it is still possible in many jurisdictions to receive alimony after an annulment. Grounds for an annulment may include fraud and impotence, among others.

Separation

A legal separation occurs where the court legally recognizes the parties as living apart. Such separation may also include orders for temporary alimony, child custody, and child support.

Alimony

Alimony consists of court-ordered payments, temporary or permanent, from one spouse to the other for support and maintenance during separation or after divorce. Once only paid by the male to the female, many states now allow for alimony to be paid to either party. Alimony can be for *reimbursement*, paying for previous support or assistance, or for *rehabilitation*, aiding the spouse—usually on a short-term basis—during education, child rearing, or job searching. Permanent alimony often ceases upon remarriage. *Marvin v. Marvin,* (p. 256) accepted the concept of "palimony," enforcing express or implied agreements between unmarried cohabitants.

Division of Property

What is "property"? On what basis should it be divided? If one individual makes a greater financial contribution to the family assets should that person receive a greater share upon dissolution of the marriage? How should the nonfinancial contributions of a spouse, such as raising children, making a home, entertaining business associates, and providing emotional support be valued? In those states that call for an equitable distribution of marital assets, the contested property divisions are at the discretion of the judge, who may or may not be obliged to consider nonfinancial contributions. In community property states, one-half of all property acquired during marriage is usually awarded to each ex-spouse upon divorce.[7] Yet even in community property states, Weitzman argues that divorcing women and children experience a drastic decline in their standard of living while divorcing men experience a sharp increase (Weitzman, 1985: 339).

A sometimes difficult issue is what constitutes property. In the following case, the N.Y. Court of Appeals found that a medical license constitutes marital property and could be given a present monetary value based on future projections of earnings.

O'BRIEN v. O'BRIEN
66 N.Y.2d 576, 489 N.E.2d 712 (1985)
N.Y. COURT OF APPEALS

SIMONS, JUDGE.

In this divorce action, the parties' only asset of any consequence is the husband's newly acquired license to practice medicine. The principal issue presented is whether that license, acquired during their marriage, is marital property subject to equitable distribution under domestic Relations Law § 236(B)(5). Supreme Court held that it was and accordingly made a distributive award in defendant's favor.***On appeal to the Appellate Division, a majority of that court held that plaintiff's medical license is not marital property and that defendant was not entitled to an award for the expert witness fees.***

We now hold that plaintiff's medical license constitutes "marital property" within the meaning of Domestic Relations Law § 236(B)(1)(c) and that it is therefore subject to equitable distribution pursuant to subdivision 5 of that part.***

Plaintiff and defendant married on April 3, 1971. At the time both were employed as teachers at the same private school. Defendant had a bachelor's degree and a temporary teaching certificate but required 18 months of postgraduate classes at an approximate cost of $3,000, excluding living expenses, to obtain permanent certification in New York. She claimed, and the trial court found, that she had relinquished the opportunity to obtain permanent certification while plaintiff pursued his education. At the time of the marriage, plaintiff had completed only three and one-half years of college but shortly afterward he returned to school at night to earn his bachelor's degree and to complete sufficient premedical courses to enter medical school. In September 1973 the parties moved to Guadalajara, Mexico, where plaintiff became a full-time medical student. While he pursued his studies defendant held several teaching and tutorial positions and contributed her earnings to their joint expenses. The parties returned to New York in December 1976 so that plaintiff could complete the last two semesters of medical school and internship training here. After they returned, defendant resumed her former teaching position and she remained in it at the time this action was commenced. Plaintiff was licensed to practice medicine in October 1980. He commenced this action for divorce two months later. At the time of trial, he was a resident in general surgery.

During the marriage both parties contributed to paying the living and educational expenses and they received additional help from both of their families. They disagreed on the amounts of their respective contributions but it is undisputed that in addition to performing household work and managing the family finances defendant was gainfully employed throughout the marriage, that she contributed all of her earnings to their living and educational expenses and that her financial contributions exceeded those of plaintiff. The trial court found that she had contributed 76% of the parties' income exclusive of a $10,000 student loan obtained by defendant. Finding that plaintiff's medical degree and license are marital property, the court received evidence of its value and ordered a distributive award to defendant.

Defendant presented expert testimony that the present value of plaintiff's medical license was $472,000. Her expert testified that he arrived at this figure by comparing the average income of a college graduate and that of a general surgeon between 1985, when plaintiff's residency would end, and 2012, when he would reach age 65. After considering Federal income taxes, an inflation rate of 10% and a real interest rate of 3% he capitalized the difference in average earnings and reduced the amount to present value. He also gave his opinion that the present value of defendant's contribution to plaintiff's medical education was $103,390. Plaintiff offered no expert testimony on the subject.

The court, after considering the life-style that plaintiff would enjoy from the enhanced earning potential his medical license would bring and defendant's contributions and efforts toward attainment of it, made a distributive award to her of $188,800, representing 40% of the value of the license.***

The Equitable Distribution Law contemplates only two classes of property: marital property and separate property (Domestic Relations Law § 236[B][1][c], [d]). The former, which is subject to equitable distribution, is defined broadly as "*all* property acquired by either or both spouses during the marriage and before the execution of a separation agreement or the commencement of a matrimonial action, *regardless of the form in which title is held*" (Domestic Relations Law § 236[B][1][c] [emphasis added]; *see* § 236[B][5][b], [c]). Plaintiff does not contend that his license is excluded from distribution because it is separate property; rather, he claims that it is not property at all but represents a personal attainment in acquiring knowledge.***

Section 236 provides that in making an equitable distribution of marital property, "the court shall consider:***(6) any equitable claim to, interest in, or direct or indirect contribution made to the acquisition of such marital property by the party not having title, including joint efforts or expenditures and contributions and services as a spouse, parent, wage earner, and homemaker, and *to the career or career potential* of the other party [and]***(9) the impossibility or difficulty of evaluating any component asset or any interest in a business, corporation or *profession*" (Domestic Relations Law § 236[B][5][d][6], [9] [emphasis added]). Where equitable distribution of marital property is appropriate but "the distribution of an interest in a business, corporation or *profession* would be contrary to law" the court shall make a distributive award in lieu of an actual distribution of the property (Domestic Relations Law § 236[B][5][e] [emphasis added]. The words mean exactly what they say: that an interest in a profession or professional career potential is marital property which may be represented by direct or indirect contributions of the non-title-holding spouse, including financial contributions and nonfinancial contributions made by caring for the home and family.***

The determination that a professional license is marital property is also consistent with the conceptual base upon which the statute rests. As this case demonstrates, few undertakings during a marriage better qualify as the type of joint effort that the statute's economic partnership theory is intended to address than contributions toward one spouse's acquisition of a professional license. Working spouses are often required to contribute substantial income as wage earners, sacrifice their own educational or career goals and opportunities for child rearing, perform the bulk of household duties and responsibilities and forego the acquisition of marital assets that could have been accumulated if the professional spouse had been employed rather than occupied with the study and training necessary to acquire a professional license. In this case, nearly all of the parties' nine-year marriage was devoted to the acquisition of plaintiff's medical license and defendant played a major role in that project. She worked continuously during the marriage and contributed all of her earnings to their joint effort, she sacrificed her own educational and career opportunities, and she traveled with plaintiff to Mexico for three and one-half years while he attended medical school there. The Legislature has decided, by its explicit reference in the statute to the contributions of one spouse to the other's profession or career (*see*, Domestic Relations Law §236[B][5][d][6], [9]; [e]), that these contributions represent investments in the economic partnership of the marriage and that the product of the parties' joint efforts, the professional license, should be considered marital property.***

Turning to the question of valuation, it has been suggested that even if a professional license is considered marital property, the working spouse is entitled only to reimbursement of his or her direct financial contributions (*see*, Note, *Equitable Distribution of Degrees and Licenses: Two Theories Toward Compensating*

Spousal Contributions, 49 Brooklyn L.Rev. 301, 317–322). By parity of reasoning, a spouse's down payment on real estate or contribution to the purchase of securities would be limited to the money contributed, without any remuneration for any incremental value in the asset because of price appreciation. Such a result is completely at odds with the statute's requirement that the court give full consideration to both direct and indirect contributions "made to the acquisition of such marital property by the party not having title, including joint *efforts* or expenditures and *contributions and services as a spouse, parent,* wage earner *and homemaker"* (Domestic Relations Law § 236[B][5][d][6] [emphasis added]). If the license is marital property, then the working spouse is entitled to an equitable portion of it, not a return of funds advanced. Its value is the enhanced earning capacity it affords the holder and although fixing the present value of that enhanced earning capacity may present problems, the problems are not insurmountable. Certainly they are no more difficult than computing tort damages for wrongful death or diminished earning capacity resulting from injury and they differ only in degree from the problems presented when valuing a professional practice for purposes of a distributive award, something the courts have not hesitated to do.***

Accordingly, in view of our holding that plaintiff's license to practice medicine is marital property, the order of the Appellate Division should be modified, with costs to defendant, by reinstating the judgment***

MEYER, JUDGE (concurring).

I concur in Judge Simons' opinion but write separately to point up for consideration by the Legislature the potential for unfairness involved in distributive awards based upon a license of a professional still in training.***

The present case points up the problem. A medical license is but a step toward the practice ultimately engaged in by its holder, which follows after internship, residency and, for particular specialties, board certification. Here it is undisputed that plaintiff was in a residency for general surgery at the time of the trial, but had the previous year done a residency in internal medicine. Defendant's expert based his opinion on the difference between the average income of a general surgeon and that of a college graduate of plaintiff's age and life expectancy, which the trial judge utilized, impliedly finding that plaintiff would engage in a surgical practice despite plaintiff's testimony that he was dissatisfied with the general surgery program he was in and was attempting to return to the internal medicine training he had been in the previous year. The trial judge had the right, of course, to discredit that testimony, but the point is that equitable distribution was not intended to permit a judge to make a career decision for a licensed spouse still in training. Yet the degree of speculation involved in the award made is emphasized by the testimony of the expert on which it was based. Asked whether his assumptions and calculations were in any way speculative, he replied: "Yes. They're speculative to the extent of, will Dr. O'Brien practice medicine? Will Dr. O'Brien earn more or less than the average surgeon earns? Will Dr. O'Brien live to age sixty-five? Will Dr. O'Brien have a heart attack or will he be injured in an automobile accident? Will he be disabled? I mean, there is a degree of speculation."***

The equitable distribution provisions of the Domestic Relations Law were intended to provide flexibility so that equity could be done. But if the assumption as to career choice on which a distributive award payable over a number of years is based turns out not to be the fact (as, for example, should a general surgery trainee accidentally lose the use of his hand), it should be possible for the court to revise the distributive award to conform to the fact.***

Notes and Issues for Discussion

1. In *Mahoney v. Mahoney*, 453 A.2d 527 (1982), the New Jersey Supreme Court found that an M.B.A. degree was not marital property, noting that calculating the present value of projected future earnings was "little more than guesswork." The court did, however, introduce the concept of reimbursement alimony, through which the former spouse could recoup her past expenses associated with her ex-husband's degree. Is an M.B.A. degree more difficult to value than a professional practice?
2. Under the Retirement Equity Act amendments to the Employment Retirement Income Security Act, 29 U.S.C. § 1001 *et seq.*, pension accumulations are subject to distribution to nonparticipants if there is a qualified domestic relations order.

Prenuptial Contracts

In *DeLorean v. DeLorean*, 211 N.J. Super 432, 511 A.2d 1257 (1986), the court was faced with a prenuptial contract which stated "any and all property, income and earnings acquired by each before and after the marriage shall be the separate property of the person acquiring same, without any rights, title or control vesting in the other person." Finding the contract was not unconscionable, the wife was not subject to duress, had consulted an attorney prior to signing the contract (who advised her not to sign), and was aware in a general sense of her intended husband's wealth although unaware his assets exceeded $20 million, the court upheld the contract.

Child Support

Child support generally reflects a calculation of the child's needs and the parents' ability to pay, and although later modifications are possible, requires estimates of current and projections of future expenses. Without careful attention these costs may be substantially underestimated, since they include far more than food, clothing, and shelter. While there is wide discretion in awarding child support, there is a move toward using established formulas based on relative incomes and number of children.[8] Should child support extend beyond the age of majority? States vary, with some doing so, sometimes until completion of college, while others do not.[9]

Enforcement of child support orders remains a major hurdle.

> There are basically three reasons child support is difficult to enforce. First, the father may not have the resources to make the payments. Second, the mother may have great difficulty in locating the father. . . . Third, even if the father can be located, if he now resides in a state different from that where the mother and child are found, there are substantial difficulties relating to interstate enforcement. (Mnookin and Weisberg, 1989: 234)

Among important legislation in this area is the Uniform Reciprocal Enforcement of Support Act, now in effect in every state, which provides for the enforcement of out-of-state support orders. The Federal Child Support Act of 1974, 42 U.S.C. § 659, allows for the garnishment of federal payments. Under the Omnibus Budget Reconciliation Act of 1981 (P.L. 97–35) past due child payments can be deducted from federal income tax refunds. The Child Support Enforcement Amendments of 1984 (P.L. 98–378) allow for automatic withholding of overdue support from all wages.

Child Custody and Visitation

With the awarding of custody, one parent is usually given the power to make decisions for the child, unless otherwise specified in the custody order. These decisions may include schooling, religious instruction, medical care, and normal day-to-day life decisions. While the noncustodial parent may offer suggestions and express wishes, the final decision-making authority resides with the custodial parent. One exception to this general rule is joint custody, where often there is a sharing of decision-making power. Legal custody generally has to do with decision making. It may correspond to physical custody, a determination of the child's living arrangements, but it need not. The child's preferences may be considered, especially preferences of older children, but they need not be determinative. Traditionally, under the "tender years" doctrine, custody of younger children was usually awarded to the mother. Recently many states have moved away from this approach, placing both parents on more equal footing, with the custody decision based on a determination of what would be in the best interests of the child.

BEST INTEREST STANDARD

"Best interests" may include a number of factors, ranging from the fitness of the parents and their ability to care for the child to considerations such as life-styles, religious preference, and sexual orientation. These factors may come into play in the initial custody award, or in later requests for modification of the award due to subsequent changes. Consider the following cases.

JARRETT v. JARRETT
78 Ill.2d 337, 400 N.E.2d 421 (1979)
ILLINOIS SUPREME COURT

UNDERWOOD, JUSTICE.

On December 6, 1976, Jacqueline Jarrett received a divorce from Walter Jarrett in the circuit court of Cook County on grounds of extreme and repeated mental cruelty. The divorce decree, by agreement, also awarded Jacqueline custody of the three Jarrett children subject to the father's right of visitation at reasonable times. Seven months later, alleging changed conditions, Walter petitioned the circuit court to modify the divorce decree and award him custody of the children. The circuit court granted his petition subject to the mother's right of visitation at reasonable times, but a majority of the appellate court reversed and we granted leave to appeal.

During their marriage, Walter and Jacqueline had three daughters, who, at the time of the divorce, were 12, 10 and 7 years old. In addition to custody of the children, the divorce decree also awarded Jacqueline the use of the family home, and child support; Walter received visitation rights at all reasonable times and usually had the children from Saturday evening to Sunday evening. In April 1977, five months after the divorce, Jacqueline informed Walter that she planned to have her boyfriend, Wayne Hammon, move into the family home with her. Walter protested, but Hammon moved in on May 1, 1977. Jacqueline and Hammon thereafter cohabited in the Jarrett home but did not marry.

The children, who were not "overly enthused" when they first learned that Hammon would move into the family home with them, asked Jacqueline if she intended to marry Hammon, but Jacqueline responded that she did not know. At the modification hearing Jacqueline testified that she did not want to remarry because it was too soon after her divorce; because she did not believe that a marriage license makes a relationship; and because the divorce decree required her to sell the family home within six months after remarriage. She did not want to sell the house because the children did not want to move and she could not afford to do so. Jacqueline explained to the children that some people thought it was wrong for an unmarried man and woman to live together but she thought that what mattered was that they loved each other. Jacqueline testified that she told some neighbors that Hammon would move in with her but she had not received any adverse comments. Jacqueline further testified that the children seemed to develop an affectionate relationship with Hammon, who played with them, helped them with their homework, and verbally disciplined them. Both Jacqueline and Hammon testified at the hearing that they did not at that time have any plans to marry. In oral argument before this court Jacqueline's counsel conceded that she and Hammon were still living together unmarried.

Walter Jarrett testified that he thought Jacqueline's living arrangements created a moral environment which was not a proper one in which to raise three young girls. He also testified that the children were always clean, healthy, and well dressed and well nourished when he picked them up, and that when he talked with his oldest daughter, Kathleen, she did not object to Jacqueline's living arrangement.

The circuit court found that it was "necessary for the moral and spiritual well-being and development" of the children that Walter receive custody. In reversing, the appellate court reasoned that the record did not reveal any negative effects on the children caused by Jacqueline's cohabitation with Hammon, and that the circuit court had not found Jacqueline unfit. It declined to consider potential future harmful effects of the cohabitation on the children.***

The chief issue in this case is whether a change of custody predicated upon the open and continuing cohabitation of the custodial parent with a member of the opposite sex is contrary to the manifest weight of the evidence in the absence of any tangible evidence of contemporaneous adverse effect upon the minor children. Considering the principles previously enunciated, and the statutory provisions, and prior decisions of the courts of this State, we conclude that under the facts in this case the trial court properly transferred custody of the Jarrett children from Jacqueline to Walter Jarrett.

The relevant standards of conduct are expressed in the statutes of this State: Section 11–8 of the Criminal Code of 1961 (Ill.Rev.Stat.1977, ch. 38, par. 11–8) provides that "[a]ny person who cohabits or has sexual intercourse with another not his spouse commits fornication if the behavior is open and notorious." In *Hewitt v. Hewitt* (1979), 77 Ill.2d 49, 61–62 we emphasized the refusal of the General Assembly in enacting the new Illinois Marriage and Dissolution of Marriage Act to sanction any nonmarital relationships and its declaration of the purpose to "strengthen and preserve the integrity of marriage and safeguard family relationships" (Ill.Rev.Stat. 1977, ch. 40, par. 102(2)).

Jacqueline argues, however, that her conduct does not affront public morality because such conduct is now widely accepted, and cites 1978 Census Bureau statistics that show 1.1 million households composed of an unmarried man and woman, close to a quarter of which also include at least one child. This is essentially the same argument we rejected last term in *Hewitt v. Hewitt*, and it is equally unpersuasive here. The number of people living in such households forms only a small percentage of the adult population, but more to the point, the statutory interpretation urged upon us by Jacqueline simply nullifies the fornication statute. The logical conclusion of her argument is that the statutory prohibitions are void as to those who believe the proscribed acts are not immoral, or, for one reason or another, need not be heeded. So stated, of course, the argument defeats itself. The rules which our society enacts for the governance of its members are not limited to those who agree with those rules—they are equally binding on the dissenters. The fornication statute and the Illinois Marriage and Dissolution of Marriage Act evidence the relevant moral standards of this State, as declared by our legislature. The open and notorious limitation on the former's prohibitions reflects both a disinclination to criminalize purely private relationships and a recognition that open fornication represents a graver threat to public morality than private violations. Conduct of that nature, when it is open, not only violates the statutorily expressed moral standards of the State, but also encourages others to violate those standards, and debases public morality. While we agree that the statute does not penalize conduct which is essentially private and discreet, Jacqueline's conduct has been neither, for she has discussed this relationship and her rationalization of it with at least her children, her former husband and her neighbors. It is, in our judgment, clear that her conduct offends prevailing public policy.

Jacqueline's disregard for existing standards of conduct instructs her children, by example, that they, too, may ignore them and could well encourage the children to engage in similar activity in the future. That factor, of course, supports the trial court's conclusion that their daily presence in that environment was injurious to the moral well-being and development of the children.***

While our comments have focused upon the moral hazards, we are not convinced that open cohabitation does not also affect the mental and emotional health of the children. Jacqueline's testimony at the hearing indicated that when her children originally learned that Wayne Hammon would move in with them, they initially expected that she would marry him. It is difficult to predict what psychological effects or problems may later develop from their efforts to overcome the disparity between their concepts of propriety and their mother's conduct. Nor will their attempts to adjust to this new environment occur in a vacuum. Jacqueline's domestic arrangements are known to her neighbors and their children; testimony at the hearing indicated that Wayne Hammon played with the Jarrett children and their friends at the Jarrett home and also engaged in other activities with them. If the Jarrett children remained in that situation, they might well be compelled to try to explain Hammon's presence to their friends and, perhaps, to endure their taunts and jibes. In a case such as this the trial judge must also weigh these imponderables, and he is not limited to examining the children for current physical manifestations of emotional or mental difficulties.

Accordingly, we reverse the judgment of the appellate court and affirm the judgment of the circuit court of Cook County.

GOLDENHERSH, CHIEF JUSTICE, with whom THOMAS J. MORAN, JUSTICE, joins, dissenting:

The majority states, "The chief issue in this case is whether a change of custody predicated upon the open and continuing cohabitation of the custodial parent with a member of the opposite sex is contrary to the manifest weight of the evidence in the absence of any tangible evidence of contemporaneous adverse effect upon the minor children." An examination of the opinion fails to reveal any other issue, and the effect of the decision is that the plaintiff's cohabitation with Hammon *per se* was sufficient grounds for changing the custody order previously entered. This record shows clearly that the children were healthy, well adjusted, and well cared for, and it should be noted that both the circuit and appellate courts made no finding that plaintiff was an unfit mother. The majority, too, makes no such finding and based its decision on a nebulous concept of injury to the children's "moral well-being and development." I question that any competent sociologist would attribute the increase of "live in" unmarried couples to parental example.

The fragility of its conclusion concerning "prevailing public policy" is demonstrated by the majority's reliance on cases decided by this court in 1852 (*Searls v. People*, 13 Ill. 597) and 1902 (*Lyman v. People*, 198 Ill. 344, 64 N.E. 974), and an appellate court decision (*People v. Potter* (1943), 319 Ill. App. 409, 49 N.E.2d 307) which, rather than "prevailing public policy," more clearly indicates the prejudice extant in that period against interracial sexual relations.

As the appellate court pointed out, the courts should not impose the personal preferences and standards of the judiciary in the decision of this case. Courts are uniquely equipped to decide legal issues and are well advised to leave to the theologians the question of the morality of the living arrangement into which the plaintiff had entered.

As a legal matter, simply stated, the majority has held that on the basis of her presumptive guilt of fornication, a Class B misdemeanor, plaintiff, although not declared to be an unfit mother, has forfeited the right to have the custody of her children. This finding flies in the face of the established rule that, in order to modify or amend an award of custody, the evidence must show that the parent to whom custody of the children was originally awarded is unfit to retain custody, or that a change of conditions makes a change of custody in their best interests. This record fails to show either. Mr. Justice Moran and I dissent and would affirm the decision of the appellate court.

MORAN, JUSTICE, with whom GOLDENHERSH, CHIEF JUSTICE, joins, dissenting:
I join in the dissent of the chief justice, but also dissent separately. My primary disagreement with the majority lies with its countenancing a change of custody based solely on a *conclusive presumption* that harm to the Jarrett children stemmed from Jacqueline's living arrangements. The majority purports to follow the Illinois Marriage and Dissolution of Marriage Act. Yet, under that act, only on the basis of fact can there be a finding that a change in circumstances has occurred and that modification of the prior custody judgment is necessary to serve the best interest of the children. The court is not to consider conduct of a custodian if that conduct does not affect his relationship to the child. In this case, not one scintilla of actual or statistical evidence of harm or danger to the children has been presented. To the contrary, all of the evidence of record, as related by the majority, indicates that under Jacqueline's custodianship the children's welfare and needs were met. Also, the trial court expressly declined to find Jacqueline unfit. Nevertheless, the majority's finding of a violation of the seldom-enforced fornication statute effectively foreclosed any further consideration of the custody issue. Instead of focusing solely on the best interest of the children—the "guiding star"— the majority has utilized child custody as a vehicle to punish Jacqueline for her "misconduct." Such selective enforcement of a statute is inappropriate and, especially in the child-custody context, unfortunate.***

M.A.B. v. R.B.
134 Misc.2d 317, 510 N.Y.S.2d 960 (1986)
NEW YORK SUPREME COURT

Morton I. Willen, J.

The plaintiff mother in this proceeding, M.A.B., applied to the court in June 1985, seeking to modify a judgment of divorce entered June 14, 1984. She wishes the court to permit her to move to Florida with her three children. The defendant father, R.B., cross-moved for a modification of the same divorce judgment, seeking to have sole custody of their 12-year-old son, B., awarded to him. He does not seek custody of the two younger children and opposes their removal to Florida.***

The parties were married in 1970, separated in 1978 and divorced in 1984. There are three infant issue of the marriage, B., born November 27, 1973, J., born February 22, 1976, and T., born July 2, 1977. The judgment of divorce incorporated the parties' stipulation which included the provision of joint custody of their three children but that the children were to reside with plaintiff mother permanently in the State of New York. In general, the parties have followed this custodial arrangement. There was a five-month period between February and June 1985, when B. resided with his father.

While the marriage between the parties was dissolved in an uncontested proceeding by reason of the abandonment of the mother by the father, the record indicates other problems in the marriage caused the breakup.

In May 1978, the defendant revealed to the plaintiff that he was a homosexual. Thereafter, the parties had a trial separation during which period they sought marital counseling. Ultimately the defendant indicated that he "could not in good conscience return" to their home and since 1978 has chosen to live with a male partner.

Since 1973, some five years prior to the revelation and separation, the mother has had severe health problems which she testified caused her to be hospitalized as an in-patient about 80 times in the past 10 years. These frequent hospitalizations have often resulted in the children being cared for by her parents, the defendant or his parents.

At the outset it is important to note that both parents love B. very much and B., in an in camera interview, stated he knew his parents loved him and that he also loved both of them. He also stated his strong desire to remain with his mother expressing embarrassment and discomfort with the fact of his father's homosexuality. Unfortunately, B. is a troubled young man. He admits to having school troubles as early as first grade, coinciding approximately with his parents' separation. The mother testified that he got "harder and harder" to handle shortly after the parties divorced. School records indicate that he has been suspended from school numbers of times in recent years for being a poor school citizen (i.e., mooning the class, leaving class without permission, giving the finger, causing class disturbances, fighting, cutting class and sticking a classmate with a compass point). School records further indicate that B. did not pass any of his major seventh grade courses this year, with the exception of a "D" in one course and an "A" in physical education. B. was referred to the school's Committee on the Handicapped in early 1986. The Committee did not classify him as educationally handicapped but judged that he had a serious lack of impulse control causing problems in school. The Committee urged counseling to focus on control of impulses and growth of self-esteem. B.'s out-of-school behavior has also been troublesome at times. At trial his mother testified that at age 10 he used alcohol which he took from the house. During the same year, B. removed $10 or $20 from his mother's household which he gave to a friend for purchase of marihuana.

The father testified that in November 1984, upon returning from a European business trip, four calls from B.'s school were on his telephone answering machine. The father called Dr. Wayne Warren, then B.'s psychologist, about B.'s school suspensions. Dr. Warren, whose services were obtained by the mother when the school principal recommended counseling, saw the parents for some 3 or 4 sessions, was made aware of the family situation including the father's homosexuality. The father indicated to Dr. Warren that he could change his job situation and travel less in order to be more available to help B. He asked Dr. Warren if it would be beneficial to B. if he were to move in with him. At a meeting in January 1985, of both parents, Dr. Warren, and B., the father presented the mother with the idea, recommended by Dr. Warren, that B. live with him. Initially, she agreed it would be positive, but then objected to the idea due to the fact that the father's live-in partner would continue living there. The mother testified that three weeks later, in February 1985, she called the father saying that B. could stay with him on a trial basis to see if it would help him psychologically. The father testified that she called to say she had been hasty in her objections that she could no longer handle B., and that B. could move in with him. Dr. Warren testified that he recommended that B. live with the father because B. was having problems in and out of school and that the mother was overwhelmed and could no longer handle him. In February 1985, B. went to live with his father where he remained until June 1985.

While in his father's custody, B. was subjected to a more structured environment. Consistency improved. The father took a demotion on his job to be local and more available day to day for B.***A letter from the school principal on June 18, 1985, to the father contained her comment: "It is interesting to note that from April through June of this year, during the time B. was living with you his behavior was improved, indicated by the lack of referrals***Thank you so much for all your understanding and cooperation." In June 1985, after a confrontation between the mother and the father about the mother's planned relocation to Florida, during which the father announced his intention to fight the planned move, the mother refused to return B. to the father. Since June 1985, around the time this action was commenced, B. has been in the physical custody of his mother.

It is important to note that the school recommended counseling for B. and that B. stopped therapy in August 1985, shortly after he returned to her. The mother testified that it was painful for B. to talk with anyone but her, that she could not get him to go to therapy anymore, and that she became his therapist. She stated: "After we talk, he feels better. I consider me to be his therapist." Evidently the boy's problems became worse by the end of the trial in May 1986, and the mother found another therapist for the child. However, again the mother gave in to the boy's desire that he be allowed to terminate therapy. While all of this was going on the boy was dropping one summer session course, barely getting by in another and the subject of further disciplinary proceedings at his school.

The father maintains that it would be in B.'s best interest if an award of physical custody was made to him. The court agrees, and in so doing follows the standard enunciated in *Friederwitzer v Friederwitzer* (55 NY2d 89, 95): "The standard ultimately to be applied remains the best interests of the child when all of the applicable factors are considered, not whether there exists one or more circumstances that can be denominated extraordinary." The record indicates that B. fared far better with his father than with his mother. B.'s father altered his job position to be more available to him. B.'s mother is frequently hospitalized (25 to 30 times in the last two years) with colitis and other ailments for periods of 1 to 2 weeks during which time B.'s care is left to the grandparents and friends. B. needs professional counseling, something which he has resisted for over a year, with the mother's complicity, believing herself to be an adequate substitute, during which period B.'s behavior in school and home have deteriorated severely. That B. needs a guiding hand to see him through his difficulties in school is clear. His father has provided guidance by his effective use of the card-point system and his frequent contact with school officials, teachers, counselors and psychologists. B. has had problems on school field trips, even when accompanied by his mother. However, on a fifth grade trip to the Statue of Liberty when his father acted as a group leader B. and his classmates wrote the father letters of thanks. On March 18, 1985, B. wrote to his father: "My classmates loved the trip and thought it was terrific***You made that day a nice day for everyone in my group. They all are telling me to pick them for my group if you have another trip. Love, B."

***B.'s father has demonstrated appropriate discipline and consistency which is needed by B. at this time in his life.

In contrast, B.'s mother has been unable to sustain the requisite wherewithal to deal effectively with the child's manipulative tendencies.

The mother testified that her frequent and severe health problems are a physical result of finding out that her husband had a male lover. Undoubtedly this is a contributing factor. However, the record indicates that she has had 80 hospitalizations since 1976, that her health problems date back to 1973, shortly after the birth of B. and predate her knowledge of her former husband's homosexuality. Her medical problems are of such severity that she is totally disabled and receives $820 per month in disability payments. She testified she suffers from peritonitis, endomytriosis and colitis. She has had eight operations in 10 years, seven abdominal, one chest, and some 80 in-patient hospitalizations over this period and is on a large number of medications, pain-killers, mild tranquilizers, zyloprim, tranzene and percoset.

The mother contends that B. is an impressionable adolescent who is well aware of, and strongly rejects, his father's homosexuality. She argues that it is unavoidable that the father's homosexuality would adversely affect B. if physical custody were awarded to the father. The evidence is to the contrary. The father's behavior has been discreet, not flamboyant. His relationship with his partner is apparently stable and of eight years' duration. Testimony was given and not challenged that neither had engaged in any other homosexual relationships. The father acknowledges that B.'s sexual orientation is heterosexual, and he has stated that he has no intention of interfering with this. That B. has conflicts with regard to his father's homosexuality may not be ignored. These conflicts create anxiety which Dr. Warren testified require further therapy to be worked through. B. is difficult and defiant and acts out his anxieties. However, B.'s acting out behavior far outdates his awareness of his father's sexual orientation, and, according to his former therapist, the boy faces not only this problem but the mother's repeated hospitalizations as a source of major anxiety. B. has a tendency to blame himself for his father's homosexuality and for his mother's ill health, which Dr. Warren testified was understandable, if not normal. Accordingly, the court finds that the father's homosexuality and the mother's poor health have had an adverse effect upon B. Given the realities of reactions that may be anticipated from B.'s peers, the taunting, teasing and ostracism, B. will have genuine social pressure to grapple with and will require strength to integrate the fact of his father's homosexuality into his own life. To accept that these problems are inevitable is, however, a long distance from saying that the father's homosexual *conduct* has had an adverse effect upon B.

The court in *M.P. v S.P.* (169 NJ Super 425, 436–439, 404 A2d 1256, 1262–1263) addressed this issue:

"Plaintiff's argument overlooks, too, the fact that the children's exposure to embarrassment is not dependent upon the identity of the parent with whom they happen to reside. Their discomfiture, if any, comes about not because of living with defendant, but because she is their mother, because she is a lesbian, and because the community will not accept her. Neither prejudices of the small community in which they live nor the curiosity of their peers about the defendant's sexual nature will be abated by a change of custody. Hard facts must be faced. These are matters which courts cannot control, and there is little to gain by creating an artificial world where the children may dream that life is different than it is.

"Furthermore, the law governing grants of custody does not yield to such narrow considerations. Of overriding importance is that within the context of a loving and supportive relationship there is no reason to think that the girls will be unable to manage whatever anxieties may flow from the community's disapproval of their mother***

"If defendant retains custody, it may be that because the community is intolerant of her differences these girls may sometimes have to bear themselves with greater than ordinary fortitude. But this does not necessarily portend that their moral welfare or safety will be jeopardized. It is just as reasonable to expect that they will emerge better equipped to search out their own standards of right and wrong, better able to perceive that the majority is not always correct in its moral judgments, and better able to understand the importance of conforming their beliefs to the requirements of reason and tested knowledge, not the constraints of currently popular sentiment or prejudice.

"Taking the children from defendant can be done only at the cost of sacrificing those very qualities they will find most sustaining in meeting the challenges inevitably ahead. Instead of forbearance and feelings of protectiveness, it will foster in them a sense of shame for their mother. Instead of courage and the precept that people of integrity do not shrink from bigots, it counsels that easy option of shirking difficult problems and following the course of expedience. Lastly, it diminishes their regard for the rule of human behavior, everywhere accepted, that we do not forsake those to whom we are indebted for love and nurture solely because they are held in low esteem by others.

"We conclude that the children's best interests will be disserved by undermining in this way their growth as mature and principled adults. Extensive evidence in the record upon which we have not commented amply confirms the trial judge's finding that defendant is a worthy mother. Nothing suggests that her homosexual preference in itself presents any threat of harm to her daughters or that in the ordinary course of their development they will be unable to deal with whatever vexation may be caused to their spirits by the community."

Supportive of this view is the decision of the United States Supreme Court in *Palmore v Sidoti* (466 US 429, 433 [1984]) wherein it was stated: "[The issue is] whether***private biases and the possible injury they might inflict are permissible consideration for removal of an infant child from the custody of its natural mother. We have little difficulty concluding that they are not. The Constitution cannot control such prejudices but neither can it tolerate them. Private biases may be outside the reach of the law, but the law cannot, directly or indirectly, give them effect."

One commentator has recently outlined the reasons why homosexual parents are often denied custody. "The reasons given boil down to a few arguments: if gay parents have custody, they will molest the children; if gay parents have custody, they will turn the children into homosexuals; if gay parents have custody, they will perform sex acts in front of the children; if gay parents have custody, the children will be harmed because of the immoral environment." (Rivera, *Queer Law: Sexual Orientation Law In the Mid-Eighties*, 11 U Dayton L Rev 275, 329.) Until the 1970's, few homosexual parents were successful in custody cases.***

Since Domestic Relations Law § 240(1) gives the court great discretion in making custody decisions, Judges often seek expert opinions. The court here relies on the testimony of Dr. Wayne Warren, B.'s former therapist. Dr. Warren saw B. 42 times and the parents six times from June 1984, until August 1985. In February 1985, he recommended that B. live with his homosexual father because he offered more consistency. The court is also mindful of the expert opinions from two cases already mentioned regarding the effect that homosexuality has on parenting skills. In *Bezio* the court relied on the testimony of Dr. Alexandra Kaplan, a clinical psychologist and professor of psychology at the University of Massachusetts: "'There is no evidence at all that sexual preference of adults in the home has any detrimental impact on children . . . [M]any other issues influence child rearing. Sexual preference per se is typically not one of them***[M]ost children raised in homosexual situation[s] become heterosexual as adults . . . There is no evidence that children who are raised with a loving couple of the same sex are any more disturbed, unhealthy, [or] maladjusted than children raised with a loving couple of mixed sex.'"

In *Doe* the court said: "Four psychiatrists testified at trial. As put by the trial judge, and the record supports him, 'three of these people were of the opinion that the [homosexual] wife's lifestyle, in and of itself, would not adversely affect the minor child should the wife be awarded some form of custody.' [Note: The fourth psychiatrist was not credible because he had no supporting studies and his exposure to homosexual parents was limited.] Further, one of these three witnesses testified to a study he had conducted comparing single parent heterosexuals with minor children to single homosexual parents with minor children. He found 'no difference in the minor children and no evidence of sexual dysfunction to a minor child reared by a single homosexual parent.'"

The court finds that R.B. is a caring, worthy father. His homosexuality is not flaunted and has no adverse deleterious effect on his 12-year-old son. In view of the cases cited, the court finds that it is impermissible as a matter of law to decide the question of custody on the basis of the father's sexual orientation. The guiding consideration must be B.'s best interest. At this time, B.'s needs can best be met by his father. B. shall reside permanently with his father, R.B., in the State of New York. R.B. shall have day-to-day control over B.'s actions and M.A.B., the boy's mother, shall have liberal visitation with B. away from the custodial residence. The parents shall consult with each other with reference to items of major importance affecting the health, welfare and education of B., especially counseling. Both parents shall have input on all major decisions involving B.

Notes and Issues for Discussion

1. The *Jarrett* case illustrates the wide latitude trial courts have in making not only original custody determinations but also modifications. What is potential harm to the three children? Are there indications that Jacqueline and Wayne's relationship has harmed them to date? The court observes "While . . . the statute does not penalize conduct which is essentially private and discreet, Jacqueline's conduct has been neither, for she has discussed this relationship and her rationalization of it with at least her children, her former husband and her neighbors. It is, in our judgment, clear that her conduct offends prevailing public policy." What do you think?

2. In situations involving gay or lesbian parents, courts are divided, some holding as in *M.A.B.* that homosexuality is not relevant in determining best interests, others holding that it is. See for example, *Roe v. Roe*, 228 Va. 722, 324 S.E.2d 691 at 694 (1985), where the court said of a homosexual father: "The father's continuous exposure of the child to his immoral and illicit relationship renders him an unfit and improper custodian as a matter of law."

3. The *M.A.B.* court refused to allow M.A.B. to modify the divorce judgment and move with the remaining children to Florida: "Both parents need to be near B., J., and T., and the children need to be near their parents." 134 Misc. 2d. at 332.

4. In *Stewart v. Stewart*, 521 N.E. 956 (1988), the Indiana Court of Appeals reversed a lower court order terminating visitation rights of a father who tested positive for HIV. The court noted that the trial court had inaccurately stated, "What you have proved is that Mr. Stewart has AIDS, and even if, even if there's a one percent chance that this child is going to contract it from him, I'm not going to expose her to it." The appeals court said, "[I]n light of the medical evidence presented, the complete termination of visitation was an extreme and unwarranted action. When courts are confronted with new situations and problems regarding visitation, they must be sure that the action corresponds to the danger presented. Many parents suffer from varying degrees of handicaps and illnesses. Yet those parents cannot be deprived of all visitation with their children merely because some danger exists. The level of danger must be examined and appropriate precautions taken. Only in this way can both the parent's visitation rights and the child's health and welfare be fairly and fully protected. This was not done in the present case." 521 N.E. at 965.

In the following case, the issues include the validity of a surrogate mother contract and the custody of the child who was born.

MATTER OF BABY M.
109 N.J. 396, 537 A.2d 1227 (1988)
NEW JERSEY SUPREME COURT

WILENTZ, C.J.

In this matter the Court is asked to determine the validity of a contract that purports to provide a new way of bringing children into a family. For a fee of $10,000, a woman agrees to be artificially inseminated with the semen of another woman's husband; she is to conceive a child, carry it to term, and after its birth surrender it to the natural father and his wife. The intent of the contract is that the child's natural mother will thereafter be forever separated from her child. The wife is to adopt the child, and she and the natural father are to be regarded as its parents for all purposes. The contract providing for this is called a "surrogacy contract," the natural mother inappropriately called the "surrogate mother."

We invalidate the surrogacy contract because it conflicts with the law and public policy of this State. While we recognize the depth of the yearning of infertile couples to have their own children, we find the payment of money to a "surrogate" mother illegal, perhaps criminal, and potentially degrading to women. Although in this case we grant custody to the natural father, the evidence having clearly proved such custody to be in the best interests of the infant, we void both the termination of the surrogate mother's parental rights and the adoption of the child by the wife/stepparent. We thus restore the "surrogate" as the mother of the child. We remand the issue of the natural mother's visitation rights to the trial court, since that issue was not reached below and the record before us is not sufficient to permit us to decide it *de novo*.

We find no offense to our present laws where a woman voluntarily and without payment agrees to act as a "surrogate" mother, provided that she is not subject to a binding agreement to surrender her child. Moreover, our holding today does not preclude the Legislature from altering the current statutory scheme, within constitutional limits, so as to permit surrogacy contracts. Under current law, however, the surrogacy agreement before us is illegal and invalid.

In February 1985, William Stern and Mary Beth Whitehead entered into a surrogacy contract. It recited that Stern's wife, Elizabeth, was infertile, that they wanted a child, and that Mrs. Whitehead was willing to provide that child as the mother with Mr. Stern as the father.

The contract provided that through artificial insemination using Mr. Stern's sperm, Mrs. Whitehead would become pregnant, carry the child to term, bear it, deliver it to the Sterns, and thereafter do whatever was necessary to terminate her maternal rights so that Mrs. Stern could thereafter adopt the child. Mrs. Whitehead's husband, Richard, was also a party to the contract; Mrs. Stern was not. Mr. Whitehead promised to do all acts necessary to rebut the presumption of paternity under the Parentage Act. *N.J.S.A.* 9:17–43a(1), –44a. Although Mrs. Stern was not a party to the surrogacy agreement, the contract gave her sole custody of the child in the event of Mr. Stern's death. Mrs. Stern's status as a nonparty to the surrogate parenting agreement presumably was to avoid the application of the baby-selling statute to this arrangement. *N.J.S.A.* 9:3-54.

Mr. Stern, on his part, agreed to attempt the artificial insemination and to pay Mrs. Whitehead $10,000 after the child's birth, on its delivery to him. In a separate contract, Mr. Stern agreed to pay $7,500 to the Infertility Center of New York ("ICNY"). The Center's advertising campaigns solicit surrogate mothers and encourage infertile couples to consider surrogacy. ICNY arranged for the surrogacy contract by bringing the parties together, explaining the process to them, furnishing the contractual form, and providing legal counsel.

The history of the parties' involvement in this arrangement suggests their good faith. William and Elizabeth Stern were married in July 1974, having met at the University of Michigan, where both were Ph.D. candidates. Due to financial considerations and Mrs. Stern's pursuit of a medical degree and residency, they decided to defer starting a family until 1981. Before then, however, Mrs. Stern learned that she might have multiple sclerosis and that the disease in some cases renders pregnancy a serious health risk. Her anxiety appears to have exceeded the actual risk, which current medical authorities assess as minimal. Nonetheless that anxiety was evidently quite real, Mrs. Stern fearing that pregnancy might precipitate blindness, paraplegia, or other forms of debilitation. Based on the perceived risk, the Sterns decided to forego having their own children. The decision had special significance for Mr. Stern. Most of his family had been destroyed in the Holocaust. As the family's only survivor, he very much wanted to continue his bloodline.

Initially the Sterns considered adoption, but were discouraged by the substantial delay apparently involved and by the potential problems they saw arising from their age and their differing religious backgrounds. They were most eager for some other means to start a family.

The paths of Mrs. Whitehead and the Sterns to surrogacy were similar. Both responded to advertising by ICNY. The Sterns' response, following their inquiries into adoption, was the result of their long-standing decision to have a child. Mrs. Whitehead's response apparently resulted from her sympathy with family members and others who could have no children (she stated that she wanted to give another couple the "gift of life"); she also wanted the $10,000 to help her family.

Both parties, undoubtedly because of their own self-interest, were less sensitive to the implications of the transaction than they might otherwise have been. Mrs. Whitehead, for instance, appears not to have been concerned about whether the Sterns would make good parents for her child; the Sterns, on their part, while conscious of the obvious possibility that surrendering the child might cause grief to Mrs. Whitehead, overcame their qualms because of their desire for a child. At any rate, both the Sterns and Mrs. Whitehead were committed to the arrangement; both thought it right and constructive.***On February 6, 1985, Mr. Stern and Mr. and Mrs. Whitehead executed the surrogate parenting agreement. After several artificial inseminations over a period of months, Mrs. Whitehead became pregnant. The pregnancy was uneventful and on March 27, 1986, Baby M was born.***

Mrs. Whitehead realized, almost from the moment of birth, that she could not part with this child. She had felt a bond with it even during pregnancy. Some indication of the attachment was conveyed to the Sterns at the hospital when they told Mrs. Whitehead what they were going to name the baby. She apparently broke into tears and indicated that she did not know if she could give up the child. She talked about how the baby looked like her other daughter, and made it clear that she was experiencing great difficulty with the decision.

Nonetheless, Mrs. Whitehead was, for the moment, true to her word. Despite powerful inclinations to the contrary, she turned her child over to the Sterns on March 30 at the Whiteheads' home.***

Later in the evening of March 30, Mrs. Whitehead became deeply disturbed, disconsolate, stricken with unbearable sadness. She had to have her child. She could not eat, sleep, or concentrate on anything other than her need for her baby. The next day she went to the Sterns' home and told them how much she was suffering.

The depth of Mrs. Whitehead's despair surprised and frightened the Sterns. She told them that she could not live without her baby, that she must have her, even if only for one week, that thereafter she would surrender her child. The Sterns, concerned that Mrs. Whitehead might indeed commit suicide, not wanting under any circumstances to risk that, and in any event believing that Mrs. Whitehead would keep her word, turned the child over to her. It was not until four months later, after a series of attempts to regain possession of the child, that Melissa was returned to the Sterns, having been forcibly removed from the home where she was then living with Mr. and Mrs. Whitehead, the home in Florida owned by Mary Beth Whitehead's parents.

The struggle over Baby M began when it became apparent that Mrs. Whitehead could not return the child to Mr. Stern. Due to Mrs. Whitehead's refusal to relinquish the baby, Mr. Stern filed a complaint seeking enforcement of the surrogacy contract.***

The Whiteheads immediately fled to Florida with Baby M. They stayed initially with Mrs. Whitehead's parents, where one of Mrs. Whitehead's children had been living. For the next three months, the Whiteheads and Melissa lived at roughly twenty different hotels, motels, and homes in order to avoid apprehension. From time to time Mrs. Whitehead would call Mr. Stern to discuss the matter; the conversations, recorded by Mr. Stern on advice of counsel, show an escalating dispute about rights, morality, and power, accompanied by threats of Mrs. Whitehead to kill herself, to kill the child, and falsely to accuse Mr. Stern of sexually molesting Mrs. Whitehead's other daughter.

Eventually the Sterns discovered where the Whiteheads were staying, commenced supplementary proceedings in Florida, and obtained an order requiring the Whiteheads to turn over the child. Police in Florida enforced the order, forcibly removing the child from her grandparents' home. She was soon thereafter brought to New Jersey, and turned over to the Sterns.***

The trial took thirty-two days over a period of more than two months. It included numerous interlocutory appeals and attempted interlocutory appeals. There were twenty-three witnesses to the facts recited above and fifteen expert witnesses, eleven testifying on the issue of custody and four on the subject of Mrs. Stern's multiple sclerosis; the bulk of the testimony was devoted to determining the parenting arrangement most compatible with the child's best interests. Soon after the conclusion of the trial, the trial court announced its opinion from the bench. It held that the surrogacy contract was valid; ordered that Mrs. Whitehead's parental rights be terminated and that sole custody of the child be granted to Mr. Stern; and, after hearing brief testimony from Mrs. Stern, immediately entered an order allowing the adoption of Melissa by Mrs. Stern, all in accordance with the surrogacy contract. Pending the outcome of the appeal, we granted a continuation of visitation to Mrs. Whitehead, although slightly more limited than the visitation allowed during the trial.

Although clearly expressing its view that the surrogacy contract was valid, the trial court devoted the major portion of its opinion to the question of the baby's best interests. The inconsistency is apparent. The surrogacy contract calls for the surrender of the child to the Sterns, permanent and sole custody in the Sterns, and termination of Mrs. Whitehead's parental rights, all without qualification, all regardless of any evaluation of the best interests of the child.***

On the question of best interests—and we agree, but for different reasons, that custody was the critical issue—the court's analysis of the testimony was perceptive, demonstrating both its understanding of the case and its considerable experience in these matters. We agree substantially with both its analysis and conclusions on the matter of custody.***

Having decided that the surrogacy contract is illegal and unenforceable, we now must decide the custody question without regard to the provisions of the surrogacy contract that would give Mr. Stern sole and permanent custody.***

There were eleven experts who testified concerning the child's best interests, either directly or in connection with matters related to that issue. Our reading of the record persuades us that the trial court's decision awarding custody to the Sterns (technically to Mr. Stern) should be affirmed since "its findings . . . could reasonably have been reached on sufficient credible evidence present in the record."***

Our custody conclusion is based on strongly persuasive testimony contrasting both the family life of the Whiteheads and the Sterns and the personalities and characters of the individuals. The stability of the Whitehead family life was doubtful at the time of trial. Their finances were in serious trouble (foreclosure by Mrs. Whitehead's sister on a second mortgage was in process). Mr. Whitehead's employment, though relatively steady, was always at risk because of his alcoholism, a condition that he seems not to have been able to confront effectively. Mrs. Whitehead had not worked for quite some time, her last two employments having been part-time. One of the Whiteheads' positive attributes was their ability to bring up two children, and apparently well, even in so vulnerable a household. Yet substantial question was raised even about that aspect of their home life. The expert testimony contained criticism of Mrs. Whitehead's handling of her son's educational difficulties. Certain of the experts noted that Mrs. Whitehead perceived herself as omnipotent and omniscient concerning her children. She knew what they were thinking, what they wanted, and she spoke for them. As to Melissa, Mrs. Whitehead expressed the view that she alone knew what that child's cries and sounds meant. Her inconsistent stories about various things engendered grave doubts about her ability to explain honestly and sensitively to Baby M—and at the right time—the nature of her origin. Although faith in professional counseling is not a *sine qua non* of parenting, several experts believed that Mrs. Whitehead's contempt for professional help, especially professional psychological help, coincided with her feelings of omnipotence in a way that could be devastating to a child who most likely will need such help. In short, while love and affection there would be, Baby M's life with the Whiteheads promised to be too closely controlled by Mrs. Whitehead. The prospects for wholesome, independent psychological growth and development would be at serious risk.

The Sterns have no other children, but all indications are that their household and their personalities promise a much more likely foundation for Melissa to grow and thrive. There *is* a track record of sorts—during the one-and-a-half years of custody Baby M has done very well, and the relationship between both Mr. and Mrs. Stern and the baby has become very strong. The household is stable, and likely to remain so. Their finances are more than adequate, their circle of friends supportive, and their marriage happy. Most important, they are loving, giving, nurturing, and open-minded people. They have demonstrated the wish and ability to nurture and protect Melissa, yet at the same time to encourage her independence. Their lack of experience is more than made up for by a willingness to learn and to listen, a willingness that is enhanced by their professional training, especially Mrs. Stern's experience as a pediatrician. They are honest; they can recognize error, deal with it, and learn from it. They will try to determine rationally the best way to cope with problems in their relationship with

Melissa. When the time comes to tell her about her origins, they will probably have found a means of doing so that accords with the best interests of Baby M. All in all, Melissa's future appears solid, happy, and promising with them.

Based on all of this we have concluded, independent of the trial court's identical conclusion, that Melissa's best interests call for custody in the Sterns. Our above-mentioned disagreements with the trial court do not, as we have noted, in any way diminish our concurrence with its conclusions. We feel, however, that those disagreements are important enough to be stated. They are disagreements about the evaluation of conduct. They also may provide some insight about the potential consequences of surrogacy.

It seems to us that given her predicament, Mrs. Whitehead was rather harshly judged—both by the trial court and by some of the experts. She was guilty of a breach of contract, and indeed, she did break a very important promise, but we think it is expecting something well beyond normal human capabilities to suggest that this mother should have parted with her newly born infant without a struggle. Other than survival, what stronger force is there? We do not know of, and cannot conceive of, any other case where a perfectly fit mother was expected to surrender her newly born infant, perhaps forever, and was then told she was a bad mother because she did not. We know of no authority suggesting that the moral quality of her act in those circumstances should be judged by referring to a contract made before she became pregnant. We do not countenance, and would never countenance, violating a court order as Mrs. Whitehead did, even a court order that is wrong; but her resistance to an order that she surrender her infant, possibly forever, merits a measure of understanding. We do not find it so clear that her efforts to keep her infant, when measured against the Sterns' efforts to take her away, make one, rather than the other, the wrongdoer. The Sterns suffered, but so did she. And if we go beyond suffering to an evaluation of the human stakes involved in the struggle, how much weight should be given to her nine months of pregnancy, the labor of childbirth, the risk to her life, compared to the payment of money, the anticipation of a child and the donation of sperm?***

We have a further concern regarding the trial court's emphasis on the Sterns' interest in Melissa's education as compared to the Whiteheads'. That this difference is a legitimate factor to be considered we have no doubt. But it should not be overlooked that a best-interests test is designed to create not a new member of the intelligentsia but rather a well-integrated person who might reasonably be expected to be happy with life. "Best interests" does not contain within it any idealized lifestyle; the question boils down to a judgment, consisting of many factors, about the likely future happiness of a human being. Stability, love, family happiness, tolerance, and, ultimately, support of independence—all rank much higher in predicting future happiness than the likelihood of a college education. We do not mean to suggest that the trial court would disagree. We simply want to dispel any possible misunderstanding on the issue.

Even allowing for these differences, the facts, the experts' opinions, and the trial court's analysis of both argue strongly in favor of custody in the Sterns. Mary Beth Whitehead's family life, into which Baby M would be placed, was anything but secure—the quality Melissa needs most. And today it may be even less so. Furthermore, the evidence and expert opinion based on it reveal personality characteristics, mentioned above, that might threaten the child's best development. The Sterns promise a secure home, with an understanding relationship that allows nurturing and independent growth to develop together. Although there is no substitute for reading the entire record, including the review of every word of each experts' testimony and reports, a summary of their conclusions is revealing. Six experts testified for Mrs. Whitehead: one favored joint custody, clearly unwarranted in this case; one simply rebutted an opposing expert's claim that Mary Beth Whitehead had a recognized personality disorder; one testified to the adverse impact of separation on *Mrs. Whitehead*; one testified about the evils of adoption and, to him, the probable analogous evils of surrogacy; one spoke only on the question of whether Mrs. Whitehead's consent in the surrogacy agreement was "informed consent"; and one spelled out the strong bond between mother and child. None of them unequivocally stated, or even necessarily implied, an opinion that custody in the Whiteheads was in the best interests of Melissa—the ultimate issue. The Sterns' experts, both well qualified—as were the Whiteheads'—concluded that the best interests of Melissa required custody in Mr. Stern. Most convincingly, the three experts chosen by the court-appointed guardian *ad litem* of Baby M, each clearly free of all bias and interest, unanimously and persuasively recommended custody in the Sterns.***

Notes and Issues for Discussion

1. The *Baby M.* case was returned to the trial court, which allowed Mary Beth Whitehead substantial visitation, starting with once a week and after a year increasing to two days a week with an overnight and time in the summer.
2. While the court found the contract in Baby M. illegal on statutory and public policy grounds, it also said that such contracts, as long as there was no money paid and as long as the mother retained her parental rights, would be valid. In reality is there anything left of surrogate contracts in the state?
3. States differ on surrogate contracts, some approving them, others like New Jersey holding them invalid unless very restrictive conditions are met. New Hampshire (N.H. Rev. Stat. §168-B:16) and Virginia (Va. Code Ann. §20-156) legalize surrogate contracts. What arguments can you make for validating surrogate contracts? Holding them invalid? Does the fact that the prospective surrogate mother is competent and understands the agreement make a difference? Or should the state have a policy that under no conditions allows these agreements?

The issue in the following case is whether a former same-sex cohabitee who helped raise a child born through artificial insemination has standing as a *de facto* parent to seek visitation rights under the New York statute.

ALLISON D. v. VIRGINIA M.
77 N.Y.2d 651, 572 N.E.2d 27 (1991)
NEW YORK COURT OF APPEALS

PER CURIAM.

At issue in this case is whether petitioner, a biological stranger to a child who is properly in the custody of his biological mother, has standing to seek visitation with the child under Domestic Relations Law §70. Petitioner relies on both her established relationship with the child and her alleged agreement with the biological mother to support her claim that she has standing. We agree with the Appellate Division, that, although petitioner apparently nurtured a close and loving relationship with the child, she is not a parent within the meaning of Domestic Relations Law §70. Accordingly, we affirm.

Petitioner Alison D. and respondent Virginia M. established a relationship in September 1977 and began living together in March 1978. In March 1980, they decided to have a child and agreed that respondent would be artificially inseminated. Together, they planned for the conception and birth of the child and agreed to share jointly all rights and responsibilities of childrearing. In July 1981, respondent gave birth to a baby boy, A.D.M., who was given petitioner's last name as his middle name and respondent's last name became his last name. Petitioner shared in all birthing expenses and, after A.D.M.'s birth, continued to provide for his support. During A.D.M.'s first two years, petitioner and respondent jointly cared for and made decisions regarding the child.

In November 1983, when the child was 2 years and 4 months old, petitioner and respondent terminated their relationship and petitioner moved out of the home they jointly owned. Petitioner and respondent agreed to a visitation schedule whereby petitioner continued to see the child a few times a week. Petitioner also agreed to continue to pay one half of the mortgage and major household expenses. By this time, the child had referred to both respondent and petitioner as "mommy." Petitioner's visitation with the child continued until 1986, at which time respondent bought out petitioner's interest in the house and then began to restrict petitioner's visitation with the child. In 1987 petitioner moved to Ireland to pursue career opportunities, but continued her attempts to communicate with the child. Thereafter, respondent terminated all contact between petitioner and the child, returning all of petitioner's gifts and letters. No dispute exists that respondent is a fit parent. Petitioner commenced this proceeding seeking visitation rights pursuant to Domestic Relations Law §70.

Supreme Court dismissed the proceeding concluding that petitioner is not a parent under Domestic Relations Law §70 and, given the concession that respondent is a fit parent, petitioner is not entitled to seek visitation pursuant to section 70. The Appellate Division affirmed, with one Justice dissenting, and granted leave to appeal to our Court.

Pursuant to Domestic Relations Law §70 "either parent may apply to the supreme court for a writ of habeas corpus to have such minor child brought before such court; and [the court] may award the natural guardianship, charge and custody of such child to either parent***as the case may require." Although the Court is mindful of petitioner's understandable concern for and interest in the child and of her expectation and desire that her contact with the child would continue, she has no right under Domestic Relations Law §70 to seek visitation and, thereby, limit or diminish the right of the concededly fit biological parent to choose with whom her child associates. She is not a "parent" within the meaning of section 70.

Petitioner concedes that she is not the child's "parent"; that is, she is not the biological mother of the child nor is she a legal parent by virtue of an adoption. Rather she claims to have acted as a "de facto" parent or that she should be viewed as a parent "by estoppel." Therefore, she claims she has standing to seek visitation rights. These claims, however, are insufficient under section 70. Traditionally, in this State it is the child's mother and father who, assuming fitness, have the right to the care and custody of their child, even in situations where the nonparent has exercised some control over the child with the parents' consent. "It has long been recognized that, as between a parent and a third person, parental custody of a child may not be displaced absent grievous cause or necessity" (*Matter of Ronald FF. v. Cindy GG.* 70 N.Y.2d at 144). To allow the courts to award visitation—a limited form of custody—to a third person would necessarily impair the parents' right to custody and control. Petitioner concedes that respondent is a fit parent. Therefore she has no right to petition the court to displace the choice made by this fit parent in deciding what is in the child's best interests.

Section 70 gives *parents* the right to bring proceedings to ensure their proper exercise of their care, custody and control. Where the Legislature deemed it appropriate, it gave other categories of persons standing to seek visitation and it gave the courts the power to determine whether an award of visitation would be in the child's best interests (*see, e.g.,* Domestic Relations Law §71 [special proceeding or habeas corpus to obtain visitation rights for siblings]; §72 [special proceeding or habeas corpus to obtain visitation rights for grandparents]. We decline petitioner's invitation to read the term parent in section 70 to include categories of nonparents who have developed a relationship with a child or who have had prior relationships with a child's parents and who wish to continue visitation with the child. While one may dispute in an individual case whether it would be beneficial to a child to have continued contact with a nonparent, the Legislature did not in section 70 give such nonparent the opportunity to compel a fit parent to allow them to do so.***

Notes and Issues for Discussion

1. In her dissent, Judge Kaye argues, "The court's decision, fixing biology as the key to visitation rights, has impact far beyond this particular controversy, one that may affect a wide spectrum of relationships. . . . Estimates that more than 15.5 million children do not live with two biological

parents, and that as many as 8 to 10 million children are born into families with a gay or lesbian parent suggest just how widespread the impact may be. . . . But the impact of today's decision falls hardest on the children of those relationships, limiting their opportunity to maintain bonds that may be crucial to their development." 572 N.E.2d at 30.

2. Allison D. had minimal contact with A.D.M. since 1986, a period of five years. Does this make a difference? Compare a similar biological parent, who unless shown to be unfit, in all probability would be allowed to resume contact with the child after a five year absence. Should they be treated differently?

3. In *Nancy S. v. Michele G.*, 279 Cal.Rptr. 212 (1991), a California Appellate court reached a similar conclusion, noting "We agree with appellant that the absence of any legal formalization of her relationship to the children has resulted in a tragic situation. As is always the case, it is the children who will suffer the most as a result of the inability of the adults, who they love and need, to reach an agreement. We do not, however, agree that the only way to avoid such an unfortunate situation is for the courts to adopt appellant's novel theory by which a nonparent can acquire the rights of a parent, and then face years of unraveling the complex, practical, social and constitutional ramifications of this expansion of the definition of parent." In a footnote, the court observed: "Although the validity of an adoption in these circumstances is not before us, we note that Civil Code section 221 provides, in part, that '[a]ny unmarried minor child may be adopted by any adult person . . .' We see nothing in these provisions that would preclude a child from being jointly adopted by someone of the same sex as the natural parent." 279 Cal.Rptr. at 219. A few states prohibit adoption by homosexuals. For example, in Florida, "no person eligible to adopt under this statute may adopt if that person is a homosexual." Fla. Stat. Ann. 63-042.

4. Mary K. and Victoria T. decided that Mary should be artificially inseminated and they would raise the child together. They chose Jhordan C. as the sperm donor and Mary K., a nurse, inseminated herself. Jhordan remained in contact with Mary after she became pregnant, purchased gifts for the baby, and offered to set up a trust fund for the child. Devin was born and over Mary's objections Jhordan visited him some five times, and a monthly visitation was agreed to. Mary stopped the visits and Jhordan filed for visitation rights. The California court upheld visitation rights for Jhordan:

"Mary and Victoria contend that they and Devin compose a family unit and that trial court's ruling constitutes an infringement upon a right they have to family autonomy, encompassed by the constitutional right to privacy. But this argument begs the question of which persons comprise the family in this case for purposes of judicial intervention. Characterization of the family unit must precede consideration of whether family autonomy has been infringed.

The semen donor here was permitted to develop a social relationship with Mary and Devin as the child's father. During Mary's pregnancy Jhordan maintained contact with her. They visited each other several times, and Mary did not object to Jhordan's collection of baby equipment or the creation of a trust fund for the child. Mary permitted Jhordan to visit Devin on the day after the child's birth and allowed monthly visits thereafter. The record demonstrates no clear understanding that Jhordan's role would be limited to provision of semen and that he would have no parental relationship with Devin; indeed the parties' conduct indicates otherwise. . . ." (*Jhordan C. v. Mary K.*, 224 Cal.Rptr. 530, at 536 (1986).

JOINT CUSTODY

In awards of joint custody, both parents have the same decision-making powers as before. In some states, joint custody is a preference, in others it is an option.[10]

In either situation, cooperation and communication between the parties is required. In *Beck v. Beck*, 86 N.J. 480 (1981), the court discussed some considerations:

The most troublesome aspect of a joint custody decree is the additional requirement that the parent exhibit a potential for cooperation in matters of child rearing. This feature does not translate into a requirement that the parents have an amicable relationship. Although such a positive relationship is preferable, a successful joint custody arrangement requires only that the parents be able to isolate their personal conflicts from their roles as parents and that the children be spared whatever resentments and rancor the parents may harbor.

. . . [T]he physical custody element of a joint custody award requires examination of practical considerations such as the financial status of the parents, the proximity of their respective homes, the demands of parental employment, and the age and number of children. Joint physical custody necessarily places an additional financial burden on the family. Although exact duplication of facilities and furnishings is not necessary, the trial court should insure that the children can be adequately cared for in two homes. The geographical proximity of the two homes is an important factor to the extent that it impinges on school arrangements, the children's access to relatives and friends, . . . and the ease of travel between the two homes. Parental employment is significant for its effect on a parent's ability properly to care for the children and maintain a relationship with them. 86 N.J. at 498–500.

CHILDREN AND THE LAW

Generally parents make most decisions for their children free from interference by the state, in part shielded by a Fourteenth Amendment privacy right (see page 248). Yet the state may exercise its authority for the protection of the child, for example through restricting child labor, or for the furtherance of legitimate aims, such as mandatory education laws. Where parents are seen as failing to exercise their lawful authority, as in juvenile delinquency, or where the parents abuse their authority, as in child abuse or neglect, the state may intervene. Here two areas will be examined that clearly identify the conflicts and tensions among children, parents, and the state, the juvenile court and the public school.

Underlying the following discussion are two themes. One is *autonomy*, the idea that children are persons with their own interests, rights, and abilities to make decisions. Another is *paternalism*, the idea that adults (or the state) know what is best for children and should make decisions on their behalf, even if these decisions are inconsistent with what the child wishes. For example, in *Tinker v. Des Moines School District*, a First Amendment free expression case, the court upheld the right of students to wear black armbands to school protesting the Vietnam war. Yet in *Hazelwood School District v. Kuhlmeier* the court upheld the right of a school principal to censor a student newspaper. Similarly, *Carey v. Population Services International*, 431 U.S. 678 (1977), invalidated a law forbidding the sale of contraceptives to minors, while *Ginsburg v. New York*, 390 U.S. 629 (1968), upheld a New York statute forbidding the sale of obscenity to minors.[11]

What rights do children have independent of their parents? Case law is divided on this point. Traditionally the law has taken a paternalistic approach, where decisions made for children by their parents are accepted by courts to be in best interests of the child. In a few areas, such as abortion, an unemancipated minor has the right to make decisions without parental consent.

The Juvenile Court[12]

DELINQUENT AND STATUS OFFENSES

All states specify a range of offenses which if committed by a juvenile are categorized as juvenile delinquency. Generally these approximate adult criminal offenses, with one main difference being the range of sanctions available if a juvenile court determines the juvenile committed the offense as charged. Juvenile court sanctions may be more or less severe than comparable adult court penalties, and the court is given wide latitude to determine what is most appropriate with a view toward rehabilitation rather than punishment.

A separate group of offenses are specific only to minors, and are often referred to as juvenile status offenses. They include truancy, incorrigibility, running away from home, and immoral conduct. Although often imprecise, these categories have been upheld as not being unconstitutionally vague. States have different nomenclature for juvenile status offenses, such as Minors in Need of Supervision (MINS), Persons in Need of Supervision (PINS), and Children in Need of Supervision (CHINS), indicating their fundamental difference from delinquency.

Some juveniles may be tried as adults, however, if—based on factors such as severity of the offense, age, past record, and lack of potential for rehabilitation—they have been waived by the juvenile court to an adult court.[13] In these cases, the juveniles have all the procedural protections of an adult charged with a similar offense, and, if found guilty, could be sentenced as an adult.

JUVENILE COURT PROCEDURES

Generally, there are separate juvenile court hearings for adjudication and disposition, paralleling adult criminal court's trial and sentencing phases. Until 1967 most juvenile court proceedings were informal and most of the procedural protections available to adults in criminal courts were not afforded to juveniles. In *In re Gault*, the Supreme Court changed this, finding that a number of procedural protections were required by the Constitution. Noting that the Constitution applies to children as well as adults, the court held that juveniles were entitled to adequate notice, representation by counsel, confrontation and cross-examination of witnesses, and to be protected by the privilege against self-incrimination.

IN RE GAULT
387 U.S. 1 (1967)
U.S. SUPREME COURT

MR. JUSTICE FORTAS delivered the opinion of the Court.

This is an appeal***from a judgment of the Supreme Court of Arizona affirming the dismissal of a petition for a writ of habeas corpus. The petition sought the release of Gerald Francis Gault, appellants' 15-year-old son, who had been committed as a juvenile delinquent to the State Industrial School by the Juvenile Court of Gila County, Arizona.***

On Monday, June 8, 1964, at about 10 a.m., Gerald Francis Gault and a friend, Ronald Lewis, were taken into custody by the Sheriff of Gila County. Gerald was then still subject to a six months' probation order which had been entered on February 25, 1964, as a result of his having been in the company of another boy who had stolen a wallet from a lady's purse. The police action on June 8 was taken as the result of a verbal complaint by a neighbor of the boys, Mrs. Cook, about a telephone call made to her in which the caller or callers made lewd or indecent remarks. It will suffice for purposes of this opinion to say that the remarks or questions put to her were of the irritatingly offensive, adolescent, sex variety.

At the time Gerald was picked up, his mother and father were both at work. No notice that Gerald was being taken into custody was left at the home. No other steps were taken to advise them that their son had, in effect, been arrested. Gerald was taken to the Children's Detention Home. When his mother arrived home at 6 o'clock, Gerald was not there. Gerald's older brother was sent to look for him at the trailer home of the Lewis family. He apparently learned then that Gerald was in custody. He so informed his mother. The two of them went to the Detention Home. The deputy probation officer, Flagg, who was also superintendent of the Detention Home, told Mrs. Gault "why Jerry was there" and said that a hearing would be held at Juvenile Court at 3 o'clock the following day, June 9.

Officer Flagg filed a petition with the court on the hearing day, June 9, 1964. It was not served on the Gaults. Indeed, none of them saw this petition until the habeas corpus hearing on August 17, 1964. The petition was entirely formal. It made no reference to any factual basis for the judicial action which it initiated. It recited only that "said minor is under the age of eighteen years, and is in need of the protection of this Honorable Court; [and that] said minor is a delinquent minor." It prayed for a hearing and an order regarding "the care and custody of said minor." Officer Flagg executed a formal affidavit in support of the petition.

On June 9, Gerald, his mother, his older brother, and Probation Officers Flagg and Henderson appeared before the Juvenile Judge in chambers. Gerald's father was not there. He was at work out of the city. Mrs. Cook, the complainant, was not there. No one was sworn at this hearing. No transcript or recording was made. No memorandum or record of the substance of the proceedings was prepared. Our information about the proceedings and the subsequent hearing on June 15, derives entirely from the testimony of the Juvenile Court Judge, Mr. and Mrs. Gault and Officer Flagg at the habeas corpus proceeding conducted two months later. From this, it appears that at the June 9 hearing Gerald was questioned by the judge about the telephone call. There was conflict as to what he said. His mother recalled that Gerald said he only dialed Mrs. Cook's number and handed the telephone to his friend, Ronald. Officer Flagg recalled that Gerald had admitted making the lewd remarks. Judge McGhee testified that Gerald "admitted making one of these [lewd] statements." At the conclusion of the hearing, the judge said he would "think about it." Gerald was taken back to the Detention Home. He was not sent to his own home with his parents. On June 11 or 12, after having been detained since June 8, Gerald was released and driven home. There is no explanation in the record as to why he was kept in the Detention Home or why he was released. At 5 p.m. on the day of Gerald's release, Mrs. Gault received a note signed by Officer Flagg. It was on plain paper, not letterhead. Its entire text was as follows:

"Mrs. Gault:
"Judge McGHEE has set Monday June 15, 1964 at 11:00 A.M. as the date and time for further Hearings on Gerald's delinquency
"/s/Flagg"

At the appointed time on Monday, June 15, Gerald, his father and mother, Ronald Lewis and his father, and Officer Flagg and Henderson were present before Judge McGhee. Witnesses at the habeas corpus proceeding differed in their recollections of Gerald's testimony at the June 15 hearing. Mrs. and Mrs. Gault recalled that Gerald again testified that he had only dialed the number and that the other boy had made the remarks. Officer Flagg agreed that at this hearing Gerald did not admit making the lewd remarks. But Judge McGhee recalled that "there was some admission again of some of the lewd statements. He—he didn't admit any of the more serious lewd statements." Again, the complainant, Mrs. Cook, was not present. Mrs. Gault asked that Mrs. Cook be present "so she could see which boy that done the talking, the dirty talking over the phone." The Juvenile Judge said "she didn't have to be present at that hearing." The judge did not speak to Mrs. Cook or communicate with her at any time. Probation Officer Flagg had talked to her once—over the telephone on June 9.

At this June 15 hearing a "referral report" made by the probation officers was filed with the court, although not disclosed to Gerald or his parents. This listed the charge as "Lewd Phone Calls." At the conclusion of the hearing, the judge committed Gerald as a juvenile delinquent to the State Industrial School "for the period of his minority [that is, until 21], unless sooner discharged."***

At the habeas corpus hearing on August 17, Judge McGhee was vigorously cross-examined as to the basis for his actions. He testified that he had taken into account the fact that Gerald was on probation. He was asked "under what section of***the code you found the boy delinquent?"***In substance, he concluded that Gerald came within ARS §8-201, subsec. 6(a), which specifies that a "delinquent child" includes one "who has violated a law of the state or an ordinance or regulation of a political subdivision thereof." The law which Gerald was found to have violated is ARS §13-377. This section of the Arizona Criminal Code provides that a person who "in the presence or hearing of any woman or child***uses vulgar, abusive or obscene language, is guilty of a misdemeanor***." The penalty specified in the Criminal Code, which would apply to an adult, is $5 to $50, or imprisonment for not more than two months. The judge also testified that he acted under ARS §8-201, subsec. 6(d) which includes in the definition of a "delinquent child" one who, as the judge phrased it, is "habitually involved in immoral matters."

***As to these proceedings, there appears to be little current dissent from the proposition that the Due Process Clause has a role to play. The problem is to ascertain the precise impact of the due process requirement upon such proceedings.

From the inception of the juvenile court system, wide differences have been tolerated—indeed insisted upon—between the procedural rights accorded to adults and those of juveniles. In practically all jurisdictions, there are rights granted to adults which are withheld from juveniles. In addition to the specific problems involved in the present case, for example, it has been held that the juvenile is not entitled to bail, to indictment by grand jury, to a public trial or to trial by jury. It is frequent practice that rules governing the arrest and interrogation of adults by the police are not observed in the case of juveniles.

The history and theory underlying this development are well-known, but a recapitulation is necessary for purposes of this opinion.***

The early reformers were appalled by adult procedures and penalties, and by the fact that children could be given long prison sentences and mixed in jails with hardened criminals. They were profoundly convinced that society's duty to the child could not be confined by the concept of justice alone. They believed that society's role was not to ascertain whether the child was "guilty" or "innocent," but "What is he, how has he become what he is, and what had best be done in his interest and in the interest of the state to save him from a downward career." The child—essentially good, as they saw it—was to be made "to feel that he is the object of [the state's] care and solicitude," not that he was under arrest or on trial. The rules of criminal procedure were therefore altogether inapplicable. The apparent rigidities, technicalities, and harshness which they observed in both substantive and procedural criminal law were therefore to be discarded. The idea of crime and punishment was to be abandoned. The child was to be "treated" and "rehabilitated" and the procedures, from apprehension through institutionalization, were to be "clinical" rather than punitive.***

The right of the state, as *parens patriae*, to deny to the child procedural rights available to his elders was elaborated by the assertion that a child, unlike an adult, has a right "not to liberty but to custody." He can be made to attorn to his parents, to go to school, etc. If his parents default in effectively performing their custodial functions—that is, if the child is "delinquent"—the state may intervene. In doing so, it does not deprive the child of any rights, because he has none. It merely provides the "custody" to which the child is entitled. On this basis, proceedings involving juveniles were described as "civil" not "criminal" and therefore not subject to the requirements which restrict the state when it seeks to deprive a person of his liberty.***

Ultimately, however, we confront the reality of that portion of the Juvenile Court process with which we deal in this case. A boy is charged with misconduct. The boy is committed to an institution where he may be restrained of liberty for years.***

If Gerald had been over 18, he would not have been subject to the Juvenile Court proceedings. For the particular offense immediately involved, the maximum punishment would have been a fine of $5 to $50, or imprisonment in jail for not more than two months. Instead, he was committed to custody for a maximum of six years. If he had been over 18 and had committed an offense to which such a sentence might apply, he would have been entitled to substantial rights under the Constitution of the United States as well as under Arizona's laws and constitution. The United States Constitution would guarantee him rights and protections with respect to arrest, search, and seizure, and pretrial interrogation. It would assure him of specific notice of the charges and adequate time to decide his course of action and to prepare his defense. He would be entitled to clear advice that he could be represented by counsel, and, at least if a felony were involved, the State would be required to provide counsel if his parents were unable to afford it. If the court acted on the basis of his confession, careful procedures would be required to assure its voluntariness. If the case went to trial, confrontation and opportunity for cross-examination would be guaranteed.***

We now turn to the specific issues which are presented to us in the present case.

NOTICE OF CHARGES

Appellants allege that the Arizona Juvenile Code is unconstitutional or alternatively that the proceedings before the Juvenile Court were constitutionally defective because of failure to provide adequate notice of the hearings.***

We cannot agree***that adequate notice was given in this case. Notice, to comply with due process requirements, must be given sufficiently in advance of scheduled court proceedings so that reasonable opportunity to prepare will be afforded, and it must "set forth the alleged misconduct with particularity."***

RIGHT TO COUNSEL

Appellants charge that the Juvenile Court proceedings were fatally defective because the court did not advise Gerald or his parents of their right to counsel, and proceeded with the hearing, the adjudication of delinquency and the order of commitment in the absence of counsel for the child and his parents or an express waiver of the right thereto. The Supreme Court of Arizona pointed out that "[t]here is disagreement [among the various jurisdictions] as to whether the court must advise the infant that he has a right to counsel." It referred to a provision of the Juvenile Code which it characterized as requiring "that the probation officer shall look after the interests of neglected delinquent and dependent children," including representing their interests in Court. We do not agree. Probation officers in the Arizona scheme, are also arresting officers. They initiate proceedings and file petitions which they verify, as here, alleging the delinquency of the child; and they testify, as here, against the child. And here the probation officer was also superintendent of the Detention Home. The probation officer cannot act as counsel for the child. His role in the adjudicatory hearing, by statute and in fact, is as arresting officer and witness against the child. Nor can the judge represent the child. There is no material difference in this respect between adult and juvenile proceedings of the sort here involved. In adult proceedings, this contention has been foreclosed by decisions of this Court. A proceeding where the issue is whether the child will be found to be "delinquent" and subjected to the loss of his liberty for years is comparable in seriousness to a felony prosecution. The juvenile needs the assistance of counsel to cope with problems of law, to make skilled inquiry into the facts, to insist upon regularity of the proceedings, and to ascertain whether he has a defense and to prepare and submit it.***

We conclude that the Due Process Clause of the Fourteenth Amendment requires that in respect of proceedings to determine delinquency which may result in commitment to an institution in which the juvenile's freedom is curtailed, the child and his parents must be notified of the child's right to be represented by counsel retained by them, or if they are unable to afford counsel, that counsel will be appointed to represent the child.***

CONFRONTATION, SELF-INCRIMINATION, CROSS-EXAMINATION

Appellants urge that the writ of habeas corpus should have been granted because of the denial of the rights of confrontation and cross-examination in the Juvenile Court hearings, and because the privilege against self-incrimination was not observed. The Juvenile Court Judge testified at the habeas corpus hearing that he had proceeded on the basis of Gerald's admission at the two hearings. Appellants attack this on the ground that the admissions were obtained in disregard of the privilege against self-incrimination. If the confession is disregarded, appellants argue that the delinquency conclusion, since it was fundamentally based on a finding that Gerald had made lewd remarks during the phone call to Mrs. Cook, is fatally defective for failure to accord the rights of confrontation and cross-examination which the Due Process Clause of the Fourteenth Amendment of the Federal Constitution guarantees in state proceedings generally.

Our first question, then, is whether Gerald's admission was improperly obtained and relied on as the basis of decision, in conflict with the Federal Constitution.***

It would indeed be surprising if the privilege against self-incrimination were available to hardened criminals but not to children. The language of the Fifth Amendment, applicable to the States by operation of the Fourteenth Amendment, is unequivocal and without exception. And the scope of the privilege is comprehensive.***

Against the application to juveniles of the right to silence, it is argued that juvenile proceedings are "civil" and not "criminal," and therefore the privilege should not apply. It is true that the statement of the privilege in the Fifth Amendment, which is applicable to the States by reason of the Fourteenth Amendment, is that no person "shall be compelled in any *criminal case* to be a witness against himself."***

It would be entirely unrealistic to carve out of the Fifth Amendment all statements by juveniles on the ground that these cannot lead to "criminal" involvement. In the first place, juvenile proceedings to determine "delinquency," which may lead to commitment to a state institution, must be regarded as "criminal" for purposes of the privilege against self-incrimination. To hold otherwise would be to disregard substance because of the feeble enticement of the "civil" label-of-convenience which has been attached to juvenile proceedings.***

It is also urged, as the Supreme Court of Arizona here asserted, that the juvenile and presumably his parents should not be advised of the juvenile's right to silence because confession is good for the child as the commencement of the assumed therapy of the juvenile court process, and he should be encouraged to assume an attitude of trust and confidence toward the officials of the juvenile process. This proposition has been subjected to widespread challenge on the basis of current reappraisals of the rhetoric and realities of the handling of juvenile offenders.***

We conclude that the constitutional privilege against self-incrimination is applicable in the case of juveniles as it is with respect to adults.

We now hold that, absent a valid confession, a determination of delinquency and an order of commitment to a state institution cannot be sustained in the absence of sworn testimony subjected to the opportunity for cross-examination in accordance with our law and constitutional requirements.

For the reasons stated, the judgment of the Supreme Court of Arizona is reversed and the case remanded for further proceedings not inconsistent with this opinion. It is so ordered.

Notes and Issues for Discussion

1. What notice did Mrs. Gault receive? Who was present at the hearings? Was the complainant, Mrs. Cook, required by law to be present? What roles did Officer Flagg serve?
2. Gault was accused of making lewd or indecent remarks, and for this he was sentenced to a State Industrial School for a maximum of six years—until he became twenty-one. If he had been an adult he could have been sentenced to a five-to-fifty-dollar fine and up to two months in jail. What is the rationale for such a great discrepancy between juvenile and adult?
3. What is the question to be decided in the *Gault* case before the U.S. Supreme Court? Is it whether or not Gault made the phone call? Whether or not Judge McGhee acted illegally and in violation of the Arizona law in the way he ran the hearings? Or is it whether or not the legal proceedings called for in Arizona and followed by Judge McGhee violated Gerald Gault's constitutional right to due process?
4. As a model of due process, *Gault* extends to juveniles in juvenile court many of the protections available to adults in criminal court. Since that decision, juvenile delinquents have been given many but not all the protections provided to adult criminals. In *In re Winship*, 397 U.S. 358 (1970), the Court held that the degree of proof in juvenile delinquency proceedings should be beyond a reasonable doubt. In *McKeiver v. Pa.*, 403 U.S. 528 (1971), the Court held that there was no constitutional right to a jury trial in juvenile court.

Public Schools

DISCRIMINATION AND FUNDING

In *Brown v. Board of Education*, 347 U.S. 483 (1954), the Supreme Court in a decision with far-reaching consequences for public education held that the legal segregation of public schools was an unconstitutional violation of the Equal Protection Clause of the Fourteenth Amendment. The Court said:

We come then to the question presented: Does segregation of children in public schools solely on the basis of race, even though the physical facilities and other 'tangible' factors may be equal, deprive the children of the minority group of equal educational opportunities? We believe it does. 347 U.S. at 493.

While a series of later decisions reinforced this position, the Supreme Court has held that an education itself is not a fundamental right under the Constitution. *San Antonio Independent School District v. Rodriguez*, 411 U.S. 1 (1973). The Civil Rights Act of 1964, 42 U.S.C. § 2000 *et seq.*, provided funds for school integration and for withholding funds from schools that discriminate on the basis of race.

SUSPENSIONS AND DISCIPLINE

We saw in Chapter 3 that school suspensions conflict with a student's property right to an education under the Fourteenth Amendment and that a student facing a suspension of ten days or less is entitled to adequate notice and a hearing. *Goss v. Lopez*, 419 U.S. 565 (1975). In *Ingraham v. Wright*, the Court held that corporal punishment in the public school does not violate the constitutional prohibition of cruel and unusual punishment.

INGRAHAM v. WRIGHT
430 U.S. 651 (1977)
U.S. SUPREME COURT

MR. JUSTICE POWELL delivered the opinion of the Court.

This case presents questions concerning the use of corporal punishment in public schools: First, whether the paddling of students as a means of maintaining school discipline constitutes cruel and unusual punishment in violation of the Eighth Amendment; and, second, to the extent that paddling is constitutionally permissible, whether the Due Process Clause of the Fourteenth Amendment requires prior notice and an opportunity to be heard.

Petitioners James Ingraham and Roosevelt Andrews filed the complaint in this case on January 7, 1971, in the United States District Court for the Southern District of Florida. At the time both were enrolled in the Charles R. Drew Junior High School in Dade County, Fla., Ingraham in the eighth grade and Andrews in the ninth.***

Petitioners' evidence may be summarized briefly. In the 1970–1971 school year many of the 237 schools in Dade County used corporal punishment as a means of maintaining discipline pursuant to Florida legislation and a local School Board regulation. The statute then in effect authorized limited corporal punishment by negative inference, proscribing punishment which was "degrading or unduly severe," or which was inflicted without prior consultation with the principal or the teacher in charge of the school. Fla. Stat. Ann. § 232.27 (1961). The regulation, Dade County School Board Policy 5144, contained explicit directions and limitations. The authorized punishment consisted of paddling the recalcitrant student on the buttocks with a flat wooden paddle measuring less than two feet long, three to four inches wide, and about one-half inch thick. The normal punishment was limited to one to five "licks" or blows with the paddle and resulted in no apparent physical injury to the student. School authorities viewed corporal punishment as a less drastic means of discipline than suspension or expulsion. Contrary to the procedural requirements of the statute and regulation, teachers often paddled students on their own authority without first consulting the principal.

Petitioners focused on Drew Junior High School, the school in which both Ingraham and Andrews were enrolled in the fall of 1970. In an apparent reference to Drew, the District Court found that "[t]he instances of punishment which could be characterized as severe, accepting the students' testimony as credible, took place in one junior high school." The evidence, consisting mainly of the testimony of 16 students, suggests that the regime at Drew was exceptionally harsh. The testimony of Ingraham and Andrews, in support of their individual claims for damages, is illustrative. Because he was slow to respond to his teacher's instructions, Ingraham was subjected to more than 20 licks with a paddle while being held over a table in the principal's office. The paddling was so severe that he suffered a hematoma requiring medical attention and keeping him out of school for several days. Andrews was paddled several times for minor infractions. On two occasions he was struck on his arms, once depriving him of the full use of his arm for a week.

The District Court made no findings on the credibility of the students' testimony. Rather, assuming their testimony to be credible, the court found no constitutional basis for relief.***

A panel of the Court of Appeals voted to reverse. The panel concluded that the punishment was so severe and oppressive as to violate the Eighth and Fourteenth Amendments, and that the procedures outlined in Policy 5144 failed to satisfy the requirements of the Due Process Clause. Upon rehearing, the en banc court rejected these conclusions and affirmed the judgment of the District Court.***

In addressing the scope of the Eighth Amendment's prohibition on cruel and unusual punishment, this Court has found it useful to refer to "[t]raditional common-law concepts," *Powell v. Texas*, 392 U.S. 514, 535 (1968) (plurality opinion), and to the "attitude[s] which our society has traditionally taken." *Id.*, at 531. So, too, in defining the requirements of procedural due process under the Fifth and Fourteenth Amendments, the Court has been attuned to what "has always been the law of the land," and to "traditional ideas of fair procedure." We therefore begin by examining the way in which our traditions and our laws have responded to the use of corporal punishment in public schools.

The use of corporal punishment in this country as a means of disciplining schoolchildren dates back to the colonial period. It has survived the transformation of primary and secondary education from the colonial's reliance on optional private arrangements to our present system of compulsory education and dependence on public schools. Despite the general abandonment of corporal punishment as a means of punishing criminal offenders, the practice continues to play a role in the public education of schoolchildren in most parts of the country.

Professional and public opinion is sharply divided on the practice, and has been for more than a century. Yet we can discern no trend toward its elimination.

At common law a single principle has governed the use of corporal punishment since before the American Revolution: Teachers may impose reasonable but not excessive force to discipline a child.***The basic doctrine has not changed. The prevalent rule in this country today privileges such force as a teacher or administrator "reasonably believes to be necessary for [the child's] proper control, training, or education." Restatement (Second) of Torts § 147 (2) (1965); see id., § 153(2). To the extent that the force is excessive or unreasonable, the educator in virtually all States is subject to possible civil and criminal liability.***

Of the 23 States that have addressed the problem through legislation, 21 have authorized the moderate use of corporal punishment in public schools. Of these States only a few have elaborated on the common-law test of reasonableness, typically providing for approval or notification of the child's parents, or for infliction of punishment only by the principal or in the presence of an adult witness. Only two States, Massachusetts and New Jersey, have prohibited all corporal punishment in their public schools. Where the legislatures have not acted, the state courts have uniformly preserved the common-law rule permitting teachers to use reasonable force in disciplining children in their charge.

Against this background of historical and contemporary approval of reasonable corporal punishment, we turn to the constitutional questions before us.

The Eighth Amendment provides: "Excessive bail shall not be required, nor excessive fines imposed, nor cruel and unusual punishments inflicted." Bail, fines, and punishment traditionally have been associated with the criminal process, and by subjecting the three to parallel limitations the text of the Amendment suggests an intention to limit the power of those entrusted with the criminal-law function of government. An examination of the history of the Amendment and the decisions of this Court construing the proscription against cruel and unusual punishment confirms that it was designed to protect those convicted of crimes. We adhere to this long-standing limitation and hold that the Eighth Amendment does not apply to the paddling of children as a means of maintaining discipline in public schools.***

Petitioners acknowledge that the original design of the Cruel and Unusual Punishment Clause was to limit criminal punishments, but urge nonetheless that the prohibition should be extended to ban the paddling of schoolchildren. Observing that the Framers of the Eighth Amendment could not have envisioned our present system of public and compulsory education, with its opportunities for noncriminal punishments, petitioners contend that extension of the prohibition against cruel punishments is necessary lest we afford greater protection to criminals than to schoolchildren. It would be anomalous, they say, if schoolchildren could be beaten without constitutional redress, while hardened criminals suffering the same beatings at the hands of their jailers might have a valid claim under the Eighth Amendment. See *Jackson* v. *Bishop*, 404 F.2d 571 (CA8 1968). Whatever force this logic may have in other settings, we find it an inadequate basis for wrenching the Eighth Amendment from its historical context and extending it to traditional disciplinary practices in the public schools.***

The schoolchild has little need for the protection of the Eighth Amendment.

Though attendance may not always be voluntary, the public school remains an open institution. Except perhaps when very young, the child is not physically restrained from leaving school during school hours; and at the end of the school day, the child is invariably free to return home. Even while at school, the child brings with him the support of family and friends and is rarely apart from teachers and other pupils who may witness and protest any instances of mistreatment.

The openness of the public school and its supervision by the community afford significant safeguards against the kinds of abuses from which the Eighth Amendment protects the prisoner. In virtually every community where corporal punishment is permitted in the schools, these safeguards are reinforced by the legal constraints of the common law. Public school teachers and administrators are privileged at common law to inflict only such corporal punishment as is reasonably necessary for the proper education and discipline of the child; any punishment going beyond the privilege may result in both civil and criminal liability. As long as the schools are open to public scrutiny, there is no reason to believe that the common-law constraints will not effectively remedy and deter excesses such as those alleged in this case.

We conclude that when public school teachers or administrators impose disciplinary corporal punishment, the Eighth Amendment is inapplicable.***

Notes and Issues for Discussion

1. Among the more populous states now permitting corporal punishment in the schools are California (with prior parental approval) (Cal. Educ. Code §§49000-49001, Florida (Fla. Stat. Ann. §232.27), Illinois (Ill. Ann. Stat. ch. 122, §§24-24, 34-84a), Michigan, (Mich. Stats. Ann. §340.756), North Carolina (N.C. Gen. Stat. §115-146), Ohio (Ohio Rev. Code Ann. §3319.41), and Pennsylvania, (Pa. Stat. Ann. Tit. 24, §13-1317).

2. While the majority opinion relied on the openness of the public school and common law remedies to safeguard students against abuses, Justice White in his dissent pointed out that one student had received fifty licks with a paddle for making an obscene phone call. Moreover, "under Florida law, a student punished for an act he did not commit cannot recover damages from a teacher 'proceeding in utmost good faith . . . on the reports and advice of others'; the student has no remedy at all for punishment imposed on the basis of mistaken facts, at least as long as the punishment was reasonable from the point of view of the disciplinarian. . . ." 430 U.S. at 693–4. In a footnote, Justice White questions whether there can be any recovery for excessive corporal punishment under Florida law due to good faith and sovereign immunities. 430 U.S. at 693, Note 11.

3. In another part of the opinion, the court held that a hearing prior to the punishment was unnecessary: "This judgment must be viewed in light of the disciplinary problems commonplace in the schools. . . . The court has repeatedly emphasized the need for affirming the comprehensive authority of the States and of school officials, consistent with fundamental constitutional safeguards, to prescribe and control conduct in the schools. . . .

[T]he risk of error that may result in violation of a schoolchild's substantive rights can only be regarded as minimal. Imposing additional administrative safeguards as a constitutional requirement might reduce that risk marginally, but it would also entail a significant intrusion into an area of primary educational responsibility." 430 U.S. at 682.

4. Several subsequent cases have held there may be recovery for excessive corporal punishment under the Fourteenth Amendment. See *Hall v. Tawney*, 621 F.2d 607 (1980), and *Garcia by Garcia v. Miera*, 817 F.2d 650 (1988).

5. Students have fewer protections than adults in the area of searches. In *New Jersey v. T.L.O.*, 469 U.S. 325 (1985), after two girls were found smoking in a school lavatory in violation of a school rule, they were taken to the principal's office. T.L.O. insisted she was not smoking. The school administrator demanded to inspect her purse and found cigarettes and cigarette rolling papers. Suspecting marijuana use, he looked further finding marijuana, drug-related equipment, a roll of one dollar bills and a list of students. The Court found the search did not violate the Fourth Amendment prohibition against illegal searches. Balancing the student's privacy interest with the need to maintain order and discipline, the Court said: "The school setting . . . requires some modification of the level of suspicion of illicit activity needed to justify a search. . . . We . . . [conclude] that the accommodation of the privacy interests of school children with the substantial need of teachers and administrators for freedom to maintain order in the schools does not require strict adherence to the requirement that searches be based on probable cause to believe that the subject of the search has violated or is violating the law. Rather, the legality of a search of a student should depend simply on the reasonableness, under all the circumstances, of the search. . . . Under ordinary circumstances, a search of a student by a teacher or other school official will be 'justified at its inception' when there are reasonable grounds for suspecting that the search will turn up evidence that the student has violated or is violating either the law or the rules of the school. Such a search will be permissible in its scope when the measures adopted are reasonably related to the objectives of the search and not excessively intrusive in light of the age and sex of the student and the nature of the infraction." 469 U.S. at 340–342.

FREE SPEECH IN THE SCHOOL

Justice Fortas wrote in the *Tinker* case (below):

It can hardly be argued that either students or teachers shed their constitutional rights to freedom of speech or expression at the schoolhouse gate.

A series of court cases after *Tinker* has shown that while this basic principle remains, the right of free expression for students in schools is limited, and depends on the form and content of the expression and the audience.

TINKER *v. DES MOINES INDEP. COMMUNITY SCHOOL DIST.*
393 U.S. 503 (1969)
U. S. SUPREME COURT

MR. JUSTICE FORTAS delivered the opinion of the Court.

Petitioner John F. Tinker, 15 years old, and petitioner Christopher Eckhardt, 16 years old, attended high schools in Des Moines, Iowa. Petitioner Mary Beth Tinker, John's sister, was a 13-year-old student in junior high school.

In December 1965, a group of adults and students in Des Moines held a meeting at the Eckhardt home. The group determined to publicize their objections to the hostilities in Vietnam and their support for a truce by wearing black armbands during the holiday season and by fasting on December 16 and New Year's Eve. Petitioners and their parents had previously engaged in similar activities, and they decided to participate in the program.

The principals of the Des Moines schools became aware of the plan to wear armbands. On December 14, 1965, they met and adopted a policy that any student wearing an armband to school would be asked to remove it, and if he refused he would be suspended until he returned without the armband. Petitioners were aware of the regulation that the school authorities adopted.

On December 16, Mary Beth and Christopher wore black armbands to their schools. John Tinker wore his armband the next day. They were all sent home and suspended from school until they would come back without their armbands. They did not return to school until after the planned period for wearing armbands had expired—that is, until after New Year's Day.

This complaint was filed in the United States District Court by petitioners, through their fathers, under § 1983 of Title 42 of the United States Code. It prayed for an injunction restraining the respondent school officials and the respondent members of the board of directors of the school district from disciplining the petitioners, and it sought nominal damages. After an evidentiary hearing the District Court dismissed the complaint.***

On appeal, the Court of Appeals for the Eighth Circuit considered the case en banc. The court was equally divided, and the District Court's decision was accordingly affirmed, without opinion.***

First Amendment rights, applied in light of the special characteristics of the school environment, are available to teachers and students. It can hardly be argued that either students or teachers shed their constitutional rights to freedom of speech or expression at the schoolhouse gate. This has been the unmistakable holding of this Court for almost 50 years.***

On the other hand, the Court has repeatedly emphasized the need for affirming the comprehensive authority of the States and of school officials, consistent with fundamental constitutional safeguards, to proscribe and control conduct in the schools. Our problem lies in the area where students in the exercise of First Amendment rights collide with the rules of the school authorities.***

Only a few of the 18,000 students in the school system wore the black armbands. Only five students were suspended for wearing them. There is no indication that the work of the schools or any class was disrupted. Outside the classrooms, a few students made hostile remarks to the children wearing armbands, but there were no threats or acts of violence on school premises.

The District Court concluded that the action of the school authorities was reasonable because it was based upon their fear of a disturbance from the wearing of the armbands. But, in our system, undifferentiated fear or apprehension of disturbance is not enough to overcome the right to freedom of expression. Any departure from absolute regimentation may cause trouble. Any variation from the majority's opinion may inspire fear. Any word spoken, in class, in the lunchroom, or on the campus, that deviates from the views of another person may start an argument or cause a disturbance. But our Constitution says we must take this risk, and our history says that it is this sort of hazardous freedom—this kind of openness—that is the basis of our national strength and of the independence and vigor of Americans who grow up and live in this relatively permissive, often disputatious, society.

In order for the State in the person of school officials to justify prohibition of a particular expression of opinion, it must be able to show that its action was caused by something more than a mere desire to avoid the discomfort and unpleasantness that always accompany an unpopular viewpoint. Certainly where there is no finding and no showing that engaging in of the forbidden conduct would "materially and substantially interfere with the requirements of appropriate discipline in the operation of the school," the prohibition cannot be sustained.

In the present case, the District Court made no such finding, and our independent examination of the record fails to yield evidence that the school authorities had reason to anticipate that the wearing of armbands would substantially interfere with the work of the school or impinge upon the rights of other students. Even an official memorandum prepared after the suspension that listed the reasons for the ban on wearing the armbands made no reference to the anticipation of such disruption.

On the contrary, the action of the school authorities appears to have been based upon an urgent wish to avoid the controversy which might result from the expression, even by the silent symbol of armbands, of opposition to this Nation's part in the conflagration in Vietnam.***

It is also relevant that the school authorities did not purport to prohibit the wearing of all symbols of political or controversial significance. The record shows that students in some of the schools wore buttons relating to national political campaigns, and some even wore the Iron Cross, traditionally a symbol of Nazism. The order prohibiting the wearing of armbands did not extend to these. Instead, a particular symbol—black armbands worn to exhibit opposition to this Nation's involvement in Vietnam—was singled out for prohibition. Clearly, the prohibition of expression of one particular opinion, at least without evidence that it is necessary to avoid material and substantial interference with schoolwork or discipline, is not constitutionally permissible.

In our system, state-operated schools may not be enclaves of totalitarianism. School officials do not possess absolute authority over their students. Students in school as well as out of school are "persons" under our Constitution. They are possessed of fundamental rights which the State must respect, just as they themselves must respect their obligations to the State. In our system, students may not be regarded as closed-circuit recipients of only that which the State chooses to communicate. They may not be confined to the expression of those sentiments that are official approved. In the absence of a specific showing of constitutionally valid reasons to regulate their speech, students are entitled to freedom of expression of their views.***

As we have discussed, the record does not demonstrate any facts which might reasonably have led school authorities to forecast substantial disruption of or material interference with school activities, and no disturbances or disorders on the school premises in fact occurred. These petitioners merely went about their ordained rounds in school. Their deviation consisted only in wearing on their sleeve a band of black cloth, not more than two inches wide. They wore it to exhibit their disapproval of the Vietnam hostilities and their advocacy of a truce, to make their views known, and, by their example, to influence others to adopt them. They neither interrupted school activities nor sought to intrude in the school affairs or the lives of others. They caused discussion outside of the class rooms, but no interference with work and no disorder. In the circumstances, our Constitution does not permit officials of the State to deny their form of expression.

Notes and Issues for Discussion

1. What if the school district banned all political symbols? Would it be on stronger ground for banning the armbands? What if the schools were afraid of disruptions and riots? Would this make a difference?

2. In his dissent, Justice Black noted that the youngest of the protesting students was eight years old and in second grade, and another was eleven years old and in fifth grade. Mr. Tinker was a minister paid by the American Friends Service Committee and another student's mother was an official in a peace organization. Should this make a difference? Is the *Tinker* case about free expression of students or their parents?

3. Later cases have identified limits to free expression in the schools. In *Bethel School Dist. No. 403 v. Fraser*, 478 U.S. 675 (1986), the Court upheld the suspension of a high school student. While the school disciplinary code prohibited obscenity, the student's speech was sexually suggestive but not obscene. The student made a nominating speech for a school election before 600 high school students, some as young as fourteen. The speech evoked reactions from some students that included bewilderment and embarrassment. The Supreme Court distinguished the case from *Tinker*

both in terms of the content of the speech "offensively lewd and indecent" and in the reaction it caused. "The First Amendment does not prevent the school officials from determining that to permit a vulgar and lewd speech such as respondent's would undermine the school's basic educational mission. A high school assembly or classroom is no place for a sexually explicit monologue directed toward an unsuspecting audience of teenage students."

In his dissent, Justice Stevens said: "It does seem to me, however, that if a student is to be punished for using offensive speech, he is entitled to fair notice of the scope of the prohibition and the consequences of its violation. . . . This respondent was an outstanding young man with a fine academic record . . . chosen by the student body to speak at the school's commencement exercises. . . . [This] indicates that he was probably in a better position to determine whether an audience composed of 600 of his contemporaries would be offended by the use of a four-letter word—or a sexual metaphor—than a group of judges who are at least two generations and 3,000 miles away from the scene of the crime. The fact that the speech may not have been offensive to his audience—or that he honestly believed that it would be inoffensive—does not mean that he had a constitutional right to deliver it. For the school—not the student—must prescribe rules of conduct in an educational institution. But it does mean that he should not be disciplined for speaking frankly in a school assembly if he had no reason to anticipate punitive consequences." 478 U.S. at 675. The Justice also observed the Appeals Court had noted there was no evidence that any students found the speech offensive.

4. In *Hazelwood School District v. Kuhlmeier*, 484 U.S. 260 (1988), the Court found that the deletion of two pages of material from a school newspaper by the school principal was not a violation of the First Amendment. The excised material dealt with pregnancy and divorce, and among the reasons for the deletions were the pregnant students might have been identifiable despite aliases, and references to sexual activity and birth control were inappropriate for younger students. Citing *Fraser, Tinker*, and *T.L.O.*, the Court noted that "First Amendment rights of students in public schools are not automatically coextensive with the rights of adults in other settings and must be applied in light of the special characteristics of the school environment. A school need not tolerate student speech that is inconsistent with its basic educational mission, even though the government could not censor similar speech outside the school. . . . We thus recognize that the determination of what matter of speech in the classroom or in school assembly is inappropriate properly rests with the school board rather than with the federal courts." 484 U.S. at 266–267. The Court distinguished *Tinker* in that it related to personal expression, as opposed to the content of a school-sponsored publication. After *Fraser* and *Kuhlmeier*, what speech and expression remains protected in the public schools—what is left of *Tinker*?

The Rights of Children

In most of the decisions presented so far, the interests of the child and parent are the same. Both Gerald Gault and his parents sought due process in the Arizona juvenile court. The Tinker children and their parents wanted to protest. Neither the children nor their parents in *Ingraham* favored corporal punishment in the schools. But what if the interests of parent and child collide? Do children have rights independent of and perhaps in conflict with their parent's wishes? In *Wisconsin v. Yoder*, the Supreme Court upheld the right of Amish people to refuse to send their children to public school after eighth grade in violation of Wisconsin's compulsory education act, finding this choice as part of their free exercise of religion. In his dissenting opinion, Justice Douglas presented the potential conflict between children and parents, arguing that on such as important issue as their education, the children should be heard.

WISCONSIN v. YODER
406 U.S. 205 (1972)
U.S. SUPREME COURT

MR. JUSTICE DOUGLAS, dissenting in part.

I agree with the Court that the religious scruples of the Amish are opposed to the education of their children beyond the grade schools, yet I disagree with the Court's conclusion that the matter is within the dispensation of parents alone. The Court's analysis assumes that the only interests at stake in the case are those of the Amish parents on the one hand, and those of the State on the other. The difficulty with this approach is that, despite the Court's claim, the parents are seeking to vindicate not only their own free exercise claims, but also those of their high-school-age children.***Although the lower courts and a majority of this Court assume an identity of interest between parent and child, it is clear that they have treated the religious interest of the child as a factor in the analysis.***

If the parents in this case are allowed a religious exemption, the inevitable effect is to impose the parents' notions of religious duty upon their children. Where the child is mature enough to express potentially conflicting desires, it would be an invasion of the child's rights to permit such an imposition without canvassing his views. As in *Prince* v. *Massachusetts*, 321 U.S. 158, it is an imposition resulting from this very litigation. As the child has no other effective forum, it is in this litigation that his rights should be considered. And, if an Amish child desires to attend high school, and is mature enough to have that desire respected, the State may well be able to override the parents' religiously motivated objections.***

On this important and vital matter of education, I think the children should be entitled to be heard. While the parents, absent dissent, normally speak for the entire family, the education of the child is a matter on which the child will often have decided views. He may want to be a pianist or an astronaut or an oceanographer. To do so he will have to break from the Amish tradition.

It is the future of the student, not the future of the parents, that is imperiled by today's decision. If a parent keeps his child out of school beyond the grade school, then the child will be forever barred from entry into the new and amazing world of diversity that we have today. The child may decide that that is the preferred course, or he may rebel. It is the student's judgment, not his parents', that is essential if we are to give full meaning to what we have said about the Bill of Rights and of the right of students to be masters of their own destiny.[1] If he is harnessed to the Amish way of life by those in authority over him and if his education is truncated, his entire life may be stunted and deformed. The child, therefore, should be given an opportunity to be heard before the State gives the exemption which we honor today.

Notes and Issues for Discussion

1. The issue of autonomy vs. parental decision making has appeared in other areas, notably a minor's right to an abortion and civil commitment of minors. Upholding a minor's right to an abortion, the Court has approved various restrictions such a parental notification and a judicial bypass. See generally, p.197. The Court has generally supported parental decision-making. See *Parham*, p. 387.

2. In *In re Snyder*, 532 P. 2d 278 (1975), Cynthia Nell Snyder, a sixteen-year-old girl who found living at home intolerable, sought the assistance of a youth advocacy group which filed a petition in juvenile court that Cynthia was incorrigible and should be removed from her home. The parents opposed the petition. At the trial, Cynthia stated "I just absolutely refuse to go back there, I can't live with them." The trial court, taking testimony from Cynthia, her family, and various professionals found Cynthia to be incorrigible and that she did not have to return home. The Washington Supreme Court upheld the decision.

3. In April, 1992, Gregory K., an eleven-year-old boy who had been in foster care for almost three years, filed a petition to terminate his biological parents' rights so that he could be adopted by his foster parents. The trial court found Gregory had standing and approved the petition. A Florida appellate court found Gregory had no standing, and the issue is currently

---

[1] The court below brushed aside the students' interests with the offhand comment that "[w]hen a child reaches the age of judgment, he can choose for himself his religion." But there is nothing in this record to indicate that the moral and intellectual judgment demanded of the student by the question in this case is beyond his capacity. Children far younger than the 14- and 15-year-olds involved here are regularly permitted to testify in custody and other proceedings. Indeed, the failure to call the affected child in a custody hearing is often reversible error. Moreover, there is substantial agreement among child psychologists and sociologists that the moral and intellectual maturity of the 14-year-old approaches that of the adult. The maturity of Amish youth, who identify with and assume adult roles from early childhood, is certainly not less than that of children in the general population.

on appeal to the Florida Supreme Court. See Russ, "Through the Eyes of a Child, 'Gregory K.': A Child's Right to Be Heard," 27 *Fam. Law Q.* 365, Fall 1993.

SELECTED REFERENCES

Areen, J. *Family Law-Cases and Materials* (2nd ed., 1985 with 1991 Supplement).

Clark, H. *Law of Domestic Relations* (1987).

Lambda Legal Defense and Education Fund. *Domestic Partnership: Issues and Legislation* (1992).

Mnookin, R. H. "Child custody adjudication: Judicial functions in the face of indeterminacy", 39 *Law and Contemporary Problems* 226 (1975).

Mnookin, R. H., and Weisberg, D. K. *Child, Family and State* (2nd ed., 1989).

Note, "A more perfect union: Legal and social analysis of domestic partnership ordinances," 92 *Columbia L.R.* 1164 (1992).

Note, "Developments in the law: Sexual orientation and the law," 102 *Harvard L.R.* 617 (1989).

U.S. Bureau of the Census, *Statistical Abstracts of the United States* (1993).

Walker, T., and Lindad, E. "Family law in the fifty states: An overview," 26 *Family L.Q.* 319 (1993).

Weitzman, L. *The Divorce Revolution* (1985).

CHAPTER 10

FAMILIES AND CHILDREN II

Child Abuse, Termination of Parental Rights, Foster Care, and Domestic Violence

CHILD ABUSE AND NEGLECT

In 1990, there were over 2.5 million reports of suspected abuse and neglect in America, about half involving neglect and half involving physical or sexual abuse (Myers, 1992). While some claim these figures are inflated (Pride, 1986), there is no denying that child abuse is a serious national problem. Of these instances reported, a considerably lesser number were substantiated. Of those that were not substantiated, a number probably were abuse cases, but lacked sufficient proof.[1]

For the health and human services professional important legal issues concern identifying child abuse, mandatory reporting, immunity for good faith reporting, liability for failure to report, the impact of privileged communications, and courtroom testimony in child abuse proceedings. In this discussion, both abuse and neglect will, except when noted, be included within the term child abuse.

Defining Child Abuse

State child abuse statutory definitions range from brief to lengthy and complex. Some states differentiate between abuse—more serious harm or that involving nonaccidental physical injury—and neglect—less serious harm or that involving a failure to care, supervise, provide necessities or treatment. Some states limit child abuse to actions or inaction by a parent, guardian, or person with custody or control. Others include the acts of any adult. Some states include abuse in institutional settings such as schools, residential centers, state institutions, and day care centers. Types of abuse in civil statutes may include physical or emotional harm, child endangerment, failure to supervise, abandonment, sexual abuse, and failure to provide food, clothing, shelter, or medical treatment. Some state statutes add several qualifications such as a provision that the parent or guardian must be financially able to provide the missing care, or exceptions for reasonable physical discipline or good faith religious care through faith healing.[2]

The Oregon statute is an example of a relatively uncomplicated definition:

(a) Any physical injury to a child which has been caused by other than accidental means, including any injury which appears to be at variance with the explanation given of the injury. (b) Neglect which leads to physical harm. . . . (c) Sexual molestation. Ore. Rev. Stats. §418.740.

In contrast, the New York statute typifies the more complex:

"Abused child" means a child less than eighteen years of age whose parent or other person legally responsible for his care

(i) inflicts or allows to be inflicted upon such child physical injury by other than accidental means which causes or creates a substantial risk of death, or serious or protracted disfigurement, or protracted impairment of physical or emotional health or protracted loss or impairment of the function of any bodily organ, or

(ii) creates or allows to be created a substantial risk of physical injury to such child by other than accidental means which would be likely to cause death or serious or protracted disfigurement, or protracted impairment of physical or emotional health or protracted loss or impairment of the function of any bodily organ, or

(iii) commits or allows to be committed, a sex offense against such child, as defined in the penal law, provided however, that the corroboration requirements contained therein shall not apply to proceedings under this article.

"Neglected child" means a child less than eighteen years of age

(i) whose physical, mental or emotional condition has been impaired or is in imminent danger of becoming impaired as a result of a failure of his parent or other person legally responsible for his care to exercise a minimum degree of care

(A) in supplying the child with adequate food, clothing, shelter or education in accordance with the provisions of . . . the educational law, or medical, dental, optometrical or surgical care, though financially able to do so or offered financial or other reasonable means to do so; or

(B) in providing the child with proper supervision or guardianship, by unreasonably inflicting or allowing to be inflicted harm, or a substantial risk thereof, including the infliction of excessive corporal punishment; or by misusing a drug or drugs; or by misusing alcoholic beverages to the extent that he loses self-control of his actions; or by any other acts of a similarly serious nature requiring aid of the court; provided, however, that where the respondent is voluntarily and regularly participating in a rehabilitative program, evidence that the respondent has repeatedly misused a drug or drugs or alcoholic beverages to the extent that he loses self-control of his actions shall not establish that the child is a neglected child in the absence of evidence establishing that the child's physical, mental, or emotional condition has been impaired or is in imminent danger of becoming impaired as set forth in paragraph (i) of this subdivision; or

(ii) who has been abandoned. . . . N.Y. Soc. Serv. Law §1012.[3]

The New York statute lists the misuse of drugs and alcohol as grounds for neglect. A growing number of states now include exposure to drugs *in utero* as child abuse and neglect, and some states have proceeded criminally against drug abusing pregnant women, on grounds such as criminal neglect or distribution of drugs to a minor.[4]

Mandatory Reporting of Child Abuse

Every state has a child abuse mandatory reporting law. Failure to report may subject an individual to criminal or civil actions. Conversely, in many states, good faith reporting of child abuse carries with it an immunity to any suit, civil or criminal.

About one-third of the states have universal reporting, requiring any person to report. These statutes take one of two general forms. A few states such as New Jersey simply require any person with belief or suspicion to report: "Any person having a reasonable cause to believe that a child has been subjected to child abuse . . . shall report . . ." N.J.S.A. 9:6–8.10. More frequently, the statutes will identify specific individuals who must report and then conclude with a statement that any person is required to report (Cole, 1987).

The remaining states do not have universal reporting requirements, but instead list individuals mandated to report. Many states require specific professionals such as physicians, nurses, mental health professionals, teachers, and social workers to report child abuse. In some states, the list is lengthy.

For example, New York requires reports from

> any physician; surgeon; medical examiner; coroner; dentist; dental hygienist; osteopath; optometrist; chiropractor; podiatrist; resident; intern; psychologist; registered nurse; hospital personnel; a Christian Science practitioner; school official; social services worker; day care center worker; provider of daily or group family day care; employee or volunteer in a residential care facility . . . or another child care or foster care worker; mental health professional; peace officer; police officer; district attorney or assistant district attorney; investigator . . . or other law enforcement official. N.Y. Soc. Serv. Law §413.

Thus virtually every state either through a universal reporting requirement or by identification of specific professions mandates all health and human services professionals to report abuse or neglect if they have the requisite degree of knowledge.[5]

A recurring problem is the conflict between mandatory reporting laws and state confidentiality and privilege laws prohibiting disclosure of certain communications between patients, clients, and certain professionals. Many states specifically exempt child abuse reporting from the privileged communications, but others do not make this distinction. Sometimes a limited range of professionals are exempted from the child abuse reporting laws. For example, Washington exempts clergypersons from reporting; Oregon exempts the reporting of child abuse disclosed in privileged communications made to psychiatrists, psychologists, clergy and attorneys; and Maryland exempts mandatory reporting of disclosures of abuse made by sex offenders in treatment.[6]

Determinations of Abuse

DEGREE OF CERTAINTY

How sure must the professional be that abuse has taken place before reporting? Some professionals concerned about the consequences of having a child welfare case opened are reluctant to file a report unless the abuse is a virtual certainty. But no mandatory reporting statute has this requirement. While states vary in the degree of certainty needed to report, none require proof beyond a reasonable doubt or even probable cause. Some states only require a suspicion that the abuse has taken place; many specify a reasonable cause to believe, a reasonable belief, a reasonable cause to suspect, or a reasonable suspicion as the requisite level of knowledge.[7] These less demanding levels require a lesser degree of certainty that the abuse or neglect has taken place.

Nor does the health and human services professional need to investigate reasonable suspicions before reporting. State child welfare agencies have the mandated duty to investigate suspected child abuse.

ELEMENTS OF ABUSE AND NEGLECT

Consider the following cases. Was there reportable abuse? Were there sufficient grounds for going to court?

IN RE VULON CHILDREN
288 N.Y.S.2d 203 (1968)
NEW YORK FAMILY COURT

NANETTE DEMBITZ, JUDGE.

This neglect proceeding was initiated by a caseworker of the Bureau of Child Welfare of New York City, by a petition praying for a determination that the three Vulon children are neglected by both their father and mother within the meaning of article 3 of the Family Court Act. At the close of a lengthy hearing, the petition was dismissed.

Once a determination of neglect is made, the Court acquires not only broad authority to control the life of the family but even to deprive the parents of their cardinal right to the custody of their children (New York Family Court Act, secs. 353 to 355, Family Court Rules, rules 3.6, 3.7). Accordingly, a finding of neglect cannot be made lightly; the Court should exercise "its jurisdiction to interfere with parental guardianship reluctantly, and only upon strong and convincing proof of unfitness on the part of the parent or material benefit to the child."

This standard of judicial caution must be observed in applying this Court's mandate to dismiss a neglect petition if its allegations "are not established, or if the court concludes that its aid is not required on the record before it***" (Family Court Act, sec. 351). The Court dismissed the petition herein on both of these grounds.

The hearing showed without contradiction—and indeed from the mouths of petitioner's own witnesses—that Mr. and Mrs. Vulon are hard-working and devoted parents with an intact family, who maintain a well-kept apartment. The children—Maurice, 13, Marie, 10, and Michelle, 8, all attending a Catholic school, have good school records with respect to both studies and behavior, and are not known to have ever been the subject of any type of complaint at school or in the community. The Court's interview with the children (in the presence of the attorneys for all parties) revealed them to be well-spoken, well-dressed, well-groomed, and apparently well cared for. How then did this family become involved with the City's Bureau of Child Welfare?

The Bureau's petition alleges that the three children are left alone and unattended from 3:30 to 5:30 P.M. on week-days; that after Michelle was admitted to Lincoln Hospital "with severe injury to the vaginal area***the hospital reported

Michelle as an abused child whose injuries were most likely the result of rape, and the circumstances surrounding this incident were unexplained by the parents." The undisputed evidence shows that these allegations are misleading in significant respects.

Both Mr. and Mrs. Vulon work to support the family, Mrs. Vulon as an IBM key punch operator. She arrives home from work at 5:30 or a few minutes before. The three children generally return from school between 3:30 and 4:30 and then stay in the apartment doing homework. It is questionable whether it would constitute "neglect" to leave habitually well-behaved children of ages 13, 10 and 8, unattended in an apparently secure apartment in the afternoon for the two hours alleged in the petition; possibly self-responsibility to this limited extent, in a family where parents show an over-all affection and concern, may not only be harmless but beneficial. In any event, Mrs. Vulon testified without contradiction that since the troubling incident here involved she had secured some one to stay in the apartment in the afternoons until she returns from work. Thus there is no evidence that the children are likely to be unattended; this Court's statutory mandate is—as in legal principle it must be—to determine whether, despite any past deficiency, children are at the time of the hearing suffering or are likely to suffer from neglect (Family Court Act, sec. 312).

The evidence showed that on the afternoon of the incident in issue—which was a partial school holiday—Maurice was in and out of the home doing errands, Marie was washing dishes, and Michelle was first using the vacuum cleaner and then taking a bath, Marie heard Michelle exclaim from the bathroom and saw she was bleeding. Mrs. Vulon came home shortly thereafter, and although the bleeding was not extreme took Michelle to Prospect Hospital. There, because no physician was available, she was referred to Lincoln Hospital. By the time of her arrival at Lincoln the bleeding was more profuse and a physician recommended a surgical procedure under anesthesia for remedial and exploratory purposes. One source of suspicion against the family appears to have been that Mrs. Vulon did not immediately consent to surgery for her daughter; she testified that she had wanted to wait for her husband to arrive from Prospect Hospital, where he had expected to meet them. (Mrs. Vulon, who emigrated from Haiti in 1958, speaks poor English). The father arrived shortly; consent was given forthwith; and the child's condition was soon remedied.

The Lincoln Hospital physician called by petitioner testified that the bleeding was attributable to a laceration of the vagina of about an inch; that he could not estimate the source of the laceration with any certainty except that rape probably was *not* the cause; that the condition was probably due to "trauma" of some other type and could have been self-inflicted.

The erroneous suspicion of rape—which persisted apparently because of a failure to consult this knowledgeable physician—underlay petitioner's allegation as to the parents' failure to explain the circumstances of Michelle's bleeding. Mrs. Vulon did explain the circumstances to petitioner and other interrogators to the extent she could ascertain them from the children. There is no indication that she knew or could have known anything more than she recounted. What she failed to do was to accept the mistaken allegation of rape and to aid the Bureau in its exploration of this suspicion. According to petitioner, the parents "refused to believe that their child had been raped. They stated that they would not go into any conversation about rape with their children. They explained that in their country, a child did not learn about sex until the child was about 15 years of age; nor did the mother want me to discuss this with the child."

No doubt Mrs. Vulon's perturbation (described by petitioner) about the erroneous rape theory was due in part to the great damage that this charge would have inflicted on Maurice, the only suspect, who was an exemplary student in a Catholic school, aspiring to the priesthood. Though Mrs. Vulon apparently was herself concerned and frustrated that she was unable to ascertain the exact source of Michelle's bleeding, it was to the benefit rather than the detriment of her children that she refused to succumb to the mistaken suspicion of rape or to give it further currency.

Petitioner's attorney argued that neglect should be inferred from the parental failure to explain the basis for Michelle's bleeding. When there is insufficient evidence as to whether or not parents are responsible for a child's injury, an inference of parental abuse or lack of attention may, under special circumstances, be drawn from the injury itself coupled with the lack of explanation (for example, when a young baby has recurrent fractures, explicable only by either blows or serious falls). In the case at bar, however, it cannot be inferred—nor has it even been suggested—that the parents contributed directly to Michelle's condition (which the father believed, perhaps correctly, was due to some esoteric disease process). Further, considering the now-established improbability of rape and the possibility of a self-inflicted wound, it appears unlikely that Michelle's situation would have been any different if an adult had been in the apartment. In any event, any possible fault in supervisory care has been remedied, as noted above.

Prosecution of this petition was largely attributable, it is clear, to the parents' refusal of the Bureau's request that they consent to their children's examination by the Court psychiatrist. Such examination apparently was viewed in part by the Bureau as a possible method of determining whether Maurice committed the non-existent rape. So intent was the Bureau on its proposal that its attorney approached the Court ex parte before the hearing to ask it to order such examinations.

The failure to seek psychiatric aid was not alleged in the petition and therefore cannot, under the Family Court Act, the CPLR, or the due process guarantee of the Constitution be passed upon in this proceeding as an element of neglect. Even if properly alleged, however, the parents' rejection of psychiatric aid would not under the circumstances of this case and with the suspicion of rape eliminated, constitute neglect. The Vulons believe that their children's welfare will not be served by probing into the frightening episode of Michelle's bleeding by social workers or psychiatrists, and indeed indicate that the repetitive references to the incident to which the children have already been subjected were detrimental.

This judge personally has confidence in the psychiatric method and in free discussion with children of sex-related experiences. However, one cannot say that this approach has been so successful with our youth that the State can force parents—particularly in a family with a distinctive cultural pattern—to accept it, unless the need and the likelihood of benefit is clear.

It is the function of the trial court "which has seen and heard the witnesses" to determine whether neglect exists. This Court believes from observation of these parents and children that they have an affectionate, mutually-respecting and beneficial relationship. A good faith appraisal by responsible and concerned parents, such as the Vulons, of the best way to handle a problem of child development on which reasonable men can differ in their value judgments, is not neglect. While it is necessary and proper to conduct some investigation of whether Michelle's unusual condition indicated abuse or lack of care, the State cannot, without more justification than here appears, override the liberty of the parents, protected by the Constitution, to bring up their children as they think best.

Notes and Issues for Discussion

1. It appears that there was no abuse or rape and that the injury to Michelle was "probably due to trauma" and "could have been self-inflicted." What was the alleged neglect in the *Vulon* case? A failure to supervise? The injury to Michelle? Parental failure to explain Michelle's injury? Perhaps all three?

2. The case was probably reported by the hospital. If you were the hospital professional receiving the case would you report it to Protective Services? If upon further investigation you concluded that the injury was most likely self-inflicted, would you report?

3. If you worked for the protective services agency and you received the hospital report, do you think there is sufficient information for an investigation?

4. If the issue is a failure to supervise, does it make a difference whether the parents are not at home between 3:30 and 5:30 because they are at work or at the nearest tavern? Whether the children are well cared for or not?

5. In *In re H. Children,* 317 N.Y.S. 2d 535 (1970), the court found neglect because a married woman was living with her five minor children and another man, despite testimony that the children were well cared for. The court observed "Isolated instances of infidelity can be overlooked . . . but for a married woman to live with a man with five minor children of her undissolved marriage transcends the area of an isolated occurrence. . . . The gods visit the sins of the fathers upon the children. Here the sins of the mother are being visited upon the children and as *parens patriae* we are duty bound to intervene." 317 N.Y.S. 2d at 537. The case was decided some twenty years ago. Could it still occur? What if the mother lived with her female lover or the father had the children and lived with a male lover? How would courts in your jurisdiction respond today?

6. Beneath the rationale of the *In re H.* court lies an important point: trial courts have broad discretion in applying child abuse and neglect laws, and a judge's view of morality may be an important factor.

MATTER OF HOFBAUER
47 N.Y.2d 648, 393 N.E.2d 1009 (1979)
NEW YORK COURT OF APPEALS

JASEN, JUDGE.

This appeal involves the issue whether a child suffering from Hodgkin's disease whose parents failed to follow the recommendation of an attending physician to have their child treated by radiation and chemotherapy, but, rather, placed their child under the care of physicians advocating nutritional or metabolic therapy, including injections of laetrile, is a "neglected child" within the meaning of section 1012 of the Family Court Act. This case does not involve the legality of the use of laetrile per se in this State inasmuch as neither party contends that a duly licensed New York physician may not administer laetrile to his or her own patients. Nor is this an action brought against a physician to test the validity of his determination to treat Hodgkin's disease by prescribing metabolic therapy and injections of laetrile. Rather, the issue presented for our determination is whether the parents of a child afflicted with Hodgkin's disease have failed to exercise a minimum degree of care in supplying their child with adequate medical care by entrusting the child's physical well-being to a duly licensed physician who advocates a treatment not widely embraced by the medical community.

The relevant facts are as follows: In October, 1977, Joseph Hofbauer, then a seven-year-old child, was diagnosed as suffering from Hodgkin's disease, a disease which is almost always fatal if left untreated. The then attending physician, Dr. Arthur Cohn, recommended that Joseph be seen by an oncologist or hematologist for further treatment which would have included radiation treatments and possibly chemotherapy, the conventional modes of treatment. Joseph's parents, however, after making numerous inquiries, rejected Dr. Cohn's advice and elected to take Joseph to Fairfield Medical Clinic in Jamaica where a course of nutritional or metabolic therapy, including injections of laetrile, was initiated.

Upon Joseph's return home to Saratoga County in November, 1977, the instant neglect proceeding was commenced, pursuant to article 10 of the Family Court Act, upon the filing of a petition in Family Court by the Saratoga County Commissioner of Social Services. The petition alleged, in substance, that Joseph's parents neglected their son by their failure to follow the advice of Dr. Cohn with respect to treatment and, instead, chose a course of treatment for Joseph in the form of nutritional therapy and laetrile. A preliminary hearing was held and the court, finding "that there exists the probability of neglect of [Joseph] by his parents," ordered that Joseph be temporarily removed from the custody of his parents and placed in St. Peter's Hospital in Albany.

Thereafter, Joseph's parents made an application to have Joseph returned to their custody. A hearing was duly commenced in December, 1977, but the proceeding was suspended for six months when a stipulation was entered into by the parties returning Joseph to the custody and care of his parents, and authorizing Joseph to come under the care of Dr. Michael Schachter, a physician duly licensed in New York who is a proponent of metabolic therapy. The stipulation further provided that at least one other physician would be consulted regularly, with medical reports to be submitted to the court periodically.

At the direction of the Appellate Division, a fact-finding hearing on the merits of this case was conducted by Family Court in June, 1978. A review of the testimony adduced at the hearing reveals a sharp conflict in medical opinion as to the effectiveness of the treatment being administered to Joseph. The physicians produced by appellants testified, in substance, that radiation and chemotherapy were the accepted methods of treating Hodgkin's disease and that nutritional therapy was an inadequate and ineffective mode of treatment. In addition, two physicians, who by stipulation examined Joseph during the hearing, testified, in essence, that there had been a progression of the disease and denounced the treatment being rendered to Joseph as ineffective.

Two physicians produced by respondents, however, testified that they prescribed nutritional therapy for cancer patients and considered such therapy as a beneficial and effective mode of treatment, although they did not preclude the use of conventional therapy—radiation treatments and chemotherapy—in some cases.

Dr. Schachter, the attending physician, then testified that in his opinion Joseph was responding well to the nutritional therapy and that both his appetite and energy levels were good. Dr. Schachter further stated that he had consulted with numerous other physicians concerning Joseph's treatment, and that he never ruled out the possibility of conventional treatment if the boy's condition appeared to be deteriorating beyond control. Significantly, Joseph's father also testified that he would allow his son to be treated by conventional means if Dr. Schachter so advised. Both appellants' and respondents' witnesses testified as to the potentially dangerous side effects of radiation treatments and chemotherapy which could include, among other things, fibrosis of the body organs, swelling of the heart, impairment of the growth centers and leukemia.

Family Court, finding that Joseph's mother and father are concerned and loving parents who have employed conscientious efforts to secure for their child a viable alternative of medical treatment administered by a duly licensed physician, found that Joseph was not a neglected child within the meaning of section 1012 of the Family Court Act and dismissed the petitions. On appeal, a unanimous Appellate Division affirmed. Leave to appeal to this court was granted by the Appellate Division. There should be an affirmance.

Our threshold task in this case is, by necessity, the identification of the standard of neglect against which the facts of this case may be measured. So far as is material for the issue under consideration, a neglected child is defined, by statute, to "[mean] a child less than eighteen years of age whose physical***condition has been impaired or is in imminent danger of becoming impaired as a result of the failure of his parent***to exercise a minimum degree of care in supplying the child with adequate***medical***care, though financially able to do so." (Family Ct. Act, §1012, subd. [f], par. [i], cl. [A].)

A reading of this statutory provision makes it clear that the Legislature has imposed upon the parents of a child the nondelegable affirmative duty to provide their child with adequate medical care. What constitutes adequate medical care, however, cannot be judged in a vacuum free from external influences, but, rather, each case must be decided on its own particular facts. In this regard, we deem certain factors significant in determining whether Joseph was afforded adequate medical care.

It is readily apparent that the phrase "adequate medical care" does not require a parent to beckon the assistance of a physician for every trifling affliction which a child may suffer for everyday experience teaches us that many of a child's ills may be overcome by simple household nursing. We believe, however, that the statute does require a parent to entrust the child's care to that of a physician when such course would be undertaken by an ordinarily prudent and loving parent, "solicitous for the welfare of his child and anxious to promote [the child's] recovery." This obligation, however, is not without qualification.

It surely cannot be disputed that every parent has a fundamental right to rear its child. While this right is not absolute inasmuch as the State, as *parens patriae*, may intervene to ensure that a child's health or welfare is not being seriously jeopardized by a parent's fault or omission, great deference must be accorded a parent's choice as to the mode of medical treatment to be undertaken and the physician selected to administer the same.

In this regard, it is important to stress that a parent, in making the sensitive decision as to how the child should be treated, may rely upon the recommendations and competency of the attending physician if he or she is duly licensed to practice medicine in this State, for "[i]f a physician is licensed by the State, he is recognized by the State as capable of exercising acceptable clinical judgment."

Ultimately, however, the most significant factor in determining whether a child is being deprived of adequate medical care, and, thus, a neglected child within the meaning of the statute, is whether the parents have provided an acceptable course of medical treatment for their child in light of all the surrounding circumstances. This inquiry cannot be posed in terms of whether the parent has made a "right" or a "wrong" decision, for the present state of the practice of medicine, despite its vast advances, very seldom permits such definitive conclusions. Nor can a court assume the role of a surrogate parent and establish as the objective criteria with which to evaluate a parent's decision its own judgment as to the exact method or degree of medical treatment which should be provided, for such standard is fraught with subjectivity. Rather, in our view, the court's inquiry should be whether the parents, once having sought accredited medical assistance and having been made aware of the seriousness of their child's affliction and the possibility of cure if a certain mode of treatment is undertaken, have provided for their child a treatment which is recommended by their physician and which has not been totally rejected by all responsible medical authority.

With these considerations in mind and cognizant that the State has the burden of demonstrating neglect, we now examine the facts of this case. It is abundantly clear that this is not a case where the parents, for religious reasons, refused necessary medical procedures for their child, nor is this a case where the parents have made a irreversible decision to deprive their child of a certain mode of treatment. Indeed, this is not a case where the child is receiving no medical treatment, for the record discloses that Joseph's mother and father were concerned and loving parents who sought qualified medical assistance for their child.

Rather, appellants predicate their charge of neglect upon the basis that Joseph's parents have selected for their child a mode of treatment which is inadequate and ineffective. Both courts below found, however—and we conclude that these findings are supported by the record—that numerous qualified doctors have been consulted by Dr. Schachter and have contributed to the child's care; that the parents have both serious and justifiable concerns about the deleterious effects of radiation treatments and chemotherapy; that there is medical proof that the nutritional treatment being administered Joseph was controlling his condition and that such treatment is not as toxic as is the conventional treatment; and that conventional treatments will be administered to the child if his condition so warrants. In light of these affirmed findings of fact, we are unable to conclude, as a matter of law, that Joseph's parents have not undertaken reasonable efforts to ensure that acceptable medical treatment is being provided their child.

Notes and Issues for Discussion

1. Medical choices by parents for children raise difficult issues. In *Hofbauer*, the choice was between alternate medical approaches, one traditional, the other nontraditional. The traditional approach, often effective at early stages of Hodgkin's disease, is accompanied by many documented side effects. Should a protective services agency attempt to balance these? How untraditional can nontraditional treatment be? Important to the *Hofbauer* decision were the findings that there was professional medical care for Joseph and the parents agreed to use traditional medical treatment if Joseph's condition warranted it.

2. Christian Scientists believe in faith healing. Jehovah's Witnesses believe that blood transfusions are forbidden by the Bible and contaminate the body. What happens when the child needs medical care that violates the parent's religious beliefs? Under what conditions may the state intervene? What rights do the parents have? The child? Often the outcome seems to depend on the court and jurisdiction. One important factor is whether the medical intervention is required to save the child's life. A number of jurisdictions have approved state action where lifesaving medical procedures are necessary. See, for example, *State v. Perricone*, 37 N.J. 463 (1962), and *People ex rel. Wallace v. Labrenz*, 411 Ill. 618. Where the intervention is not lifesaving, courts vary. In *In re Seiferth*, 300 N.Y. 80 (1955), the New York court upheld the parent and child's decisions not to have invasive surgery; In *Matter of Sampson*, 29 N.Y. 2d 900 (1972), the same court upheld non-lifesaving medical intervention by the state. See also *Guardianship of Philip B.*, p. 435.

3. Should the court have asked Joseph, age seven, what he wanted? What if Joseph were seventeen? In *In re Green*, 448 Pa. 338 (1972), the court was asked to appoint a guardian to consent to surgery for Ricky Green, a sixteen-year-old boy who had a severe curvature of the spine. The medical testimony was that with surgery Ricky had a good chance to become am-

bulatory, but without it he probably would be bedridden for life. Ricky's mother, a Jehovah's Witness, objected to surgery on religious grounds. The majority of the Pennsylvania Supreme Court said that if the condition was not life-threatening, the parent's religious wishes should generally prevail. However, they voted to send the case back to trial to determine the child's wishes. At the rehearing, Ricky, now seventeen, rejected the surgery and the court concurred. The Pennsylvania Supreme Court upheld this decision. *In re Green*, 452 Pa. 373 (1973).

Should this decision be left to the child? Can he make an independent choice? The dissent in the original case argued this was an unfair burden on Ricky: "We are herein dealing with a young boy who has been crippled most of his life, consequently, he has been under the direct control and guidance of his parents for that time. To now presume that he could make an independent decision as to what is best for his welfare and health is not reasonable. . . . Moreover, the mandate of this Court presents this youth with a most painful choice between the wishes of his parents and their religious convictions on the one hand, and his chance for a normal healthy life on the other hand. We should not confront him with this dilemma."

4. In *Walker v. Superior Court*, 253 Cal. Rptr. 1 (1988), the California Supreme Court upheld a manslaughter conviction of a Christian Scientist whose four-year-old daughter died of acute purulent meningitis when her parents provided only treatment by a faith healer and Scientist nurse. The Court found no exemption from prosecution in state law and based on *Prince v. Massachusetts*, 321 U.S. 158 (1944), held that the First Amendment Free Exercise of Religion Clause did not bar prosecution. "Parents may be free to become martyrs themselves. But it does not follow they are free, in identical circumstances to make martyrs of their children before they have reached the age of full legal discretion when they can make that choice for themselves." 321 U.S. 158 at 170. See also *Commonwealth v. Barnhart*, 497 A.2d 616, where the Pennsylvania Supreme Court upheld a manslaughter conviction for failure to treat cancer in a two-year-old for religious reasons. The family were third generation members of the Faith Tabernacle Church which rejects medical treatment and believes "life rests in God's hands."

Civil Liability for Failure to Diagnose or Report Child Abuse

Failure to report child abuse may subject the health and human services professional to civil or criminal actions. Criminal penalties for failure to report range from fines to imprisonment. Civil liability for failure to diagnose a battered child syndrome or failure to report child abuse has been established in both case law and by statute in some states. In *Landeroos v. Flood*, 551 P.2d 389 (1976), the California court held there could be civil liability for failure to diagnose the battered child syndrome. Some states establish civil liability by statute. See for example N.Y. Soc. Serv. Law §420.2.

Child Abuse Hearings

The abuse of a child can be a violation of the state's civil or criminal statutes, or both. Civil and criminal proceedings are separate, with different courts, types of proceedings, degrees of proof, and outcomes.

In civil hearings the issue is whether the child is an abused child under the state civil child abuse statute, and if so, what the disposition should be. Dispositions include out-of-home placement for a period of time, provision of services to the family, and mandatory counseling, among others, depending upon the state. Civil child abuse hearings usually take place in a family or juvenile court with a judge as the decision maker, although in some states a jury may decide civil child abuse cases. Usually the civil proceedings are brought by a legal representative of the state child welfare agency. Depending on the state, counsel may be provided for the indigent parent and the child. Civil court proceedings may be more informal than those in criminal court. The degree of proof necessary for finding abuse is that found in most civil proceedings: preponderance of the evidence.

Various exceptions exist to the general rule that excludes hearsay, those out of court statements by other than the witness offered as proof. In *People in the Interest of O.E.P.*, 654 P.2d 312 (1982), the court found a child's statements indicating sexual abuse by her mother and a companion made to her foster mother and to a social worker were admissible as exceptions to hearsay. The court held that the statements qualified under the "excited utterance" exception: "A statement relating to a startling event or condition made while the declarant was under the stress of excitement caused by the event or condition," (654 P.2d at 317), although they were made at a later time and in response to questioning. Depending on the jurisdiction, contemporaneous memoranda, notes, photographs or other written entries may be admissible. This points to the importance of careful, accurate, and timely record keeping by the professional.

In contrast, the issue in criminal child abuse trials is whether or not the defendant is guilty of abusing a child in violation of the state's criminal code. The criminal case is brought by the county prosecutor or similar government official responsible for filing criminal cases. A defendant found guilty faces the sentencing outcomes for criminal trials: incarceration, probation, fines, and so forth. The trial takes place in criminal court before a judge and, if the defendant wishes, a jury. Under *Gideon v. Wainwright*, counsel must be provided to a defendant if indigent. The child rarely has counsel and is usually not a legal party to the proceeding, but may be called as a witness. The proceedings are formal and rules of evidence for criminal trials are strictly followed. Proof must be beyond a reasonable doubt as in any criminal proceeding.[8]

A criminal child abuse case will often be heard by judge and jury, and the child witness is often called to testify in open court. Under the Fifth Amendment Confrontation Clause, the accused in a criminal trial has the right to confront the accuser. However, for the child victim, the consequences of open court testimony and facing the alleged perpetrator, who may be a friend or close relative, can be traumatic. Several approaches have been adopted to try to balance the rights of the accused with the potential harm to the child witness, ranging from closed circuit broadcasting of out-of-court testimony to blocking the view of the child so the accused cannot be seen. In *Coy v. Iowa*, 487 U.S. 1012 (1988), the Supreme Court voided an Iowa statute designed to protect the child witness as a violation of the Confrontation Clause. Justice O'Connor filed a concurring opinion noting that Confrontation Clause rights "are not absolute but rather may give way in an appropriate case to other competing interests. . . ." In *Maryland v. Craig* these "competing interests" were held to outweigh the defendant's interest in face-to-face confrontation.

MARYLAND v. CRAIG
497 U.S. 836 (1990)
U.S. SUPREME COURT

JUSTICE O'CONNOR delivered the opinion of the Court.

This case requires us to decide whether the Confrontation Clause of the Sixth Amendment categorically prohibits a child witness in a child abuse case from testifying against a defendant at trial, outside the defendant's physical presence, by one-way closed circuit television.

In October 1986, a Howard County grand jury charged respondent, Sandra Ann Craig, with child abuse, first and second degree sexual offenses, perverted sexual practice, assault, and battery. The named victim in each count was Brooke Etze, a six-year-old child who, from August 1984 to June 1986, had attended a kindergarten and prekindergarten center owned and operated by Craig.

In March 1987, before the case went to trial, the State sought to invoke a Maryland statutory procedure that permits a judge to receive, by one-way closed circuit television, the testimony of a child witness who is alleged to be a victim of child abuse.[1] To invoke the procedure, the trial judge must first "determin[e] that

---

[1]Section 9-102 of the Courts and Judicial Proceedings Article of the Annotated Code of Maryland (1989) provides in full:

"(a)(1) In a case of abuse of a child as defined in §5-701 of the Family Law Article or Article 27, §35A of the Code, a court may order that the testimony of a child victim be taken outside the courtroom and shown in the courtroom by means of a closed circuit television if:

"(i) The testimony is taken during the proceeding; and

testimony by the child victim in the courtroom will result in the child suffering serious emotional distress such that the child cannot reasonably communicate." Once the procedure is invoked, the child witness, prosecutor, and defense counsel withdraw to a separate room; the judge, jury, and defendant remain in the courtroom. The child witness is then examined and cross-examined in the separate room, while a video monitor records and displays the witness' testimony to those in the courtroom. During this time the witness cannot see the defendant. The defendant remains in electronic communication with defense counsel, and objections may be made and ruled on as if the witness were testifying in the courtroom.

In support of its motion invoking the one-way closed circuit television procedure, the State presented expert testimony that Brooke, as well as a number of other children who were alleged to have been sexually abused by Craig, would suffer "serious emotional distress such that [they could not] reasonably communicate," §9-102(a)(1)(ii), if required to testify in the courtroom. The Maryland Court of Appeals characterized the evidence as follows:

> "The expert testimony in each case suggested that each child would have some or considerable difficulty in testifying in Craig's presence. For example, as to one child, the expert said that what 'would cause him the most anxiety would be to testify in front of Mrs. Craig. . . .' The child 'wouldn't be able to communicate effectively.' As to another, an expert said she 'would probably stop talking and she would withdraw and curl up.' With respect to two others, the testimony was that one would 'become highly agitated, that he may refuse to talk or if he did talk, that he would choose his subject regardless of the questions' while the other would 'become extremely timid and unwilling to talk.'"

"(ii) The judge determines that testimony by the child victim in the courtroom will result in the child suffering serious emotional distress such that the child cannot reasonably communicate.

"(2) Only the prosecuting attorney, the attorney for the defendant, and the judge may question the child.

"(3) The operators of the closed circuit television shall make every effort to be unobtrusive.

"(b)(1) Only the following persons may be in the room with the child when the child testifies by closed circuit television:

"(i) The prosecuting attorney;

"(ii) The attorney for the defendant;

"(iii) The operators of the closed circuit television equipment; and

"(iv) Unless the defendant objects, any person whose presence, in the opinion of the court, contributes to the well-being of the child, including a person who has dealt with the child in a therapeutic setting concerning the abuse.

"(2) During the child's testimony by closed circuit television, the judge and the defendant shall be in the courtroom.

"(3) The judge and the defendant shall be allowed to communicate with the persons in the room where the child is testifying by any appropriate electronic method.

"(c) The provisions of this section do not apply if the defendant is an attorney pro se.

"(d) This section may not be interpreted to preclude, for purposes of identification of a defendant, the presence of both the victim and the defendant in the courtroom at the same time.

Craig objected to the use of the procedure on Confrontation Clause grounds, but the trial court rejected that contention, concluding that although the statute "take[s] away the right of the defendant to be face to face with his or her accuser," the defendant retains the "essence of the right of confrontation," including the right to observe, cross-examine, and have the jury view the demeanor of the witness. The trial court further found that, "based upon the evidence presented . . . the testimony of each of these children in a courtroom will result in each child suffering serious emotional distress . . . such that each of these children cannot reasonably communicate." The trial court then found Brooke and three other children competent to testify and accordingly permitted them to testify against Craig via the one-way closed circuit television procedure. The jury convicted Craig on all counts, and the Maryland Court of Special Appeals affirmed the convictions.

The Court of Appeals of Maryland reversed and remanded for a new trial. The Court of Appeals rejected Craig's argument that the Confrontation Clause requires in all cases a face-to-face courtroom encounter between the accused and his accusers, but concluded:

"[U]nder §9-102(a)(1)(ii), the operative 'serious emotional distress' which renders a child victim unable to 'reasonably communicate' must be determined to arise, at least primarily, from face-to-face confrontation with the defendant. Thus, we construe the phrase 'in the courtroom' as meaning, for sixth amendment and [state constitution] confrontation purposes, 'in the courtroom in the presence of the defendant.' Unless prevention of 'eyeball-to-eyeball' confrontation is necessary to obtain the trial testimony of the child, the defendant cannot be denied that right."

Reviewing the trial court's finding and the evidence presented in support of the §9-102 procedure, the Court of Appeals held that, "as [it] read Coy [v Iowa, 487 US 1012 (1988)], the showing made by the State was insufficient to reach the high threshold required by that case before §9-102 may be invoked."

We granted certiorari to resolve the important Confrontation Clause issues raised by this case.

The Confrontation Clause of the Sixth Amendment, made applicable to the States through the Fourteenth Amendment, provides: "In all criminal prosecutions, the accused shall enjoy the right . . . to be confronted with the witnesses against him."

The central concern of the Confrontation Clause is to ensure the reliability of the evidence against a criminal defendant by subjecting it to rigorous testing in the context of an adversary proceeding before the trier of fact. The word "confront," after all, also means a clashing of forces or ideas, thus carrying with it the notion of adversariness. As we noted in our earliest case interpreting the Clause:

"The primary object of the constitutional provision in question was to prevent depositions or ex parte affidavits, such as were sometimes admitted in civil cases, being used against the prisoner in lieu of a personal examination and cross-examination of the witness in which the accused has an opportunity, not only of testing the recollection and sifting the conscience of the witness, but of compelling him to stand face to face with the jury in order that they may look at him, and judge by his demeanor upon the stand and the manner in which he gives his testimony whether he is worthy of belief."

As this description indicates, the right guaranteed by the Confrontation Clause includes not only a "personal examination," but also "(1) insures that the witness will give his statements under oath—thus impressing him with the seriousness of the matter and guarding against the lie by the possibility of a penalty for perjury; (2) forces the witness to submit to cross-examination, the 'greatest legal engine ever invented for the discovery of truth'; [and] (3) permits the jury that is to decide the defendant's fate to observe the demeanor of the witness in making his statement, thus aiding the jury in assessing his credibility."

The combined effect of these elements of confrontation—physical presence, oath, cross-examination, and observation of demeanor by the trier of fact—serves the purposes of the Confrontation Clause by ensuring that evidence admitted against an accused is reliable and subject to the rigorous adversarial testing that is the norm of Anglo-American criminal proceedings.

Although face-to-face confrontation forms "the core of the values furthered by the Confrontation Clause," we have nevertheless recognized that it is not the sine qua non of the confrontation right. See Delaware v Fensterer, 474 US 15, 22 (1985) ("[T]he Confrontation Clause is generally satisfied when the defense is given a full and fair opportunity to probe and expose [testimonial] infirmities [such as forgetfulness, confusion, or evasion] through cross-examination, thereby calling to the attention of the factfinder the reasons for giving scant weight to the witness' testimony"); Roberts, at 69 (oath, cross-examination, and demeanor provide "all that the Sixth Amendment demands: 'substantial compliance with the purposes behind the confrontation requirement'") see also Stincer, at 739–744 (confrontation right not violated by exclusion of defendant from competency hearing of child witnesses, where defendant had opportunity for full and effective cross-examination at trial).

In sum, our precedents establish that "the Confrontation Clause reflects a *preference* for face-to-face confrontation at trial," Roberts, at 63 (emphasis added), a preference that "must occasionally give way to considerations of public policy and the necessities of the case."

Maryland's statutory procedure, when invoked, prevents a child witness from seeing the defendant as he or she testifies against the defendant at trial. We find it significant, however, that Maryland's procedure preserves all of the other elements of the confrontation right: the child witness must be competent to testify and must testify under oath; the defendant retains full opportunity for contemporaneous cross-examination; and the judge, jury, and defendant are able to view (albeit by video monitor) the demeanor (and body) of the witness as he or she testifies. Although we are mindful of the many subtle effects face-to-face confrontation may have on an adversary criminal proceeding, the presence of these other elements of confrontation—oath, cross-examination, and observation of the witness' demeanor—adequately ensures that the testimony is both reliable and subject to rigorous adversarial testing in a manner functionally equivalent to that accorded live, in-person testimony. These safeguards of reliability and adversariness render the use of such a procedure a far cry from the undisputed prohibition of the Confrontation Clause: trial by ex parte affidavit or inquisition.

The critical inquiry in this case, therefore, is whether use of the procedure is necessary to further an important state interest. The State contends that it has a substantial interest in protecting children who are allegedly victims of child abuse from the trauma of testifying against the alleged perpetrator and that its statutory procedure for receiving testimony from such witnesses is necessary to further that interest.

We have of course recognized that a State's interest in "the protection of minor victims of sex crimes from further trauma and embarrassment" is a "compelling" one.

We likewise conclude today that a State's interest in the physical and psychological well-being of child abuse victims may be sufficiently important to outweigh, at least in some cases, a defendant's right to face his or her accusers in court. That a significant majority of States has enacted statutes to protect child witnesses from the trauma of giving testimony in child abuse cases attests to the widespread belief in the importance of such a public policy. See Coy, 487 US, at 1022–1023 (concurring opinion) ("Many States have determined that a child victim may suffer trauma from exposure to the harsh atmosphere of the typical courtroom and have undertaken to shield the child through a variety of ameliorative measures"). Thirty-seven States, for example, permit the use of videotaped testimony of sexually abused children; 24 States have authorized the use of one-way closed circuit television testimony in child abuse cases, and 8 States authorize the use of a two-way system in which the child-witness is permitted to see the courtroom and the defendant on a video monitor and in which the jury and judge is permitted to view the child during the testimony.

The statute at issue in this case, for example, was specifically intended "to safeguard the physical and psychological well-being of child victims by avoiding, or at least minimizing, the emotional trauma produced by testifying." Wildermuth v State, 310 Md 496, 518, 530 A2d 275, 286 (1987). The Wildermuth court noted:

> "In Maryland, the Governor's Task Force on Child Abuse in its Interim Report (Nov. 1984) documented the existence of the [child abuse] problem in our State. It brought the picture up to date in its Final Report. In the first six months of 1985, investigations of child abuse were 12 percent more numerous than during the same period of 1984. In 1979, 4,615 cases of child abuse were investigated; in 1984, 8,321. Final Report at iii. In its Interim Report at 2, the Commission proposed legislation that, with some changes, became §9-102. The proposal was 'aimed at alleviating the trauma to a child victim in the courtroom atmosphere by allowing the child's testimony to be obtained outside of the courtroom.' Id., at 2. This would both protect the child and enhance the public interest by encouraging effective prosecution of the alleged abuser." Id., at 517, 530 A2d, at 285.

Given the State's traditional and "'transcendent interest in protecting the welfare of children,'" Ginsberg, 390 US, at 640, 20 L Ed 2d 195, 88 S Ct 1274 (citation omitted), and buttressed by the growing body of academic literature documenting the psychological trauma suffered by child abuse victims who must testify in court, see Brief for American Psychological Association as Amicus Curiae 7-13; G. Goodman et al., Emotional Effects of Criminal Court Testimony on Child Sexual Assault Victims, Final Report to the National Institute of Justice (presented as conference paper at annual convention of American Psychological Assn., Aug 1989), we will not second-guess the considered judgment of the Maryland Legislature regarding the importance of its interest in protecting child abuse victims from the emotional trauma of testifying. Accordingly, we hold that, if the State makes an adequate showing of necessity, the state interest in protecting child witnesses from the trauma of testifying in a child abuse case is sufficiently important to justify the use of a special procedure that permits a child witness in such cases to testify at trial against a defendant in the absence of face-to-face confrontation with the defendant.

Notes and Issues for Discussion

1. At least twenty-six states now permit testimony via closed circuit television or behind screens. For a typical statute, see New Jersey Statutes 2A:84A-32.4. In *State v. Crandall*,120 N.J. 649 (1990), the court mandated a judicial interview with the child witness to ascertain the need for closed circuit testimony; in *State v. Michaels*, 264 N.J. Super. 579 (1993), the court reversed a child sexual abuse conviction because the court relied on expert witness testimony that the children would be harmed by in-court testimony and failed to interview each child witness prior to testifying.

2. When is a child competent to testify? How young may a child be and still be competent to testify? There appears to be no minimum age. Myers (1992) cites cases where two- and three-year-olds were found competent to testify, as well as one case where out-of-court statements of an eighteen-month-old child were not allowed. "To testify as a witness, a child must posses certain characteristics, including capacity to observe, sufficient intelligence, adequate memory, ability to communicate, awareness of the difference between truth and falsehood, and appreciation of the obligation to speak the truth in court. A child of any age who possess the requisite characteristics may testify." (Myers, 1992: 60–61). A few states presume children below a certain age are incompetent and cannot testify without examination and permission of the court. See, generally, Myers, 1992:Chapter 2.

3. A number of states have extended the statute of limitations for prosecuting child sexual abuse cases beyond those set for most criminal offenses. Health and human services professionals should ascertain the statute of limitations in their states.[9]

Civil Liability for Commission of Child Abuse

An individual who commits child abuse also may be liable for monetary damages in a separate civil action. Damage awards could include medical or psychological treatment, and pain and suffering. Most civil damage actions are governed by a statute of limitations barring recovery unless an action has been filed within a stated period of time. In the case of children, the usual statute of limitations extends to one to three years after the child attains majority.

In the case of child sexual abuse, in some jurisdictions the statute of limitations does not run until the time an individual becomes aware that the abuse has occurred or that harm has been done. In *Mary V. v. John D.*, 264 Cal. Rptr. 633 (1990), the court applied the doctrine of delayed discovery where the victim alleged she had repressed all knowledge of the abuse which occurred at age four or five until the age of twenty-three when she attended a group counseling session and there recalled it:

> We are called upon to decide upon the relative importance of, on one hand, a defendant's right to be free from stale claims, which are difficult to defend and sometimes rest entirely on subjective evidence, and on the other hand, a plaintiff's right to seek redress for an outrageous violation against her which she has allegedly repressed until recently, through no fault of her own and as a direct result of the alleged abuse. In our mind, the deciding factor ought to be whether the repression occurred before the plaintiff was of age and then continued until a recent time. Under those circumstances, it would be most unfair to the plaintiff not to toll the statute. Accrual of a minor's cause of action is postponed until majority partly because it is expected that she is not in a position to assert her rights before that time. No more can she assert her rights if, when she reaches majority, she is wholly unaware of the facts constituting her cause of action because of the operation of a psychological mechanism which is directly caused by alleged tortious acts. 264 Cal. Rptr. at 638–639.[10]

TERMINATION OF PARENTAL RIGHTS

Severing all legal bonds between parent and child is a serious step. In termination proceedings (sometimes known as guardianship or permanent managing conservatorship, among other terms), a court permanently and totally severs all legal rights of the parent or guardian in the child. These rights may be vested in another through adoption, or remain with the state.

Degree of Proof

Because of the severe loss involved, the Supreme Court has mandated a demanding standard of proof in these proceedings, at least clear and convincing evidence. See *Santosky v. Kramer*, 445 U.S. 745 (1982). Under the Indian Child Welfare Act, 25 U.S.C. §1901 *et seq.*, a more stringent standard, beyond a reasonable doubt, is required for terminations of parental rights of Native Americans.

Right to Counsel

Counsel is not constitutionally required in termination proceedings and states vary, some providing separate counsel to each parent and the child, others providing no legal representation. See *Lassiter v. Department of Social Services*, p. 28.

Standards for Termination

Standards for termination vary across the states, but usually are tied to parental unfitness, abandonment and the best interests of the child standards. In the following two cases, what standards are used?

D.Y.F.S. v. A.W.
103 N.J. 591, 512 A.2d 438 (1986)
N.J. SUPREME COURT

O'HERN, J.

This appeal concerns the standard for termination of parental rights under N.J.S.A. 30:4C–15 and–20. We hold that the trial court incorrectly emphasized the economic and social disadvantages of respondent-parents as factors that excused or outweighed in significance the essentially uncontradicted showing of serious harm suffered by the children as a result of a lack of nurturing care in the home.

At issue is the well-being of seven members of a troubled family in one of our urban centers. The parents, Robert and Adrian, are now 35 and 30 years of age, respectively. Both have limited backgrounds and abilities. Robert, the father, has been diagnosed as having a borderline personality disorder and Adrian has been diagnosed as having pronounced limitations that affect her judgment and capacity to care for her children. Robert struggles to be economically independent by working in a local restaurant.***The couple had their first child, Ennett, in 1974. In June of 1975, DYFS received a complaint from Robert's mother, alleging that Adrian had abandoned Ennett. DYFS workers found Adrian in a hospital. She was severely injured. She attributed her injuries to an assault by Robert. Upon release from the hospital, DYFS assisted Adrian in moving herself and Ennett to her mother's home. Eventually both Adrian and Ennett moved back in with Robert.

In June 1976, a welfare board worker referred Adrian and Ennett to DYFS. Mother and daughter were removed from the home; Adrian, however, returned the next day. In July of 1976, Adrian signed a placement agreement whereby Ennett would be cared for by her paternal great grandmother. DYFS continued to supervise Ennett but lost touch with the parents.

The Division regained contact with the couple in 1977. Though Robert allegedly continued to beat her, Adrian married him in October 1977. In March 1978, they resumed care of Ennett under the supervision of DYFS.

In September 1978, a daughter, Kimberly, was born. In November of 1978, Adrian asked DYFS to remove herself and the two girls from the home due to her own fears for the safety and well-being of the children. She claimed that her husband not only beat her but also had threatened to kill her with a knife. After a week in a shelter, she returned home with the children. The DYFS worker who tried to do a follow-up visit was told by Robert that he would kill the worker if he returned again.

In December 1978, the two girls were placed in foster care with the agreement of their parents. Ennett, then four years old, showed signs of physical injury as well as severe emotional disorder. At that time, the DYFS worker had been repeatedly informed by Adrian that her husband assaulted her and that she feared for her own safety. The worker had seen Robert in a variety of moods ranging from despair to rage. Intense hostility was the dominant tone of what the worker viewed as a violent, unpredictable personality. Adrian was seen as an extremely passive, unassuming person who did not appear to be able to function outside of the confines of her present marital situation. She described to the worker the frequency and increased intensity of beatings by her husband, from whom she was unable to sever her ties.

DYFS contends that it tried thereafter to help the parents resume the care of their children but the efforts were unsuccessful. They remained in foster care. Two boys, Robert and Michael, were born in 1979 and 1980. Soon after Michael's birth, a DYFS worker visited the home and was told by Robert that DYFS could keep the girls but he would "kill anyone who tries to take the boys."***

The girls continued to be separated from and were not seen by their parents for over a year. The parents continued to reject all of DYFS's attempts to provide homemaker services, counseling, and visits with the girls. DYFS workers who visited the home in 1981 found it in "total disarray." In early 1982, Adrian gave birth to a fifth child, a boy, Jacob. Jacob died in September 1982. Faced with information that the infant's death was not accidental, a DYFS caseworker went to the home and found what she considered to be appalling conditions of neglect. The two young boys who were with their parents showed minor signs of physical neglect but major signs of a lack of emotional and developmental growth. On October 7, 1982, on DYFS's motion, an order was entered placing Robert and Michael under the care, custody, and supervision of the Division. The two boys were placed in foster care.

Despite the problems, DYFS sought to work with the parents to facilitate returning the boys and eventually reuniting the entire family. Jacob's death was confirmed as not being the result of foul play; it was attributed to sudden-infant-death syndrome. DYFS arranged for supervised visitation with the children at a child-care center and sought to built, at least in Adrian, a greater strength and ability to provide care for the children. Until 1984, the Division continued to help the parents but all efforts appeared unsuccessful. Of both parents, one witness later concluded:

> [T]heir comprehension is on the level of a child basically. Their judgment, insight, understanding, ability to predict from one step to the next, ability to perceive what is happening and understand what is going on are very, very limited compared to other adults of their age.

Finally, in July 1984, their last child, Joseph, was born. Because of concern for his health, Joseph was immediately placed under DYFS's care.

Following a two-day trial in October 1984, the Family Part reserved decision on the question whether parental rights should be terminated. The trial judge issued a decision from the bench on January 25, 1985. Regrettably, Ennett and Kimberly's foster mother died before the court reached its decision. The court deferred decision on the two girls pending evaluation of their relationship with their new foster mother, though the court indicated its belief that they too should ultimately be returned to the natural parents. As for the boys, however, the court found it was in their best interests that they be returned to their natural parents. In its view the events were beyond the control of the parents: "[The] most that can be said combining the assessments of parents and children is that they are victims of cultural and financial deprivation." The court further emphasized that DYFS had made "no attempt***to***keep the family unit integral." The three boys were ordered returned to their parents with the direction that they be placed under the protective supervision of DYFS for one year. The trial court's decision was stayed pending appeal. The Appellate Division affirmed the judgment in an unreported opinion.

Termination of parental rights presents the legal system with an almost insoluble dilemma. On the one hand, we emphasize the inviolability of the family unit, noting that "[t]he rights to conceive and to raise one's children have been deemed 'essential,'***'basic civil rights of man,'***and '[r]ights for more precious***than property rights'***." *Stanley v. Illinois*, 405 U.S. 645, 651 (1972). The interests of parents in this relationship have thus been deemed fundamental and are constitutionally protected. On the other hand, it has been recognized "that a state is not without constitutional control over parental discretion in dealing with children when their physical or mental health is jeopardized."

***In this case we focus upon subsection (c) of *N.J.S.A.* 30:4C–15, which provides that if "the best interests of any child under the care or custody of the [Division] require that he be placed under the guardianship[,]" then the Division may petition the court for termination of parental rights.

> If upon the completion of such hearing the court is satisfied that the best interests of such child require that he be placed under proper guardianship,

such court shall make an order terminating parental rights and committing such child to the guardianship and control of the [Division], and such child shall thereupon become the legal ward of [the Division], and [the Division] shall be the legal guardian of such child for all purposes, including the placement of such child for adoption. [*N.J.S.A.* 30:4C–20.]***

We emphasize at the outset that the "best interests" of a child can never mean the better interests of the child. It is not a choice between a home with all the amenities and a simple apartment, or an upbringing with the classics on the bookshelf as opposed to the mass media, or even between parents or providers of vastly unequal skills.***

To the basic focus upon the injury to the child we would add what we believe is implicit—that in a termination proceeding a trial court would determine that:

(1) *The child's health and development have been or will be seriously impaired by the parental relationship.*

The primary focus of the court should be upon harm for which there is "unambiguous and universal social condemnation." Paramount examples of such condemnation are evident in the context of physical and sexual abuse. For example, *N.J.S.A.* 30:4C–15(a) authorizes termination of parental rights when a judgment of conviction has been entered based on abuse, abandonment, neglect of, or cruelty to the child. In Title 9, the definition of "abused or neglected child" includes "a child***whose parent***inflicts or allows to be inflicted upon such child***protracted impairment of***emotional health***or a child whose***mental, or emotional condition has been impaired or is in imminent danger of becoming impaired as the result of the failure of his parent***to exercise a minimum degree of care***." *N.J.S.A.* 9:6–8.21. Serious emotional injury and developmental retardation should thus be regarded as constituting an injury to the child.

Not every injury—real or imagined—to the child's psyche satisfies the test. Still, in some cases, the potential for emotional injury can be the crucial factor in child placement.***The potential return of a child to a parent maybe so injurious that it would bar such an alternative. In this case, for example, visits with his parents have allegedly disturbed Michael. The trial court therefore must consider the potential for serious psychological damage to the child.***

(2) *The parents are unable or unwilling to eliminate the harm and delaying permanent placement will add to the harm.*

We must emphasize that what is at stake here is not that a parent lacks the financial wherewithal to elevate the child's intellectual stimulation. The Supreme Court of California has put it thus: "It is true that [the natural mother] was poor, but the hallmark of an effective parent has never been the parent's bank account. Children can be and are loved and nurtured in poverty-stricken families and deprived and neglected in affluent homes.

In our view, this record simply demonstrates an extreme case of deficient parenting." *In re Laura F.*, 33 Cal.3d 826, 837. In referring to the parents' role, we are not concerned here with what may be called "inadequate parenting." Hence, a court should focus upon whether, within this setting, the parents are giving the child the nurture and affection that money cannot provide.

A court analyzing the ability of the parents to give their children care should not look at the parents to determine whether they are themselves unfit or whether they are the victims of social circumstances beyond their control; it should only determine whether it is reasonably foreseeable that the parents can cease to inflict harm upon the children entrusted to their care. No more and no less is required of them than that they will not place their children in substantial jeopardy to physical or mental health. There is a natural tendency to want to continue working with the parents to restore the family unit. How long a court should be willing to wait, however, depends in part on the age of the child.

(3) *The court has considered alternatives to termination.*

***A court should require as part of the case in chief consideration of the plan that was developed for the child. As noted, there is a great tension here because, to the extent that adults—and when we speak of adults we mean courts, social workers, and therapists—delay the permanent decision, they lose sight of the child's concept of time. *See* J. Goldstein, A. Freud, and A. Solnit, *Beyond the Best Interests of the Child* 43 (1973) ("Three months may not be a long time for an adult decisionmaker. For a young child it may be forever"). A common alternative is placement with a relative or relatives.

Some factors that suggest that efforts to reunite the family "are no longer reasonable" include "parents [who] refuse to engage in therapy or other services;***parents [who] cannot benefit from therapy or instruction due to mental retardation or psychosis;***parents [who] threaten workers, child, foster parents, or therapists;***another child in the home is abused or neglected and taken into care;***[and the] child shows serious adverse reaction to contact with parent***." Ducote, *Why States Don't Terminate Parental Rights, Justice for Children* 3 (Winter 1986). We expect that in most cases the court will be presented with a record that will have adequately canvassed the alternatives to termination of parental rights.

(4) *The termination of parental rights will not do more harm than good.*

While this may appear to be nothing more than a tautological statement, what the concept conveys is that termination of parental rights will result, among other things, in a permanent resolution of the child's status. Some have suggested that "[a] decision to terminate parental rights should not simply extinguish an unsuccessful parent-child relationship without making provision for***a more promising relationship***[in] the child's future***." Ketcham and Babcock, *Statutory Standards for the Involuntary Termination of Parental Rights*, 29 Rutgers L.Rev. 530, 542–43 (1976).

If one thing is clear, it is that the child deeply needs association with a nurturing adult. Since it seems generally agreed that permanence in itself is an important part of that nurture, a court must carefully weigh that aspect of the child's life.***

> It is an unfortunate truth that not all children, who are "freed" from their legal relationship with their parents, find the state and permanent situation that is desired even though this is the implicit promise made by the state when it seeks to terminate the parent-child relationship. Multiple placements and impermanent situations sometimes mark the state's guardianship of a child. This unstable situation is frequently detrimental to a child. Indeed, the detriment may be greater than keeping the parent-child relationship intact since the child's psychological and emotional bond to the parent may have been broken with nothing substituted in its place.
> [*In re Angelia P.*, 28 *Cal.*3d 908, 930 (1981) (Bird, C.J., concurring and dissenting)].

Naturally, there will be circumstances when the termination of parental rights must precede the permanency plan. A multiply-handicapped child or a young adolescent might not be adoptable at the time of the termination proceedings. In other cases, the court will have to consider whether the child has already developed "a filial relationship [with another]***that***cannot be destroyed or changed without some risk of emotional harm to the child." *Sees v. Baber, supra*, 74 N.J. at 222. Just such a relationship was recognized in *Sorentino II* as warranting, with proper notice, a termination of parental rights. As we have seen in this case, the filial relationship that the girls had developed with their foster mother was ended by her untimely death. In other cases, the court may consider whether placement with an extended-family member can give the child both continuing nurture and roots.

These then are the standards that should be followed in a termination case.***

The primary focus of the trial testimony was upon the injuries that the children of this family had suffered. Although there is a regrettable cultural cast to the words chosen by the experts to convey the significance of their findings, it is clear to us that they did not intend to express a cultural bias against the economic, racial, or ethnic conditions in which they found these children.

What the witnesses sought to convey when they spoke of "cultural deprivation," lack of exposure to "language stimulation," and the failure to offer a "culturally rich and stimulating home environment" was not that the children did not speak in polysyllables but rather that they had little or no vocabulary at all; not that they were incapable of advanced reasoning but that they failed to grasp the most basic of concepts—that an object rolled under a table would remain there though not visible; not that they could not discern a work of art but that they could not relate to familiar objects such as blocks and squares.

We can share the concerns of the trial court that there not be any cultural bias. Still, we cannot avert our eyes from the grave injury that these children have suffered. We are sympathetic to the plight of these parents, who may suffer because of the larger faults of society. Nevertheless, we do not believe that their economic or social circumstances were proven to be the cause of their children's condition. The regrettable injury to the growth and development of the children was due not to economic deprivation or lack of resources but to a fundamental lack of the most precious of all resources, the attention and concern of a caring family.

As to Ennett and Kimberly, the proofs were most demonstrative. There was proof that Ennett suffered from a severe disability bordering on psychosis that was attributed to her early exposure to violence in the home. She was described as "starving for attention." Returning her to a home not purged of all violence would be, in the view of the witnesses, fatal. At the time of trial, the only home that Kimberly had ever known was her foster mother's. There was a "very intense emotional bond between these two girls" (Kimberly and Ennett). The clinical psychologist who testified at trial concluded that the two girls clearly needed to remain together. In Kimberly's case, then, were she returned to her parents at the time of trial, she would have suffered the emotional loss of both her foster mother, whom she called "grandma," and her sister. Her relationship with her sister remains critical.

As to the boys, Robert was "significantly developmentally delayed." He was already a year behind in his ability to form the simplest perceptions of the world about him; he would be "not capable of independent living unless changes were made." In Michael's case, a "continued lack of exposure [to nurturing care] would eventually doom him."

As tragic as the consequences to the parents of the loss of their children may be, we cannot ignore evidence of serious injury. It is inappropriate to disregard a clear and essentially undisputed showing of such injury and its probable consequences because society may have been unfair to the parents.

Nor do we believe it appropriate to consider as a factor mitigating or excusing the showing of injury to the children that, in the case of Robert and Michael, their placement had not been successful, or that following the death of Ennett and Kimberly's foster mother there had been difficulties with the new foster parent. These are the inevitable consequence of temporary living arrangements.***

Finally, what concerns us most about the case is that there was simply no evidence of any realistic likelihood that the parents would ever be capable of caring for the children. We cannot determine how much the inability of the parents to transfer affection or care to their children may be attributed to the parents' being short-changed by either nature or society. We are confronted with a situation in which children have been injured. We know that we must balance this injury with the realization that the natural family or its extension will, in many cases, be the best resource that society can afford children. But here there is simply no evidence that the parents will be able to care for the children in the near future. Time is running out for these children.***

The trial court here, however, relied on inappropriate factors in reaching its determination. The court emphasized that respondents were disadvantaged and DYFS had difficulties in placing the children. These are not legal factors relevant to the four-part standard for termination except insofar as the parents' condition might bear upon their ability to cease to harm their children.***Had the court made affirmative findings that the children had not suffered substantial emotional or developmental injury, that the parents would soon resume an appropriate nurturing role with assistance from DYFS or another agency, or that termination would affirmatively harm the children, such findings could warrant the disposition made. However, as noted, we do not read the trial record or the opinion below to embrace these findings.***

The judgment of the Appellate Division is reversed.

Notes and Issues for Discussion

1. Does termination in this case focus on physical abuse or emotional and psychological neglect? What was the evidence of physical abuse? Of neglect? Do you think parental rights should have been terminated?
2. Contested termination proceedings may take years. What happens to the children during this time? In the *A.W.* case, the children were under supervision of the child welfare agency for most of their lives. What policies would argue for an earlier termination. What policies would argue for proceeding slowly?
3. Note that Robert has a diagnosis of "borderline personality disorder" and Adrian has "pronounced limitations that affect her capacity to care for her children." Should these factors be weighed in the termination calculus? Parental mental retardation or mental illness alone would not appear sufficient to terminate rights. However if the condition sufficiently impairs ability to care for the child or otherwise endangers the child, courts will intervene. (See Myers, 1992:181–182; but see also Sackett, 1992, who argues it is often difficult to determine how much a handicap may be a factor in terminations.)

IN INTEREST OF S.H.A.
728 S.W.2d 73 (1987)
TEXAS APPELLATE COURT

SCALES, JUSTICE.

Appellants, A_____ A_____ and S_____ A_____ ("the parents") appeal from the trial court's judgment terminating their parental rights to their son ("the child").***We overrule the parents' points of error and affirm the judgment of the trial court.

The record reflects that the parents are illegal aliens who came to the United States in 1981. The child, the parents' fourth, was born in the United States on February 12, 1982. The father has been employed, from time to time, working as a construction worker and as a dishwasher at a restaurant. The family's economic situation was characterized by several witnesses as "low-income." At the time of trial in March 1985, the parents had another child. The parents do not speak English, and they testified at trial through an interpreter.

The child's situation was first brought to the attention of Child Welfare in 1983, when the child was approximately sixteen months old. The child had been hospitalized in May 1983 for an ear infection and anemia. The treating physician notified the public health department about the child's condition. Consequently, Barbara Brown, a public health nurse, visited the child's home on May 25, just after the child was released from the hospital. Brown testified that the child was filthy; that he was crying; and that he was eating cookies off of the dirty floor. Brown discussed the child's medication and the need to improve the child's hygiene with the mother. Brown stated that the mother "seemed disinterested in anything I had to say."

After the mother did not keep another appointment for the child at the public health clinic, Brown rescheduled the child's appointment for June 22. Brown performed nutritional, medical, and developmental tests on the child. The child was 28 inches in height and weighed sixteen pounds, eight ounces. This height and weight is below the thirtieth percentile for an average sixteen-month-old infant, and Brown testified that "that is a medical definition for failure to thrive." The statistics indicated that "the child was not growing as a normal child should." The mother told Brown that she fed the child about one-half gallon of milk each day; tortillas; soup once a week; eggs about four times a week; chicken once a week; occasionally fruits and cheese; and soup and beans. Brown stated that this was not a proper diet for an infant. Brown advised the mother that the child should be hospitalized immediately. Brown referred the family to a federally funded program that offers food to infants, and also made a referral to Child Welfare.

As a consequence of Brown's referral, Melba Martinez, an "in-take" worker for Child Welfare, visited the parents' home on June 23. Martinez testified that the child appeared very thin, very weak, and sluggish; his rib cage showed; he had a "protruding stomach or abdomen"; and his face "looked very sad." The older children appeared to be relatively healthy. The mother told Martinez that she fed the child twice a day, and that she fed him "sopas," a mixture of rice and pasta. Martinez expressed concern about the child's health to the mother, but the mother felt that the child was "just naturally thin, as one of her other children had been." Martinez testified that the mother "did not appear to understand that she needed to be concerned." As a result of the home visit, Martinez arranged for food to be provided to the family and to take the child to see a doctor. The next day, June 24, Martinez transported the mother and the child to Children's Medical Center.

The child was hospitalized on June 24 at Parkland Hospital for six days for treatment of the burn on his arm and an ear infection. Part of the diagnosis was that the child was a "failure to thrive" child, and Dr. Paul Prescott was called in as a consultant on the child's case. Dr. Prescott testified that failure to thrive "means a child is not living up to his own growth potential."***

Dr. Prescott stated that once failure to thrive is diagnosed, medical causes are ruled out first. Here, the child's failure to thrive was not due to medical reasons. Dr. Prescott testified that the cause of this child's failure to thrive was malnutrition.***

Mario Zuniga was assigned to this case in July 1983 as the permanent case-worker for Child Welfare. He testified at trial that his role was to help the family create a safe environment for the child, so that the child could be returned to the family. Zuniga first visited the parents' home after the child had been placed in foster care. Zuniga stated that the house was unsanitary and that he located a better apartment for the family near a day-care center. He arranged for and transported the mother and the other children to doctors' appointments. Zuniga obtained soap for the family; gave them a heater; provided diapers and formula for the baby, and some clothing and toys for the older children. Zuniga stated that the mother, with four small children at home excluding the child in issue, was "very overloaded" and "very, very depressed." Child Welfare arranged for the three older children to be placed in a nearby day-care center operated by Child Care Dallas. Zuniga testified that the older children in the family were being cared for, as far as Child Welfare was concerned, because they were receiving meals at day care.

From June 30 to December 4, 1983, the child remained in foster care. During this time, various workers from Child Welfare and Child Care Dallas worked with the family and offered support services to the family. The agencies arranged for the parents to attend parenting skills classes; the mother went to four out of the five classes, and the father attended one class.

On December 4, 1983, Child Welfare, in accordance with its goal of keeping the child with his natural parents if possible, returned the child to the parents' home. However, the child was removed and placed in foster care again on December 29.***

Zuniga testified that he went to the parents' home on December 29 to take the mother and the new baby to a doctor's appointment, as had been pre-arranged with the mother. When he arrived, he found the family car was gone from the driveway, the parents were not there, and the child, with a "real deep gash over his eye," was lying on a bed. The child was "glassy-eyed" and did not respond to Zuniga when he walked into the room. The child had on a dirty diaper. A "young girl," apparently a baby-sitter, was at the home; Zuniga stated that she "appeared to be mentally retarded." The girl told Zuniga: "They want you to take [the child] to the hospital." Zuniga took the new baby to her doctor's appointment and then took the child to Parkland Hospital.

Zuniga's case notes state that the treating physician at Parkland told Zuniga that the injury had occurred at least one day earlier; that the parents should have immediately sought medical treatment; and that it was too late to put stitches in the cut.***

The following day, Zuniga met with the mother and father at the Child Welfare Office. Zuniga testified that the father was "very angry" because "it was not that bad of an accident, [and] that we had no business going in there and taking the child out, and that these things happen all the time." Zuniga's report states: "The parents stated that they had not taken [the child] to the hospital since they were out looking for money to borrow to pay for the rent and that [the child] had sustained that injury jumping off a bed." The mother testified at trial that she and the father had gone to look for "money and transportation" to take the child to a doctor.

***Section 15.02, which provides for the involuntary termination of parental rights, states in pertinent part:

A petition requesting termination of the parent-child relationship with respect to a parent who is not the petitioner may be granted if the court finds that:
(1) the parent has:

***

(D) knowingly placed or knowingly allowed the child to remain in conditions or surroundings which endanger the physical or emotional well-being of the child; or
(E) engaged in conduct or knowingly placed the child with persons who engaged in conduct which endangers the physical or emotional well-being of the child;

***

and in addition, the court further finds that
(2) termination is in the best interest of the child.

TEX.FAM.CODE ANN. §15.02.
In order to terminate parental rights under section 15.02, there must be both a finding that the parent has committed one of the enumerated acts under section 15.02(1) and a finding that termination is in the best interest of the child.***

With these principles in mind, we believe the evidence in this case supports the jury's findings that the parents engaged in conduct which endangered the child's physical and emotional well-being.***

The evidence in this case which supports the jury's findings reflects parental conduct which endangered the child's physical and emotional well-being. First, the parents did not give the child enough food or did not properly feed the child. There is little direct evidence as to what foods were fed to the child on a daily basis. The mother told one worker that she fed the child "sopas" twice a day; she told another worker that she regularly fed the child milk, tortillas, soup, and beans, and occasionally fed him soup, eggs, chicken, fruit, and cheese. There is, however, ample circumstantial evidence which shows that the parents did not provide the child with enough food or nutritionally adequate food, and circumstantial evidence may be sufficient to prove the grounds for termination under section 15.02.***

Second, the parents engaged in conduct which endangered the physical well-being of the child in that they did not seek appropriate medical treatment for the child. The record is replete with testimony that the mother missed doctors' appointments for the child on several occasions.***

Moreover, after the child was injured in December 1983, the parents did not take the child to the doctor immediately after the injury or the next day. There is testimony from which the jury may have inferred that, instead of learning to take the child to the doctor when he was ill or injured, the parents had come to rely on the social workers to take care of the child's injuries.

Thus, we hold that there is some evidence to support the jury's findings in special issues numbers two and five that the parents engaged in conduct which endangered the child's physical and emotional well-being. The record reflects that the parents did not properly feed the child and did not seek appropriate medical treatment for the child. This is conduct which, the evidence shows, endangered the child's physical and emotional well-being.***

We hold that the evidence was sufficient to support the jury findings that termination of parental rights would be in the best interest of the child.

McCLUNG, JUSTICE, dissenting.

***

In order to terminate parental rights there must be a finding of specific conduct under section 15.02 *and* a finding that termination is in the best interest of the child. *Richardson v. Green,* 677 S.W.2d 497, 499 (Tex.1984); *Wiley v. Spratley,* 543 S.W.2d 349, 351 (Tex.1976). Both of these requirements must be proven by clear and convincing evidence independently of each other.***

I conclude that the evidence is insufficient to support either of the affirmative findings.***

These parents have five children. The older three were examined and found not to be malnourished. These children are all in school and in day care *provided by Child Welfare.* Indeed, as pointed out by the majority, a social worker for Child Welfare testified that the other children were being adequately cared for *because* they were receiving meals at day care. Child Care Dallas, a United Way agency, offered to enroll this child in their special programs with his brothers and sisters but Child Welfare refused, opting instead to pursue termination of the parents' rights. The youngest child, born after the time that this child was removed from the home, is also adequately nourished. This is due to the parents' improved financial condition and parenting skills.

While in the parents' home, this child was fed a diet consisting primarily of dairy and cheese products as well as a dish called "sopas," described as "like rice, pastas, baked with spices." This diet was said to be nutritionally inadequate for the child both for the inadequacy of the portions and the lack of meat and vegetable items. The parents were getting free milk, dairy and cereal products from the "WIC" program. Consequently, the child's diet consisted heavily of milk and dairy products. The only form of assistance the family was receiving in the way of food was free milk, cheese and cereal. It naturally follows that the child's diet was heavy on milk and dairy products. As the parents were not receiving free meat and vegetable products, likewise, the child was not being fed a diet replete with meat and vegetables. The parents were not American citizens so the family was unable to get government assistance in the form of welfare benefits, food stamps and medical care paid for by the federal government.

The inadequacy of the meal portions was caused by the family's poverty. The lack of nutritionally balanced meals was also caused by poverty as well as the ignorance of the parents in the proper proportion of food groups to be fed to an infant of that age. The pediatrician that examined, tested, and followed the child's progress in the hospital stated conclusively that any failure of the child to meet his optimum growth potential was solely the result of malnutrition. Further, he excluded physical or emotional abuse by the parents and the home environment along some 500 other possible causes, stating, "In that particular child, it was 100–percent nutrition." In this regard, the record reflects that the other children were as thin as this child at his age. It is also interesting to note the child's nutritional state did not originally so concern Child Welfare that they thought termination was needed. Child Welfare originally returned the child to the home even after he was found to be undernourished. This child's nutritional woes were exacerbated by his eating habits. One foster parent testified that the child refused to eat during his stay with her family and that she, therefore, had to forcefeed him. This behavior was consistent with the parents' testimony of their difficulty in getting the child to eat.***

An examination of the only remaining basis on which termination was sought finds it to be lacking as well. The child was again removed from the home and termination proceedings brought when the child was discovered by a social worker to be suffering from a gash over his eye. The babysitter in the home at that time told the social worker that the parents wanted the social worker to take the child to the hospital. The parents testified that they did not take the child to the hospital because they were out looking for money to buy food and they knew that the social worker was coming by the next day and he could take the child to the doctor. The social worker further testified that the injury was an accident resulting from the active nature of the child, and that the parents had tried to reach him about the accident when it happened at 8:30 p.m. the evening before his scheduled visit but that he was unavailable. There was no evidence that this wound was life-threatening, or that the one-day delay was an impediment to treatment. Indeed, there was no evidence that this delay had any ill effects at all on the child.

It must be remembered that these parents are undocumented aliens from Mexico, unable to speak English. There was evidence that test scores show them to be mentally retarded. The parents are uneducated, ill-trained, and scared of deportation. The record shows that the social workers assigned to this family performed many tasks for them. The workers found them a place to live, brought food and appliances they needed, and generally tended to their needs. It would seem quite natural for these parents to grow dependent upon this individual. When this child needed medical attention the parents quite naturally looked to their "guardian and provider" for help. While these workers' substantial efforts to assist the family in whatever way possible are to be applauded and encouraged, it is cruel and unfair to allow these parents to become dependent on the Child Welfare Department and then have the department use acts of the parents caused by this dependency as a basis for terminating their parental rights.

Notes and Issues for Discussion

1. The termination decision was based on a failure to thrive due to malnourishment and medical neglect. As in *A.W.* do you think the limitations of the parents can be used as a basis for termination? Can poverty?
2. Opposing the state's witnesses were workers and supervisors from a pri-

vate child welfare agency who argued that with proper support services, the child could be returned home. They argued that the child could enter a day home program and the agency could provide services to the family.
3. One of the considerations of the *A.W.* case was that the termination not result in greater harm to the child. S.H.A. will probably continue in one or more foster care homes unless he is adopted or institutionalized. His siblings remain with his parents. Is S.H.A. better off? Worse off?
4. What are the costs to the state? If S.H.A. isn't adopted, isn't it likely that thirteen years of foster care or institutions will cost substantially more than the provision of in-home services? Should this be a factor?

FOSTER CARE AND ADOPTION

Foster care has been seen as a temporary condition, in which children reside for a relatively short period of time until they are either reunited with their families or placed in adoptive homes. The reality is quite different. In *Smith v. Org. of Foster Families For Equality and Reform*, 431 U.S. 816 (1977), the Court noted:

"It is certainly true that the poor resort to foster care more often than other citizens. For example, over 50% of all children in foster care in New York City are from female-headed families receiving Aid to Families with Dependent Children. Minority families are more likely to turn to foster care; 52.3% of the children in foster care are black and 25.5% are Puerto Rican. This disproportionate resort to foster care by the poor and victims of discrimination doubtless reflects in part the greater likelihood of disruption of poverty stricken families. . . . The poor have little choice but to submit to state-supervised child care when family crises strike.

The extent to which supposedly "voluntary" placements are in fact voluntary has been questioned. . . . For example, it has been said that many "voluntary" placements are in fact coerced by threat of neglect proceedings and are not in fact voluntary in the sense of the product of an informed consent. . . .

The District Court found as a fact that the median time spent in foster care in New York was over four years. Indeed, many children apparently remain in this "limbo" indefinitely. The District Court also found that the longer a child remains in foster care, the more likely it is that he will never leave: "the probability of a foster child being returned to his biological parents declined markedly after the first year in foster care.". . . . It is not surprising then that many children, particularly those that enter foster care at a very early age and have little or no contact with their natural parents . . . often develop deep emotional ties with their foster parents.

Yet such ties do not seem to be regarded as obstacles to transfer of the child from one foster placement to another. The record in this case indicates that nearly 60% of the children in foster care in New York City have experienced more than one placement, and about 28% have experienced three or more. 431 U.S. at 833-837.

Legal issues permeate foster care, including opening, supervising, and closing foster homes, placing and removing foster children, and state and foster parent liability.[11]

Although the state creates a family by placement of foster children, case law indicates that the foster family is less of a family than a biological or adoptive one, and has fewer rights. In the *Smith v. OFFER* case above, a group of New York foster parents challenged procedures for removing children from foster homes, including a postremoval hearing when requested. The parents requested an automatic preremoval hearing for removal to another foster home where children have been in a foster home for over a year, arguing that a "psychological family" has been created, with a recognizable constitutional liberty interest protection. The Supreme Court did not reach the liberty issue, but found the New York procedures constitutionally adequate.

Can the state remove foster children even if the foster parents are providing adequate care? Consider the following case:

DRUMMOND v. FULTON CO. DEPT. OF FAMILY & CHILDREN'S SERVICES
563 F.2d 1200 (1977)
U.S. COURT OF APPEALS

RONEY, CIRCUIT JUDGE:

Plaintiffs, Robert and Mildred Drummond, a white couple, acted as state-designated foster parents of a mixed race child for over two years. When the defendant state adoption agency decided to remove the child for permanent placement in another home, plaintiffs commenced this action under 42 U.S.C.A. §1983. Alleging denial of their rights under both the equal protection and the due process clauses of the Fourteenth Amendment, they sought preliminary and permanent injunctive relief, which was denied by the district court. Although a panel of this Court reversed, the full Court finds no deprivation of constitutional rights and affirms the dismissal of plaintiff's complaint.

In December 1973 in an emergency situation, a one-month-old mixed race child named Timmy was placed for temporary care in the home of Mr. and Mrs. Drummond by the Fulton County children's service agency.***

Within a year, the Drummonds had become sufficiently attached to Timmy to request permission to adopt him. The Drummonds had not signed an agreement that they would not try to adopt their foster child, as is common practice with many placement agencies. Although the level of care provided by them as foster parents had consistently been rated excellent, there was an emerging consensus within the defendant child placement agency charged with Timmy's care that it would be best to look elsewhere for a permanent adoptive home.***

The child was not legally freed for adoption by the Georgia courts until September 1975. Because this signaled the end of any attempt to return Timmy to his natural mother, the agency began a more focused consideration of what ultimate placement would be best for Timmy. After a number of discussions with the Drummonds, a final decision-making meeting was held in November 1975 with 19 agency employees present. Although the Drummonds were not present at this meeting, caseworkers who had dealt with them during the past two years did attend. As a result of that meeting a final agency decision was made to remove Timmy from the Drummond home and to deny the Drummonds' adoption application. It is clear that the race of the Drummonds and of Timmy and the racial attitudes of the parties were given substantial weight in coming to this conclusion. The agency employees were also aware that as Timmy grew older he would retain the characteristics of his black father. A few months later the plaintiffs filed suit.***

After hearing six witnesses and arguments of counsel the court, by verbal order, dismissed the complaint on the merits. In rendering that decision, the court made the following finding:

> It is obvious that race did enter into the decision of the Department. . . . [I]t appears to the Court . . . that the consideration of race was properly directed to the best interest of the child and was not an automatic-type of thing or of placement, that is, that all blacks go to black families, all whites go to white families, and all mixed children go to black families, which would be prohibited.

On appeal counsel was appointed to represent Timmy's separate interest in this litigation.

The case as now presented to the *en banc* Court formulates four major issues for resolution: (1) did the action of the defendant constitute a denial of equal protection; (2) do the Drummonds have a protected liberty or property right in their relationship with Timmy; (3) does Timmy have such a right; and (4) if such rights exist, how much procedural protection is required in order to safeguard them?

The Drummonds and counsel for Timmy contend that the state denied them equal protection of the laws because of the extent to which race was considered in making the adoption decision. Although the complaint alleged that race was the sole determining factor, the district court found that this was not the case, and the finding was not clearly erroneous. The argument has thus centered on the question of whether a state agency, charged with the responsibility of placing for adoption a child in its custody, may take into consideration the race of the child and the race of the prospective adoptive parents without violating the equal protection clause of the United States Constitution.

The manner in which race was considered in this case frames the precise issue before us. The district court found that race was not used in an automatic fashion. The Drummonds' application was not automatically rejected on racial grounds. This finding may not be disturbed here because not clearly erroneous. But can race be taken into account, perhaps decisively if it is the factor which tips the balance between two potential families, where it is not used automatically? We conclude, as did another court which grappled with the problem, that "the difficulties inherent in interracial adoption" justify the consideration of "race as a relevant factor in adoption, . . ." *Compos v. McKeithen*, 341 F.Supp. 264, 266 (E.D.La.1972).

In this regard, the Supreme Court has recently provided some guidance. It appears that even if government activity has a racially disproportionate impact, the impact alone does not sustain a claim of racial discrimination. "Proof of racially discriminatory intent or purpose is required to show a violation. . . ." *Arlington Heights v. Metropolitan Housing Corp.*, 429 U.S. 252, 265 (1977). There has been no suggestion before this Court that the defendants had any purposes other than to act in the best interest of the child when it considered race.***

In concluding that there has been no denial of equal protection in these circumstances, we note the following factors.

First, consideration of race in the child placement process suggests no racial slur or stigma in connection with any race. It is a natural thing for children to be raised by parents of their same ethnic background.

Second, no case has been cited to the Court suggesting that it is impermissible to consider race in adoption placement. The only cases which have addressed this problem indicate that, while the automatic use of race is barred, the use of race as one of the factors in making the ultimate decision is legitimate.

Third, the professional literature on the subject of transracial child placement stresses the importance of considering the racial attitudes of potential parents. The constitutional strictures against racial discrimination are not mandates to ignore the accumulated experience of unbiased professionals. A couple has no right to adopt a child it is not equipped to rear, and according to the professional literature race bears directly on that inquiry. From the child's perspective, the consideration of race is simply another facet of finding him the best possible home. Rather than eliminating certain categories of homes from consideration it avoids the potentially tragic possibility of placing a child in a home with parents who will not be able to cope with the child's problems.

Fourth, in the analogous inquiry over the permissibility of considering the religion of would-be adoptive parents, numerous courts have found no constitutional infirmity. Those cases make the same distinction as this Court makes in the racial context. So long as religion is not an automatic factor, its consideration as one of a number of factors is unobjectionable.

Finally, adoption agencies quite frequently try to place a child where he can most easily become a normal family member. The duplication of his natural biological environment is a part of that program. Such factors as age, hair color, eye color and facial features of parents and child are considered in reaching a decision. This flows from the belief that a child and adoptive parents can best adjust to a normal family relationship if the child is placed with adoptive parents who could have actually parented him. To permit consideration of physical characteristics necessarily carries with it permission to consider racial characteristics. This

Court does not have the professional expertise to assess the wisdom of that type of inquiry, but it is our province to conclude, as we do today, that the use of race as one of those factors is not unconstitutional.

In order to make out a claim of deprivation of Fourteenth Amendment due process rights a plaintiff must demonstrate first, that he has been deprived of liberty or property in the constitutional sense, and second, that the procedure used to deprive him of that interest was constitutionally deficient.

The Drummonds assert two possible constitutional liberty and property interests. The first involves a concept which plaintiffs have denominated the "psychological family"; the second, a stigma to their reputation alleged to accrue upon the rejection by the agency of their application to adopt Timmy.

Plaintiffs maintain that during the period Timmy lived with them mutual feelings of love and dependence developed which are analogous to those found in most biological families. By so characterizing their home situation they seek to come within the protection which courts have afforded to the family unit. They assert that their relationship to Timmy is part of the familial right to privacy which is a protected interest under the Fourteenth Amendment. As the "psychological parents" of Timmy, they claim entitlement to the parental rights referred to in numerous decisions.

The argument that foster parents possess such a protected interest was placed squarely before, and discussed by, the Supreme Court in its recent decision in *Smith v. Organization of Foster Families for Equality & Reform*, 431 U.S. 816 (1977) [hereinafter *OFFER*]. Although the Supreme Court did not find it necessary to resolve whether such an interest exists, Justice Brennan's discussion of that claim is helpful to our analysis. He first considered the elements which have traditionally been thought to define the concept of "family." Of course, the Court recognized that "the importance of the familial relationship, to the individuals involved and to the society, stems from the emotional attachments that derive from the intimacy of daily association." Nonetheless, the Court then noted several differences between foster and natural families, particularly the fact that the foster parent relationship has its genesis in state law, unlike the biological relationship, and that with foster parents there is often a natural parent seeking to assert a competing liberty interest.

We conclude that there is no such constitutionally protected interest in the context of this case. An understanding of the role of the foster parent in a child placement helps make this conclusion plain. In the search for adoptive parents, thorough investigations are made so that long range considerations may be given substantial weight.***

During this process in Georgia, children are placed in foster homes as an alternative to institutional care for what is clearly designed as a transitional phase in the child's life. Foster parents are thus considered only on the basis of the quality of temporary care they can be expected to provide. Therefore, in the eyes of the state, which creates the foster relationship, the relationship is considered temporary at the outset and gives rise to no state created rights in the foster parents.***

Notes and Issues for Discussion

1. What is the argument of the state? Of the Drummonds? Does Timmy have an independent interest? What would you argue on his behalf? Who do you think should prevail? Why?

2. The National Association of Black Social Workers adopted a position opposing transracial adoptions in 1972. The Child Welfare League of America's Standards for Adoption Service state "Children in need of adoption have a right to be placed in a family that reflects their ethnicity or race . . ." (C.W.L.A. Standards, 1988). A number of states have adoption statutes with a same race preference. For example, Minnesota requires "due consideration of the child's race or ethnic heritage" and specifies a preference for adoption by parents of the same race or ethnic heritage. Minn. Stat. §259.28.

3. In *Mississippi Band of Choctaw Indians v. Holyfield*, 490 U.S. 30 (1989), a Native American couple consented to the adoption of their twin children born off the reservation and the adoption was finalized by a Mississippi state court. The Choctaw tribe went to court to vacate the adoption under the Indian Child Welfare Act which gives exclusive tribal jurisdiction over child custody proceedings involving Native American children domiciled on the reservation. The Supreme Court found the children were domiciled on the reservation and upheld tribal jurisdiction: "We are not unaware that over three years have passed since the twin babies were born and placed in the Holyfield home. . . . Whatever feelings we might have as to where the twins should live, however, it is not for us to decide that question. . . . The law places that decision in the hands of the Choctaw tribal court. . . . It is not ours to say whether the trauma that might result from removing these children from their adoptive family should outweigh the interest of the Tribe—and perhaps the children themselves—in having them raised as part of the Choctaw community." 490 U.S. at 53.

4. How final are surrenders of children and adoptions? There is no easy answer. In *Sorentino v. Family & Children's Soc. of Elizabeth*, 74 N.J. 314 (1977), the court refused to return a child to her biological parents after several years in foster care on the grounds of psychological bonding, although the original surrender was illegal and coerced. In *Matter of Baby M* (p. 283), the court refused to honor a surrogacy contract and terminate the parental rights of the surrogate mother.

5. For confidentiality of adoption records, see p. VI-6.

DOMESTIC VIOLENCE

In *State v. Kelly*, 97 N.J. 178 (1984), the New Jersey Supreme Court observes: "It is clear that the American home, once assumed to be the cornerstone of our society, is often a violent place." 97 N.J. at 178. Domestic violence is now recognized as a major social problem, with anywhere from two million to forty million victims.[12] Several studies suggest at least 15 percent of all married couples experienced at least one incident of violence within the previous year, with women the primary victims. There may be substantial underreporting.[13] (Waits, 1985: 273).

Domestic Violence Statutes

Every state has enacted legislation to prevent domestic violence and aid victims. (Note, "History of Abuse," 1989: 1002). The statutes are designed to protect the victim, punish the abuser, and provide shelter and services for abused spouses. They are similar in that they define the acts which constitute domestic violence, identify who is covered by the statues, provide for temporary relief through the issuance of a temporary restraining order and then, along with procedures for hearings, provide for a range of possible relief including permanent restraining orders and monetary awards.

> The design of domestic violence legislation generally includes a definition of those individuals entitled to protection under the statute, provisions for temporary or emergency relief, issuance of a protective order and notice to victims under the act. . . . In addition, varying from state to state, one will find protection for police officers from civil liability and the ability to arrest without a warrant, monetary compensation for the victim for physical injuries incurred and court ordered counseling for the parties concerned. (Lengyel, 1990: 62)

Protection is generally limited to adults or emancipated minors, with child protection coming under state child abuse statutes. States appear to be divided between limiting protection to opposite sex cohabitants or including same sex couples.[14]

In Wisconsin, protection applies to adult family or household members, with adult family member defined as spouse, parent, child, or blood relation, and household member defined as "a person currently or formerly residing in a place of abode with another person." Wis. Stat. Ann. §813.12. In New Jersey:

> "Victim of domestic violence" means . . . any person who is 18 years of age or older or who is an emancipated minor and who has been subjected to domestic violence by a spouse, former spouse, or any other person who is a present or former household member or a person with whom the victim has a child in common. N.J.S.A. 2C:25–19.

States vary in defining what constitutes domestic violence. In New Jersey, for example, domestic violence is "the occurrence of one or more of the following acts inflicted upon a person protected under this act by an adult or an emancipated minor" and includes homicide, assault, terroristic threats, kidnapping, criminal restraint, false imprisonment, sexual assault, criminal sexual contact, lewdness, criminal mischief, burglary, criminal trespass and harassment. N.J.S.A. 2C:25–19.

One problematic issue is how discretionary an arrest should be. In the New Jersey statute, arrests are mandatory under certain conditions, including where there are signs of injury caused by domestic violence, or there are warrants or court orders in effect, and is discretionary where there is probable cause to believe that domestic violence has occurred. N.J.S.A. 2C:25–22. In a number of states, arrest is not mandatory and is left to the discretion of the investigating officer. Many states provide for civil immunity for arrests made under the statutes if the enforcement is in good faith.

Central to the domestic violence legislation is the issuance of protective orders, temporary or permanent. These orders may prohibit the defendant from harming, threatening, or having contact with the plaintiff and their children, or from returning to the family home. Other relief includes orders for child custody, visitation, medical expenses, financial support, and mandatory counseling, depending on the jurisdiction. Failure to abide by these orders may place the defendant in contempt of court and subject to fines or imprisonment (Lengyel, 1990).

Notes and Issues for Discussion

1. What constitutes domestic violence? The use of physical force is probably the most commonly reported act of domestic violence. But as the New Jersey statute indicates, domestic violence can be far broader, extending to lewdness, burglary, and harassment as well as physical force. What are the limits of domestic violence? Does any family quarrel constitute domestic violence? Because of the wide variations, health and human services professionals and administrators should ascertain the legal criteria for domestic violence in their state.

2. Can domestic violence in the presence of children also be child abuse? Can it be argued that for a child to be living with domestic violence constitutes emotional harm even if the child is not physically touched? Could there be emotional abuse or neglect?

3. Consider the following requirement for notice to domestic violence victims:

   "You have the right to go to court to get an order called a temporary restraining order, also called a TRO, which may protect you from more abuse by your attacker. The officer who handed you this card can tell you how to get a TRO.

The kinds of things a judge can order in a TRO may include:

(1) That your attacker is temporarily forbidden from entering the home you live in;

(2) That your attacker is temporarily forbidden from having contact with you or your relatives;

(3) That your attacker is temporarily forbidden from bothering you at work;

(4) That your attacker has to pay temporary child support or support for you;

(5) That you be given temporary custody of your children;

(6) That your attacker pay you back any money you have to spend for medical treatment or repairs because of the violence.

There are other things the court can order, and the court clerk will explain the procedure to you and will help you fill out the papers for a TRO.

You also have the right to file a criminal complaint against your attacker. The police officer who gave you this paper will tell you how to file a criminal complaint.

On weekends, holidays and other times when the courts are closed, you still have a right to get a TRO. The police officer who gave you this paper can help you get in touch with a judge who can give you a TRO." N.J.S.A. 2C:25-23.

The notice is to be printed in English and Spanish, given to the victim at the time of the incident and explained by the police officer. Is it informative? Clear? Would domestic violence victims understand it? What are the requirements in your state?

4. A temporary restraining order may be obtained in many jurisdictions by one party appearing before a judge. The other party need not be present and in fact need not have prior notice of the proceeding. Is this *ex parte* appearance fair? In *Schramek v. Bohren*, 429 NW 2d 501 (1988), the Wisconsin Supreme Court upheld the constitutionality of *ex parte* orders.

5. How effective are the statutes? Violations of temporary and permanent restraining orders may constitute contempt of court, resulting in fines or incarceration. However, their enforcement depends on police or court action: "Protection orders, however, are beset with practical difficulties. They are frequently violated, rarely produce an arrest for violation, and often fail to prevent further violence." (Note, "Developments in the Law," 1993: 1510).

6. Domestic violence shelters provide temporary housing for victims of domestic violence and their children often in a location unknown to the defendant. What are the provisions for shelter in your state? For the provision of services to domestic violence victims? Are they adequate? Are there limits on how long a victim may reside in a shelter? What happens after the limits are reached?

Self-Defense and the Battered Spouse Syndrome

There may come a time when a victim of domestic violence can endure no more and leaves the relationship. However, many of those who leave return, and many others do not leave at all. Sometimes the domestic violence victim responds by injuring or even killing the abuser. Is this response justified? It is self-defense? Murder?

One problem in these situations is that it is often difficult for a judge or jury to understand why a person would remain in or return to an abusive situation, and why the person would believe they had no alternative but to retaliate. A growing number of states permit the use of expert testimony to educate the judge or jury on these points.

STATE v. KELLY
97 N.J. 178, 478 A.2d 364 (1984)
NEW JERSEY SUPREME COURT

WILENTZ, C.J.

The central issue before us is whether expert testimony about the battered-woman's syndrome is admissible to help establish a claim of self-defense in a homicide case. The question is one of first impression in this state. We hold, based on the limited record before us (the State not having had a full opportunity to prove the contrary), that the battered-woman's syndrome is an appropriate subject for expert testimony; that the experts' conclusions, despite the relative newness of the field, are sufficiently reliable under New Jersey's standards for scientific testimony; and that defendant's expert was sufficiently qualified. Accordingly, we reverse and remand for a new trial. If on retrial after a full examination of these issues the evidence continues to support these conclusions, the expert's testimony on the battered-woman's syndrome shall be admitted as relevant to the honesty and reasonableness of defendant's belief that deadly force was necessary to protect her against death or serious bodily harm.

On May 24, 1980, defendant, Gladys Kelly, stabbed her husband, Ernest, with a pair of scissors. He died shortly thereafter at a nearby hospital. The couple had been married for seven years, during which time Ernest had periodically attacked Gladys. According to Ms. Kelly, he assaulted her that afternoon, and she stabbed him in self-defense, fearing that he would kill her if she did not act.

Ms. Kelly was indicted for murder. At trial, she did not deny stabbing her husband, but asserted that her action was in self-defense. To establish the requisite state of mind for her self-defense claim, Ms. Kelly called Dr. Lois Veronen as an expert witness to testify about the battered-woman's syndrome. After hearing a lengthy voir dire examination of Dr. Veronen, the trial court ruled that expert testimony concerning the syndrome was inadmissible on the self-defense issue under *State v. Bess*, 53 N.J. 10 (1968). Apparently the court believed that the sole purpose of this testimony was to explain and justify defendant's perception of the danger rather than to show the objective reasonableness of that perception.

Ms. Kelly was convicted of reckless manslaughter. In an unreported decision relying in part on *Bess*, the Appellate Division affirmed the conviction. We granted certification, and now reverse.***

The Kellys had a stormy marriage. Some of the details of their relationship, especially the stabbing, are disputed. The following is Ms. Kelly's version of what happened—a version that the jury could have accepted and, if they had, a version that would make the proffered expert testimony not only relevant, but critical.

The day after the marriage, Mr. Kelly got drunk and knocked Ms. Kelly down. Although a period of calm followed the initial attack, the next seven years were accompanied by periodic and frequent beatings, sometimes as often as once a week. During the attacks, which generally occurred when Mr. Kelly was drunk, he threatened to kill Ms. Kelly and to cut off parts of her body if she tried to leave him. Mr. Kelly often moved out of the house after an attack, later returning with a promise that he would change his ways. Until the day of the homicide, only one of the attacks had taken place in public.

The day before the stabbing, Gladys and Ernest went shopping. They did not have enough money to buy food for the entire week, so Ernest said he would give his wife more money the next day.

The following morning he left for work. Ms. Kelly next saw her husband late that afternoon at a friend's house. She had gone there with her daughter, Annette, to ask Ernest for money to buy food. He told her to wait until they got home, and shortly thereafter the Kellys left. After walking past several houses, Mr. Kelly, who was drunk, angrily asked "What the hell did you come around here for?" He then grabbed the collar of her dress, and the two fell to the ground. He choked her by pushing his fingers against her throat, punched or hit her face, and bit her leg.

A crowd gathered on the street. Two men from the crowd separated them, just as Gladys felt that she was "passing out" from being choked. Fearing that Annette had been pushed around in the crowd, Gladys then left to look for her. Upon finding Annette, defendant noticed that Annette had defendant's pocketbook. Gladys had dropped it during the fight. Annette had retrieved it and gave her mother the pocketbook.

After finding her daughter, Ms. Kelly then observed Mr. Kelly running toward her with his hands raised. Within seconds he was right next to her. Unsure of whether he had armed himself while she was looking for their daughter, and thinking that he had come back to kill her, she grabbed a pair of scissors from her pocketbook. She tried to scare him away, but instead stabbed him.[1]

---

[1]This version of the homicide—with a drunk Mr. Kelly as the aggressor both in pushing Ms. Kelly to the ground and again in rushing at her with his hands in a threatening position after the two had been separated—is sharply disputed by the State. The prosecution presented testimony intended to show that the initial scuffle was started by Gladys; that upon disentanglement, while she was restrained by bystanders, she stated that she intended to kill Ernest; that she then chased after him, and upon catching up with him stabbed him with a pair of scissors taken from her pocketbook.

The central question in this case is whether the trial court erred in its exclusion of expert testimony on the battered-woman's syndrome. That testimony was intended to explain defendant's state of mind and bolster her claim of self-defense. We shall first examine the nature of the battered-woman's syndrome and then consider the expert testimony proffered in this case and its relevancy.

In the past decade social scientists and the legal community began to examine the forces that generate and perpetuate wife beating and violence in the family. What has been revealed is that the problem affects many more people than had been thought and that the victims of the violence are not only the battered family members (almost always either the wife or the children). There are also many other strangers to the family who feel the devastating impact, often in the form of violence, of the psychological damage suffered by the victims.

Due to the high increase of unreported abuse (the FBI and other law enforcement experts believe that wife abuse is the most unreported crime in the United States), estimates vary of the number of American women who are beaten regularly by their husband, boyfriend, or the dominant male figure in their lives. One recent estimate puts the number of women beaten yearly at over one million. See *California Advisory Comm'n on Family Law, Domestic Violence* app. F at 119 (1st report 1978). The state police statistics show more than 18,000 *reported* cases of domestic violence in New Jersey during the first nine months of 1983, in 83% of which the victim was female. It is clear that the American home, once assumed to be the cornerstone of our society, is often a violent place.

While common law notions that assigned an inferior status to women, and to wives in particular, no longer represent the state of the law as reflected in statutes and cases, many commentators assert that a bias against battered women still exists, institutionalized in the attitudes of law enforcement agencies unwilling to pursue or uninterested in pursuing wife beating cases.

Another problem is the currency enjoyed by stereotypes and myths concerning the characteristics of battered women and their reasons for staying in battering relationships. Some popular misconceptions about battered women include the beliefs that they are masochistic and actually enjoy their beatings, that they purposely provoke their husbands into violent behavior, and, most critically, as we shall soon see, that women who remain in battering relationships are free to leave their abusers at any time. *See L. Walker, The Battered Woman* at 19–31 (1979).

As these cases so tragically suggest, not only do many women suffer physical abuse at the hands of their mates, but a significant number of women kill (or are killed by) their husbands. In 1978, murders between husband and wife or girlfriend and boyfriend constituted 13% of all murders committed in the United States. Undoubtedly some of these arose from battering incidents. *Federal Bureau of Investigation, Crime in the United States 1978* (1978). Men were the victims in 48% of these killings. *Id.*

As the problem of battered women has begun to receive more attention, sociologists and psychologists have begun to focus on the effects a sustained pattern of physical and psychological abuse can have on a woman. The effects of such abuse are what some scientific observers have termed "the battered-woman's syndrome," a series of common characteristics that appear in women who are abused physically and psychologically over an extended period of time by the dominant male figure in their lives. Dr. Lenore Walker, a prominent writer on the battered-woman's syndrome, defines the battered woman as one

> who is repeatedly subjected to any forceful physical or psychological be-havior by a man in order to coerce her to do something he wants her to do without concern for her rights. Battered women include wives or women in any form of intimate relationships with men. Furthermore, in order to be classified as a battered woman, the couple must go through the battering cycle at least twice. Any woman may find herself in an abusive relationship with a man once. If it occurs a second time, and she remains in the situa-tion, she is defined as a battered woman. [L. Walker, supra, at xv.]

According to Dr. Walker, relationships characterized by physical abuse tend to develop battering cycles. Violent behavior directed at the woman occurs in three distinct and repetitive stages that vary both in duration and intensity depending on the individuals involved. L. Walker, supra, at 55–70.

Phase one of the battering cycle is referred to as the "tension-building stage," during which the battering male engages in minor battering incidents and ver-bal abuse while the woman, beset by fear and tension, attempts to be as placat-ing and passive as possible in order to stave off more serious violence. Id. at 56–59.

Phase two of the battering cycle is the "acute battering incident." At some point during phase one, the tension between the battered woman and the bat-terer becomes intolerable and more serious violence inevitable. The triggering event that initiates phase two is most often an internal or external event in the life of the battering male, but provocation for more severe violence is sometimes provided by the woman who can no longer tolerate or control her phase-one anger and anxiety. Id. at 59–65.

Phase three of the battering cycle is characterized by extreme contrition and loving behavior on the part of the battering male. During this period the man will often mix his pleas for forgiveness and protestations of devotion with promises to seek professional help, to stop drinking, and to refrain from further violence. For some couples, this period of relative calm may last as long as several months, but in a battering relationship the affection and contrition of the man will even-tually fade and phase one of the cycle will start anew. Id. at 65–70.

The cyclical nature of battering behavior helps explain why more women sim-ply do not leave their abusers. The loving behavior demonstrated by the batterer during phase three reinforces whatever hopes these women might have for their mate's reform and keeps them bound to the relationship. R. Langley & R. Levy, Wife Beating: The Silent Crisis 112–14 (1977).

Some women may even perceive the battering cycle as normal, especially if they grew up in a violent household. Battered Women, A Psychosociological Study of Domestic Violence 60 (M. Roy ed. 1977); D. Martin, Battered Wives, 60 (1981). Or they may simply not wish to acknowledge the reality of their situation. T. David-son, Conjugal Crime, at 50 (1978) ("The middle-class battered wife's response to her situation tends to be withdrawal, silence and denial . . .").

Other women, however, become so demoralized and degraded by the fact that they cannot predict or control the violence that they sink into a state of psychological paralysis and become unable to take any action at all to improve or alter the situation. There is a tendency in battered women to believe in the omnipotence or strength of their battering husbands and thus to feel that any attempt to resist them is hopeless. *L. Walker, supra.,* at 75.

In addition to these psychological impacts, external social and economic factors often make it difficult for some women to extricate themselves from battering relationships. A woman without independent financial resources who wishes to leave her husband often finds it difficult to do so because of a lack of material and social resources.

Even with the progress of the last decade, women typically make less money and hold less prestigious jobs than men, and are more responsible for child care. Thus, in a violent confrontation where the first reaction might be to flee, women realize soon that there may be no place to go. Moreover, the stigma that attaches to a woman who leaves the family unit without her children undoubtedly acts as a further deterrent to moving out.

In addition, battered women, when they want to leave the relationship, are typically unwilling to reach out and confide in their friends, family, or the police, either out of shame and humiliation, fear of reprisal by their husband, or the feeling they will not be believed.

Dr. Walker and other commentators have identified several common personality traits of the battered woman: low self-esteem, traditional beliefs about the home, the family, and the female sex role, tremendous feelings of guilt that their marriages are failing, and the tendency to accept responsibility for the batterer's actions. *L. Walker, supra,* at 35–36.

Finally, battered women are often hesitant to leave a battering relationship because, in addition to their hope of reform on the part of their spouse, they harbor a deep concern about the possible response leaving might provoke in their mates. They literally become trapped by their own fear. Case histories are replete with instances in which a battered wife left her husband only to have him pursue her and subject her to an even more brutal attack. *D. Martin, supra,* at 76–79.

The combination of all these symptoms—resulting from sustained psychological and physical trauma compounded by aggravating social and economic factors—constitutes the battered-woman's syndrome. Only by understanding these unique pressures that force battered women to remain with their mates, despite their long-standing and reasonable fear of severe bodily harm and the isolation that being a battered woman creates, can a battered woman's state of mind be accurately and fairly understood.

The voir dire testimony of Dr. Veronen, sought to be introduced by defendant Gladys Kelly, conformed essentially to this outline of the battered-woman's syndrome. Dr. Veronen, after establishing her credentials, described in general terms the component parts of the battered-woman's syndrome and its effects on a woman's physical and mental health. The witness then documented, based on her own considerable experience in counseling, treating, and studying battered women, and her familiarity with the work of others in the field, the feelings of anxiety, self-blame, isolation, and, above all, fear that plagues these women and leaves them prey to a psychological paralysis that hinders their ability to break free or seek help.

Dr. Veronen stated that the problems of battered women are aggravated by a lack of understanding among the general public concerning both the prevalence of violence against women and the nature of battering relationships. She cited several myths concerning battered women that enjoy popular acceptance—primarily that such women are masochistic and enjoy the abuse they receive and that they are free to leave their husbands but choose not to.

Dr. Veronen described the various psychological tests and examinations she had performed in connection with her independent research. These tests and their methodology, including their interpretation, are, according to Dr. Veronen, widely accepted by clinical psychologists. Applying this methodology to defendant (who was subjected to all of the tests, including a five-hour interview), Dr. Veronen concluded that defendant was a battered woman and subject to the battered-woman's syndrome.***

Gladys Kelly claims that she stabbed her husband in self-defense, believing he was about to kill her. The gist of the State's case was that Gladys Kelly was the aggressor, that she consciously intended to kill her husband, and that she certainly was not acting in self-defense.

The credibility of Gladys Kelly is a critical issue in this case. If the jury does not believe Gladys Kelly's account, it cannot find she acted in self-defense. The expert testimony offered was directly relevant to one of the critical elements of that account, namely, what Gladys Kelly believed at the time of the stabbing, and was thus material to establish the honesty of her stated belief that she was in imminent danger of death.

As can be seen from our discussion of the expert testimony, Dr. Veronen would have bolstered Gladys Kelly's credibility. Specifically, by showing that her experience, although concededly difficult to comprehend, was common to that of other women who had been in similarly abusive relationships, Dr. Veronen would have helped the jury understand that Gladys Kelly could have honestly feared that she would suffer serious bodily harm from her husband's attacks, yet still remain with him. This, in turn, would support Ms. Kelly's testimony about her state of mind (that is, that she honestly feared serious bodily harm) at the time of the stabbing.

On the facts in this case, we find that the expert testimony was relevant to Gladys Kelly's state of mind, namely it was admissible to show she *honestly* believed she was in imminent danger of death.***

Notes and Issues for Discussion

1. Gladys Kelly says she remained in an abusive relationship for seven years. Under the theory of the battered spouse syndrome, is this believable? Why?

2. A majority of states now accept the battered spouse syndrome as an appropriate subject for expert testimony. See, for example, *Ibn-Tamas v. U.S.*,

407 A.2d 626 (D.C. Circuit); *Smith v. State*, 277 S.E. 2d 678 (Georgia). Citing the *Kelly* case, Ohio recently reversed a decision that expert testimony in this area was unnecessary, and now accepts expert testimony. See *State v. Koss*, 551 N.E.2d 970 (Ohio 1990). Some jurisdictions have refused to admit expert testimony on the battered spouse syndrome. See *Buhrie v. Wyoming*, 627 P.2d 1374 (Wyoming 1981); *Hill v. State*, 507 So.2d 554 (Ala. 1986), while others have not decided the issue. What are some arguments in favor of accepting battered spouse syndrome testimony? What are some arguments against?

3. Another issue is whether a subjective or objective standard should be used—whether the standard of perceiving oneself to be in danger should be that of a reasonable person who was the victim of domestic violence—an objective standard—or that of the particular victim—a subjective standard. In *State v. Koss* (above), the Ohio Supreme Court held the following trial court instruction to the jury on the reasonable person standard was proper: "In determining whether the Defendant had reasonable grounds for an honest belief that she was in imminent danger, you must put yourself in the position of the Defendant, with her characteristics, knowledge, or lack of knowledge, and under the same circumstances and conditions that surrounded the Defendant at the time. You must consider the conduct of Michael Koss and determine if such acts and works caused the defendant to reasonably and honestly believe that she was about to be killed or to receive great bodily harm." 551 N.E. 2d at 973.

Liability for Failure to Enforce Domestic Violence Laws

An ongoing problem with domestic violence has been the reluctance of some law enforcement agents to acknowledge the violence and protect the victim. A number of lawsuits have been filed against police for a failure to enforce domestic violence statutes and protect victims with mixed results. In the *Watson* case recovery was allowed under federal law. However, in several recent cases recovery has been denied on the basis of the Supreme Court's *DeShanney* holding (see p. 558). As the *Sorichetti* case (below) indicates, there may be recovery under state law.

WATSON v. CITY OF KANSAS CITY
857 F.2d 690 (1988)
U.S. COURT OF APPEALS

TACHA, CIRCUIT JUDGE.

This case involves claims arising out of the alleged failure to provide police protection to a victim of domestic violence and her son. The plaintiff, Nancy Watson, filed a federal civil rights action against the City of Kansas City, Kansas (City), its police chief, and a number of officers. She also alleged state law violations. The district court granted the defendants' motion for summary judgment on all claims and denied plaintiff's motion for reconsideration. Plaintiff appeals. We affirm in part and reverse in part.

This case involves a long history of domestic violence. Because the record must be viewed in the light most favorable to the nonmoving party, we present, briefly, the plaintiff's version of the facts. Nancy and Ed Watson, Jr., were married for the first time on August 9, 1979. At that time, Nancy Watson already had a son, Jason Fitch, who was three years old. Nancy and Ed Watson had a daughter, Andrea, born on December 7, 1979. Ed Watson was a police officer with the Kansas City, Kansas Police Department (Police Department) from September 4, 1973, until his death on January 20, 1984. The Watsons experienced marital difficulties during their marriage, and Ed Watson physically abused his wife. Nancy Watson filed for divorce on January 6, 1981, and obtained a restraining order against Ed Watson. In February, 1981, Nancy Watson dismissed the divorce proceedings, but the Watsons were ultimately divorced on November 20, 1981.

Nancy Watson did not report to the police all of the incidents of abuse that occurred during this period. She did, however, report at least one incident. A few days before the divorce, Ed Watson shook a knife at her. She ran next door and called the police. Captain Hooks and some other officers responded. According to Nancy Watson, Captain Hooks told her, "Mrs. Watson, if you ever call the police again, I will see to it that you are arrested and you'll never see those two kids again."

On September 10, 1981, shortly before he and his wife were divorced, Ed Watson received severe head and facial injuries in a motorcycle accident. After the accident, his coworkers noticed and reported that he suffered from memory loss and confusion, and experienced periods where he seemed to be in a daze. As a result of these reports, the police department ordered Ed Watson to undergo psychological evaluation. He was approved to return to full-time work as a patrolman.

In July, 1982, Nancy and Ed Watson began seeing each other again. During this period, Ed Watson was not abusive; he maintained that he had reformed. On August 9, 1982, Nancy and Ed Watson were remarried. The first instance of physical abuse during the second marriage occurred on February 7, 1983. After that, Ed Watson went to their home many times while he was on duty and abused Nancy Watson.

On October 29, 1983, Ed Watson severely beat Nancy Watson with a flashlight. She required inpatient treatment at the University of Kansas Medical Center. She did not report this beating to the police immediately because she was afraid her children would be taken away from her as Captain Hooks had threatened.

On November 20, 1983, Ed Watson came home while he was on a break and brought with him an order from a fast food restaurant. Jason Fitch ate some of the food and vomited. Ed Watson struck his stepson several times and forced him to eat the regurgitated food. He also struck Nancy Watson. After Ed Watson left, Nancy Watson called the Police Department. She informed Sergeant Wilkerson of what had happened. She also informed him of the October 29th incident when Ed Watson had beaten her with a flashlight. She asked that Ed Watson be arrested. Ed Watson was not arrested, but Officer Golubski took an offense report.

On November 21, 1983, Nancy Watson gave a statement to Detective Sands concerning the events of the previous day as well as the October 29 attack with the flashlight. She also signed a formal complaint against Ed Watson. The offense report and Nancy Watson's statement were referred to the Internal Affairs Unit of the Police Department, and an investigation was begun. According to the Police Department's Internal Investigation Procedures, a Criminal Investigation Unit in the detective division is to investigate alleged violations of criminal laws. The Internal Affairs Unit is to investigate complaints not amounting to violation of criminal laws. On approximately December 15, 1983, the Internal Affairs Unit delivered its file to the Wyandotte County District Attorney's Office for possible criminal action. The Police Department took no disciplinary action during the investigation.

Mark Frey of the Kansas Social and Rehabilitation Service was assigned to investigate the child abuse charges. The Police Department told him not to contact Ed Watson.

On November 28, 1983, Nancy Watson filed for divorce. The court issued an order providing that Nancy Watson was to have the use, occupancy, and control of the parties' residence and restraining the parties from molesting or interfering with the privacy of the other.

On December 15, 1983, Ed Watson went to the family's residence where he held Nancy Watson and the children until December 18. On December 18, Nancy Watson called the police and requested assistance because Ed Watson had forced his way into the house, put a gun to her head, and threatened to kill both her and himself. Several police officers responded to the call shortly after Ed Watson returned to the house. Nancy Watson told the officers about the restraining order and requested that Ed Watson be arrested. Although Sergeant Cheek maintains that Nancy Watson did not request that Ed Watson be arrested, Officer Bradley testified that she wanted to press charges. Also, despite the existence of physical evidence, Bradley testified that he made no investigation of forced entry. He testified that an officer normally investigates the scene but that he did not do so because he was there "investigating a domestic disturbance, it was not classified as a forced entry. . . ." The officers took no action and were preparing to leave when Nancy Watson called an abuse hotline. She described the situation and gave the names of the officers present. The officers then made a report but refused to arrest Ed Watson or order him to leave. When, after two hours, it became apparent that the officers would take no further action, Nancy Watson requested that she and her children be taken to a shelter for battered women. Nancy Watson later moved back home and had the locks changed.

On the evening of January 19, 1984, Nancy Watson and the children were driving home from the grocery store when they noticed Ed Watson following them. Nancy Watson drove directly to the police station and honked for assistance. Sergeant Woolery came out, and Nancy Watson told him that Ed Watson was following her. She asked Woolery to detain her husband so that she and the children could get home, and Sergeant Woolery told her that he would detain him. Woolery was aware of the Internal Affairs investigation. Nancy Watson drove directly home. However, when she and the children arrived, Ed Watson was already there. He forced the family into the house, locked deadbolt locks, and ripped out the telephones. He locked the children in their room and raped Nancy Watson. After the rape, he beat and stabbed her. When the knife he was using broke, he left her to go to the kitchen to get another one. While he was in the kitchen, Nancy Watson tried unsuccessfully to get out of the house through the front door. She then jumped through a picture window onto the front law. Ed Watson followed her through the window. A neighbor heard the disturbance and called the police. Ed Watson left in his car. One officer who responded to the call said to Nancy Watson that the whole situation was her fault because she had married Ed Watson. Three hours later it was discovered that Ed Watson had committed suicide at his brother's home. After Watson's death, Lieutenant Miller, the Police Department's public information officer and Ed Watson's former supervisor, told a *Kansas City Star* reporter that Ed Watson "was like a time bomb waiting to go off."

Nancy Watson filed suit under 42 U.S.C. §1983 claiming that the Police Department and the various individual police officers violated her right to equal protection under the law. She also filed suit under the Kansas Tort Claims Act.

***To establish a cause of action under section 1983, a plaintiff must allege (1) deprivation of a federal right by (2) a person acting under color of state law. In this case, Nancy Watson has alleged that the defendants' custom and policy of not providing assistance to victims of abuse by spouses in the same manner as other victims of assault deprived her of the equal protection of laws guaranteed by the fourteenth amendment.

The defendants do not contest that action under color of state law has occurred. Nor do they contest that failing to provide police protection is subject to the equal protection clause under section 1983. Although there is no general constitutional right to police protection, the state may not discriminate in providing such protection.***

We will first address the plaintiff's section 1983 claim against the City and several police officers acting in their official capacities, including the Police Chief, Alan Meyers.***

Nancy Watson's claim does not involve a *law* which discriminates against victims of domestic violence. Rather she claims that the Police Department follows an unwritten *policy* or *custom* of responding differently and thus affording less protection to victims of domestic violence. It is well settled that the city may be liable for the plaintiff's injuries only if she can establish that her injuries were the result of an unconstitutional municipal policy or custom.

Much of plaintiff's evidence regarding what happened consists of her testimony in the form of her deposition. Defendants in most instances deny or contradict her version of the various events. Therefore factual disputes clearly exist. However, these factual disputes are immaterial if the plaintiff has offered insufficient evidence for a jury to find in her favor regarding discriminatory policy and intent. Normally a plaintiff must point to facts outside the plaintiff's own case to support the allegation of an unconstitutional municipal policy. We have examined the record and find that the plaintiff has presented sufficient evidence that could allow a jury to find in her favor on her section 1983 claim.

First, the plaintiff has presented evidence showing that out of 608 nondomestic assault cases in Kansas City, Kansas, from January 1, 1983, to September 8, 1983, where there was a known perpetrator, there were 186 arrests for an arrest rate of 31%. Out of 369 domestic assaults, there were only 69 arrests for a rate of 16%.

The defendants argue that these statistics should not be considered. Apparently their argument is that the statistics are irrelevant and therefore inadmissible because they fail to take into account whether probable cause to arrest was present.***

We find no merit in defendants' argument. Whether or not probable cause exists is not susceptible to statistical quantification. It represents a judgment call on the part of the officer or officers at the scene taking into account the particular circumstances. Although there are clearly guidelines, much depends on the individual officers' assessment. In the context of assaults, it is possible or perhaps even probable that officers' assessments as to whether probable cause exists are colored by whether the disturbance is domestic or nondomestic. The determination of whether probable cause exists may be subject to the same allegedly unconstitutional policy that leads to the discrepancy in arrest rates between domestic and nondomestic situations here.***

Furthermore, the plaintiff's version of events regarding her own situation, if believed, may demonstrate a pattern of deliberate indifference on the part of the Police Department. Such a pattern, when examined in the context of other evidence the plaintiff has presented, constitutes evidence of a custom or policy. In *Thurman,* the plaintiff alleged that she requested assistance from the police many times over an eight month period because of threats upon her life by her estranged husband. She made several attempts to file complaints against her husband which were ignored or rejected by the police department. In considering the defendants' motion to dismiss, the court held that such a pattern raises an inference of a municipal custom or policy. In the present case, we need not decide whether demonstration of such a pattern, by itself, could establish an unconstitutional municipal custom or policy. We note, however, that this is an equal protection claim, and because there is no general constitutional right to police protection, *Bartalone,* 643 F.Supp. at 577; *Lowers,* 627 F.Supp. at 246, the plaintiff must demonstrate that she was treated differently because of her membership in a certain class. We doubt whether evidence of deliberate indifference in the plaintiff's case alone would be sufficient evidence of *different* treatment. We do find, however, that taken with the other evidence plaintiff has proffered, a pattern such as the one alleged by plaintiff in this case constitutes some evidence of custom or policy.

When all of the plaintiff's evidence is considered, it is sufficient, if believed, to support a jury finding that the City and Police Department followed a policy or custom of affording less protection to victims of domestic violence than to victims of nondomestic attacks. Furthermore, a jury could infer, based on this evidence, that the City and Police Department acted with a discriminatory motive in pursuing this policy, and that her injuries were a result of the policy.

The district court therefore erred in granting summary judgment to the City.***

The basis for the district court's order granting summary judgment for defendants in their individual capacities is unclear. The court's decision appears to have been based in part on its disposition of the "municipal policy or custom" claim. The court did not address the defendants' claim for qualified immunity. Given our reversal of the district court's conclusion regarding the claim against the City, the court on remand should determine whether qualified immunity shields these individual defendants notwithstanding the presence of a section 1983 claim against the city. In making this determination the court must decide whether the actions of these defendants violate "clearly established statutory or constitutional rights of which a reasonable person would have known." *Harlow v. Fitzgerald*, 457 U.S. 800, 818 (1982).

SORICHETTI v. CITY OF NEW YORK
65 N.Y.2d 461, 482 N.E.2d 70 (1985)
N.Y. COURT OF APPEALS

ALEXANDER, JUDGE.

This action was commenced against the City of New York (City) by Dina Sorichetti, an infant, and her mother, Josephine Sorichetti, to recover damages resulting from injuries inflicted on Dina by her father, Frank Sorichetti. Plaintiff's theory of recovery is that the City, through the New York City Police Department, negligently failed to take Frank Sorichetti into custody or otherwise prevent his assault upon his daughter after being informed that he may have violated a Family Court order of protection and that he had threatened to do harm to the infant.***

A jury thereafter returned a verdict in plaintiff's favor in the amount of $3,000,000 for the infant and $40,000 for the mother.***

To uphold the award of damages in this case, we must determine whether a special relationship existed between the infant and the municipality by virtue of (1) the issuance of a judicial order of protection directing Frank Sorichetti to refrain from threatening or assaulting his wife and providing that the order constituted authority for a peace officer to arrest a person charged with violating its terms; and (2) the police department's knowledge of Frank Sorichetti's history of assaultive and abusive conduct toward his family and his immediate threats of harm to his daughter and its response to Josephine Sorichetti's pleas for assistance.

Josephine and Frank Sorichetti were married in 1949, and had three children, the youngest being Dina, who was born in 1969. It appears that Frank drank excessively and that the couple's relationship was quite stormy, with Frank becoming violent and abusive when under the influence of alcohol. In January 1975, Josephine obtained an order of protection in Family Court following a particularly violent incident in which her husband had threatened her and punched her in the chest so forcefully as to send her "flying across the room." The order recited that Frank was forbidden to assault, menace, harass, endanger, threaten or act in a disorderly manner toward" Josephine. By June 1975, Frank's drinking and abusiveness had intensified. Consequently, Josephine moved out of their residence and took her own apartment. Upon her return in early July to obtain her personal belongings, Frank attacked her with a butcher knife, cutting her hand, which required suturing, and threatened to kill her and the children. The police were summoned from the 43rd precinct, but Frank had fled by the time they arrived. A second order of protection was issued by Family Court and a complaint filed in Criminal Court by Josephine. Frank was arrested by detectives from the 43rd precinct, but Josephine subsequently dropped both the Family Court and criminal charges based on Frank's promise to reform.

Frank's drinking and violent behavior continued, however, and in September 1975, Josephine served divorce papers on him. Frank became enraged and proceeded to destroy the contents of their apartment. He broke every piece of furniture, cut up clothes belonging to his wife and Dina, threw the food out of the refrigerator and bent every knife and fork. The police from the 43rd precinct were summoned, but they refused to arrest Frank because "he lived there."

Family Court entered a third order of protection that also ordered Frank Sorichetti to stay away from Josephine's home. During the ensuing months, Frank continued to harass his wife and daughter, following them in the mornings as they walked to Dina's school and threatening that they "were Sorichettis" and were going to "die Sorichettis," and that he was going to "bury them." Josephine reported these incidents to the 43rd precinct. Additionally, Frank created disturbances at Josephine's place of employment on a number of occasions with the result that she was discharged. On October 9, 1975, Frank was arrested by officers of the 43rd precinct for driving while intoxicated.

On November 6, 1975, Josephine and Frank appeared in Family Court where the order of protection was made final for one year. Included in the order was a provision granting Frank visitation privileges with his daughter each weekend from 10:00 a.m. Saturday until 6:00 p.m. Sunday. It was agreed that Dina would be picked up and dropped off at the 43rd precinct. As required by Family Court Act §168, the order also recited that: "[T]he presentation of this Certificate to any Peace Officer shall constitute authority for said Peace Officer to take into custody the person charged with violating the terms of such Order of Protection and bring said person before this Court and otherwise, so far as lies within his power, to aid the Petitioner in securing the protection such Order was intended to afford."

On the following weekend, Josephine delivered Dina to her husband in front of the 43rd precinct at the appointed time. As he walked away with the child, Frank turned to Josephine and shouted, "You, I'm going to kill you." Pointing to his daughter, he said, "You see Dina; you better do the sign of the cross before this weekend is up." He then made the sign of the cross on himself. Josephine understood her husband's statements and actions to be a death threat, and she immediately entered the police station and reported the incident to the officer at the desk. She showed him the order of protection and reported that her husband had just threatened her and her child. She requested that the officer "pick up Dina and arrest Frank." She also reported the past history of violence inflicted by

Frank. The officer told Josephine that because her husband had not "hurt her bodily—did not touch her" there was nothing the police could do. Josephine then returned home.

At 5:30 p.m. the following day, Sunday, Josephine returned to the station house. She was distraught, agitated and crying. She approached the officer at the front desk and demanded that the police pick up Dina and arrest her husband who was then living with his sister some five minutes from the precinct. She showed the officer the order of protection and related the threats made the previous morning as well as the prior incidents and Frank's history of drinking and abusive behavior. The officer testified that he told Josephine that if "he didn't drop her off in a reasonable time, we would send a radio car out."

The officer referred Josephine to Lieutenant Leon Granello, to whom she detailed the prior events. He dismissed the protective order as "only a piece of paper" that "means nothing" and told Josephine to wait outside until 6:00. At 6:00 p.m., Josephine returned to the Lieutenant who told her, "why don't you wait a few minutes***Maybe he took her to a movie. He'll be back. Don't worry about it." Josephine made several similar requests, but each time was told "to just wait. We'll just wait." In the meantime, at about 5:20 or 5:30, Officer John Hobbie arrived at the station house. He recognized Josephine, who by then was hysterical, from prior incidents involving the Sorichettis. Specifically, just a few months previously, on June 28, 1975, Hobbie had intervened in an altercation in which Frank, while intoxicated and being abusive, had tried to pull Dina away from a babysitter, cursing and saying, "if I don't have her, the mother shouldn't have her." Hobbie had taken Frank, Dina and the babysitter to the 43rd precinct, where a decision was made not to let Frank have the child. Frank had started cursing and became loud and abusive. He calmed down somewhat when threatened with removal from the station house, and left when told that the police were holding the child until her mother arrived. In a second incident on October 9, 1975, Officer Hobbie transferred Frank to a hospital for detoxification following Frank's arrest by officers of the 43rd precinct for driving while intoxicated.

After speaking with Josephine on November 9, 1975, Officer Hobbie informed Lieutenant Granello of his prior experience with Frank. He told the Lieutenant that Sorichetti was a "very violent man" and that Dina was "petrified" of him. Officer Hobbie recommended that a patrol car be sent to Sorichetti's home. Lieutenant Granello rejected this suggestion, contending initially that no patrol cars were available and later that "not enough time ha[d] gone by."

At 6:30, Lieutenant Granello suggested that Josephine call home to see if Dina had been dropped off there. She did so and was informed that the child was not there. She continued to plead that the officer take immediate action. The Lieutenant again told Josephine "Let's just wait." At 7:00, the Lieutenant told Josephine to leave her phone number and to go home, and that he would call her if Sorichetti showed up. She did as suggested.

At about the same time, Frank Sorichetti's sister entered her apartment and found him passed out on the floor with an empty whiskey bottle and pill bottle nearby. The woman also found Dina, who was severely injured. Between 6:55 and 7:00 p.m., Sorichetti had attacked the infant repeatedly with a fork, a knife and a screwdriver and had attempted to saw off her leg. Police from the 43rd precinct, responding to a 911 call, arrived within five minutes and rushed the child, who was in a coma, to the hospital. The infant plaintiff was hospitalized for 40 days and remains permanently disabled. Frank Sorichetti was convicted of attempted murder, and is currently serving a prison sentence.

The infant and her mother commenced this action against the City to recover damages for Dina's injuries and for the mother's loss of services.***

A municipality cannot be held liable for injuries resulting from a failure to provide adequate police protection absent a special relationship existing between the municipality and the injured party. Indeed, where there is no special relationship, a municipality does not owe a duty to its citizens in the performance of governmental functions, and thus courts will not examine the "reasonableness" of the municipality's actions.***

In several extraordinary instances, a special relationship has been found which imposes a duty on a municipality to provide reasonable police protection to an individual. For example, in *Schuster v. City of New York*, 5 N.Y.2d 75, the City was held liable when a citizen collaborated with the police in the arrest of a dangerous fugitive and was thereafter denied protection after he received death threats, which were successfully carried out. Similarly, in *De long v. County of Erie* (60 N.Y.2d 296), we imposed a special duty of care on a municipality toward a woman who called 911 for police assistance, was told that assistance would be forthcoming, and in reliance on this assurance exposed herself to danger that resulted in her death.

A key element in each of these cases***is some direct contact between agents of the municipality and the injured party.

In the present case, we hold that a special relationship existed between the City and Dina Sorichetti which arose out of (1) the order of protection; (2) the police department's knowledge of Frank Sorichetti's violent history, gained through and verified both by its actual dealings with him, the existence of the order of protection, and its knowledge of the specific situation in which the infant had been placed; (3) its response to Josephine Sorichetti's pleas for assistance on the day of the assault; and (4) Mrs. Sorichetti's reasonable expectation of police protection.

In enacting Family Court Act §168, the Legislature intended to encourage police involvement in domestic matters, an area in which the police traditionally have exhibited a reluctance to intervene. The statute does not evince a legislative determination that the scope of municipal tort liability attendant upon traditional governmental activities, such as police protection, should be extended to an entire class. By its terms, section 168 provides that a certificate of protection "shall constitute authority" for a peace officer to take into custody one who reasonably appears to have violated the order. As such, it "broadens the circumstances under which a peace officer may take a person into custody beyond those enumerated in Article 140 of the Criminal Procedure Law." When presented with an order of protection, a police officer is not mandated to make an arrest. Nonetheless, such presentation along with an allegation that the order has been violated obligates the officer to investigate and take appropriate action.***

The fact that an injury occurs because of a violation of an order of protection does not in itself create municipal liability. An arrest may not be warranted in each case, and the failure of the police to take such action will not alone be determinative of the reasonableness of their conduct. But when the police are made aware of a possible violation, they are obligated to respond and investigate, and their actions will be subject to a "reasonableness" review in a negligence action.

As the jury in this case found, the 43rd precinct police had particular knowledge of Frank Sorichetti's abusiveness, assaultiveness and chronic alcoholism. This knowledge was obtained by direct experience emanating from Sorichetti's past arrests and the numerous instances in which they had intervened in disturbances caused by Sorichetti. Indeed, on the day of the assault, the precinct's supervising officer, Lieutenant Granello, was specifically and emphatically informed by one of his officers that Sorichetti was a "very violent man" whose threats should not be taken lightly, and was given information relating to Sorichetti's past violence. In addition, the certificate of protection represented a judicial affirmation of the seriousness of Sorichetti's past conduct.

Aside from their awareness of the threatmaker's violent propensity, a critical factor in the creation of a special duty of protection herein is the police officers' conduct toward Josephine on the evening of November 9th. When she first approached the front-desk officer at 5:30, Josephine was told that if Sorichetti did not arrive within a reasonable time the police would send a patrol car out. Thereafter, the Lieutenant told Josephine to "wait outside" until 6:00, creating the clear impression that at that time, when Sorichetti's failure to return would be a violation of the order of protection, some action would be taken. From this point on, the police repeatedly told Josephine to "wait awhile longer," never dispelling the notion that they would provide assistance at some reasonable time, until she was finally told at 7:00 to "go home." Josephine, in her helpless and distraught state, had no alternative but to seek the assistance of the police to assure her daughter's safety. The passage of time was critical inasmuch as the assault did not take place until approximately 6:55.

***Under the circumstances presented on this appeal, we hold that a special relationship existed between the police and Josephine and her six-year-old daughter such that the jury could properly consider whether the police conduct satisfied the duty of care owing to Dina.

Notes and Issues for Discussion

1. Courts have taken different positions on the liability issue under federal law. In *Thurman v. City of Torrington*, 595 F.Supp. 1521 (1984), the court found liability for failure to enforce the domestic violence statute, basing the decision on gender-based discrimination under the Equal Protection clause. However, in *McKee v. Rockwell*, 877 F.2d 409 (1989), the Fifth Circuit found no liability, holding the police had no duty to protect the public in general. The decision was based on the U.S. Supreme Court's recent holding in *DeShaney v. Winnebago Soc. Serv.*, where the Court held the state

had no responsibility to protect a child living at home supervised by a protective services worker. (See p. 558). See also *Balistreri v. Pacifica Police Dep't.*, 901 F.2d 696, reversing a previous circuit panel and denying recovery.

2. Note the use of arrest data in *Watson*. While not sufficient alone they point to a differential arrest pattern for domestic violence. An arrest is only made upon probable cause. The city argues that there are fewer arrests in domestic violence cases because there is less often probable cause present. The court points out that even if there is less probable cause in domestic violence disputes, this may result from a biased judgment by the arresting officer.

3. Liability under state laws will depend upon sovereign immunity considerations and whether the police have only a general duty to society but not to specific individuals. Unless there is a specific duty, there probably can be no breach and therefore no cause of action.

4. In *Sorichetti*, the appellate court modified the reward, reducing it to $2 million. The *Sorichetti* court says that an injury occurring because of a violation of an order of protection does not automatically create liability. The test is whether the police were reasonable in their response and investigation. What would have been reasonable actions in this case?

SELECTED REFERENCES

Areen, J. *Family Law: Cases and Materials* (2nd ed. 1985, with 1991 Supplement).

Besharov, D. *The Vulnerable Social Worker* (1985).

Cole, W. A. "Religious confidentiality and the reporting of child abuse: A statutory and constitutional analysis," 21 *Columbia J. Law and Social Problems* 1 (1987).

Hefler, R., and Kempe, R. (Eds.). *The Battered Child* (4th ed., 1987).

Langan, P. A. and Innes, C. A. *Special Report: Preventing Domestic Violence Against Women* (U.S. Department of Justice, 1986).

Lengyel, L. B. "Survey of state domestic violence legislation," 11 *Legal Reference Service. Q.* 59 (1990).

Myers, J. E. B. *Evidence in Child Abuse and Neglect Cases* (2nd ed. 1992).

———. "A survey of child abuse and neglect reporting statutes," 10 *J. Juvenile Law* 1 (1986).

Note, "Developments in the law—legal response to domestic violence," 106 *Harv. L. Rev.* 1498 (1993).

Note, "History of abuse: Societal, judicial and legislative responses to the problem of wife beating," 23 *Suffolk U. L. R.* 983 (1989).

Pride, M. *The Child Abuse Industry* (1986).

Sackett, R. S. "Terminating parental rights of the handicapped," 25 *Family L. Q.* 253 (1992).

U.S. Commission of Civil Rights. *Under the Rule of Thumb: Battered Women and the Administration of Justice* (1982).

Waits, K. "The criminal justice system: Response to batterers," 60 *Washington L.R.* 267 (1985).

Walker, L. *Battered Wife Syndrome* (1984).

CHAPTER 11

LAW AND THE MENTALLY ILL

LEGAL ISSUES IN THE MENTAL HEALTH SYSTEM

This chapter will examine some legal issues particularly relevant to health and human services professionals in the mental health field: voluntary admission, involuntary commitment, commitment of children, patients rights, constitutional rights to liberty and treatment, the right to refuse medication, and legal issues pertaining to those who are both mentally ill and have committed criminal acts.

One of the most dramatic changes in mental health is the sharp decrease in state mental hospital populations. Between 1956 and 1980, the census of state mental hospitals dropped from about 550,000 to around 130,000.[1] Several factors have contributed to this decline. A key reason has been the broad acceptance of the philosophy of deinstitutionalization, which is tied to the legal concept of least restrictive confinement. Although the U.S. Supreme Court has never embraced this as a constitutional requirement, most states now include the concept in either case or statutory law.[2] Related to the deinstitutionalization movement is the growth of psychotropic drugs as a treatment modality, allowing many mentally ill individuals to become stabilized and live in the community, coupled with substantial federal funding for community mental health centers and the enactment of short-term civil commitment statutes.[3] Finally, most states have modified their civil commitment laws to require proof of dangerousness along with mental illness before an involuntary commitment can be ordered. The result of these movements, laws, and funding patterns is that now individuals who are mentally ill may reside in many locations, including institutions, psychiatric wards of general hospitals, halfway houses, community programs, at home, or may live in rooming houses, boarding homes, or on the streets.

ENTRANCE INTO THE MENTAL HEALTH SYSTEM

The two main pathways into the mental health systems are voluntary admission and involuntary civil commitment. In a voluntarily admission, the patient requests admission or signs admittance forms and the hospital accepts the patient. In the involuntary civil commitment proceeding, based on the findings of a formal hearing the patient is committed to the mental hospital for an indefinite duration. Ideally the voluntary admission entails informed consent, and the involuntary proceeding is based on a thorough evaluation and a fair hearing. Questions have been raised as to how voluntary are many voluntary admissions, and how adequate are the involuntary commitment proceedings.[4]

Commitments also may be on a short-term basis for emergencies, detention, or for observation, any of which may be extended for longer periods through the more elaborate involuntary commitment proceeding. Voluntarily admitted adults may leave at any time, but often the hospital has the option of extending commitment by initiating involuntary proceedings.

VOLUNTARY ADMISSION

Almost one-half of all admissions to public mental hospitals are voluntary.[5]

Brakel notes that voluntary admission procedures are generally classified into three types: (1) informal admission procedures, (2) traditional voluntary admission procedures, and (3) third-party voluntary procedures. (Brakel, et al., 1985: 177.)

> The informal procedures, in their relative absence of administrative red tape and lack of pre- and post-admission legal constraints to which the person seeking admission is subjected, are the most truly voluntary, but their availability and use in the various states is limited. The traditional voluntary admission scheme deviates from the pure voluntary model in the retention provisions found in most states as well as in the elements of pressure that sometimes accompanies the admission decision. (Brakel, et al., 1985: 177)

In an informal voluntary admission the patient simply asks for admission and at a later time can ask for release:

> (a) Any person desiring admission to a mental health facility for treatment of a mental illness may be admitted upon his request without making formal application therefore if, after examination, the director of the facility considers that person clinically suitable for admission upon an informal basis.
> (b) Each patient admitted under this Section shall be informed in writing and orally at the time of admission of his right to be discharged from the facility at any time during the normal daily day-shift hours of

operation, which shall include but need not be limited to 9 A.M. to 5 P.M. Such right to be discharged shall commence with the first day-shift hours of operation after his admission. Illinois Stat. Ann. ch. 91 1/2 §3.300.

In a traditional or formal voluntary admission, the mentally ill patient signs into the mental health facility on a voluntary basis and can sign out at will. As noted, most states provide for delay in release during which the hospital can initiate involuntarily proceedings if it is believed the patient meets involuntarily commitment standards. States may require mental illness and dangerousness as standards for voluntary admission or may only require that the individual be in need of treatment.

Key elements of a voluntary admission, then, are those for informed consent: disclosure, capacity, and the absence of coercion. The individual signing in does so knowingly, freely, and is aware of the consequences.

Some states try to insure that the admission is truly voluntary. In New York the voluntary admission procedures require

that the applicant have the ability to understand (1) that the institution to which he is applying for admission is a mental institution, (2) that he is applying for voluntary admission and (3) what the nature of voluntary status is, including the meaning of provisions governing release and conversion to involuntary status. N.Y. Mental Hyg. Law §§9.13(a), 9.17(a), and 15.13(a).

The following notes address the voluntary admission aspects of the Supreme Court's decision, *Zinermon v. Burch*, 494 U.S. 113 (1990). The Zinermon case is found on p. 169.

Notes and Issues for Discussion

1. What is the potential impact of the *Zinermon* decision on voluntary admissions? At its narrowest, the case only applies to the relatively uncommon Florida statutory scheme which specifically requires informed consent for voluntary admissions, and only deals with the use of preadmission safeguards to insure that the patient is capable of giving that consent. In the opinion, the Court specifically avoids the broader issues of substantive or procedural due process in voluntary admissions.

2. Consider Justice Blackmun's observation:
   "The risk is that some persons who come into Florida's mental health facilities will apparently be willing to sign forms authorizing admission and treatment, but will be incompetent to give the 'express and informed consent' required. . . . Indeed, the very nature of mental illness makes it

foreseeable that a person needing mental health care will be unable to understand any proffered 'explanation and disclosure of the subject matter' of the forms that person is asked to sign and will be unable 'to make a knowing and willful decision' whether to consent to admission." 494 U.S. at 133.

While this is not the holding of the case, and technically is called "*obiter dictum*," or observations not part of the holding, couldn't this apply to virtually any voluntary admission of the mentally ill?[6] If a later court adopted this perspective on voluntary admissions, what would be the ramifications?

3. If Florida had not used a voluntary commitment, they would have had to use the involuntary commitment route, showing that Burch was both mentally ill and dangerous based on clear and convincing proof. There is, as the court notes, some likelihood that with these standards Burch is not committable.

INVOLUNTARY CIVIL COMMITMENT

The primary alternative to voluntary admission is through the involuntary civil commitment process. While short-term involuntary commitments may be possible without a court order, extended involuntary commitments now require a hearing in all states, usually before a judge. The state can civilly commit an individual who has not committed a crime under either its police powers to protect society or its *parens patriae* powers to protect the disabled individual (Brakel, *et al.*, 1985: 24).

Commitment Standards

Many states now require proof of both mental illness and dangerousness for commitment, although some states only require that the individual be mentally ill and in need of treatment. The danger may be to others, self, or property; in addition, an inability to provide for basic needs is a commitment standard in some states. The terms "mental illness" and "dangerous" may be defined in detail or left with little clarification. States have generally moved away from a simple commitment formulation linking some undefined mental illness with a need for treatment and toward more complex formulations of mental illness, disorder, and impairment, and sometimes specific criteria for dangerousness (Brakel, *et al.*, 1985: Chapter 2).

The most significant change in the judicial commitment criteria over the past decade has been the rise of "dangerous" to most prominent. . . . Where dangerousness is a necessary condition for commitment, as it is in some 25 states, it raises the aforementioned question of whether the statutes are too tightly drawn to reach those who need institutionalization and to keep the integrity of the law intact." (Brakel, *et al.*, 1985: 34)

The Pennsylvania statute is an example of one that requires recent dangerous acts as a requirement for commitment as a danger to others:

(a) Whenever a person is severely mentally disabled and in need of immediate treatment, he may be made subject to involuntary emergency examination and treatment. A person is severely mentally disabled when, as a result of mental illness, his capacity to exercise self-control, judgment and discretion in the conduct of his affairs and social relations or to care for his own personal needs is so lessened that he poses a clear and present danger of harm to others or to himself.

(b)(1) Clear and present danger to others shall be shown by establishing that within the past 30 days the person had inflicted or attempted to inflict serious bodily harm on another and that there is a reasonable probability that such conduct will be repeated. . . . For the purposes of this section, a clear and present danger to others may be demonstrated by proof that the person has made threats of harm and has committed acts in furtherance of the threat to commit harm. Pa. Stat. Ann. Tit. 50 §7301.

Compare Arizona, where a person is deemed a danger to others when:

the judgment of a person who has a mental disorder is so impaired that he is unable to understand his need for treatment and as a result of his mental disorder his continued behavior can reasonably be expected, on the basis of competent medical opinion, to result in serious physical harm." Ariz. Rev. Stats. §36-501.

Other criteria for commitment are a danger to self or to property. Danger to self might be an actual physical danger or the inability to provide for basic needs, and may be described in such terms as "in need of treatment," or "gravely disabled."

Questions also persist about the two other major criteria, mental illness and inability to provide for one's basic needs. Whether these terms in themselves have adequate content remains an open issue. . . . In a very basic sense, these criteria are no less troublesome than the dangerous standard: the medical knowledge necessary to define precisely and to clearly identify mental illness is lacking, the sociological expertise or consensus for determining who needs treatment or who cannot provide for himself remains conspicuously absent, and the law's capacity to address the issue, to the extent that it is founded on inadequate socio-medical knowledge (and must resort to essentially political judgment for want of scientific fact) will continue to be suspect. (Brakel, *et al.*, 1985, 36–37)

Notes and Issues for Discussion

1. Note that the Pennsylvania commitment statute requires a recent overt dangerous act or specific threats to commit harm. Is this too restrictive? Conversely, is the Arizona formulation too loose? If the issue is over- or underinclusion, which is safer for society? More protective of the mentally ill individual? How do you balance these two considerations?
2. In the Pennsylvania statute, clear and present danger to self "shall be shown by establishing that within the past 30 days:

   (i) the person has acted in such manner as to evidence that he would be unable, without care, supervision and the continued assistance of others, to satisfy his need for nourishment, personal or medical care, shelter, or self-protection and safety, and that there is a reasonable probability that death, serious bodily injury or serious physical debilitation would ensue within 30 days unless adequate treatment were afforded under this act; or

   (ii) the person has attempted suicide and that there is the reasonable probability of suicide unless adequate treatment is afforded under this act. For the purposes of this subsection, a clear and present danger may be demonstrated by the proof that the person has made threats to commit suicide and has committed acts which are in furtherance of the threat to commit suicide; or

   (iii) the person has substantially mutilated himself or attempted to mutilate himself substantially and there is the reasonable probability of mutilation unless adequate treatment is afforded under this act. For purposes of this subsection, a clear and present danger shall be established by proof that the person has made threats to commit mutilation and has committed acts which are in furtherance of the threat to commit mutilation." Pa. Stat. Ann. Tit. 50 §7301 (b)(2)(II). Is this too specific, or does it prevent unnecessary commitments?
3. Gravely disabled or unable to provide for basic needs are additional or alternative commitment standards in a number of states. See for example, Arizona (Ariz. Rev. Stat. Ann. §36-540[A]), Colorado (Colo. Rev. Stat. §27-10-109[1][a]), and Washington (Wash. Rev. Code Ann. §71.05.280[4]).

INVOLUNTARY COMMITMENT HEARINGS

Involuntary commitment hearings may take place in a public courtroom, the judge's chambers, or at the mental health facility, depending upon the state.

Usually the hearing is before a judge. Commitment generally requires certification by one or more physicians or psychiatrists, and/or testimony by one of these individuals that the individual is mentally ill and dangerous. Several studies of civil commitment proceedings have noted their brevity.

The degree of procedural protection provided varies across the states. Since the proceedings are civil and not criminal, routine criminal court procedures which are constitutionally mandated for those facing loss of liberty—such as *Miranda* warnings (*Miranda v. Arizona*, 384 U.S. 436 [1967]), confrontation and cross-examination, privileges against self-incrimination, proof beyond a reasonable doubt, and a right to counsel—do not automatically apply in civil commitments. Virtually all states require notice and allow the presence of counsel, and many provide for the personal appearance of the patient and a right to confront and cross-examine. Some states allow jury trials. In a move away from indeterminate commitment, many states now require periodic reviews or recommitment hearings. In some states, however, involuntary commitment to a mental hospital remains indeterminate and could last for days, weeks, years, or a lifetime.

DANGEROUSNESS

A critical element in most civil commitment statutes is dangerousness.

BAREFOOT v. ESTELLE
463 U.S. 880 (1982)
U.S. SUPREME COURT

JUSTICE WHITE delivered the opinion of the Court.
***

On November 14, 1978, petitioner was convicted of the capital murder of a police officer in Bell County, Tex. A separate sentencing hearing before the same jury was then held to determine whether the death penalty should be imposed. Under Tex. Code Crim. Proc. Ann., Art. 37.071 (Vernon 1981), two special questions were to be submitted to the jury: whether the conduct causing death was "committed deliberately and with reasonable expectation that the death of the deceased or another would result"; and whether "there is a probability that the defendant would commit criminal acts of violence that would constitute a continuing threat to society." The State introduced into evidence petitioner's prior convictions and his reputation for lawlessness. The State also called two psychiatrists, John Holbrook and James Grigson, who, in response to hypothetical questions, testified that petitioner would probably commit further acts of violence and represent a continuing threat to society. The jury answered both of the questions put to them in the affirmative, a result which required the imposition of the death penalty.***

An application for habeas corpus to the Texas Court of Criminal Appeals was denied on October 7, 1981, whereafter a petition for habeas corpus was filed in the United States District Court for the Western District of Texas. Among other issues, petitioner raised the same claims with respect to the use of psychiatric testimony that he had presented to the state courts. The District Court stayed petitioner's execution pending action on the petition. An evidentiary hearing was held on July 28, 1982, at which petitioner was represented by competent counsel. On November 9, 1982, the District Court filed its findings and conclusions, rejecting each of the several grounds asserted by petitioner. The writ was accordingly denied.***

Petitioner's merits submission is that his death sentence must be set aside because the Constitution of the United States barred the testimony of the two psychiatrists who testified against him at the punishment hearing. There are several aspects to this claim. First, it is urged that psychiatrists, individually and as a group, are incompetent to predict with an acceptable degree of reliability that a particular criminal will commit other crimes in the future and so represent a danger to the community.***

Acceptance of petitioner's position that expert testimony about future dangerousness is far too unreliable to be admissible would immediately call into question those other contexts in which predictions of future behavior are constantly made. For example, in *O'Connor* v. *Donaldson*, 422 U. S. 563, 576 (1975), we held that a nondangerous mental hospital patient could not be held in confinement against his will. Later, speaking about the requirements for civil commitments, we said:

> "There may be factual issues in a commitment proceeding, but the factual aspects represent only the beginning of the inquiry. Whether the individual is mentally ill and dangerous to either himself or others and is in need of confined therapy turns on the *meaning* of the facts which must be interpreted by expert psychiatrists and psychologists." *Addington* v. *Texas*, 441 U. S. 418, 429 (1979).

In the second place, the rules of evidence generally extant at the federal and state levels anticipate that relevant, unprivileged evidence should be admitted and its weight left to the factfinder, who would have the benefit of cross-examination and contrary evidence by the opposing party. Psychiatric testimony predicting dangerousness may be countered not only as erroneous in a particular case but also as generally so unreliable that it should be ignored. If the jury may make up its mind about future dangerousness unaided by psychiatric testimony, jurors should not be barred from hearing the views of the State's psychiatrists along with opposing views of the defendant's doctors.

Third, petitioner's view mirrors the position expressed in the *amicus* brief of the American Psychiatric Association (APA). As indicated above, however, the same view was presented and rejected in *Estelle v. Smith*. We are no more convinced now that the view of the APA should be converted into a constitutional rule barring an entire category of expert testimony. We are not persuaded that such testimony is almost entirely unreliable and that the factfinder and the adversary system will not be competent to uncover, recognize, and take due account of its shortcomings.

The *amicus* does not suggest that there are not other views held by members of the Association or of the profession generally. Indeed, as this case and others indicate, there are those doctors who are quite willing to testify at the sentencing hearing, who think, and will say, that they know what they are talking about, and who expressly disagree with the Association's point of view. Furthermore, their qualifications as experts are regularly accepted by the courts. If they are so obviously wrong and should be discredited, there should be no insuperable problem in doing so by calling members of the Association who are of that view and who confidently assert that opinion in their *amicus* brief. Neither petitioner nor the Association suggests that psychiatrists are always wrong with respect to future dangerousness, only most of the time. Yet the submission is that this category of testimony should be excised entirely from all trials. We are unconvinced, however, at least as of now, that the adversary process cannot be trusted to sort out the reliable from the unreliable evidence and opinion about future dangerousness, particularly when the convicted felon has the opportunity to present his own side of the case.

We are unaware of and have not been cited to any case, federal or state, that has adopted the categorical views of the Association. Certainly it was presented and rejected at every stage of the present proceeding. After listening to the two schools of thought testify not only generally but also about the petitioner and his criminal record, the District Court found:

"The majority of psychiatric experts agree that where there is a pattern of repetitive assaultive and violent conduct, the accuracy of psychiatric predictions of future dangerousness dramatically rises. The accuracy of this conclusion is reaffirmed by the expert medical testimony in this case at the evidentiary hearing. . . . It would appear that Petitioner's complaint is not the diagnosis and prediction made by Drs. Holbrook and Grigson at the punishment phase of his trial, but that Dr. Grigson expressed extreme certainty in his diagnosis and prediction. . . . In any event, the differences among the experts were quantitative, not qualitative. The differences in opinion go to the weight [of the evidence] and not the admissibility of such testimony. . . . Such disputes are within the province of the jury to resolve. Indeed, it is a fundamental premise of our entire system of criminal jurisprudence that the purpose of the jury is to sort out the true testimony from the false, the important matters from the unimportant matters, and, when called upon to do so, to give greater credence to one party's expert witnesses than another's. Such matters occur routinely in the American judicial system, both civil and criminal." (footnote omitted).

We agree with the District Court, as well as with the Court of Appeals' judges who dealt with the merits of the issue and agreed with the District Court in this respect.***

JUSTICE BLACKMUN, with whom JUSTICE BRENNAN and JUSTICE MARSHALL join as to Parts I–IV, dissenting.

***

To obtain a death sentence in Texas, the State is required to prove beyond a reasonable doubt that "there is a probability that the defendant would commit criminal acts of violence that would constitute a continuing threat to society." Tex. Code Crim. Proc. Ann., Art. 37.071(b)(2) (Vernon 1981). As a practical matter, this prediction of future dangerousness was the only issue to be decided by Barefoot's sentencing jury.

At the sentencing hearing, the State established that Barefoot had two prior convictions for drug offenses and two prior convictions for unlawful possession of firearms. None of these convictions involved acts of violence. At the guilt stage of the trial, for the limited purpose of establishing that the crime was committed in order to evade police custody, the State had presented evidence that Barefoot had escaped from jail in New Mexico where he was being held on charges of statutory rape and unlawful restraint of a minor child with intent to commit sexual penetration against the child's will. The prosecution also called several character witnesses at the sentencing hearing, from towns in five States. Without mentioning particular examples of Barefoot's conduct, these witnesses testified that Barefoot's reputation for being a peaceable and law-abiding citizen was bad in their respective communities.

Last, the prosecution called Doctors Holbrook and Grigson, whose testimony extended over more than half the hearing. Neither had examined Barefoot or requested the opportunity to examine him. In the presence of the jury, and over defense counsel's objection, each was qualified as an expert psychiatrist witness. Doctor Holbrook detailed at length his training and experience as a psychiatrist, which included a position as chief of psychiatric services at the Texas Department of Corrections. He explained that he had previously performed many "criminal evaluations," and that he subsequently took the post at the Department of Corrections to observe the subjects of these evaluations so that he could "be certain those opinions that [he] had were accurate at the time of trial and pretrial." He then informed the jury that it was "within [his] *capacity as a doctor of psychiatry* to predict the future dangerousness of an individual within a *reasonable medical certainty*," (emphasis supplied), and that he could give "*an expert medical opinion* that would be *within reasonable psychiatric certainty* as to whether or not that individual would be dangerous to the degree that there would be a probability that that person would commit criminal acts of violence in the future that would constitute a continuing threat to society," (emphasis supplied).

Doctor Grigson also detailed his training and medical experience, which, he said, included examination of "between thirty and forty thousand individuals," including 8,000 charged with felonies, and at least 300 charged with murder. He testified that with enough information he would be able to "give *a medical opinion within reasonable psychiatric certainty* as to the psychological or psychiatric makeup of an individual," (emphasis supplied), and that this skill was "particular to the field of psychiatry and not to the average layman."

Each psychiatrist then was given an extended hypothetical question asking him to assume as true about Barefoot the four prior convictions for nonviolent offences, the bad reputation for being law-abiding in various communities, the New Mexico escape, the events surrounding the murder for which he was on trial and, in Doctor Grigson's Case, the New Mexico arrest. On the basis of the hypothetical question, Doctor Holbrook diagnosed Barefoot "within a reasonable psychiatr[ic] certainty," as a "criminal sociopath." He testified that he knew of no treatment that could change this condition, and that the condition would not change for the better but "may become accelerated" in the next few years. Finally, Doctor Holbrook testified that, "within reasonable psychiatric certainty," there was "a probability that the Thomas A. Barefoot in that hypothetical will commit criminal acts of violence in the future that would constitute a continuing threat to society," and that his opinion would not change if the "society" at issue was that within Texas prisons rather than society outside prison.

Doctor Grigson then testified that, on the basis of the hypothetical question, he could diagnose Barefoot "within reasonable psychiatric certainty" as an individual with "a fairly classical, typical, sociopathic personality disorder." He placed Barefoot in the "most severe category" of sociopaths (on a scale of one to ten, Barefoot was "above ten"), and stated that there was no known cure for the condition. Finally, Doctor Grigson testified that whether Barefoot was in society at large or in a prison society there was a *"one hundred percent and absolute"* chance that Barefoot would commit future acts of criminal violence that would constitute a continuing threat to society. (emphasis supplied).***

The American Psychiatric Association (APA), participating in this case as *amicus curiae*, informs us that "[t]he unreliability of psychiatric predictions of long-term future dangerousness is by now an established fact within the profession." The APA's best estimate is that *two out of three* predictions of long-term future violence made by psychiatrists are wrong. The Court does not dispute this proposition, and indeed it could not do so; the evidence is overwhelming. For example, the APA's Draft Report of the Task Force on the Role of Psychiatry in the Sentencing Process (1983) states that "[c]onsiderable evidence has been accumulated by now to demonstrate that long-term prediction by psychiatrists of future violence is an extremely inaccurate process." John Monahan, recognized as "the leading thinker on this issue" even by the State's expert witness at Barefoot's federal habeas corpus hearing, concludes that "the 'best' clinical research currently in existence indicates that psychiatrists and psychologists are accurate in no more than one out of three predictions of violent behavior," even among populations of individuals who are mentally ill and have committed violence in the past. J. Monahan, The Clinical Prediction of Violent Behavior 47–49 (1981) (emphasis deleted). Another study has found it impossible to identify any subclass of offenders "whose members have a greater-than-even chance of engaging again in an assaultive act." Wenk, Robison, & Smith, Can Violence Be Predicted?, 18 Crime & Delinquency 393, 394 (1972). Yet another commentator observes: "In general, mental health professionals ... are more likely to be wrong than right when they predict legally relevant behavior. When predicting violence, dangerousness, and suicide, they are far more likely to be wrong than right." Morse, Crazy Behavior, Morals, and Science: An Analysis of Mental Health Law, 51 S. Cal. L. Rev. 527, 600 (1978). Neither the Court nor the State of Texas has cited a single reputable scientific source contradicting the unanimous conclusion of professionals in this field that psychiatric predictions of long-term future violence are wrong more often than they are right.

The APA also concludes, as do researchers that have studied the issue, that psychiatrists simply have no expertise in predicting long-term future dangerousness. A layman with access to relevant statistics can do at least as well and possibly better; psychiatric training is not relevant to the factors that validly can be employed to make such predictions, and psychiatrists consistently err on the side of overpredicting violence. Thus, while Doctors Grigson and Holbrook were presented by the State and by self-proclamation as experts at predicting future dangerousness, the scientific literature makes crystal clear that they had no expertise whatever. Despite their claims that they were able to predict Barefoot's future behavior "within reasonable psychiatric certainty," or to a "one hundred percent and absolute" certainty, there was in fact no more than a one in three chance that they were correct.***

Notes and Issues for Discussion

1. What is the role of the expert testimony in this case? What are the conclusions of the experts? On what are these conclusions based?
2. Note that the experts never examined Barefoot and were responding to hypothetical questions. Answers to hypothetical questions are acceptable in court.
3. What is the American Psychiatric Association's position on predictions of dangerousness? The state's expert testified there was a "one hundred percent and absolute" probability that Barefoot would commit future violence if he was ever released. Justice Blackmun points to studies claiming that psychiatric predictions of dangerousness have a one in three chance of being correct. Validity of predictions of dangerous continue to be debated. See, for example, McNeil and Binder, 1987.

STANDARD OF PROOF

In *Addington v. Texas*, 441 U.S. 418 (1978), the Supreme Court held that a clear and convincing standard was constitutionally adequate for civil commitments. This is less proof than is necessary in a criminal trial, but more than required in most civil proceedings. Currently, at least thirty-one states have adopted the clear and convincing standard, and a few others adhere to the more demanding beyond a reasonable doubt standard (Brakel, *et al.*, 1985: 67).

CIVIL COMMITMENT OF MINORS

Civil commitment of minors presents some difficult issues. Minors, unless emancipated, generally are considered legally incompetent and lack most legal decision-making powers. Some states permit older minors to admit themselves voluntarily to mental hospitals and may provide legal representation, but many permit a parent to sign the minor into the institution regardless of the minor's wishes. Legally this is a voluntary admission, since the parent, as guardian, is making the decision. Consequently, release is not the minor's decision, but lies with the parent and the institution. In the absence of a parent, a legal guardian has the same power. As long as the parent and minor are in agreement, there is no problem. In some jurisdictions, however, when the two disagree, the parent, supported by the institution, will prevail.

PARHAM v. J.L. AND J.R.
442 U.S. 584 (1979)
U.S. SUPREME COURT

MR. CHIEF JUSTICE BURGER delivered the opinion of the Court.

The question presented in this appeal is what process is constitutionally due a minor child whose parents or guardian seek state administered institutional mental health care for the child and specifically whether an adversary proceeding is required prior to or after the commitment.***

J. L., a plaintiff before the District Court who is now deceased, was admitted in 1970 at the age of 6 years to Central State Regional Hospital in Milledgeville, Ga. Prior to his admission, J. L. had received outpatient treatment at the hospital for over two months. J. L.'s mother then requested the hospital to admit him indefinitely.

The admitting physician interviewed J. L. and his parents. He learned that J. L.'s natural parents had divorced and his mother had remarried. He also learned that J. L. had been expelled from school because he was uncontrollable. He accepted the parents' representation that the boy had been extremely aggressive and diagnosed the child as having a "hyperkinetic reaction of childhood."

J. L.'s mother and stepfather agreed to participate in family therapy during the time their son was hospitalized. Under this program, J. L. was permitted to go home for short stays. Apparently his behavior during these visits was erratic. After several months, the parents requested discontinuance of the program.

In 1972, the child was returned to his mother and stepfather on a furlough basis, *i.e.*, he would live at home but go to school at the hospital. The parents found they were unable to control J. L. to their satisfaction, and this created family stress. Within two months, they requested his readmission to Central State. J. L.'s parents relinquished their parental rights to the county in 1974.

Although several hospital employees recommended that J. L. should be placed in a special foster home with "a warm, supported, truly involved couple," the Department of Family and Children Services was unable to place him in such a setting. On October 24, 1975, J. L. (with J. R.) filed this suit requesting an order of the court placing him in a less drastic environment suitable to his needs.

(c) Appellee J. R. was declared a neglected child by the county and removed from his natural parents when he was 3 months old. He was placed in seven different foster homes in succession prior to his admission to Central State Hospital at the age of 7.

Immediately preceding his hospitalization, J. R. received outpatient treatment at a county mental health center for several months. He then began attending school where he was so disruptive and incorrigible that he could not conform to normal behavior patterns. Because of his abnormal behavior, J. R.'s seventh set of foster parents requested his removal from their home. The Department of Family and Children Services then sought his admission at Central State. The agency provided the hospital with a complete sociomedical history at the time of his admission. In addition, three separate interviews were conducted with J. R. by the admission team of the hospital.

It was determined that he was borderline retarded, and suffered an "unsocialized, aggressive reaction of childhood." It was recommended unanimously that he would "benefit from the structured environment" of the hospital and would "enjoy living and playing with boys of the same age."

J. R.'s progress was re-examined periodically. In addition, unsuccessful efforts were made by the Department of Family and Children Services during his stay at the hospital to place J. R. in various foster homes. On October 24, 1975, J. R. (with J. L.) filed this suit requesting an order of the court placing him in a less drastic environment suitable to his needs.

(d) Georgia Code § 88-503.1 (1975) provides for the voluntary admission to a state regional hospital of children such as J. L. and J. R. Under that provision, admission begins with an application for hospitalization signed by a "parent or guardian." Upon application, the superintendent of each hospital is given the power to admit temporarily any child for "observation and diagnosis." If, after observation, the superintendent finds "evidence of mental illness" and that the child is "suitable for treatment" in the hospital, then the child may be admitted "for such period and under such conditions as may be authorized by law."

Georgia's mental health statute also provides for the discharge of voluntary patients. Any child who has been hospitalized for more than five days may be discharged at the request of a parent or guardian. § 88-503.3 (a) (1975). Even without a request for discharge, however, the superintendent of each regional hospital has an affirmative duty to release any child "who has recovered from his mental illness or who has sufficiently improved that the superintendent determines that hospitalization of the patient is no longer desirable." § 88-503.2 (1975).***

In holding unconstitutional Georgia's statutory procedure for voluntary commitment of juveniles, the District Court first determined that commitment to any of the eight regional hospitals constitutes a severe deprivation of a child's liberty. The court defined this liberty interest in terms of both freedom from bodily restraint and freedom from the "emotional and psychic harm" caused by the institutionalization. Having determined that a liberty interest is implicated by a child's admission to a mental hospital, the court considered what process is required to protect that interest. It held that the process due "includes at least the right after notice to be heard before an impartial tribunal."

In requiring the prescribed hearing, the court rejected Georgia's argument that no adversary-type hearing was required since the State was merely assisting parents who could not afford private care by making available treatment similar to that offered in private hospitals and by private physicians. The court acknowledged that most parents who seek to have their children admitted to a state mental hospital do so in good faith. It, however, relied on one of appellees' witnesses who expressed an opinion that "some still look upon mental hospitals as a 'dumping ground.'"***

The parties agree that our prior holdings have set out a general approach for testing challenged state procedures under a due process claim. Assuming the existence of a protectible property or liberty interest, the Court has required a balancing of a number of factors:

> "First, the private interest that will be affected by the official action; second, the risk of an erroneous deprivation of such interest through the procedures used, and the probable value, if any, of additional or substitute procedural safeguards; and finally, the Government's interest, including the function involved and the fiscal and administrative burdens that the additional or substitute procedural requirement would entail."***

(a) It is not disputed that a child, in common with adults, has a substantial liberty interest in not being confined unnecessarily for medical treatment and that the state's involvement in the commitment decision constitutes state action under the Fourteenth Amendment. We also recognize that commitment sometimes produces adverse social consequences for the child because of the reaction of some to the discovery that the child has received psychiatric care.*** For purposes of this decision, we assume that a child has a protectible interest not only in being free of unnecessary bodily restraints but also in not being labeled erroneously by some persons because of an improper decision by the state hospital superintendent.

(b) We next deal with the interests of the parents who have decided, on the basis of their observations and independent professional recommendations, that their child needs institutional care, Appellees argue that the constitutional rights of the child are of such magnitude and the likelihood of parental abuse is so great that the parents' traditional interests in and responsibility for the upbringing of their child must be subordinated at least to the extent of providing a formal adversary hearing prior to a voluntary commitment.

Our jurisprudence historically has reflected Western civilization concepts of the family as a unit with broad parental authority over minor children. Our cases have consistently followed that course; our constitutional system long ago rejected any notion that a child is "the mere creature of the State" and, on the contrary, asserted that parents generally "have the right, coupled with the high duty, to recognize and prepare [their children] for additional obligations." Surely, this includes a "high duty" to recognize symptoms of illness and to seek and follow medical advice. The law's concept of the family rests on a presumption that parents possess what a child lacks in maturity, experience, and capacity for judgment required for making life's difficult decisions. More important, historically it has recognized that natural bonds of affection lead parents to act in the best interests of their children.*** Simply because the decision of a parent is not agreeable to a child or because it involves risks does not automatically transfer the power to make that decision from the parents to some agency or officer of the state. The same characterizations can be made for a tonsillectomy, appendectomy, or other medical procedure. Most children, even in adolescence, simply are not able to make sound judgments concerning many decisions, including their need for medical care or treatment. Parents can and must make those judgments.****

(c) The State obviously has a significant interest in confining the use of its costly mental health facilities to cases of genuine need. The Georgia program seeks first to determine whether the patient seeking admission has an illness that calls for inpatient treatment. To accomplish this purpose, the State has charged the superintendents of each regional hospital with the responsibility for determining, before authorizing an admission, whether a prospective patient is mentally ill and whether the patient will likely benefit from hospital care. In addition, the State has imposed a continuing duty on hospital superintendents to release any patient who has recovered to the point where hospitalization is no longer needed.***

The State also has a genuine interest in allocating priority to the diagnosis and treatment of patients as soon as they are admitted to a hospital rather than to time-consuming procedural minuets before the admission. One factor that must be considered is the utilization of the time of psychiatrists, psychologists, and other behavioral specialists in preparing for and participating in hearings rather than performing the task for which their special training has fitted them. Behavioral experts in courtrooms and hearings are of little help to patients.***

(d) We now turn to consideration of what process protects adequately the child's constitutional rights by reducing risks of error without unduly trenching on traditional parental authority and without undercutting "efforts to further the legitimate interests of both the state and the patient that are served by" voluntary commitments. We conclude that the risk of error inherent in the parental decision to have a child institutionalized for mental health care is sufficiently great that some kind of inquiry should be made by a "neutral factfinder" to determine whether the statutory requirements for admission are satisfied. That inquiry must carefully probe the child's background using all available sources, including, but not limited to, parents, schools, and other social agencies. Of course, the review must also include an interview with the child. It is necessary that the decisionmaker have the authority to refuse to admit any child who does not satisfy the medical standards for admission. Finally, it is necessary that the child's continuing need for commitment be reviewed periodically by a similarly independent procedure.

We are satisfied that such procedures will protect the child from an erroneous admission decision in a way that neither unduly burdens the states nor inhibits parental decisions to seek state help.

Due process has never been thought to require that the neutral and detached trier of fact be law trained or a judicial or administrative officer. Surely, this is the case as to medical decisions, for "neither judges nor administrative hearing officers are better qualified than psychiatrists to render psychiatric judgments." Thus, a staff physician will suffice, so long as he or she is free to evaluate independently the child's mental and emotional condition and need for treatment.

It is not necessary that the deciding physician conduct a formal or quasi-formal hearing. A state is free to require such a hearing, but due process is not violated by use of informal, traditional medical investigative techniques.*** In general, we are satisfied that an independent medical decisionmaking process, which includes the thorough psychiatric investigation described earlier, followed by additional periodic review of a child's condition, will protect children who should not be admitted; we do not believe the risks of error in that process would be significantly reduced by a more formal, judicial-type hearing.***

Notes and Issues for Discussion

1. J. L. came from a broken home, had been "aggressive," "uncontrollable," expelled from school, and was diagnosed as having a "hyperkinetic reaction to childhood." Was J. L. mentally ill? In need of institutional care? J. R. was neglected, in seven foster homes, "disruptive," "incorrigible," and "suffered from an 'unsocialized, aggressive reaction to childhood.'" Was J. R. mentally ill? In need of institutional care?
2. A challenge to the former Pennsylvania civil commitment statute was brought in *Bartley v. Kremens*, 402 F. Supp. 1039 (1975), by a class of minors including those committed by their parents for "running away, robbing a gas station, stealing in general, chasing and striking a girl, arson, delinquent behavior in general, truancy, physical ailments such as colitis and weight loss, school phobia, and drug overdose." 402 F. Supp. at 1044. The statute was found unconstitutional by the Federal District Court. Pennsylvania then modified its statute so that children over fourteen no longer required a parent to sign them into or out of state mental hospitals. The revised statute was upheld by the U.S. Supreme Court in *Secretary of Public Welfare v. Institutionalized Juveniles*, 442 U.S. 640 (1979), a companion case to *Parham*.
3. The California Supreme Court held that a statute similar to Georgia's was unconstitutional. See *In re Roger S.*, 569 P.2d 1286 (Cal. 1977).

THE MENTALLY ILL CRIMINAL OFFENDER

Whether an individual charged with a crime is unable, due to a present mental disability, to assist in the preparation or the conduct of the ensuing criminal trial is a different legal issue from whether or not the individual was suffering from a mental disability at the time of the criminal act. The issue in the former is whether the individual is competent to stand trial, the issue in the latter is whether the individual should be found not guilty by reason of insanity.

Incompetence to Stand Trial

The outcome of a finding that someone is not competent to stand trial may result in that individual being held in a maximum security facility or mental hospital until competence is regained. Brakel (1985) indicates that most individuals found incompetent to stand trial are restored to competence through medication within three months, but theoretically the individual could be held for an extended period.[7] In *Jackson v. Indiana*, 406 U.S. 715 (1972), the Court held that Indiana could not indefinitely hold a retarded deaf-mute charged with purse snatching and found to be incompetent to stand trial without instituting a civil commitment proceeding.[8]

The Insanity Defense

If the individual was suffering from a mental disability at the time of the criminal act, the issue is whether the person's mental state falls within the state's insanity defense standard. This standard takes various formulations, but the basic underlying concept is that lacking criminal intent and therefore responsibility, a person should not be punished for otherwise criminal acts.

A number of states still use the M'Naghten Rule, formulated in England in the 1840s. This rule holds that to be not guilty by reason of insanity, it must be shown that:

> at the time of the committing of the act, the party accused was labouring under such a defect of reason from the disease of the mind, as not to know the nature and quality of the act he was doing, or, if he did know it, that he did not know he was doing what was wrong. *M'Naghten's Case*, 8 Eng. Rep. 718 at 722.

For the federal standard, see the Comprehensive Crime Control Act of 1984, P.L. 98-473, 98 Stat. 1837 (1984).

Civil Commitment of the Mentally Ill Criminal Offender

Of increasing concern is the sexual offender who has been convicted, has served a prison term, has been released into the community, and may still be dangerous.[9] Under many civil commitment statutes which require evidence of recent dangerous behavior, incarcerated offenders often are not committable. Washington and some other states have enacted statutes that allow for postrelease confinement of such individuals through special civil commitment proceedings.[10]

Washington defines a "sexually violent predator" as "any person who has been convicted of or charged with a crime of sexual violence and suffers from a mental abnormality or personality disorder which makes the person likely to engage in predatory acts of sexual violence." Wash. Rev. Code § 71.09.020(1).

"Sexually violent offense" includes various acts: of rape, indecent liberties, incest, or child molestation, or murder, assault, kidnapping, burglary if determined beyond a reasonable doubt to be sexually motivated. Wash. Rev. Code § 71.09.020(4).

The act permits the state to file a petition when the sentence of a person has expired or will expire, alleging that the individual may be a sexually violent predator. If there is probable cause, a trial is held to determine if the person is a sexually violent predator. The defendant is provided counsel and the state must prove its case beyond a reasonable doubt. If the judge or jury determines the individual is a sexually violent predator, "the person shall be committed to the custody of the department of social and health services in a secure facility for control, care, and treatment until such time as the person's mental abnormality or personality disorder has so changed that the person is safe to be at large." Wash. Rev. Code § 71.09.050.

Notes and Issues for Discussion

1. Washington's act followed the rape and sexual mutilation of a young boy by a released prisoner with a long criminal record including kidnapping and assaulting juveniles. Although a prison psychiatrist reported he had unusual sadistic sexual fantasies and an intent to follow through, the prisoner was released and not civilly committed because he had committed no "recent overt act" as required for civil commitment. The prisoner had been incarcerated for ten years. The incident occurred two years after his release.[11]
2. Are the rights of the alleged sexually violent predator protected?
3. Note that the standard of proof is beyond a reasonable doubt that the person who has committed a past act suffers from a mental abnormality such

that the person is likely to engage in predatory acts of sexual violence. What kinds of proof would establish this?

4. If psychiatrists have difficulty predicting dangerous behavior in general, is it any easier predicting sexually violent behavior? Harder?

PATIENTS' RIGHTS

Rights of mental hospital patients are protected by federal constitutional law and federal and state statutes. A number of states follow the federal model and have enacted codes of patients' rights. While each state has its own approach, most states now presume patient competence unless incompetence has been proven and entitle patients to exercise their civil rights, including a right to vote. Some codes provide for rights to privacy, visitation, uncensored mail and telephone communication, communication with an attorney, religious freedom, and require the least restrictive living arrangement possible in light of the patient's condition. Most states also protect patients from excessive medication, restraint, and seclusion. Many prohibit sterilization, psychosurgery, shock treatment, or research without patient or guardian informed consent. Some provide specific penalties if these rights are denied or violated, others do not. (See, generally, Brakel, *et al.*, 1985: Chapter 5).

In the Appendix to *Wyatt v. Stickney*, a case holding there is a constitutional right to treatment for involuntarily committed mental hospital patients in Alabama, Judge Johnson set forth minimum constitutional standards for adequate treatment.

WYATT v. STICKNEY
344 F.Supp. 373 (1972)
U.S. DISTRICT COURT

JOHNSON, CHIEF JUDGE.

This class action originally was filed on October 23, 1970, in behalf of patients involuntarily confined for mental treatment purposes at Bryce Hospital, Tuscaloosa, Alabama. On March 12, 1971, in a formal opinion and decree, this Court held that these involuntarily committed patients "unquestionably have a constitutional right to receive such individual treatment as will give each of them a realistic opportunity to be cured or to improve his or her mental condition." The Court further held that patients at Bryce were being denied their right to treatment and that defendants, per their request, would be allowed six months in which to raise the level of care at Bryce to the constitutionally required minimum. Wyatt v. Stickney, 325 F.Supp. 781 (M.D.Ala. 1971). In this decree, the Court ordered defendants to file reports defining the mission and functions of Bryce Hospital, specifying the objective and subjective standards required to furnish adequate care to the treatable mentally ill and detailing the hospital's progress toward the implementation of minimum constitutional standards.

***Generally, the Court found that defendants' treatment program was deficient in three fundamental areas. It failed to provide: (1) a humane psychological and physical environment, (2) qualified staff in numbers sufficient to administer adequate treatment and (3) individualized treatment plans. More specifically, the Court found that many conditions, such as nontherapeutic, uncompensated work assignments, and the absence of any semblance of privacy, constituted dehumanizing factors contributing to the degeneration of the patients' self-esteem. The physical facilities at Bryce were overcrowded and plagued by fire and other emergency hazards. The Court found also that most staff members were poorly trained and that staffing ratios were so inadequate as to render the administration of effective treatment impossible. The Court concluded, therefore, that whatever treatment was provided at Bryce was grossly deficient and failed to satisfy minimum medical and constitutional standards. Based upon this conclusion, the Court ordered that a formal hearing be held at which the parties and amici would have the opportunity to submit proposed standards for constitutionally adequate treatment and to present expert testimony in support of their proposals.

Pursuant to this order, a hearing was held at which the foremost authorities on mental health in the United States appeared and testified as to the minimum medical and constitutional requisites for public institutions, such as Bryce and Searcy, designed to treat the mentally ill. At this hearing, the parties and amici submitted their proposed standards, and now have filed briefs in support of them. Moreover, the parties and amici have stipulated to a broad spectrum of conditions they feel are mandatory for a constitutionally acceptable minimum treatment program. This Court, having considered the evidence in the case, as well as the briefs, proposed standards and stipulations of the parties, has concluded that the standards set out in Appendix A to this decree are medical and constitutional minimums. Consequently, the Court will order their implementation.

APPENDIX A
MINIMUM CONSTITUTIONAL STANDARDS FOR ADEQUATE TREATMENT OF THE MENTALLY ILL

I. *Definitions:*

    a. "Hospital"—Bryce and Searcy Hospitals.

    b. "Patients"—all persons who are now confined and all persons who may in the future be confined at Bryce and Searcy Hospitals pursuant to an involuntary civil commitment procedure.

    c. "Qualified Mental Health Professional"—

      (1) a psychiatrist with three years of residency training in psychiatry;

      (2) a psychologist with a doctoral degree from an accredited program;

      (3) a social worker with a master's degree from an accredited program and two years of clinical experience under the supervision of a Qualified Mental Health Professional;

      (4) a registered nurse with a graduate degree in psychiatric nursing and two years of clinical experience under the supervision of a Qualified Mental Health Professional.

d. "Non-Professional Staff Member"—an employee of the hospital, other than a Qualified Mental Health Professional, whose duties require contact with or supervision of patients.

II. *Human Psychological and Physical Environment*
   1. Patients have a right to privacy and dignity.
   2. Patients have a right to the least restrictive conditions necessary to achieve the purposes of commitment.
   3. No person shall be deemed incompetent to manage his affairs, to contract, to hold professional or occupational or vehicle operator's licenses, to marry and obtain a divorce, to register and vote, or to make a will *solely* by reason of his admission or commitment to the hospital.
   4. Patients shall have the same rights to visitation and telephone communications as patients at other public hospitals, except to the extent that the Qualified Mental Health Professional responsible for formulation of a particular patient's treatment plan writes an order imposing special restrictions. The written order must be renewed after each periodic review of the treatment plan if any restrictions are to be continued. Patients shall have an unrestricted right to visitation with attorneys and with private physicians and other health professionals.
   5. Patients shall have an unrestricted right to send sealed mail. Patients shall have an unrestricted right to receive sealed mail from their attorneys, private physicians, and other mental health professionals, from courts, and government officials. Patients shall have a right to receive sealed mail from others, except to the extent that the Qualified Mental Health Professional responsible for formulation of a particular patient's treatment plan writes an order imposing special restrictions on receipt of sealed mail. The written order must be renewed after each periodic review of the treatment plan if any restrictions are to be continued.
   6. Patients have a right to be free from unnecessary or excessive medication. No medication shall be administered unless at the written order of a physician. The superintendent of the hospital and the attending physician shall be responsible for all medication given or administered to a patient. The use of medication shall not exceed standards of use that are advocated by the United States Food and Drug Administration. Notation of each individual's medication shall be kept in his medical records. At least weekly the attending physician shall review the drug regimen of each patient under his care.. All prescriptions shall be written with a termination date, which shall not exceed 30 days. Medication shall not be used as punishment, for the convenience of staff, as a substitute for program, or in quantities that interfere with the patient's treatment program.
   7. Patients have a right to be free from physical restraint and isolation. Except for emergency situations, in which it is likely that patients could harm themselves or others and in which less restrictive means of restraint are not feasible, patients may be physically restrained or placed in isolation only on a Qualified Mental-Health Professional's written order which explains the ra-

tionale for such action. The written order may be entered only after the Qualified Mental Health Professional has personally seen the patient concerned and evaluated whatever episode or situation is said to call for restraint or isolation. Emergency use of restraints or isolation shall be for no more than one hour, by which time a Qualified Mental Health Professional shall have been consulted and shall have entered an appropriate order in writing. Such written order shall be effective for no more than 24 hours and must be renewed if restraint and isolation are to be continued. While in restraint or isolation the patient must be seen by qualified ward personnel who will chart the patient's physical condition (if it is compromised) and psychiatric condition every hour. The patient must have bathroom privileges every hour and must be bathed every 12 hours.

8. Patients shall have a right not to be subjected to experimental research without the express and informed consent of the patient, if the patient is able to give such consent, and of his guardian or next of kin, after opportunities for consultation with independent specialists and with legal counsel. Such proposed research shall first have been reviewed and approved by the institution's Human Rights Committee before such consent shall be sought. Prior to such approval the Committee shall determine that such research complies with the principles of the Statement on the Use of Human Subjects for Research of the American Association on Mental Deficiency and with the principles for research involving human subjects required by the United States Department of Health, Education and Welfare for projects supported by that agency.

9. Patients have a right not to be subjected to treatment procedures such as lobotomy, electro-convulsive treatment, adversive reinforcement conditioning or other unusual or hazardous treatment procedures without their express and informed consent after consultation with counsel or interested party of the patient's choice.

10. Patients have a right to receive prompt and adequate medical treatment for any physical ailments.

11. Patients have a right to wear their own clothes and to keep and use their own personal possessions except insofar as such clothes or personal possessions may be determined by a Qualified Mental Health Professional to be dangerous or otherwise inappropriate to the treatment regimen.

12. The hospital has an obligation to supply an adequate allowance of clothing to any patients who do not have suitable clothing of their own. Patients shall have the opportunity to select from various types of neat, clean, and seasonable clothing. Such clothing shall be considered the patient's throughout his stay in the hospital.

13. The hospital shall make provision for the laundering of patient clothing.

14. Patients have a right to regular physical exercise several times a week. Moreover, it shall be the duty of the hospital to provide facilities and equipment for such exercise.

15. Patients have a right to be outdoors at regular and frequent intervals in the absence of medical considerations.

16. The right to religious worship shall be accorded to each patient who desires such opportunities. Provisions for such worship shall be made available to all patients on a nondiscriminatory basis. No individual shall be coerced into engaging in any religious activities.

17. The institution shall provide, with adequate supervision, suitable opportunities for the patient's interaction with members of the opposite sex.***

Notes and Issues for Discussion

1. Many of the *Wyatt* standards were codified in state law and are also found in the Bill of Rights in the Federal Mental Health Systems Act, 42 U.S.C. §9501.
2. Other *Wyatt* standards not included here pertain to patient labor, physical conditions including minimum dayroom and bedroom space, minimum staff-patient ratios, food and nutritional requirements, individualized treatment plans, and record keeping.
3. Note the comprehensiveness and specificity of the standards. Is this "overkill" or necessary to implement changes? How would you document that the *Wyatt* standards were being met?
4. Not addressed in *Wyatt* is the cost of implementing the standards. Generally courts have been reluctant to enter into the funding arena.

A Constitutional Right to Liberty

Kenneth Donaldson was held involuntarily in a Florida mental hospital without treatment for fifteen years. He sued based on a deprivation of liberty. In its decision, the Supreme Court held that involuntarily committed mental patients have a constitutional right to liberty.

O'CONNOR v. DONALDSON
422 U.S. 563 (1975)
U.S. SUPREME COURT

MR. JUSTICE STEWART delivered the opinion of the Court.

The respondent, Kenneth Donaldson, was civilly committed to confinement as a mental patient in the Florida State Hospital at Chattahoochee in January 1957. He was kept in custody there against his will for nearly 15 years. The petitioner, Dr. J. B O'Connor, was the hospital's superintendent during most of this period. Throughout his confinement Donaldson repeatedly, but unsuccessfully, demanded his release, claiming that he was dangerous to no one, that he was not mentally ill, and that, at any rate, the hospital was not providing treatment for his supposed illness. Finally, in February 1971, Donaldson brought this lawsuit under 42 U. S. C. § 1983, in the United States District Court for the Northern District of Florida, alleging that O'Connor, and other members of the hospital staff named as defendants, had intentionally and maliciously deprived him of his constitutional right to liberty. After a four-day trial, the jury returned a verdict assessing both compensatory and punitive damages against O'Connor and a codefendant. The Court of Appeals for the Fifth Circuit affirmed the judgment. We granted O'Connor's petition for certiorari, because of the important constitutional questions seemingly presented.

Donaldson's commitment was initiated by his father, who thought that his son was suffering from "delusions." After hearings before a county judge of Pinellas County, Fla., Donaldson was found to be suffering from "paranoid schizophrenia" and was committed for "care, maintenance, and treatment" pursuant to Florida statutory provisions that have since been repealed.***

The evidence at the trial showed that the hospital staff had the power to release a patient, not dangerous to himself or others, even if he remained mentally ill and had been lawfully committed. Despite many requests, O'Connor refused to allow that power to be exercised in Donaldson's case. At the trial, O'Connor indicated that he had believed that Donaldson would have been unable to make a "successful adjustment outside the institution," but could not recall the basis for that conclusion. O'Connor retired as superintendent shortly before this suit was filed. A few months thereafter, and before the trial, Donaldson secured his release and a judicial restoration of competency, with the support of the hospital staff.

The testimony at the trial demonstrated, without contradiction, that Donaldson had posed no danger to others during his long confinement, or indeed at any point in his life. O'Connor himself conceded that he had no personal or secondhand knowledge that Donaldson had ever committed a dangerous act. There was no evidence that Donaldson had ever been suicidal or been thought likely to inflict injury upon himself. One of O'Connor's codefendants acknowledged that Donaldson could have earned his own living outside the hospital. He had done so for some 14 years before his commitment, and immediately upon his release he secured a responsible job in hotel administration.

Furthermore, Donaldson's frequent requests for release had been supported by responsible persons willing to provide him any care he might need on release. In 1963, for example, a representative of Helping Hands, Inc., a halfway house for mental patients, wrote O'Connor asking him to release Donaldson to its care. The request was accompanied by a supporting letter from the Minneapolis Clinic of Psychiatry and Neurology, which a codefendant conceded was a "good clinic." O'Connor rejected the offer, replying that Donaldson could be released only to his parents. That rule was apparently of O'Connor's own making. At the time, Donaldson was 55 years old, and, as O'Connor knew, Donaldson's parents were too elderly and infirm to take responsibility for him. Moreover, in his continuing correspondence with Donaldson's parents, O'Connor never informed them of the Helping Hands offer. In addition, on four separate occasions between 1964 and 1968, John Lembcke, a college classmate of Donaldson's and a longtime family friend, asked O'Connor to release Donaldson to his care. On each occasion O'Connor refused. The record shows that Lembcke was a serious and responsible person, who was willing and able to assume responsibility for Donaldson's welfare.

The evidence showed that Donaldson's confinement was a simple regime of enforced custodial care, not a program designed to alleviate or cure his supposed illness. Numerous witnesses, including one of O'Connor's codefendants, testified that Donaldson had received nothing but custodial care while at the hospital. O'Connor described Donaldson's treatment as "milieu therapy." But witnesses from the hospital staff conceded that, in the context of this case, "milieu therapy" was a euphemism for confinement in the "milieu" of a mental hospital. For substantial periods, Donaldson was simply kept in a large room that housed 60 patients, many of whom were under criminal commitment. Donaldson's requests for ground privileges, occupational training, and an opportunity to discuss his case with O'Connor or other staff members were repeatedly denied.

At the trial, O'Connor's principal defense was that he had acted in good faith and was therefore immune from any liability for monetary damages. His position, in short, was that state law, which he had believed valid, had authorized indefinite custodial confinement of the "sick," even if they were not given treatment and their release could harm no one.

The trial judge instructed the members of the jury that they should find that O'Connor had violated Donaldson's constitutional right to liberty if they found that he had

> confined [Donaldson] against his will, knowing that he was not mentally ill or dangerous or knowing that if mentally ill he was not receiving treatment for his alleged mental illness.***

The jury returned a verdict for Donaldson against O'Connor and a codefendant, and awarded damages of $38,500, including $10,000 in punitive damages.

***As we view it, this case raises a single, relatively simple, but nonetheless important question concerning every man's constitutional right to liberty.

The jury found that Donaldson was neither dangerous to himself nor dangerous to others, and also found that, if mentally ill, Donaldson had not received treatment.***

A finding of "mental illness" alone cannot justify a State's locking a person up against his will and keeping him indefinitely in simple custodial confinement. Assuming that that term can be given a reasonably precise content and that the "mentally ill" can be identified with reasonable accuracy, there is still no constitutional basis for confining such persons involuntarily if they are dangerous to no one and can live safely in freedom.

May the State confine the mentally ill merely to ensure them a living standard superior to that they enjoy in the private community? That the State has a proper interest in providing care and assistance to the unfortunate goes without saying. But the mere presence of mental illness does not disqualify a person from preferring his home to the comforts of an institution. Moreover, while the State may arguably confine a person to save him from harm, incarceration is rarely if ever a necessary condition for raising the living standards of those capable of surviving safely in freedom, on their own or with the help of family or friends.

May the State fence in the harmless mentally ill solely to save its citizens from exposure to those whose ways are different? One might as well ask if the State, to avoid public unease, could incarcerate all who are physically unattractive or socially eccentric. Mere public intolerance or animosity cannot constitutionally justify the deprivation of a person's physical liberty.

In short, a State cannot constitutionally confine without more a nondangerous individual who is capable of surviving safely in freedom by himself or with the help of willing and responsible family members or friends. Since the jury found, upon ample evidence, that O'Connor, as an agent of the State, knowingly did so confine Donaldson, it properly concluded that O'Connor violated Donaldson's constitutional right to freedom. ***

Notes and Issues for Discussion

1. " . . . [T]here still is no constitutional basis for confining such persons involuntarily if they are dangerous to no one and can live safely in freedom." The *Donaldson* case has been read to require a finding of dangerousness before there can be involuntary civil commitment.
2. The Court states: "In short, a state cannot constitutionally confine without more a nondangerous individual who is capable of surviving safely in freedom by himself or with the help of willing and responsible family members or friends." 422 U.S. at 576. Without more what? One of the argument's raised by Donaldson was that he was receiving no treatment. Can a state confine someone who is nondangerous if treatment is provided?
3. The case was remanded for further consideration in light of another Supreme Court decision, *Wood v. Strickland*, 420 U.S. 308 (1975). The award to Donaldson was upheld.

A Constitutional Right to Treatment

To date, while much has been written in the legal literature, the Supreme Court has not addressed the constitutional right to treatment issue.[12] Several lower court decisions have found such a right in the Constitution. See *Rouse v. Cameron*, 373 F. 2d 451 (1967), and *Wyatt v. Stickney*, 325 F. Supp. 781 (1971), affirmed as *Wyatt v. Aderholt*, 503 F.2d 1305 (1974).

Donaldson began as a right to treatment, not a right to liberty case, and at the appellate level, the federal circuit court wrote a lengthy decision in which it found a constitutional right to treatment. See *Donaldson v. O'Connor*, 493 F.2d 507 (1974). The Supreme Court majority opinion did not address this issue, although Chief Justice Burger wrote a lengthy concurring opinion rejecting the concept.[13]

The Right to Refuse Treatment

Several federal courts have addressed the related issue of an involuntarily committed mental hospital patient's constitutional right to refuse treatment, and more specifically the right to refuse medication. In *Rennie v. Klein*, the Third Circuit modified but upheld a district court decision, stating that involuntarily committed patients had a "constitutional right to refuse antipsychotic drugs that may have permanently disabling side effects. The state may override that right when the patient is a danger to himself or others, but in non-emergency situations must first provide procedural due process." 653 F.2d at 838.

RENNIE v. KLEIN
653 F.2d 836 (1981)
U.S. COURT OF APPEALS

WEIS, CIRCUIT JUDGE.

This appeal requires us to define the legal rights of the mentally ill with respect to the care and treatment supplied by the state. We hold that mental patients who are committed involuntarily to state institutions nevertheless retain a constitutional right to refuse antipsychotic drugs that may have permanently disabling side effects. The state may override that right when the patient is a danger to himself or others, but in non-emergency situations must first provide procedural due process. We further determine that the informal administrative procedures established by New Jersey meet constitutional standards, and accordingly, modify a district court injunction that required a formal adversary hearing and other measures before a patient's refusal can be overridden.

John Rennie has been a patient at the Ancora Psychiatric Hospital, a state institution in New Jersey, on numerous occasions since 1973. In several instances, powerful antipsychotic drugs have been administered to him against his will. He brought suit in the district court alleging several violations of his constitutional rights and later amended the complaint to assert a class action. The district court defined a qualified constitutional right to refuse treatment and issued a preliminary injunction directing New Jersey to establish an independent review mechanism that went beyond procedures already prescribed by the state.

Rennie is a forty year old divorced man, a former pilot and flight instructor. In 1971 he first showed symptoms of mental illness, which became more serious in 1973 when his twin brother was killed. Shortly thereafter, Rennie was admitted for the first time to Ancora, one of five hospitals for the mentally ill operated by the state of New Jersey. He was depressed and suicidal and was diagnosed as a paranoid schizophrenic. At various times during his stays, Rennie refused to accept prescribed drugs despite the hospital staff's insistence that it has a right to medicate him against his will. During his twelfth admission to Ancora, which began in August 1976 after an involuntary commitment proceeding, Rennie instituted the suit that is the subject of this appeal.

Rennie's complaint charged the defendants with violating a number of his constitutional rights. By agreement of the parties, the litigation has focused exclusively on motions for preliminary injunctions with respect to the right to refuse treatment, leaving other issues for future determination.***

There are essentially two questions presented on this appeal. First, whether compulsory medication of involuntarily committed mental patients violates a liberty interest protected by the fourteenth amendment. Second, if such an interest exists, what procedures must the state follow to protect it.***

An individual who has not been committed to a mental institution has a right to refuse medication sought to be administered against his will. The state cannot ignore due process and simply seize a person and administer drugs to him without his consent. The case before us is one step removed, since it involves the right of an individual to refuse treatment after he has been confined to a mental institution. Such a commitment requires a proceeding in conformity with procedural due process which, under New Jersey law, requires the state to prove that "the institutionalization of the patients is required by reason of his being a danger to himself or others or property if he is not so confined." N.J. Civil Practice Rule 4:74-7(f).

An involuntary civil commitment in itself entails "a massive curtailment of liberty." *Humphrey v. Cady,* 405 U.S. 504, 509 (1972). We must determine, then, whether, as the state argues, the freedom to refuse medication normally possessed by an individual is extinguished by involuntary civil commitment, or whether the patient "retain[s] a residuum of liberty that would be infringed" by compulsory medication "without complying with minimum requirements of due process."

We are not persuaded by the state's argument that involuntary commitment takes away all aspects of a person's liberty interest. In our view, the patient's liberty is diminished only to the extent necessary to allow for confinement by the state so as to prevent him from being a danger to himself or to others.***

The extent to which the plaintiffs' liberty interest is invaded by compulsory medication appears dramatically from the record here. All the antipsychotic drugs induce a variety of disorders of the central nervous system as side effects. Most serious among these is tardive dyskinesia, a potentially permanent disorder. It is "characterized by rhythmical, repetitive, involuntary movements of the tongue, face, mouth, or jaw, sometimes accompanied by other bizarre muscular activity." *Rennie v. Klein,* 462 F.Supp. at 1138. More common, but less serious than tardive dyskinesia, are akinesia and akathesia. The former can induce a state of diminished spontaneity, physical weakness and muscle fatigue. The latter is "a subjective state and refers to an inability to be still; a motor restlessness which may produce a shaking of the hands or arms or feet or an irresistible desire to keep walking or tapping the feet." *Id.* Both of these disorders usually disappear either during or shortly after the course of medication. They can sometimes be controlled by anticholinergic or antiparkinsonian medications.***

The impact of these side effects was highlighted by the testimony of several patients at the institutions. An older woman described involuntary jaw movements as a result of tardive dyskinesia so severe that she could not be fitted with dentures. As a result she is restricted to a diet of ground food. One young woman told of feeling sedated by the antipsychotic drugs to the point where she would sleep most of the day. Others testified to severe discomfort in response to the drugs.

The record convinces us that there is a difference of constitutional significance between simple involuntary confinement to a mental institution and commitment combined with enforced administration of antipsychotic drugs. It implicates the "right to be free from, and to obtain judicial relief for, unjustified intrusions on personal security." This intrusion rises to the level of a liberty interest warranting the protection of the due process clause of the fourteenth amendment.***

Having concluded that the patient has a constitutional right to be free from treatment that poses substantial risks to his well-being, we must consider the scope of that right. Like most rights, it is not absolute, but is limited by other legitimate governmental concerns and obligations. The administration of drugs generally is a recognized adjunct to the treatment of the mentally ill and indeed may be required by the state as a concomitant of its power to commit involuntarily.***

The deprivation of liberty imposed by the state must not exceed that required by needed care or legitimate administrative concerns. What is at issue here is the administration of drugs—psychotropics—with the very real possibility of damaging results accompanying their use so that "the cure [c]ould be worse than the illness." *Rennie v. Klein*, 462 F.Supp. at 1146. To protect the liberty interest in the face of such a threat, the least intrusive infringement is required.***

Just as the power to confine is accepted, but its nature limited, so may involuntary administration of drugs be justified only when accompanied by appropriate restrictions. The involuntarily committed patient retains a "residuum of liberty," and he correspondingly retains the right to be free from "unjustified intrusions on [his] personal security." That concept has sometimes been paired with the "least intrusive means" when objections to forced administration of drugs are raised. *See e.g., Rogers v. Okin*, 634 F.2d 650 (1st Cir. 1980), *cert. granted*— U.S.—, 101 S.Ct. 1972, 68 L.Ed.2d 293 (1981).***

The least intrusive means standard does not prohibit all intrusions. It merely directs attention to and requires avoidance of those which are unnecessary or whose cost benefit ratios, weighed from the patient's standpoint, are unacceptable. There must be a careful balancing of the patient's interest with those to be furthered by administering the psychotropic drug.***

It must be observed that emergency conditions, for example, may require that more discretion be granted the attending physician. In the case of antipsychotic drugs, it would appear that treatment for a limited period is not as likely to have as intrusive an effect upon the patient as administration for an extended time. This, moreover emphasizes that the least intrusive standard is generally applicable to a regimen or treatment program rather than individual dosages. We emphasize that the emergency treatment provisions are not at issue in this case.

Having concluded that a constitutional right to refuse treatment exists, it is necessary to consider whether the due process safeguards imposed by the district court were proper.

Initially, we recognize that the decision to administer drugs depends upon a medical judgment based upon a variety of facts, such as the need for the drugs and their probable effects on the patient, including the possibility of side effects.

Matters such as the likelihood of violence on the part of the patient; his previous reaction to acute psychotropic drugs, if any; the duration of previous drug therapy; the prognosis for improvement or stability; alternative medications; close confinement or other alternatives; and other factors too numerous to mention here, all enter into the decision-making. The nature of these elements makes it plain that the determination must be made on an individual basis. Due process procedures must therefore provide an opportunity for the exercise of professional judgment in these circumstances.

From a legal standpoint, the outline of due process protections that must guide state agency proceedings are summarized in *Matthews v. Eldridge*, 424 U.S. 319 (1976). The Court listed three factors for consideration: (1) the private interest; (2) the risk of an erroneous decision through the procedures used as well as the value of the any of additional or substituted safeguards; and (3) the governmental interest, including fiscal and administrative burdens that other procedural requirements would impose. These guidelines permit flexibility to adjust to a variety of circumstances, such as the employment of professional judgment, and do not mandate adherence to rigid, traditionally adversary proceedings. Against this background, we turn to the administrative provisions adopted by the State.

***Administrative Bulletin 78-3, issued soon after this litigation began, incorporates many of the provisions found in the statute and, while not conceding the right of involuntarily committed patients to refuse drugs, also defines the need for compulsory medication. For those not adjudicated incompetent, medication may be imposed involuntarily in some limited, non-emergency situations. If, without it, the patient is incapable of participating in any treatment plan that will give him a realistic opportunity to improve his condition, or if it will shorten the required commitment time, or if there is a significant possibility that the patient will harm himself or others before his condition improves, drugs may be administered.

Procedurally, the Bulletin sets up a mechanism through which a decision to administer drugs against a patient's will shall be made and reviewed. At the first level, when a patient refuses to accept medication, the treating physician must explain to the patient the nature of his condition, the rationale for using the particular drug, and the risks or benefits of it as well as those of alternative treatments. If the patient still declines, the matter is discussed at a meeting of the patient's treatment team, which is composed of the treating physician and other hospital personnel, such as psychologists, social workers, and nurses who have regular contact with the patient. The patient is to be present at this meeting if his condition permits.

If, after the team meeting, the impasse remains, the medical director of the hospital or his designee must personally examine the patient and review the record. In the event the director agrees with the physician's assessment of the need for involuntary treatment, medication may then be administered. The medical director is also authorized, but not required, to retain an independent psychiatrist to evaluate the patient's need for medication. Finally, the director is required to make a weekly review of the treatment program of each patient who is being drugged against his will to determine whether the compulsory treatment is still necessary. In addition, the district court found that the Division of

Mental Health and Hospitals had adopted a practice, not incorporated in the Bulletin, of having all cases of compulsory medication reviewed by a division director or another physician in the division's central office.***

We are acutely aware of the finite state resources available for the care of the mentally ill. Diversion of these funds to finance nonessential administrative procedures, however beneficial and desirable, will not provide help for the patient's most critical needs.

The New Jersey regulations provide a series of informal consultations and reviews to determine from a medical standpoint whether administration of the drugs is necessary. To the extent that other treatment possibilities are discussed and discarded, the process also provides a reasonable exploration of the least intrusive means. The participants in the procedure are mental health professionals, rather than judges who have doffed their black robes and donned white coats. Nevertheless, the regulations and the statutes adequately focus the administrative proceedings on the facts that shape the constitutional standard and thereby protect the patients' interests at stake.

We are persuaded, therefore, that the procedures established in Bulletin 78-3 are consistent with constitutional guarantees and the district court erred in applying the appropriate legal standard.***

Notes and Issues for Discussion

1. *Rennie* was later remanded by the U.S. Supreme Court, *Rennie v. Klein,* 458 U.S. 1119 (1982). In a rehearing, the circuit court once again found a qualified constitutional right to refuse medication. See *Rennie v. Klein,* 720 F.2d 261 (1983).
2. For a similar case in the First Circuit, see *Rogers v. Okin,* 634 F.2d 650 (1980), remanded as *Mills v. Rogers* 457 U.S. 291 (1982).
3. Given the Supreme Court's reliance on professional judgement in *Youngberg v. Romeo* (p. 417) it is unclear how much effect these cases have. The more typical pattern is for courts now to rely on state constitutional law or statutory law to find a right to treatment. See *Rogers v. Commissioner of Dep't of Mental Health,* 458 N.E.2d 308 (Mass. 1983), and *Rivers v. Katz,* 495 N.E.2d 337 (N.Y. 1986).

SELECTED REFERENCES

Birnbaum, M. "The right to treatment," 46 *A.B.A.J.* 449 (1960).

Brakel, S. J., Perry, and Weiner, *The Mentally Disabled and the Law* (3rd ed., 1985).

McNeil, D., and Binder, R. "Predictive validity of judgements of dangerous in emergency civil commitment," 144 *Am. J. Psychiatry* 197 (1987).

Reed, S. C., and Lewis, D. A. "The negotiation of voluntary admission in Chicago's state mental hospitals," 18 *J. Psychiatry and Law* 137 (1990).

Reisner, R., and Slobogen, C. *Law and the Mental Health System* (2nd ed., 1990).

CHAPTER 12

LEGAL ISSUES FOR INDIVIDUALS WITH DISABILITIES

In its legislative findings accompanying the Americans with Disabilities Act (A.D.A.), Congress reported that some 43 million Americans have one or more physical or mental disability, with the numbers increasing as the population ages. In addition, Congress found that these groups have historically tended to be isolated, segregated, and discriminated against and that much of this discrimination continues today. 42 U.S.C. §12101.

A number of major federal statutes apply to individuals with disabilities. Among the most important are the Architectural Barriers Act of 1968, the Rehabilitation Act of 1973, the Education of Handicapped Children Act of 1975, now amended as the Individuals with Disabilities Education Act, The Developmentally Disabled Assistance and Bill of Rights Act of 1978, and the Americans with Disabilities Act of 1990. In addition, important amendments were added in the Rehabilitation Comprehensive Services and Developmental Disabilities Amendments Act of 1978.[1] While these statutes cannot be covered in detail, some major provisions and related court decisions will be addressed.

FEDERAL STATUTES

Barrier-Free Access

The Architectural Barriers Act of 1968, 42 U.S.C. §4151 *et seq.*, implemented through the Architectural and Transportation Compliance Board, sets standards for barrier-free access to any federally financed, federally constructed, or federally leased building or facility the "intended use for which either will require that such building or facility be accessible to the public, or may result in the employment or residence therein of physically handicapped persons . . ." 42 U.S.C. §4151, and requires that standards be set for design, construction, and alterations "to insure wherever possible that physically handicapped persons will have ready access to, and use of, such buildings."[2]

Definitions and Rights of the Developmentally Disabled

The Developmentally Disabled Assistance and Bill of Rights Act, 42 U.S.C. §6000 *et seq.*, provides a functional definition of developmental disabilities, which states must adopt to receive federal funding. According to the act:

Developmental disability means a severe, chronic disability of a person which:
(1) is attributable to a mental or physical impairment or combination of mental or physical impairments;
(2) is manifest before age 22;
(3) is likely to continue indefinitely;
(4) results in substantial functional limitations in three or more of the following areas of major life activity, that is, self-care, receptive and expressive language, learning, mobility, self-direction and capacity for independent living or economic self-sufficiency; and
(5) reflects the need for a combination and sequence of special interdisciplinary or generic care, treatment or other services which are of lifelong or extended duration and are individually planned and coordinated. Developmental disability includes but is not limited to severe disabilities attributable to mental retardation, autism, cerebral palsy, epilepsy, spina bifida and other neurological impairments where the above criteria are met. . . ." 42 U.S.C. §6000.

Section 504 of the Rehabilitation Act

Until the passage of the American with Disabilities Act, Section 504 of the Rehabilitation Act of 1973 was a primary vehicle to protect disabled individuals against discrimination:

No otherwise qualified handicapped individual . . . shall, solely by reason of his handicap, be excluded from participation in, be denied the benefits of, or be subjected to discrimination under any program or activity receiving Federal financial assistance. 29 U.S.C. §794.[3]

Among the key issues are who qualifies as a "handicapped individual" and what is the meaning of "otherwise qualified."

SCHOOL BOARD OF NASSAU CO. v. ARLINE
480 U.S. 273 (1987)
U.S. SUPREME COURT

JUSTICE BRENNAN delivered the opinion of the Court.

Section 504 of the Rehabilitation Act of 1973, prohibits a federally funded state program from discriminating against a handicapped individual solely by reason of his or her handicap. This case presents the questions whether a person afflicted with tuberculosis, a contagious disease, may be considered a "handicapped individual" within the meaning of §504 of the Act, and, if so, whether such an individual is "otherwise qualified" to teach elementary school.

From 1966 until 1979, respondent Gene Arline taught elementary school in Nassau County, Florida. She was discharged in 1979 after suffering a third relapse of tuberculosis within two years. After she was denied relief in state administrative proceedings, she brought suit in federal court, alleging that the School Board's decision to dismiss her because of her tuberculosis violated § 504 of the Act.

A trial was held in the District Court, at which the principal medical evidence was provided by Marianne McEuen, M.D., an assistant director of the Community Tuberculosis Control Service of the Florida Department of Health and Rehabilitative Services. According to the medical records reviewed by Dr. McEuen, Arline was hospitalized for tuberculosis in 1957. For the next twenty years, Arline's disease was in remission. Then, in 1977, a culture revealed that tuberculosis was again active in her system; cultures taken in March 1978 and in November 1978 were also positive.

The superintendent of schools for Nassau County, Craig Marsh, then testified as to the School Board's response to Arline's medical reports. After both her second relapse, in the Spring of 1978, and her third relapse in November 1978, the School Board suspended Arline with pay for the remainder of the school year. At the end of the 1978–1979 school year, the School Board held a hearing, after which it discharged Arline, "not because she had done anything wrong," but because of the "continued reoccurrence [sic] of tuberculosis."

In her trial memorandum, Arline argued that it was "not disputed that the [School Board dismissed her] solely on the basis of her illness. Since the illness in this case qualifies the Plaintiff as a 'handicapped person' it is clear that she was dismissed solely as a result of her handicap in violation of Section 504." The District Court held, however, that although there was "[n]o question that she suffers a handicap," Arline was nevertheless not "a handicapped person under the terms of that statute." The court found it "difficult . . . to conceive that Congress intended contagious diseases to be included within the definition of a handicapped person." The court then went on to state that, "even assuming" that a person with a contagious disease could be deemed a handicapped person, Arline was not "qualified" to teach elementary school.

The Court of Appeals reversed, holding that "persons with contagious diseases are within the coverage of section 504," and that Arline's condition "falls . . . neatly within the statutory and regulatory framework" of the Act. The court remanded the case "for further findings as to whether the risks of infection precluded Mrs. Arline from being 'otherwise qualified' for her job and, if so, whether it was possible to make some reasonable accommodation for her in that teaching position" or in some other position. We granted certiorari, and now affirm.

In enacting and amending the Act, Congress enlisted all programs receiving federal funds in an effort "to share with handicapped Americans the opportunities for an education, transportation, housing, health care, and jobs that other Americans take for granted." To that end, Congress not only increased federal support for vocational rehabilitation, but also addressed the broader problem of discrimination against the handicapped by including § 504, an antidiscrimination provision patterned after Title VI of the Civil Rights of 1964. Section 504 of the Rehabilitation Act reads in pertinent part:

> "No otherwise qualified handicapped individual in the United States, as defined in section 706(7) of this title, shall, solely by reason of his handicap, be excluded from participation in, be denied the benefits of, or be subjected to discrimination under any program or activity receiving Federal financial assistance. . . ." 29 USC § 794.

In 1974 Congress expanded the definition of "handicapped individual" for use in § 504 to read as follows:

> "[A]ny person who (i) has a physical or mental impairment which substantially limits one or more of such person's major life activities, (ii) has a record of such an impairment, or (iii) is regarded as having such an impairment." 29 USC § 706(7)(B).

The amended definition reflected Congress' concern with protecting the handicapped against discrimination stemming not only from simple prejudice, but from "archaic attitudes and laws" and from "the fact that the American people are simply unfamiliar with and insensitive to the difficulties confront[ing] individuals with handicaps." S Rep No. 93-1297, p 50 (1974). To combat the effects of erroneous but nevertheless prevalent perceptions about the handicapped, Congress expanded the definition of "handicapped individual" so as to preclude discrimination against "[a] person who has a record of, or is regarded as having, an impairment [but who] may at present have no actual incapacity at all." Southeastern Community College v Davis, 442 US 397, 405-406, n 6 (1979).

In determining whether a particular individual is handicapped as defined by the Act, the regulations promulgated by the Department of Health and Human Services are of significant assistance. As we have previously recognized, these regulations were drafted with the oversight and approval of Congress; they provide "an important source of guidance on the meaning of § 504." The regulations are particularly significant here because they define two critical terms used in the statutory definition of handicapped individual. "Physical impairment" is defined as follows:

"[A]ny physiological disorder or condition, cosmetic disfigurement, or anatomical loss affecting one or more of the following body systems: neurological; musculoskeletal; special sense organs; respiratory, including speech organs; cardiovascular; reproductive, digestive, genitourinary; hemic and lymphatic; skin; and endocrine." 45 CFR § 84.3(j)(2)(i) (1985).

In addition, the regulations define "major life activities" as:

"functions such as caring for one's self, performing manual tasks, walking, seeing, hearing, speaking, breathing, learning, and working." § 84.3j(2)(ii).

Within this statutory and regulatory framework, then, we must consider whether Arline can be considered a handicapped individual. According to the testimony of Dr. McEuen, Arline suffered tuberculosis "in an acute form in such a degree that it affected her respiratory system," and was hospitalized for this condition. Arline thus had a physical impairment as that term is defined by the regulations, since she had a "physiological disorder or condition . . . affecting [her] . . . respiratory [system]." 45 CFR § 84.3(j)(2)(i) (1985). This impairment was serious enough to require hospitalization, a fact more than sufficient to establish that one or more of her major life activities were substantially limited by her impairment. Thus, Arline's hospitalization for tuberculosis in 1957 suffices to establish that she has a "record of . . . impairment" within the meaning of 29 USC § 706(7)(b)(ii), and is therefore a handicapped individual.

Petitioners concede that a contagious disease may constitute a handicapping condition to the extent that it leaves a person with "diminished physical or mental capabilities," and concede that Arline's hospitalization for tuberculosis in 1957 demonstrates that she has a record of a physical impairment. Petitioners maintain, however, Arline's record of impairment is irrelevant in this case, since the School Board dismissed Arline not because of her diminished physical capabilities, but because of the threat that her relapses of tuberculosis posed to the health of others.

We do not agree with petitioners that, in defining a handicapped individual under § 504, the contagious effects of a disease can be meaningfully distinguished from the disease's physical effects on a claimant in a case such as this. Arline's contagiousness and her physical impairment each resulted from the same underlying condition, tuberculosis. It would be unfair to allow an employer to seize upon the distinction between the effects of a disease on others and the effects of a disease on a patient and use that distinction to justify discriminatory treatment.[1]

---

[1] The United States argues that it is possible for a person to be simply a carrier of a disease, that is, to be capable of spreading a disease without having a "physical impairment" or suffering from any other symptoms associated with the disease. The United States contends that this is true in the case of some carriers of the Acquired Immune Deficiency Syndrome (AIDS) virus. From this premise the United States concludes that discrimination solely on the basis of contagiousness is never discrimination on the basis of a handicap. The argument is misplaced in this

Nothing in the legislative history of § 504 suggests that Congress intended such a result. That history demonstrates that Congress was as concerned about the effect of an impairment on others as it was about its effect on the individual. Congress extended coverage, in 29 USC § 706(7)(B)(iii), to those individuals who are simply "regarded as having" a physical or mental impairment. The Senate Report provides as an example of a person who would be covered under this subsection "a person with some kind of visible physical impairment which in fact does not substantially limit that person's functioning." Such an impairment might not diminish a person's physical or mental capabilities, but could nevertheless substantially limit that person's ability to work as a result of the negative reactions of others to the impairment.

Allowing discrimination based on the contagious effects of a physical impairment would be inconsistent with the basic purpose of § 504, which is to ensure that handicapped individuals are not denied jobs or other benefits because of the prejudiced attitudes or the ignorance of others. By amending the definition of "handicapped individual" to include not only those who are actually physically impaired, but also those who are regarded as impaired and who, as a result, are substantially limited in a major life activity, Congress acknowledged that society's accumulated myths and fears about disability and disease are as handicapping as are the physical limitations that flow from actual impairment. Few aspects of a handicap give rise to the same level of public fear and misapprehension as contagiousness. Even those who suffer or have recovered from such noninfectious diseases as epilepsy or cancer have faced discrimination based on the irrational fear that they might be contagious. The Act is carefully structured to replace such reflexive reactions to actual or perceived handicaps with actions based on reasoned and medically sound judgments: the definition of "handicapped individual" is broad, but only those individuals who are both handicapped *and* otherwise qualified are eligible for relief. The fact that *some* persons who have contagious diseases may pose a serious health threat to others under certain circumstances does not justify excluding from the coverage of the Act *all* persons with actual or perceived contagious diseases. Such exclusion would mean that those accused of being contagious would never have the opportunity to have their condition evaluated in light of medical evidence and a determination made as to whether they were "otherwise qualified." Rather, they would be vulnerable to discrimination on the basis of mythology—precisely the type of injury Congress sought to prevent. We conclude that the fact that a person with a record of a physical impairment is also contagious does not suffice to remove that person from coverage under § 504.

The remaining question is whether Arline is otherwise qualified for the job of elementary schoolteacher. To answer this question in most cases, the district court will need to conduct an individualized inquiry and make appropriate find-

---

case, because the handicap here, tuberculosis, gave rise both to a physical impairment *and* to contagiousness. This case does not present, and we therefore do not reach, the questions whether a carrier of a contagious disease such as AIDS could be considered to have a physical impairment, or whether such a person could be considered, solely on the basis of contagiousness, a handicapped person as defined by the Act.

ings of fact. Such an inquiry is essential if § 504 is to achieve its goal of protecting handicapped individuals from deprivations based on prejudice, stereotypes, or unfounded fear, while giving appropriate weight to such legitimate concerns of grantees as avoiding exposing others to significant health and safety risks. The basic factors to be considered in conducting this inquiry are well established. In the context of the employment of a person handicapped with a contagious disease, we agree with *amicus* American Medical Association that this inquiry should include

> "[findings of] facts, based on reasonable medical judgments given the state of medical knowledge, about (a) the nature of the risk (how the disease is transmitted), (b) the duration of the risk (how long is the carrier infectious), (c) the severity of the risk (what is the potential harm to third parties) and (d) the probabilities the disease will be transmitted and will cause varying degrees of harm." Brief for American Medical Association as *Amicus Curiae* 19.

In making these findings, courts normally should defer to the reasonable medical judgments of public health officials. The next step in the "otherwise-qualified" inquiry is for the court to evaluate, in light of these medical findings, whether the employer could reasonably accommodate the employee under the established standards for that inquiry.

Because of the paucity of factual findings by the District Court, we, like the Court of Appeals, are unable at this stage of the proceedings to resolve whether Arline is "otherwise qualified" for her job. The District Court made no findings as to the duration and severity of Arline's condition, nor as to the probability that she would transmit the disease. Nor did the court determine whether Arline was contagious at the time she was discharged, or whether the School Board could have reasonably accommodated her. Accordingly, the resolution of whether Arline was otherwise qualified requires further findings of fact.

We hold that a person suffering from the contagious disease of tuberculosis can be a handicapped person within the meaning of § 504 of the Rehabilitation Act of 1973, and that respondent Arline is such a person. We remand the case to the District Court to determine whether Arline is otherwise qualified for her position. The judgment of the Court of Appeals is affirmed.

Notes and Issues for Discussion

1. Note the expanded congressional definition of a handicapped individual, which includes not only those with handicaps or those with a record of handicaps, but also those who are "regarded as having such an impairment." This inclusion of those without any incapacity who are viewed as handicapped was, according to the Court, added to combat erroneous perceptions and stereotypes which result in discrimination.
2. In the congressional definition of a handicapped person, a physical or mental impairment is one that "substantially limits one or more of such

person's major life activities. . . ." In the Code of Federal Regulations, major life activities include "functions such as caring for one's self, performing manual tasks, walking, seeing, hearing, speaking, breathing, learning, and working." 45 C.F.R. §84.3(j)(2)(ii). Note the breadth of this provision. Arline was hospitalized once in 1957 because of respiratory problems stemming from her tuberculosis. The Court finds that sufficient to establish a record of limitation of a major life activity.

3. Also consider the breadth of "physical impairment": "[A]ny physiological disorder or condition, cosmetic disfigurement, or anatomical loss affecting one or more of the following body systems: neurological; musculoskeletal; special sense organs; respiratory, including speech organs; cardiovascular; reproductive, digestive, genitourinary; hemic and lymphatic; skin; and endocrine." 45 C.F.R. §84.3(j)(2)(i).

4. The school board argued that Arline was not dismissed because of her impairment, but because with a relapse she could become a danger to the health of others. The Court refuses to make a distinction between an impairment and its possible health dangers. This could be an important point. While the Court in a footnote excludes persons with AIDS from its decision, the difference does not appear great. See *Chalk v. U.S. District Court*, p. 467.

5. Is Arline "otherwise qualified" to teach? We don't know, since the case is sent back to decide this issue. It appears that this will turn on possible contagion and transmission of the disease, as well as whether the school board could make "reasonable accommodations."

The Americans with Disabilities Act (A.D.A.)

Perhaps the most comprehensive legislation protecting the rights of persons with disabilities is the Americans with Disabilities Act of 1990, 42 U.S.C. §§12101-12514. Using language similar to that found in the Rehabilitation Act of 1973, the act extends protections to the disabled in employment, public services, public accommodations, and telecommunications. Title I generally prohibits employment discrimination and will apply to all public and private employers with fifteen or more full-time employees over twenty calendar weeks in the current or preceding year. Exceptions include the federal government (covered under the Rehabilitation Act of 1973) and certain private and religious organizations. Title II prohibits discrimination in public services, and applies to most transportation services. Title III forbids discrimination against persons with disabilities in a range of public accommodations and services operated by private entities, including most lodging establishments, restaurants, shopping centers, and retail establishments. Also identified as public accommodations are professional offices of health care providers, hospitals, and a number of other health and human service agencies.[4] Key here is whether the necessary modification is "readily achievable" as defined by the statute. Title IV applies to telecommunications and Title V contains miscellaneous provisions.

For the purposes of the Act, disability is defined as:

(A) a physical or mental impairment that substantially limits one or more of the major life activities of such individual;
(B) a record of such an impairment; or
(C) being regarded as having such an impairment. 42 U.S.C. §12102.

Because of space limitations, only Title I pertaining to employment will be discussed in depth here. However, the health and human services professional should be aware of the scope of Title II, which will significantly affect access by the disabled to all forms of public transport, Title III, which forbids discrimination in most public and many private accommodations, and Title IV pertaining to telecommunications for individuals with disabilities and closed-captioning for federally funded public service announcements. Some of the Title III antidiscrimination provisions are discussed in relation to persons with AIDS in Chapter 13. While the effective date of the legislation is 1992, various provisions are further delayed in their implementation. The health and human services professional should be aware of the regulations interpreting and clarifying the provisions and should refer to current regulations to understand fully the effect of the legislation.

Essentially Title I of the A.D.A. prohibits discrimination against a "qualified individual with a disability" who is capable of performing the "essential functions" of an employment position. The prohibition against discrimination extends to job applications, hiring, promotions, discharge, compensation, training, and other areas. The employer must make a "reasonable accommodation" for the disabled individual, including restructuring jobs, modifying work schedules, and modifying and adjusting equipment and materials or, where appropriate, using interpreters or readers. 42 U.S.C. §12111–12112.[5] However, if the employer can show "undue hardship" as defined, such accommodations need not be made. 42 U.S.C. §12113.[6]

Along with definitions of disability and discrimination, key terms used in determining whether or not discrimination has taken place include who is a "qualified individual with a disability," what constitutes a "reasonable accommodation," what are "essential functions," and what is included under "undue hardship." Some of these terms have been the subject of interpretation and litigation in the Rehabilitation Act of 1973 and probably will be further interpreted and clarified in rules and litigation surrounding this act.

A key task for the employer is to identify "essential functions" of a position and to document them prior to advertising or interviewing applicants.

This written description shall be considered evidence of essential functions of the position (§12111), and will be used as a basis for judging what a reasonable accommodation is, and when there is undue hardship.[7]

A defense to a charge of discrimination may be that the challenged application of qualifications, standards, tests, or selection criteria is job-related and consistent with business necessity and its performance cannot be accomplished by reasonable accommodation (§12113).[8]

In addition, certain individuals are excluded unless otherwise disabled. These include those engaging in the illegal use of drugs, homosexuals, bisexuals, transvestites, and various other groups (§§12114, 12211). Of interest here is the law in relation to substance abuse. Under §12114, although an employee or applicant currently engaging in the illegal use of drugs is excluded from the coverage of the act if the employer acts on the basis of this use, a user of illegal drugs who is participating in or who has successfully completed a drug rehabilitation program and is no longer using the drugs is not excluded. In addition, the employer may hold the illegal user of drugs or an alcoholic to the same standards applied to other employees, even though the unsatisfactory performance is related to drug use or alcoholism.[9]

THE RIGHT TO HABILITATION

In *Halderman v. Pennhurst State School*, 446 F. Supp 1295 (1977), the district court found a constitutional right to habilitation—defined as education, training, and care to enable mentally retarded citizens to reach their maximum development. In a lengthy opinion filled with descriptions of the unsafe and unsanitary conditions at the Pennsylvania school, including lack of staff, absence of programs, repeated physical injuries suffered by patients, and an actual deterioration of patient performance over time, the court found that Pennhurst residents could not achieve habilitation at the institution. The judge ordered a halt to commitments, mandated and later implemented a plan to close the institution and place the residents in the community. The state appealed, joined by the southeastern Pennsylvania counties within the Pennhurst catchment area. At the federal circuit court level, the lower court decision was upheld on statutory not constitutional grounds. The circuit court relied on the Developmentally Disabled Assistance and Bill of Rights Act, 42 U.S.C. §6000 *et seq.*, which contains the provision:

(1) Persons with developmental disabilities have a right to appropriate treatment, services and habilitation. . . . (2) The treatment, services and habilitation for a person with developmental disabilities should be designed to maximize the developmental potential of the person and

should be provided in the setting that is least restrictive of the person's liberty. 42 U.S.C. §6010.

Another modification by the court was that admissions to Pennhurst could continue on a limited basis. *Halderman v. Pennhurst*, 612 F.2d 84 (1979). The case was appealed to the U.S. Supreme Court. The Court reversed and remanded, holding that there was no statutory basis for a right to habilitation since the intent of Congress in the Developmentally Disabled Assistance Act was only to provide funding to the states for programs and not to establish new rights for the developmentally disabled. *Pennhurst State School v. Halderman*, 451 U.S. 1 (1981).

The case was reheard at the federal court of appeals and district levels, and alternate grounds were found for the order. The trial court had created the position of Special Master to oversee community placement of all residents and the closing of the institution. During the various appeals, the master continued with community placement, and some ten years after the original case was filed, Pennhurst was closed. In the following case, a Pennhurst patient sued for damages for breach of his constitutional rights.

YOUNGBERG v. ROMEO
457 U.S. 307 (1981)
U.S. SUPREME COURT

JUSTICE POWELL delivered the opinion of the Court.

The question presented is whether respondent, involuntarily committed to a state institution for the mentally retarded, has substantive rights under the Due Process Clause of the Fourteenth Amendment to (i) safe conditions of confinement; (ii) freedom from bodily restraints; and (iii) training or "habilitation."[1] Respondent sued under 42 USC § 1983 [42 USCS § 1983] three administrators of the institution, claiming damages for the alleged breach of his constitutional rights.

Respondent Nicholas Romeo is profoundly retarded. Although 33 years old, he has the mental capacity of an eighteen-month-old child, with an I.Q. between 8 and 10. He cannot talk and lacks the most basic self-care skills. Until he was 26, respondent lived with his parents in Philadelphia. But after the death of his father in May 1974, his mother was unable to care for him. Within two weeks of the father's death, respondent's mother sought his temporary admission to a nearby Pennsylvania hospital.

---

[1] The American Psychiatric Association explains that "[t]he word 'habilitation,' . . . is commonly used to refer to programs for the mentally-retarded because mental retardation is . . . a learning disability and training impairment rather than an illness. . . . [T]he principal focus of habilitation is upon training and development of needed skills." Brief of American Psychiatric Association as Amicus Curiae, at 4, n 1.

Shortly thereafter, she asked the Philadelphia County Court of Common Pleas to admit Romeo to a state facility on a permanent basis. Her petition to the court explained that she was unable to care for Romeo or control his violence. As part of the commitment process, Romeo was examined by a physician and a psychologist. They both certified that respondent was severely retarded and unable to care for himself. On June 11, 1974, the Court of Common Pleas committed respondent to the Pennhurst State School and Hospital, pursuant to the applicable involuntary commitment provision of the Pennsylvania Mental Health and Mental Retardation Act, Pa Stat Ann tit 50 § 4406.

At Pennhurst, Romeo was injured on numerous occasions, both by his own violence and by the reactions of other residents to him. Respondent's mother became concerned about these injuries. After objecting to respondent's treatment several times, she filed this complaint on November 4, 1976, in the United States District Court for the Eastern District of Pennsylvania as his next friend. The complaint alleged that "[d]uring the period July, 1974 to the present, plaintiff has suffered injuries on at least sixty-three occasions." The complaint originally sought damages and injunctive relief from Pennhurst's director and two supervisors; it alleged that these officials knew, or should have known, that Romeo was suffering injuries and that they failed to institute appropriate preventive procedures, thus violating his rights under the Eighth and Fourteenth Amendments.

Thereafter, in late 1976, Romeo was transferred from his ward to the hospital for treatment of a broken arm. While in the infirmary, and by order of a doctor, he was physically restrained during portions of each day. These restraints were ordered by Dr. Gabroy, not a defendant here, to protect Romeo and others in the hospital, some of whom were in traction or were being treated intravenously. Although respondent normally would have returned to his ward when his arm healed, the parties to this litigation agreed that he should remain in the hospital due to the pending law suit. Nevertheless, in December 1977, a second amended complaint was filed alleging that the defendants were restraining respondent for prolonged periods on a routine basis. The second amended complaint also added a claim for damages to compensate Romeo for the defendants' failure to provide him with appropriate "treatment or programs for his mental retardation."**

An eight-day jury trial was held in April 1978. Petitioners introduced evidence that respondent participated in several programs teaching basic self-care skills. A comprehensive behavior-modification program was designed by staff members to reduce Romeo's aggressive behavior, but that program was never implemented because of his mother's objections. Respondent introduced evidence of his injuries and of conditions in his unit.

***The jury returned a verdict for the defendants, on which judgment was entered.

The Court of Appeals for the Third Circuit, sitting en banc, reversed and remanded for a new trial. 644 F2d 147 (1980). The court held that the Eighth Amendment, prohibiting cruel and unusual punishment of those convicted of crimes, was not an appropriate source for determining the rights of the involuntarily committed. Rather, the Fourteenth Amendment and the liberty interest protected by that amendment provided the proper constitutional basis for these rights. In applying the Fourteenth Amendment, the court found that the involuntarily committed retain liberty interests in freedom of movement and in personal security. These were "fundamental liberties" that can be limited only by an "overriding, nonpunitive" state interest. 644 F2d, at 157–158 (footnote omitted). It further found that the involuntarily committed have a liberty interest in habilitation designed to "treat" their mental retardation.***

We granted the petition for certiorari because of the importance of the question presented to the administration of state institutions for the mentally retarded.***

We consider here for the first time the substantive rights of involuntarily-committed mentally retarded persons under the Fourteenth Amendment to the Constitution. In this case, respondent has been committed under the laws of Pennsylvania, and he does not challenge the commitment. Rather, he argues that he has a constitutionally protected liberty interest in safety, freedom of movement, and training within the institution; and that petitioners infringed these rights by failing to provide constitutionally required conditions of confinement.

The mere fact that Romeo has been committed under proper procedures does not deprive him of all substantive liberty interests under the Fourteenth Amendment. Indeed, the state concedes that respondent has a right to adequate food, shelter, clothing, and medical care. We must decide whether liberty interests also exist in safety, freedom of movement, and training. If such interests do exist, we must further decide whether they have been infringed in this case.

Respondent's first two claims involve liberty interests recognized by prior decisions of this Court, interests that involuntary commitment proceedings do not extinguish. The first is a claim to safe conditions. In the past, this Court has noted that the right to personal security constitutes an "historic liberty interest" protected substantively by the Due Process Clause. And that right is not extinguished by lawful confinement, even for penal purposes. If it is cruel and unusual punishment to hold convicted criminals in unsafe conditions, it must be unconstitutional to confine the involuntarily committed—who may not be punished at all—in unsafe conditions.

Next, respondent claims a right to freedom from bodily restraint. In other contexts, the existence of such an interest is clear in the prior decisions of this Court. Indeed, "[l]iberty from bodily restraint always has been recognized as the core of the liberty protected by the Due Process Clause from arbitrary governmental action." Greenholtz v Nebraska Penal Inmates, 442 US 1, 18 (1979) (Powell, J., concurring). This interest survives criminal conviction and incarceration. Similarly, it must also survive involuntary commitment.

Respondent's remaining claim is more troubling. In his words, he asserts a "constitutional right to minimally adequate habilitation." This is a substantive due process claim that is said to be grounded in the liberty component of the Due Process Clause of the Fourteenth Amendment. The term "habilitation," used in psychiatry, is not defined precisely or consistently in the opinions below or in the briefs of the parties or the amici.[2] As noted previously, the term refers to "training and development of needed skills." Respondent emphasizes that the right he asserts is for "minimal" training, and he would leave the type and extent of train-

[2] Professionals in the habilitation of the mentally retarded disagree strongly on the question whether effective training of all severely or profoundly retarded individuals is even possible.

ing to be determined on a case-by-case basis "in light of present medical or other scientific knowledge."

In addressing the asserted right to training, we start from established principles. As a general matter, a State is under no constitutional duty to provide substantive services for those within its border. When a person is institutionalized—and wholly dependent on the State—it is conceded by petitioner that a duty to provide certain services and care does exist, although even then a State necessarily has considerable discretion in determining the nature and scope of its responsibilities.***

Respondent, in light of the severe character of his retardation, concedes that no amount of training will make possible his release. And he does not argue that if he were still at home, the State would have an obligation to provide training at its expense. The record reveals that respondent's primary needs are bodily safety and a minimum of physical restraint, and respondent clearly claims training related to these needs. As we have recognized that there is a constitutionally protected liberty interest in safety and freedom from restraint, training may be necessary to avoid unconstitutional infringement of those rights. On the basis of the record before us, it is quite uncertain whether respondent seeks any "habilitation" or training unrelated to safety and freedom from bodily restraints. In his brief to this Court, Romeo indicates that even the self-care programs he seeks are needed to reduce his aggressive behavior. And in his offer of proof to the trial court, respondent repeatedly indicated that, if allowed to testify, his experts would show that additional training programs, including self-care programs, were needed to reduce Romeo's aggressive behavior. If, as seems the case, respondent seeks only training related to safety and freedom from restraints, this case does not present the difficult question whether a mentally retarded person, involuntarily committed to a state institution, has some general constitutional right to training per se, even when no type or amount of training would lead to freedom.

Chief Judge Seitz, in language apparently adopted by respondent, observed:

"I believe that the plaintiff has a constitutional right to minimally adequate care and treatment. The existence of a constitutional right to care and treatment is no longer a novel legal proposition." 644 F2d, ——.

Chief Judge Seitz did not identify or otherwise define—beyond the right to reasonable safety and freedom from physical restraint—the "minimally adequate care and treatment" that appropriately may be required for this respondent. In the circumstances presented by this case, and on the basis of the record developed to date, we agree with his view and conclude that respondent's liberty interests require the State to provide minimally adequate or reasonable training to ensure safety and freedom from undue restraint. In view of the kinds of treatment sought by respondent and the evidence of record, we need go no further in this case.

We have established that Romeo retains liberty interests in safety and freedom from bodily restraint. Yet these interests are not absolute; indeed to some extent they are in conflict. In operating an institution such as Pennhurst, there are occasions in which it is necessary for the State to restrain the movement of residents—for example, to protect them as well as others from violence. Similar restraints may also be appropriate in a training program. And an institution cannot protect its residents from all danger of violence if it is to permit them to have any freedom of movement. The question then is not simply whether a liberty interest has been infringed but whether the extent or nature of the restraint or lack of absolute safety is such as to violate due process.

In determining whether a substantive right protected by the Due Process Clause has been violated, it is necessary to balance "the liberty of the individual" and "the demands of an organized society." Poe v Ullman, 367 US 497, 522 (1961). In seeking this balance in other cases, the Court has weighed the individual's interest in liberty against the State's asserted reasons for restraining individual liberty.***

We think the standard articulated by Chief Judge Seitz affords the necessary guidance and reflects the proper balance between the legitimate interests of the State and the rights of the involuntarily committed to reasonable conditions of safety and freedom from unreasonable restraints. He would have held that "the Constitution only requires that the courts make certain that professional judgment in fact was exercised. It is not appropriate for the courts to specify which of several professionally acceptable choices should have been made." Persons who have been involuntarily committed are entitled to more considerate treatment and conditions of confinement than criminals whose conditions of confinement are designed to punish. At the same time, this standard is lower than the "compelling" or "substantial" necessity tests the Court of Appeals would require a state to meet to justify use of restraints or conditions of less than absolute safety. We think this requirement would place an undue burden on the administration of institutions such as Pennhurst and also would restrict unnecessarily the exercise of professional judgment as to the needs of residents.

Moreover, we agree that respondent is entitled to minimally adequate training. In this case, the minimally adequate training required by the Constitution is such training as may be reasonable in light of respondent's liberty interests in safety and freedom from unreasonable restraints. In determining what is "reasonable"—in this and in any case presenting a claim for training by a state—we emphasize that courts must show deference to the judgment exercised by a qualified professional. By so limiting judicial review of challenges to conditions in state institutions, interference by the federal judiciary with the internal operations of these institutions should be minimized.[3] Moreover, there certainly is no reason to think judges or juries are better qualified than appropriate professionals in making such decisions. See Parham v J.R., 442 US 584, 607 (1979). (Courts should not "'second-guess the expert administrators on matters on which they are better informed.'"). For these reasons, the decision, if made by a professional, is presumptively valid; liability may be imposed only when the decision by the

---

[3] See Parham v J.R., 442 US, at 808 n 16, (In limiting judicial review of medical decisions made by professionals, "it is incumbent on courts to design procedures that protect the rights of individuals without unduly burdening the legitimate efforts of the states to deal with difficult social problems.")

professional is such a substantial departure from accepted professional judgment, practice or standards as to demonstrate that the person responsible actually did not base the decision on such a judgment. In an action for damages against a professional in his individual capacity, however, the professional will not be liable if he was unable to satisfy his normal professional standards because of budgetary constraints; in such a situation, good-faith immunity would bar liability.***

Respondent thus enjoys constitutionally protected interests in conditions of reasonable care and safety, reasonably non-restrictive confinement conditions, and such training as may be required by these interests. Such conditions of confinement would comport fully with the purpose of respondent's commitment. In determining whether the state has met its obligations in these respects, decisions made by the appropriate professional are entitled to a presumption of correctness. Such a presumption is necessary to enable institutions of this type—often, unfortunately, overcrowded and understaffed—to continue to function. A single professional may have to make decisions with respect to a number of residents with widely varying needs and problems in the course of a normal day. The administrators, and particularly professional personnel, should not be required to make each decision in the shadow of an action for damages.

In this case, we conclude that the jury was erroneously instructed on the assumption that the proper standard of liability was that of the Eighth Amendment. Accordingly, we vacate the decision of the Court of Appeals and remand for further proceedings consistent with this decision.

Notes and Issues for Discussion

1. How does the court define "habilitation"? How does it differ from "treatment" as defined in the Appendix to *Wyatt v. Stickney*, p. 394.
2. *Youngberg* is one of the few Supreme Court decisions addressing the rights of retarded citizens. The Court finds a right of safety and freedom from restraint, and "minimally adequate or reasonable training" to accomplish these. What do you think these rights mean for patients and clients? What kinds of programs or training would achieve these goals?
3. An important point in *Youngberg* is that it is left to the professional to decide what is "reasonable," and that professional decision is presumed valid. Liability exists only "when the decision . . . is such a substantial departure from accepted professional judgment, practice, or standards as to demonstrate that the person responsible actually did not base the decision on such a judgment" and even if there were a substantial departure from accepted professional judgment, budgetary constraints are a valid defense. This case along with *Parham v. J.L. and J.R.* (p. 387) has been relied upon to support the view that parental and professional decisions are presumed valid. After this decision, when would Romeo have a valid claim for damages?

STERILIZATION DECISIONS

As discussed in Chapter 8, the involuntary sterilization of incompetent individuals is a highly controversial issue and this is no less true for the developmentally disabled. In *Buck v. Bell*, 274 U.S. 200 (1927), the Supreme Court upheld Virginia's statute permitting the involuntary sterilization of an allegedly retarded woman to prevent her from giving birth to more retarded children. While involuntary sterilizations now are rare, the question remains under what conditions a developmentally disabled individual may be sterilized. Put another way, if a competent individual can exercise the right to undergo a sterilization, how can that right be exercised for an incompetent one?

IN RE GRADY
85 N.J. 235, 426 A.2d 467 (1981)
NEW JERSEY SUPREME COURT

PASHMAN, J.

As once before in *In re Quinlan*, 70 N.J. 10 (1976), we again examine a disturbing paradox: how we can preserve the personal freedom of one incapable of exercising it by allowing others to make a profoundly personal decision on her behalf. In *Quinlan* this Court held that a comatose person kept alive by extraordinary means shall have a guardian appointed who would decide whether to discontinue those means. The question now before us is closely related: under what conditions should a court appoint a guardian who may authorize the sterilization of a woman who is severely mentally impaired.

Lee Ann Grady is a 19-year-old mentally impaired woman seriously afflicted with Down's syndrome. Within a few days of her birth, Lee Ann's parents decided not to place her in an institution but to care for her at home.***

Her formal education has consisted of special programs within the public schools. Over the years she has been tested by school personnel, who have recommended that she continue to participate in the special classes. Although unable to read words, she does recognize the letters of the alphabet. She has moderate success in writing her name. She has some ability to count low numbers, but it is not clear whether she counts by rote or with awareness of the function of numbers. In her conversation she often fails to form complete sentences.

At home Lee Ann's activities include playing simple games, watching television, and taking short walks. She is capable of performing tasks such as folding laundry and dusting. She can dress herself, but she cannot select clothes appropriate for the season or matching in color. She is able to bathe herself but needs help regulating the temperature of the water. She can open and warm a can of soup but has difficulty in controlling the heat of the stove burner. Her physical limitations have kept her from learning to ride a bicycle, to catch a ball or to jump rope. But she goes bowling occasionally, and she likes to swim.

Because Lee Ann does not suffer from some of the physical ailments associated with Down's syndrome, her life expectancy is about normal. Her physical maturation has not deviated significantly from that of other adolescents.

Although in a physical sense her sexual development has kept pace with that of others her age, Lee Ann's severe mental impairment has prevented the emotional and social development of sexuality. She has no significant understanding of sexual relationships or marriage. If she became pregnant, she would neither understand her condition nor be able to make decisions about it. Her lack of awareness could lead to severe health problems. It is uncontradicted that she would not be able to care for a baby alone. Indeed, she will probably need lifetime supervision to care for her own needs.

Recognizing her sexual growth, the Gradys have provided birth control pills for Lee Ann during the past four years. Although there is no evidence that Lee Ann has engaged in sexual activity or has any interest in doing so, her parents believe that contraception is an appropriate precaution to exercise under the circumstances of their daughter's life.

As Lee Ann has approached the age of 20—when she will leave her special class in the public school system—the Gradys have given more thought to her future. The parents fear they will predecease their daughter and she will be unable to live independently. Thus they have sought to attain for her a life less dependent on her family. The Gradys wish to place Lee Ann in a sheltered work group and eventually in a group home for retarded adults. But the parents see dependable and continuous contraception as a prerequisite to any such change in their daughter's environment. With the advice of their doctor, they sought to have Lee Ann sterilized at Morristown Memorial Hospital. The hospital refused to permit the operation.

The Gradys requested such authorization from the Superior Court, Chancery Division. They sought appointment of a special guardian with authority to consent on Lee Ann's behalf to a conventional sterilization procedure known as a tubal ligation.*** After considering all the evidence, Judge Polow rendered judgment allowing the parents to exercise substituted consent for Lee Ann to be sterilized.

Although we agree with much of the trial court opinion, the standard we establish today for judicial authorization of sterilization differs from that applied by the trial court. Therefore, we vacate the judgment of the Superior Court, Chancery Division, and remand for application of the new standard to the facts of this case.

We are well aware that the decision before us is awesome. Sterilization may be said to destroy an important part of a person's social and biological identity—the ability to reproduce. It affects not only the health and welfare of the individual but the well-being of all society. Any legal discussion of sterilization must begin with an acknowledgment that the right to procreate is "fundamental to the very existence and survival of the race." *Skinner v. Oklahoma*, 316 U.S. 535 (1942). This right is "a basic liberty" of which the individual is "forever deprived" through unwanted sterilization. *Id.***

Sterilization has a sordid past in this country—especially from the viewpoint of the mentally retarded. In the early part of this century many states enacted compulsory sterilization laws as an easy answer to the problems and costs of caring for the misfortune of society. Lawmakers may have sincerely believed that the social welfare would improve if fewer handicapped people were born, but they were too quick to accept unproven scientific theories of eugenics. In the United States Supreme Court, a compulsory sterilization law withstood a challenge that such legislation unconstitutionally infringes upon liberty protected by the due process clause. In *Buck v. Bell*, 274 *U.S.* 200 (1927), the Court upheld a law authorizing the compulsory sterilization of a mentally impaired woman for no more compelling reason than to prevent another generation of "imbeciles." Compulsory, eugenic sterilization would have to overcome much higher constitutional hurdles today.

Half a century later, we have serious doubts about the scientific validity of eugenic sterilization, as well as its morality. Yet compulsory sterilization is not altogether part of the past. Many of our sister states have not abandoned their compulsory sterilization laws. Nothing we say today should be interpreted as approval of compulsory sterilization *for any purpose.*

The case before us presents a situation that is difficult to characterize as either "compulsory" or "voluntary." "Compulsory" would refer to a sterilization that the state imposes despite objections by the person to be sterilized or one who represents his interests. Here, however, Lee Ann's parents and her guardian *ad litem* all agree that sterilization is in her best interests, and while the state may be acting in the constitutional sense, it would not be compelling sterilization. Lee Ann herself can comprehend neither the problem nor the proposed solution; without any such understanding it is difficult to say that sterilization would be against her will. Yet for this same reason, the label "voluntary" is equally inappropriate. Since Lee Ann is without the capacity for giving informed consent, any explanation of the proposed sterilization could only mislead her. Thus, what is proposed for Lee Ann is best described as neither "compulsory" nor "voluntary," but as lacking personal consent because of a legal disability.

We believe that an individual's constitutional right of privacy includes the right to undergo sterilization voluntarily.

Having recognized that both a right to be sterilized and a right to procreate exist, we face the problem, as in *Quinlan*, that Lee Ann Grady is not competent to exercise either of her constitutional rights. What is at stake is not simply a right to obtain contraception or to attempt procreation. Implicit in both these complementary liberties is the right to make a meaningful choice between them. Yet because of her severe mental impairment, Lee Ann does not have the ability to make a choice between sterilization and procreation, or between sterilization and other methods of contraception—a choice which she would presumably make in her "best interests" had she such ability. But her inability should not result in the forfeit of this constitutional interest or of the effective protection of her "best interests." If the decision whether or not to procreate is "a valuable incident of her right of privacy, as we believe it to be, then it should not be discarded solely on the basis that her condition prevents her conscious exercise of the choice." *Quinlan, supra,* at 41. To preserve that right and the benefits that a meaningful decision would bring to her life, it may be necessary to assert it on her behalf.

We need not determine here the full range of persons who may assert such a right on behalf of the incompetent. The parents are unquestionably eligible to do so. The question of who besides the parents has standing to represent the purported interests of the incompetent can await future determination. Nevertheless, we believe that an appropriate court must make the final determination whether consent to sterilization should be given on behalf of an incompetent individual. It must be the court's judgment, and not just the parents' good faith decision, that substitutes for the incompetent's consent. To the extent that the trial court held otherwise, we disagree.

We realize that this holding is a departure from *Quinlan*. In *Quinlan* we found that the only practical way to preserve the comatose patient's right to discontinue artificial life-support was to allow the guardian and family "to render their best judgment, subject to . . . qualifications . . . , as to whether she would exercise it in these circumstances." 70 *N.J.* at 41. But Quinlan concerned a very special situation. The alternatives available there were much more clear-cut than those here. The patient could continue to live indefinitely in a coma with the support of artificial apparatus or she could have the apparatus removed and allow natural forces to take over, probably resulting in her death. This choice is not conducive to detached evaluation and resolution by the person exercising it in behalf of the patient. A decision to choose life or death will rely on instinct more than reasoned calculation. Other than considering the medical opinions to determine the chances of the patient's future recovery, there are few factors for a court to weigh in deciding what is in the incompetent's best interest. The Court in *Quinlan* thought it best to defer to the parents' judgment as long as safeguards were observed. Also, the Court was not made aware in that case of any history of abuse in such decisions.

In contrast, sterilization of incompetents, especially the mentally impaired, has been subject to abuse in the past. We must ensure that the law does not allow abuse to continue. Since the sterilization decision involves a variety of factors well suited to rational development in judicial proceedings, a court can take cognizance of these factors and reach a fair decision of what is the incompetent's best interest.***

Our discussion thus far leads to the following conclusions. The right to choose among procreation, sterilization and other methods of contraception is an important privacy right of all individuals. Our courts must preserve that right. Where an incompetent person lacks the mental capacity to make that choice, a court should ensure the exercise of that right on behalf of the incompetent in a manner that reflects his or her best interests.***

We now consider the standards a court must apply in determining whether to authorize sterilization.***

First, it is ultimately the duty of the court rather than the parents to determine the need for sterilization.***

Second, we fully endorse the procedural safeguards employed by the trial court. In every case where application is made for authorization to sterilize an allegedly incompetent person, the court should appoint an independent guardian *ad litem* as soon as possible. The guardian must have full opportunity to meet with the incompetent person, to present proofs and cross-examine witnesses at the hearing, and to represent zealously the interests of his ward in other appropriate ways.

In addition, the court should receive independent medical and psychological evaluations by qualified professionals.***

The incompetent person need not be present at the proceedings if the court determines that his presence would not be useful in protecting his rights. Nevertheless, the trial judge should personally meet with the individual to obtain his own impressions of competency. This meeting need not be conducted formally and can occur in any convenient and appropriate place, such as chambers, counsel's office, an institution or the incompetent person's home. The incompetent person should be given every opportunity to express his own views about the judicial proceedings and the prospect of sterilization.

Third, the trial judge must find that the individual lacks capacity to make a decision about sterilization and that the incapacity is not likely to change in the foreseeable future. Many mentally impaired persons and others with legal disabilities are capable of making their own decisions regarding procreation and sterilization. We emphasize that there are widely different degrees of mental retardation. The fact that a person is legally incompetent for some purposes, cf. R. 4:83 (action for guardianship of incompetent), does not mean that he lacks the capacity to make a decision about sterilization. The trial court should be reluctant to substitute its consent for any person who may be capable of making a decision for himself. Therefore, the proponent of sterilization should have the burden of proving by *clear and convincing evidence* that the person to be sterilized lacks the capacity to consent or withhold consent.

Fourth, the trial court must be persuaded by *clear and convincing* proof that sterilization is in the incompetent person's best interests. To determine those interests, the court should consider at least the following factors:

(1) The possibility that the incompetent person can become pregnant. There need be no showing that pregnancy is likely. The court can presume fertility if the medical evidence indicates normal development of sexual organs and the evidence does not otherwise raise doubts about fertility.

(2) The possibility that the incompetent person will experience trauma or psychological damage if she becomes pregnant or gives birth, and, conversely, the possibility of trauma or psychological damage from the sterilization operation.

(3) The likelihood that the individual will voluntarily engage in sexual activity or be exposed to situations where sexual intercourse is imposed upon her.

(4) The inability of the incompetent person to understand reproduction or contraception and the likely permanence of that inability.

(5) The feasibility and medical advisability of less drastic means of contraception, both at the present time and under foreseeable future circumstances.

(6) The advisability of sterilization at the time of the application rather than in the future. While sterilization should not be postponed until unwanted pregnancy occurs, the court should be cautious not to authorize sterilization before it clearly has become an advisable procedure.

(7) The ability of the incompetent person to care for a child, or the possibility that the incompetent may at some future date be able to marry and, with a spouse, care for a child.

(8) Evidence that scientific or medical advances may occur within the foresee-

able future which will make possible either improvement of the individual's condition or alternative and less drastic sterilization procedures.

(9) A demonstration that the proponents of sterilization are seeking it in good faith and that their primary concern is for the best interests of the incompetent person rather than their own or the public's convenience.

These factors should each be given appropriate weight as the particular circumstances dictate. The list is not meant to be exclusive. The ultimate criterion is the best interests of the incompetent person.***

While the trial court applied the clear and convincing standard of proof to its finding of incapacity, it apparently did not utilize that standard for its other findings. Our decision today requires that the clear and convincing standard of proof apply as well to the finding that sterilization is in the best interests of the incompetent person. Also, because we have established a stricter standard for determining best interests than that applied by the trial court, we do not know how the court below weighed the factors discussed in this opinion. It is necessary, therefore, to remand to the Chancery Division for application of the new standard to the facts of this case.

Notes and Issues for Discussion

1. Where does the *Grady* court find a right to sterilization? If this right exists for a competent individual, does it exist for an incompetent one? The court views Lee Ann's proposed sterilization as neither compulsory nor voluntary. Do you agree?
2. Why do Lee Ann's parents want to have her sterilized? Are these valid concerns? What are the countervailing arguments?
3. One of the factors in the decision is Lee Ann's predicted inability to care for a possible child. The inability of an individual who is not retarded to care for a child or a past pattern of serious abuse to a child would not legally justify sterilization. Is this case different? Why?
4. The standard used in *Grady* is that of "best interests." What factors do the court see as important in determining Lee Ann's best interests? Do you agree? Are there others?
5. The trial court must make the final sterilization decision. What kinds of evidence could you supply the court to help in making this decision? Would it make a difference if the individual were sexually active? Unsupervised for periods of time? What kinds of documentation should you keep?
6. Lee Ann has spent her life with her parents, who, although caring, may have overprotected her and restricted her development. If so, it is possible that she is capable of functioning at a much higher level. Should this be considered?
7. In *Matter of Moe*, 432 N.E. 2d 712, the Massachusetts Supreme Court approved a mother's request for the sterilization of her retarded adult daughter, given the pseudonym Mary Moe. The court relied on the theory of substituted judgment, that is, what decision would be made by the in-

competent if she were competent. Is this a viable approach? Consider the dissenting opinion of Justice Nolan:

"I dissent. Sterilization is a species of self mutilation which is almost always irreversible. Its effect is to deprive the sterilized person of her or his capacity to beget or bear a child. We do not deal here with what has been described as therapeutic sterilization in which as a secondary effect to an operative procedure which is necessary to save the life of a person such person is rendered sterile (e.g., cancer of a reproductive organ may require its surgical removal).

The court today has decided that the probate judge has the power to divine the wishes of a severely mentally retarded woman who 'currently functions at the level of a four year old' as to whether she should permit herself to be rendered forever incapable of conceiving and bearing a child. To say the least, this is an impossible task. . . .

The court speaks of human dignity in connection with the free choice to be sterilized. It is difficult to think of an experience more degrading to human dignity than a sterilization ordered by a judge who is empowered by the court to read the heart and mind of the incompetent ward and forever bar the ward from bringing forth a child." 432 N.E.2d at 724. Do you agree?

MATTER OF ROMERO
790 P.2d 819 (1990)
COLORADO SUPREME COURT

JUSTICE LOHR delivered the Opinion of the Court.

This case involves a guardian's petition seeking a court order authorizing sterilization of her ward, an incapacitated adult woman. After an evidentiary hearing, the Delta County District Court issued the sterilization order. We reverse the district court's order.

LaVista Romero is a thirty-seven-year-old woman, who is the mother of two children. When Ms. Romero was thirty-three years old, she suffered oxygen deprivation from complications associated with diabetes, and brain damage resulted. On October 8, 1985, Shirley J. Harvey, Ms. Romero's mother, petitioned the Delta County District Court to have Ms. Romero declared an incapacitated person and to have herself appointed guardian. The court entered the requested order.

On June 14, 1988, Ms. Harvey petitioned the Delta County District Court to order sterilization of Ms. Romero. A guardian ad litem was appointed for Ms. Romero, and on August 31, 1988, the court held an evidentiary hearing. After hearing the testimony of Ms. Harvey, Ms. Romero, three doctors, and a social worker on the staff of the nursing home where Ms. Romero resided, the court ordered that Ms. Romero be sterilized.

This appeal was then filed on Ms. Romero's behalf.

No Colorado statute authorizes district courts to act on petitions for sterilization in circumstances applicable to Ms. Romero. We have held, however, that district courts have jurisdiction to act on petitions for sterilization of incompetent persons under the courts' *parens patriae* authority.***

The threshold consideration in a trial court's determination whether to order sterilization of an incapacitated person is whether that individual is competent to grant or withhold consent to the sterilization procedure. Before a district court may consider whether sterilization is medically essential or in the individual's best interest, the petitioner must prove *by clear and convincing evidence* that the individual is incompetent to make a decision about sterilization and that the individual's capacity to make such a decision is not likely to improve in the future.

An individual who is incompetent to make some decisions is not necessarily incompetent to make all decisions. Implicit in our holding in *In re A.W.* was a recognition that some mentally retarded individuals are competent to grant or withhold consent to sterilization. Many mentally retarded individuals are, in fact, capable of understanding the implications of sterilization and the responsibilities of parenthood, and are competent to make a decision regarding sterilization.

An individual should be deemed competent to grant or withhold consent if the individual understands the nature of the district court's proceedings, the relationship between sexual activity and reproduction and the consequences of the sterilization procedure. To be competent, an individual need not have a technical understanding of bodily functions or fully understand the medical complications or risks involved in the sterilization procedure. Nor must the person comprehend all the risks of pregnancy and childbirth in order to be considered competent to grant or withhold consent to sterilization. The fact that a court finds the decision an individual would make to be unreasonable is not enough to find the individual incompetent.***

Although the district court found Ms. Romero incompetent to grant or withhold consent knowingly, we find that conclusion to be unsupported by clear and convincing evidence. The evidence was that Ms. Romero has an intelligence quotient (IQ) of approximately 74, which is higher than individuals who are classified as mentally retarded. Individuals with similar IQs often hold jobs and live independently. *DSM-III-R* at 31.

Ms. Romero testified at the district court hearing in an articulate manner. Her testimony demonstrates that she understood the nature of the court's proceedings. Both her testimony and that of Dr. Paula Trautner, a psychiatrist, reflect that she understands the relationship between sexual intercourse and pregnancy. Ms. Romero further demonstrated an understanding of the consequences of a tubal ligation. She expressed clearly her desire to remain capable of having another child.

Dr. Trautner was the only witness the petitioner offered to testify on the issue of competency. She testified in general terms that Ms. Romero is subject to rapid changes in mood, has poor social judgment, has episodes of anger and apathy, is sometimes paranoid, and has difficulty thinking abstractly. Although Dr. Trautner concluded that Ms. Romero is not competent to consent to sterilization, her only explanation for this conclusion was that Ms. Romero "doesn't look at things in terms of future consequences." In short, Dr. Trautner's testimony does not indicate that Ms. Romero is incapable of understanding the nature of the court proceedings, the relationship between sexual intercourse and pregnancy, or the consequences of sterilization .

Most of the testimony at the hearing focused on the reasonableness of Ms. Romero's decision to oppose sterilization and the extent of her understanding of the risks of pregnancy and childbirth rather than on her competence to grant or withhold consent. Various experts who testified concluded that it would be unwise for Ms. Romero to try to have another child, and the district court found that to be true. The witnesses expressed the belief that Ms. Romero's desire to bear a child is unreasonable. Although Ms. Romero has not indicated any intention to become pregnant in the near future, she has clearly articulated her desire to remain capable of having children. She would like another child if and when she is able to leave the nursing home at which she now lives and if her diabetes becomes more manageable. Dr. Trautner testified that Ms. Romero is not realistic in assessing the risks of pregnancy and child birth or in making a judgment based on those risks, but Dr. Trautner did not state that Ms. Romero is unaware of those risks. Moreover, Ms. Romero's statement that she would like to have a child when and if her diabetes is cured indicates her understanding that pregnancy at this time would be risky.

In the final analysis, however, a court's role is not to pass judgment upon the wisdom of Ms. Romero's decision or the importance she assigns to potential risks and benefits. If Ms. Romero is competent to make a decision, she must remain free to do so, even if that means making a decision that many would consider unwise.

In summary, we find the trial court's determination that Ms. Romero is incompetent to grant or withhold consent to sterilization to be unsupported by clear and convincing evidence and, therefore, we reverse the trial court's sterilization order.

JUSTICE MULLARKEY, dissenting:

I respectfully dissent.

I agree with the majority's conclusion that *In re A.W.*, 637 P.2d 366 (Colo. 1981), set the appropriate procedure for the trial court to follow in deciding whether to order the sterilization of La Vista Romero. *In re A.W.* provides a clear list of steps which should be followed by the district court in making such determinations. Prior to deciding the primary issue of whether to order sterilization of an incapacitated person, the district court must make the following preliminary determinations: First, the trial judge should talk to the individual in order to observe the person's physical and mental conditions; along these lines, the individual's wishes are relevant although not conclusive and should be weighed heavily. Second, the district court must determine by clear and convincing evidence that the person is incapable of making a decision about sterilization and that the person's capacity is unlikely to improve in the future. Third, the person must be proven capable of reproduction. Once a district court makes the preliminary determinations, the court must find by clear and convincing evidence that sterilization is medically essential.

The majority adopts the following test for determining an individual's capacity to make a decision about sterilization:

An individual should be deemed competent to grant or withhold consent [to sterilization] if the individual understands the nature of the district court's proceedings, the relationship between sexual activity and repro- duction and the consequences of the sterilization procedure.

Maj. op. at 823.

Shirley Harvey, Romero's mother and guardian, argues that the test of com- petency in this context requires an inquiry into the individual's capacity to un- derstand the risks of pregnancy and childbirth. Without discussion, the majority apparently rejects Harvey's argument and states that the individual need not "comprehend all the risks of pregnancy and childbirth in order to be considered competent to grant or withhold consent to sterilization." Maj. op. at 823.

In its application of the test, however, the majority addresses Romero's un- derstanding of the risks of pregnancy and childbirth. The majority interprets the record as supporting the conclusion that Romero is aware of and understands the risks of pregnancy and childbirth which she is willing to undertake in the future, and it notes that Romero's psychiatrist, Dr. Paula Trautner, "did not state that Ms. Romero is unaware of those risks." The majority supports its conclusion that Romero is aware and understands the risks of pregnancy by her statement that she would like to have a child when her diabetes is cured. The majority's analy- sis of Romero's understanding of the risks of pregnancy and childbirth shows me that such awareness is an inherent part of determining the individual's under- standing of "the consequences of sterilization," which is part of the majority's test. A sexually active, fertile woman assumes the risks of becoming pregnant and bearing a child, and a woman's capacity to understand such risks as applied to herself, therefore, should enter into the court's assessment of her ability to make a sterilization decision.

The record as a whole does not support the conclusion that Romero was able to understand or actually understood the risks which pregnancy and childbirth posed to her because of her age and her severe diabetic condition. Dr. Trautner testified as to Romero's understanding of the physical consequences of preg- nancy and said that "[b]asically her response is she had babies before and she can do it again and that there should not be any major problems. So, in other words, she does not have a good understanding of how the pregnancy would affect the diabetes at this point." Furthermore, when Romero was on the stand she testified as follows:

Q. Do you understand if you got pregnant that it might be risky for your health?

A. No.

Q. Because you've got diabetes it might make it unsafe for you to be pregnant?

A. It didn't hurt me the first time. I mean the second time is what I should say.

Q. Even if there was a risk would you want to get pregnant and have another baby?

A. Not at the nursing home, no.

Q. What about if you are out of the nursing home? What if you were married to Dean?

A. Yes, I would want a baby then.
Q. Even though it would be risky for you?
A. Yes. I'll take that chance.

Later the trial judge questioned Romero about her understanding of the risks involved in pregnancy and she testified as follows:

Q. You've told us that you want to have a child.
A. Yes.
Q. And the doctors have been telling me here today in the hearing that that would be very dangerous for you to do. In fact, it could be threatening to your health, or even to your life. Did you hear that testimony?
A. Yes.
Q. Does that make you feel maybe you should be more cautious or maybe you shouldn't have a baby because of what they have said?
A. No.
Q. Why is that?
A. Because I want one bad enough.
Q. Realizing that it could even kill you?
A. Yes, sir.

It appears that Romero could not connect her diabetic condition with the risks of pregnancy and childbirth. Romero asserted that pregnancy would "not be bad" for her and that her past difficulty in childbirth and the premature birth of her second child were not a result of her diabetes but rather due to her smoking. She also indicated that her diabetic condition would not be a serious limitation on her being pregnant because in the meantime a cure would be found for diabetes.

In my opinion, Romero's statements indicate that she lacks the capacity to understand the risks involved in pregnancy. Her responses to questions imply that she has an illusory view of her disease and its implications. The attorneys and medical experts at the hearing repeatedly emphasized the dangers that pregnancy and childbirth entailed, but her responses indicated that she could not relate the dangers to herself and her particular situation. Although she did state that she would like to have a child when her diabetes was cured, the context of her statement indicated her unrealistic, and perhaps wishful, assessment of her situation.

An evaluation of Romero's capacity to understand the risks of pregnancy should include consideration of whether she could comprehend the risks at a future date when she was not in the courtroom being reminded constantly of the risks. Dr. Trautner testified that Romero is subject to rapid mood changes and has difficulty thinking abstractly or in terms of future consequences. Dr. Trautner's testimony is, thus, relevant to an evaluation of Romero's capacity to understand the risks.

I would include the individual's capacity to understand the risks of pregnancy and childbirth in the test for determining one's competence to make a decision regarding sterilization. Capacity to understand, not perfect knowledge, should be the key. As the majority correctly points out at page 822, competency must be determined in context and an individual is not necessarily incompetent for all purposes. When sterilization is the issue, it is not enough for the incapacitated person to understand the nature of the district court's proceedings, the relationship between sexual activity and reproduction and the consequences of the sterilization procedure. The individual also must be able to understand the risks of childbirth and pregnancy in order to decide whether to be sterilized.

I also dissent from the majority's disposition of this case. This is a significant issue which this court addresses for the first time. The majority develops a test which was not available when the case was tried. An appellate court is in a poor position to evaluate Romero's testimony and demeanor which obviously are critical in determining her competence. The best course is to remand the case for retrial so that relevant evidence may be presented and the trial court can make the initial determination of Romero's competency under the new standard.

Notes and Issues for Discussion

1. *Grady* concerns the sterilization of an individual with developmental disabilities. *Romero* deals with the sterilization of an individual who became disabled later in life. How else are the facts of the two cases different?
2. The physician testifying to LaVista Romero's lack of competence stated she "is subject to rapid changes in mood, has poor social judgement, has episodes of anger and apathy, is sometimes paranoid, and has difficulty thinking abstractly," and "doesn't look at things in terms of future consequences." Does this make her incompetent?
3. The dissent argues that Ms. Romero doesn't understand the risks of pregnancy: "A sexually active, fertile woman assumes the risks of becoming pregnant and bearing a child, and a woman's capacity to understand such risks as applied to herself, therefore, should enter into the court's assessment of her ability to make a sterilization decision." What do you think?
4. As a health and human services professional what would you recommend to the court in this case? In the *Grady* case?

MAKING DECISIONS FOR THE DISABLED CHILD

Courts will generally accept health care decisions parents make for their minor children except in cases of life or death. (See generally p. 228). The following case is uncommon in that the court allowed a third party, volunteers who had established a relationship with the disabled child, to intervene and overrule the parent's medical decisions.

GUARDIANSHIP OF PHILLIP B., A MINOR
188 Cal. Rptr. 781 (1983)
CALIFORNIA SUPREME COURT

RACANELLI, PRESIDING JUSTICE.

Few human experiences evoke the poignancy of a filial relationship and the pathos attendant upon its disruption in society's effort to afford every child a meaningful chance to live life to its fullest promise. This appeal, posing a sensitive confrontation between the fundamental right of parental custody and the well being of a retarded child, reflects the deeply ingrained concern that the needs of the child remain paramount in the judicial monitoring of custody. In reaching our decision to affirm, we neither suggest nor imply that appellants' subjectively motivated custodial objectives affront conventional norms of parental fitness; rather, we determine only that on the unusual factual record before us, the challenged order of guardianship must be upheld in order to avert potential harm to the minor ward likely to result from appellants' continuing custody and to subserve his best interest.***

Phillip B. was born on October 16, 1966, with Down's Syndrome, a chromosomal anomaly—usually the presence of an extra chromosome attached to the number 21 pair—resulting in varying degrees of mental retardation and a number of abnormal physical characteristics. Down's Syndrome reported occurs in approximately ⅒ of 1 percent of live births.

Appellants, deeply distraught over Phillip's disability, decided upon institutionalization, a course of action recommended by a state social worker and approved by appellants' pediatrician. A few days later, Phillip was transferred from the hospital to a licensed board and care facility for disabled youngsters. Although the facility was clean, it offered no structured educational or developmental programs and required that all the children (up to 8 years of age) sleep in cribs. Appellants initially visited Phillip frequently; but soon their visits became less frequent and they became more detached from him.

When Phillip was three years old a pediatrician informed appellants that Phillip had a congenital heart defect, a condition afflicting half of Down's Syndrome children. Open heart surgery was suggested when Phillip attained age six. However, appellants took no action to investigate or remedy the suspected medical problem.

At appellants' request, a state social worker arranged for Phillip's transfer in January, 1972, to We Care, a licensed residential facility for developmentally disabled children located in San Jose, where he remained up to the time of trial.

In April 1972, We Care employed Jeanne Haight (later to become program director and assistant administrator of the facility) to organize a volunteer program. Mrs. Haight quickly noticed Phillip's debilitated condition. She found him unusually small and thin for his age (five); he was not toilet trained and wore diapers, still slept in a crib, walked like a toddler, and crawled down stairs only inches high. His speech was limited and mostly unintelligible; his teeth were in poor condition.

Mrs. Haight, who undertook a recruitment program for volunteers, soon recruited respondent Patsy H.***

Mrs. H., initially assigned to work with Phillip and another child, assisted Phillip in experimenting with basic sensory experiences, improving body coordination, and in overcoming his fear of steps. Mr. H. and one of the H. children helped fence the yard area, put in a lawn, a sandbox, and install some climbing equipment.***

Respondents continued working with Phillip coordinating their efforts with his classroom lessons. Among other things, they concentrated on development of feeding skills and toilet training and Mr. H. and the two eldest children gradually became more involved in the volunteer program.***

A pattern of physical and emotional detachment from their son was developed by appellants over the next several years. In contrast, during the same period, respondents established a close and caring relationship with Phillip. Beginning in December, 1972, Phillip became a frequent visitor at respondents' home; with appellants' consent, Phillip was permitted to spend weekends with respondents, a practice which continued regularly and often included weekday evenings. At the same time, respondents maintained frequent contact with Phillip at We Care as regular volunteer visitors. Meanwhile, appellants visited Phillip at the facility only a few times a year; however, no overnight home visits occurred until after the underlying litigation ensued.

Respondents played an active role in Phillip's behavioral development and educational training. They consistently supplemented basic skills training given Phillip at We Care.

Phillip was openly accepted as a member of the H. family whom he came to love and trust. He eventually had his own bedroom; he was included in sharing household chores. Mr. H. set up a workbench for Phillip and helped him make simple wooden toys; they attended special Boy Scout meetings together. And Phillip regularly participated in family outings. Phillip referred to the H. residence as "my house." When Phillip began to refer to the H. as "Mom" and "Dad," they initially discouraged the familiar reference, eventually succeeding in persuading Phillip to use the discriminate references "Mama Pat" and "Dada Bert" and "Mama B." and "Daddy B." Both Mrs. Haight and Phillip's teacher observed significant improvements in Phillip's development and behavior. Phillip had developed, in Mrs. Haight's opinion, "true love and strong [emotional] feelings" for respondents.

Meanwhile, appellants continued to remain physically and emotionally detached from Phillip.***

In matters of Phillip's health care needs, appellants manifested a reluctant—if not neglectful—concern. When Dr. Gathman, a pediatric cardiologist, diagnosed a ventricular septal defect in Phillip's heart in early 1973 and recommended catheterization (a medically accepted pre-surgery procedure to measure pressure and to examine the interior of the heart), appellants refused their consent.

In the spring of 1977, Dr. Gathman again recommended heart catheterization in connection with the anticipated use of general anesthesia during Phillip's major dental surgery. Appellants consented to the preoperative procedure which revealed that the heart defect was surgically correctible with a maximum risk factor of 5 percent. At a conference attended by appellants and Mrs. Haight in June, 1977, Dr. Gathman recommended corrective surgery in order to avoid a progressively deteriorating condition resulting in a "bed-to-chair existence" and the probability of death before the age of 30.*** Later that summer, appellants decided—without obtaining an independent medical consultation—against surgery. Appellants' stated reason was that Dr. Gathman had "painted" an inaccurate picture of the situation. They felt that surgery would be merely life-prolonging rather than life-saving, presenting the possibility that they would be unable to care for Phillip during his later years. A few months later, in early 1978, appellants' decision was challenged in a juvenile dependency proceeding initiated by the district attorney on the ground that the withholding of surgery constituted neglect within the meaning of Welfare and Institutions Code section 300, subdivision (b); the juvenile court's dismissal of the action on the basis of inconclusive evidence was ultimately sustained on appeal.

In September, 1978, upon hearing from a staff member of We Care that Phillip had been regularly spending weekends at respondents' home, Mr. B. promptly forbade Phillip's removal from the facility (except for medical purposes and school attendance) and requested that respondents be denied personal visits with Phillip at We Care. Although respondents continued to visit Phillip daily at the facility, the abrupt cessation of home visits produced regressive changes in Phillip's behavior: he began acting out violently when respondents prepared to leave, begging to be taken "home"; he resorted to profanity; he became sullen and withdrawn when respondents were gone; bed-wetting regularly occurred, a recognized symptom of emotional disturbance in children. He began to blame himself for the apparent rejection by respondents; he began playing with matches and on one occasion he set his clothes afire; on another, he rode his tricycle to respondents' residence a few blocks away proclaiming on arrival that he was "home." He continuously pleaded to return home with respondents. Many of the behavioral changes continued to the time of trial.***

The trial court expressly found that an award of custody to appellants would be harmful to Phillip in light of the psychological or "de facto" parental relationship established between him and respondents.***

Appellants vigorously challenge the evidence and finding that respondents have become Phillip's de facto or psychological parents since he did not reside with them full-time, as underscored in previous California decisions which have recognized de facto parenthood. They argue that the subjective concept of psychological parenthood, relying on such nebulous factors as "love and affection" is susceptible to abuse and requires the countervailing element of objectivity provided by a showing of the child's long-term residency in the home of the claimed psychological parent.

We disagree. Adoption of the proposed standard would require this court to endorse a novel doctrine of child psychology unsupported either by a demonstrated general acceptance in the field of psychology or by the record before us. Although psychological parenthood is said to result from "day-to-day attention to [the child's] needs for physical care, nourishment, comfort, affection, and stimulation," appellants fail to point to any authority or body of professional opinion that equates daily attention with full-time residency. To the contrary, the record contains uncontradicted expert testimony that while psychological parenthood usually will require residency on a "24-hour basis," it is not an absolute requirement; further, that the frequency and quality of Phillip's weekend visits with respondents, together with the regular weekday visits at We Care, provided an adequate foundation to establish the crucial parent-child relationship.***

Appellants also challenge the sufficiency of the evidence to support the finding that their retention of custody would have been detrimental to Phillip. In making the critical finding, the trial court correctly applied the "clear and convincing" standard of proof necessary to protect the fundamental rights of parents in all cases involving a nonparent's bid for custody.***

The record contains abundant evidence that appellants' retention of custody would cause Phillip profound emotional harm. Notwithstanding Phillip's strong emotional ties with respondents, appellants abruptly foreclosed home visits and set out to end all contact between them. When Phillip's home visits terminated in 1978, he displayed many signs of severe emotional trauma: he appeared depressed and withdrawn and became visibly distressed at being unable to return to "my house," a request he steadily voiced up until trial. He became enuretic, which a psychologist, Dr. Edward Becking, testified indicates emotional stress in children. Dr. Becking testified to other signs of emotional disturbance which were present nearly three years after the termination of home visits.***

There was uncontroverted expert testimony that Phillip would sustain further emotional trauma in the event of total separation from respondents: that testimony indicated that, as with all children, Phillip needs love and affection, and he would be profoundly hurt if he were deprived of the existing psychological parental relationship with respondents in favor of maintaining unity with his biological parents.

Phillip's conduct unmistakably demonstrated that he derived none of the emotional benefits attending a close parental relationship largely as a result of appellants' individualized decision to abandon that traditional supporting role. Dr. Becking testified that no "bonding or attachment" has occurred between Phillip and his biological parents, a result palpably consistent with appellants' view that Phillip had none of the emotional needs uniquely filled by natural parents. We conclude that such substantial evidence adequately supports the finding that parental custody would have resulted in harmful deprivation of these human needs contrary to Phillip's best interest.***

We strongly emphasize, as the trial court correctly concluded, that the fact of detriment *cannot* be proved solely by evidence that the biological parent has elected to institutionalize a handicapped child, or that nonparents are able and willing to offer the child the advantages of their home in lieu of institutional placement. Sound reasons may exist justifying institutionalization of a handicapped child. But the totality of the evidence under review permits of no rational conclusion other than that the detriment caused Phillip, and its possible recurrence, was due not to appellants' choice to institutionalize but their calculated decision to remain emotionally and physically detached—abdicating the conventional role of competent decisionmaker in times of demonstrated need—thus effectively depriving him of *any* of the substantial benefits of a true parental relationship. *It is the emotional abandonment of Phillip, not his institutionalization,* which inevitably has created the unusual circumstances which led to the award of limited custody to respondents. We do not question the sincerity of appellants' belief that their approach to Phillip's welfare was in their combined best interests. But the record is replete with substantial and credible evidence supporting the trial court's determination, tested by the standard of clear and convincing proof, that appellants' retention of custody has caused and will continue to cause serious detriment to Phillip and that his best interests will be served through the guardianship award of custody to respondents. In light of such compelling circumstances, no legal basis is shown to disturb that carefully considered determination.***

Notes and Issues for Discussion

1. After the volunteers were appointed guardians of Phillip, a heart catheterization was performed, later followed by successful open heart surgery. Phillip then lived with the volunteer family, attended school, was learning to read, and worked in a cafeteria. See Mnookin, "The Guardianship of Phillip B.: Jay Spears' achievement," 40 *Stan L. Rev.* 841 (1988).
2. You are a professional at Phillip's residential facility. Would you encourage volunteers to establish close ties with Phillip? Discourage close ties? What would you tell the biological parents?
3. If you were asked to testify in a similar situation, what types of information do you see as particularly relevant? Would that information be routinely recorded? By whom?

Education of Children with Disabilities[10]

The Education of Handicapped Children Act of 1975, 20 U.S. §1400 *et seq.* (now titled the Individuals with Disabilities Education Act or IDEA), with its various amendments and related state statutes, remains a keystone in laws for the education of disabled children. To qualify for federal monies under the act, a state must demonstrate that there is "in effect a policy that assures all children with disabilities the right to a free appropriate public education" 20 U.S.C. §1412(1), follow a list of priorities among children with disabilities, and must establish

> procedures to assure that, to the maximum extent appropriate, children with disabilities, including children in public or private institutions or other care facilities, are educated with children who are not disabled, and that special classes, separate schooling, or other removal of children with disabilities from the regular educational environment occurs

only when the nature or severity of the disability is such that education in regular classes with the use of supplementary aids and services cannot be achieved satisfactorily. 20 U.S.C. §1412(5).

The act has a number of key definitions: "Children with disabilities" are

children (i) with mental retardation, hearing impairments including deafness, speech or language impairments, visual impairments including blindness, serious emotional disturbance, orthopedic impairments, autism, traumatic brain injury, or other health impairments, or specific learning disabilities; and (ii) who, by reason thereof, need special education and related services. 20 U.S.C. §1401(a)(1)(A).[11]

"Special education" is

specially designed instruction, at no cost to parents or guardians, to meet the unique needs of a child with a disability including (A) instruction conducted in the classroom, in the home, in hospitals and institutions, and in other settings; and (B) instruction in physical education. 20 U.S.C. §1401(a)(16).

"Related services" are

transportation, and such developmental, corrective, and other supportive services (including speech, pathology and audiology, psychological services, physical and occupational therapy, recreation including therapeutic recreation, social work services, counseling services, including rehabilitation counseling, and medical services, except that such medical services shall be for diagnostic and evaluative purposes only) as may be required to assist a child with a disability to benefit from special education and includes early identification and assessment of disabling conditions in children. 20 U.S.C. §1401(a)(17).

"Free appropriate public education" is

special education and related services which (A) have been provided at public expense, under public supervision and direction and without charge, (B) meet the standards of the state education agency, (C) include an appropriate preschool, elementary, or secondary school education in the State involved, and (D) are provided in conformity with the individualized education program. . . . 20 U.S.C. §1401(a)(18).

"Transition services" are

a coordinated set of activities for a student designed within an outcome-oriented process, which promotes movement from school to post-school activities, including post-secondary education, vocational training, integrated employment (including supported employment), continuing and adult education, adult services, independent living, or community participation. The coordinated set of activities shall be based upon the individual student's needs, taking into account the student's preferences and interests, and shall include instruction, community experiences, the development of employment and other post-school adult living objectives, and when appropriate, acquisition of daily living skills and functional vocational evaluation. 20 U.S.C. §1401(a)(19).

"Individualized education program" is

a written statement for each child with a disability developed in any meeting by a representative of the local education agency or intermediate educational unit who shall be qualified to provide, or supervise the provision of, specially designed instruction to meet the unique needs of children with disabilities, the teacher, the parents or guardian of such child, and wherever appropriate, such child, which statement shall include (A) a statement of the present levels of educational performance of such child, (B) a statement of the annual goals, including short-term instructional objectives, (C) a statement of the specific education services to be provided to such child, and the extent to which such child will be able to participate in regular educational programs, (D) a statement of the needed transition services for students beginning no later than age 16 and annually thereafter (and, when determined appropriate, for the individual beginning at 14 or younger), including, when appropriate, a statement of the interagency responsibilities or linkages (or both) before the student leaves the school setting, (E) the projected date for initiation and anticipated duration of such services, and (F) appropriate objective criteria and evaluation procedures and schedules for determining, on at least an annual basis, whether instructional objectives are being achieved. 20 U.S.C. §1401(a)(20).

Among the major provisions of the act are the provision of free appropriate education and related services to children with disabilities, the mainstreaming of children with disabilities into regular classrooms, and the development and implementation of individualized education programs (IEP) for children with disabilities. Under §1415 of the act, parents are provided an opportunity to "examine all relevant records with respect to the identification, evaluation, and educational placement of the child," "obtain an independent educational evaluation of the child," and receive written prior notice when the educational agency "proposes to initiate or change or refuses to initiate or change" programs. Parents are afforded an opportunity to present complaints and can request "an impartial due process hearing" with appeal to the state educational agency. Parents have the right to bring counsel or an advisor to confront and cross-examine, the right to a written or electronic record of the hearing, and the right to written findings of fact and decisions. 20 U.S.C. §1415.

In *Hendrick Hudson Dist. Bd. of Ed. v. Rowley*, 458 U.S. 176 (1982), the Supreme Court clarified the meaning of "free appropriate public education." The IEP for Amy Rowley, a first grade student with a substantial hearing impairment, called for the provision of a hearing aid, which according to the Court "would amplify words spoken into a wireless receiver by the teacher or fellow students during certain classroom activities." Her parents objected to the hearing aid and requested that she be provided a sign-language interpreter. The Board of Education refused.

The district court, in a decision upheld by the circuit court of appeals, found Amy "performs better than the average child in her class and is advancing easily from grade to grade," "that she understands considerably less of what goes on in class than she could if she were not deaf," and "is not learning as much, or performing as well academically, as she would without her handicap," and held that she was not receiving a free appropriate education defined as "an opportunity to achieve full potential commensurate with the opportunity provided to other children." 458 U.S. at 185–186.

The Supreme Court reversed, holding that under the act, Congress intended that ". . . the requirement that a State provide specialized educational services to handicapped children generates no additional requirement that the services so provided be sufficient to maximize each child's potential 'commensurate with the opportunities provided other children.'" Instead, all that is needed is "access to specialized instruction and related services which are individually designed to provide educational benefit to the handicapped child." The Court also noted:

> When that "mainstreaming" preference of the act has been met and a child is being educated in the regular classroom of a public school system, the system itself monitors the educational progress of the child. Regular examinations are administered, grades are awarded, and yearly advancement to higher grade levels is permitted for those children who attain an adequate knowledge of course material. The grading and advancement system thus constitutes an important factor in determining educational benefit. 458 U.S. at 198–203.

Notes and Issues for Discussion

1. How realistic is the Court's assessment of grades and advancement as indicators of educational benefit or public school success?

2. Can parents be reimbursed for private school expenses if they disagree with an IEP calling for public school education? In *Florence County v. Carter*, 126 L.Ed.2d 284 (1993), parents of Shannon Carter, a ninth grade learning disabled child, challenged an IEP providing three periods of individualized instruction per week in public schools and enrolled her in a private school. The private school specialized in the education of children with disabilities, provided Shannon "an excellent education" and "low teacher-student ratios," and she made "significant progress." The school board refused to pay for private education and the parents sued for reimbursement for tuition and other costs, arguing the child was entitled to a "free and appropriate public education" under the IDEA. The school board argued that the IEP was adequate and in any case the private school was not state approved. The Supreme Court upheld the right of parents to be reimbursed for private school education under the IDEA where the IEP is inadequate. Although the Court made it clear that parents who similarly challenge IEPs do so at their own financial risk, courts are "authorized to grant such relief as the court determines is appropriate," considering all relevant factors including the reasonableness of the cost. The Court also noted:

   "The school district also claims that allowing reimbursement for parents such a Shannon's puts an unreasonable burden on financially strapped local education authorities. . . .

   There is no doubt that Congress has imposed a significant financial burden on States and school districts that participate in IDEA. Yet public educational authorities who want to avoid reimbursing parents for private education of a disabled child can do one of two things: give the child a free appropriate public education in a public setting, or place the child in an appropriate private setting of the state's choice. This is IDEA's mandate, and school officials who conform to it need not worry about reimbursement claims." 126 L.Ed.2d at 293-294.

SELECTED REFERENCE

Brakel, *et al. The Mentally Disabled and the Law* (1985).

CHAPTER 13

AIDS AND THE LAW

Over the last decade, the spread of HIV and AIDS has grown to epidemic proportions. The World Health Organization estimates that 12 to 14 million individuals across the world are infected with HIV, and about one million of those live in North America (*Newsweek*, March 22, 1993). It predicts 30 million to 40 million cases by the year 2000. (*New York Times*, June 1, 1993). Within the United States, the Centers for Disease Control reported 161,073 cases of AIDS in the United States at the end of 1990, and estimated there would be an additional 400,000 cases reported by the end of 1993, resulting in around 300,000 deaths.[1] While AIDS cuts across all social classes, income groups, ages, racial and ethnic compositions, and affects both sexes, in the United States, two populations—intravenous drug users and homosexual males—remain most at risk.[2]

In his provocative work *And the Band Played On*, Randy Shilts traces the slow response of the federal government and others to the AIDS crisis.[3] Within the legal literature, scant attention was paid to AIDS as a legal issue until the late 1980s.[4] However, the early 1990s saw an explosion in the AIDS legal literature, reflecting both increased concern and growing legal complexities.

AIDS AS A LEGAL CATEGORY

AIDS as a legal area has come so recently and rapidly upon the scene that it does not fit neatly into a single legal category, but overlaps a number of areas, including public health law, civil rights law, privacy law, and law for the disabled. The areas are potentially in conflict, and the resulting laws applicable to those infected with AIDS reflect these tensions.

If AIDS were only a public health issue, then it could be treated as a communicable disease. It would fall within that area of public health law that mandates state protection of the public from the spread of contagious and communicable diseases. In some instances, the law allows for mandatory testing, isolation, quarantining, contact tracing, and notification to those who have come into contact with the diseased person.

If AIDS were only a privacy issue, then the infected individual could have a right to privacy such that the AIDS condition could not be disclosed without informed consent and the confidentiality of the condition would be preserved.

If AIDS were only a civil rights issue, the AIDS-infected person could retain all civil rights as does any other competent person and would be able to bear children, make contracts, vote, work or attend school, and otherwise carry out life free from discrimination.

If AIDS were a only a disabilities issue, then persons with AIDS could be entitled to the benefits and protections available to other disabled individuals.

Since AIDS falls within all these categories and others, with their inherent conflicts, the legislatures and courts are left with the work of resolving these clashes within a legal and political context made more complicated by public fears, changes in public attitudes, and new medical information about the AIDS virus and its treatment. In the discussion that follows, the health and human services professional should keep in mind that due to these conflicts and uncertainties, the law around AIDS is particularly unsettled and undergoing rapid change.

LEGAL ISSUES

Health and human services professionals may be confronted with a number of AIDS-related legal issues, among them:

1. Privacy rights, the confidentiality of persons with AIDS, and liability— both civil and criminal—for wrongful disclosure of this information

2. Mandatory blood testing for AIDS or HIV

3. Disclosure of AIDS test results

4. Discrimination against persons with AIDS, particularly in employment, education, and health care.

Many other AIDS issues remain beyond the scope of this text, but the health and human services professional may need to explore the areas of provision or denial of health care; life and health insurance; civil and criminal liability for transmission of AIDS; family law issues including divorce, child custody, visitation, and foster care; termination-of-life and estate-planning issues for persons with AIDS, including wills and living wills; and liability for faulty AIDS diagnoses, including failure to diagnose AIDS and erroneous positive diagnoses.[5] Many of these issues are addressed in several source books listed at the conclusion of the chapter.

TRANSMISSION OF AIDS

In *Chalk v. U.S. District Court* (see p. 467) the court noted:

> Transmission of HIV is known to occur in three ways: (1) through inti-
> mate sexual contact with an infected person; (2) through invasive expo-
> sure to contaminated blood or certain other bodily fluids; or (3) through
> perinatal exposure (i.e. from mother to infant). Although HIV has been
> isolated in several bodily fluids, epidemiologic evidence has implicated
> only blood, semen, vaginal secretions, and possibly breast milk in
> transmission. Extensive and numerous studies have consistently found
> no apparent risk of HIV infection to individuals exposed through close,
> nonsexual contact with AIDS patients. 840 F.2d at 706.

While HIV may also be present in other bodily fluids, including saliva, there is currently no evidence of transmission by means of these fluids. Nonetheless, criminal actions have been brought against those with AIDS who have bitten another with the intent to spread the virus, and in California, Proposition 96 enacted in 1988 provides for the mandatory testing and disclosure of HIV information when saliva or other bodily fluids are transferred by biting, scratching, or spitting on police, fire fighters, or emergency medical personnel. Cal. Health and Safety Code §199.97. See *Johnetta J. v. Municipal Court*, 267 Cal. Rptr. 666 (1990), upholding that law.

PRIVACY AND CONFIDENTIALITY

At least forty states have statutes protecting the confidentiality of AIDS and HIV information. Among these are California (Cal. Health and Safety Code §§199.20–199.44); New York (N.Y. Pub. Health §§2780–2787); and Massachusetts (Mass. Pub. Health ch. 111 §70F).[6] In addition, the release of HIV information without informed consent within federally funded programs is a violation of the Privacy Act of 1974 (5 U.S.C.§552a), and within federally funded drug and alcohol programs is a violation of 42 U.S.C. §290ee-3 and 42 U.S.C. §290dd-3. (See p. 124.) Depending upon the jurisdiction, release of the information may result in civil or criminal liability. See, for example, Cal. Health and Safety Code §199.21, Michigan Stats. §333.5131(8).[7] However, a growing number of states now permit limited disclosure of AIDS and HIV information in certain situations. (See p. 460.)

Liability for Disclosure

In *Doe v. Borough of Barrington* (p. 110), the court held that the Doe family had a right of privacy such that the AIDS-infected condition of Jane Doe's husband could not be revealed to others without consent, and held that the police violated the family's constitutional right of privacy in releasing this information. The court rejected the police officer's argument that disclosure of the AIDS condition to a neighbor was justified to protect the health of others, and found that absent a training program on AIDS and confidentiality the municipality could be held liable for damages. Consider the following:

BEHRINGER ESTATE v. PRINCETON MEDICAL CENTER
249 N.J. Super. 59, 592 A.2d 1251 (1991)
NEW JERSEY SUPERIOR COURT, LAW DIVISION

CARCHMAN, J.S.C.

Plaintiff, William H. Behringer, was a patient at defendant Medical Center at Princeton (the medical center) when on June 17, 1987, he tested positive for the Human Immunodeficiency Virus (HIV), and combined with Pneumocystis Carinii Pneumonia (PCP), was diagnosed as suffering from Acquired Immunodeficiency Syndrome (AIDS). At the time, plaintiff, an otolaryngologist (ENT) and plastic surgeon, was also a member of the staff at the medical center. Within hours of his discharge from the medical center on June 18, 1987, plaintiff received numerous phone calls from well-wishers indicating a concern for his welfare but also demonstrating an awareness of his illness. Most of these callers were also members of the medical staff at the medical center. Other calls were received from friends in the community. Within days, similar calls were received from patients. Within a few weeks of his diagnosis, plaintiff's surgical privileges at the medical center were suspended. From the date of his diagnosis until his death on July 2, 1989, plaintiff did not perform any further surgery at the medical center, his practice declined and he suffered both emotionally and financially.

Plaintiff brings this action seeking damages for: (1) a breach of the medical center's and named employees' duty to maintain confidentiality of plaintiff's diagnosis and test results, and (2) a violation of the New Jersey Law Against Discrimination, N.J.S.A. 10:5–1 *et seq.*, as a result of the imposition of conditions on plaintiff's continued performance of surgical procedures at the medical center, revocation of plaintiff's surgical privileges and breach of confidentiality.***

Plaintiff, a board-certified ENT surgeon, developed a successful practice during his ten years in the Princeton area. His practice extended beyond the limited area of ear, nose and throat surgery and included a practice in facial plastic surgery. He served as an attending physician at the Medical Center since 1979 and performed surgery at the medical center since 1981.

In early June 1987, plaintiff felt ill. He complained of various symptoms and treated himself. Acknowledging no improvement, plaintiff consulted with a physician-friend (the treating physician). On June 16, 1987, plaintiff's companion arrived at plaintiff's home and observed that plaintiff was in distress. A call was made to the treating physician, and at approximately 11:00 p.m., plaintiff and his companion proceeded to the medical center emergency room, where plaintiff was examined initially by a number of residents and, thereafter, by the treating physician. The treating physician advised plaintiff that a pulmonary consultation was necessary, and a pulmonary specialist proceeded to examine plaintiff. A determination was made to perform a bronchoscopy—a diagnostic procedure involving bronchial washings—to establish the existence of PCP, a conclusive indicator of AIDS. The pulmonary consultant assumed that plaintiff, as a physician, knew the implications of PCP and its relationship to AIDS. In addition, the treating physician ordered a blood study including a test to determine whether plaintiff was infected with HIV—the cause of AIDS.

Plaintiff's companion has no recollection of specific information being transmitted to plaintiff regarding the HIV test, nor does she recollect any specific "counselling" or explanation being given to plaintiff about the significance, impact or confidentiality of a positive result of the HIV test.

***During the morning of June 17, 1987, plaintiff submitted to a bronchoscopy and returned to his room in the afternoon, where he was described as "sedated" and "out of it." Later that day, the pulmonary consultant reported to plaintiff that the results of the tests were positive for PCP, and he concluded that this information was new to plaintiff. Early that evening, the treating physician returned to plaintiff's room, and in the presence of plaintiff's companion, informed plaintiff that the HIV test was positive. Plaintiff was also informed that he had AIDS. Plaintiff's reaction, according to plaintiff's companion, was one of shock and dismay. His emotions ranged from concern about his health to fear of the impact of this information on his practice. Plaintiff's companion described her initial response as "who else knew?" The treating physician responded that he had told his wife; both plaintiff and his companion, close personal friends of both the treating physician and his wife, responded that "they understood."

It was readily apparent to all persons involved at this point that plaintiff's presence in the medical center was cause for concern. An infectious disease consultant and staff epidemiologist suggested to plaintiff that he transfer to Lenox Hill Hospital in New York or other available hospitals in the area. After inquiry, it was determined that no other beds were available. This concern for an immediate transfer appeared to be two-fold—to ensure the best available treatment for plaintiff (the treating physician suggested that AZT treatment be considered) and to prevent plaintiff's diagnosis from becoming public. It is apparent that all parties involved to this point—plaintiff, the treating physician, the epidemiologist and plaintiff's companion— fully understood the implications of the AIDS diagnosis becoming a matter of public knowledge. A determination was made that plaintiff would leave the hospital and be treated at home. Plaintiff was discharged from the hospital on the afternoon of June 18, 1987. To minimize the significance of his condition, plaintiff walked out of the hospital rather than following the normal medical center practice of being wheeled out.

Plaintiff's concern about public knowledge of the diagnosis was not misplaced. Upon his arrival home, plaintiff and his companion received a series of phone calls. Calls were received from various doctors who practiced at the medical center with plaintiff. All doctors, in addition to being professional colleagues, were social friends, but none were involved with the care and treatment of plaintiff. All indicated in various ways that they were aware of the diagnosis. Statements were made either directly to plaintiff's companion or by insinuation, such as an inquiry as to whether the companion was "tested." She did not deny references to the diagnosis but admits that she "tacitly acknowledged the diagnosis in one instance by silence." During the evening of June 18, she received a call from social non-medical friends who indicated their knowledge of the diagnosis and expressed support to her and plaintiff. She indicated that the relationships with various neighbors and friends changed as a result of the diagnosis. There was less social contact and communication and what she perceived as a significant diminution in the popularity of plaintiff.

Plaintiff's condition and the growing awareness of that condition in the community impacted upon not only plaintiff's social relationships but, more significantly, on his practice as well. In July 1987, plaintiff returned to his office practice. During his short absence from his office and in the ensuing months, calls were received at his practice from doctors and patients alike who indicated an awareness of plaintiff's condition and in many cases, requested transfer of files or indicated no further interest in being treated by plaintiff. At one point plaintiff's companion instructed Jeannie Weinstein, plaintiff's receptionist, not to confirm any information regarding AIDS, and "instruct patients that plaintiff did not have AIDS." Over an extended period of time, the practice diminished as more of plaintiff's patients became aware of his condition.

Cancellations continued at an exceedingly high rate. The effect of plaintiff's condition was not limited simply to patient relationships, but affected employees as well. As early as June 18, 1987, Weinstein, a long-standing employee of plaintiff, received an office telephone call from a local physician inquiring as to whether plaintiff had AIDS. Weinstein responded that she knew nothing about it but, thereafter, met with other employees in the office and told them of the phone call. During the two-week period after this call, some 15 to 20 calls were received from various patients indicating knowledge of plaintiff's condition. An extensive list was prepared by Weinstein indicating cancellation of appointments and patient requests for records. The list, for reasons not sufficiently explained, was kept only until September 1987, when the listing stopped. During this period, three employees left plaintiff's employ and a replacement employee left one day after being hired upon learning that plaintiff had contracted AIDS. During the two years following his AIDS diagnosis, plaintiff suffered from an ulcer, was hospitalized for one week for a virus, and as a result of his AIDS condition, lost sight in one eye. Plaintiff continued in an office practice until his death on July 2, 1989.***

The administration of plaintiff's blood test, resulting in a finding of HIV positivity, warrants a critical examination of the testing procedures and efforts made by medical center to insure confidentiality of results.

In 1985, the medical center began testing blood for HIV seropositivity for its blood bank. Since HIV testing was available for blood donors, HIV testing was also made available to staff physicians, both for inpatients and outpatients. Initially, the reporting procedures for both inpatients and outpatients required the physician to submit the blood to the laboratory with only a code number. After the test was completed, the results were returned to the physician under the code number, without the patient's name. This procedure was approved by the New Jersey Department of Health.

By 1986, many hospitals began to realize that the established procedures were unworkable for inpatients. In 1986, a meeting was held by the New Jersey Department of Health, which was attended by representatives of many New Jersey hospitals, including Pachter of the medical center. The consensus at the meeting was that inpatient testing could not be conducted under a code-number system for a variety of reasons including lack of cooperation by members of the medical staff. In addition, it was felt that HIV positive status was an important medical fact that should be included within a patient's medical chart.

In response to this meeting, the department of health issued new guidelines in October 1986 dealing with the reporting of HIV results for hospital inpatients. The new guidelines included the following:

1) Testing facilities must make reasonable efforts to maintain confidentiality.

2) For in-patients and clinic out patients, specimens may be received with the patient's name on them. These specimens must be encoded, (e.g., assignment of lab I.D. numbers) in the laboratory before testing occurs, so that test results do not appear with the patient's name in the laboratory's work records. The results of these assays may be placed on the patient chart in the same manner as other routine tests.

These stated procedures were designed to recognize and deal appropriately with the issue of confidentiality. While health care facilities recognized the need for confidentiality, an additional, yet critical, element of HIV-test protocol required communication with the patient. This communication took the form of pre-test counselling of patients prior to the administration of the HIV test.

Pre-test counselling for HIV blood tests has been the standard of practice since the beginning of HIV testing. Such counselling includes discussion about the disclosure of test results and an identification of those having access to test results. Before HIV tests are given, patients are counselled as to the privacy and confidentiality implications of being identified as HIV-infected. These implications are explained to symptomatic and asymptomatic patients alike. Members of the medical center's department of laboratories attended New Jersey Department of Health seminars prior to June 1987, at which pre-test counselling was addressed.***

While no question was raised at trial that the responsibility for pre-test counselling appropriately rested with the treating physician, the record is devoid of any suggestion that any pre-test counselling of plaintiff, either in oral or written form, took place during the period June 16 to June 18, 1987. While plaintiff was, by profession, a physician, he was, during this period, a patient at the medical center. No one in this litigation suggests that plaintiff was not entitled to all of the protections afforded any other patient. The informed consent form promulgated by the department of laboratories at the medical center and signed by plaintiff, does little to correct this apparent deficiency. The form provides as follows:

CONSENT FORM. . . .

I William Behringer hereby give my consent to the Medical Center at Princeton to have my blood tested for antibodies to HTLV III Virus as ordered by my physician. The results of the test will be reported only to the ordering physician.

Date <u>6/17/87</u>   Patient signature <u>(s)William</u>
                                                                 <u>Behringer</u>
                              Witness <u>(illegible)</u>

                              PATIENT CODE NO. <u>865353</u>

The test was ordered by the treating physician on admission and administered sometime on June 17, 1987. The informed consent form indicated a time of 1:00 p.m. At approximately 2:00 p.m., the infectious disease specialist went to the department of laboratories at the medical center to determine the status of plaintiff's HIV blood test. Upon learning that the test had not been conducted, the infectious disease specialist asked Lee to conduct the test on an expedited basis. Lee agreed and instructed the blood bank supervisor to conduct the test as soon as possible. Plaintiff's name was identified to the supervisor by the infectious disease consultant and Lee. Since plaintiff's blood sample was already in the lab, the sample had been given a code number, and plaintiff's name was removed from the sample. Plaintiff's name and code number had been placed in a locked filing cabinet pursuant to laboratory procedures. The supervisor went to the locked file cabinet, looked up plaintiff's name and obtained the code number for his blood sample. The blood sample was then located by reference to the code number and was given to a laboratory technician with instructions to conduct the HIV test. This occurred sometime between 2:30 and 3:30 p.m. The technician was not provided with the name of the patient for whom the HIV test was being conducted.

Since the technician left work at 3:30 p.m. each day and since the test takes approximately four hours, she did not conclude the test and thus did not learn the results. The test was concluded by the supervisor at approximately 6:00 p.m., at which time the results, which were positive, were relinked to plaintiff's name in the record maintained in the locked file cabinet pursuant to the standard procedures followed by the department of laboratories.***

On June 18, 1987, pursuant to normal procedures, the department of laboratories ran a follow-up confirmation HIV test. The result was again positive and a preprinted form was prepared indicating a positive result. The preprinted form was taken by the supervisor and presented to Pachter, who signed it.

Normal procedures within the department of laboratories called for the test result to be taken by a blood-bank technician and hand-carried to the patient's chart and placed in the section of the chart designated for laboratory results. All other laboratory test results are placed in the patient's medical chart by clerical personnel. This special procedure for HIV test results was implemented by the department of laboratories as an additional safeguard for patient confidentiality.

The above procedure was not immediately carried out but was delayed in an effort to protect plaintiff's confidentiality. In a telephone conversation during the afternoon of June 18, the treating physician and Pachter agreed that since plaintiff was to be discharged from the medical center late that afternoon, the HIV test results should be held back and charted as late in the day as possible. Therefore, consistent with the agreement reached with the treating physician, Pachter instructed the supervisor to hand-carry the result to the patient's chart just before she left for the day.*** She, without commenting on the HIV test or the results, placed the test results in the section of the chart designated for laboratory results.

At approximately 4:30 p.m. on June 18, 1987, plaintiff was discharged from the medical center.

While there is some dispute as to the propriety of charting as an acceptable medical practice, the medical center felt there were safeguards in the general confidentiality guidelines set forth in its by-laws and employee manuals. According to stated policy, charts were limited to those persons having patient-care responsibility, but in practical terms, the charts were available to any doctor, nurse or other hospital personnel. Despite the CDC's recommendation that access to HIV results be limited, the medical center had no policy physically restricting access to the HIV test results or the charts containing the results to those involved with the particular patient's care. In addition, the broad confidentiality policies of the medical center specifically restrict HCWs from discussing patient's charts with other HCWs.

The employees of the medical center were not given any instructions advising them of the confidentiality of HIV test results. The department of laboratories of the medical center took no steps to ensure that HIV test results were kept confidential by other departments of the medical center after being placed in patient charts. Under Lee, the department of laboratories ran no confidentiality training programs despite the fact that it was responsible for HIV testing.

Plaintiff's medical chart was kept at the nurses' station on the floor on which plaintiff was an inpatient. Not only was the HIV result charted, but his AIDS diagnosis was noted at numerous places therein. No effort was made to keep knowledge of this diagnosis limited to persons involved in plaintiff's care. There was no written or verbal restriction against any HCW involved in plaintiff's care discussing plaintiff's diagnosis with other medical center employees. Employees not involved in his care did learn of plaintiff's diagnosis. Employees of the medical center who had been plaintiff's patients ceased going to him for medical services. Given the significance of a physician-patient with a diagnosis of AIDS and the lack of special procedures directed at securing confidentiality, the inevitable happened.***

Plaintiff asserts that the medical center, Doody and Lee breached a duty of confidentiality in failing to restrict access to plaintiff's medical records, thus causing widespread and improper dissemination of information about plaintiff's medical condition. Plaintiff argues that as a result of this breach of confidentiality, his ability to practice was impaired so significantly that his medical practice was damaged, if not destroyed. Plaintiff's confidentiality-based claims arise out of his status as a *patient*. While plaintiff was unable to identify specifically the actual sources of the disclosure of his diagnosis, he argues that the medical center's failure to implement meaningful restrictions on access to his medical records is sufficient to establish liability. In sum, he urges that the failure of the medical center to take reasonable precautions regarding access to his records establishes liability. Defendants argue that any disclosure by its employees or others outside of its control is beyond its responsibility and cannot be the basis of liability.

The physician-patient privilege has a strong tradition in New Jersey. The privilege imposes an obligation on the physician to maintain the confidentiality of a patient's communications. This obligation of confidentiality applies to patient records and information and applies not only to physicians but to hospitals as well. This duty of confidentiality has been the subject of legislative codification which reflects the public policy of this State. *N.J.S.A.* 2A:84A–22.1 *et seq.****

It is against this basic policy and statutory framework that the conduct of a hospital dealing with an AIDS patient must be measured.***

The medical center's disregard for the importance of preserving the confidentiality of plaintiff's patient medical records was evident even before the charting of the HIV test results. A review of plaintiff's hospital chart reveals not only the HIV test results, but the results of the bronchoscopy—PCP—which all concede was a definitive diagnosis of AIDS. While the medical center argues that the decision regarding charting is one for the physicians to make, the medical center cannot avoid liability on that basis. It is not the charting *per se* that generates the issue; it is the easy *accessibility* to the charts and the lack of any meaningful medical center policy or procedure to limit access that causes the breach to occur. Where the impact of such accessibility is so clearly foreseeable, it is incumbent on the medical center, as the custodian of the charts, to take such reasonable measures as are necessary to insure that confidentiality. Failure to take such steps is negligence.*** Insuring confidentiality even by medical center employees required more, in the present case, than simply instructing employees that medical records are confidential. The charts are kept under the control of the medical center with full knowledge of the accessibility of such charts to virtually all medical center personnel whether authorized or not. Little, if any, action was taken to establish any policy or procedure for dealing with a chart such as plaintiff's.***

Because the stakes are so high in the case of a physician being treated at his own hospital, it is imperative that the hospital take reasonable steps to insure the confidentiality of not only an HIV test result, but a diagnosis which is conclusive of AIDS, such as PCP. These precautions may include a securing of the chart, with access only to those HCWs demonstrating to designated record-keepers a bona-fide need to know, or utilizing sequestration procedures for those portions of the record containing such information. While a designation in a chart of sequestered information such as a diagnosis or test result may lead to speculation or rumor among persons not having access to the chart, this speculation is an acceptable cost to prevent free access to a chart where real information improperly disseminated will cause untold harm. This court recognizes that in some circumstances, such as rounds at a teaching hospital, exposure to a patient's records must be greater than to solely physicians or students directly involved in the patient's care. It is incumbent upon the hospital to impress upon these physicians or students the significance of maintaining the confidentiality of patient records.

***The confidentiality breached in the present case is simply grist for a gossip mill with little concern for the impact of disclosure on the patient. While one can legitimately question the good judgment of a practicing physician choosing to undergo HIV testing or a bronchoscopy procedure at the same hospital where he practices, this apparent error in judgment does not relieve the medical center of its underlying obligation—to protect its patients against the dissemination of confidential information. It makes little difference to identify those who "spread the news." The information was too easily available, too titillating to disregard. All that was required was a glance at a chart, and the written words became whispers and the whispers became roars. And common sense told all that this would happen.

This court holds that the failure of the medical center and Lee as director of the department of laboratories, who were together responsible for developing the misstated informed consent form, the counselling procedure and implementation of the charting protocol, to take reasonable steps to maintain the confidentiality of plaintiff's medical records, while plaintiff was a patient, was a breach of the medical center's duty and obligation to keep such records confidential. The medical center is liable for damages caused by this breach.***

Notes and Issues for Discussion

1. What are the possible sources of breaches of confidentiality in this case—where might have the information about Behringer's AIDS condition come from?
2. In discussing the medical chart, kept at the nurses' station on the patient's floor, the court notes, "While there is some dispute as to the propriety of charting as an acceptable medical practice, the medical center felt there were safeguards in the general confidentiality guidelines set forth in its by-laws and employee manuals." Note that access to medical charts was limited by policy to those having patient-care responsibilities, but in reality, "the charts were available to any doctor, nurse or other hospital personnel." Given this, how confidential was the chart?
3. Consider also the attending physician's concern for protecting confidentiality and the steps taken to further this, including transfer to another hospital, the patient's release, and delaying the charting of the medical information. Don't these indicate the physician's concern about the hospital's ability to preserve confidentiality?
4. After Dr. Doody, the hospital administrator, initially revoked Behringer's surgical privileges, the hospital reinstated them conditioned upon a newly developed policy on physicians with AIDS. That policy dictated that the physician obtain an informed consent for surgery from any patient, notifying them that the physician was as AIDS carrier and informing them of the possible consequences. This policy was probably developed to protect the patients and to protect the hospital from liability. Are there other ways of protecting the patients? The hospital? Note that while this was a general policy, the only physician it currently applied to was Behringer. Is requiring such an informed consent merely an indirect way

to accomplish what Doody originally did—bar Behringer from surgical practice at the Medical Center?

5. What steps does your agency take to protect the confidentiality of an AIDS-infected patient or client? Are there written policies? In light of the *Barrington* and *Behringer* cases, are they adequate?

6. However, disclosure may be permitted for some purposes. In *State v. Stark,* 832 P.2d 109 (1992), a Washington appellate court permitted the disclosure of a confidential HIV test to a prosecutor to prohibit the individual from continuing to engage in "behavior dangerous to the public health." Stark was found guilty of intentionally exposing his sexual partners to HIV.

MANDATORY BLOOD TESTING

Despite general and specific privacy and confidentiality provisions protecting persons with AIDS, a number of states permit mandatory blood testing for the AIDS virus without informed consent in specific situations. Mandatory testing is also permissible for members of the U.S. Armed Forces and federal prisoners.[8] Various proposals have been advanced for mandatory premarital AIDS testing, and some states now mandate testing for prostitutes, some sexual offenders, health care workers, children going into foster care, and infants of drug abusing mothers. While confidentiality of this information is generally protected, disclosures are permitted in some situations.

The following case presents arguments for prohibiting blanket AIDS testing in the workplace without informed consent. Some states forbid such testing by statute. In *Glover,* the court refused to permit the testing, calling it an unreasonable bodily search and an ineffective way to control the spread of the virus.

GLOVER v. EASTERN NEBRASKA COMMUNITY OFFICE OF RETARDATION
686 F. Supp. 243 (1988)
U.S. DISTRICT COURT

STROM, CHIEF JUDGE.

The controversy in this case surrounds the Chronic Infectious Disease Policy No. 8.85 (the policy) adopted by the governing board of defendant Eastern Nebraska Human Services Agency (ENHSA) which requires certain employees to submit to mandatory testing for tuberculosis (TB), hepatitis B (HBV), and human immunodeficiency virus (HIV). The policy also contains a reporting requirement for employees who know or suspect they have any of the diseases and a disclosure requirement for employees who are hospitalized or receiving treatment for any of the diseases. This Court issued a temporary restraining order on December 7, 1987, restraining all testing for HIV and the reporting and disclosure requirements for all of the specified diseases. A revised policy was adopted on January 20, 1988, and it is the subject of this action.***

The policy in question requires employees in certain identified positions to submit to mandatory testing for tuberculosis (TB), the hepatitis B virus (HBV) and the human immunodeficiency virus (HIV or the AIDS virus), or be subjected to discipline for refusal to test.

The testing requirement will be applied annually if recommended by the agency's medical consultant to employees in the identified positions, and ENHSA reserves the right under the policy to require employees testing positive for TB, HBV or HIV to be tested more frequently than annually.

The policy also requires employees in the identified positions who know or suspect that they have a chronic infectious disease, as identified in the policy, to inform the ENCOR employee relations officer immediately. Failure to inform will result in disciplinary action which may include termination.

The policy requires employees in the identified positions hospitalized or receiving treatment for a chronic infectious disease, as identified in the policy, to submit the medical records relating to treatment for the disease to the ENCOR employee relations officer, if requested. [The disclosure requirement, Policy, Par. III(b)]. Curtis Starks, the affirmative action director and employee relations officer at ENHSA, will have responsibility for notifying ENCOR employees in the identified positions of positive test results.

The Eastern Nebraska Community Office of Retardation (ENCOR), a sub agency of the Eastern Nebraska Human Services Agency (ENHSA) is a community based program which provides residential, vocational and other specialized services for the mentally retarded. ENCOR serves approximately six hundred clients who are mentally retarded, ranging from the mild to the profound level of retardation. ENCOR's client based foundation respects the individual rights of its clients, and the agency works diligently to insure that these rights are upheld on behalf of these clients. ENCOR's philosophy recognizes the dignity of risk, thus permitting its clients to live life with all its inherent risks, as they live in a community setting.***

ENCOR began its concern with the AIDS virus as a result of general publicity about the AIDS problem.***

In July of 1987, ENCOR's concern with AIDS became more acute when it learned that two clients from the Omaha Manor facility, a private facility that had recently closed, who were transferred to the Beatrice State Development Center, tested positive for the AIDS virus. Even though these clients were eventually found to not have the virus, the intense concern had taken root at ENCOR.

In September of 1987, an ENCOR employee, unrelated to the Omaha Manor incident, died from AIDS. At this point, the ENHSA governing board instructed Executive Director Donald Moray to develop a policy for mandatory AIDS testing of employees. The original policy was announced and challenged by the ENCOR employees. After this Court restrained the policy, and pending the trial on the merits, the policy was reviewed and some aspects were changed. The new policy, effective January 20, 1988, states that the persons holding or applying for the following titles must undergo testing: home teacher, residential associate, residential assistant, vocational program manager, vocational production manager, registered nurse, and licensed practical nurse. The policy also states that new positions may be added to the list. The rationale behind testing staff members in the identified positions is that these positions involve extensive contact with clients. The evidence in this case, however, shows that staff members who hold non-test positions have also been the recipients of bites and scratches from ENCOR clients.

The evidence shows that the ENCOR staff member who died from AIDS was involved in numerous incidents where he was bitten, scratched, pinched, kicked and hit by clients. When this staff member died from AIDS, however, ENCOR did not follow up on the clients involved in any of these incidents, nor did they notify these clients or their guardians that ENCOR believed they were potentially at risk of contracting the AIDS virus because of the contact with this staff member.***

There is some evidence of sexual abuse of clients at ENCOR. These incidents, however, are not limited to staff/client contacts, of which there are few reported incidents. The testimony of the ENCOR staff members, Executive Director Moray, and Deputy Director Brinker are all in agreement and establish that there is not a sexual abuse problem at ENCOR.

The AIDS virus may be detected by two medical tests, the enzyme-linked immunoassay test (ELISA) or the confirmatory test, the Western blot. Both of these tests are blood tests which determine the presence of antibodies to the AIDS virus.

The ELISA test is a simple blood test which can detect the presence of antibodies to HIV. A positive ELISA test, however, does not mean that a person has AIDS; it merely signifies that, if the test results are accurate, the person has been exposed to the virus. A positive result on an ELISA test is not a finding that is reportable to the CDC for this positive finding is "not evidence of AIDS, but evidence of the agent of AIDS."

If the ELISA test is repeatedly reactive, the employee will be given the confirmatory Western blot examination. The confirmatory Western blot test is a more specific test which identifies antibodies to HIV antigens. The test, if positive for HIV, will show a pattern of distinctive bands appearing at certain points on a paper strip which correspond to those bands on a strip associated with HIV. There is a lack of consensus among laboratories, however, as to the point on the bands that indicate the presence of HIV.

The ELISA test has a significant number of false positives. The Western blot is a more reliable test with far fewer false positive results, yet they do occur. False positives occur as a result of laboratory error, either labeling errors or technical errors, previous illness, pregnancy, and because other retroviruses have the same molecular weight as the AIDS virus and can mimic a positive finding.

The State of Nebraska is a low prevalence area for the AIDS virus, that is, the amount of the disease in the State is low. As such, the predictive value of a positive result in any individual test is low, because the few positive test results that occur will contain some false positives. Thus, the percentage of false positives in a low prevalence community will be much higher than in a high prevalence community.

The medically indicated reasons for HIV testing are: (a) as an adjunct to the medical workup of a patient who may be infected, (b) for epidemiological purposes to establish the level of infection in a community, and (c) as a device used in conjunction with counseling those in high risk groups to stimulate them to change their high-risk behaviors. Testing in isolation as provided in ENCOR's policy does not serve these purposes.

The ELISA and Western blot tests are innocuous in themselves; however, the ramification of these tests gives rise to serious problems. A positive report of an HIV test is a "very foreboding kind of message." The reaction of patients to this news is devastation. If not handled properly, it can lead to disastrous results, including suicide. Because of the foreboding message that accompanies a positive HIV test result, some people simply do not want to know if they are infected.

In this case, the ENCOR employees who test positive would receive this devastating message from Curtis Starks, the affirmative action and employee relations officer at ENHSA. If Mr. Starks is unavailable, the personnel director will deliver the test results to employees. In addition, tested employees will not have the option of not being told of their test results.***

The evidence establishes that the risk of transmission of the AIDS virus from staff to client, assuming a staff member is infected with HIV, in the ENCOR environment is extremely low, approaching zero. The medical evidence is undisputed that the disease is not contracted by casual contact. The risk of transmission of the disease to clients as a result of a client biting or scratching a staff member, and potentially drawing blood, is extraordinarily low, also approaching zero. The risk of transmission of the virus from staff to client due to the staff member attending to a client's personal hygiene needs is zero. Further, there is absolutely no evidence of drug use or needle sharing at ENCOR, nor is there a problem of sexual abuse of clients by staff.

In short, the evidence in this case establishes that the risk of transmission of the HIV virus at ENCOR is minuscule at best and will have little, if any, effect in preventing the spread of HIV or in protecting the clients. Further, from a medical viewpoint, this policy is not necessary to protect clients from any medical risks.

This case raises issues involving the Fourth Amendment rights of public employees. The Fourth Amendment to the United States Constitution protects the "right of the people to be secure in their persons, houses, papers, and effects, against unreasonable searches and seizures. . .," rights which are implicated only if the conduct at issue infringes "an expectation of privacy that society is prepared to consider reasonable." *O'Connor v. Ortega*,—U.S.—, 107 S.Ct. 1492, 1497 (1987). The Fourth Amendment is enforceable against the states through the Fourteenth amendment and seeks to "safeguard the privacy and security of individuals against arbitrary invasions by governmental officials." *McDonell v. Hunter*, 809 F.2d 1302, 1305 (8th Cir.1987)

Individuals have a reasonable expectation of privacy in the personal information their body fluids contain. Compulsory administration of a blood test "plainly involves the broadly conceived reach of a search and seizure under the Fourth Amendment." *Schmerber v. California*, 384 U.S. 757, 767 (1966). The mandatory testing required by the policy involves an involuntary intrusion into the body by the State for the purposes of withdrawing blood and constitutes a search and seizure for purposes of the Fourth Amendment. Having determined that the mandatory blood tests required by the policy constitutes a search and seizure, this Court must then determine whether the search meets the Fourth Amendment test of reasonableness.

To determine the appropriate standard of reasonableness in this matter, this Court must balance the "nature and quality of the intrusion on the individual's Fourth Amendment interests against the importance of the governmental interests alleged to justify the intrusion." *O'Connor*, 107 S.Ct. at 1499. In this matter, the Court must balance the ENCOR employees' reasonable expectations of privacy with ENCOR's interest in a safe training and living environment for all developmentally disabled persons receiving services from the agency.

That the AIDS "epidemic" is a matter of great concern to the public and to the government is a matter of common knowledge. The presently devastating character of this disease is frightening to everyone. It is in such circumstances that governmental units, the public, and most importantly, the courts, do not overreact and permit unreasonable invasions into a carefully formulated and preserved constitutional right as a response to this concern. Thus the Court is guided by the standard which requires that "both the inception and the scope of the intrusion must be reasonable." *O'Connor v. Ortega*, 107 S.Ct. at 1503. After careful consideration, the Court finds that the mandatory blood testing policy is not justified at its inception and constitutes an unreasonable search and seizure in violation of the Fourth Amendment to the United States Constitution.

ENHSA's justification for the testing is the pursuit of a safe work environment for all employees and a safe training and living environment for its clients. The medical evidence, however, demonstrates that even if staff members were infected with a chronic infectious disease, the risk to ENHSA's clients is extremely low and approaches zero. The medical evidence is overwhelming that the risk of transmission of the AIDS virus in the ENCOR work place is trivial to the point of non-existence. Such a theoretical risk does not justify a policy which interferes with the constitutional rights of the staff members.

Although the pursuit of a safe work environment for employees and a safe training and living environment for all clients is a worthy one, the policy does not reasonably serve that purpose. There is simply no real basis to be concerned that clients are at risk of contracting the AIDS virus at the work place. These clients are not in danger of contracting the AIDS virus from staff members and such an unreasonable fear cannot justify a policy which intrudes on staff members' constitutionally protected rights.

There was testimony in this case that there can be no guarantee that the ENCOR clients could not possibly contract the AIDS virus, and thus the policy is necessary because of the devastating consequences of the disease. This overly cautious, "better to be safe than sorry" approach, however, is impermissible as it infringes on the constitutional rights of the staff members to be free from unreasonable searches and seizures.

In addition, the mandatory testing of staff members is not an effective way to prevent the spread of the disease. This policy simply ignores the current state of medical knowledge which establishes that the AIDS virus is not contracted by casual contact. The defendants are simply asking that this Court approve their policy because it is better to be safe than sorry. Donald Moray, the Executive Director of ENCOR, stated that his paramount concern was to "protect clients at all cost." This approach is impermissible for "at all cost" in this case includes the violation of the plaintiffs' constitutional rights.

The Court is convinced that the evidence, considered in its entirety, leads to the conclusion that the policy was prompted by concerns about the AIDS virus, formulated with little or erroneous medical knowledge, and is a constitutionally impermissible reaction to a devastating disease with no known cure. The risk of transmission of the disease from the staff to the clients at ENCOR is minuscule, trivial, extremely low, extraordinarily low, theoretical, and approaches zero. Such a risk does not justify the implementation of such a sweeping policy which ignores and violates the staff members' constitutional rights.***

Accordingly, a separate order will be issued this date in conformity with this opinion enjoining the defendant from implementing ENHSA policy 8.85, the chronic infectious disease policy.

Notes and Issues for Discussion

1. What were the court's reasons for not permitting blanket testing in *Glover*? Do you agree?
2. The *Glover* court also held that mandatory testing of staff for HBV (hepatitis B virus) was not justified because other protective measures were available, including HBV immunization of clients or treating a not-immunized exposed client with hepatitis B immune globulin.

DISCLOSURE OF AIDS OR HIV

A growing number of states not only mandate some AIDS testing but permit the disclosure of a person's AIDS/HIV condition under limited circumstances.

Disclosure to Spouse or Sexual Partner

Among those permitting disclosure to a spouse or a sexual partner are California (Cal. Health and Safety Code §199.25), Connecticut (Conn. Acts §246), Florida (Fla. Stats. §455.2416, Maryland, (Md. Laws §783); Michigan (Mich. Stats. §331.513), Pennsylvania (Pa. Stats. Tit. 35 §7609), and Texas (Tex. Health and Safety Code Ann. §81.103), as well as the Veterans Administration (38 U.S.C. §4132).

The California statute provides for immunity from civil or criminal liability for physicians and surgeons:

[N]o physician and surgeon who has the results of a confirmed positive test to detect infection by the probable causative agent of acquired immune deficiency syndrome of a patient under his or her care shall be held criminally or civilly liable for disclosing to a person reasonably believed to be the spouse, or to a person reasonably believed to be a sexual partner or a person with whom the patient has shared the use of hypodermic needles, or to the county health officer, that the patient has tested positive on a test to detect infection by the probable causative agent of acquired immune deficiency syndrome, except that no physician and surgeon shall disclose any identifying information about the individual believed to be infected. Cal. Health and Safety Code §199.25(a).

Disclosure may not be made unless the physician and surgeon

has first discussed the test results with the patient and offered the patient appropriate educational and psychological counseling, which shall include information on the risks of transmitting the human immunodeficiency virus to other people and methods of avoiding those risks, and has attempted to obtain the patient's voluntary consent for notification of his or her contacts. The physician and surgeon shall notify the patient of his or her intent to notify the patient's contacts prior to any notification. When the information is disclosed . . . the physician and surgeon shall refer that person for appropriate care, counseling, and followup. . . . Cal. Health and Safety Code §199.25(b).

Disclosure is

permissive on the part of the attending physician. . . . No physician has a duty to notify any person of the fact that a patient is reasonably believed to be infected by the probable causative agent of acquired immune deficiency syndrome. Cal. Health and Safety Code §199.25(c).

Within the Veterans Administration system, notification may be made to a spouse or sexual partner that a patient is infected with HIV under certain conditions. The VA hospital exception provides that if the patient refuses to inform a spouse or sexual partner, and the professional believes the individual is at risk,

. . . subject to paragraph (2), a physician or a professional counselor may disclose information or records indicating that a patient or subject is infected with the human immunodeficiency virus if the disclosure is made to (A) the spouse of the patient or subject, or (B) to an individual who the patient or subject has, during the process of professional counseling or of testing to determine whether the patient or subject is infected with such virus, identified as being a sexual partner of such patient or subject.

(2)(A) A disclosure under paragraph (1) may be made only if the physician or counselor, after making reasonable efforts to counsel and encourage the patient or subject to provide the information to the spouse or sexual partner, reasonably believes that the patient or subject will not provide the information to the spouse or sexual partner and that the disclosure is necessary to protect the health of the spouse or sexual partner. 38 U.S.C. §7332(f)(1).

The two statutes have significant differences: The VA statute includes professional counselors as well as physicians within those who may disclose. The California statute is more detailed, is clearer about immunity from liability, includes needle-sharing partners, requires patient notification, forbids disclosing identifying information, and mandates referral for counseling and follow-up.

Disclosure to Patients or Clients

Following the Kimberly Bergalis case in Florida, in which a young patient was apparently infected with AIDS by her dentist, there has been growing pressure for AIDS testing and the regulation of HIV-infected health care workers, including restricting the performance of invasive procedures, notifying patients of the health care workers' condition and obtaining informed consent prior to surgical procedures.

APPLICATION OF MILTON S. HERSHEY MEDICAL CENTER
595 A.2d 1290 (1990)
PENNSYLVANIA SUPERIOR COURT

POPOVICH, JUDGE.

This appeal involves a delicate issue of first impression in this Commonwealth. We are asked to decide whether the trial court correctly permitted two hospitals to disclose the identity of a member of their staffs who tested positive for the Human Immunodeficiency Virus (HIV). The physician, whose pseudonym John Doe has become familiar to this Court, was an obsterics/gynecology resident working alternately between the Milton S. Hershey Medical Center to the Pennsylvania State University ("Hershey Medical Center") and the Harrisburg Hospital. Dr. Doe, during an invasive, internal procedure, sustained a cut through his surgical glove and exposed a patient to his infected blood. Although the risk that the patient contracted the HIV infection was minimal, the possibility was there and, thus, litigation ensued. The outcome was the trial court's order compelling disclosure of Dr. Doe's name and certain medical information to a limited populace. This appeal followed.

Because the specific facts of this case are so important to our discussion, we take this opportunity to detail its history more fully. Dr. Doe was a resident physician participating in a four year program involving obstetrics and gynecology. On May 19, 1991, during the course of an invasive operative procedure, Dr. Doe was accidentally cut by the attending physician. The record does not indicate whether there was an actual transfer of blood between Dr. Doe and the patient. It appears that there was not, although no one can be certain.

The following day, Dr. Doe voluntarily submitted to blood testing for the HIV virus. On May 21, 1991, Dr. Doe was informed that the test results were positive. At that time, Dr. Doe voluntarily withdrew from participation in further surgical procedures. An additional test called the Western Blot was performed on Dr. Doe's blood. The results, which were returned on May 28, 1991, confirmed that Dr. Doe was HIV positive. Dr. Doe informed the appropriate officials of his condition and pursued a voluntary leave of absence.

After investigation, Hershey Medical Center identified 279 patients who had been involved to some degree with Dr. Doe in the course of their medical treatment. Likewise, Harrisburg Hospital identified 168 patients who had been in contact with Dr. Doe since the time of his joint residency. As Dr. Doe points out, the nature and degree of his participation in the medical treatments were not presented to either the trial court or this Court. Unfortunately, as has been explained to this Court during oral arguments, the hospital records do not necessarily reflect each time a physician is cut; nor do they particularize the distinct role played by each physician during a surgical procedure. Thus, every patient who reasonably may have been exposed to Dr. Doe's condition was included in the statistics outlined above.

Both Hershey Medical Center and Harrisburg Hospital filed petitions alleging that there was a "compelling need" to disclose information regarding Dr. Doe's condition to the patients potentially affected by contact with him, as well as to certain staff members. The hospitals proceeded under The Confidentiality of HIV-Related Information Act ("The Act"), 35 P.S. §§7601–7612, particularly § 7608(a)(2). They argued, *inter alia*, that disclosure of Dr. Doe's identity was necessary to prevent the spread of the AIDS disease. Most basically, the hospitals felt it their duty to inform the possibly affected individuals of their potential exposure to HIV and to offer them treatment, testing and counseling.

In addition, the hospitals believed that there was a compelling need to disclose Dr. Doe's name to the other treating physicians in the department, so that those physicians could contact their patients in the event that Dr. Doe assisted in any invasive procedures which involved them. Finally, the hospitals felt that a limited disclosure was necessary to protect the other health professionals from stigmatism and to alleviate any "mass hysteria" that could result from a general disclosure. By providing the patients with adequate and sound information, at least those who were not involved with the obstetrics/gynecology division could be assured that they were not at risk to contract the HIV virus. In response, Dr. Doe asserted his right to privacy and argued that a compelling need did not exist tantamount to justifying the disclosure of his HIV-related information.

The trial court issued an order allowing limited disclosure on June 14, 1991. The order was accompanied by an opinion. That day, Dr. Doe filed a notice of appeal to this Court.

The issue presented for our review is whether the hospitals sustained their burden of demonstrating a "compelling need" for the disclosure of Dr. Doe's HIV status in light of the strong proscriptions against disclosure under the Act. The trial court, after weighing the competing needs of public disclosure versus the doctor's privacy interest, found that the hospitals had met the test and ordered that Dr. Doe's identity and his HIV-related information be revealed, selectively.***

The Confidentiality of HIV-Related Information Act, was promulgated to promote voluntary blood testing to limit the spread of the Acquired Immune Deficiency Syndrome (AIDS). In the interest of furthering public health, the Act assures that information gained as a result of the HIV testing will remain confidential.*** The disclosure of an individual's HIV-related status is subject to stringent regulation and few exceptions.***

As with most rules, however, there are provisions for special circumstances. This case represents one of them.

***Section 7 of the Act dictates that those in possession of confidential information relating to an individual's HIV status must respect an obligation of confidentiality. Specifically, it provides, in pertinent part:

> No person or employee, or agent of such person, who obtains confidential HIV-related information in the course of providing any health or social service or pursuant to a release of confidential HIV-related information under subsection (c) may disclose or be compelled to disclose the information, except to the following persons: [. . . .] (10)[a] person allowed access to the information by a court order issued pursuant to section 8 [35 P.S. §7608].

Dr. Doe did not consent to the disclosure of his identity or health status. Thus, the hospitals invoked the language of Section 8(a)(2) of the Act which reads:

> (a) Order to Disclose.—No court may issue an order to allow access to confidential HIV-related information unless the court finds, upon application, that one of the following conditions exists: [. . . .] (2) The person seeking to disclose the information has a compelling need to do so.

35 P.S. §7608(a)(2). The general term "compelling need" may encompass any number of circumstances. The Act provides us with a standard for assessing "compelling need," but fails to define the phrase or set forth examples of what would constitute it. Under 36 P.S. §7608(c), to determine the existence of "compelling need" the courts must engage in a balancing analysis. "In assessing compelling need for subsections (a) and (b), the court shall weigh the need for

disclosure against the privacy interest of the individual and the public interests which may be harmed by disclosure."

Given the infectious nature of the HIV virus, coupled with the fact that full blown AIDS is in all cases fatal, there is no question that Hershey Medical Center and Harrisburg Hospital were faced with a grave dilemma. Unquestionably, medical professionals have a duty to insure the health of their patients to the best of their capabilities.*** Surely, when individuals visit their doctors, they do not expect to confront a risk of illness different from that which they already suffer. A hospital, which invites the sick and infirm, impliedly assures its patients that they will receive safe and adequate medical care. Thus, there is instilled public confidence in the health care system. It is understandable that Hershey Medical Center and Harrisburg Hospital were concerned about their obligations to their patients. At the same time, the Act in question affords confidentiality to those carrying the HIV virus.

In this case, we have an added factor to consider. The physician who was infected by this potentially contagious and ultimately deadly virus, was involved in invasive surgical procedures where the risk of sustaining cuts and exposing patients to tainted blood was high. According to researchers, while the chances of transmitting the HIV virus via surgical procedures is very slim—one commentator has estimated the chances to be $\frac{1}{48,000}$—the potential is nevertheless there. When one begins to calculate how many individuals may be subjected to the same risk by the same medical worker, multiplied by the aggregate of infected health care professionals, the numbers become staggering.

Surely, it is no consolation to the one or two individuals who become infected after innocently consenting to medical care by an unhealthy doctor that they were part of a rare statistic.

Here, given the nature of Dr. Doe's residency and his involvement with the surgical teams at two hospitals, it is beyond dispute that the appellees demonstrated a compelling need for disclosure.***

Dr. Doe strenuously argues that to allow future disclosures will be counterproductive and will discourage health professionals from seeking voluntary HIV testing. He contends that the facts here did not warrant the trial court's remedy and that if disclosure is permitted under the instant facts, the harm to the public interest in future like circumstances will be severe. Summarizing, Dr. Doe states:

> The public will be given a message that having an HIV-infected physician, per se, creates a risk of AIDS. Hospitals in the future will risk liability if they fail to follow through with similar unsubstantiated notifications to patients. The already high cost of medical care will be increased because of needless repetitious HIV testing. The high cost of medical malpractice insurance will be increased by imposing a notification standard which goes beyond a [sound] public health policy, and physicians and other health care workers will be discouraged from treating those infected with HIV.

***After weighing the competing interests in this case, we find that the scales tip in favor of the public health, regardless of the small potential for transmittal of the fatal virus.

Notes and Issues for Discussion

1. What are the arguments for disclosure of Dr. Doe's AIDS condition? Against disclosure?
2. The hospital disclosed nonidentifying information to the 450 patients with whom Dr. Doe had some involvement, and in addition, notified the other treating physicians of Dr. Doe's condition and identity. The disclosure was necessary "to protect the other health professionals from stigmatism and to alleviate mass hysteria." What do you think?
3. *Love v. Superior Court*, 276 Cal. Rptr. 660 (1990), upheld a California statute requiring mandatory AIDS testing for those convicted of prostitution, which is coupled to a law providing that if a prostitute tests positive for HIV, subsequent prostitution convictions will become felonies.
4. In another section of the *Behringer Estate v. Princeton Medical Center* decision, the court upheld a hospital policy which required Behringer to obtain informed consent from patients before invasive surgery, informing them of his AIDS condition. The Centers for Disease Control (CDC) have at various times supported and opposed this approach. In 1991, the CDC recommended that health care workers performing exposure-prone procedures should ascertain their HIV status and if HIV positive should not perform such procedures without patient informed consent. (CDC Guidelines, 1991). In 1988, the American Medical Association's Council on Ethical and Judicial Affairs adopted the position that an HIV-infected physician "should not engage in any activity that creates a risk of transmission for others."

DISCRIMINATION AGAINST PERSONS WITH AIDS

As was seen in Chapter 12, both §504 of the Rehabilitation Act of 1973, 29 U.S.C. §794, and the Americans with Disabilities Act of 1990, 42 U.S.C. §12101 *et seq.*, prohibit discrimination in the workplace against individuals with disabilities. In *Arline v. School Board of Nassau County* (see p. 409), the Supreme Court found that Arline's recurring tuberculosis was a handicapping condition that qualified her for protection under §504. In a footnote to that decision, the Court refused to address whether persons with AIDS are covered under §504. To date the U.S. Supreme Court has not dealt with the issue, however a number of lower courts have found that persons with AIDS or HIV come within the criteria of a person with a disability and qualify for protection under §504. Since the A.D.A. provides similar protections to many non-federally funded workplaces, presumably these protections would extend to covered employees.

Discrimination in the Workplace

The *Chalk* decision is one of the early cases that extends §504 protections to those with AIDS.

CHALK v. U.S. DISTRICT COURT
840 F.2d 701 (1988)
U.S. COURT OF APPEALS

POOLE, CIRCUIT JUDGE.

Petitioner Vincent L. Chalk is a certified teacher of hearing-impaired students in the Orange County Department of Education. In February of 1987, Chalk was diagnosed as having Acquired Immune Deficiency Syndrome (AIDS). Subsequently, the Department reassigned Chalk to an administrative position and barred him from teaching in the classroom. Chalk then filed this action in the district court, claiming that the Department's action violated §504 of the Rehabilitation Act of 1973, 29 U.S.C.A. §794 (West Supp.1987), as amended, which proscribes recipients of federal funds from discriminating against otherwise qualified handicapped persons.

Chalk's motion for a preliminary injunction ordering his reinstatement was denied by the district court, and Chalk brought this appeal. After hearing oral argument, we issued an order reversing the district court and directing it to issue the preliminary injunction. In this opinion, we now set forth in full the reasons underlying our reversal.

Petitioner Chalk has been teaching hearing-impaired students in the Orange County schools for approximately six years. In February 1987, Chalk was hospitalized with pneumocystis carinii pneumonia and was diagnosed as having AIDS. On April 20, after eight weeks of treatment and recuperation, he was found fit for duty and released to return to work by his personal physician, Dr. Andrew Siskind. The Department, however, placed him on administrative leave pending the opinion of Dr. Thomas J. Prendergast, the Director of Epidemiology and Disease Control for the Orange County Health Care Agency. On May 22, Dr. Prendergast informed the Department that "[n]othing in his [Chalk's] role as a teacher should place his students or others in the school at any risk of acquiring HIV infection."

Chalk agreed to remain on administrative leave through the end of the school year in June. On August 5, Chalk and representatives of the Department met to discuss his return to the classroom. The Department offered Chalk an administrative position at the same rate of pay and benefits, with the option of working either at the Department's offices or at his home, and informed him that if he insisted on returning to the classroom, it would file an action for declaratory relief. Chalk refused the offer. On August 6, the Department filed an action in the Orange County Superior Court, and Chalk filed this action in the district court seeking a preliminary and permanent injunction barring the Department from excluding him from classroom duties.***

Chalk bases his claim on section 504 of the Rehabilitation Act of 1973, 29 U.S.C. §794, as amended (the Act), which provides:

> No otherwise qualified individual with handicaps . . . shall, solely by reason of his handicap, be excluded from the participation in . . . or be subjected to discrimination under any program or activity receiving Federal financial assistance . . .

As the district court recognized, the Supreme Court recently held that section 504 is fully applicable to individuals who suffer from contagious diseases. *School Bd. of Nassau County v. Arline.*—U.S.—, 107 S.Ct. 1123 (1987).***

In applying this standard to the facts before it, the Court recognized the difficult circumstances which confront a handicapped person, an employer, and the public in dealing with the possibility of contagion in the workplace. The problem is in reconciling the needs for protection of other persons, continuation of the work mission, and reasonable accommodation—if possible —of the afflicted individual. The Court effected this reconciliation by formulating a standard for determining when a contagious disease would prevent an individual from being "otherwise qualified":

> A person who poses a significant risk of communicating an infectious disease to others in the workplace will not be otherwise qualified for his or her job if reasonable accommodation will not eliminate that risk. The Act would not require a school board to place a teacher with active, contagious tuberculosis in a classroom with elementary school children.

The application of this standard requires, in most cases, an individualized inquiry and appropriate findings of fact, so that "§504 [may] achieve its goal of protecting handicapped individuals from deprivations based on prejudice, stereotypes, or unfounded fear, while giving appropriate weight to such legitimate concerns of grantees as avoiding exposing others to significant health and safety risks." *Id.* at 1131. Specifically, *Arline* requires a trial court to make findings regarding four factors: "(a) the nature of the risk (how the disease is transmitted), (b) the duration of the risk (how long is the carrier infectious), (c) the severity of the risk (what is the potential harm to third parties) and (d) the probabilities the disease will be transmitted and will cause varying degrees of harm." Findings regarding these factors should be based "on reasonable medical judgments given the state of medical knowledge," and courts should give particular deference to the judgments of public health officials.

Chalk submitted in evidence to the district court, and that court accepted, more than 100 articles from prestigious medical journals and the declarations of five experts on AIDS, including two public health officials of Los Angeles County. Those submissions reveal an overwhelming evidentiary consensus of medical and scientific opinion regarding the nature and transmission of AIDS. AIDS is caused by infection of the individual with HIV, a retrovirus that penetrates chromosomes of certain human cells that combat infection throughout the body. Individuals who become infected with HIV may remain without symptoms for an extended period of time. When the disease takes hold, however, a number of symptoms can occur, including swollen lymph nodes, fever, weight loss, fatigue and night sweats. Eventually, the virus destroys its host cells, thereby weakening the victim's immune system. When the immune system is in a compromised state, the victim becomes susceptible to a variety of so-called "opportunistic infections," many of which can prove fatal.

Transmission of HIV is known to occur in three ways: (1) through intimate sexual contact with an infected person, (2) through invasive exposure to contaminated blood or certain other bodily fluids; or (3) through perinatal exposure (ie., from mother to infant). Although HIV has been isolated in several body fluids, epidemiologic evidence has implicated only blood, semen, vaginal secretions, and possibly breast milk in transmission. Extensive and numerous studies have consistently found no apparent risk of HIV infection to individuals exposed through close, non-sexual contact with AIDS patients.

Based on the accumulated body of medical evidence, the Surgeon General of the United States has concluded:

> There is no known risk of non-sexual infection in most of the situations we encounter in our daily lives. We know that family members living with individuals who have the AIDS virus do not become infected except through sexual contact. There is no evidence of transmission (spread) of AIDS virus by everyday contact even though these family members shared food, towels, cups, razors, even toothbrushes, and kissed each other.

The only opposing medical opinion submitted by the Department was that of one witness, Dr. Steven Armentrout, that "there is a probability, small though it is, that there are vectors of transmission as yet not clearly defined." He elaborated on his opinion as follows:

> I believe, sincerely believe that there is a significant, and significant here— it's significant even though it's small, potential for transmission of AIDS in ways which we have not yet determined and, therefore, may pose a risk . . . If they don't occur now, it is my firm belief that with the almost inevitable mutation of the virus, they will occur. And when that does occur, they certainly could be—there can be a potential threat.

Asked whether there was a scientific basis for such a hypothesis, Dr. Armentrout indicated that he had "no scientific evidence that would enable me to answer that or to have an opinion. . . . What we're saying is that we haven't proved scientifically a vector."

The district judge addressed each of the four *Arline* factors in his ruling. He found that the duration of the risk was long and the severity was "catastrophic," but that scientifically established methods of transmission were unlikely to occur and that the probability of harm was minimal. He therefore concluded that Chalk "may very well win ultimately." Nonetheless, the district judge expressed skepticism about the current state of medical knowledge. He was troubled that there might be something yet unknown to science that might do harm. He said:

> Now, here, according to present knowledge, the risk probably is not great because of the limited ways that medical science believes the disease is transmitted. But, of course, if it is transmitted the result is horrendous.
>
> It seems to me the problem is that we simply do not know enough about AIDS to be *completely certain*. The plaintiff has submitted massive documentation tending to show a minimal risk. . . . But in any event, the risk is small—risk of infection through casual contact. . . . The incubation period is reported to be seven years. We have been studying this only for six. And I do not in any sense mean to be an alarmist. I—I reiterate, I think the risk is small. The likelihood is that the medical profession knows exactly what it's talking about. But I think it's too early to draw a definite conclusion, as far as this case is concerned, about the extent of the risk.

This language demonstrates that the district court failed to follow the legal standards set forth in *Arline* and improperly placed an impossible burden of proof on the petitioner. Little in science can be proved with complete certainty, and section 504 does not require such a test. As authoritatively construed by the Supreme Court, section 504 allows the exclusion of an employee only if there is "a *significant* risk of communicating an infectious disease to others." *Arline,* 107 S.Ct. at 1131 n. 16 (emphasis added). In addition, *Arline* admonishes courts that they "should defer to the reasonable medical judgments of public health officials." The district judge ignored these admonitions. Instead, he rejected the overwhelming consensus of medical opinion and improperly relied on speculation for which there was no credible support in the record.

That Chalk demonstrates a strong probability of success on the merits is supported by the three published opinions brought to our attention dealing with AIDS discrimination under section 504.***

Viewing Chalk's submissions in light of these cases, it is clear that he has amply demonstrated a strong probability of success on the merits. We hold that it was error to require that every theoretical possibility of harm be disproved.***

We conclude that petitioner met all of the requirements necessary to receive a preliminary injunction. We therefore reverse the district court's order and remand this action with direction to enter a preliminary injunction ordering defendants forthwith to restore petitioner to his former duties as a teacher of hearing-impaired children in the Orange County Department of Education.

Notes and Issues for Discussion

1. The district judge held that as long as there was any risk of transmission—unless one could be completely certain that was no possibility of infection—then Chalk could be removed from the classroom. What does the appellate court find wrong with this approach? What do you think?
2. In a footnote to the case, the court observes, "there is no evidence . . . that

Chalk is currently suffering from any opportunistic infections." The court indicated that if he later developed a communicable disease it would be appropriate under *Arline* to treat him as any other teacher with a communicable infection.

3. In *Leckelt v. Board of Commissioners*, 909 F.2d 820 (1990), the court upheld the dismissal of a nurse because he refused to divulge the results of an AIDS test. He had previously been identified as a homosexual and the roommate of a patient who had recently died of AIDS. The court held there was no violation of §504 because the dismissal was for insubordination, not because of an AIDS condition. What if Leckelt gave the hospital the results and he was HIV positive? Could they fire him? Reassign him?

Discrimination in the Schools

The plight of Ryan White, a young student who contracted AIDS through a blood transfusion and was repeatedly denied admittance to public schools, illustrates some of the problems of children with AIDS. A number of cases have been litigated, with the final decision usually allowing the child to enter or remain in school, often on the legal grounds of discrimination against a person with a disability.

DOE v. DOLTON ELEMENTARY SCHOOL DIST. NO. 148
694 F.Supp. 440 (1988)
U.S. DISTRICT COURT

NORGLE, DISTRICT JUDGE.

This is a motion for a preliminary injunction to return Student # 9387, a student who has Acquired Immune Deficiency Syndrome ("AIDS"), to his regular classes as a full-time student. *See* Fed.R.Civ.P. 65(a). For the following reasons, the motion is granted.

AIDS is a disease caused by a retrovirus that invades certain body cells which are vital to the immune system. Eventually, the virus kills its host cells, resulting in a decrease in the body's ability to combat disease.

An AIDS victim initially becomes a carrier of the AIDS virus. The carrier can transmit the virus to others, but is himself asymptomatic. It is, however, generally agreed that more than fifty percent of the carriers of the AIDS virus will eventually contract the AIDS disease.

A person has AIDS Related Complex ("ARC") when he carries the AIDS virus and exhibits symptoms of a weakened immune system. This indicates that the person is no longer a mere "carrier"; he has been attacked by the virus: The ARC symptoms can be fatal. Once a person's immune system is weakened, he is susceptible to diseases which uninfected persons' immune systems can easily fight off. Such diseases are labeled "opportunistic infections." Once a person contracts an opportunistic infection, he is diagnosed as having the AIDS disease. The opportunistic infections cause most AIDS deaths. A person with AIDS can contract any of a number of opportunistic infections; AIDS is a syndrome, and thus affects individuals in various ways. Furthermore, there is no known cure for AIDS, and the disease is believed to be fatal in every instance. A carrier of the AIDS virus may contract the AIDS disease without ever exhibiting symptoms of ARC.

The AIDS virus is transmitted through exchange of bodily fluids: blood, semen, and vaginal/cervical secretions. The virus has been found in saliva and tears, but the concentration is so low and the virus so fragile that the possibility of transmission through those fluids is remote. No known cases of transmission through saliva or tears have been reported. As a result, the AIDS virus is transmitted by intimate sexual contact, blood transfusions, and use of contaminated drug needles. It may also be passed from infected mothers to fetuses or to infants through breast feeding, and, in a few instances, from patients to hospital personnel in accidental fluid exchanges.

Student # 9387 ("the Student") is enrolled in Dolton Elementary School District # 148, Cook County, Illinois ("the School District"). The Student is twelve years old. He underwent open heart surgery three times as a child, at ages three months, three years and six years.

In July, 1986, the Student was hospitalized for rash and high fever of unknown origin. The fever subsided and he was well for two weeks. He then developed thrush, fever, and a swollen cheek and lip. He was readmitted to the hospital, where he was diagnosed as infected with the Human Immunodeficiency Virus ("HIV") (HIV is the AIDS virus). The doctors concluded that he must have contracted the virus through blood transfusions during one or more of the operations. The court is not required to determine the correctness of these conclusions. As of September 10, 1987, the Student was diagnosed as an asymptomatic carrier of the AIDS virus. However, by October, 1987, the time of the filing of this lawsuit, the Student had ARC.

In February, 1988, the Student's attending physician, Dr. Raoul Wolf, diagnosed him as having AIDS. The Student had exhibited symptoms of diarrhea, fever, thrush, loss of weight, infections in the form of cellulitis of his episodes (inflammations), pneumonia, and a T-4 (white blood) cell level below normal.

At last report, however, the Student exhibited no pneumonia. He had, however, cold sore on the upper lip, and oral thrush. He had no diarrhea or other abnormal bodily secretions. He has never exhibited aggressive, abnormal, or antisocial behavior.

On September 28, 1987, upon being informed that the Student was infected with the AIDS virus, the Board of Education of the School District excluded the Student from attending the school's regular education classes and extracurricular activities. On October 8, 1987, the Student filed an eight count complaint alleging various federal and state constitutional and statutory violations. Subsequently, the present Motion for Preliminary Injunction was filed asserting that 1) the School District, as a recipient of federal aid, had violated Section 504 of the Federal Rehabilitation Act of 1973, 29 U.S.C. §794, which prohibits recipients of such aid from discriminating against handicapped individuals, and 2) it had violated the Student's right to an equal education in the free schools of the State of Illinois, as guaranteed by Section 10-20.12 of the Illinois School Code, Ill.Rev.Stat. ch. 122, ¶ 10–20.12 (1985).

By late October, 1987, the School District received the written medical reports of Dr. Wolf and Dr. Kenneth Rich, the School District's physician. The medical reports were in complete agreement. Both concluded no known medical reason existed for excluding the student from school, given his condition at the time.

On January 15, 1988, the School District's Clinical Psychologist, Barry Zaransky, Psy.D., evaluated the Student. Dr. Zaransky's report indicated that the Student was capable of regular classroom attendance and that his exclusion from the classroom was contributing to a loss of self-esteem.

Pursuant to Rule 706 of the Federal Rules of Evidence, the court appointed Dr. Robert Murphy, Director of the AIDS Clinic at Northwestern University Medical School, as its medical expert. Dr. Murphy examined the Student, the Student's medical records, and the medical authorities submitted by the parties. Dr. Murphy's June 8, 1988 report to the court was in accord with those of the parties' medical experts. Dr. Murphy found there was no medical reason for excluding the Student from a regular classroom environment, so long as the Student had no open lesions, sores or other illnesses.***

Here, the Student's claim is based primarily on 29 U.S.C. §794, §504 of the Rehabilitation Act of 1973, which states in pertinent part:

> No otherwise qualified handicapped individual in the United States, as defined in section 706(7) of this title, shall, solely by reason of his handicap, be excluded from the participation in, be denied the benefits of, or be subjected to discrimination under any program or activity receiving Federal financial assistance. . . .

Therefore, in order for the Student to prevail on the merits, the court must find that the Student is a "handicapped individual" and is "otherwise qualified" to attend school under Section 504.

Section 706(7)(B) defines "handicapped individual" as any person who "(i) has a physical . . . impairment which substantially limits one or more of [his or her] major life activities, (ii) has a record of such an impairment, or (iii) is regarded as having such an impairment." 29 U.S.C. §706(7)(B). The court finds the Student is likely to be considered a handicapped individual under the third definition: "regarded" as having a physical impairment which substantially limits his life activities.

Supreme Court has stated that

> . . . [the] basic purpose of §504 . . . is to ensure that handicapped individuals are not denied jobs or other benefits because of the prejudiced attitudes or the ignorance of others. By amending the definition of "handicapped individual" to include not only those who are actually physically impaired, but also those who are regarded as impaired and who, as a result, are substantially limited in a major life activity, Congress acknowledged that society's accumulated myths and fears about disability and disease are as handicapping as are the physical limitations that flow from actual impair-

ment. Few aspects of a handicap give rise to the same level of public fear and misapprehension as contagiousness. Even those who suffer or have recovered from such noninfectious diseases as epilepsy or cancer have faced discrimination based on the irrational fear that they might be contagious. The Act is carefully structured to replace such reflexive reactions to actual or perceived handicaps with actions based on reasoned and medically sound judgments. . . .

School Board of Nassau County v. Arline, 480 U.S. 273 (1987). Following this reasoning, the Court held that the mere fact that a disease is contagious does not exclude the disease carrier from the definition of "handicapped individual" (although contagiousness could make the individual not "otherwise qualified," depending on the circumstances). *Id.* 107 S.Ct. at 1130.[1] However, the reasoning is readily applicable to the plight of a victim of AIDS. Surely no physical problem has created greater public fear and misapprehension than AIDS. That fear includes a perception that a person with AIDS is substantially impaired in his ability to interact with others, e.g., to attend public school. Such interaction is a major life activity.

Congress has wisely determined that the courts shall protect individuals from reflexive reactions to their actual or perceived handicaps. While AIDS is a serious problem which demands immediate attention, only reasoned and medically sound judgments shall prevail. Therefore, the court holds the Student is likely to prevail in establishing he is a "handicapped individual," protected under §706(7)(B)(iii).[2]

The Student may also be viewed as "handicapped individual" because he "has a physical impairment which substantially limits one or more . . . major life activities." 29 U.S.C. §706(7)(B)(i). The phrase "physical impairment" means "any physiological disorder or condition, cosmetic disfigurement, or anatomical loss affecting one or more of the following body systems: . . . respiratory; . . . reproductive; . . . digestive; . . . hemic and lymphatic. . . ." 45 C.F.R. §84.3(j)(2)(i).

The parties agree the Student has AIDS, as found by Dr. Wolf. Given that finding alone, the Student has a substantial likelihood of demonstrating that he has a physiological disorder of his hemic, lymphatic and reproductive systems. AIDS destroys white blood cells, including lymphocytes (white blood cells produced by the lymphatic system). Therefore, AIDS creates a physiological disorder of the hemic (blood) and lymphatic systems. Furthermore, the AIDS victim has a disorder of the reproductive system in that he or she cannot engage in reproductive activity without endangering the lives of both the offspring and the other parent. In

[1] The Supreme Court declined to decide, since the case did not present the question, whether a carrier of AIDS could be considered to have a physical impairment, or whether such a person could be considered, solely on the basis of contagiousness, a handicapped person as defined by the Act. *Arline*, 107 S.Ct. at 1128 n. 7.

[2] The fact that the Student has a contagious disease in no way affects the court's holding that the Student is likely to be considered a handicapped individual. Persons with contagious diseases are not necessarily excluded from the purview of the Rehabilitation Act. *Arline*, 107 S.Ct. at 1130; *Chalk v. United States District Court of California*, 840 F.2d 701 (9th Cir.1988).

addition, this student had pneumonia, a physiological disorder of the respiratory system. He also had diarrhea and weight loss, disorders of the digestive system.

These physiological disorders substantially limit major life activities of the Student. His involvement in contact sports is limited to that of an observer, forcing him to sit on the side while his classmates engage in these activities. Also, he may not engage in reproductive functions without endangering the lives of others. While the Student may not yet be of an age where such activity is appropriate, the mere prospect of such a limitation is certain to restrict social interaction with those of the opposite sex.***

The next determination involves whether Student # 9387 is "otherwise qualified" to attend school. As set out in *Chalk:*

> A person who poses a significant risk of communicating an infectious disease to others in the workplace will not be otherwise qualified for his or her job if reasonable accommodation will not eliminate that risk.

840 F.2d at 705, *quoting, Arline,* 107 S.Ct. at 1131 n. 16. Similarly, the Student is otherwise qualified unless he poses a significant risk of infecting teachers and fellow students. In deciding this issue, *Arline* required that this court make findings regarding four factors: "(a) the nature of the risk (how the disease is transmitted), (b) the duration of the risk (how long is the carrier infectious), (c) the severity of the risk (what is the potential harm to third parties) and (d) the probabilities the disease will be transmitted and will cause varying degrees of harm." *Arline,* 107 S.Ct. at 1131. Further, in making these findings, a district court should give particular deference to the pronouncements of public health officials. *Chalk* also adopted this analysis. 840 F.2d at 705–06.

In this case, the court finds there is no significant risk of transmission of AIDS in the classroom setting. Plaintiffs and defendants have each submitted reports from medical experts. The court appointed a third expert. All three are in agreement. Dr. Murphy, the court appointed expert, stated:

> Infection with the Human Immunodeficiency Virus (HIV-I) does not present a hazard to others in the school or workplace (except in a hospital setting). There is very strong scientific evidence that the HIV-I virus is not transmitted through touching, sharing toys, playground equipment, bathrooms, water fountains or through other types of "casual contact." Even siblings of infected children who have bathed together and shared toothbrushes do not appear to be at risk. . . . Allowing [the Student] access to school poses no significant risk to classmates, teachers or other personnel.

The opinions of public health officials are in agreement with Dr. Murphy. Based on the accumulated body of medical evidence, the Surgeon General of the United States has concluded:

> There is no known risk of non-sexual infection in most of the situations we encounter in our daily lives. We know that family members living with in-

dividuals who have the AIDS virus do not become infected except through sexual contact. There is no evidence of transmission (spread) of the AIDS virus by everyday contact even though these family members shared food, towels, cups, razors, even toothbrushes, and kissed each other.

U.S. Public Health Service, *Surgeon General's Report on Acquired Immune Deficiency*, at 13 (1986). Regarding the classroom environment specifically, the Surgeon General found:

> None of the identified cases of AIDS in the United States are known or are suspected to have been transmitted from one child to another in school, day care or foster care settings. Transmission would necessitate exposure of open cuts to the blood or other body fluids of the infected child, a highly unlikely occurrence. Even then, routine safety procedures for handling blood or other body fluids . . . would be effective in preventing transmission from children with AIDS to other children in school. . . . Casual social contact between children and persons infected with AIDS virus is not dangerous.***

The School District asserts that the Student will not suffer irreparable harm because he has had and could continue to have homebound education.[3] The School District employees' admissions, however are inconsistent with this assertion. The Superintendent for the School District admitted at his deposition that attendance in the normal school environment is superior, in educational terms, to the "homebound" education the Student has been receiving. He stated that group interaction, class discussion, and learning different points of view are advantages of classroom participation which are unavailable to those receiving homebound education. Nor would homebound students have access to a library, chemistry lab or biology lab. This testimony clearly demonstrates the educational benefits of the school environment are far superior to those derived from two (2) hours of daily homebound education.

Dr. Zaransky, the staff psychologist for the School District, following an extensive evaluation of Student # 9387, concluded:

> The Student's considerable self-focus at this time would also appear to indicate that it would, indeed, be in his best interest to become involved in things outside the home in an effort to reduce the self-focus and direct his attention to other age-appropriate things.***

[3] Homebound education consists of a teacher going to a student's home during normal class days and giving him individualized instruction for several hours.

Notes and Issues for Discussion

1. For similar holdings based on AIDS as a handicap protected under section 504, see *Thomas v. Atascadero Unified School District*, 662 F. Supp. 376 (C.D.Cal. 1987), and *District 27 Community School Board v. Board of Education*, 502 N.Y.S.2d 325 (1986). For a decision based on administrative law, see *Board of Education v. Cooperman*, 523 A.2d 655 (N.J. 1987).

Discrimination in Health Care Agencies

May a health and human services professional refuse to treat a client or patient with AIDS or HIV? May the professional refuse to treat for no reason?

Some professions directly address the AIDS treatment issue in their codes of ethics. For example, in the interpretations to the American Dental Association Code of Ethics, it is clear that the refusal to treat a HIV infected patient is a violation of the A.D.A.'s code of ethics. Article VI of the American Medical Association's Principles of Medical Ethics provides: "A physician shall, in the provision of appropriate patient care, except in emergencies, be free to choose whom to serve" (Beauchamp and Childress, 1983: 332). However, the AMA Council on Ethical and Judicial Affairs has stated: "A physician may not ethically refuse to treat a patient whose condition is within the physician's current realm of competence solely because the patient is seropositive," basing this on the ethical principle "When an epidemic prevails, a physician must continue his labors without regard to the risks to his own health" and an ethical prohibition of discrimination (AMA Council, 1988: 1360). Many professional associations, however, have not taken a stand on the issue.

Under the anti-patient dumping provisions of the Emergency Medical Treatment and Active Labor Act, 42 U.S.C. §1395dd, health care facilities receiving federal funds are prohibited from refusing to provide treatment to patients needing emergency medical treatment.

In *Glanz v. Vernick*, 756 F. Supp. 632 (1991), a physician working in a hospital clinic refused to perform elective surgery on a patient because he had tested positive for HIV. The patient alleged discrimination under §504 of the Rehabilitation Act. The hospital claimed no liability because the physician was an independent contractor, not an employee. The court found that the hospital did exercise control over its physicians and since it was receiving federal funds, it was in violation of §504. However, the court held that since the physician did not receive federal monies, he could not be held liable under §504.

The Americans with Disabilities Act, 42 U.S.C. §12100 *et seq.*, prohibits discrimination against the disabled in public accommodations:

No individual shall be discriminated against on the basis of disability in the full and equal enjoyment of the goods, services, facilities, privileges, advantages, or accommodations of any place of public accommodation by any person who owns, leases (or leases to), or operates a place of public accommodation. 42 U.S.C. §12168.

Among places of public accommodations are the "professional office of a health care provider, hospital, or other service establishment," 42 U.S.C. §12167(7)(F), and "a day care center, senior citizen center, homeless shelter, food bank, adoption agency or other social service center establishment." §12167(7)(K).

Under this statute, federal funding is not a requirement. Would Dr. Vernick be required to treat AIDS patients at the hospital or at a professional office? Perhaps. However, the A.D.A. also contains an escape:

Nothing in this subchapter shall require an entity to permit an individual to participate in or benefit from the goods, services, privileges, advantages and accommodations of such entity where such individual poses a direct threat to the health or safety of others." 42 U.S.C. 12182(b)(3).[9]

SELECTED REFERENCES

AMA Council on Ethical and Judicial Affairs, "Ethical issues involved in the growing AIDS crisis," 259 *JAMA* 1360–1361 (1988).

Beauchamp, T., and Childress, J. *Principles of Biomedical Ethics* (1983).

Brandt, A. *No Magic Bullet* (1987).

Center for Disease Control, "Guidelines," 40 *Morbidity and Mortality Weekly* 1 (1991).

Center for Disease Control, *HIV/AIDS Surveillance Year End Report* 3 (1991).

Dalton, H. L. and Burris, S. (Eds.) *AIDS and the Law: A Guide for the Public* (1987).

Dornette, W. H. L. *AIDS and the Law* (1987).

Gostin, L. "Hospitals, health care professionals, and AIDS: The 'right to know' the health status of professionals and patients," in "Symposium on AIDS and the rights and obligations of health care workers," 48 *Maryland L.R.* 1 (1989).

McDonald, B. A., "Ethical problems for physicians raised by AIDS and HIV infection: Conflicting legal obligations of confidentiality and disclosure," 22 *U. C. Davis L. R.* 557 (1989).

Note, "Between a rock and a hard place: AIDS and the conflicting physician's duties of preventing disease transmission and safeguarding confidentiality," 76 *Georgetown L. J.* 169 (1987).

Note, "Access to medical care after the A.D.A.," 18 *Am. J. of Law and Medicine* 233 (1992).

Shilts, R. *And the Band Played On* (1987).

Waxman, H. A., "Lawyers, clients, and AIDS: Some notes from the trenches," in "Current legal issues in AIDS: A symposium," 49 *Ohio St. L.J.* 877 (1989).

PART IV

LAW IN PROFESSIONAL PRACTICE

Workplace and Courtroom Issues, Malpractice and Administrative Liability

Part IV addresses some key legal issues becoming increasingly common in professional practice.

In Chapter 14, some legal issues in the workplace are discussed. Sexual harassment is a topic of growing concern in the health and human services, both because of its prevalence and because of the costs to workers and agencies. Two types of sexual harassment—*quid pro quo* and hostile environment—are examined. Employer liability and steps to prevent harassment and protect the employer are addressed next. Drug testing in the workplace remains a controversial topic, in both the public and private sectors. Finally, the law relating to employee assistance programs is surveyed.

Chapter 15 deals with malpractice and liability issues for both practitioners and administrators. First the elements of malpractice are discussed in light of relevant malpractice cases. Then the related topic of administrative liability is examined, including liability for actions of workers, supervisor liability, and liability under 42 U.S.C §1983. Finally some limits to liability are examined, including the absence of duty to protect private citizens and sovereign immunity, and some steps to prevent malpractice are discussed.

481

Chapter 16 discusses courtroom testimony for both lay and expert witnesses. Courtroom conduct and rules of evidence, particularly hearsay evidence, are examined. Expert witness testimony is addressed in detail, including qualifying the professional as an expert, and the content of expert testimony. Reliability of expert testimony is a controversial issue and is discussed in light of two types of expert testimony, one relating to battered children—the battered child syndrome—and the other relating to a child's accommodation to sexual abuse, the Child Sexual Abuse Accommodation Syndrome. The former is accepted by courts as a reliable indicator that abuse has occurred, while courts generally use the latter only to explain a child's behavior and not as a predictor of sexual abuse.

CHAPTER 14

LAW IN THE WORKPLACE

Sexual Harassment, Drug Testing, and
Employee Assistance Programs

This chapter will address three particularly important areas of workplace law: sexual harassment, drug testing, and the law as it relates to employee assistance programs. The first two are the subjects of widespread litigation and concern, the last is a rapidly growing area in the health and human services.

SEXUAL HARASSMENT

Sexual harassment is a topic of growing concern in business, education, and the health and human services. While Judge Clarence Thomas's Supreme Court confirmation hearings may have greatly increased public awareness, the problem of sexual harassment is not new.[1] Most litigation has been focused on workplace harassment, but sexual harassment in education is a growing concern.

Available data indicate that unwelcome sexual behavior pervades the workplace. A 1981 Merit Systems Protection Board survey found that 42 percent of female employees and 15 percent of male employees reported workplace sexual harassment within a two-year period, and a more recent update showed little change (Feldman, 1987; Champagne and McAfee, 1989). In a 1988 Survey by *Working Women*, 90 percent of the *Fortune* 500 companies received sexual harassment complaints and over one third had been sued (Koen, 1990).[2]

Litigated cases compiled in the *Fair Employment Practices Cases* (FEP) between 1988 and 1990 include charges of rape, attempted rape, and other sexual attacks; threats of violence; indecent exposure, kissing, fondling, massaging, touching and rubbing; propositions, sexual advances, sexual remarks, insults, innuendos, jokes and suggestions; posting obscene pictures and cartoons, and mailing pornography (*FEP Cases*, 1988–1990; Strauss, 1990). The vast majority of sexual harassment complaints are filed by women against men. However, there are a number of cases of males complaining of harassment by females, as well as males claiming harassment by other males, and females claiming harassment by other females. Most claims are made by workers against supervisors (Koen, 1990).

While most of the literature has focused on sexual harassment in business, health and human services agencies are not immune. Recent defendants have included public schools, correctional departments, public administrative agencies, courts, veterans hospitals, public hospitals, mental health clinics, and public housing authorities (*FEP Cases*, 1988-1990).

SEXUAL HARASSMENT AND THE LAW

The law pertaining to sexual harassment in the workplace is complex and changing. An increasing number of cases are being litigated around what constitutes sexual harassment, what proofs are necessary, what steps should have been taken to rectify it, and supervisor and employer liability. Most claims are brought under federal law, but there are state law remedies as well. While earlier federal remedies were limited to cessation of the harassment, reasonable attorney's fees, and, where appropriate, reinstatement and back wages, recent amendments to the Civil Rights Act now permit substantial monetary recoveries in some cases. Actions brought under state antidiscrimination laws or state tort laws have resulted in large awards.

One reason definitions of sexual harassment are unclear is that the law itself remains vague. A primary vehicle for sexual harassment complaints, Title VII of the Civil Rights Act of 1964, never uses the term "sexual harassment." Title VII was originally enacted to prohibit workplace discrimination on the basis of race, religion, gender or national origin.[3] Thus it states:

> It shall be an unlawful employment practice for an employer—(1) to fail or refuse to hire or to discharge any individual, or otherwise to discriminate against any individual with respect to his compensation, terms, conditions or privileges of employment because of such individual's race, color, religion, sex or national origin. . . . 42 U.S.C. sec. 2000e-2(a)(1).

Early sexual harassment cases were dismissed on the grounds that sexual harassment was not part of Title VII discrimination on the basis of sex. Among reasons for rejecting claims were lack of legislative intent, that the actions were personal and not reflective of employers' policies, and that to hold otherwise would produce a flood of federal cases[4] (Paul, 1990: 338–339)

By the early 1970s, courts began to extend the Title VII sex discrimination provisions to cover instances of sexual harassment.[5] These cases involved what has been termed *quid pro quo* (literally, "this for that") harassment, where the demand for sexual favors was linked to employment decisions such as promotions and compensation. Typically *quid pro quo* harassment involved supervisors making demands upon supervisees. Sexual harassment without a *quid pro quo* was not addressed.

The 1981 decision *Bundy v. Jackson*, 641 F.2d 934 (1981), recognized a different kind of sexual harassment, called *hostile environment*.[6] The concept was elaborated in *Henson v. City of Dundee*, which involved both hostile environment and *quid pro quo* harassment.

HENSON v. CITY OF DUNDEE
682 F.2d 897 (1982)
U.S. COURT OF APPEALS

VANCE, CIRCUIT JUDGE.

In deciding this appeal, we must determine the proper application of Title VII principles to claims of sexual harassment at the workplace. Appellant, Barbara Henson, filed a Title VII action against the City of Dundee, Florida alleging sexual harassment on her job with the police department. At the close of appellant's case, the district court entered judgment for the city of Dundee and this appeal followed.

Henson was hired as a dispatcher in the five-officer Dundee police department on January 14, 1975. Her position was funded by the federal government under the Comprehensive Employment Training Act (CETA). There were five other CETA employees who worked as dispatchers for the department, one female employee who generally worked with Henson during her shift, Carolyn Dicks, and four male employees.

Henson claims that during the two years she worked for the Dundee police department, she and her female coworker were subjected to sexual harassment by the chief of the Dundee police department, John Sellgren. She alleges that this harassment ultimately led her to resign under duress on January 28, 1977. In May 1977 Henson filed a complaint against the City of Dundee with the Equal Employment Opportunity Commission (E.E.O.C.) alleging sexual harassment. The E.E.O.C. issued a right to sue letter on January 31, 1978 and Henson filed this suit in the middle district of Florida in March.***

Henson contends that a plaintiff states a claim under Title VII by alleging that sexual harassment perpetrated or condoned by an employer has created a hostile or offensive work environment. She argues that the trial court erred by holding that a Title VII plaintiff must allege in addition that she suffered some tangible job detriment as a result of working in such an environment. We agree that under certain circumstances the creation of an offensive or hostile work environment due to sexual harassment can violate Title VII irrespective of whether the complainant suffers tangible job detriment. We therefore reverse the district court's order as to this claim and remand for a new trial on Henson's work environment claim.

Title VII prohibits employment discrimination on the basis of gender, and seeks to remove arbitrary barriers to sexual equality at the workplace with respect to "compensation, terms, conditions, or privileges of employment." 42 U.S.C. §2000e-2(a)(1); *Griggs v. Duke Power Co.*, 401 U.S. 424, 431 (1971). The former fifth circuit has held that "terms, conditions, or privileges of employment" include the state of psychological well being at the workplace. In the area of race discrimination, Judge Goldberg stated:

> the phrase "terms, conditions, or privileges of employment" in [Title VII] is an expansive concept which sweeps within its protective ambit the practice of creating a working environment heavily charged with ethnic or racial discrimination.

Rogers v. EEOC, 454 F.2d 234, 238 (5th Cir. 1971). Therefore, courts have held that an employer violates Title VII simply by creating or condoning an environment at the workplace which significantly and adversely affects an employee because of his race or ethnicity, regardless of any other tangible job detriment to the protected employee.

Sexual harassment which creates a hostile or offensive environment for members of one sex is every bit the arbitrary barrier to sexual equality at the workplace that racial harassment is to racial equality. Surely, a requirement that a man or woman run a gauntlet of sexual abuse in return for the privilege of being allowed to work and make a living can be as demeaning and disconcerting as the harshest of racial epithets. A pattern of sexual harassment inflicted upon an employee because of her sex is a pattern of behavior that inflicts disparate treatment upon a member of one sex with respect to terms, conditions, or privileges of employment. There is no requirement that an employee subjected to such disparate treatment prove in addition that she has suffered tangible job detriment.***

Of course, neither the courts nor the E.E.O.C. have suggested that every instance of sexual harassment gives rise to a Title VII claim against an employer for a hostile work environment. Rather, the plaintiff must allege and prove a number of elements in order to establish her claim. These elements include the following:

(1) *The employee belongs to a protected group.* As in other cases of sexual discrimination, this requires a simple stipulation that the employee is a man or a woman.

(2) *The employee was subject to unwelcome sexual harassment.* The E.E.O.C. regulations helpfully define the type of conduct that may constitute sexual harassment: "sexual advances, requests for sexual favors, and other verbal or physical conduct of a sexual nature. . . ." 29 C.F.R. §1604.11(a) (1981). In order to constitute harassment, this conduct must be unwelcome in the sense that the employee did not solicit or incite it, and in the sense that the employee regarded the conduct as undesirable or offensive.***

(3) *The harassment complained of was based upon sex.* The essence of a disparate treatment claim under Title VII is that an employee or applicant is intentionally singled out for adverse treatment on the basis of a prohibited criterion. In proving a hostile work environment due to sexual harassment, therefore, the plaintiff must show that but for the fact of her sex, she would not have been the object of harassment.

In the typical case in which a male supervisor makes sexual overtures to a female worker, it is obvious that the supervisor did not treat male employees in a similar fashion. It will therefore be a simple matter for the plaintiff to prove that but for her sex, she would not have been subjected to sexual harassment. However, there may be cases in which a supervisor makes sexual overtures to workers of both sexes or where the conduct complained of is equally offensive to male and female workers. In such cases, the sexual harassment would not be based upon sex because men and women are accorded like treatment.***

(4) *The harassment complained of affected a "term, condition, or privilege" of employment.* The former fifth circuit has held that the state of psychological well being is a term, condition, or privilege of employment within the meaning of Title VII. The court in *Rogers* made it clear, however, that the "mere utterance of an ethnic or racial epithet which engenders offensive feelings in an employee" does not affect the terms, conditions, or privileges of employment to a sufficiently significant degree to violate Title VII. For sexual harassment to state a claim under Title VII, it must be sufficiently pervasive so as to alter the conditions of employment and create an abusive working environment. Whether sexual harassment at the workplace is sufficiently severe and persistent to affect seriously the psychological well being of employees is a question to be determined with regard to the totality of the circumstances.***

In this case, Henson has made a prima facie showing of all elements necessary to establish a violation of Title VII. Dismissal of her claim was therefore erroneous. She is entitled to prove her claim on remand to the district court for a new trial.

Notes and Issues for Discussion

1. *Henson* sets forth four criteria for proof of sexual harassment which have been widely accepted:
   "(1) The employee belongs to a protected group. . . .
   (2) The employee was subject to unwelcome sexual harassment. . . .
   (3) The harassment complained of was based upon sex. . . .
   (4) The harassment complained of affected a 'term, condition, or privilege' of employment . . . as to alter the conditions of employment and create an abusive working environment."
   Most problematic are showing that the conduct was unwelcome and that it was sufficiently pervasive to alter the conditions of employment.

The complainant must establish that the conduct at issue was unwelcome sexual harassment. Without physical evidence or the presence of a third party, there may be problems of proof. Some form of contemporaneous documentation or remarks to friends or co-workers could provide useful evidence. It is also important that the complainant did not incite the conduct. It is not clear what the court means by "solicit or incite," but it seems to indicate a willingness to accept testimony about the complainant's behavior. The conduct in question must be regarded by the complainant as unwelcome, in the sense of "undesirable or offensive."

The *Henson* criteria also require that the harassment be more than a "mere utterance which engenders offensive feelings" and must actually create an abusive working environment. The court indicates the conduct must be "severe and persistent to affect seriously the psychological well being of the employee." For a recent Supreme Court discussion of this issue, see *Harris v. Forklift Systems, Inc.*, 126 L.Ed.2d 295 (1993), p. 493 below.

2. *Henson* also raises the issue of employer liability, or *respondeat superior*. "Where ... the plaintiff seeks to hold the employer responsible for the hostile environment created by the plaintiff's supervisor or co-worker, she must show that the employer knew or should have known of the harassment in question and failed to take prompt remedial action." See p. 500.

ESTABLISHING SEXUAL HARASSMENT

Health and human services professionals who may face harassment or be called on to assist victims should understand the process of bringing a sexual harassment claim, keeping in mind the importance of documentation and proof.

The procedures for a Title VII harassment claim are set forth in federal statutes and regulations. Important elements include a requirement that sexual harassment claims brought before the Equal Employment Opportunity Commission (EEOC) must be filed with the Commission within 180 days (or, if the complaint has been filed with a state or local agency, within 300 days after occurrence or within thirty days after receiving notice that the state or local agency has terminated proceedings, whichever is earlier). 42 U.S.C. §2000e-5(e). The commission serves notice of the charge upon the employer within ten days and investigates. If there is not "reasonable cause to believe the charge is true" it will dismiss. If there is reasonable cause, the commission is empowered to eliminate the practice by "informal methods" of "conference, conciliation, and persuasion." These informal discussions may not be made public without consent of the persons involved. 42 U.S.C. §2000e-5(b). Failing conciliation efforts, the Commission may bring a civil action. 42 U.S.C. §2000e-5(f)(1).[7]

TYPES OF SEXUAL HARASSMENT

Courts have recognized two types of sexual harassment, *quid pro quo* harassment and hostile environment harassment. Each is distinct in content and type of available relief.

Quid Pro Quo Sexual Harassment

As *Henson* illustrates, *quid pro quo* harassment usually occurs when the employer or supervisor makes employment benefits contingent upon sexual favors or denies benefits due to a refusal to engage in sexual activity. Typical is *Williams v. Saxbe*, 413 F. Supp. 654 (1976), where the court found sexual harassment when a female employee was dismissed after she refused the sexual advances of a supervisor.

A different situation was presented in *King v. Palmer*, 778 F.2d 878 (1985), where the court found *quid pro quo* harassment when one employee was promoted based on her sexual relationship with her supervisor and another employee was denied promotion. The evidence showed that the promoted employee was a poor worker, had an inferior work record, and was promoted to a new position solely because of her sexual relationship with her supervisor. The complaining employee who was not promoted was never directly harassed by the supervisor. However, the court said that the promotion based on a sexual relationship had the effect of denying promotion to the complaining employee and was therefore sexual harassment.

Hostile Environment Sexual Harassment

MERITOR SAVINGS v. VINSON
477 U.S. 57 (1985)
U.S. SUPREME COURT

JUSTICE REHNQUIST delivered the opinion of the Court.

This case represents important questions concerning claims of workplace "sexual harassment" brought under Title VII of the Civil Rights Act of 1964, 78 Stat. 253, as amended, 42 U.S.C. §2000e *et seq.*

In 1974, respondent Mechelle Vinson met Sidney Taylor, a vice president of what is now petitioner Meritor Savings Bank (bank) and manager of one of its branch offices. When respondent asked whether she might obtain employment at the bank, Taylor gave her an application, which she completed and returned the next day; later that same day Taylor called her to say that she had been hired. With Taylor as her supervisor, respondent started as a teller-trainee, and thereafter was promoted to teller, head teller, and assistant branch manager. She worked at the same branch for four years, and it is undisputed that her advancement there was based on merit alone. In September 1978, respondent notified Taylor that she was taking sick leave for an indefinite period. On November 1, 1978, the bank discharged her for excessive use of that leave.

Respondent brought this action against Taylor and the bank, claiming that during her four years at the bank she had "constantly been subjected to sexual harassment" by Taylor in violation of Title VII. She sought injunctive relief, compensatory and punitive damages against Taylor and the bank, and attorney's fees.

At the 11-day bench trial, the parties presented conflicting testimony about Taylor's behavior during respondent's employment. Respondent testified that during her probationary period as a teller-trainee, Taylor treated her in a fatherly way and made no sexual advances. Shortly thereafter, however, he invited her out to dinner and, during the course of the meal, suggested that they go to a motel to have sexual relations. At first she refused, but out of what she described as fear of losing her job she eventually agreed. According to respondent, Taylor thereafter made repeated demands upon her for sexual favors, usually at the branch, both during and after business hours; she estimated that over the next several years she had intercourse with him some 40 or 50 times. In addition, respondent testified that Taylor fondled her in front of other employees, followed her into the women's restroom when she went there alone, exposed himself to her, and even forcibly raped her on several occasions. These activities ceased after 1977, respondent stated, when she started going with a steady boyfriend.***

Taylor denied respondent's allegations of sexual activity, testifying that he never fondled her, never made suggestive remarks to her, never engaged in sexual intercourse with her, and never asked her to do so. He contended instead that respondent made her accusations in response to a business-related dispute. The bank also denied respondent's allegations and asserted that any sexual harassment by Taylor was unknown to the bank and engaged in without its consent or approval.***

Title VII of the Civil Rights Act of 1964 makes it "an unlawful employment practice for an employer . . . to discriminate against any individual with respect to his compensation, terms, conditions, or privileges of employment, because of such individual's race, color, religion, sex, or national origin." 42 U.S.C. §2000e-2(a)(1). The prohibition against discrimination based on sex was added to Title VII at the last minute on the floor of the House of Representatives. 110 Cong. Rec. 2577–2584 (1964). The principal argument in opposition to the amendment was that "sex discrimination" was sufficiently different from other types of discrimination that it ought to receive separate legislative treatment. This argument was defeated, the bill quickly passed as amended, and we are left with little legislative history to guide us in interpreting the Act's prohibition against discrimination based on "sex."

Respondent argues, and the Court of Appeals held, that unwelcome sexual advances that create an offensive or hostile working environment violate Title VII. Without question, when a supervisor sexually harasses a subordinate because of the subordinate's sex, that supervisor "discriminate[s]" on the basis of sex. Petitioner apparently does not challenge this proposition. It contends instead that in prohibiting discrimination with respect to "compensation, terms, conditions, or privileges" of employment, Congress was concerned with what petitioner describes as "tangible loss" of "an economic character," not "purely psychological aspects of the workplace environment." In support of this claim petitioner observes that in both the legislative history of Title VII and this Court's Title VII decisions, the focus has been on tangible, economic barriers erected by discrimination.

We reject petitioner's view. First, the language of Title VII is not limited to "economic" or "tangible" discrimination. The phrase "terms, conditions, or privileges of employment" evinces a congressional intent "'to strike at the entire spectrum of disparate treatment of men and women'" in employment.***

Second, in 1980 the EEOC issued Guidelines specifying that "sexual harassment," as there defined, is a form of sex discrimination prohibited by Title VII.***

In defining "sexual harassment," the Guidelines first describe the kinds of workplace conduct that may be actionable under Title VII. These include "[u]nwelcome sexual advances, requests for sexual favors, and other verbal or physical conduct of a sexual nature." 29 CFR §1604.11(a) (1985). Relevant to the charges at issue in this case, the Guidelines provide that such sexual misconduct constitutes prohibited "sexual harassment," whether or not it is directly linked to the grant or denial of an economic *quid pro quo*, where "such conduct has the purpose or effect of unreasonably interfering with an individual's work performance or creating an intimidating, hostile, or offensive working environment." §1604.11(a)(3).***

Since the Guidelines were issued, courts have uniformly held, and we agree, that a plaintiff may establish a violation of Title VII by proving that discrimination based on sex has created a hostile or abusive work environment. As the Court of Appeals for the Eleventh Circuit wrote in *Henson v. Dundee*, 682 F.2d 897, 902 (1982):

"Sexual harassment which creates a hostile or offensive environment for members of one sex is every bit the arbitrary barrier to sexual equality at the workplace that racial harassment is to racial equality. Surely, a requirement that a man or woman run a gauntlet of sexual abuse in return for the privilege of being allowed to work and make a living can be as demeaning and disconcerting as the harshest of racial epithets."

Of course, as the courts in both *Rogers* and *Henson* recognized, not all workplace conduct that may be described as "harassment" affects a "term, condition, or privilege" of employment within the meaning of Title VII. See *Rogers v. EEOC, supra*, at 238 ("mere utterance of an ethnic or racial epithet which engenders offensive feelings in an employee" would not affect the conditions of employment to sufficiently significant degree to violate Title VII); *Henson*, 682 F.2d, at 904 (quoting same). For sexual harassment to be actionable, it must be sufficiently severe or pervasive "to alter the conditions of [the victim's] employment and create an abusive working environment." *Ibid.* Respondent's allegations in this case—which include not only pervasive harassment but also criminal conduct of the most serious nature—are plainly sufficient to state a claim for "hostile environment" sexual harassment.

The question remains, however, whether the District Court's ultimate finding that respondent "was not the victim of sexual harassment," effectively disposed of respondent's claim. The Court of Appeals recognized, we think correctly, that this ultimate finding was likely based on one or both of two erroneous views of the law. First, the District Court apparently believed that a claim for sexual harassment will not lie absent an *economic* effect on the complainant's employment. ("It is without question that sexual harassment of female employees in which they are asked or required to submit to sexual demands as a *condition to obtain employment or to maintain employment or to obtain promotions* falls within protection of Title VII") (emphasis added). Since it appears that the District Court made its findings without ever considering the "hostile environment" theory of sexual harassment, the Court of Appeals' decision to remand was correct.

Second, the District Court's conclusion that no actionable harassment occurred might have rested on its earlier "finding" that "[i]f [respondent] and Taylor did engage in an intimate or sexual relationship . . . , that relationship was a voluntary one." But the fact that sex-related conduct was "voluntary," in the sense that the complainant was not forced to participate against her will, is not a defense to a sexual harassment suit brought under Title VII. The gravamen of any sexual harassment claim is that the alleged sexual advances were "unwelcome." 29 CFR §1604.11(a) (1985). While the question whether particular conduct was indeed unwelcome presents difficult problems of proof and turns largely on credibility determinations committed to the trier of fact, the District Court in this case erroneously focused on the "voluntariness" of respondent's participation in the claimed sexual episodes. The correct inquiry is whether respondent by her conduct indicated that the alleged sexual advances were unwelcome, not whether her actual participation in sexual intercourse was voluntary.

Petitioner contends that even if this case must be remanded to the District Court, the Court of Appeals erred in one of the terms of its remand. Specifically, the Court of Appeals stated that testimony about respondent's "dress and personal fantasies," which the District Court apparently admitted into evidence, "had no place in this litigation." The apparent ground for this conclusion was that respondent's voluntariness *vel non* in submitting to Taylor's advances was immaterial to her sexual harassment claim. While "voluntariness" in the sense of consent is not a defense to such a claim, it does not follow that a complainant's sexually provocative speech or dress is irrelevant as a matter of law in determining whether he or she found particular sexual advances unwelcome. To the contrary, such evidence is obviously relevant. The EEOC Guidelines emphasize that the trier of fact must determine the existence of sexual harassment in light of "the record as a whole" and "the totality of circumstances, such as the nature of the sexual advances and the context in which the alleged incidents occurred." 29 CFR §1604.11(b) (1985). Respondent's claim that any marginal relevance of the evidence in question was outweighed by the potential for unfair prejudice is the sort of argument properly addressed to the District Court. In this case the District Court concluded that the evidence should be admitted, and the Court of Appeals' contrary conclusion was based upon the erroneous, categorical view that testimony about provocative dress and publicly expressed sexual fantasies "had no place in this litigation." While the District Court must carefully weigh the applicable considerations in deciding whether to admit evidence of this kind, there is no *per se* rule against its admissibility.

Although the District Court concluded that respondent had not proved a violation of Title VII, it nevertheless went on to consider the question of the bank's liability. Finding that "the bank was without notice" of Taylor's alleged conduct, and that notice to Taylor was not the equivalent of notice to the bank, the court concluded that the bank therefore could not be held liable for Taylor's alleged actions. The Court of Appeals took the opposite view, holding that an employer is strictly liable for a hostile environment created by a supervisor's sexual advances, even though the employer neither knew nor reasonably could have known of the alleged misconduct. The court held that a supervisor, whether or not he possesses the authority to hire, fire, or promote, is necessarily an "agent" of his employer for all Title VII purposes, since "even the appearance" of such authority may enable him to impose himself on his subordinates.***

This debate over the appropriate standard for employer liability has a rather abstract quality about it given the state of the record in this case. We do not know at this stage whether Taylor made any sexual advances toward respondent at all, let alone whether those advances were unwelcome, whether they were sufficiently pervasive to constitute a condition of employment, or whether they were "so pervasive and so long continuing . . . that the employer must have become conscious of [them]," *Taylor* v. *Jones*, 653 F.2d 1193, 1197–1199 (CA 8 1981) (holding employer liable for racially hostile working environment based on constructive knowledge).

We therefore decline the parties' invitation to issue a definitive rule on employer liability, but we do agree with the EEOC that Congress wanted courts to look to agency principles for guidance in this area. While such common-law principles may not be transferable in all their particulars to Title VII, Congress' decision to define "employer" to include any "agent" of an employer, 42 U.S.C. §2000e(b), surely evinces an intent to place some limits on the acts of employees for which employers under Title VII are to be held responsible. For this reason, we hold that the Court of Appeals erred in concluding that employers are always automatically liable for sexual harassment by their supervisors. For the same reason, absence of notice to an employer does not necessarily insulate that employer from liability.

Finally, we reject petitioner's view that the mere existence of a grievance procedure and a policy against discrimination, coupled with respondent's failure to invoke that procedure, must insulate petitioner from liability. While those facts are plainly relevant, the situation before us demonstrates why they are not necessarily dispositive. Petitioner's general nondiscrimination policy did not address sexual harassment in particular, and thus did not alert employees to their employer's interest in correcting that form of discrimination. Moreover, the bank's grievance procedure apparently required an employee to complain first to her supervisor, in this case Taylor. Since Taylor was the alleged perpetrator, it is not altogether surprising that respondent failed to invoke the procedure and report her grievance to him. Petitioner's contention that respondent's failure should insulate it from liability might be substantially stronger if its procedures were better calculated to encourage victims of harassment to come forward.

In sum, we hold that a claim of "hostile environment" sex discrimination is actionable under Title VII, that the District Court's findings were insufficient to dispose of respondent's hostile environment claim, and that the District Court did not err in admitting testimony about respondent's sexually provocative speech and dress. As to employer liability, we conclude that the Court of Appeals was wrong to entirely disregard agency principles and impose absolute liability on employers for the acts of their supervisors, regardless of the circumstances of a particular case.

Accordingly, the judgment of the Court of Appeals reversing the judgment of the District Court is affirmed, and the case is remanded for further proceedings consistent with this opinion.

Notes and Issues for Discussion

1. "For sexual harassment to be actionable it must be sufficiently severe or pervasive 'to alter the conditions of [the victim's] employment and create an abusive working environment.'" Are Mechelle Vinson's allegations sufficient to establish harassment? Would an occasional offensive comment be sufficient?

2. The Court makes a distinction between "voluntary" conduct, and "unwelcome" conduct. The Court states the "correct inquiry is whether respondent by her conduct indicated that the alleged sexual advances were unwelcome, not whether her actual participation in sexual intercourse was voluntary." Given this standard, offensive conduct would not seem to qualify as sexual harassment unless the victim indicated it was unwelcome. What would be some indications that conduct was unwelcome? What advice would you give about how to respond to unwelcome advances; how to document them; how to document that the unwelcome nature of the advance was made clear?

3. While voluntariness in terms of consent is not the issue, the court says "it does not follow that a complainant's sexually provocative speech or dress is irrelevant as a matter of law in determining whether he or she found the particular sexual advances unwelcome." The advantage for the defendant is that this testimony can be used to counter a claim of unwelcome conduct, but there are obvious costs for the complainant. Might allowing this evidence deter some complainants?

4. To establish unwelcome conduct, the complainant may need to show that it was made clear that the conduct was not acceptable and that the complainant requested that it cease. Copies of letters or notes to this effect would be helpful, as would statements in the presence of third parties.

5. For employer liability issues, see p. 501.

6. In *Harris v. Forklift Systems Inc.*, 126 L.Ed.2d 295 (1993), the U.S. Supreme Court somewhat clarified the standard for sexual harassment. In finding that an offensive work environment need not seriously affect the em-

ployee's physiological well-being or lead the plaintiff to suffer psychological injury, Justice O'Connor wrote:

"The phrase 'terms, conditions or privileges of employment " evinces a congressional intent 'to strike at the entire spectrum of disparate treatment of men and women' in employment. . . . When the workplace is permeated with 'discriminatory intimidation, ridicule and insult' that is 'sufficiently severe or pervasive to alter the conditions of the victim's employment and create an abusive working environment,' Title VII is violated.

This standard, which we reaffirm today, takes a middle path between making actionable any conduct that is merely offensive and requiring the conduct cause psychological injury. As we pointed out in Meritor, 'mere utterance of an . . . epithet which engenders offensive feelings in an employee' does not sufficiently affect the conditions of employment to implicate Title VII. Conduct that is not severe or pervasive enough to create an objectively hostile or abusive work environment—an environment that a reasonable person could find hostile or abusive—is beyond Title VII's purview. Likewise if the victim does not subjectively perceive the environment to be abusive, the conduct has not actually altered the conditions of the victim's employment, and there is no Title VII violation.

But Title VII comes into play before the harassing conduct leads to a nervous breakdown. A discriminatorily abusive work environment, even one that does not seriously affect employees' psychological well-being can and often will detract from employees' job performance, discourage employees from remaining on the job, or keep them from advancing in their careers." (126 L.Ed.2d 301-302).

INDIRECT HOSTILE ENVIRONMENT SEXUAL HARASSMENT

"Even a woman who was never herself the object of harassment might have a Title VII claim if she were forced to work in an atmosphere in which such harassment was pervasive." *Broderick v. Ruder*, 685 F.Supp. 1269 at 1278 (D.D.C. 1988) citing *Vinson v. Taylor*, 753 F.2d at 146. *Broderick* raises a different type of hostile environment issue. Catherine Broderick was a staff attorney at the Washington Regional Office (WRO) of the Securities and Exchange Commission. Initially her work was well received, but over time her performance ratings fell from "superior" to "unacceptable" and she was threatened with discharge. Broderick in turn charged that she was retaliated against because she had complained of the sexual activity at her office. While there were some allegations of sexual advances made toward Broderick, her primary complaint was that the office was permeated with sexual advances, sexual relationships, extensive drinking, and frequent partying during office hours. Many of the sexual relationships were between supervisors and supervisees. The district court held that there was hostile environment sexual harassment:

> Ms. Broderick established a *prima facie* case of sexual harassment because of having to work in a hostile work environment. The evidence at trial established that such conduct of a sexual nature was so pervasive at the WRO that it can reasonably be said that such conduct created a hostile or offensive work environment which affected the motivation and work performance of those who found such conduct repugnant and offensive. . . . (*Broderick*, 685 F. Supp. at 1278).

Thus hostile environment harassment may include either activities focused directly upon the individual or a generally offensive climate.

WHAT CONSTITUTES A "REASONABLE PERSON" AND AN ABUSIVE WORK ENVIRONMENT"?

One unresolved issue is how to assess the effect of the alleged harassment on the individual. The comments and actions of a sexual nature that one individual might find deeply offensive could seem harmless, humorous, or flattering to another. Many courts have opted for an objective "reasonable person" standard, holding that if a reasonable person in the plaintiff's situation would have felt harassed then there could be a valid claim. However, the gender of the hypothetical reasonable "person" has not been resolved. One federal circuit court using the reasonable person standard found no harassment when a woman in an all-male environment was subjected to an atmosphere of nude posters and particularly obscene language. See *Rabidue v. Osceola Refining Co.*, 805 F.2d. 611 (1986). In *Ellison v. Brady*, the court used the standard of a "reasonable woman" to determine if the conduct was offensive.

ELLISON v. BRADY
924 F. 2d 872 (1991)
U.S. COURT OF APPEALS

BEEZER, Circuit Judge.

Kerry Ellison appeals the district court's order granting summary judgment to the Secretary of the Treasury on her sexual harassment action brought under Title VII of the Civil Rights Act of 1964.***

Kerry Ellison worked as a revenue agent for the Internal Revenue Service in San Mateo, California. During her initial training in 1984 she met Sterling Gray, another trainee, who was also assigned to the San Mateo office. The two coworkers never became friends, and they did not work closely together.

Gray's desk was twenty feet from Ellison's desk, two rows behind and one row over. Revenue agents in the San Mateo office often went to lunch in groups. In June of 1986 when no one else was in the office, Gray asked Ellison to lunch. She accepted. Gray had to pick up his son's forgotten lunch, so they stopped by Gray's house. He gave Ellison a tour of his house.

Ellison alleges that after the June lunch Gray started to pester her with unnecessary questions and hang around her desk. On October 9, 1986, Gray asked Ellison out for a drink after work. She declined, but she suggested that they have lunch the following week. She did not want to have lunch alone with him, and she tried to stay away from the office during lunch time.

On October 22, 1986 Gray handed Ellison a note he wrote on a telephone message slip which read:

> I cried over you last night and I'm totally drained today. I have never been in such constant term oil (sic). Thank you for talking with me. I could not stand to feel your hatred for another day.

When Ellison realized that Gray wrote the note, she became shocked and frightened and left the room. Gray followed her into the hallway and demanded that she talk to him, but she left the building.

Ellison later showed the note to Bonnie Miller, who supervised both Ellison and Gray. Miller said "this is sexual harassment." Ellison asked Miller not to do anything about it. She wanted to try to handle it herself. Ellison asked a male coworker to talk to Gray, to tell him that she was not interested in him and to leave her alone. The next day, Thursday, Gray called in sick.

Ellison did not work on Friday, and on the following Monday, she started four weeks of training in St. Louis, Missouri. Gray mailed her a card and a typed, single-spaced, three-page letter. She describes this letter as "twenty times, a hundred times weirder" than the prior one. Gray wrote, in part:

> I know that you are worth knowing with or without sex. . . . Leaving aside the hassles and disasters of recent weeks. I have enjoyed you so much over these past few months. Watching you. Experiencing you from O so far away. Admiring your style and elan. . . . Don't you think it odd that two people who have never even talked together, alone, are striking off such intense sparks . . . I will [write] another letter in the near future.

Explaining her reaction, Ellison stated: "I just thought he was crazy. I thought he was nuts. I didn't know what he would do next. I was frightened."

She immediately telephoned Miller. Ellison told her supervisor that she was frightened and really upset. She requested that Miller transfer either her or Gray because she would not be comfortable working in the same office with him. Miller asked Ellison to send a copy of the card and letter to San Mateo.

Miller then telephoned her supervisor, Joe Benton, and discussed the problem. That same day she had a counseling session with Gray. She informed him that he was entitled to union representation. During this meeting, she told Gray to leave Ellison alone.

At Benton's request, Miller apprised the labor relations department of the situation. She also reminded Gray many times over the next few weeks that he must not contact Ellison in any way. Gray subsequently transferred to the San Francisco office on November 24, 1986. Ellison returned from St. Louis in late November and did not discuss the matter further with Miller.

After three weeks in San Francisco, Gray filed union grievances requesting a return to the San Mateo office. The IRS and the union settled the grievances in Gray's favor, agreeing to allow him to transfer back to the San Mateo office provided that he spend four more months in San Francisco and promise not to bother Ellison. On January 28, 1987, Ellison first learned of Gray's request in a letter from Miller explaining that Gray would return to the San Mateo office. The letter indicated that management decided to resolve Ellison's problem with a six-month separation, and that it would take additional action if the problem recurred.

After receiving the letter, Ellison was "frantic." She filed a formal complaint alleging sexual harassment on January 30, 1987 with the IRS. She also obtained permission to transfer to San Francisco temporarily when Gray returned.

Gray sought joint counseling. He wrote Ellison another letter which still sought to maintain the idea that he and Ellison had some type of relationship.***

Ellison filed a complaint in September of 1987 in federal district court. The court granted the government's motion for summary judgment on the ground that Ellison had failed to state a prima facie case of sexual harassment due to a hostile working environment. Ellison appeals.***

Congress added the word "sex" to Title VII of the Civil Rights Act of 1964 at the last minute on the floor of the House of Representatives. Virtually no legislative history provides guidance to courts interpreting the prohibition of sex discrimination. In *Meritor Savings Bank v. Vinson*, 477 U.S. 57 (1986), the Supreme Court held that sexual harassment constitutes sex discrimination in violation of Title VII.***

Courts have recognized different forms of sexual harassment. In "quid pro quo" cases, employers condition employment benefits on sexual favors. In "hostile environment" cases, employees work in offensive or abusive environments.***

The parties ask us to determine if Gray's conduct, as alleged by Ellison, was sufficiently severe or pervasive to alter the conditions of Ellison's employment and create an abusive working environment. The district court, with little Ninth Circuit case law to look to for guidance, held that Ellison did not state a prima facie case of sexual harassment due to a hostile working environment. It believed that Gray's conduct was "isolated and genuinely trivial." We disagree.***

We have closely examined *Meritor* and our previous cases, and we believe that Gray's conduct was sufficiently severe and pervasive to alter the conditions of Ellison's employment and create an abusive working environment. We first note that the required showing of severity or seriousness of the harassing conduct varies inversely with the pervasiveness or frequency of the conduct.***

Next, we believe that in evaluating the severity and pervasiveness of sexual harassment, we should focus on the perspective of the victim. If we only examined whether a reasonable person would engage in allegedly harassing conduct, we would run the risk of reinforcing the prevailing level of discrimination. Harassers could continue to harass merely because a particular discriminatory practice was common, and victims of harassment would have no remedy.

We therefore prefer to analyze harassment from the victim's perspective. A complete understanding of the victim's view requires, among other things, an analysis of the different perspectives of men and women. Conduct that many men consider unobjectionable may offend many women. *See, e.g., Lipsett v. University of Puerto Rico,* 864 F.2d 881, 898 (1st Cir. 1988) ("A male supervisor might believe, for example, that it is legitimate for him to tell a female subordinate that she has a 'great figure' or 'nice legs.' The female subordinate, however, may find such comments offensive").***

We realize that there is a broad range of viewpoints among women as a group, but we believe that many women share common concerns which men do not necessarily share. For example, because women are disproportionately victims of rape and sexual assault, women have a stronger incentive to be concerned with sexual behavior. Women who are victims of mild forms of sexual harassment may understandably worry whether a harasser's conduct is merely a prelude to violent sexual assault. Men, who are rarely victims of sexual assault, may view sexual conduct in a vacuum without a full appreciation of the social setting or the underlying threat of violence that a woman may perceive.

In order to shield employers from having to accommodate the idiosyncratic concerns of the rare hyper-sensitive employee, we hold that a female plaintiff states a prima facie case of hostile environment sexual harassment when she alleges conduct which a reasonable woman would consider sufficiently severe or pervasive to alter the conditions of employment and create an abusive working environment.***

We adopt the perspective of a reasonable woman primarily because we believe that a sex-blind reasonable person standard tends to be male-biased and tends to systematically ignore the experiences of women. The reasonable woman standard does not establish a higher level of protection for women than men.***Instead, a gender-conscious examination of sexual harassment enables women to participate in the workplace on an equal footing with men. By acknowledging and not trivializing the effects of sexual harassment on reasonable women, courts can work towards ensuring that neither men nor women will have to "run a gauntlet of sexual abuse in return for the privilege of being allowed to work and make a living." *Henson v. Dundee,* 682 F.2d 897, 902 (11th Cir. 1982).

We note that the reasonable victim standard we adopt today classifies conduct as unlawful sexual harassment even when harassers do not realize that their conduct creates a hostile working environment. Well-intentioned compliments by co-workers or supervisors can form the basis of a sexual harassment cause of action if a reasonable victim of the same sex as the plaintiff would consider the comments sufficiently severe or pervasive to alter a condition of employment and create an abusive working environment. That is because Title VII is not a fault-based tort scheme. "Title VII aimed at the consequences or effects of an employment practice and not at the ... motivation" of co-workers or employers. *Rogers,* 454 F.2d at 239; *see also Griggs v. Duke Power Co.,* 401 U.S. 424, 432, 91 S.Ct.

849, 854, 28 L.Ed.2d 158 (1971) (the absence of discriminatory intent does not re-
deem an otherwise unlawful employment practice). To avoid liability under Title
VII, employers may have to educate and sensitize their workforce to eliminate
conduct which a reasonable victim would consider unlawful sexual harassment.
See 29 C.F.R. §1604.11(f) ("Prevention is the best tool for the elimination of sexual
harassment.")

The facts of this case illustrate the importance of considering the victim's perspective. Analyzing the facts from the alleged harasser's viewpoint, Gray could
be portrayed as a modern-day Cyrano de Bergerac wishing no more than to woo
Ellison with his words. There is no evidence that Gray harbored ill will toward
Ellison. He even offered in his "love letter" to leave her alone if she wished. Examined in this light, it is not difficult to see why the district court characterized
Gray's conduct as isolated and trivial.

Ellison, however, did not consider the acts to be trivial. Gray's first note
shocked and frightened her. After receiving the three-page letter, she became really upset and frightened again. She immediately requested that she or Gray be
transferred. Her supervisor's prompt response suggests that she too did not consider the conduct trivial. When Ellison learned that Gray arranged to return to
San Mateo, she immediately asked to transfer, and she immediately filed an official complaint.

We cannot say as a matter of law that Ellison's reaction was idiosyncratic or
hyper-sensitive. We believe that a reasonable woman could have had a similar reaction. After receiving the first bizarre note from Gray, a person she barely knew,
Ellison asked a co-worker to tell Gray to leave her alone. Despite her request,
Gray sent her a long, passionate, disturbing letter. He told her he had been
"watching" and "experiencing" her; he made repeated references to sex; he said
he would write again. Ellison had no way of knowing what Gray would do next.
A reasonable woman could consider Gray's conduct, as alleged by Ellison, sufficiently severe and pervasive to alter a condition of employment and create an
abusive working environment.

Notes and Issues for Discussion

1. What is Gray accused of? Is this harassment? Is it sexual harassment? Do
   you think it is offensive? Would a reasonable person find it offensive?
2. The court adopts the perspective of a reasonable person of the same sex as
   the complainant, here a female. What are the arguments in favor of a "reasonable woman" or "reasonable man" standard to decide if the conduct
   altered employment conditions and produced an abusive working environment? Note the court's comment: "Well-intentioned compliments by
   co-workers or supervisors can form the basis of a sexual harassment cause
   of action if a reasonable victim of the same sex as the plaintiff would consider the comments sufficiently severe or pervasive to alter a condition of
   employment and create an abusive working environment."
3. What if the complainant was particularly sensitive to certain words or
   conduct which a reasonable person of the same sex would not find offen-

sive? Should there be a subjective standard rather than an objective one? Several courts have adopted such a standard.[8]

EMPLOYER LIABILITY

The costs of sexual harassment to an employer are high. If a health and human services agency loses or settles a case prior to trial, possible costs include damages, both plaintiff and defendant attorney fees, and plaintiff's reinstatement and back pay. Awards cited in cases and in the literature have run into tens of thousands and on occasion into the hundreds of thousands of dollars. Even if the human services agency wins a harassment suit, there are the costs of attorney fees and the administrator's time and effort in preparation. In either situation there are real but hidden costs in morale, productivity, and adverse publicity.

Perhaps the easiest way to minimize these costs is for the administrator to make every effort to insure that harassment does not take place. The EEOC guidelines state:

> Prevention is the best tool for the elimination of sexual harassment. An employer should take all steps necessary to prevent harassment such as affirmatively raising the subject, expressing strong disapproval, developing appropriate sanctions, informing employees of their rights to raise and how to raise the issue of harassment under Title VII and developing methods to sensitize all concerned. 29 CFR §1604.11 (f).

While these guidelines do not have the force of law, it would be prudent for an employer to consider them. Developing clear policies and giving appropriate staff training seem particularly important.

One problem for administrators is where to draw the line in terms of regulating speech or behavior. A strong argument can be made that sexually offensive speech or conduct in the workplace, much like racially offensive speech or conduct, falls outside general First Amendment protections (Strauss, 1990). At the same time, an administration that attempts to constrain after-hours, nonwork-related conduct or speech would seem to intrude upon individuals' privacy rights.[9] Between these are what may or may not be "welcome" sexual advances, speech, or conduct.

If harassment does occur, then the administrator should have a viable grievance system to handle complaints. In *Meritor*, the Supreme Court said the bank was deficient both in policies and procedures:

> Petitioner's general nondiscrimination policy did not address sexual harassment in particular, and thus did not alert employees to their em-

ployer's interest in correcting that form of discrimination. . . . Moreover, the bank's grievance procedure apparently required an employee
to complain first to her supervisor, in this case Taylor. Since Taylor was
the alleged perpetrator, it is not altogether surprising that respondent
failed to invoke the procedure. . . ." 477 U.S. at 72.

A grievance procedure allowing alternative routes to register complaints
appears necessary to avoid the problem of the harassing supervisor.
  If there is a complaint, the cases suggest that prompt action by the administration is called for (Jennings and Clapp, 1989). This would include an impartial investigation of the complaint, and if valid, immediate action.

DORNHECKER v. MALIBU GRAND PRIX CORP.
828 F.2d 307 (1987)
U.S. COURT OF APPEALS

EDITH H. JONES, CIRCUIT JUDGE.
  The behavior of a co-worker at the Malibu Grand Prix Corporation proved too
racy for Marvelle Dornhecker. She worked there in a corporate staff position for
four days in December 1984 before resigning because of sexual harassment to
which, she felt, the company was insensitive. This Title VII lawsuit followed, and
the district court awarded her $25,000 compensatory damages. Malibu appeals.
  We shall assume, without deciding, that Mrs. Dornhecker was the victim of
unwelcome sexual harassment that was sufficiently pervasive to alter the conditions of her employment and create an abusive working environment. *Meritor
Savings Bank, FSB v. Vinson*, 477 U.S. 57 (1986). The perpetrator was one Robert
Rockefeller, a contract consultant to the corporation in marketing, who was
slated to attend a series of out-of-town presentations with Mrs. Dornhecker and
other Malibu representatives during December 1984. Rockefeller's conduct in the
presence of Mrs. Dornhecker was public, clownish and boorish. During two days
of her first business trip with the company to Cincinnati and Miami, Rockefeller
put his hands on her hips in an airport ticket line and dropped his pants in front
of the passengers while waiting to board the airplane. He touched her breasts. Finally, when a number of Malibu employees attended a business dinner at the
Downunder Restaurant in Fort Lauderdale, he put his stocking feet on a cocktail
table directly in front of her and "playfully" choked her when she complained.
The co-workers were appalled.
  The events most pertinent to this appeal commenced when Mrs. Dornhecker,
overcome by Rockefeller's disgusting lack of professionalism, rushed to the
ladies' room immediately after this last incident and dissolved, in her words, into
hysterical tears. Her immediate supervisor, Krysia Swift, followed and tried to
console her. Although Swift had not seen the choking incident, she agreed to talk
to the company president about it. The next morning, December 6, Mrs. Dornhecker herself addressed Peabody, the president, and the court found that he

"told Plaintiff that she would not have to work with Rockefeller after the Florida trip." The Florida presentations were then scheduled to last one-and-a-half more days. It is undisputed that Rockefeller did not attend the remaining presentations in Fort Lauderdale, and his contract with Malibu went un-renewed at the end of December. Mrs. Dornhecker was not present to savor these events: she believed management was unresponsive, and shortly after talking to Peabody on December 6, she left Fort Lauderdale, explaining her departure only with a brief note in her supervisor's hotel mail slot.

The critical issue in this case for purposes of Title VII liability is whether Malibu, knowing about Mrs. Dornhecker's claims of sexual harassment, failed to take prompt remedial action. The district court found that Malibu did not. This is clearly erroneous. Since the demise of the institution of dueling, society has seldom provided instantaneous redress for dishonorable conduct. In this case, the district court found that Malibu's president personally reassured Mrs. Dornhecker that Rockefeller would not be working with her after the Florida trip. This assurance occurred approximately 12 hours after Mrs. Dornhecker had tearfully confronted Krysia Swift in the ladies' room and first acquainted her with Rockefeller's behavior. Considered in terms of the speed with which the company addressed Mrs. Dornhecker's complaint or the length of time it proposed to resolve that complaint, Malibu's remedial action was unusually prompt.

Mrs. Dornhecker resigned before she ever saw or worked with Rockefeller again after dinner at the Downunder Restaurant. Thus, we do not know whether Rockefeller, ashamed by his performance or by conversation with Malibu employees, or by the prospect of being summarily booted out of the rest of the business trip, might have left Mrs. Dornhecker alone for the remaining one-and-a-half days in Florida. Where the offending conduct spanned only two days to begin with, it is not unreasonable for the company to offer ending it virtually overnight. And, although we do not condone Rockefeller's conduct, it was not as aggressive or coercive as that underlying a number of hostile sexual environment claims that have been unsuccessful in court. Mrs. Dornhecker was not propositioned, she was not forced to respond to Rockefeller, she was not placed in any threatening situation. The company's remedy to Mrs. Dornhecker's complaint may be assessed proportionately to the seriousness of the offense. A company's lines of command, organizational format and immediate business demands cannot be wholly extracted from the analysis of its manner and promptness in resolving a claim of sexual harassment. The remedy was prompt.

Malibu's handling of the problem was also decisive. Ordinarily, an organization requires time to respond to embarrassing, emotional and often litigation-spawning claims of sexual harassment. Careers and corporate image rest on the company's handling of such charges. Here, Krysia Swift witnessed an hysterical outpouring from Mrs. Dornhecker, whom she had known and worked with for only two days, and whose reaction to offensive conduct Swift could hardly have been expected to assess in a moment. Whether Swift brushed off the charges or was just trying to defuse Mrs. Dornhecker's condition in the ladies' room is unclear but irrelevant. The next morning Peabody informed Mrs. Dornhecker that Rockefeller would only work with her one-and-a-half more days. Had Malibu believed it needed more time to consider Mrs. Dornhecker's complaints or what

504   LAW IN PROFESSIONAL PRACTICE

to do about them, it would have been reasonable. Rockefeller, despite his faults, had helped to purchase Malibu for its owners and held an employment contract. In this case, one cannot reasonably demand the employer to ignore its experience with the alleged offender or to examine a charge of sexual harassment based on one side of the story, in a vacuum. Malibu speedily evaluated Mrs. Dornhecker's complaints.

The judgment of the district court is reversed.

Notes and Issues for Discussion

1. What steps did Malibu take upon learning of the harassment? Are these sufficient?
2. In *Steele v. Offshore Shipbuilding Inc.* (CA 11, 3/15/89, 49 *FEP Cases* 522), the employer was held not liable, when after learning of the harassment it sent an equal employment opportunity officer to interview the employees, reprimanded the perpetrator, and assured the employees that the harassment would cease.
3. Conversely, in *Waltman v. International Paper Co.* (CA 5, 6/16/89, 50 *FEP Cases* 179) the employer allegedly did not reprimand an employee, conducted no investigation beyond a discussion with a supervisor, and then transferred the complainant. The court held the employer could be found liable for not taking steps which would reasonably halt the harassment.
4. A more complex situation occurred in *Paroline v. UNISYS Corp.*, 879 F.2d 100 (1989). UNISYS's supervisor, Moore, had a history of sexually harassing employees, and had been previously reprimanded. He made sexually suggestive remarks to Paroline, engaged in unwelcome physical contact, and on one day drove her home and kissed and fondled her. Paroline complained and UNISYS management warned Moore in writing that if the actions recurred he would be fired, instructed him to seek counseling and to limit his contact with female employees to official company business. Paroline argued that UNISYS's actions were inadequate, and also that given Moore's past history UNISYS should have taken adequate steps to prevent the harassment from taking place. The circuit court reversed a summary judgment for UNISYS and remanded the case for a hearing, noting that there were adequate grounds for finding UNISYS's actions inadequate and for finding that UNISYS had a duty to prevent the harassment from taking place.

Liability issues are complicated by variations in state laws and differing interpretations of the scope of Title VII. There is general agreement that in cases of *quid pro quo* harassment, the employer is liable under agency principles whether or not it knew of the harassment. In *Meritor*, the Supreme Court noted:

Examination of those principles has led the EEOC to the view that where a supervisor exercises the authority actually delegated to him by his employer, by making or threatening to make decisions affecting the employment status of his subordinates, such actions are properly imputed to the employer whose delegation of authority empowered the supervisor to undertake them. . . . Thus the courts have consistently held employers liable for the discriminatory discharges of employees by supervisory personnel, whether or not the employer knew, should have known, or approved of the supervisor's actions. 477 U.S. at 70.

In cases of hostile environment harassment, courts are less likely to find employers automatically liable unless the employer had no policies about sexual harassment or grievance procedures were deficient or absent. However, if the employer has notice of the harassment or should have known that it was occurring, the likelihood of liability is greater.

The scope of Title VII liability is limited by the Civil Rights Act of 1964 and its 1991 amendments. The 1964 act was enacted to rectify various types of workplace discrimination and most courts have held that the a plaintiff can only obtain reinstatement, back pay, reasonable attorney's fees, and injunctive and other equitable relief under its provisions. 42 U.S.C. §2000e-5(g). The 1991 amendments allow compensatory and punitive damages if "the respondent engaged in a discriminatory practice . . . with malice or with reckless indifference. . . ." In such cases punitive and compensatory damage awards are limited by the size of the of the organization and range from $50,000 for those ranging from 15 to 100 employees to $300,000 for those with over 500 employees. Governments, governmental agencies, and political subdivisions are excluded. 42 U.S.C. §1981a(b).

Alternate grounds for suit include the U.S. Constitution, state constitutions, state tort actions and violations of civil rights under 42 U.S.C. §1983 (Cohen, 1987). These actions could result in extensive damage awards, including both punitive and compensatory damages depending upon the law. Which of these laws apply or even whether they apply is a complex issue and may depend upon interpretations of federal and state law, whether agency principles and the doctrine of *respondeat superior* apply, whether the agency is public, private, or nonprofit, or whether the actions complained of fall within sovereign immunity or state tort claims acts. Competent legal advice may be crucial, since the potential liability could run to thousands of dollars.

One cannot easily predict when or to what extent liability will occur. However, case law suggests that the wise administrator will at a minimum (1) promulgate policies and grievance procedures along the lines indicated; (2) institute staff training programs, and update and repeat them periodically; and (3) when harassment complaints are filed investigate promptly, and if the complaints have merit, take prompt disciplinary action.

Sexual Harassment in Education

In *Franklin v. Gwinnett County Pub. Schools*, 117 L. Ed. 2d 208 (1992), the suit was for monetary damages under Title IX:

> According to the complaint . . . Franklin was subjected to continual sexual harassment beginning in the autumn of her tenth grade year (1986) from Andrew Hill, a sports coach and teacher employed by the district. Among other allegations, Franklin avers that Hill engaged her in sexually-oriented conversation . . . , forcibly kissed her . . . , telephoned her at home and asked if she would meet him socially . . . , and on three occasions in her junior year, Hill interrupted a class, requested that the teacher excuse Franklin, and took her to a private office where he subjected her to coercive intercourse. . . . The complaint further alleges that though they became aware of and investigated Hill's sexual harassment of Franklin and other female students, teachers and administrators took no action to halt it and discouraged Franklin from pressing charges against Hill. On April 14, 1988, Hill resigned on the condition that all matters pending against him be dropped. The school thereupon closed its investigation. 117 L.Ed. 2d 215.

The Court held there could be monetary damages awarded for sexual harassment in a public high school under Title IX of the Educational Amendments of 1972, 20 U.S.C. §1681-1688. Title IX provides in part:

> No person in the United States shall, on the basis of sex, be excluded from participation in, be denied the benefits of, or be subjected to discrimination under any education program or activity receiving Federal financial assistance. 20 U.S.C. §1681(a).

DRUG TESTING IN THE WORKPLACE

The increased concern over workplace substance abuse has resulted in a variety of policies banning possession or use of drugs or alcohol in the workplace and testing employees for drug abuse. Testing may be based on reasonable cause, it may be random, or it may be required of all employees or job applicants. Courts have generally held that drug testing conducted by governmental entities constitutes a search within the meaning of the Fourth Amendment and therefore invokes the Fourth Amendment prohibition on unreasonable searches and seizures applied to the states through the Fourteenth Amendment. Conversely, drug testing by private employers generally does not involve Fourth Amendment protections since there is no requisite state action.

Public Sector Drug Testing

Generally, courts have invalidated random governmental drug testing, instead requiring that there be reasonable cause for the search. Exceptions include drug tests in the U.S. Armed Forces, in federal and state corrections agencies, and in public programs dealing with narcotics offenders.

CAPUA v. CITY OF PLAINFIELD
643 F. Supp. 1507 (1986)
U.S. DISTRICT COURT

SAROKIN, DISTRICT JUDGE.

In the face of widespread use of drugs and its intrusion into the workplace, it is tempting to turn to mass testing as a solution. The issue presented by this case is the constitutionality of such testing of current employees by governmental entities.***Whether such testing may be done in the private sector or be imposed as a condition of accepting employment, even in the public sector, is not here presented. Government has a vital interest in making certain that its employees, particularly those whose impairment endangers their co-workers or the public, are free of drugs. But the question posed by this litigation challenges the means by which that laudable goal is attained, not the goal itself.

Urine testing involves one of the most private functions, a function traditionally performed in private, and indeed, usually prohibited in public. The proposed test, in order to ensure its reliability, requires the presence of another when the specimen is created and frequently reveals information about one's health unrelated to the use of drugs. If the tests are positive, it may affect one's employment status and even result in criminal prosecution.

We would be appalled at the spectre of the police spying on employees during their free time and then reporting their activities to their employers. Drug testing is a form of surveillance, albeit a technological one. Nonetheless, it reports on a person's off-duty activities just as surely as someone had been present and watching. It is George Orwell's "Big Brother" Society come to life.

To argue that it is the only practical means of discovering drug abuse is not sufficient. We do not permit a search of every house on a block merely because there is reason to believe that *one* contains evidence of criminal activity. No prohibition more significantly distinguishes our democracy from a totalitarian government than that which bars warrantless searches and seizures. Nor can the success of massive testing justify its use. We would not condone the beatings of suspects and the admissibility of their confessions merely because a large number of convictions resulted.***

On May 26, 1986 all fire fighters and fire officers employed by the defendant, City of Plainfield, were ordered to submit to a surprise urinalysis test. At 7:00

A.M. on May 26, the Plainfield Fire Chief and Plainfield Director of Public Affairs and Safety entered the city fire station, secured and locked all station doors and awakened the fire fighters present on the premises. Each fire department employee was required to submit a urine sample while under the surveillance and supervision of bonded testing agents employed by the city. Defendants repeated a substantially similar procedure on May 28 and June 12, 1986 until approximately all of the 103 employees of the Plainfield Fire Department were tested.

Prior to May 26, the Plainfield fire employees had no notice of defendant's intent to conduct mass urinalysis. Such urinalysis had not been provided for in the collective bargaining agreement between the fire fighters and the City. Nor was there any written directive, order, departmental policy or basis for such testing and prescribing appropriate standards and procedures for collecting, testing, and utilizing the information derived.

Between July 10 and July 14, 1986, sixteen firefighting personnel were advised that their respective urinalysis had proved positive for the presence of controlled dangerous substances. They were immediately terminated without pay. Those who tested positive were not informed of the particular substance found in their urine or of its concentration. Neither were they provided copies of the actual laboratory results. Written complaints were served ten days later on July 24, 1986, charging these fire fighters with numerous violations including "commission of a criminal act".***

Plaintiffs bring this action pursuant to 42 U.S.C. §1983, seeking declaratory and injunctive relief. They seek to have the urine testing declared unconstitutional and to enjoin the City of Plainfield and its agents from further conducting standardless, department-wide urine testing in violation of the Fourth Amendment. The parties have agreed to submit the mater for a final determination on the record before the court conceding that no actual issues exist which would require a hearing.

The Fourth Amendment to the United States Constitution states:

> The right of the people to be secure in their persons, houses, papers and effects, against unreasonable searches and seizures, shall not be violated . . .

The essential purpose of the Fourth Amendment is to "impose a standard of reasonableness upon the exercise of discretion by government officials" in order to "safeguard the privacy and security of individuals against arbitrary invasions by government officials."***The constitutional issue here arises only if the Fourth Amendment is implicated by defendant's conduct. The threshold question then is whether urinalysis constitutes a search and seizure within the meaning of the Fourth Amendment.

Courts have clearly established that individuals retain an expectation of privacy and a right to be free from government intrusion in the integrity of their own bodies.***

The "taking" of urine has been likened to the involuntary taking of blood which the Supreme Court found to constitute a search and seizure within the Fourth Amendment. Though urine, unlike blood, is routinely discharged from the body so that no actual intrusion is required for its collection, it is normally discharged and disposed of under circumstances that merit protection from arbitrary interference.

Both blood and urine can be analyzed in a medical laboratory to discover numerous physiological facts about the person from whom it came, including but not limited to recent ingestion of alcohol or drugs. "One does not reasonably expect to discharge urine under circumstances making it available to others to collect and analyze in order to discover the personal physiological secrets it holds." *McDonnell v. Hunter,* 612 F.Supp. 1122, 1127 (D.Iowa 1985). As with blood, each individual has a reasonable expectation of privacy in the personal "information" bodily fluids contain. For these reasons, governmental taking of a urine specimen constitutes a search and seizure within the meaning of the Fourth Amendment.***

Having determined that urine testing constitutes a search and seizure, this court must now evaluate defendants' search under the Fourth Amendment's dictates. The fundamental command of the Fourth Amendment is that searches and seizures be "reasonable." What is reasonable depends upon the context in which a search takes place. Ordinarily a search requires both a warrant and probable cause to qualify as constitutionally reasonable. Yet the Supreme Court has stated that neither element is "an irreducible requirement of a valid search." *New Jersey v. TLO, supra,* 105 S.Ct. at 743. Instead, the ultimate determination of a search's reasonableness requires a judicious balancing of the intrusiveness of the search against its promotion of a legitimate governmental interest.

This Court must determine whether the intrusion occasioned by compelling members of the Plainfield Fire Department to submit to compulsory urine testing is sufficiently justified by the governmental interest in ferreting out drugs so as to be "reasonable" within the meaning of the Fourth Amendment.

The degree of intrusion engendered by any search must be viewed in the context of the individual's legitimate expectation of privacy.***

Applied to the facts at hand, defendants' mass urine testing program subjected plaintiffs to a relatively high degree of bodily intrusion. As stated earlier, while urine is routinely discharged from the body, it is generally discharged and disposed of under circumstances that warrant a legitimate expectation of privacy. The act itself, totally apart from what it may reveal, is traditionally private. Facilities both at home and in places of public accommodation recognize this privacy tradition. In addition, society has generally condemned and prohibited the act in public. The "interests of human dignity and privacy" which compelled Justice Brennan to find mandatory blood extractions greatly intrusive, are implicated with equally compelling force when individuals are directed to urinate in the presence of a government agent. The requirement of surveillance during urine collection forces those tested to expose parts of their anatomy to the testing official in a manner akin to strip search exposure. Body surveillance is considered essential and standard operating procedure in the administration of urine drug tests, thus heightening the intrusiveness of these searches. A urine test done under close surveillance of a government representative, regardless of how professionally or courteously conducted, is likely to be a very embarrassing and humiliating experience.

Defendants contend that fire fighters, as public servants, have a diminished expectation of privacy, or in fact, no expectation of privacy at all with respect to job-related inquiries by the municipality. As employer, the City bears ultimate responsibility for insuring that its firefighting force is fully capable of protecting the welfare and public safety of Plainfield's citizenry. Consequently, defendants claim that their interest in the discovery and elimination of drug abuse among fire personnel overrides any privacy rights fire fighters may have.***

The City of Plainfield proceeded in its urine testing campaign without any specific information or independent knowledge that any individual fire department employee was under the influence of drugs. None of the 103 individual fire fighters compelled to submit to urine testing had received prior notice that their job performance was below standard. None of the 103 fire fighters tested were under investigation for drug use on the job. There was not an increased incidence of fire-related accidents or complaints of inadequate fire protection from the community. Defendants had no general job-related basis for instituting this mass urinalysis, much less any individualized basis.

The deleterious effects of drug consumption upon public safety officers' ability to properly perform their duties is undeniably an issue legitimately within the City's concern. But the merits of the City's efforts to assure that all fire fighters are free from drug induced impairments and capable to perform their public service is not at issue in this case. Rather the question to be answered is whether the means chosen by the City to achieve this laudable goal are "reasonable" within the meaning of the Fourth Amendment. This court is impelled to conclude that they are not.

As justification for undertaking the department-wide search, defendants explain that the widespread, large scale drug use in all segments of the population leads to the "reasonable and logical inference that some of those affected may ultimately be employed in a public-safety capacity." *See* Brief Submitted on Behalf of Defendants at 14. Defendants contend that mass round-up urinalysis is the most efficient way to detect drug use.

It is beyond dispute that the taking and testing of urine samples achieves the city's desired goal, namely the identification of employees who use drugs. But under the law, the results achieved cannot justify the means utilized and the constitutionality of a search cannot rest on its fruits.

The sweeping manner in which defendants set about to accomplish their goals violated the fire fighter's individual liberties. As to each individual tested the search was unreasonable because defendants lacked any specific suspicion as to that fire fighter.***

The invidious effect of such mass, round-up urinalysis is that it casually sweeps up the innocent with the guilty and willingly sacrifices each individual's Fourth Amendment rights in the name of some larger public interest. The City of Plainfield essentially presumed the guilt of each person tested. The burden was shifted onto each fire fighter to submit to a highly intrusive urine test in order to vindicate his or her innocence. Such an unfounded presumption of guilt is contrary to the protections against arbitrary and intrusive government interference set forth in the Constitution. Although plaintiffs' privacy and liberty interests may be diminished on the job, these interests are not extinguished and therefore must be accorded some constitutional protection.***

The Fourth Amendment allows defendants to demand urine of an employee only on the basis of a reasonable suspicion predicated upon specific facts and reasonable inferences drawn from those facts in light of experience. The reasonable suspicion standard requires individualized suspicion, specifically directed to the person who is targeted for the search.***Absent a requirement of individualized suspicion, the Fourth Amendment would cease to protect against arbitrary government intrusion.***

A balancing of the state's interest against the significant invasion of privacy occasioned by the urine testing requires a determination that defendants' conduct was unreasonable and violative of the Fourth Amendment.***

This court finds that plaintiffs have met their burden of demonstrating that defendant City of Plainfield and its agents violated their constitutional rights by instituting compulsory, departmentwide, urine testing absent individualized reasonable, suspicion.

Notes and Issues for Discussion

1. The drug testing was without individual suspicion and without notice. The court states that the Fourth Amendment search must be based on a "reasonable suspicion predicated on specific facts and reasonable inferences." What would be some reasonable suspicions? How would you document them?
2. Plainfield argues that the widespread use of drugs leads to a "reasonable and logical inference that some of those affected may ultimately be employed in a public-safety capacity." Would this logical inference lead to testing in public health agencies? Public human service agencies?
3. In *Policemen's Benevolent Assn. of N.J. v. Washington Twp.*, 672 F. Supp. 799 (1987), a mandatory random drug testing program was found in violation of the Fourth Amendment.
4. In *Shoemaker v. Handel*, 795 F.2d 1136, the court upheld random drug testing of jockeys on the basis of a diminished privacy right because of the high degree of state regulation of the racing industry and the need to assure the integrity of persons involved in horse racing.

TREASURY EMPLOYEES v. VON RAAB
489 U.S. 656 (1988)
U.S. SUPREME COURT

JUSTICE KENNEDY delivered the opinion of the Court.

We granted certiorari to decide whether it violates the Fourth Amendment for the United States Customs Service to require a urinalysis test from employees who seek transfer or promotion to certain positions.

The United States Customs Service, a bureau of the Department of Treasury, is the federal agency responsible for processing persons, carriers, cargo, and mail into the United States, collecting revenue from imports, and enforcing customs and related laws. An important responsibility of the Service is the interdiction and seizure of contraband, including illegal drugs.

In May 1986, the Commissioner announced implementation of the drug-testing program. Drug tests were made a condition of placement or employment for positions that meet one or more of three criteria. The first is direct involvement in drug interdiction or enforcement of related laws, an activity the Commissioner deemed fraught with obvious dangers to the mission of the agency and the lives of customs agents. The second criterion is a requirement that the incumbent carry firearms, as the Commissioner concluded that "[p]ublic safety demands that employees who carry deadly arms and are prepared to make instant life or death decisions be drug free." The third criterion is a requirement for the incumbent to handle "classified" material, which the Commissioner determined might fall into the hands of smugglers if accessible to employees who, by reason of their own illegal drug use, are susceptible to bribery or blackmail.***

After an employee qualifies for a position covered by the Customs testing program, the Service advises him by letter that his final selection is contingent upon successful completion of drug screening. An independent contractor contacts the employee to fix the time and place for collecting the sample. On reporting for the test, the employee must produce photographic identification and remove any outer garments, such as a coat or a jacket, and personal belongings. The employee may produce the sample behind a partition, or in the privacy of a bathroom stall if he so chooses. To ensure against adulteration of the specimen, or substitution of a sample from another person, a monitor of the same sex as the employee remains close at hand to listen for the normal sounds of urination. Dye is added to the toilet water to prevent the employee from using the water to adulterate the sample.

Upon receiving the specimen, the monitor inspects it to ensure its proper temperature and color, places a tamper-proof custody seal over the container, and affixes an identification label indicating the date and the individual's specimen number. The employee signs a chain-of-custody form, which is initialed by the monitor, and the urine sample is placed in a plastic bag, sealed, and submitted to a laboratory.

The laboratory tests the sample for the presence of marijuana, cocaine, opiates, amphetamines, and phenyclidine. Two tests are used. An initial screening test uses the enzyme-multiplied-immunoassay technique (EMIT). Any specimen that is identified as positive on this initial test must then be confirmed using gas chromatography/mass spectrometry (GC/MS). Confirmed positive results are reported to a "Medical Review Officer," "[a] licensed physician ... who has knowledge of substance abuse disorders and has appropriate medical training to interpret and evaluate the individual's positive test result together with his or her medical history and any other relevant biomedical information." HHS Reg §1.2, 53 Fed Reg 11980 (1988); HHS Reg §2.4(g), id., at 11983. After verifying the positive result, the Medical Review Officer transmits it to the agency.

Customs employees who test positive for drugs and who can offer no satisfactory explanation are subject to dismissal from the Service. Test results may not, however, be turned over to any other agency, including criminal prosecutors, without the employee's written consent.

Petitioners, a union of federal employees and a union official, commenced this suit in the United States District Court for the Eastern District of Louisiana on behalf of current Customs Service employees who seek covered positions. Petitioners alleged that the Customs Service drug-testing program violated, inter alia, the Fourth Amendment. The District Court agreed.***The court enjoined the drug testing program, and ordered the Customs Service not to require drug tests of any applicants for covered positions.

A divided panel of the United States Court of Appeals for the Fifth Circuit vacated the injunction.

***We now affirm so much of the judgment of the court of appeals as upheld the testing of employees directly involved in drug interdiction or required to carry firearms. We vacate the judgment to the extent it upheld the testing of applicants for positions requiring the incumbent to handle classified materials, and remand for further proceedings.

In Skinner v Railway Labor Executives' Assn., ante, at ———, 103 L Ed 2d 639, 109 S Ct ———, decided today, we hold that federal regulations requiring employees of private railroads to produce urine samples for chemical testing implicate the Fourth Amendment, as those tests invade reasonable expectations of privacy.

While we have often emphasized, and reiterate today, that a search must be supported, as a general matter, by a warrant issued upon probable cause, our decision in Railway Labor Executives reaffirms the longstanding principle that neither a warrant nor probable cause, nor, indeed, any measure of individualized suspicion, is an indispensable component of reasonableness in every circumstance. As we note in Railway Labor Executives, our cases establish that where a Fourth Amendment intrusion serves special government needs, beyond the normal need for law enforcement, it is necessary to balance the individual's privacy expectations against the Government's interests to determine whether it is impractical to require a warrant or some level of individualized suspicion in the particular context.

***Our precedents have settled that, in certain limited circumstances, the Government's need to discover such latent or hidden conditions, or to prevent their development, is sufficiently compelling to justify the intrusion on privacy entailed by conducting such searches without any measure of individualized suspicion. E.g., Railway Labor Executives, ante, at ———, 103 L Ed 2d 639, 109 S Ct ———. We think the Government's need to conduct the suspicionless searches required by the Customs program outweighs the privacy interests of employees engaged directly in drug interdiction, and of those who otherwise are required to carry firearms.

The Customs Service is our Nation's first line of defense against one of the greatest problems affecting the health and welfare of our population. We have adverted before to "the veritable national crisis in law enforcement caused by smuggling of illicit narcotics." United States v Montoya de Hernandez, 473 US

531, 538 (1985). Our cases also reflect the traffickers' seemingly inexhaustible repertoire of deceptive practices and elaborate schemes for importing narcotics.***

Many of the Service's employees are often exposed to this criminal element and to the controlled substances they seek to smuggle into the country. The physical safety of these employees may be threatened, and many may be tempted not only by bribes from the traffickers with whom they deal, but also by their own access to vast sources of valuable contraband seized and controlled by the Service. The Commissioner indicated below that "Customs [o]fficers have been shot, stabbed, run over, dragged by automobiles, and assaulted with blunt objects while performing their duties." At least nine officers have died in the line of duty since 1974. He also noted that Customs officers have been the targets of bribery by drug smugglers on numerous occasions, and several have been removed from the Service for accepting bribes and other integrity violations. See also Customs USA, Fiscal Year 1987, at 31 (reporting internal investigations that resulted in the arrest of 24 employees and 54 civilians); Customs USA, Fiscal Year 1986, p 32 (reporting that 334 criminal and serious integrity investigations were conducted during the fiscal year, resulting in the arrest of 37 employees and 17 civilians); Customs USA, Fiscal Year 1985, at 32 (reporting that 284 criminal and serious integrity investigations were conducted during the 1985 fiscal year, resulting in the arrest of 15 employees and 51 civilians).

It is readily apparent that the Government has a compelling interest in ensuring that front-line interdiction personnel are physically fit, and have unimpeachable integrity and judgment.***This national interest in self protection could be irreparably damaged if those charged with safeguarding it were, because of their own drug use, unsympathetic to their mission of interdicting narcotics. A drug user's indifference to the Service's basic mission or, even worse, his active complicity with the malefactors, can facilitate importation of sizable drug shipments or block apprehension of dangerous criminals. The public interest demands effective measures to bar drug users from positions directly involving the interdiction of illegal drugs.

The public interest likewise demands effective measures to prevent the promotion of drug users to positions that require the incumbent to carry a firearm, even if the incumbent is not engaged directly in the interdiction of drugs. Customs employees who may use deadly force plainly "discharge duties fraught with such risks of injury to others that even a momentary lapse of attention can have disastrous consequences." Railway Labor Executives, ante, at ———, 103 L Ed 2d 639, 109 S Ct ———. We agree with the Government that the public should not bear the risk that employees who may suffer from impaired perception and judgment will be promoted to positions where they may need to employ deadly force. Indeed, ensuring against the creation of this dangerous risk will itself further Fourth Amendment values, as the use of deadly force may violate the Fourth Amendment in certain circumstances.

Against these valid public interests we must weigh the interference with individual liberty that results from requiring these classes of employees to undergo a urine test. The interference with individual privacy that results from the collection of a urine sample for subsequent chemical analysis could be substantial in some circumstances. We have recognized, however, that the "operational realities of the workplace" may render entirely reasonable certain work-related intrusions by supervisors and co-workers that might be viewed as unreasonable in other contexts. While these operational realities will rarely affect an employee's expectations of privacy with respect to searches of his person, or of personal effects that the employee may bring to the workplace, it is plain that certain forms of public employment may diminish privacy expectations even with respect to such personal searches. Employees of the United States Mint, for example, should expect to be subject to certain routine personal searches when they leave the workplace every day.***

We think Customs employees who are directly involved in the interdiction of illegal drugs or who are required to carry firearms in the line of duty likewise have a diminished expectation of privacy in respect to the intrusions occasioned by a urine test. Unlike most private citizens or government employees in general, employees involved in drug interdiction reasonably should expect effective inquiry into their fitness and probity. Much the same is true of employees who are required to carry firearms. Because successful performance of their duties depends uniquely on their judgment and dexterity, these employees cannot reasonably expect to keep from the Service personal information that bears directly on their fitness. While reasonable tests designed to elicit this information doubtless infringe some privacy expectations, we do not believe these expectations outweigh the Government's compelling interest in safety and in the integrity of our borders.***

In sum, we believe the Government has demonstrated that its compelling interests in safeguarding our borders and the public safety outweigh the privacy expectations of employees who seek to be promoted to positions that directly involve the interdiction of illegal drugs or that require the incumbent to carry a firearm. We hold that the testing of these employees is reasonable under the Fourth Amendment.

Notes and Issues for Discussion

1. In *Capua* the drug testing was unreasonable and unconstitutional. *Von Raab* upholds governmental testing. How are the two cases different?
2. In *Von Raab*, the search is warrantless, without suspicion or probable cause. It is constitutionally acceptable because of the balancing of employee privacy rights with the nature of the employment.
3. On the same day the court decided *Skinner v. Railway Labor Executives Assn.*, 489 U.S. 602 (1988). In that case the Court upheld federal regulations mandating blood and urine testing of covered employees involved in certain train accidents. The Court held that the tests were governed by the Fourth Amendment, but that public safety could take precedence over private interests.
4. In *American Postal Workers Union v. Frank*, 725 F. Supp. 87 (1989), the court distinguished the U.S. Postal Service from the railroads in *Skinner* and the Customs Service in *Von Raab*. The court noted that the postal service is not a highly regulated industry like the railroads, and postal workers do not

carry firearms or interdict drugs as do Customs employees. The court found the drug testing regulations unconstitutional under the Fourth Amendment.

Drug-Free Workplace Act

The Drug-Free Workplace Act, effective in 1989, applies to federal agencies, certain federal contractors, and agencies receiving federal funds. Its provisions are limited in scope in that the act does not require testing for substance abuse, prohibit workers from coming to work under the influence of drugs, or require the establishment of employee assistance programs (EAPs). Among its provisions are requirements that the employer

1. notify employees that the unlawful manufacture, distribution, dispensation, or use of a controlled substance is prohibited, and the actions that can be taken for violation;
2. establish a drug-free awareness program, including informing employees of the existence of drug counseling or EAP programs;
3. require employees as a condition of employment to notify the employer of any criminal drug conviction occurring in the workplace within five days;
4. requiring employers to sanction these employees or to require participation in a drug abuse assistance or rehabilitation program. 41 U.S.C. §701 *et seq.*

Drug Testing in the Private Sector

A 1987 study of employer drug testing found that 40 percent of the companies surveyed use drug tests to test either current employees or job applicants. Of the other 60 percent, over half were considering the implementation of drug tests (Abbey and Redel, 1991:239). Since private employers are generally not covered by the Fourth Amendment, constitutional restrictions on private employer drug testing are limited.

Additional restrictions may be found in state law. A number of states now regulate drug testing and the use of private workplace tests to some extent.[10] There have been proposals for federal regulation of private sector drug testing that would preempt conflicting state law and provide uniformity.[11]

Employee dismissals following drug testing have resulted in actions for emotional distress, invasion of privacy, and wrongful discharge and have resulted in some substantial damage awards.[12]

Outside of these restrictions, mandatory drug testing has been held as an appropriate subject for collective bargaining, with those not covered by collective bargaining agreements and job applicants tested as the employer wishes (Abbey and Redel, 1991).

EMPLOYEE ASSISTANCE PROGRAMS

An increasing number of public and private employers are establishing employee assistance programs, resulting in greater utilization of health and human services professionals. The EAPs may be within or outside the agency, and may provide referrals or programs. Many of the EAPs are primarily focused on alcohol and drug abuse, but they may extend to a number of health and social problems.

The EAP and the Law

The EAP professional-client relationship is regulated by laws pertaining to privacy, confidentiality, duty to protect, informed consent, and AIDS among others. EAP workers may be governed by the codes of ethics of relevant professional associations. Violations of these laws and codes may result in malpractice, and perhaps supervisory or administrative liability.

Confidentiality and Privacy

Confidentiality and privacy of EAP records and client information may fall under the Privacy Act of 1974 (5 U.S.C. §552a), confidentiality of federally funded drug and alcohol programs (42 U.S.C. §290ee-3 and §290dd-3), state confidentiality statutes, or state privilege statutes where applicable. If the EAP is a federal program, or federally funded or assisted, federal confidentiality laws will apply. Promises or assurances of confidentiality to the EAP client will in many cases create a confidential relationship. In addition, confidentiality may be seen as implicit in the EAP professional-client relationship. Release of information should be predicated on a valid waiver by the client.

As with confidentiality and privacy in general, there are limits. The EAP professional is usually mandated to report to the appropriate agency disclosures of suspected child abuse. Some states also mandate disclosure of elder abuse, institutional abuse, or abuse of handicapped persons. In many states, the professional may have to take steps to protect an intended victim or the client from probable harm. Some states may also require disclosure of certain criminal acts. Disclosure of an AIDS or HIV positive condition to a spouse or sexual partner without informed consent creates the same sort of dilemma for the EAP professional as it does for other health and human services professionals. Unless there is a law permitting such disclosure, revealing this information to another for that person's protection is a violation of the client's confidentiality and privacy rights. On the other hand, disclosure when the professional believes that the other person is at risk may be an ethical or moral obligation. Informing the EAP client of the limits of confidentiality at the outset of the relationship will ease later mandated disclosures. Whether the EAP is an internal or external program, information received in confidence should not be released to the employer without a waiver by the client.

Release of any confidential information should be based on a valid waiver by the client unless mandated by law. The waiver should include what is to be released, when, to whom, for what purpose, and for what period of time.

Informed Consent

The EAP professional should obtain an informed consent prior to treatment, based on adequate disclosure, a capacity to understand, and the absence of coercion. Where the employee is required to seek treatment or treatment is a condition of continued employment, there may be questions about degree of voluntariness in consent for treatment.

Liability Issues

The EAP professional faces the same liability issues discussed in the following chapter that most health and human services professionals face. Whether the standard for unintentional wrongs is negligence or malpractice will depend on whether or not the EAP professional is regarded as a member of a group whose professional standard calls for a higher degree of skill. Use of community or national standards of conduct will depend upon the jurisdiction. Common malpractice or liability actions may include failure to protect another or the client, lack of informed consent, failure to treat, failure to refer or improper referral, breach of confidentiality or invasion of privacy, faulty diagnosis, abandonment, wrongful treatment or sexual misconduct. Actions may also be brought for breach of contract, breach of a fiduciary duty, or intentional harm. Inadequate supervision, failure to supervise, or, where applicable, vicarious liability may result in supervisory liability.

In *Wangen v. Knudson*, 428 N.W. 2d 242, the South Dakota Supreme Court upheld Wangen's award against an EAP counselor, Wangen's supervisor, and their employers. After Wangen had been hospitalized for depression, his wife expressed concern about his drinking to his supervisor. The supervisor referred Wangen to an EAP counselor who told Wangen that he was an alcoholic and would have to undergo a thirty-day inpatient treatment for alcoholism or be fired. The conversation took place in front of the supervisor. When Wangen later phoned to ask for a postponement until his psychologist could discuss his case with the EAP counselor, the counselor included Wangen's supervisor in the telephone conversation and told Wangen he was fired, although this was untrue.

The court held that an award of $130,000 for compensatory and punitive damages was not excessive.

SELECTED REFERENCES

Abbey, A., and Redel, C. "Drug testing in the workplace: Public and private sector employers and the courts," 42 *Labor L.J.* 239 (1991).

Champagne, P., and McAfee, R. B. "Auditing sexual harassment," 68 *Personnel J.* 124 (1989).

Cohen, C. "Legal dilemmas in sexual harassment cases," 38 *Labor L.J.* 681 (1987).

Feldman, D. "Sexual harassment: Policies and prevention," 64 *Personnel J.* 12 (1987).

Jennings, K., and Clapp, M. "Harassed and harassing employees' rights in sexual discrimination cases," 40 *Labor L.J.* 756 (1989).

Koen, C. "Sexual harassment claims stem from hostile work environment," 69 *Personnel J.* 88 (1990).

MacKinnon, C. *Sexual Harassment of Working Women* (1979).

Note, "Employer: Beware of 'Hostile Environment' Sexual Harassment," 26 *Duquesne Law Review* 461 (1988).

Nye, S. G. *Employee Assistance Law Answer Book* (1990, and 1992 supp.).

Olsen, J. J. "A comprehensive review of private sector drug testing law," 8 *Hofstra Labor L.J.* 223 (1991).

Paul, E. F. "Sexual harassment as sex discrimination: A defective paradigm," 8 *Yale L. and Policy R.* 333 (1990).

Strauss, M. "Sexist speech in the workplace," 25 *Harvard Civil Rights and Civil Liberties L. R.* 1 (1990).

CHAPTER 15

MALPRACTICE AND ADMINISTRATIVE LIABILITY

Malpractice and liability issues remain a major concern of the health and human services professional. While the greatest number of malpractice actions occurs in the medical arena, other malpractice actions have involved a broad range of professionals, including psychiatrists, psychologists, psychotherapists, clergypersons, social workers, and probation and parole officers. Some authorities argue that outside of medicine the importance of malpractice in the health and human services has been overstated (Saltzman and Proch, 1990; Jones and Alcabes, 1989), while others warn of increasing numbers of legal actions against health and human services professionals (Bernstein, 1978, 1981; Besharov, 1985; Cohen, 1979; Robertson, 1988).

As a policy matter, some authorities have suggested that health and human services professionals should be protected from most malpractice claims and held harmless for their actions because much of their work involves risk taking with a probability of good-faith erroneous decisions while trying to benefit patients and clients. They argue that the threat of malpractice claims will cause professionals to avoid taking chances and perhaps even refuse to serve high-risk clients, thus doing a disservice to patient and client populations (Besharov, 1984). Others have argued for increasingly strict standards of professional liability as one way to insure accountability and provide a higher quality of services for the client and patient populations (Horowitz and Davidson, 1981; Furrow, 1980).

RANGE OF MALPRACTICE ACTIONS

According to an American Psychological Association survey, sexual contact with clients constituted 18.5 percent of all successful malpractice cases brought against psychologists between 1976 and 1986, and awards from these actions totaled 45.8 percent of all malpractice claims paid by psychologists' insurance companies. Other frequent claims included errors in treatment, evaluation and diagnosis; death of a patient; breach of confidentiality; disputes over fees; defamation; violations of civil rights; and assault and battery (Austin, Moline, and Williams, 1990: 16–17).[1] A survey of claims against a major insurer of social workers over a twenty-year period showed similar results: Sexual impropriety was the most common claim, followed by incorrect treatment, improper placement, breach of confidentiality, and death of a patient (Besharov, 1985: 3).

While outside of the field of medicine there are relatively few reported malpractice cases in the health and human services, this low number may be misleading since many malpractice and liability actions are settled prior to court or go unreported. Whether or not malpractice and liability claims are or will soon reach "crisis" proportions, the health and human services professional needs to be aware of the major issues and existing case law. Malpractice suits can result in major financial losses and damage to the professional's reputation, and they can take a toll in time, money, energy, and distraction from normal work.

THE LEGAL CONTEXT OF MALPRACTICE

At its broadest, malpractice includes all forms of professional misconduct. Malpractice can be defined as

> [p]rofessional misconduct or unreasonable lack of skill. . . . Failure of one rendering professional services to exercise that degree of skill and learning commonly applied under all the circumstances in the community by the average prudent reputable member of the profession with the result of injury, loss or damage to the recipient of those services or to those entitled to rely upon them. (Black's *Law Dictionary*, 1991)

Many malpractice and liability issues lie within the legal area of tort law (pertaining to civil wrongs), which includes both intentional and unintentional harms. Within the area of unintentional harm lies the field of negligence, which technically includes malpractice actions. In addition, there are other types of professional legal liability including breach of contract, violation of a fiduciary duty, invasion of privacy, defamation, and violation of constitutional rights.

Negligence and Malpractice

Negligence has been defined as conduct "which falls below the standard established by law for the protection of others against unreasonable risk of

harm." (Restatement of the Law, Second, Torts 2d §282.)[2]
A key element of negligence is that the harm is unintentional:

> In negligence, the actor does not desire to bring about the consequences which follow, nor does he know that they are substantially certain to occur, or believe that they will. There is merely a risk of such consequences, sufficiently great to lead a reasonable person in his position to anticipate them, and to guard against them. (Keeton *et al.*, 1984: 169)

If a professional acts in a negligent manner it is malpractice; if the individual is not a professional, there may still be liability, but it would fall within simple negligence, not malpractice. This distinction is important because it determines the standard of performance used to determine liability (and may affect the statute of limitations that will apply). For the nonprofessional, the standard is that of a reasonable person exercising due care. For the professional, the standard is a more demanding one, that of a reasonable professional drawing upon the skill and training typical of the profession. Thus technically to establish malpractice, the plaintiff needs first to show that the defendant is in fact a professional—perhaps licensed by some public or quasi-public authority or the recipient of an advanced degree from a professional school—and then show that the conduct in question falls outside that of a reasonable professional in similar circumstances.[3] Of course, action or inaction by one who does not legally qualify as a "professional" may still be subject to liability in negligence.

BASIC CONCEPTS

Generally, for a successful malpractice action based in negligence, the plaintiff must establish four elements:

1. The existence of a legal duty to the patient or client
2. A breach of that duty through action or inaction
3. Actual harm or damage incurred by the patient or client
4. A causal connection between the breach of duty and the resulting harm or damage (Keeton *et al.*, 1984: 164–165; Schutz, 1982: 2–10).[4]

Duty

A duty, in negligence cases, may be defined as an obligation, to which the law will give recognition and effect, to conform to a particular standard of conduct toward another. (Keeton *et al.*, 1984: 356)

A professional relationship (or the belief in one) is probably sufficient to establish a duty, although the duty may be limited to the scope of the profession. For example, a therapist has a duty to provide adequate therapy or treatment, but not a duty to provide adequate religious or nutritional instruction.

Several important cases have extended the concept of duty beyond the professional relationship. The *Tarasoff* case in California and case law and statutes in many other jurisdictions have extended a duty to protect readily identifiable—and sometimes unidentified—third parties who are not part of the professional relationship. In these jurisdictions, the professional must take affirmative steps to protect even though there is no professional relationship. (See, generally, Chapter 6.)

Breach of Duty

A breach of duty may occur through professional action or inaction, sometimes known as commission or omission.[5] In either case, an external comparative standard is generally used to determine whether or not there was a breach of the duty owed.[6] While the standard used in most negligence actions is that of a reasonable person of average ability, the skilled professional is held to a higher standard reflecting that person's greater knowledge, skill, and training. In some jurisdictions, this is a *community standard*, where the professional's action is measured against the actions of similar professionals in the same or similar communities. In other jurisdictions, a broader *national standard* is used, where the actions of the professional are measured against the standards of the profession at large.[7] These standards may be established through testimony by expert witnesses, licensure statutes, and sometimes professional codes of ethics.[8]

Where there are several acceptable schools of thought within a profession, the professional is usually judged by the standards of the school with which that individual identifies (Keeton, *et al.*, 1984: 187). However, in some of the health and human services, it may be difficult to establish that the professional identifies with one particular school, or what the standards are for a particular school. This may make it more difficult for a plaintiff to establish that the conduct was outside that required by the profession.

Harm or Injury

Even if there is a duty and a breach of that duty, no action for malpractice will lie if there is not some demonstrable harm or injury. The injury may be physical or mental, and may be to the patient or client or may extend to someone in close proximity. The simplest situation involves actual physical injury, for example, stemming from improper therapy or treatment. The physical injury might be accompanied by emotional harm, which is recognized in many jurisdictions as an additional grounds for recovery. However, if the emotional harm is not directly linked to any physical harm, or where it is related to a preexisting condition, some jurisdictions may not allow recovery on the grounds that it is too difficult to prove the connection to the improper treatment. (See generally, Keeton, *et al.*, 1984: 54 *ff.*, 361 *ff.*) A different order of harm occurs when another person, perhaps a spouse or other family member, is present when the injury to the client or patient takes place or observes the individual in great distress and claims to have been harmed by the experience. Some jurisdictions will allow recovery on this basis as well (Keeton, *et al.*, 1984: 65–66, 365 *ff.*).

Direct or Proximate Cause

Finally, for recovery, the harm or injury must result from or have a causal relation with the breach of duty. Legally the breach must be the "proximate" cause of the harm, where proximate means closest in causal connection: "That which, in a natural and continuous sequence, unbroken by an efficient intervening cause, produces injury . . ." (Black's *Law Dictionary*, 1991). If, for example, a patient in therapy threatened suicide in such a way that a reasonable professional would believe the threat valid and would have taken steps to protect the patient, but no action was taken, and the patient left the office and, before anything else occurred, attempted suicide and was injured or killed. Here, there is a very strong case for liability based on a breach of duty which was the proximate cause of the injury. However, in the same situation if the patient attempted suicide in the following month, and lost a job or was divorced in the meantime, there is a much weaker case for liability because of the difficulty in demonstrating an uninterrupted causal link between the professional's failure to take steps to protect the individual and the later harm. If the suicide was attempted in the following year it would be very hard to prove that nothing intervened to break the causal link. (See generally, Keeton, *et al.*, 1984: Chapter 7.)

Monetary Awards

Monetary awards for malpractice are generally in the form of compensatory damages to the individual for losses suffered because of the malpractice, and can include out-of-pocket costs for loss of earnings, medical and mental health expenses, the cost of the inadequate services rendered, and compensation for loss of future earnings and pain and suffering.[9] In addition, damage awards could compensate others related to the injured party, including compensation for loss of consortium, loss of support, or—in the event of a fatality—wrongful death.

SPECIFIC MALPRACTICE AND LIABILITY ACTIONS

Given the variety and complexity of activities in which health and human services professionals are engaged, the possibility for malpractice and other liability actions always exists. The following discussion is not intended to be all-inclusive, but instead to give examples of some of the more frequent types of malpractice actions and the issues involved in them. Several areas—such as violations of privacy and confidentiality, and the duty to warn about a dangerous patient—have been discussed in detail elsewhere and will only be touched upon.[10]

Self-Inflicted Harm

Failing to prevent suicide or other self-inflicted injury by a patient or client is a frequent malpractice claim. Once a duty is established the issues usually are if there was a breach of duty and if the breach was the proximate cause of the injury.

As a first step, the health and human services professional must make a reasonable diagnosis whether or not the patient or client is potentially suicidal or otherwise dangerous to self. This would include an assessment of statements and prior actions, along with information such as statements by others, existence and content of a plan to commit the act, and the availability of a means to carry out the threatened action. If a reasonable professional would believe that the individual was dangerous to self, then appropriate supervision, treatment, or referral would need to be provided. However, this does not mean that the health and human services professional is liable for every instance of self-inflicted harm. Calculated risks that can be shown to be part of a treatment philosophy or plan are permitted; errors that a reasonable professional might make are not actionable; extended twenty-four surveillance often is not practicable.

INADEQUATE DIAGNOSIS

BAKER v. UNITED STATES
226 F. Supp. 129 (1964)
U.S. DISTRICT COURT

STEPHENSON, CHIEF JUDGE.

This action was brought by Mrs. Kenneth Baker as legal guardian for Kenneth Baker, an incompetent, against the United States of America under the provisions of the Federal Tort Claims Act, Title 28 U.S.C.A., §1346(b) and §§2671–2680. Plaintiff seeks to recover damages in the sum of $100,000 for injuries allegedly sustained by her ward in attempting to commit suicide by jumping into a concrete window well on the grounds of the Veterans Administration Hospital at Iowa City, Iowa, where said ward was under psychiatric treatment. In addition plaintiff, individually, seeks damages in the sum of $25,000 for loss of consortium.***

Plaintiff's ward, Kenneth Baker (hereinafter referred to as the patient) was referred to the Veterans Administration Hospital in Iowa City, Iowa, on August 23, 1960, by his attending physician, Dr. C. E. Schrock, M.D. The patient, then 61 years of age, had been under Dr. Schrock's care for approximately 60 days prior thereto. In a medical certificate accompanying the patient's written application for admission to the V.A. Hospital, Dr. Schrock indicated the following:

> Brief History: Progressive symptoms of depression past three months. Suicidal content evident, no real response to imipramine medication to date.
> Symptoms: Depressed, self accusatory, sleep disturbance and periods of confusion. Suicidal content.
> Diagnosis: Involuntary psychotic reaction.

The patient's wife testified that at the time of patient's application for admission she conferred with Dr. James A. Kennedy, M.D. (then acting Chief of the Neuropsychiatric Service at the V.A. Hospital) and advised him that there was a suicidal tendency on the part of her husband and told him about finding a gun her husband had hid in one of the buildings on the farm about three weeks before. Dr. Kennedy interviewed the patient for an hour to an hour and a half, visited with the patient's wife and brother, examined the admitting certificate above referred to, and advised the patient's wife that the patient would be admitted.***Dr. Kennedy then ordered his admission to Ward 10E, an open ward, because as the doctor testified "in my opinion he did not present himself as a suicidal risk." The patient remained on this open ward on the 10th floor for the next three days and had free access to go to the 3rd floor for meals, to the canteen, and to go outside. On August 27, 1960, the patient left the ward on the 10th floor voluntarily and went to the grounds immediately outside the hospital building. At about 7:30 p.m., the patient jumped into a window well 13 feet deep in an obvious suicide attempt. He suffered scalp wounds, fractures of the left clavicle, the

8th, 9th and 10th ribs, and the left transverse processes of the 3rd, 4th and 5th lumbar vertebral bodies. About six hours later the patient suffered an occlusion of the left carotid artery. Thereafter the patient suffered a complete paralysis of his right side. On April 19, 1961, the patient was removed to Restopia, a private nursing home, where he now remains. The patient is completely and permanently disabled both mentally and physically and requires constant nursing attendance.

In considering the various allegations of negligence it should first be observed that there is no evidence indicating that hospital employees failed to carry out the orders of Dr. Kennedy or any other physicians in the care of the patient. Failure on the part of hospital employees to carry out the instructions of a patient's physician may constitute a violation of the standard of care required of hospitals. Neither is there evidence indicating any appreciable change in the patient's condition from the time of his admission to the time of the suicidal attempt which might require action on the part of hospital employees not covered by Dr. Kennedy's instructions. It should also now be observed that the window well into which the patient leaped was enclosed by a heavy mesh wire fence which was at least three feet high. This was not a case of the patient falling into the window well but the injury was caused by a deliberate leap of the patient over the fence into the window well.***

The negligence, if any, which was the proximate cause of the patient's injuries arises out of the failure of Dr. Kennedy to properly diagnose the patient as a sufficient suicide risk so as to require closer supervision than was furnished by the immediate assignment of the patient to an open ward. A closed ward on the 9th floor was available to which patients were assigned when close supervision was deemed advisable. The issues are: What standard of care was required of the hospital and its staff: Was that standard of care violated in assigning the patient to an open ward?

There appear to be no Iowa cases involving the standard of care required of mental hospitals toward their patients. But it appears generally, that the care required of a hospital includes giving such care to a patient as the hospital knew or in the exercise of reasonable care should have known was required. This duty is measured by the degree of care, skill and diligence customarily exercised by hospitals generally in the community. A hospital is not an insurer of a patient's safety and is not required to guard against that which a reasonable person under the circumstances would not anticipate.***

***Was the doctor negligent? In Wilson v. Corbin, 241 Iowa 593, 599 (1950), the Iowa Supreme Court said:

> "A physician is bound to use that degree of knowledge, skill, care, and attention ordinarily exercised by physicians under like circumstances and in like localities. He does not impliedly guarantee results.
>
> "Of course malpractice may consist in lack of skill or care in diagnosis as well as in treatment.
>
> "A patient is entitled to a thorough and careful examination such as his condition and attending circumstances will permit, with such diligence and methods of diagnosis as are usually approved and practiced by physi-

cians of ordinary learning, judgment and skill in the community or similar
localities. A physician does not insure the correctness of his diagnosis."***

In the case at hand plaintiff offered evidence of practices followed at the State
University of Iowa Psychopathic Hospital in the same city and during the same
period of time as here involved. In this connection Dr. Paul Huston, Director of
that hospital since 1956, testified as follows:

"A   The first step would have been to establish the diagnosis and to determine if in fact this man was depressed, as the note from the referring physician had indicated. Since the referring physician had indicated that there
was suicidal content to this man's thinking, we would have paid particular
attention to this in order to determine what kind of precautions would be
necessary in handling the case.
    "Q   And what kind of precautions would be used until it was found
definitely he was subject to that suicidal content or was not?
    "A   Well, this varies some. It depends upon the presence or absence of
the suicidal content. If present, this means certain precautions. If they are
absent, then precautions aren't generally taken. If one is unsure, one is apt
to be conservative and keep the patient under observation for a few days
and try to determine whether there are suicidal thoughts in the patient's
mind. Now as to the exact nature of precautions, this means generally that
the patient is never let out of somebody's sight, out of sight of an employee
of the hospital, a nurse or an attendant. It means that he does not have access to materials which he could readily destroy himself with—knives, razors, belts, and so on. If the suicidal intent is prominent, then an attendant
even accompanies the patient to the bathroom. He isn't left alone, you see.
So that it varies, depending upon the degree or judgment of the degree of
the suicidal impulse and whether it's present or not.
    "Q   Doctor, would a patient such as referred to there in Exhibit 1 have
been given free access to go and come from his quarters and freedom of the
building and grounds at the Psychopathic Hospital during the month of
August, 1960?
    "A   This would be very difficult to determine. The patient, when he ar-
rived at the hospital, may not have been as depressed as was indicated by
the referral note from Doctor Schrock. In Doctor Kennedy's report, he made
a very definite attempt to determine the depth of the depression. He
brought out that there had been history of it and that there were certain
signs present now. But this comes, in the end, to a matter of judgment. It's
entirely possible to miss a depression or suicidal thought on the first examination. On the other hand, if the referring physician has referred to this,
then one is perhaps inclined to be more conservative and take extra precautions. So that, this is an extraordinarily difficult question to answer, you
see.
    "Q   Well, ordinarily, doctor, what would be the practice in a case such as
Mr. Baker where there is suicidal content indicated by the referring doctor?
    "A   We would have taken this very seriously.

"Q   And what procedure would have been followed in regard to his care and treatment there at the Psychopathic Hospital during that time?

"A   I think we would have been conservative in our approach to it.

"Q   And what do you mean by that?

"A   Well, I can't say for sure, I didn't see the patient, you see. But we possibly would have written in the note 'suicidal precautions' at least for a few days until we got a chance to know this patient better, and this would have meant that he would have been under observation and that somebody would have watched him closely all the time.

***

"Q   To summarize your testimony then, doctor, in this particular case, such as Mr. Baker, you would have been on the conservative side as I understand your testimony. Is that correct?

"A   Yes, I think so. If you are going to err, err on the conservative side, I feel. But again let me emphasize, I wasn't there, I didn't examine the patient. It's impossible to say what I would have done had I seen him, you see."

Dr. H. J. Madsen, Director of the 1540 bed Neuropsychiatric Veterans Hospital at Knoxville, Iowa, expressed the opinion that the patient received perfectly acceptable psychiatric care.

In reviewing the conduct of Dr. Kennedy it will be considered that he was aware of Dr. Schrock's note on the medical certificate as to the patient's mental condition prior to admission and the statement made by the patient's wife concerning the finding of a hidden gun, as heretofore related. It will also be considered that the doctor conducted a lengthy interview and examination of the patient and made his own judgment that the circumstances did not require assignment of the patient to a closed ward or that other precautions be taken. Without reviewing all of the facts in detail it is sufficient to state that the Court finds that Dr. Kennedy exercised the proper standard of care required under the circumstances. Calculated risks of necessity must be taken if the modern and enlightened treatment of the mentally ill is to be pursued intelligently and rationally. Neither the hospital nor the doctor are insurers of the patient's health and safety. They can only be required to use that degree of knowledge, skill, care and attention exercised by others in like circumstances.

The foregoing memorandum shall constitute the Court's findings of fact and conclusions of law as provided by Rule 52, Federal Rules of Civil Procedure. Judgment will be entered for the defendant.

Notes and Issues for Discussion

1. Liability in this case is limited to the physician's diagnosis, which led him to recommend an open ward. What evidence was there that the patient was suicidal? That he was not?
2. The standard used by the court is a community standard and appears to be one of reasonable care. The court relies on a prior case, *Wilson v. Corbin*,

41 N.W. 2d 702, to identify several elements: (1) use of knowledge, skill, care, and attention ordinarily exercised in a similar locality; (2) no guarantee of results; (3) extension of liability to diagnosis as well as treatment; and (4) use of a thorough and careful examination as warranted by the patient's condition and circumstances, using the diligence and diagnostic methods as are ordinarily practiced.

3. How does the plaintiff attempt to prove malpractice? The physician to defend himself? What are the positions of the experts? How effective is the plaintiff's expert? What does the court identify as the important considerations in finding no malpractice? Do you agree?

4. What kind of documentation would you have made? Would you have consulted with another professional? In light of the attending physician's certification and the warning by the patient's wife, wouldn't you have been particularly careful?

5. What policies does your agency have concerning treatment decisions and care of patients who have been identified by others as possible suicide risks?

INADEQUATE SUPERVISION AND PROTECTION

The following two cases present similar situations. In one, recovery by the plaintiff is allowed, in the other it is denied. How do the cases differ?

COMISKEY v. STATE
418 N.Y.S.2d 233 (1979)
NEW YORK SUPREME COURT, APPELLATE DIVISION

MEMORANDUM DECISION.

Appeal from a judgment, entered August 28, 1978, upon a decision of the Court of Claims.

This is an action for conscious pain and suffering and wrongful death of a decedent based upon the alleged negligence of the State. The decedent was a patient at the Central Islip State Hospital where he was initially admitted on November 22, 1970. Claimant maintains that the State was negligent in failing to properly supervise decedent and in permitting him to leave the hospital grounds unaccompanied. The court found for the claimant on the ground that an attendant who knew of decedent's suicidal tendencies and who had been directed to keep decedent under close supervision took no action to prevent decedent from leaving the premises for lunch.

The record reveals that on three previous occasions while a patient of the hospital decedent attempted suicide, that on March 16, 1976 he was in one of his depressed moods and asked to be put in a locked ward because he wanted to hurt himself, and that on March 18, 1976 he was still in a depressed mood. The record also reveals that decedent was the holder of an honor card which permitted him free access to the hospital grounds but not to leave without permission, and that on March 19, 1976 decedent told his attendant that he was going off the premises to have lunch at a nearby restaurant. Later that day decedent jumped in front of a subway train and received certain injuries resulting in his death. Death was listed as suicide.

While the State is not required to have someone watch a patient 24 hours a day, it is required to exercise reasonable care in restraining, supervising and protecting mentally deficient persons to prevent injury to themselves and others. A fair reading of this record demonstrates that the State had knowledge of decedent's proclivities to elope and his tendency to attempt suicide. There is, in our view, therefore, ample evidence in the record to support the court's determination that the State was negligent and that the negligence was a proximate cause of decedent's death. The judgment should be affirmed.

WILSON v. STATE
491 N.Y.S.2d 818 (1985)
NEW YORK SUPREME COURT, APPELLATE DIVISION

MEMORANDUM BY THE COURT.

In a claim to recover damages for personal injuries, claimant appeals from a judgment of the Court of Claims, dated April 4, 1984, which dismissed his claim after a trial.

Judgment affirmed, without costs or disbursements.

On or about February 11, 1981, claimant was admitted to a locked ward at the South Beach Psychiatric Center and placed under constant observation after he attempted to commit suicide by consuming an overdose of antidepressant medication. Claimant, then approximately 21 years of age, had been treated at the center on several occasions in the past after other attempts to take his life. Some weeks later, claimant's treatment team, which included a psychiatrist, a psychiatric social worker and several mental health assistants, determined that claimant should be transferred to an open living unit and granted him "grounds privileges" as part of a treatment plan designed to restore and strengthen his self esteem and confidence. On the evening of April 8, 1981, claimant left the hospital grounds without permission and once again attempted to commit suicide, this time by throwing himself in front of a train. His claim against the State for the resulting injuries was dismissed after a trial. We affirm.

Claimant's allegation of negligence against the State lies in the determination to grant him grounds privileges, a decision which he argues was medically unsound in light of his psychiatric record. At trial, claimant's expert witness testified that he would classify the claimant as a very high risk for suicide, and that it was dangerous to award such a patient grounds privileges. The expert also voiced disagreement with the psychiatric center's choice to assign the claimant to a female therapist, as well as the failure to involve his parents more directly in the treatment program.

It is well established that doctors, or the State that employs them, cannot be held responsible for damages resulting from honest errors in professional judgment. Thus, in order for liability to ensue in this instant case, it must be shown that the decision to grant the claimant grounds privileges was "something less than a professional medical determination" (*Bell v. New York City Health & Hosps. Corp.*, 90 A.D.2d 270, 282, 456 N.Y.S.2d 787). He cannot prevail merely by showing that another physician would have recommended another form of treatment.

The record contains no evidence that the conclusion reached at the South Beach Psychiatric Center to the effect that the claimant was no longer suicidal was improperly arrived at. Unfortunately, the prediction of the future course of a mental illness sometimes involves "a measure of calculated risk" (*Taig v. State of New York*, 241 N.Y.S.2d 495). Nor can we consider as negligent the failure of the hospital to obtain the entire medical record of the claimant's stay at another mental health institution. The center possessed sufficient medical information on the claimant's condition through the records of its prior years of periodic treatment of the claimant.

Notes and Issues for Discussion

1. In *Comiskey*, the patient had made three previous suicide attempts. He was depressed and had asked to be put in a locked ward because he might hurt himself. Two days later, he was allowed off grounds and killed himself. Did the patient present a suicide risk? Does it matter if the previous suicide attempts were recent or long ago?

2. "While the State is not required to have someone watch the patient 24 hours a day . . . it is required to exercise reasonable care in restraining, supervising and protecting mentally deficient persons to prevent injury to themselves and others." What is reasonable care in the *Comiskey* case? Limiting the patient to the hospital grounds? Placing him in a locked ward? If you were the professional in charge in *Comiskey* and had determined that it was not in the patient's best interests to revoke the honor card, what kinds of information would you record?

3. Note the existence of a treatment plan in *Wilson*, "designed to restore and strengthen his self esteem and confidence." What bearing does this have on the court's decision? Was there such a plan in *Comiskey*? In *Taig v. State of New York*, 241 N.Y.S.2d 495 (1963), the court observed: "The prediction of the future course of a mental illness is a professional judgement of high responsibility and in some instances it involves a measure of calculated risk. If a liability were imposed on the physician or the State each time the prediction of future course of mental disease was wrong, few releases could ever be made and the hope of recovery and rehabilitation of a vast number of patients would be impeded and frustrated. . . ." 241 N.Y.S.2d 496.

4. In *Eady v. Alter*, 380 N.Y.S.2d 737 (1976), the decedent was admitted to the defendant hospital for bronchitis. While there, he began to act "very nervous," and on the night in question led a fellow patient to a window and "asked him whether he wanted to go home with him." An intern was

called, who transferred the other patient and recorded "pt is getting nervous. had shaking all body and tried to jump out from window with other patient in same room," but did nothing more. Soon after, the decedent committed suicide by jumping from the window. The court found the hospital liable: "What is relevant is that his state of mind manifested the potential to do himself harm, and that the intern, believing that decedent presented a potential danger to himself, failed to act to properly restrain him from actually harming himself." 380 N.Y.S. 2d at 739.

5. In *Hilscher v. State*, 314 N.Y.S.2d 904 (1970), a juvenile inmate at a State School confessed to the sheriff that he had started a number of fires in the area. He was returned to the school and the school was notified that he was suspected of starting fires. The juvenile both admitted and denied setting the fires and the school did nothing further. Three months later, the juvenile was assigned to outside work and set fire to a staff member's house. The court found the state negligent for failure to supervise the juvenile in the face of the previous warning.

In the following case, note how important the existence of proper documentation would have been. Without documentation and notes, the doctor is unable to properly defend his decision.

ABILLE v. UNITED STATES
482 F. Supp 703 (1980)
U.S. DISTRICT COURT

WILLIAM W. SCHWARZER, DISTRICT JUDGE.

This is an action brought under the Federal Tort Claims Act, 28 U.S.C. §2671, *et seq.*, arising from the wrongful death of plaintiff's husband, Manuel Abille.***

Manuel Abille was 51 years old at the time of his death. Following retirement from the U.S. Navy in 1965, he attended school in the Philippines until 1970. From 1970 to 1973 he was a merchant seaman. From 1974 until the time of his death, he was a cannery worker employed by Pacific Pearl Seafoods in Kodiak, Alaska. He was survived by his wife, then 41 years old, two daughters aged 17 and 19, and two sons aged 12 and 18.

In September, 1974, Abille had been given a prescription for the drug Reserpine for treatment of high blood pressure. On April 15, 1977, he was taken off the drug by a doctor in Kodiak, Alaska, because of increasing depression, a side effect sometimes induced by Reserpine. Abille had no history of depression or suicidal tendencies prior to taking Reserpine, and the record reflects no other contributing causes of his depression.

As a result of Abille's depression and thoughts of suicide, he voluntarily entered the psychiatric unit of the United States Air Force Hospital at Elmendorf Air Force Base, Anchorage, Alaska, on April 26, 1977. His medical history was taken the next day by Dr. Abel Hipolito, one of the three psychiatrists on the hospital staff, who then became his treating physician. Dr. Hipolito noted, among other things, the following:

> "moderate psychomotor retardation—flat affect—relating obsessive preoccupation [with] suicidal ideas for 3 weeks—hopelessness—helplessness—sleep disturbances—[decreasing] energy—self-condemnation."

He stated his conclusions:

> "1) Depressive neurosis
> 2) Hypertension
> 3) Reactive depression to Reserpine"

All psychiatric patients were assigned status levels in accordance with their condition. As a newly admitted patient, Abille was automatically assigned S-1. In that status, he was not allowed to leave the psychiatric unit without a staff escort.

The medical record contains no subsequent notations by a physician while Abille was alive. The nurse's notes for April 27 indicate only that Abille slept for only three hours the preceding night. The notes for April 28 state that Abille had a "brighter affect" and that he said he felt much better and wanted to go home, although the nurse recommended that his treatment "continue as before." On April 29, the notes state in substance that Abille had not slept well, was nervous but less depressed, resisted group therapy and wanted to discuss his problems only with the doctor. The psychiatric technician further noted that Abille was depressed and concerned about his thoughts of suicide. No further progress notes were made.

Beginning not later than Saturday, April 30, the psychiatric nurse on duty in the ward treated Abille as having been assigned S-2 status. It was the understanding of the medical and nursing staff that S-2 patients were permitted to leave the ward escorted by a staff member or patient having S-3 or S-4 status (permitting freer movement), or unescorted upon approval by the duty nurse to go to a specific place in the hospital for a specific purpose. According to a government memorandum,

> "S-2 level was assigned to patients [sic] who had been an inpatient for at least 24 hours, was not considered suicidal . . . did not exhibit behavior that might be harmful to himself or others . . ."

During the day on Saturday, April 30, the duty nurse permitted Abille to attend mass in the building unescorted. Abille returned without incident. Early on Sunday, May 1, the duty nurse permitted Abille to use his razor to shave and then to go to breakfast unescorted. Shortly after he left the ward, his body was found on the ground outside the building beneath a window of the Red Cross lounge, an unsupervised facility on the seventh floor of the hospital. He was pronounced dead shortly thereafter. The autopsy report concluded that he had committed suicide.

When the duty nurses permitted Abille to leave the ward unescorted on Saturday and Sunday, they assumed that his status had been changed from S–1 to S–2. Had he still been on S–1, they would not have given him permission. Neither of the nurses could remember how or when the status change was made, or by whom. Dr. Hipolito testified only that he authorized it, but there is no written record that he did. A medical order purporting to change Abille's status did not in fact do so; when the order was prepared on April 29, it contained no reference to S–2 status—that reference was added by a nurse on May 1, after Abille had died.

The issue before the Court is whether defendant exercised due care in protecting Abille against self-inflicted harm. The duty of a hospital and its staff to exercise reasonable care to protect suicidal patients against foreseeable harm to themselves is well-established.

Liability in this case turns on the change in Abille's status from S–1 to S–2. Three questions are raised:

1. Did Dr. Hipolito in fact change Abille's status?
2. If he did change it, did he exercise due care in doing so?
3. If he failed to exercise due care, was his negligence a proximate cause of Abille's death?

1. Did Dr. Hipolito in fact change Abille's status from S-1 to S-2?

The parties' expert witnesses agreed that the responsibility for determining the appropriate degree of security for a patient rests on the physician, and that is where the Elmendorf hospital's procedures placed it. As described by the government's witnesses, those procedures provided that a patient's status level could be changed only by a physician's medical order or by a therapeutic group or nurse's decision approved by a physician's medical order. If the change was made by a staff member other than the physician, a written medical order signed by the physician had to be issued within 24 hours.

It is not disputed that no proper medical order changing Abille's status was issued here; the April 29 order altered after Abille's death cannot be accepted as a change order. Thus, if Abille's status was changed, it was changed in a manner violating the hospital's procedures. If it was not changed, the action of the nurse permitting Abille to leave the ward unescorted violated the hospital's rules governing S–1 patients and was below the standard of care, according to both parties' expert witnesses.

The evidence which tends to show that Abille's status was changed by Dr. Hipolito is as follows:

a. The psychiatric nurses on duty April 30 and May 1 testified that there had been a staff conference concerning Abille's status, that Abille was shown on the patients' sign-in board as S–2, that he was treated accordingly, and that he would not have been permitted to leave unescorted had he still been S–1.

b. Dr. Hipolito testified on deposition that he ordered Abille's status changed from S–1 to S–2 on April 29.

The evidence which tends to show the contrary is as follows:

c. No proper written order changing Abille's status was ever issued, as required by hospital procedures.

d. In the narrative summary prepared by Dr. Hipolito on May 1, 1977, immediately following Abille's death, he noted that Abille was classified as S–1 upon admission but made no reference to any subsequent change to S–2.

e. The change of status from S–1 to S–2 was written by a nurse after Abille's death on the order issued by Dr. Hipolito on April 29.

Plaintiffs of course have the burden of proving by a preponderance of the evidence that defendant was negligent, i.e., that Abille was permitted to leave the ward unescorted when his S–1 status had not been changed by a physician. The issue of credibility is a close one. The Court finds and concludes that the evidence tending to show that Dr. Hipolito did *not* change Abille's status from S–1 to S–2 is more persuasive. In this connection, the Court notes that Dr. Hipolito did not appear to testify at the trial. Only his deposition is in evidence. On the issue whether he ordered Abille's status changed, his testimony, given in response to poorly phrased and leading questions, is unpersuasive.

One or more of the nurses may well have believed or assumed in good faith, for some reason not known to the Court, that Abille's status had been changed. The possibility of confusion in this regard was presumably one reason for the hospital's requirement of a written order signed by a physician. Their good faith error, however, in no way relieves defendant of its duty to adhere to the security requirements prescribed by the treating physician for a suicidal patient until duly changed by a physician.

The Court therefore finds and concludes that defendant's nurses were acting below the standard of care when they permitted Abille to leave the ward unescorted while he was classified S–1, his status not having been changed by a physician. Inasmuch as he had been diagnosed to be suicidal, his suicide attempt was a foreseeable risk and must therefore be considered as a proximate result of the negligent act of the nurses.

2. If Dr. Hipolito had changed Abille's status, did he exercise due care in doing so?

In the interest of judicial economy and the complete disposition of this matter, the Court will next consider the alternative theory that Dr. Hipolito changed Abille's status but was negligent in doing so.

According to plaintiffs' expert, Abille remained suicidal until the time of his death. His analysis of the contemporary progress notes of the nurses and psychiatric technicians and of Dr. Hipolito's post-mortem narrative summary shows that symptoms of a suicidal disposition continued to be displayed by Abille and recognized by the staff. He concluded that it would have been below the standard of care to permit Abille to leave the ward unescorted and, consequently, to change his status so that the nurses could permit him to do so.

Defendant's expert testified that suicidal patients present a spectrum of risk ranging from high to low. He pointed to modern psychiatric practice which favors the least restrictive alternative in protecting psychiatric patients from potential self-harm. Evaluation of the information contained in Abille's hospital records led him to conclude that the risk of suicide presented was sufficiently low to warrant a change to S–2 status.

The Court has no basis for rejecting the opinion of one expert in favor of that expressed by the other. It appears that the appropriate classification of Abille on April 29 was a matter of judgment on which reasonable and competent psychiatrists, acting within the standard of care, could differ. The evidence on this issue being equally balanced, the Court finds that plaintiffs have not sustained their burden.

The fact that Dr. Hipolito *could,* consistent with the standard of care, have changed Abille's status does not, however, establish that the manner in which he changed it was within the standard of care. Both experts agreed that changing Abille's status was a significant medical decision requiring an exercise of judgment. There is in this case no contemporary evidence that Dr. Hipolito in fact exercised his judgment.

Abille upon admission displayed the classic symptoms of a suicidal person, even if he was not a high risk candidate. The expert witnesses of both sides testified that the progress notes reflect no significant change in Abille's condition in the following three days. While the notes report an increase in energy and aggressiveness, this did not necessarily lessen the risk of suicide, for as the patient's energy level increases his ability to carry out his suicidal thoughts increases as well.

There are no progress notes prepared by Dr. Hipolito. If his contacts with Abille between April 27 and May 1 led him to form the judgment that he could, in accordance with the hospital's procedures, be classified S–2 as no longer being "suicidal [or] . . . exhibit[ing] behavior that might be harmful to himself", there is no record to that effect. The only contemporary document prepared by Dr. Hipolito after April 27 is his narrative summary compiled on May 1 following the death. In it he stated that Abille had on admission been "placed on Level S–1 (restricted to the Unit for O&E)", referred to no later change of status, and added:

"Friday, the 29th of April, 1977, was the last day I talked with or seen the patient. He verbalized his concern about his insomnia, depression and episodic suicidal ruminations."

Both parties' experts agreed and the government now appears to concede, that Dr. Hipolito's failure to keep contemporary progress notes reflecting his exercise of judgment, and the basis for it, was below the standard of care. Dr. Hipolito's deposition testimony, given in response to loosely phrased leading questions and based only on the nurses' and technician's notes and his general recollection, is insufficient to show that, if he did reclassify Abille, he did so in accordance with the standard of care and therefore does not serve to satisfy his duty to maintain adequate records.

The Court therefore finds and concludes that Dr. Hipolito's failure to maintain contemporary notes, orders or other records adequately recording and explaining his action in reclassifying Abille fell below the applicable standard of care.***

Notes and Issues for Discussion

1. The nursing staff acted as if Abille's status had been changed from escorted to unescorted status. What evidence tends show a change in status? What evidence tends to show no change? Which is more persuasive?

2. If the status was changed, is this change negligent? The court concludes that it might have been appropriate to change the patient's status, but finds there was no evidence that such a change was the result of a considered evaluation by the physician. Even if the status was changed for appropriate reasons, the physician cannot demonstrate this without adequate documentation. His failure to keep contemporaneous progress notes then leads to the conclusion that the change was negligent.

Violations of Privacy and Confidentiality

Where there is a confidential or privileged relationship, unauthorized release of confidential material may be actionable if it harms the individual. Even if there is no testimonial privilege, release of confidential information may still be actionable. In these situations, once a duty and a breach of that duty have been established, it may be difficult to prove harm, particularly if there is no physical harm, only mental distress. A knowing waiver by the patient or client is a defense to this type of action, although a disclosure of information that goes beyond the limits of the waiver will be actionable. Where the court orders the release of privileged or confidential information, there is no liability to the professional. However, if the release is requested by an attorney, the health and human services professional may not need to release the information and may face liability for an unauthorized release. (Note that there may be times when the health and human services professional is required to breach confidentiality such as disclosures of child abuse or harm to others (see, generally, Chapter 6).

MACDONALD v. CLINGER
446 N.Y.S.2d 801 (1982)
NEW YORK SUPREME COURT, APPELLATE DIVISION

DENMAN, JUSTICE.

We here consider whether a psychiatrist must respond in damages to his former patient for disclosure of personal information learned during the course of treatment and, if he must, on what theory of recovery the action may be maintained. We hold that such wrongful disclosure is a breach of the fiduciary duty of confidentiality and gives rise to a cause of action sounding in tort.

The complaint alleges that during two extended courses of treatment with defendant, a psychiatrist, plaintiff revealed intimate details about himself which defendant later divulged to plaintiff's wife without justification and without consent. As a consequence of such disclosure, plaintiff alleges that his marriage deteriorated, that he lost his job, that he suffered financial difficulty and that he was caused such severe emotional distress that he required further psychiatric treatment. The complaint set forth three causes of action: breach of an implied contract; breach of confidence in violation of public policy; and breach of the right of privacy guaranteed by article 5 of the Civil Rights Law. Defendant moved to dismiss for failure to state a cause of action, asserting that there was in reality only one theory of recovery, that of breach of confidence, and that such action could not be maintained against him because his disclosure to plaintiff's wife was justified. The court dismissed the third cause of action but denied the motion with respect to the first two causes of action and this appeal ensued.

Research reveals few cases in American jurisprudence which treat the doctor-patient privilege in this context. That is undoubtedly due to the fact that the confidentiality of the relationship is a cardinal rule of the medical profession, faithfully adhered to in most instances, and thus has come to be justifiably relied upon by patients seeking advice and treatment. This physician-patient relationship is contractual in nature, whereby the physician, in agreement to administer to the patient, impliedly covenants that the disclosures necessary to diagnosis and treatment of the patient's mental or physical condition will be kept in confidence.

Examination of cases which have addressed this problem makes it apparent that courts have immediately recognized a legally compensable injury in such wrongful disclosure based on a variety of grounds for recovery: public policy; right to privacy; breach of contract; breach of fiduciary duty.***

An excellent and carefully researched opinion exploring the legal ramifications of this confidentiality is *Doe v. Roe*, 93 Misc.2d 201, 400 N.Y.S.2d 668, a decision after a non-jury trial in which plaintiff sought injunctive relief and damages because of the verbatim publication by her former psychiatrist of extremely personal details of her life revealed during years of psychoanalysis. The court considered several proposed theories of recovery, including violation of public policy and breach of privacy rights. We agree with the court's observation that the several statutes and regulations requiring physicians to protect the confidentiality of information gained during treatment are clear evidence of the public policy of New York, but that there is a more appropriate theory of recovery than one rooted in public policy.***

The relationship of the parties here was one of trust and confidence out of which sprang a duty not to disclose. Defendant's breach was not merely a broken contractual promise but a violation of a fiduciary responsibility to plaintiff implicit in and essential to the doctor-patient relation.

Such duty, however, is not absolute, and its breach is actionable only if it is wrongful, that is to say, without justification or excuse. Although public policy favors the confidentiality described herein, there is a countervailing public interest to which it must yield in appropriate circumstances. Thus where a patient may be a danger to himself or others, a physician is required to disclose to the extent necessary to protect a threatened interest. "The protective privilege ends where the public peril begins" (*Tarasoff v. Regents of University of California*, 13 Cal.3d 177).***

Although the disclosure of medical information to a spouse may be justified under some circumstances, a more stringent standard should apply with respect to psychiatric information. One spouse often seeks counseling concerning personal problems that may affect the marital relationship. To permit disclosure to the other spouse in the absence of an overriding concern would deter the one in need from obtaining the help required. Disclosure of confidential information by a psychiatrist to a spouse will be justified whenever there is a danger to the patient, the spouse or another person; otherwise information should not be disclosed without authorization.***

Notes and Issues for Discussion

1. One issue in *MacDonald* is the appropriate theory for recovery. If a breach of contract is relied upon, this will limit the damages to actual economic loss. The court discards this approach, pointing out that the plaintiff would then be "precluded from recovering for mental distress, loss of his employment and the deterioration of his marriage." The fiduciary duty theory allows for this type of recovery.
2. If you received confidential information from a patient or client which could be damaging to that individual, can you reveal it? What if it raises questions about parental adequacy (but not child abuse) and there is a custody dispute? In *Cutter v. Brownbridge*, 228 Cal. Rptr. 545 (1986), a clinical social worker promised confidentiality, and then voluntarily provided his diagnosis and damaging personal details gathered during therapy to the attorney for the client's former wife. The information was used in support of a request to suspend visitation rights. The patient sued for damages. The appellate court held that the therapist could be liable for a violation of the constitutional right to privacy, and noted that under California law, if the client had notice of intent to provide the information to opposing counsel, thus providing him with an opportunity to challenge this move legally, the therapist could probably have avoided liability.
3. In *Doe v. Roe*, 400 N.Y.S. 668 (1971), a psychiatrist and her husband wrote a book describing their treatment of a famous patient, who was readily identifiable from the text. No permission had been obtained. The patient sued to prevent distribution of the book and to collect damages. The patient was successful although the appellate court reduced the damage award.

Failure to Protect Others from Harm

Whether there is a duty to protect a third party not part of the relationship between professional and patient or client, and if so, what steps are necessary to fulfill that duty will vary by state. See Chapter 6.

Sexual Relations with Patient or Client

Virtually every professional code of ethics forbids sexual relations between professionals and patients, although a few experts argue that sexual relations are a legitimate and effective form of therapy. Nonetheless, due to the power differentials within the relationship and the clear potential for abuse of that power, it is likely that a court will find sexual relations with a patient or client actionable as malpractice.

MAZZA v. HUFFAKER
300 S.E.2d 833 (1983)
NORTH CAROLINA APPELLATE COURT

HENDRICK, JUDGE.

***

Plaintiff suffers from manic depressive psychosis. Since 1975, he had received ongoing treatment of his illness from defendant Huffaker, a psychiatrist. As part of his treatment, plaintiff was prescribed medication by defendant Huffaker and participated in frequent and regular sessions at Huffaker's office, during which plaintiff was encouraged to have very intimate, self-revelatory, and uninhibited discussions with Huffaker. The treatment was described as "insight therapy" and "psychoanalysis." Plaintiff, in many of his sessions, for example, one on 4 May 1979, expressed to Huffaker serious concern about maintaining a healthy marital relationship with his wife, Jacqueline Mazza. Plaintiff had come to think of defendant Huffaker as his best friend. In May 1979, Jacqueline requested that she and plaintiff separate, and on 28 May 1979, plaintiff moved out of the Wood-haven Road house, in Chapel Hill, in which he, his wife, and family had lived. On 6 July 1979, plaintiff was entertaining one of his and Jacqueline's sons, with her prior agreement. Upon calling his wife at the Woodhaven Road home, at 10:40 p.m., to check with her as to whether he could bring the son back to her the next morning, plaintiff became concerned about his wife's welfare after noticing her conduct over the telephone. Plaintiff thereupon drove over to the Wood-haven Road house "to make sure everything was okay." Plaintiff observed his psychiatrist's automobile parked near the Woodhaven Road house and saw some of his psychiatrist's clothing strewn about the family room. Upon approaching and entering the locked master bedroom, plaintiff discovered his psychiatrist, Robert Huffaker, and his wife, Jacqueline Mazza, together in bed. Huffaker was naked and putting on his undershorts, and Jacqueline was naked and putting on a light housecoat.

Plaintiff also presented expert testimony tending to show the following:

Psychiatrists are physicians. The first duty of a physician to a patient is to do no harm; the second is to maintain the patient's trust and confidence in the physician. These basic duties apply and are even more stringent with psychiatrists, since a psychiatrist's patient reveals his innermost thoughts, feelings, worries, and concerns. Psychiatrists, therefore, have a strict duty not to breach the trusting relationship and must be very careful about what they say and how they influence patients. Psychiatrists have to take great care in the termination of a relationship with a patient so that the psychiatric patient, who is very sensitive, does not feel that he is abandoned or rejected. Especially in the light of the intimate relationship between psychiatrist and patient, the psychiatrist's duty once the psychiatrist-patient relationship has been established extends beyond the hospital or consulting room and includes social situations. The psychiatrist must endeavor to assure that the patient does not forget that the doctor is a doctor. A patient can be seriously harmed if the relationship changes from a therapeutic one to a social one. Special duties exist in the practice of medicine not to ruin a doctor and patient relationship, and those duties are more critical in psychiatry than in other areas of medicine. If the relationships are not terminated properly, but too abruptly, great harm can result to a patient. The psychiatrist's duty to advance his patient's interests is violated if the psychiatrist has sex with the patient's spouse; such sexual relations are not therapeutic. Sexual relations between a psychiatrist and his patient's wife would destroy the patient's trust in the psychiatrist and would destroy the doctor-patient relationship. Covert sexual relations between a psychiatrist and a patient's wife, if discovered by the patient, would make it extremely difficult for the patient to establish ever again a necessary trusting relationship with any psychiatrist, would render previous treatment useless, and would do harm to the mental well-being of the patient. A psychiatrist who becomes sexually involved with a relative of a patient is not exercising the requisite amount of skill, learning, and ability that a psychiatrist in any community in the United States ought to exercise. All the aforementioned standards and duties of physicians and psychiatrists are applicable in Chapel Hill.

There is ample evidence in the present case that the relevant standard of care applicable to Chapel Hill psychiatrists included the negative imperative that they not have sexual relations with their patients' spouses. The expert testimony tended to establish an obligation on the part of psychiatrists, as part of their duties within the patient-psychiatrist relationship, to conduct themselves in a certain way and this obligation applies even beyond the office, clinic, hospital, or laboratory.

There was abundant evidence that defendant Huffaker did not refrain from having sexual relations with the plaintiff's wife. Hence, there was expert evidence defining the applicable standard of care and evidence that defendant Huffaker violated such standard. Contrary to defendants' assertions, plaintiff thus presented sufficient evidence of the professional malpractice element of his claim.***

In their next six assignments of error, defendants challenge instructions given by the court about conduct upon which the jury could base a finding of malpractice.***

Defendants first challenge the court's instruction that the jury must find there was malpractice if it found that defendant Huffaker "abandoned Dr. Mazza as a patient." Defendant contends there was no "evidence of abandonment." There was, however, evidence in the present case that while the psychiatrist-patient relationship existed between defendant and plaintiff, defendant Huffaker had sexual relations with plaintiff's wife and in so doing acted in violation of the standard of care required of a psychiatrist. This evidence would suffice to permit the jury to find that defendant Huffaker has abruptly abandoned his patient, Dr. Mazza, and was acting as if there had been no psychiatrist-patient relationship with Dr. Mazza. The instruction on abandonment was not improper, and this assignment of error is not sustained. The above-mentioned evidence and expert testimony about the requirement of trust in a psychiatrist-patient relationship were also sufficient to permit the court to give the instruction next assigned as error, wherein the court stated the jury must find malpractice if it found defendant Huffaker "used his position of trust and confidence to harm his patient."***

Next defendant argues the court erred in instructing the jury that it should find malpractice if it determined defendant Huffaker "continued to treat Dr. Mazza after becoming emotionally and sexually involved with Dr. Mazza's wife." Defendants contend that such a determination could not be a basis for a verdict finding medical malpractice, since the existence of a psychiatrist-patient relationship between defendant Huffaker and plaintiff, at the time defendant Huffaker and plaintiff's wife were discovered in bed together by plaintiff, would not affect the character of the legal wrong done plaintiff. Defendants argue that such legal wrong would be the same as if there had been no psychiatrist-patient relationship at the time of the discovery, and the legal wrong would not be malpractice but would be criminal conversation or alienation of affections, if anything. Expert testimony in the present case, however, asserted that the existence of the psychiatrist-patient relationship is not irrelevant or superfluous, since sexual relations between a psychiatrist and his patient's wife during the term of the psychiatrist-patient relationship is a violation of the applicable standard of care for psychiatrists. This testimony sufficed to permit the court to issue the challenged instruction as a basis for malpractice. The assignment of error is overruled.

Defendants next assign error to the court's instruction that the jury must find malpractice if it determined that defendant Huffaker "failed to recognize and guard against the transfer or counter-transference phenomenon." According to expert testimony, transference is a common phenomenon in psychiatrist therapy in which the psychiatric patient transfers onto the psychiatrist emotions the patient has towards someone else. Counter-transference is a similarly common phenomenon in which the psychiatrist projects onto his patient feelings that the psychiatrist has towards someone else. Defendants first contend there was no evidence that defendant Huffaker failed to recognize and respond correctly to transference and counter-transference between Jacqueline Mazza, whom he was treating as a patient, and himself. Defendants contend secondly that even if there were such evidence, defendant Huffaker's improper response to transference or counter-transference would be the basis of a malpractice action only on behalf of Jacqueline Mazza, if anyone, and not on behalf of plaintiff.

The evidence and instructions in the present case placed central focus on the sexual relations between defendant Huffaker and the plaintiff's wife during the term of Huffaker's and plaintiff's psychiatrist-patient relationship. In light of that central focus, the instruction challenged here must also be deemed to pertain to the sexual relations between defendant Huffaker and the plaintiff's wife, with the added issues of transference and counter-transference. Hence, if the jury based its finding of malpractice on the instruction that it find malpractice if it determined defendant Huffaker reacted improperly to transference or counter-transference, then the jury necessarily found that defendant Huffaker had sexual relations with plaintiff's wife during the course of the psychiatrist-patient relationship, since such sexual relations are of what the improper reaction to transference or counter-transference consisted. This assignment of error is meritless.***

In their next assignment of error, defendants argue, "[t]he Court erred in permitting the [expert] witnesses . . . to express their opinions as to professional ethics for reason that breaches of professional ethics are not civilly actionable as malpractice, and this error . . . permitted . . . [the jury] to impose liability upon defendants for a breach of professional ethics."

As previously discussed, the professional malpractice element of an actionable malpractice claim is satisfied if it is shown that the health care provider violated the relevant standards of practice for his profession, and such standard of practice may be supplied by expert testimony. In the present case, expert testimony supplied such standard of practice and equated it with the standards of professional ethics. According to such expert testimony, the accepted standard of care are coterminous with the relevant standards of professional ethics. Hence, it was not improper for the expert witnesses to give content to the accepted standards of care by referring to the ethical standards of the profession, since expert testimony asserted that both standards are the same. Although defendants may be correct in arguing that breaches of professional ethics are not actionable in a malpractice suit when such standards differ from the reasonable standard of care imposed by tort law, their argument is unavailing in the present case, where expert testimony equated the two sets of standards. This assignment of error is overruled.***

HORAK v. BIRIS
474 N.E.2d 13 (1985)
ILLINOIS APPELLATE COURT

HOPF, JUSTICE.

In this appeal we are asked to recognize a cause of action for social worker malpractice under the facts presented in this case. Plaintiff, Harry J. Horak, Jr., filed a six-count amended complaint essentially alleging negligence and malpractice (counts I through IV) and breach of contract (counts V and VI) against defendant Dean Biris, a certified social worker, for defendant's having had sexual relations with plaintiff's wife during the course of marital counseling sought by the Horaks. Counts I through IV of the complaint were dismissed by the circuit court of Kane County based upon a Fourth District opinion, *Martino v. Family Service Agency of Adams County* (1982), 112 Ill.App.3d 593, which refused to recognize the tort of social worker malpractice under facts similar, if not identical, to those in the instant case. Plaintiff appeals from the dismissal of these counts, urging us to reject the reasoning in *Martino*. We note that counts V and VI were voluntarily nonsuited and a final and appealable order was issued as to counts I through IV.

Counts I through IV, although based on different theories, alleged the following essential facts in common: (1) that in February 1978, defendant held himself out to the general public as an expert in the field of psychology and mental therapy, and held himself out to professionally counsel individuals, couples, and groups for emotional problems, marriage difficulties, and other conditions which were treatable by the use of psychotherapy, psychiatric techniques, and mental therapy; (2) that on or about February 1978, defendant began to provide psychological counseling and psychiatric and mental therapeutic care for Dorothy Horak, plaintiff's then-wife; (3) that during his counseling defendant obtained significant information from plaintiff's wife about the personal profile of plaintiff and the Horak's marital relationship; (4) upon defendant's request and relying upon defendant's reputation in the community as a qualified psychological or mental therapist, plaintiff began a course of treatment with the defendant in October 1978, which treatments continued until March 1980 and were paid for by contractual arrangement costing approximately $170 per month; (5) that during this period, defendant had a close and confidential relationship with the plaintiff and that plaintiff therefore communicated numerous confidential facts about his life, personality, and marriage to the defendant; (6) that defendant administered a course of treatment ostensibly to cure and aid the plaintiff's sense of ill-being, but which was not in accordance with generally accepted standards of psychological, psychiatric and therapeutic care; and, (7) that defendant owed a duty to plaintiff to perform a course of treatment calculated to lead to the alleviation of plaintiff's condition of ill-being.

Counts I and IV, based upon the theories of negligence and malpractice, further alleged that in violation of defendant's aforementiond duty, defendant committed numerous negligent acts or omissions, including the following: (1) failed to inform plaintiff that a conflict of interest existed in counseling both the plaintiff and his wife; (2) failed to terminate therapy with the plaintiff as soon as he realized that a conflict of interest existed; and (3) failed to understand and guard against the transference phenomenon which occurs between psychotherapists and their patients.

Counts II and III, based respectively upon wilful and wanton and intentional conduct, alleged that defendant committed one or more of the following acts: (1) failed to provide treatment calculated to lead to the alleviation of plaintiff's condition of ill-being; (2) appeased defendant's own self-interest, in disregard and in violation of professional standards and in detriment to plaintiff's condition; (3) caused plaintiff's condition of ill-being to deteriorate while under defendant's care without providing any psychological, psychiatric or mental therapeutic treatment; and (4) began and allowed a course of treatment to continue that was of such a nature as to do great harm to plaintiff's condition of ill-being. We note that plaintiff's original two-count complaint, based upon theories of breach of fiduciary relationship and malpractice, also alleged that defendant became emotionally and romantically involved with plaintiff's then-wife, had sexual relations with her, and thereafter continued to counsel plaintiff. The act of sexual involvement with plaintiff's wife was not specifically alleged in the amended complaint but was alluded to in plaintiff's allegation regarding the transference phenomenon in counts I and IV. This allegation will be further discussed later in this opinion.***

We believe the facts alleged in the instant case, if proved, sufficiently establish a duty owed by defendant Biris to plaintiff Horak and a subsequent breach of that duty by defendant. It was alleged that plaintiff went to defendant's office, at defendant's request, to receive counseling and guidance in his personal and marital relationships, ostensibly for the purpose of improving those relationships. Defendant held himself out as a social worker licensed by the State to render such assistance and insight. His license placed him in a position of trust, the violation of which would constitute a breach of the fiduciary relationship. Such a breach has been held on several occasions to be an actionable and independent tort. Further, we think that the very nature of the therapist-patient relationship, which was alleged and admitted here, gives rise to a clear duty on the therapist's part to engage only in activity or conduct which is calculated to improve the patient's mental or emotional well-being, and to refrain from any activity or conduct which carries with it a foreseeable and unreasonable risk of mental or emotional harm to the patient.

We believe plaintiff alleged sufficient facts which, if proved and believed by the trier of fact, would establish a breach of defendant's duty to refrain from conduct that is detrimental to plaintiff's well-being. Defendant operated a facility known as the "Center for Psychotherapy," where he performed counseling services defined as "psychotherapy." He allegedly held himself out as possessing a certain expertise in the counseling and treatment of emotional and social problems. Accordingly, defendant was required to exercise that degree of skill and knowledge normally possessed by members of the social work profession practicing in the same field. (See Restatement (Second) of Torts §299A (1965).) We note that the field of practice engaged in by defendant here more closely resembles the practice of psychology rather than social work, as those two practices are currently defined in the Illinois Revised Statutes. (See Ill.Rev.Stat.1979, ch. 111, pars. 5304 and 6302.) Because of the apparent overlapping of these two fields, we think the proofs may well reveal that defendant possessed or should have possessed a basic knowledge of fundamental psychological principles which routinely come into play during marriage and family counseling. The "transference phenomenon" is apparently one such principle, and has been defined in psychiatric practice as "a phenomenonby which the patient transfers feelings towards everyone else to the doctor, who then must react with a proper response, the counter transference, in order to avoid emotional involvement and assist the patient in overcoming problems." (*Aetna Life & Casualty Co. v. McCabe* (E.D. Pa.1983), 556 F.Supp. 1342, 1346.) The mishandling of this phenomenon, which generally results in sexual relations or involvement between the psychiatrist or therapist and the patient, has uniformly been considered as malpractice or gross negligence in other jurisdictions, whether the sexual relations were prescribed by the doctor as part of the therapy, or occurred outside the scope of treatment. Accordingly, we believe that plaintiff's allegation of a mishandling of the transference phenomenon sufficiently alleges a breach of the defendant's duty here.

***Here, both the plaintiff and his wife were patients of the defendant, apparently for the common purpose of rehabilitating their marital relationship. Thus,

---

the treatment of each of the spouses would reasonably have an effect upon the other spouse and the prospects of improving the couple's marriage. To this extent, any malpractice committed by the defendant in the treatment of plaintiff's wife would clearly have an impact upon the plaintiff as well. See *Anclote Manor Foundation v. Wilkinson* (Fla.Ct.App. 1972), 263 So.2d 256, and *Andrews v. United States* (4th Cir.1984), 732 F.2d 366, both permitting recovery by the patient's husband for the therapist's malpractice towards the wife-patient.***

Insofar as damages are concerned, it is clear that if plaintiff can prove defendant's malpractice, if any, was the result of intentional conduct (as alleged in count III of plaintiff's complaint), the plaintiff would be entitled to recover for emotional distress pursuant to *Knierim v. Izzo* (1961), 22 Ill.2d 73, 174 N.E.2d 157. Plaintiff in any event would be entitled to recover actual damages, including loss of consortium.

In recognizing a cause of action for social worker malpractice under the facts presented in this case, we note that our legislature has provided for revocation of a social worker's license if he or she is found to be "unfit or incompetent by reason of gross negligence in the practice of social work." (Ill.Rev.Stat.1979, ch. 111, par. 6315(b).)

Further, these provisions, along with the code of ethics apparently adopted by the National Association of Social Workers (see *Martino*), make it clear that certain minimum standards of professional conduct do exist for social workers, contrary to the suggestion in the *Martino* decision that the propriety of a social worker's conduct would be difficult to ascertain. While it may be true that certain fields of social work (*i.e.*, community organization for social welfare, social work research, social welfare administration) may not readily lend themselves to a malpractice action, we believe that marriage and family counseling is one area of social work likely to possess more well-defined principles of social work practice because of its close association with the field of psychology. We are also of the opinion that an adoption by this court of the reasoning set forth in *Martino* would serve only to shield mental health professionals from any consequences of their actions to the detriment of those individuals who turn to them in reliance upon their professional expertise and in a good faith attempt to improve their marital and family relations. We believe such a result runs contrary to the public policy of this State as gleaned from the statutes heretofore discussed.

Notes and Issues for Discussion

1. A number of states have enacted statutes which make therapist-patient sexual relations criminal offenses. See for example, Minn. Stat. Ann. §609.344(1) which makes sexual penetration between psychotherapist and patient during psychotherapy sessions a felony. Consent by the patient is no defense. Also included is any sexual penetration occurring at any point in time between the psychotherapist and a patient or former patient when that individual "is emotionally dependent upon the psychotherapist." §609.344(1)(i). Sexual contact is classified as a lesser felony offense. §609.345(h). See, also, Cal. Bus. & Prof. Code §729, providing that sexual

exploitation by the therapist is punishable as a misdemeanor, with succeeding offenses punished by fines up to $5,000 and one year in prison. The California statute protects former patients whose therapists first terminate the psychotherapist-patient relationship and then engage in sexual relations if it can be proven that the termination was for the purpose of later sex. However, the psychotherapist can avoid liability by referring the patient to another therapist before engaging in the sex. §729(a).

2. In *Roy v. Hartogs*, 381 N.Y.S. 2d 587 (1976), the lower court rejected the psychiatrist's claim that his sexual relations with the plaintiff were part of therapy and awarded damages for malpractice. The decision was upheld with damages reduced.

3. In *Destafano v. Grabrian*, 763 P. 2d. 275 (1988), a Catholic priest who was engaging in marriage counseling with a couple began a sexual relationship with the wife. Both the husband and wife sued the priest and the diocese for compensatory and punitive damages. The trial court dismissed on the grounds of separation of church and state and the Colorado "heart balm" statute which abolished all civil actions for alienation of affection and seduction. The Supreme Court of Colorado held that the wife's claim was not barred by the First Amendment because the priest's conduct was "outside the practices and beliefs of the Catholic church," and outside the scope of his employment. The court upheld the wife's claim based on a breach of fiduciary duty and outrageous conduct (but dismissed her claim based on malpractice because of a provision in the Colorado statutes which exempts clergy from liability). The court also held that the husband had a cause of action based on breach of fiduciary duty.

4. In *Zipkin v. Freeman*, 436 S.W. 2d 753, an action against a therapist's insurer, the court found: ". . . as part of his treatment, he [the therapist] had her attend social gatherings . . . urged her to invest her money in his enterprises, induced her to transfer her affections . . . aroused her emotionally and convinced her that without him she and her children would starve. . . ." The insurance company argued that it had no liability because its policy was limited to "professional services rendered or which should have been rendered" and the doctor's actions were outside the scope of professional services. The court rejected this argument, finding that the patient's behaviors were linked to a mishandling of transference.

5. Similarly, in *L.L. v. Medical Protective Co.*, 362 N.W. 2d 174 (1984), the court reversed a summary judgment in favor of the defendant insurance company in a malpractice action for a psychiatrist engaging in sexual relations during treatment. "The issue is whether L.L.'s claim for damages resulting from Seigel's engaging in sexual acts with her during the course of her treatment is a 'claim for damages . . . based on professional services rendered or which should have been rendered.' We hold that because a psychiatrist's performance of sexual acts with a patient can constitute failure to give proper treatment, L.L.'s claim comes within the quoted policy language. We therefore reverse the judgment insofar as it dismissed the insurance company from the action and remand with in-

structions to reinstate the insurance company as a defendant." 362 N.W. 2d at 175. (Wis. App. 1984).

6. Some insurance companies have included in their policies exclusions or limits to liability coverage for sexual contact with patients or clients. See Jorgenson and Sutherland, 1993.

Liability for Nontraditional Therapy

In *Hammer v. Rosen*, 165 N.E. 2d 756 (1960), as part of therapy the psychiatrist repeatedly beat his patient. The court found a *prima facie* case of malpractice, noting some acts may be so obviously unacceptable that a court may not require expert testimony to justify such a conclusion. If a nontraditional therapy is used, documentation of reasons for its choice and for not utilizing more traditional approaches, and expert testimony showing the efficacy of the therapy in similar situations and its theoretical and scientific bases could be introduced to defend the choice.

SUPERVISORY AND ADMINISTRATIVE LIABILITY

A is negligent, B is not. 'Imputed negligence' means that, by reason of some relation existing between A and B, the negligence of A is to be charged against B, although B has played no part in it, has done nothing whatever to encourage it, or indeed has done all that he possibly can to prevent it. (Keeton, *et al.*, 1985: 499)

Under the doctrine of *respondeat superior*, a supervisor or administrator may become liable for the actions of a worker. Black's *Law Dictionary* defines *respondeat superior* as:

Let the master answer. This doctrine means that a master is liable in certain cases for the wrongful acts of his servant, and a principal for those of his agent. Under this doctrine master is responsible for want of care on the servant's part toward those to whom master owes duty to use care, provided failure of servant to use such care occurred in course of his employment. Under doctrine an employer is liable for injury to person or property of another proximately resulting from acts of employee done within scope of his employment in the employer's service. (Black's *Law Dictionary*, 1991.)

Critical here is the meaning and extent of "scope of employment."

It refers to those acts which are so closely connected with what the servant is employed to do, and so fairly and reasonably incidental to it, that they may be regarded as methods, even though quite improper ones, of carrying out the objectives of the employment. . . . It has been said that in general the servant's conduct is within the scope of his employment if it is of the kind which he is employed to perform, occurs substantially within the authorized limits of time and space, and is actuated, at least in part, by a purpose to serve the master. (Keeton, *et al.*, 1985: 502)

Depending on the court and jurisdiction, scope of employment has been defined broadly or very narrowly. At various times a master has been liable for most of his servant's wrongful acts or for almost none of them. (Keeton, *et al.*, 1985: 501–508). The following cases illustrate the issues.

SIMMONS v. UNITED STATES
805 F.2d 1345 (1986)
U.S. COURT OF APPEALS

TANG, CIRCUIT JUDGE.

***

Jerrie Simmons, a member of the Chehalis Tribe, sought mental health consultation from the Indian Health Services and was counseled by Ted Kammers, a social worker. Ms. Simmons had a history of economic deprivation and of physical, sexual and emotional abuse as a child. When she started consultation with Mr. Kammers, she was divorced and pregnant with her fourth child. Ms. Simmons saw Mr. Kammer for counseling from 1973 until August 1980 and maintained the counseling relationship through telephone contacts from then until at least July 9, 1981, the date of her last face-to-face counseling session.

In October 1978 Mr. Kammers initiated romantic contact with Ms. Simmons during a counseling session, encouraging her to act on her professed feelings of attraction to him. In January 1979 he had sexual intercourse with her during an out-of-town trip and this romantic sexual relationship continued during the course of Ms. Simmons' treatment.

In January 1980, the Tribal Chairwoman notified Mr. Kammers' supervisor, Victor Sansalone, of her concerns about the relationship between Ms. Simmons and Mr. Kammers. Sansalone took no action either to correct Mr. Kammers' improper counseling or to relieve him of his duties. In August 1980 Ms. Simmons moved to Seattle and began eventually to suffer a variety of emotional problems, ranging from anxiety to depression, which worsened until she was hospitalized for psychiatric treatment in May 1982. She finally attempted suicide in November 1982.

In February 1983 Ms. Simmons learned through psychiatric consultation with

Dr. Patricia Lipscomb, M.D., that her counselor's misconduct was the cause of her psychological problems and that her problems were due essentially to his inappropriate response to the normal "transference phenomenon" in therapy.

On May 23, 1983 Ms. Simmons filed an administrative claim under the Federal Tort Claims Act, 28 U.S.C. §§1346 and 2671-2680 (1982), based on Mr. Kammers' negligence while counseling her in his capacity as a social worker employed by a United States agency. After a bench trial, the district court entered findings and conclusions (summarized above) and judgment for Ms. Simmons, awarding her damages of $150,000. The Government timely appeals.

Transference is the term used by psychiatrists and psychologists to denote a patient's emotional reaction to a therapist and is "generally applied to the projection of feelings, thoughts and wishes onto the analyst, who has come to represent some person from the patient's past." *Stedman's Medical Dictionary* 1473 (5th Lawyers' Ed.1982). Transference "is perhaps regarded as the most significant concept in psychoanalytical therapy, and one of the most important discoveries of Freud." *Zipkin v. Freeman*, 436 S.W.2d 753, 755 n. 1 (Mo.1968) (quoting Noyes & Kolb, *Modern Clinical Psychiatry* 505 (6th ed. 1963)).***

Transference is crucial to the therapeutic process because the patient "unconsciously attributes to the psychiatrist or analyst those feelings which he may have repressed towards his own parents. . . .[I]t is through the creation, experiencing and resolution of these feelings that [the patient] becomes well." *L.L. v. Medical Protective Co.*, 362 N.W.2d 174, 177 (Wis.App.1984) (quoting D. Dawidoff, *The Malpractice of Psychiatrists* 6 (1973)). "Inappropriate emotions, both hostile and loving, directed toward the physician are recognized by the psychiatrist as constituting . . . the transference. The psychiatrist looks for manifestations of the transference, and is prepared to handle it as it develops." *L.L.*, 362 N.W.2d at 177 (quoting Heller, *Some Comments to Lawyers on the Practice of Psychiatry*, 30 Temp.L.Q. 401, 401–02 (1957)). "Understanding of transference forms a basic part of the psychoanalytic technique." *Zipkin*, 436 S.W.2d at 755 n. 1 (quoting Blakiston's *New Gould Medical Dictionary* 1260 (2d ed. 1956)). The proper therapeutic response is countertransference, a reaction which avoids emotional involvement and assists the patient in overcoming problems.

When the therapist mishandles transference and becomes sexually involved with a patient, medical authorities are nearly unanimous in considering such conduct to be malpractice. *L.L.*, 362 N.W.2d at 176–77 (citing Davidson, *Psychiatry's Problem with No Name: Therapist-Patient Sex*, 37 Am.J.Psychoanalysis 43, 48–49 (1977) ("[I]t is generally agreed that therapist-patient sex is psychologically deleterious for the involved woman patient and is unethical practice for the male practitioner."); Stone, *The Legal Implications of Sexual Activity Between Psychiatrist and Patient*, 133 Am.J.Psychiatry 1138, 1139 (1976) ("[T]he experts would . . . agree . . . that 'there are absolutely no circumstances which permit a psychiatrist to engage in sex with his patient.' All such instances constitute misuse of the transference.")). Dr. Brown explained at the trial that the reason sexual involvement with a patient is so harmful is due to the "parent-child" relationship symbolized by the transference. As she stated, "were a therapist to be sexual with a client it would be replicating at a symbolic level the situation in which a parent would be sexual with a child. The kinds of harm that can flow from those sorts of violations of trust are very similar."***

There is no question that a mental health professional's sexual involvement with a client is a breach of duty and malpractice under Washington law. But the liability of the Government for Mr. Kammers' conduct depends upon whether his conduct was within the scope of his employment. Washington agency law has long held that a master cannot excuse himself when any "authorized act was improperly or unlawfully performed" *De Leon v. Doyhof Fish Products Co.*, 104 Wash. 337, 343 (1918), nor can he excuse himself when an authorized act is done in conjunction with other acts which are within the scope of duties the employee is instructed to perform.

In a recent case discussing scope of employment, the Washington Supreme Court reiterated the test for determining whether an employee was within the course of his employment as:

> whether the employee was, at the time, engaged in the performance of the duties required of him by his contract of employment; *or* by specific direction of his employer; *or*, as sometimes stated, *whether he was engaged at the time in the furtherance of the employer's interest.****

We believe these principles support the district court's determination that Ted Kammers was acting within the scope of his employment in providing mental health counseling to Ms. Simmons, and that his unprofessional conduct in providing those services was the cause of her injury.

The Government advances five arguments against applying the doctrine of *respondeat superior* in this case. First it says Mr. Kammers' conduct was unauthorized and did not serve his employer's interests since the Government did not hire him to "have an affair" with anyone.***

In the instant case, Mr. Kammers was employed to provide mental health counseling and although he was not authorized to become sexually involved with his clients, that contact occurred in conjunction with his legitimate counseling activities and thus is within the rule of *Smith v. Leber*, 34 Wash.2d 611 (1949).

In this connection it is instructive to consider the analogous argument offered in many psychiatric malpractice cases that sexual contact with patients is unethical and unprofessional and therefore not covered by a practitioner's malpractice insurance, which typically covers only "the rendering of or failing to render professional services." *Vigilant Insurance Co. v. Employers Insurance of Wausau*, 626 F.Supp. 262, 265 (S.D.N.Y.1986). The majority of courts which have considered this question have held that the policies cover the sexual conduct "as long as the sexual conduct is related to therapy."***

For much the same reason, we believe the centrality of transference to therapy renders it impossible to separate an abuse of transference from the treatment itself. The district court correctly found that the abuse of transference occurred within the scope of Mr. Kammers' employment.

The Government's second argument is closely related to the first in that it says Mr. Kammers' allegedly negligent acts did not occur within the time and space of his employment since the instances of sexual intercourse occurred during out-of-town trips. This contention is without merit. The district court found Mr. Kammers' negligence to be his mishandling of the normal transference phenomenon. His romantic and sexual overtures, kissing and touching occurred during the therapy sessions, thus some of his negligent acts did occur during his working hours.

The Government also urges that the district court improperly made the employer's legal responsibility coextensive with the ethical standards of the mental health profession. However, the district court merely said that in this case a mental health counselor's conduct fell below widely accepted professional standards, and imposed derivative liability on his employer. The Government's assumption is that the court imposed liability on the employer for conduct outside the scope of employment, thus holding the employer to an ethical standard which governs "off duty" conduct as well as conduct within "business hours." There is no indication that the district court made these distinctions. It found Kammers' conduct to be negligent in toto, and at least some of his negligent acts occurred during therapy sessions, and all arose out of the ongoing therapy relationship he had with Ms. Simmons.

The Government apparently also argues that Mr. Kammers' conduct was not negligent and was not malpractice because he did not encourage Ms. Simmons to become sexually involved with him as a form of therapy. We have discovered no case, and the Government cites none, which suggests this is an element of the negligent act in a malpractice case. Although such a suggestion is often part of the factual pattern in such cases, it is not a necessary element of the cause of action.***

The district court's finding of supervisory negligence as a proximate cause of Ms. Simmons' injuries is a factual finding entitled to considerable deference.***

Mr. Kammers' supervisor, Victor Sansalone, was informed of the situation between the counselor and Ms. Simmons in January 1980. Since the counseling relationship continued until July 1981, the district court found Mr. Sansalone was negligent in failing to do anything to prevent further harm to Ms. Simmons.***

Although it is not clear which standard the district court applied, the factual finding of supervisory negligence is not clearly erroneous. Thus we affirm the judgment of the district court imposing liability on this ground as well.

GUTIERREZ v. THORNE
13 CONN. App. 493, 537 A. 2d 527 (1988)
CONNECTICUT APPELLATE COURT

BORDEN, JUDGE.

The plaintiff brought this action against the defendant in his capacity as commissioner of mental retardation, on the basis of injuries allegedly sustained by the plaintiff while she was a client-participant in a department program. The dispositive issues in this appeal are (1) whether it was reasonably foreseeable that a male employee of the department of mental retardation, who was assigned to supervise the plaintiff's living situation and who was supplied by the department with a key to the plaintiff's apartment, would commit a sexual assault upon the plaintiff in that apartment, and (2) whether the assault by the employee was within the scope of his employment sufficient to attribute his liability to the defendant. The trial court concluded that the documents submitted in support of and in opposition to the defendant's motion for summary judgment on both issues showed that no genuine issue of material fact existed as to these questions, and that the defendant was entitled to judgment as a matter of law. Because we conclude, under the circumstances of this case, that there exists a factual dispute as to whether the assault was reasonably foreseeable, we find error.***

The following undisputed facts were presented to the court for consideration in passing upon the defendant's motion for summary judgment. The plaintiff was referred to the department of mental retardation's central Connecticut regional center (CCRC) because an IQ test indicated that she was mildly retarded. She became a client of CCRC in the supervised apartment program in October, 1981, while living in a privately-owned apartment in Middletown. In this program, the plaintiff was to be supervised by state employees in how to keep her apartment, shop for her needs, budget her expenses, and perform other aspects of daily living.

In July, 1981, Steven Jones applied for a job as a mental retardation aide. In his application, Jones denied any criminal convictions or that any criminal charges were pending, which was verified through a state police fingerprint check. Upon being hired as a mental retardation aide, Jones went through a one-week orientation program and was supervised on a daily basis. Jones' job was to visit high-functioning retarded clients of CCRC living in supervised apartments and to assist them with budgeting and banking problems, shopping, and household management.

In December, 1981, Jones was assigned to visit the plaintiff. As a mental retardation aide, Jones was given a key to the plaintiff's apartment to enable him to enter the apartment in case of emergency. On December 19, while the plaintiff was taking a shower, Jones entered the plaintiff's apartment with the key provided to him and sexually assaulted the plaintiff. After the attack, Jones told the plaintiff that if she disclosed what had happened, she would lose her benefits. On three occasions in January, 1982, Jones returned to the plaintiff's apartment and sexually assaulted her again. Because she became afraid and upset, the plaintiff moved from her apartment and later told the police about Jones' conduct.

Jones was later arrested and pleaded guilty to two counts of sexual assault in the second degree in violation of General Statutes §53a-71(a)(2). In the twenty years in which CCRC operated a community residential program prior to 1981, no employee had ever been arrested or convicted of any crime of violence, including sexual assault, involving a CCRC client.***

We first consider whether the trial court was correct in its conclusion that the defendant is not liable to the plaintiff on a theory of respondeat superior. We conclude that the court's conclusion in this regard was correct.

"The underlying rationale of the modern doctrine of respondeat superior . . . is that 'every man who prefers to manage his affairs through others, remains bound to so manage them that third persons are not injured by any breach of legal duty on the part of such others *while they are engaged upon his business and within the scope of their authority.' Wolf v. Sulik,* 93 Conn. 431, 436, 106 A. 443

[1919]; *Durso v. A.D. Cozzolino, Inc.*, 128 Conn. 24, 27, 20 A.2d 392 [1941]. But *it must be the affairs of the principal, and not solely the affairs of the agent, which are being furthered* in order for the doctrine to apply."

In the present case, it is clear that Jones was not furthering the defendant's business interests when he sexually assaulted the plaintiff. He was engaging in criminal conduct which had no connection to the defendant's business of providing supervision and training to mentally retarded persons regarding daily living skills. Since there were no facts before the court from which it could conclude that Jones was furthering the defendant's interests, the defendant's nonliability under a respondeat superior theory was properly determined as a matter of law. The plaintiff's statement in her affidavit that Jones was "on duty" at the time of each assault, does not alter this conclusion, because his tortious conduct while on duty is not susceptible of an inference that he was acting to further his employer's interest. "'In the course of employment' means while engaged in the service of the master, and it is not synonymous with the phrase 'during the period covered by his employment.'"

Our conclusion that the trial court was correct in determining that the defendant could not be found vicariously liable based solely upon Jones' conduct does not mean, however, that the court properly granted the defendant's motion for summary judgment. The plaintiff seeks to base the defendant's liability upon allegations of negligence which flow, not solely from Jones' conduct, but also from the defendant's acts or omissions, or those of his agents other than Jones, which allegedly resulted in the injuries to the plaintiff. See footnote 1, supra. As such, the several allegations of a failure to exercise due care on the part of the defendant—each an independent claim of direct negligence—do not depend upon a successful theory of vicarious liability under the doctrine of respondeat superior. See, e.g., *Cardona v. Valentin*, supra (respondeat superior liability analyzed separately from liability for negligent failure to hire more employees); 53 Am.Jur.2d, Master and Servant §422, pp. 437–38 (theory of independent negligence becomes important where employee's act was not within scope of employment and respondeat superior liability unavailable). Therefore, the fact that the plaintiff failed to produce facts to show that Jones was acting within the scope of employment, would not entitle the defendant to judgment as a matter of law on the plaintiff's claims of negligent acts or omissions of the defendant which proximately resulted in the plaintiff's injuries.

We therefore turn to the issue of foreseeability, which was the principal basis of the trial court's decision, and which forms the crux of the appeal as presented by the parties. "The test that is often applied in determining whether there exists a duty to use care is the foreseeability of harm. 'Would the ordinarily prudent man in the position of the defendant, knowing what he knew or should have known, anticipate that harm of the general nature of that suffered was likely to result?' This does not mean foreseeability of any harm whatsoever or foreseeability that the particular injury which resulted would occur. It is, in short, the foreseeability or anticipation that harm of the general nature of that suffered would be likely to result, which gives rise to a duty to use due care, breach of which might constitute negligence."***

In the present case, we conclude that, even under facts which are not in dispute, the question of foreseeability is not such as would lead to only one conclusion; rather, under the circumstances of this case, the foreseeability of whether the defendant's conduct in permitting Jones to have a key to the plaintiff's apartment would result in a sexual assault upon the plaintiff is a question to be resolved by the trier of fact. In reaching this conclusion, we note several critical aspects of this case which must be carefully weighed, and therefore the inferences to be drawn from these facts cannot be resolved by summary judgment.

The plaintiff is a woman whose mental functioning is slightly impaired. She is a client of the department of mental retardation receiving the benefits of a state program to assist high-functioning mentally retarded persons in an independent living situation. The department of mental retardation's rules notwithstanding, the defendant, through department employees, permitted Jones, a male employee, to have complete, unfettered and unsupervised access to the plaintiff's apartment. The plaintiff was in a position where it is unlikely that she could resist Jones' entry into her private apartment. This impaired ability to resist arose both from the unrestricted nature of the access granted to Jones by virtue of his possession of a key to the plaintiff's apartment, and from the particular vulnerability of the plaintiff due to the superior power accorded Jones in his relationship with the plaintiff by virtue of their provider-client relationship, her mental impairment, and his ability to threaten a termination of her state services. Presented with these facts, the court erred in granting summary judgment because the conclusion to be drawn from these facts as to whether it was reasonably foreseeable that the plaintiff would be sexually assaulted by the defendant's employee is precisely the type of determination most appropriately left to the trier of fact.

There is error, the judgment is set aside and the case is remanded for further proceedings in accordance with law.

Notes and Issues for Discussion

1. In the *Simmons* case, the supervisor had knowledge of the employee's misconduct. Does that make a difference? In *Gutierrez*, the court found no liability on *respondeat superior* grounds, but held there could be liability on negligent breach of duty to use care in that the harm could be foreseeable.

2. Courts have taken different positions whether sexual relations can be within the "scope of employment." In *Cosgrove v. Lawrence*, 520 A.2d 844 (1986), affirmed 522 A.2d 484 (1987), the plaintiff sued the county and the county mental health center for damages resulting from seduction and wrongful sexual intercourse by their social worker employee. The court held that ". . . as a matter of law, sexual relations with plaintiff were not conduct of the kind he was employed to perform within the scope of his employment." 522 A.2d at 484. However, in the trial court decision, the court reported that "Defendant Lawrence asserts that he engaged in sexual relations for the purpose of therapy only and that he never looked forward to engaging in sexual relations with plaintiff. It is further asserted that plaintiff's specific personality disorder is the type which 'lends itself to the kind of inappropriate sexual behavior' admitted here." Should this

make a difference? The court also notes "It is conceded by all parties that this conduct is in violation of guidelines set forth in the code of ethics of the National Association of Social Workers." 520 A.2d at 845.
3. In *John R. v. Oakland Unified School District*, 48 Cal. 3d 438 (1989), the California Supreme Court found no liability for the school system under *respondeat superior* when a teacher invited a student to his home to work on a school project and then sexually molested him.
4. In *Kent v. Whitaker*, 304 P. 2d 556 (1961), the decedent was hospitalized after a suicide attempt. An intravenous feeding tube was attached and she was placed in a locked room from which her family and all visitors were excluded. Although the family had been assured she would be closely watched, she was not and committed suicide by strangling herself with the i.v. tube. The court held the hospital superintendent liable for a "failure of the specific duty of exercising reasonable care to safeguard and protect a patient with known suicidal tendencies from injuring herself." Although the superintendent had no responsibility to care for the patient in person, he had a general statutory responsibility for "admission and proper care" of patients. Additionally, the court found the superintendent liable under agency principles for the negligent actions of his employees.

VIOLATION OF CIVIL OR CONSTITUTIONAL RIGHTS; LIMITS TO LIABILITY

Under federal law, a worker, supervisor, or employer can be held liable for damages, compensatory and punitive, resulting from violations of civil and constitutional rights. Section 1983 provides:

Every person who under color of any statute, ordinance, regulation, custom or usage of any State or territory or the District of Columbia, subjects, or causes to be subjected, any citizen of the United States or other person within the jurisdiction thereof to the deprivation of any rights, privileges, or immunities secured by the Constitution and laws, shall be liable to the party injured in an action at law, suit in equity, or other proper proceeding for redress. . . . 42 U.S.C. §1983.

Previously used in a wide range of lawsuits in the health and human services (see, for example, *O'Connor v. Donaldson*, p. 398; *Halderman v. Pennhurst*, p. 416; *Youngberg v. Romeo*, p. 417, §1983 litigation, particularly involving liability of governmental authorities, is now more limited and complex.

In several decisions, the Supreme Court has restricted suits against municipalities and supervisors. Municipality liability is limited to situations where the municipality "implements or executes a policy statement, ordinance, regulation, or decision officially adopted and promulgated by that body's officers" or is a result of governmental custom. Supervisors may be personally liable for a failure to supervise or train employees, or where the supervisor knew or should have known that the action would violate the individual's constitutional rights.[11] For example in *Doe v. Borough of Barrington* (p. 00), the court found the Borough of Runnemeade liable for a failure to train about AIDS.

> In light of the duties assigned to police officers, the need for police training about AIDS is obvious. Officers frequently come into contact with members of high risk populations, such as intravenous drug users, therefore police must understand the disease and its transmission to protect themselves and the public. . . . Additionally the need for police training to keep confidential one's infection with the AIDS virus is obvious. . . . Runnemeade's failure to train officers, therefore, was likely to result in a violation of constitutional rights. The absence of training here is also a deliberate and conscious choice by the municipality. . . . Runnemeade's failure to train officers about AIDS and the need to keep confidential the identity of those known to the police to have the disease falls within the Supreme Court's definition of 'deliberate indifference' that caused the violation of the Does' constitutional rights. 729 F. Supp. at 389.

An important issue is the state's obligation to protect its citizens against acts of other private citizens. In the *DeShaney* decision (below), the Court found no liability when a county protective services agency failed to protect an abused child from his father, observing "nothing in the language of the Due Process Clause itself requires the State to protect the life, liberty, and property of its citizens against invasion by private actors." This decision also has been used by some courts as the basis for finding police not liable for a failure to protect domestic violence victims. (See generally, p. 372.)

DESHANEY v. WINNEBAGO COUNTY DEPARTMENT OF SOCIAL SERVICES
489 U.S. 189 (1989)
U.S. SUPREME COURT

CHIEF JUSTICE REHNQUIST delivered the opinion of the Court.

Petitioner is a boy who was beaten and permanently injured by his father, with whom he lived. The respondents are social workers and other local officials who received complaints that petitioner was being abused by his father and had reason to believe that this was the case, but nonetheless did not act to remove petitioner from his father's custody. Petitioner sued respondents claiming that their failure to act deprived him of his liberty in violation of the Due Process Clause of the Fourteenth Amendment to the United States Constitution. We hold that it did not.

The facts of this case are undeniably tragic. Petitioner, Joshua DeShaney was born in 1979. In 1980, a Wyoming court granted his parents a divorce and awarded custody of Joshua to his father, Randy DeShaney. The father shortly thereafter moved to Neenah, a city located in Winnebago County, Wisconsin, taking the infant DeShaney with him. There he entered into a second marriage, which also ended in divorce.

The Winnebago County authorities first learned that Joshua DeShaney might be a victim of child abuse in January 1982, when his father's second wife complained to the police, at the time of their divorce, that he had previously "hit the boy causing marks and [was] a prime case for child abuse." The Winnebago County Department of Social Services (DSS) interviewed the father, but he denied the accusations, and DSS did not pursue them further. In January 1983, Joshua was admitted to a local hospital with multiple bruises and abrasions. The examining physician suspected child abuse and notified DSS, which immediately obtained an order from a Wisconsin juvenile court placing Joshua in the temporary custody of the hospital. Three days later, the county convened an ad hoc "Child Protection Team"—consisting of a pediatrician, a psychologist, a police detective, the county's lawyer, several DSS caseworkers, and various hospital personnel—to consider Joshua's situation. At this meeting, the Team decided that there was insufficient evidence of child abuse to retain Joshua in the custody of the court. The Team did, however, decide to recommend several measures to protect Joshua, including enrolling him in a preschool program, providing his father with certain counselling services, and encouraging his father's girlfriend to move out of the home. Randy DeShaney entered into a voluntary agreement with DSS in which he promised to cooperate with them in accomplishing these goals.

Based on the recommendation of the Child Protection Team, the juvenile court dismissed the child protection case and returned Joshua to the custody of his father. A month later, emergency room personnel called the DSS caseworker handling Joshua's case to report that he had once again been treated for suspicious injuries. The caseworker concluded that there was no basis for action. For the next six months, the caseworker made monthly visits to the DeShaney home, during which she observed a number of suspicious injuries on Joshua's head; she also noticed that he had not been enrolled in school and that the girlfriend had not moved out. The caseworker dutifully recorded these incidents in her files, along with her continuing suspicions that someone in the DeShaney household was physically abusing Joshua, but she did nothing more. In November 1983, the emergency room notified DSS that Joshua had been treated once again for injuries that they believed to be caused by child abuse. On the caseworker's next two visits to the DeShaney home, she was told that Joshua was too ill to see her. Still DSS took no action.

In March 1984, Randy DeShaney beat 4-year-old Joshua so severely that he fell into a life-threatening coma. Emergency brain surgery revealed a series of hemorrhages caused by traumatic injuries to the head inflicted over a long period of time. Joshua did not die, but he suffered brain damage so severe that he is expected to spend the rest of his life confined to an institution for the profoundly retarded. Randy DeShaney was subsequently tried and convicted of child abuse.

Joshua and his mother brought this action under 42 USC §1983 [42 USCS §1983] in the United States District Court for the Eastern District of Wisconsin against respondent Winnebago County, its Department of Social Services, and various individual employees of the Department. The complaint alleged that respondents had deprived Joshua of his liberty without due process of law, in violation of his rights under the Fourteenth Amendment, by failure to intervene to protect him against a risk of violence at his father's hands of which they knew or should have known. The District Court granted summary judgment for respondents.

The Court of Appeals for the Seventh Circuit affirmed.***

The Due Process Clause of the Fourteenth Amendment provides that "[n]o State shall . . . deprive any person of life, liberty, or property, without due process of law." Petitioners contend that the State deprived Joshua of his liberty interest in "free[dom] from . . . unjustified intrusions on personal security," by failing to provide him with adequate protection against his father's violence. The claim is one invoking the substantive rather than procedural component of the Due Process Clause; petitioners do not claim that the State denied Joshua protection without according him appropriate procedural safeguards, see Morrissey v Brewer, 408 US 471, 481 (1972), but that it was categorically obligated to protect him in these circumstances, see Youngberg v Romeo, 457 US 307, 309 (1982).

But nothing in the language of the Due Process Clause itself requires the State to protect the life, liberty, and property of its citizens against invasion by private actors. The Clause is phrased as a limitation on the State's power to act, not as a guarantee of certain minimal levels of safety and security. It forbids the State itself to deprive individuals of life, liberty, or property without "due process of law," but its language cannot fairly be extended to impose an affirmative obligation on the State to ensure that those interests do not come to harm through other means. Nor does history support such an expansive reading of the constitutional text. Like its counterpart in the Fifth Amendment, the Due Process Clause of the Fourteenth Amendment was intended to prevent government "from abusing [its] power, or employing it as an instrument of oppression."***Its purpose was to protect the people from the State, not to ensure that the State protected them from each other. The Framers were content to leave the extent of governmental obligation in the latter area to the democratic political processes.***

Petitioners contend, however, that even if the Due Process Clause imposes no affirmative obligation on the State to provide the general public with adequate protective services, such a duty may arise out of certain "special relationships" created or assumed by the State with respect to particular individuals. Petitioners argue that such a "special relationship" existed here because the State knew that Joshua faced a special danger of abuse at his father's hands, and specifically proclaimed, by word and by deed, its intention to protect him against that danger. Having actually undertaken to protect Joshua from this danger—which petitioners concede the State played no part in creating—the State acquired an affirmative "duty," enforceable through the Due Process Clause, to do so in a reasonably competent fashion. Its failure to discharge that duty, so the argument goes, was an abuse of governmental power that so "shocks the conscience," *Rochin v California*, 342 US 165 (1952), as to constitute a substantive due process violation.

We reject this argument. It is true that in certain limited circumstances the Constitution imposes upon the State affirmative duties of care and protection with respect to particular individuals. In *Estelle v Gamble*, 429 US 97 (1976), we recognized that the Eighth Amendment's prohibition against cruel and unusual punishment, made applicable to the States through the Fourteenth Amendment's Due Process Clause, requires the State to provide adequate medical care to incarcerated prisoners. We reasoned that because the prisoner is unable "'by reason of the deprivation of his liberty [to] care for himself,'" it is only "'just'" that the State be required to care for him. Ibid.

In *Youngberg v Romeo*, 457 US 307 (1982), we extended this analysis beyond the Eighth Amendment setting, holding that the substantive component of the Fourteenth Amendment's Due Process Clause requires the State to provide involuntarily committed mental patients with such services as are necessary to ensure their "reasonable safety" from themselves and others.***

But these cases afford petitioners no help. Taken together, they stand only for the proposition that when the State takes a person into its custody and holds him there against his will, the Constitution imposes upon it a corresponding duty to assume some responsibility for his safety and general well-being. See *Youngberg v Romeo*, supra, at 317 ("When a person is institutionalized—and wholly dependent on the State[,] . . . a duty to provide certain services and care does exist"). The rationale for this principle is simple enough: when the State by the affirmative exercise of its power so restrains an individual's liberty that it renders him unable to care for himself, and at the same time fails to provide for his basic human needs—e.g., food, clothing, shelter, medical care, and reasonable safety—it transgresses the substantive limits on state action set by the Eighth Amendment and the Due Process Clause. The affirmative duty to protect arises not from the State's knowledge of the individual's predicament or from its expressions of intent to help him, but from the limitation which it has imposed on his freedom to act on his own behalf.***

The *Estelle-Youngberg* analysis simply has no applicability in the present case. Petitioners concede that the harms Joshua suffered did not occur while he was in the State's custody, but while he was in the custody of his natural father, who was in no sense a state actor. While the State may have been aware of the dangers that Joshua faced in the free world, it played no part in their creation, nor did it do anything to render him any more vulnerable to them. That the State once took temporary custody of Joshua does not alter the analysis, for when it returned him to his father's custody, it placed him in no worse position than that in which he would have been had it not acted at all; the State does not become the permanent guarantor of an individual's safety by having once offered him shelter. Under these circumstances, the State had no constitutional duty to protect Joshua.***

Judges and lawyers, like other humans, are moved by natural sympathy in a case like this to find a way for Joshua and his mother to receive adequate compensation for the grievous harm inflicted upon them. But before yielding to that impulse, it is well to remember once again that the harm was inflicted not by the State of Wisconsin, but by Joshua's father. The most that can be said of the state functionaries in this case is that they stood by and did nothing when suspicious circumstances dictated a more active role for them. In defense of them it must also be said that had they moved too soon to take custody of the son away from the father, they would likely have been met with charges of improperly intruding into the parent-child relationship, charges based on the same Due Process Clause that forms the basis for the present charge of failure to provide adequate protection.

The people of Wisconsin may well prefer a system of liability which would place upon the State and its officials the responsibility for failure to act in situations such as the present one. They may create such a system, if they do not have it already, by changing the tort law of the State in accordance with the regular law-making process. But they should not have it thrust upon them by this Court's expansion of the Due Process Clause of the Fourteenth Amendment.

Affirmed.

JUSTICE BRENNAN, with whom JUSTICE MARSHALL AND JUSTICE BLACKMUN join, dissenting.

"The most that can be said of the state functionaries in this case," the Court today concludes, "is that they stood by and did nothing when suspicious circumstances dictated a more active role for them." Because I believe that this description of respondents' conduct tells only part of the story and that, accordingly, the Constitution itself "dictated a more active role" for respondents in the circumstances presented here, I cannot agree that respondents had no constitutional duty to help Joshua DeShaney.***

I would begin from the opposite direction. I would focus first on the action that Wisconsin *has* taken with respect to Joshua and children like him, rather than on the actions that the State failed to take.***

Wisconsin has established a child-welfare system specifically designed to help children like Joshua. Wisconsin law places upon the local departments of social services such as respondent (DSS or Department) a duty to investigate reported instances of child abuse. See Wis Stat Ann §48.981(3) (1987 and Supp 1988–1989). While other governmental bodies and private persons are largely responsible for the reporting of possible cases of child abuse, see §48.981(2), Wisconsin law channels all such reports to the local department of social services for evaluation and, if necessary, further action. §48.981(3). Even when it is the sheriff's office or police department that receives a report of suspected child abuse, that report is referred to local social services departments for action, see §48.981(3)(a); the only exception to this occurs when the reporter fears for the child's *immediate* safety. §48.981(3)(b). In this way, Wisconsin law invites—indeed, directs—citizens and other governmental entities to depend on local departments of social services such as respondent to protect children from abuse.

The specific facts before us bear out this view of Wisconsin's system of protecting children. Each time someone voiced a suspicion that Joshua was being abused, that information was relayed to the Department for investigation and possible action. When Randy DeShaney's second wife told the police that he had "'hit the boy causing marks and [was] a prime case for child abuse,'" the police referred her complaint to DSS. When, on three separate occasions, emergency room personnel noticed suspicious injuries on Joshua's body, they went to DSS with this information. When neighbors informed the police that they had seen or heard Joshua's father or his father's lover beating or otherwise abusing Joshua, the police brought these reports to the attention of DSS. And when respondent Kemmeter, through these reports and through her own observations in the course of nearly 20 visits to the DeShaney home, compiled growing evidence that Joshua was being abused, that information stayed within the Department—chronicled by the social worker in detail that seems almost eerie in light of her failure to act upon it. (As to the extent of the social worker's involvement in and knowledge of Joshua's predicament, her reaction to the news of Joshua's last and most devastating injuries is illuminating: "I just knew the phone would ring some day and Joshua would be dead." 812 F2d 298, 300 (CA7 1987).)

Even more telling than these examples is the Department's control over the decision whether to take steps to protect a particular child from suspected abuse. While many different people contributed information and advice to this decision, it was up to the people at DSS to make the ultimate decision (subject to the approval of the local government's Corporation Counsel) whether to disturb the family's current arrangements. When Joshua first appeared at a local hospital with injuries signaling physical abuse, for example, it was DSS that made the decision to take him into temporary custody for the purpose of studying his situation—and it was DSS, acting in conjunction with the Corporation Counsel, that returned him to his father. Unfortunately for Joshua DeShaney, the buck effectively stopped with the Department.

In these circumstances, a private citizen, or even a person working in a government agency other than DSS, would doubtless feel that her job was done as soon as she had reported her suspicions of child abuse to DSS. Through its child-welfare program, in other words, the State of Wisconsin has relieved ordinary citizens and governmental bodies other than the Department of any sense of obligation to do anything more than report their suspicions of child abuse to DSS. If DSS ignores or dismisses these suspicions, no one will step in to fill the gap. Wisconsin's child-protection program thus effectively confined Joshua DeShaney within the walls of Randy DeShaney's violent home until such time as DSS took action to remove him. Conceivably, then, children like Joshua are made worse off by the existence of this program when the persons and entities charged with carrying it out fail to do their jobs.

It simply belies reality, therefore, to contend that the State "stood by and did nothing" with respect to Joshua. Through its child-protection program, the State actively intervened in Joshua's life and, by virtue of this intervention, acquired ever more certain knowledge that Joshua was in grave danger. These circumstances, in my view, plant this case solidly within the tradition of cases like Youngberg and Estelle.***

Youngberg's deference to a decisionmaker's professional judgment ensures that once a caseworker has decided, on the basis of her professional training and experience, that one course of protection is preferable for a given child, or even that no special protection is required, she will not be found liable for the harm that follows. (In this way, Youngberg's vision of substantive due process serves a purpose similar to that served by adherence to procedural norms, namely, requiring that a State actor stop and think before she acts in a way that may lead to a loss of liberty.) Moreover, that the Due Process Clause is not violated by merely negligent conduct means that a social worker who simply makes a mistake of judgment under what are admittedly complex and difficult conditions will not find herself liable in damages under §1983.

As the Court today reminds us, "the Due Process Clause of the Fourteenth Amendment was intended to prevent government 'from abusing [its] power, or employing it as an instrument of oppression.'" My disagreement with the Court arises from its failure to see that inaction can be every bit as abusive of power as action, that oppression can result when a State undertakes a vital duty and then ignores it. Today's opinion construes the Due Process Clause to permit a State to displace private sources of protection and then, at the critical moment, to shrug its shoulders and turn away from the harm that it has promised to try to prevent. Because I cannot agree that our Constitution is indifferent to such indifference, I respectfully dissent.

JUSTICE BLACKMUN, dissenting.

Today, the Court purports to be the dispassionate oracle of the law, unmoved by "natural sympathy." But, in this pretense, the Court itself retreats into a sterile formalism which prevents it from recognizing either the facts of the case before it or the legal norms that should apply to those facts. As Justice Brennan demonstrates, the facts here involve not mere passivity, but active state intervention in the life of Joshua DeShaney—intervention that triggered a fundamental duty to aid the boy once the State learned of the severe danger to which he was exposed.

The Court fails to recognize this duty because it attempts to draw a sharp and rigid line between action and inaction. But such formalistic reasoning has no place in the interpretation of the broad and stirring clauses of the Fourteenth Amendment. Indeed, I submit that these clauses were designed, at least in part, to undo the formalistic legal reasoning that infected antebellum jurisprudence, which the late Professor Robert Cover analyzed so effectively in his significant work entitled Justice Accused (1975).

Like the antebellum judges who denied relief to fugitive slaves, see id., at 119–121, the Court today claims that its decision, however harsh, is compelled by existing legal doctrine. On the contrary, the question presented by this case is an open one, and our Fourteenth Amendment precedents may be read more broadly or narrowly depending upon how one chooses to read them. Faced with the choice, I would adopt a "sympathetic" reading, one which comports with dictates of fundamental justice and recognizes that compassion need not be exiled from the province of judging. Cf. A. Stone, Law, Psychiatry, and Morality 262 (1984) ("We shall make mistakes if we go forward, but doing nothing can be the worst mistake. What is required of us is moral ambition. Until our composite sketch becomes a true portrait of humanity we must live with our uncertainty;

we will grope, we will struggle, and our compassion may be our only guide and comfort").

Poor Joshua! Victim of repeated attacks by an irresponsible, bullying, cowardly, and intemperate father, and abandoned by respondents who placed him in a dangerous predicament and who knew or learned what was going on, and yet did essentially nothing except, as the Court revealingly observes, "dutifully recorded these incidents in [their] files." It is a sad commentary upon American life, and constitutional principles—so full of late of patriotic fervor and proud proclamations about "liberty and justice for all," that this child, Joshua DeShaney, now is assigned to live out the remainder of his life profoundly retarded. Joshua and his mother, as petitioners here, deserve—but now are denied by this Court—the opportunity to have the facts of their case considered in the light of the constitutional protection that 42 USC §1983 is meant to provide.

Notes and Issues for Discussion

1. What constitutional rights do Joshua and his mother say were violated? Who violated those rights? If Joshua had been abused by a state worker or in a state-run foster home would this have made a difference?
2. *Youngberg v. Romeo* (p. 417) required the state to provide certain protections to institutionalized mentally retarded citizens, and in *Estelle v. Gamble*, 429 U.S. 97 (1976), the court mandated medical care for prisoners. Yet in *DeShaney*, "the State had no constitutional duty to protect Joshua." How do these cases differ?
3. According to the Court, the state has no obligation to protect the life, liberty, and property of its citizens against private individuals. Why not?
4. The dissent argues that the State did not just stand by and do nothing, as the majority suggests, but that it has taken an active role by creating an agency to deal with child abuse, giving this agency the responsibility for receiving abuse reports, and mandating supervision and the provision of services to abused children and families. Should this make a difference?
5. The broader constitutional point is that the Court has long regarded the Due Process Clause as a limitation on governmental action, and not as an affirmative mandate for governmental action. For a thorough analysis of the underlying issues and their relationship to disparate views of substantive due process, see Hickock and McDowell, 1993.

Sovereign Immunity

"The King can do no wrong." This rationale for holding state and federal governments immune for wrongs committed by their employees dates to early common law, and remains in effect to some degree today. However, much of sovereign immunity has been eroded, and under federal and state tort claims acts, governments consent to lawsuits in a variety of situations.

Major distinctions are between *governmental* or public functions as opposed to *proprietary* or private functions, and between *discretionary* acts involving skill and judgment as opposed to *ministerial* acts, or merely carrying out instructions.

Although the distinctions are not precise, governments are generally not liable for wrongful acts committed as part of governmental functions, or for the discretionary acts of their employees. However, there may be liability for wrongful acts occurring as part of a government's proprietary functions or employees' ministerial acts. For example, in some jurisdictions, the government is immune from liability for wrongful acts of its police or firemen, since police and fire protection are governmental functions, but wrongful acts occurring in the operation of a community hospital or a municipal utility may have no protection, since these are proprietary functions which could be performed by a private agency.

Governmental officials may have immunity for their discretionary acts such as governmental policy making or planning,[12] but acts that are "ministerial"—that is, having to do with implementation or operations—are not covered.[13] There is immunity for discretionary acts but not for ministerial ones under the Federal Tort Claims Act and some state acts. 28 U.S.C. §2680(a).

The main idea here is that certain governmental activities are legislative or executive in nature and that any judicial control of those activities, in tort or otherwise, would disrupt the balanced separation of powers of the three branches of government. (Keeton, *et al.*, 1984: 1039)

NATIONAL BANK OF SOUTH DAKOTA v. LEIR
325 N.W. 845 (1982)
SOUTH DAKOTA SUPREME COURT

MORGAN, JUSTICE.

This is an appeal from a summary judgment against the appellant, National Bank of South Dakota, guardian ad litem for D.C. and B.M., minors (guardian). Guardian sued defendant social workers for their alleged negligent placement and supervision of D.C. and B.M. in a foster home. The trial court entered summary judgment against guardian and in favor of social workers on the grounds that these social workers are immune from suit under the sovereign immunity doctrine. Guardian appeals and we reverse and remand.

In May 1975 social workers placed sisters D.C., then seven years of age, and B.M., then four years of age, in the foster home of Glenn and Ivy Brown. For the next two years, the sisters were sexually abused by their foster father, and physically abused by both of their foster parents. According to Department of Social Services' (Department) files maintained by these social workers, a number of incidents took place while the sisters were in the Brown foster home. During this time, social workers received complaints from the neighbors that the Browns were abusing D.C. and B.M. Additionally, D.C. and B.M.'s mother reported to the social workers that there were "rumors" about Glenn Brown, that B.M. was forced to sleep on the floor, and that B.M. had bruises that may be caused by abuse. Social workers, however, accepted the Browns' explanation that B.M.'s bruises resulted from her "accident prone" nature. Despite these complaints of abuse and their knowledge of Browns' animosity toward the children's mother, the social workers did not remove the children from the Browns' home.

Also during this two-year period, significant changes were noted in D.C.'s and B.M.'s behavior. According to Department's files, although D.C. previously was an excellent student, her grades dropped and in April 1977 when she was hospitalized for abdominal disorders the physician attributed her illness to emotional problems. The younger sister, B.M., lapsed into a baby role, was nasty to other children, would injure herself, continued going through eating motions when her plate was empty, and was "very destructive." At this time, one of the social workers noted in her file that she had "encouraged [Mrs. Brown] to forget about those [rumors of abuse] as [Mrs. Brown] can't do an effective job of mothering if she keeps worrying about what everyone will say."

While D.C. and B.M. were placed in the Browns' foster home, the social workers only once talked to the sisters alone and that discussion involved their mother's visitations. Although one social worker noted in her file that she had a "suspicious attitude" and "doubts about the wholesomeness of the [Brown] family situation," D.C. and B.M. were left in the Browns' care until a car accident in June 1977 in which Mrs. Brown was injured. After the car accident, the sisters were placed in a different foster home and in August 1977 they were returned to their natural mother. Shortly after the sisters were returned to their mother, they informed her of the physical and sexual abuse. Subsequently, as a result of his sexual abuse of D.C. and B.M., Glenn Brown was convicted of four counts of rape in the first degree, and two counts of indecent molestation of a minor child.

As guardian ad litem for D.C. and B.M., guardian instituted this action against social workers, alleging that social workers' neglect and violations of Department's rules and regulations made possible the continuing sexual and physical abuse of D.C. and B.M. Social workers denied the allegations and filed a motion to dismiss, asserting that they are immune from suit under the sovereign immunity principles announced in *High-Grade Oil Co. v. Sommer*, 295 N.W.2d 736 (S.D.1980). The trial court, treating the motion as one for summary judgment, granted summary judgment in favor of social workers. Guardian now appeals and the sole issue facing the court is whether social workers, as state employees, are immune from suit for acts of negligence under the sovereign immunity doctrine.***

Sovereign immunity provides the state with immunity from suit unless the state has consented to the particular suit alleged. As an outgrowth of sovereign immunity, a public officer may also be immune from suit when acting within the scope of his authority.***

After determining that this is not an action against the state, we now must determine whether this action is against social workers in their official capacities or as individuals. The immunity available to employees of governmental units is actually "an outgrowth of the doctrine of governmental immunity." *Sioux Falls Const. Co. v. City of Sioux Falls*, 297 N.W.2d at 458. In some instances, sovereign immunity will bar a suit against an employee acting within the scope of his employment. *Sioux Falls Const. Co. v. City of Sioux Falls, supra* (citing to Restatement (Second) of Torts §895D (1979)).

Whether immunity is available to a governmental employee depends upon the nature of the function exercised by the employee. Immunity extends to an employee who, while acting within the scope of his employment, exercises a discretionary function. In reviewing the discretionary versus ministerial dichotomy, we have held that a state employee who "fails to perform a merely ministerial duty, is liable for the proximate results of his failure to any person to whom he owes performance of such duty."***

In *Sioux Falls Const. Co.*, we looked to Restatement (Second) of Torts §895D (1979), in determining what is a discretionary function. The factors listed therein at comment f include:

(1) The nature and importance of the function that the officer is performing. . . .
(2) The extent to which passing judgment on the exercise of discretion by the officer will amount necessarily to passing judgment by the court on the conduct of a coordinate branch of government. . . .
(3) The extent to which the imposition of liability would impair the free exercise of his discretion by the officer. . . .
(4) The extent to which the ultimate financial responsibility will fall on the officer. . . .
(5) The likelihood that harm will result to members of the public if the action is taken. . . .
(6) The nature and seriousness of the type of harm that may be produced. . . .
(7) The availability to the injured party of other remedies and other forms of relief.***

Although we have before us a narrow issue, several other jurisdictions have addressed whether a social worker's functions on the placement, maintenance and care of children in foster care are discretionary or ministerial. These jurisdictions agree that such functions are ministerial and consequently the doctrine of sovereign immunity is not available to bar liability for negligence.

In *Elton v. County of Orange*, the California Appellate Court distinguished ministerial functions from discretionary functions in a suit by a foster child, for injuries suffered as a result of physical and mental abuse by foster parents. In holding that a cause of action was stated, the court determined that:

Decisions made with respect to the maintenance, care or supervision of [a foster child], or in connection with her placement in a particular home, may entail the exercise of discretion in a literal sense, but such determinations do not achieve the level of basic policy decisions, and thus do not [warrant immunity].

3 Cal.App.3d at 1058, 84 Cal.Rptr. at 30. Since the acts were ministerial, not discretionary, the defendants were not immune from a suit for negligence.

The Nebraska Supreme Court in *Koepf v. County of New York, supra,* also distinguished between ministerial and discretionary functions. *Koepf* involved a suit brought by a mother for the death of her minor child from a beating by a foster parent. As in *Elton, supra,* the court held that decisions involving the placement, maintenance, care or supervision of a child in a foster home are not basic policy decisions and thus do not fall within the discretionary-function exemption to immunity. Most recently, a New York Court agreed with this analysis in *Bartels v. County of Westchester.* In *Bartels,* the court held the actions of county employees in failing to supervise a foster child were ministerial in nature. Consequently, the defendants could not avoid liability for injuries sustained by the child at the hands of the foster parent.

In the present case, the action for which social workers claim immunity involve the placement and follow-up of these children in foster care. The care and placement of children is an important function and there is strong likelihood that serious harm will result to members of the public if it is performed incorrectly. Although some discretion in its literal sense is involved in foster care, social workers do not make policy decisions involving foster care placement. The criteria for placement and standards for follow-up of foster children are already established. Social workers are merely required to carry out or administer these previously established standards. The placement and follow-up of children in foster care according to preestablished standards is a routine, ministerial function.

***Since the actions for which social workers claim immunity are ministerial in nature, we hold that the doctrine of sovereign immunity does not extend to preclude a suit based upon these actions.

We reverse the circuit court's decision that this suit is barred by the doctrine of sovereign immunity and remand this case for trial on its merits.

Notes and Issues for Discussion

1. *Sinhogar v. Perry,* 427 N.Y.S.2d 216 (1980), involved a liability action against various state and city social services officials both as representatives of the government and personally for wrongful out-of-state placement of foster children. The court ruled against personal liability of the Commissioner of Social Services, holding the Commissioner was "entitled to immunity from personal liability for discretionary and quasi-judicial acts and the complaint against him in his individual capacity should have been dismissed. The general rule . . . has been stated as follows:

   A public official may be held liable in damages for a wrongful act only where such act is ministerial in nature. Where, however, an act is discretionary or quasi-judicial in nature no liability attaches even if the act was wrongfully performed. . . .

   The selection of an appropriate placement for a child, either in-state or out-of-state . . . is a matter of judgment, involving the exercise of executive discretion with due consideration to state policy, and the availability of suitable facilities and adequate funds. Even if wrong, such a decision does not give rise to personal liability." 427 N.Y.S.2d at 224.

2. In *Frank v. State*, 613 P.2d. 517 (1980), the action was against a staff psychiatrist, a contracting psychologist, and the State of Utah as owner of a university medical center for the failure to care for a suicidal patient. The court held that none of the parties had sovereign immunity, making a distinction between policy-making decisions and operational level implementation: "The exception to the statutory waiver under consideration here, however, was intended to shield those governmental acts and decisions impacting on large numbers of people in a myriad of unforeseen ways from individual and class legal action, the continual threat of which would make public administration almost impossible. The one-on-one dealings of physician and patient in no way reflect this public policy-making posture, and should not be given shelter under the Act." 613 P.2d at 520.

3. However, governmental officials are not immune for all discretionary acts. While there is often a general "good faith" immunity, this not total but is a "qualified" or limited immunity. One basic reason for a good faith immunity is to promote and protect administrative action and decision making. In actions for violations of constitutional rights, the governmental officials are granted immunity if the action was in good faith and "their conduct does not violate clearly established statutory or constitutional rights of which a reasonable person would have known." *Harlow v. Fitzgerald*, 457 U.S. 800 (1981).

4. Some states provide immunity to charitable organizations to a greater or lesser degree. However in most states this immunity is restricted. Under this doctrine not-for-profit organizations such as hospitals or family service agencies may be immune from liability under the theory that to hold them liable could threaten their charitable purposes.

PREVENTING MALPRACTICE ACTIONS

What can the health and human services professional do to protect against malpractice and liability actions? One obvious answer is to adhere to the code of ethics of the profession. Ethical conduct is not only in most cases the proper conduct, it is also defensible conduct. Conversely, conduct that violates a professional code of ethics is more often questionable and can be challenged as outside professional practice. Beyond this, it is advisable to consult with supervisors and colleagues about practice decisions and with lawyers about legal questions. Consultations may be used to defend one's choice of action, indicating it was thoughtful and considered. Finally, documentation is essential. A course of action for which the factual basis, the reasons for the actions, and any advice or expert opinion received is carefully and accurately documented will go far toward defending that action. Proper documentation need not be lengthy, but should be dated and recorded contemporaneously—as close to the event in question as possible. Memoranda memorializing the action and advice received should be retained. Where the patient or client chooses not to follow a course of treatment or action, this should be recorded along with advice given and, if possible, the reasons for rejection of that advice. These steps will go far in protecting the health and human services professional from future liability.

SELECTED REFERENCES

Applebaum, P., and Gutheil, T. *Clinical Handbook of Psychiatry and the Law* (2nd ed., 1992).

Austin, K., Moline, M., and Williams, G. *Confronting Malpractice: Legal and Ethical Dilemmas in Psychotherapy* (1990).

Bernstein, B. E. "Malpractice: future shock of the 1980's," 62 *Social Casework* 175 (1981).

———. "Malpractice: An ogre on the horizon, 23 *Social Work* 106 (1978).

Besharov, D. *The Vulnerable Social Worker: Liability for Serving Children and Families* (1985).

———. "Protecting abused and neglected children: Can law help social work?" in W. Holder and K. Hayes, *Liability in Child Protective Services* (1984).

Blum, K. "*Monell, DeShaney* and *Zinermon*: Official policy, affirmative duty, established state procedure and local government liability under Section 1983," 24 *Creighton L.Rev.* 1 (1990).

Cohen, R. *Malpractice: A Guide for Mental Health Professionals* (1979).

Furrow, B. *Malpractice in Psychotherapy* (1980).

Hickok, E., and McDowell, G. *Justice vs. Law—Courts and Politics in American Society* (1994).

Horowitz, R., and Davidson, H. "Improving the legal response of child protection agencies," 6 *Vermont L.Rev.* 381 (1981).

Jones, J., and Alcabes, A. "Clients don't sue: The invulnerable social worker," 70 *Social Casework* 414 (1989).

Jorgenson, L., and Sutherland, P. "Psychotherapist liability: What's sex got to do with it?" *Trial*, May 1993 p. 22.

Jorgenson, L., Randles, R., and Starasburger, L. "The furor over psychotherapist-patient sexual contact," 32 *William. and Mary L.R.* 645 (1991).

Keeton, W. P., Dobbs, D. B., Keeton, R. E., and Owen, D. G. *Prosser and Keeton on Torts* (5th ed., 1984).

Note, "*Respondeat superior*: A clarification and broadening of the current 'scope of employment' test," 30 *Santa Clara L. R.* 599 (1990).

Note, "'Scope of employment' redefined: holding employers vicariously liable for sexual assaults committed by their employees," 76 *Minnesota L. R.* 1513 (1992).

Pozgar, G. D. *Legal Aspects of Health Care Administration* (1990).

Robertson, J. D. Psychiatric Malpractice: Liability of Mental Health Professionals (1988).

Saltzman, A., and Proch, K. *Law in Social Work Practice* (1990).

Schutz, B. M. *Legal Liability in Psychotherapy* (1982).

Simon, R. I. *Clinical Psychiatry and the Law* (1987).

Smith, S. R. "Mental Health Malpractice," 28 *Houston L.R.* 209 (1991).

Swenson, L. C. Psychology and Law for the Helping Professions (1993).

VandeCreek, L., Knapp, S., and Herzog, C. "Malpractice risks in the treatment of dangerous patients," 24 *Psychotherapy* 145 (1987).

CHAPTER 16

COURTROOM TESTIMONY

Fact And Expert Witnesses

Professionals in the health and human services will usually appear in court to testify to facts or to provide specialized knowledge and opinions.[1] In the former capacity, the professional is testifying as a lay person, and may be asked to testify about what was seen, heard, said, or even smelled; in the latter, the professional is testifying as an expert, and may be asked to give an expert opinion or draw real or hypothetical conclusions.

FACT WITNESS TESTIMONY

A fact witness could appear in virtually any legal proceeding, on either side, to establish what occurred and what was recorded:

> The information offered by the witness must be considered by the court to be relevant, material and/or competent. Facts that are relevant are those which relate to what the lawyer is trying to prove. Material evidence is that which has important bearing on the case. Competent evidence is admissible because it is relevant, material, and capable of shedding light on the issues being litigated. (Barker and Branson, 1993).

The effectiveness of the witness will be determined by many factors, among them preparation and mastery of the material, dress and appearance, demeanor, speech, and confidence. A witness who is neat and well groomed; speaks clearly, directly, and without hesitation; remains cool and calm; recalls the facts; and acts as a professional will have a favorable impact on judge or jury. One who is sloppily or informally dressed; rambles, mumbles, hesitates, and stares at the floor; is argumentative, angry, and upset; is confused, has poor recall, and relies heavily on notes will not. The fact witness in

573

the health and human services is often the eyes and ears of the court or jury, telling, within the rules of evidence, what happened (Dickson, 1990a).

Since the courtroom is an adversary arena, after direct testimony the witness will often face cross-examination, where the opposing lawyer challenges or tries to discredit the testimony. In doing this, counsel may question the witness's preparation, experience, training, ability, record keeping, memory, veracity, biases, and professionalism—among others— in general, and what was actually seen, heard, or said in particular. Important to remember here is that everyone in the courtroom is acting a role, and in raising these challenges the opposing counsel is doing so not necessarily out of animosity or perversity, but because this is part of counsel's role. While anger may be an appropriate response to some particularly outlandish insinuations, generally a cool and calm demeanor and a direct response is most effective. Usually it is preferable to answer a question within the bounds of that question and without elaboration. If the question is not clear, the witness may ask for clarification. If time is needed to gather one's thoughts, this is possible, although testimony interrupted by lengthy pauses will be less effective. A witness who does not know the answer to a question or does not remember what occurred should say so. When ever possible, witnesses should meet with their counsel prior to testimony to plan a course of action. However, an actual rehearsal of the testimony may result in a more stilted and less effective delivery. The witness may be recalled for redirect examination if further clarification is needed, and could then face re-cross-examination (Dickson, 1990a).[2]

Rules of Evidence

Evidentiary rules may be crucial in courtroom proceedings, and the strictness with which they are applied will vary with the type of proceeding, the matter heard, and the presiding judge. Criminal trials are generally more formal and follow evidentiary rules more closely. Civil proceedings may be more informal and, depending on the subject matter and the presiding judge, rules of evidence may be relaxed. Quasi-judicial proceedings such as fair hearings or other administrative proceedings may be quite informal with wide latitude in admitting evidence.

Generally, rules of evidence, particularly in determining admissibility of evidence, are more the concern of lawyers and judges than of health and human services professionals. A good attorney will meet with the witness prior to the court appearance to discuss the testimony and its admissibility. If an attorney should attempt to introduce inadmissible testimony, the witness should not debate its admissibility on the stand. For example, a witness should not refuse to answer a question on direct on the grounds that the answer would be hearsay. This is for others to decide. If opposing counsel doesn't object, hearsay may be admitted even if it should not have been.

Hearsay Evidence

Hearsay is defined as

> [a] term applied to that species of testimony given by a witnesses who relates, not what he knows personally, but what others have told him, or what he has heard said by others. A statement, other than one made by the declarant while testifying at the trial or hearing, offered in evidence to prove the truth of the matter asserted. (Black's *Law Dictionary*, 1991)

The reason for the exclusion of most hearsay is that the individual who made the statement is not present and under oath so there is no way to establish the truth of the statement or the context in which it was made. There are, however, a number of exceptions to the hearsay rule. These range from dying declarations and declarations against interest to spontaneous declarations and excited utterances, and their admissibility will vary by jurisdiction.[3] One of the most important exceptions for the health and human services professional is that which allows for the admission of business records made in the ordinary course of business:

> Under this exception to hearsay rule, documentary evidence is admissible if identified by its entrant, or one under whose supervision it is kept and shown to be original or first permanent entry, made in routine course of business, at or near time of recorded transaction, by one having both the duty to so record and personal knowledge of transaction represented by entry. (Black's *Law Dictionary*, 1991)

Here "business" is far broader than traditional business and commerce, and generally includes records kept throughout the health and human services. Key to the exception is that the record be made in the ordinary course of business and that it be made contemporaneously—or nearly so—with the event. Events recorded at a much later time may not be admissible.[4]

THE EXPERT WITNESS

Generally only expert witnesses may give opinions and draw conclusions, although depending on the jurisdiction, a fact witness may, in light of experience and training, also be allowed to offer opinions. An expert is

[o]ne who by reason of education or specialized experience possesses superior knowledge respecting a subject about which persons having no particular training are incapable of forming an accurate opinion or deducing correct conclusions. A witness who has been qualified as an expert and who thereby will be allowed (through his/her answers to questions posed) to assist the jury in understanding complicated and technical subjects not within the understanding of the average lay person. (Black's *Law Dictionary*, 1991)

The health and human services professional might be called to provide expert testimony in a number of proceedings: divorce, child custody, or visitation; civil child abuse or termination of parental rights; domestic violence; incompetence and guardianship proceedings; mental health proceedings, including civil commitment testimony concerning dangerousness or mental illness; malpractice and liability cases; juvenile delinquency and a range of criminal actions, including child abuse, child sexual abuse, rape and sexual assaults, self-defense testimony in homicides or assaults, criminal sentencing hearings; and testimony to determine if someone is not guilty by reason of insanity or not competent to stand trial, among others.[5] In many of these, the expert could be witness for plaintiff, defendant, or could be court-appointed.

Qualifying as an Expert

Before testifying, the witness must be qualified as an expert witness by the presiding judge. While there is wide discretion in the criteria used to establish expert witness status, this usually is based on the particular knowledge, skill, experience, and training or education which makes that individual qualified to offer an opinion. To establish the witness's expertise, the attorney may inquire into past education and degrees, specializations, credentials, licenses, prizes and awards, teaching and research experience, consultations, professional memberships, published works, years of practice, number of cases examined or treated, and number of cases similar to the current case examined or treated. A current, detailed professional vita may be helpful to both counsel and the expert witness. A useful ploy for the opposition, particularly in the case of a highly qualified expert, is to concede qualifications to forestall a lengthy and impressive recital.[6] (*See* Baldwin, 1994:22–3, 22–4).

The direct examination of an expert witness begins with questions as to the witness' qualifications to testify on the subject at issue. Care must be taken when eliciting testimony as to credentials because the more the jury believes that the expert is truly knowledgeable about the precise issue that they are required to decide, the greater the weight that they will give to his opinion. It is important to demonstrate not only that the witness has theoretical knowledge of the subject as evidenced by his education, but also that he has a real practical knowledge acquired through years of employment experience. (Baldwin, 1994: 22–2)

Expert Testimony

As with fact witnesses, the effectiveness of the expert testimony often will depend upon the presentation. Baldwin notes that while a number of experts are generally held in high regard by juries,

... that initial favorable feeling can be turned into instant dislike by various attitudes the experts often display at trial. If the expert is condescending and talks to the jurors as if they were simpletons, if the expert is haughty and regards every "why do you say that," "please explain what you mean by that" question of counsel as a personal affront or as an indication of disbelief in his opinions, if the expert is supercilious, if he gives the impression that he feels he is wasting his valuable time testifying, if he shows impatience, flippancy or disdain, he will not be an effective witness. (Baldwin, 1994: 22–9).

Brodsky and Robey (1972) describe an effective expert witness as one who:

(a) obtains some relevant legal training or experience; (b) consults extensively with attorneys prior to trial; (c) is knowledgeable about specific legal issues; (d) maintains exact professional records; (e) presents clear, jargon-free reports and testimony; (f) directs testimony to the judge or jury in a persuasive manner; (g) anticipates cross-examination tactics and reacts to them without emotion; (h) assists the attorney in preparing rebuttal evidence; and (i) follows up results on the trial in order to improve the quality of future appearances. (cited in Nietzel and Dillehay, 1986: 109).

In terms of actual direct testimony, Baldwin suggests,

... the ideal answer is concise and responsive. To this end, the witness should be cautioned against:

1. volunteering any unnecessary information

2. attempting to lead the examination in any direction other than that in which counsel is going

3. making speeches

4. going off on tangents

5. trying to promote his own personality and thereby overshadowing the content of the testimony

6. showing impatience to counsel or the court

7. trying to impress the jurors with his scientific or medical knowledge by acting condescending and/or correcting counsel's mispronunciation of technical terms

8. mentioning insurance or anything which would suggest the fact of insurance unless the fact of insurance may be disclosed in your jurisdiction

9. attempting to answer questions that he does not understand or hear

10. using technical language not understandable to the average juror

11. being evasive, because he can not answer with absolute or scientific certainty

12. failing to couch his opinions in terms of the . . . certainty or probability required by your jurisdiction

13. saying "not as far as I know" when he means "no", saying "I should think so" or "That seems right to me" or any colloquialism which is intended by the witness to mean yes or no but which comes out meaning something less definite

14. expressing hostility for the defendant which can suggest that the witness has a motive to fabricate

15. expressing contempt for other experts involved in the case or for their opinions

16. offering opinions before stating that he has an opinion. . .

18. being evasive or embarrassed as to his fees for consultation and courtroom appearance. (Baldwin, 1994: 22–10).

In terms of cross-examination, Baldwin advises:

The expert witness should be cautioned against displaying hostility toward opposing counsel or obvious bias in favor of the side on whose behalf he is testifying. He should appear to be honest, cooperative and impartial.

The use of scientific or medical texts or journals to show disagreement with the testimony given on direct is a very effective impeachment technique and the witness should be prepared for it. . . .

At the pretrial conference, the expert should have supplied counsel with every piece of literature that he has had published on the subject at issue, to determine if there are any inconsistencies with the testimony as planned. If there are, the reasons for the inconsistency should be brought out on direct, as skillful opposing counsel may prevent the expert from testifying to other than the fact that there is a discrepancy between his testimony and his previous writings. (Baldwin, 1994: 22–17, 22–18)

A discussion of fees is particularly important:

Opposing counsel will frequently attempt to impeach the credibility of an expert witness by questioning him in an accusatory manner as to his fee for testifying. This kind of questioning is intended to portray the witness as a hired gun who will testify to anything because he is being paid to do so. . . .

The expert witness must be prepared in advance to state exactly how much he is paid for consultation and for court appearance. . . . The witness should make it clear that he is being paid only for his time and not for giving any particular testimony or opinion, and that he will be paid the same sum irrespective of the outcome of the litigation. A skillful cross-examiner may not permit the witness to communicate the above to the jury; however, if the witness is forthright, and matter of fact about his compensation and does not become sheepish or affronted, the jury will not give much credence to the attack. (Baldwin, 1994: 22–18, 22–19).

RELIABILITY OF EXPERT TESTIMONY

Since a judge or jury may rely heavily on the testimony of expert witnesses, the testimony must meet evidentiary standards to be admissible. How trustworthy are scientific theories and conclusions and when should they be relied upon by judge or jury? In his recent book, *Galileo's Revenge: Junk Science in the Courtroom*, Peter Huber argues that through relaxed standards for admitting expert scientific testimony, a substantial amount of unreliable evidence has been introduced in the areas of product liability and toxic harm, leading to erroneous verdicts. A similar debate goes on in the health and human services. Some scientific principles are accepted and established, others involve "novel" scientific theory and findings. Over time, novel scientific theory may become accepted to the point where a court will take judicial notice that a principle is reliable and accepted. Myers gives an example from the area of physical child abuse:

> In 1962, Kempe and his colleagues published their seminal article describing battered child syndrome. Presence of the syndrome is strong evidence that a child's injuries are nonaccidental. When prosecutors began using expert testimony on battered child syndrome, the reliability of the syndrome was open to question. At that early stage of development, battered child syndrome was properly considered a novel application of established scientific principles. The syndrome quickly gained acceptance as a reliable method of establishing nonaccidental injury, however, and courts uniformly approved admission of battered child syndrome testimony. Today, it is clear that battered child syndrome is accepted by medical science. The novelty (that is, questionable reliability) of the syndrome faded with experience. Courts take judicial notice of the reliability of battered child syndrome. Myers (1992: 258).

In *Daubert v. Merril Dow Pharmaceuticals, Inc.*, 125 L.Ed.2d 469 (1993), the U.S. Supreme Court held that the Federal Rules have superseded the more conservative common law approach that was enunciated in *Frye v. U.S.*, 293 F. 1013 (1923).

Federal Evidence Rule 702 is the basis for accepting expert testimony in the federal system and in many states:

> If scientific, technical, or other specialized knowledge will assist the trier of fact to understand the evidence or to determine a fact in issue, a witness qualified as an expert by knowledge, skill, experience, training, or education, may testify thereto in the form of an opinion or otherwise."

The more restrictive rule established in *Frye*, which is still followed in some jurisdictions, states:

> Just when a scientific principle or discovery crosses the line between the experimental and demonstrable stages is difficult to define. Somewhere in this twilight zone the evidential force of the principle must be recognized, and while courts will go a long way in admitting expert testimony deduced from a well-recognized scientific principle or discov-

ery, the thing from which the deduction is made must be sufficiently established to have gained general acceptance in the particular field in which it belongs. 293 F. 1013 at 1014.

Thus under *Frye* it is necessary to establish that a novel scientific theory or principle has gained general acceptance in the relevant scientific community to be admissible.[7]

In *Daubert*, parents of minor children born with birth defects sued the manufacturer of a prescription anti-nausea drug the mother had been taking prior to giving birth. Expert testimony for the pharmaceutical company was based on a review of all thirty published studies involving over 130,000 patients which had found that the drug was not a risk factor in human birth defects. Experts for the plaintiff, in concluding that the drug could cause birth defects, relied on test tube studies, live animal studies, chemical structure studies, and a reanalysis of epidemiological studies. The trial court held that the plaintiff's testimony was not admissible under the *Frye* rule because the evidence did not meet the standard of "sufficiently established to have general acceptance in the field to which it belongs," and the appellate court agreed.

In reversing, the Supreme Court observed:

That the Frye test was displaced by the Rules of Evidence does not mean, however, that the Rules themselves place no limits on the admissibility of purportedly scientific evidence. Nor is the trial judge disabled from screening such evidence. To the contrary, under the Rules the trial judge must ensure that any and all scientific testimony or evidence admitted is not only relevant, but reliable. . . . The subject of an expert's testimony must be "scientific . . . knowledge." The adjective "scientific" implies a grounding in the methods and procedures of science. Similarly, the word "knowledge" connotes more than subjective belief or unsupported speculation. . . . Of course it would be unreasonable to conclude that the subject of scientific testimony must be "known" to a certainty; arguably, there are no certainties in science. . . . But in order to qualify as "scientific knowledge," an inference or assertion must be derived by the scientific method. Proposed testimony must be supported by appropriate validation—i.e. "good grounds," based on what is known. 125 L.Ed.2d 480–481.

The court observed that pertinent criteria for deciding whether a theory or technique qualifies as scientific knowledge include whether it has been empirically tested and subjected to peer review and publication, the error rate of a particular technique, as well as how widely the theory or technique is accepted.

Medical and Psychological Syndromes

Health and human services experts may offer testimony on a wide range of topics. One important area that illustrates some of the problems of admissibility and reliability is that of syndromes. Syndromes have variable scientific reliability and range from those with a strong medical foundation, such as battered child syndrome, to some with both a medical and a psychological basis, such as battered spouse syndrome (see p. 357), to some which are based solely in psychology and as of today are more speculative, such as the recovered memory syndrome (see p. 334). Here we will examine two syndromes, battered child syndrome and child sexual abuse accommodation syndrome. The former is generally conceded to be a reliable indicator of nonaccidental injury to children. The latter was originally developed to explain why a pattern of behavior—a child's accommodation to sexual abuse—occurs, and many courts have refused to accept it as a reliable indicator of actual child sexual abuse. Myers (1993) distinguishes between syndrome, a "set of symptoms which occur together," and disease:

> The concepts of disease and syndrome overlap, but are not synonymous. With diseases, the cause of the malady is usually, although not always known. . . . By contrast, the cause or causes of syndromes are often unknown or obscure. (Myers, 1993: 1450–1453).

While syndromes and diseases both have diagnostic value, pointing to certain causes, Myers argues that the predictive value—that is, reliability—of syndromes is generally lower, and within syndromes there is a range of predictive power. Thus Myers compares battered child syndrome, one with a relatively high degree of predictability, with rape trauma syndrome, one with lower predictability:

> A child with battered child syndrome is very likely to have suffered nonaccidental injury. That is, battered child syndrome points convincingly to abuse. From a medical view, battered child syndrome has high diagnostic value. From a forensic point of view, battered child syndrome has high probative value. The syndrome points directly to abuse. . . . Rape trauma syndrome consists of symptoms that are caused by a number of events including, but not limited to, rape. Rape trauma syndrome points toward rape, but not as convincingly as battered child syndrome points toward child abuse. (Myers, 1993: 1454–1455)

BATTERED CHILD SYNDROME.

Many jurisdictions now accept expert medical testimony establishing a battered child syndrome, a combination of injuries which lead to the conclusion that the injuries to the child were nonaccidental.

> The battered child syndrome may occur at any age, but in general the affected children are younger than 3 years. In some instances the clinical manifestations are limited to those resulting from a single episode of trauma, but more often the child's general health is below par, and he shows evidence of neglect including poor skin hygiene, multiple soft tissue injuries, and malnutrition. One often obtains a history of previous episodes suggestive of parental neglect or trauma. A marked discrepancy between clinical findings and historical data as supplied by the parents is a major diagnostic feature of the battered child syndrome. . . . Subdural hematoma, with or without fracture of the skull is . . . an extremely frequent finding even in the absence of fractures of the long bones. . . . The characteristic distribution of these multiple fractures and the observation that the lesions are in different stages of healing are of additional value in making the diagnosis. *U.S. v. Boise,* 916 F.2d 497 at 503 (1990), citing Kempe, *et al.,* 1962: 17–18).

In a recent Massachusetts decision, an appellate court held battered child syndrome testimony admissible in a criminal prosecution. The child's parents had claimed that the child was injured falling off her potty seat and that they had broken and extracted several teeth when trying to force open her mouth because she was gagging:

> Four physicians . . . treated Laura on January 24–26. They found reason to disbelieve the parents' story linking the injuries to a minor fall. The individual findings, to which they testified, may be taken together . . . thus.
>
> There were multiple bruises, contusions, and abrasions across Laura's whole body; from the varying colors of the bruises, mostly to her head, arms, legs and back, these injuries could be assessed to range in age from several days past to within twelve to twenty-four hours.
>
> Laura had sustained fractures of the skull to the left side, of the right arm, and of the right collarbone, the first two fractures being recent and simultaneous, the third incurred somewhat earlier. The skull fracture was such as would be caused by strong trauma to the head, comparable to that which would result from a fall from a considerable height. This impact to the head had caused swelling and bleeding within the brain, which, implicating particularly the tissue on the left side, threat-

ened impairment of the child's ability to move the right side of her body as well as impairment of her speech. There also were retinal hemorrhages caused by severe force to the head.

The physician summed up the evidence in a medical diagnosis of "battered child syndrome" consisting of the six classic elements: child under three years of age; bone injuries at different times; subdural hematomas (here with the skull fracture); history given which does not fit the observed injuries; soft tissue injury; evidence of neglect. This syndrome tends to exclude the likelihood that the injuries occurred by accident. *Commonwealth v. Lazarovich*, 547 N.E.2d 940 at 943 (1989).[8]

Generally this evidence is admissible to show that injuries were not accidental but consistent with child abuse, and if they occurred in the absence of all but the perpetrator, tend to show who inflicted the injuries.[9]

CHILD SEXUAL ABUSE ACCOMMODATION SYNDROME

Myers argues that not only do syndromes vary in their predictive power, but a number of syndromes have little or no predictive value. These he terms "nondiagnostic" syndromes. One of these is "child sexual abuse accommodation syndrome" or CSAAS, which describes a way in which children adapt to ongoing sexual abuse.[10]

STATE v. J.Q.
617 A.2d. 1196 (1993)
New Jersey Supreme Court

O'HERN, J.

This appeal concerns the use of expert opinion testimony to aid jurors in the criminal trial of a child-sexual-abuse case. The specific issue concerns expert-opinion evidence premised on the Child Sexual Abuse Accommodation Syndrome (CSAAS), and whether there is a reliable scientific explanation for certain exhibited characteristics of an abused child, such as acceptance of the abuse or delayed reporting, that would help jurors understand why a child victim would not complain to a parent or other authority figure about the abuse. We hold that CSAAS has a sufficiently reliable scientific basis to allow an expert witness to describe traits found in victims of such abuse to aid jurors in evaluating specific defenses. In this case, the expert's opinion went beyond that limited scope and included opinions on commonplace issues, such as credibility assessments derived from conflicting versions of an event and not-yet scientifically established opinions on the ultimate issues that are for jury resolution. [We] agree with the Appellate Division that the introduction of such evidence was clearly capable of producing an unjust result and we thus affirm the Appellate Division's judgment ordering a new trial.

The background to the case is regrettably familiar, a story of childhoods unhinged by events so traumatic that even the participants cannot contemplate them. When first confronted with the possibility that defendant might have sexually abused his daughters, their mother was incredulous. After the girls first told their mother of the alleged abuse, she cautioned them that it was important to tell the truth about their father. The girls said that they were telling the truth. Their mother testified that she had warned her daughters never to let a stranger touch them but had never told them about sexual abuse from a father, because she never thought it could happen to her children. Defendant was equally insistent that committing sexual acts with children and, in particular, his daughters is unimaginable.

Rather than use the initials mandated by law, we shall use fictitious names to describe the parents and children involved. We shall refer to the mother as "Karen," the father as "John," and the two children as "Connie" and "Norma." The parents appear to be of different cultures—Karen is from the midwest and John is a recent arrival to the continental United States. They met in Indiana in 1973 or 1974 and started their life together there when Karen was thirteen and John was nineteen or twenty. John already had a child at that time. They soon moved to Brooklyn and later settled in Newark. Connie and Norma was born in 1977 and 1979, respectively. John and Karen never married. Theirs was a tempestuous union marked by recriminations that each had been unfaithful. Their relationship deteriorated in late 1984 when John separated from Karen.***

After the breakup, John customarily picked up the children and took them to Brooklyn for weekend visits. John was then living in a one-room apartment with another woman, whom he married in 1987. About two years after the separation, Karen learned that Norma, during play, had attempted to pull down her younger sister's underwear and touch her buttocks. Karen asked Norma where she had ever learned of such things and Norma reluctantly identified the person who had initiated her into such conduct by spelling out the word "D-A-D."

Although at first disbelieving, Karen consulted a family counselor and eventually reported the incident to the police. Both Connie and Norma reported that they had been the victims of repeated acts of sexual abuse by their father in the Newark apartment in 1984 as well as during their visits to Brooklyn. An Essex County grand jury returned an indictment charging John with acts of criminal sexual abuse in New Jersey on his children between January 1, 1984, and December 31, 1984.

At trial, both Connie and Norma described, in graphic detail, the abuses committed on them involving sexual penetration and oral sexual contact. A pediatric resident who conducted a genital examination of Norma testified that she found that the child had a stretched hymenal opening, an abnormal condition for a seven-year-old girl. The medical evidence relating to Connie, entered by way of stipulation, also revealed a stretched hymen. Karen described discharges that she had observed on Norma's underwear but said that she had attributed them to Norma's not changing her underwear.

Dr. Milchman was called to the stand again at trial and qualified, without objection, as an expert witness on child sexual abuse. She identified the child sexual abuse accommodation syndrome "as a pattern of behavior that is found to occur again and again in children who are victims of incest." She described the various aspects of CSAAS and related them to behavior she had observed in Connie and Norma. Dr. Milchman also testified about how she assesses the veracity of an alleged victim of child sexual abuse. At the conclusion of her direct testimony, Dr. Milchman stated that in her expert opinion, Connie and Norma had been sexually abused.

The theory of the defense was that Karen had put the children up to this story to avenge her loss of John.

The jury convicted defendant of multiple counts of first-degree aggravated sexual assault on Connie and Norma for various acts of penetration and oral sex, and of two counts of endangering the welfare of a child. The court sentenced defendant to thirty years' imprisonment, with ten years of parole ineligibility. The Appellate Division reversed the convictions, finding that the trial court had committed plain error in permitting the use of the CSAAS testimony to establish the credibility of the witnesses rather than for other limited purposes for which it is generally reliable, i.e., to explain secrecy, belated disclosure, and recantation by a child-sexual-abuse victim. The Appellate Division specifically held that

> syndrome evidence, including CSAAS, is not reliable to prove the occurrence of sexual abuse, and that absent a question of capacity, a social science expert lacks the qualifications to render an opinion as to the truthfulness of a statement by another witness. Because the expert in this case testified before the jury as to syndrome evidence to prove that sex abuse occurred; opined as to the truthfulness of the children (and their mother), and rendered the opinion that the children were abused based in great measure upon these two interdicted classes of evidence, we are satisfied that the admission of her testimony was error clearly capable of producing an unjust result.

We must examine the scientific premises supporting the expert's testimony and the purpose for which the testimony was used. We note first that testimony on the child sexual abuse accommodation syndrome has been placed within the category of behavioral-science testimony that describes behaviors commonly observed in sexually-abused children. Courts rarely permit the testimony for the purpose of establishing substantive evidence of abuse, but allow it to rehabilitate the victim's testimony. See Myers, 68 Neb.L.Rev. at 51, 66–69, 86–92. Roland C. Summit, M.D., has authored the most concise and seemingly most authoritative statement of CSAAS. Roland C. Summit, The Child Sexual Abuse Accommodation Syndrome, 7 Child Abuse & Neglect 177 (1983) [hereinafter Summit]. Dr. Summit explained in 1983 that although "[c]hild sexual abuse has exploded into public awareness during a span of less than five years," the awakening of interest creates new hazards for the child victim because it increases the likelihood of discovery "but fails to protect the victim against the secondary assaults of an inconsistent intervention system." Id. at 178 (emphasis omitted). Dr. Summit believed that most adults who hear a distraught child accuse a "respectable" adult of sexual abuse will fault the child. *Ibid.* The "[d]isbelief and rejection by potential adult caretakers," which in Dr. Summit's view were the too-frequent responses to reports of child sexual abuse, "increase the helplessness, hopelessness, isolation and self-blame that make up the most damaging aspects of child sexual victimization."

To remedy the systemic injury to the child that results from disbelief, Dr. Summit undertook a scientific study of child sexual-abuse victims. In publishing his results, Dr. Summit hoped "to provide a vehicle for a more sensitive, more therapeutic response to legitimate victims of child sexual abuse and to invite more active, more effective clinical advocacy for the child within the family and within the systems of child protection and criminal justice." Summit, *supra*, 7 *Child Abuse & Neglect* at 179–80. In other words, the purpose of his study was to improve the health of the child, ensure that children receive adequate treatment for what they had suffered, and guarantee that society's response be not flawed by misperceptions.

***The child sexual abuse accommodation syndrome, or CSAAS, "represents a common denominator of the most frequently observed victim behaviors." *Ibid.* CSAAS includes five categories of behavior, each of which contradicts "the most common assumptions of adults." Summit, *supra*, 7 *Child Abuse & Neglect* at 181. Of the five categories, he described two as "preconditions" to the occurrence of sexual abuse and the remaining three as "sequential contingencies" to the abuse "which take on increasingly variability and complexity." Obviously, the "preconditions" continue into and characterize the period of abuse.

The first of the preconditions is secrecy: child abuse happens only when the child is alone with the offending adult, and the experience must never be disclosed. That secrecy is frequently accompanied by threats: " 'This is our secret; nobody else will understand.' " " 'Don't tell anybody.' " " 'Nobody will believe you.' " " 'Don't tell your mother, (a) she will hate you, *** (c) she will kill you,' " and the like. Summit, *supra*, 7 *Child Abuse & Neglect* at 181. From the secrecy, the child gets the impression of danger and fearful outcome.

The second precondition is helplessness. Dr. Summit explains that the abused child's sense of helplessness is an outgrowth of the child's subordinate role in an authoritarian relationship in which the adult is entrusted with the child's care, such as the parent-child relationship. Summit, *supra*, 7 *Child Abuse & Neglect* at 182. The prevailing reality for the most frequent victim of child sexual abuse is a sense of total dependence on this powerful adult in the face of which the child's normal reaction is to "play possum." *Id.* at 182–83.

The third aspect of the syndrome, also the first of what Dr. Summit identifies as a sequential contingency, is a combination: the child feels trapped by the situation (entrapment), and that perception results in the behavior of accommodating the abuse (accommodation). Because of the child's helplessness, the only healthy option left is to survive by accepting the situation. "There is no way out, no place to run." Summit, *supra*, 7 *Child Abuse & Neglect* at 184. Adults find that hard to believe because they lack the child's perspective, but "[t]he child cannot safely conceptualize that a parent might be ruthless and self-serving; such a conclusion is tantamount to abandonment and annihilation." The roles of parent and child become reversed: it is the child who must protect the family. The abuser warns, " 'If you ever tell, they could send me to jail and put all you kids in an orphanage.' " Summit, *supra*, 7 *Child Abuse & Neglect* at 185.

The fourth aspect, then, is delayed, conflicted and unconvincing disclosure. *Id.* at 186. Most victims never disclose the sexual abuse—at least not outside the immediate family. Dr. Summit found that family conflict triggers disclosure, if ever, "only after some years of continuing sexual abuse and an eventual breakdown of accommodation mechanisms."

Allegations of sexual abuse seem so unbelievable to most that the natural reaction is to assume the claim is false, especially because the victim did not complain years ago when the alleged abuse was ongoing.***

The fifth and final aspect is retraction. Although this case does not involve retraction, that "[w]hatever a child says about sexual abuse, she is likely to reverse it" appears to be a fact. Summit, *supra*, 7 *Child Abuse & Neglect* at 188 (emphasis omitted). The post-disclosure family situation tends to confirm the victim's worst fears, which encouraged her secrecy in the first place, *i.e.*, her mother is disbelieving or hysterical, her father threatened with removal from the home, and the blame for this state of affairs placed squarely on the victim. Once again, because of the reversed roles, the child feels obligated to preserve the family, even at the expense of his or her own well being. The only "good" choice, then, is to "capitulate" and restore a lie for the family's sake.

Hence, the behavioral studies of CSAAS are designed not to provide certain evidence of guilt or innocence but rather to insure that all agencies, including the clinician, the offender, the family, and the criminal justice system, offer "the child a right to parity with adults in the struggle for credibility and advocacy." Summit, *supra*, 7 *Child Abuse & Neglect* at 191. CSAAS achieves that by providing a "common language" for analysis and a more "recognizable map" to the understanding of child abuse.

There does not appear to be a dispute about acceptance within the scientific community of the clinical theory that CSAAS identifies or describes behavioral traits commonly found in child-abuse victims. *See, e.g.*, Myers, *supra*, 68 *Neb.L.Rev.* at 66–69; Holmes, *supra*, 25 *Tulsa L.J.* at 158–59. The most pointed criticism of the theory is that the same traits may equally appear as the result of other disorders. *Holmes, supra*, 25 *Tulsa L.J.* at 158, 162–63. Even extreme poverty or psychological abuse can produce the sense of entrapment or accommodation. In other words, the existence of the symptoms does not invariably prove abuse.

Turning then to the application of the standards to the record of this trial, we find that the CSAAS evidence was not presented to the jury in accordance with its scientific theory, *i.e.*, the evidence was not offered to explain the conflicting behavioral traits in this case either of accommodation or delayed disclosure. Rather, the evidence was presented to the jury as though it were to prove directly and substantially that sexual abuse had occurred. Dr. Milchman, the prosecution's expert witness on child sexual abuse, described CSAAS as a pattern of behavior found to occur consistently in children who are victims of incest, and she outlined Dr. Summit's five-part syndrome: secrecy, helplessness, entrapment and accommodation, delayed disclosure, and retraction.

The prosecutor asked whether she had examined Connie and Norma and whether, in the course of examination, Dr. Milchman had found the children to "suffer symptoms of the child sexual abuse accommodation syndrome." (Recall that Dr. Summit describes two aspects of CSAAS, secrecy and helplessness, as "preconditions.") Dr. Milchman said that Norma had exhibited four of the symptoms: secrecy, helplessness, accommodation, and delayed disclosure. She said that Norma's crying, shaking, rubbing her hands in her eyes, and covering her face during the interview were manifestations of her feeling of helplessness towards the abusive situation and her fears, anxieties and anger which she had to suppress in order to accommodate the abuse. Technically, these interview observations do not seem to be the symptoms that Dr. Summit describes. Rather, they appear to us to be generic post-traumatic symptoms. Dr. Milchman pointed out that Norma had revealed the abuse only after questioning initiated by her mother. She also explained that Norma had stuck to her story, instead of recanting it, because nobody was pressuring or threatening her. Connie, on the other hand, had presented herself differently as a "very brassy, very assertive, very outgoing child on the surface" but "[u]nderneath there was a lot of fear and anxiety." Dr. Milchman described Connie as being entrapped and accommodating to the abuse—she complied and accepted the abuse for a long time. She also believed Connie had given a delayed disclosure. Dr. Milchman believed that Connie had kept the abuse a secret for a long time because John had threatened her and her mother with physical violence, a threat she believed because she had seen her father be violent with her mother.

The prosecution then made a transition into areas not covered by CSAAS. Dr. Milchman was presented with a series of questions based on a child's testimony concerning (1) the experience of feeling someone putting a finger inside the child's vagina, (2) the experience of feeling someone putting his tongue inside the child's mouth, and (3) graphic details concerning oral sexual contact. She was asked whether that testimony would be consistent with a child who had been sexually abused or would reflect a child's exposure to outside sources, such as watching others or watching an adult movie. Dr. Milchman said that such testimony was consistent with sexual abuse and added that the graphic details concerning oral sexual contact are not within a child's normal imagination.

The three questions presented to Dr. Milchman obviously had no relationship to CSAAS. They pose evidentiary difficulties in the absence of a more detailed record.

Yet counsel did not object to them. Perhaps counsel in such cases prefer to give a wide latitude to expert testimony rather than to appear to shield the jury from such opinion evidence. Had the expert's opinion gone no further, we would not find clear error capable of bringing about an unjust result.***

However, Dr. Milchman then proceeded to describe how one could "tell whether a child is lying." For example, a child's speaking in a mechanical way, "like it was by rote memory rather than by their own feelings," could raise the suspicion that the child was trying to remember what someone else had told him or her, thereby undermining the child's credibility. Or a child's perfectly consistent narration of all details of the story would be inconsistent, she said, with a child's natural tendency to forget minor detail. Certainly the prefatory basis of CSAAS has nothing to do with those areas of opinion.

This type of testimony equates with the kind of expertise said to relate to eyewitness testimony. Courts are frequently requested to permit expert opinion testimony on the reliability of eyewitness identification. Although *People v. McDonald*, 37 Cal. 3d 351, 208 Cal. Rptr. 236, 690 P.2d 709 (1984), allowed expert testimony from a psychologist concerning the ability of eyewitnesses to perceive, remember, and relate accurately and the distorting effects of fear and excitement, courts have sometimes hesitated to allow such testimony because it may interfere in the truthfinding function or create an unwarranted aura of expertise. Thus, if the child-sexual-abuse expert testifies that the child is "believable" or "truthful," the "courts will most likely exclude the evidence." Linda E. Carter, *Admissibility of Expert Testimony in Child Sexual Abuse Cases in California: Retire Kelly–Frye and Return to a Traditional Analysis*, 22 Loyola L.Rev. 1103, 1118 (1989).

Yet, in this case Dr. Milchman was asked, "How can you tell when a child or a victim is telling the truth about the fact that they have been sexually abused?" Although the court cautioned the jurors that it was up to them ultimately to determine that, the expert proffered a theory—again unrelated to CSAAS:

> Okay. I look for—I look for many different things. I look for whether the child appears to be sincere. I look for whether or not the feeling that they have at the time goes with what they are saying or whether it contradicts what they are saying. I go for whether there are a lot of different behaviors that all point to the same conclusion. For example, is what the child saying, does that match the demonstrations that they give when they try to explain it with their hands or with dolls, does it match the pictures that they draw for me? Does it match what they told the mother; does it match what they told the DYFS worker; does it match what they told the Prosecutor or investigator; or does it match what they told me? I look for consistency across a lot of different kinds of behaviors. *** I look for *** realistic, concrete, specific, kinds of details that are not the kinds of things that you would tend to see on a television so that any kid could pick up or any cable T.V. or movie that any kid could just pick up ***.

The final question to the witness was: "Doctor, based on your examinations of the girls can you give this jury your expert opinion as to whether or not both [Connie] and [Norma] were sexually abused?" Answer: "I believe that they were sexually abused."

At this point, whether Dr. Milchman had reached that opinion on the basis of her credibility assessments or on the basis of her understanding of CSAAS evidence is not clear to us and could not have been clear to the jury. If it were the former, it would be improper opinion evidence because it would introduce an unwarranted aura of scientific reliability to the analysis of credibility issues. If it were the latter, it would be improper opinion evidence because CSAAS is not relied on in the scientific community to detect abuse.

There has not been a showing in the record in this case, nor seemingly in other scientific literature or decisional law, of a general acceptance that would allow the use of CSAAS testimony to establish guilt or innocence. *See* David McCord, *Expert Psychological Testimony About Child Complainants in Sexual Abuse Prosecutions: A Foray into the Admissibility of Novel Psychological Evidence*, 77 J.Crim.L. &

Criminology 1, 24, 38 (1986). Such use of CSAAS evidence would present the analog to *State v. Cavallo, supra,* 88 *N.J.* 508, 443 *A.*2d 1020, and would require a study of the reliability of psychiatric or psychological testimony on the likelihood that the traits found in the victim will establish that another had engaged in the conduct that had caused the symptoms. It strikes us that the premise would be strained, at least on the basis of the Summit studies. As Myers noted:

> Summit did not intend the accommodation syndrome as a diagnostic device. The syndrome does not detect sexual abuse. Rather, it assumes the presence of abuse, and explains the child's reactions to it. Thus, child sexual abuse accommodation syndrome is not the sexual abuse analogue of battered child syndrome, which is diagnostic of physical abuse. With battered child syndrome, one reasons from type of injury to cause of injury. Thus, battered child syndrome is probative of physical abuse. With child sexual abuse accommodation syndrome, by contrast, one reasons from presence of sexual abuse to reactions to sexual abuse. Thus, the accommodation syndrome is not probative of abuse.
>
> Unfortunately, a number of mental health professionals, lawyers, and commentators drew unwarranted comparisons between battered child syndrome and child sexual abuse accommodation syndrome. This error led to considerable confusion. First, some professionals misinterpreted Summit's article, believing Summit had discovered a "syndrome" that could diagnose sexual abuse. This mistake is understandable, if not forgivable. Mental health and legal professionals working in the child abuse area had long been accustomed to thinking in terms of syndrome evidence to prove physical abuse. Battered child syndrome was an accepted diagnosis by the time Summit's accommodation syndrome came along in 1983. It was natural for professionals to transfer their understanding of battered child syndrome to this new syndrome, and to conclude that the accommodation syndrome, like battered child syndrome, could be used to detect abuse.
>
> ******
>
> *** [T]he accommodation syndrome was being asked to perform a task it could not accomplish.
>
> The accommodation syndrome has a place in the courtroom. The syndrome helps explain why many sexually abused children delay reporting their abuse, and why many children recant allegations of abuse and deny that anything occurred. If use of the syndrome is confined to these rehabilitative functions, the confusion clears, and the accommodation syndrome serves a useful forensic function. [Myers, *supra,* 68 *Neb.L.Rev.* at 67–68 (footnotes omitted).]

This we believe is the most concise summary of the proper use of CSAAS and will serve as a useful road map in the trial of such cases.***

Such use accords with the use now generally afforded to rape trauma syndrome (RTS) evidence most often in the context of adult rape. RTS describes symptoms frequently experienced by rape victims, *e.g.,* phobic reactions and sexual fears. Because RTS was developed as a therapeutic tool, not as a test to determine the existence of a past event, the California Supreme Court in *People v. Bledsoe*, 36 *Cal*.3d 236 (1984), questioned the reliability of RTS in determining whether a rape has occurred. Thus, the court held that, given the history, purpose and nature of RTS, testimony on the concept was inadmissible to prove that a rape occurred, but recognized that RTS testimony has been admitted in cases in which the alleged rapist suggests that the victim's conduct after the incident was inconsistent with her claim of rape. *Id*. 203 *Cal. Rptr.* at 457–460. In the latter context, expert testimony of RTS may play a particularly useful role by disabusing the jury of widely-held myths and misconceptions about rape and rape victims. *Id*. at 457.

Expert opinion testimony has a vital role to play in the trial of child-sexual-abuse cases. At one end of the spectrum is the clearly admissible evidence of the qualified expert with respect to the physical manifestations of sexual abuse or the child's out-of-court statements relating to a sexual offense under *Evidence Rule* 63(33) (the tender-years exception). As courts and counsel proceed further from that clearly admissible end of the spectrum, they must focus on the research basis for the proposition that the expert witness seeks to establish.

The state has argued before us that it is appropriate to admit Dr. Milchman's testimony describing CSAAS and concluding that Norma's and Connie's symptoms were consistent with sexual abuse and rendering an expert opinion that they had been sexually abused. Obviously, scientific evidence exists to aid a jury in determining whether sexual abuse has occurred. As we understand CSAAS, however, it does not purport to establish sexual abuse but helps to explain traits often found in children who have been abused. Hence we believe that in this case the "accommodation syndrome was being asked [by the State] to perform a task it could not accomplish." Myers, *supra*, 68 *Neb.L.Rev.* at 68.***

The judgment of the Appellate Division is affirmed.

Notes and Issues For Discussion

1. What is the role of the expert witness in this case? How does her role differ from that of a fact witness?

2. Dr. Milchman appears to have relied upon the child abuse sexual accommodation syndrome for several purposes, including an opinion on whether a child's graphic testimony about sexual abuse would be consistent with a child who has been sexually abused, and an opinion on whether a child who has said she was abused was telling the truth. Does the child sexual abuse accommodation syndrome provide reliable scientific evidence in these areas?

3. Does the child sexual abuse accommodation syndrome as developed by Summit diagnose the occurrence of child sexual abuse? What does it explain?

SELECTED REFERENCES

Baldwin, S. *Art of Advocacy* (1994).

Barker, R. L., and Branson, D. M. *Forensic Social Work: Legal Aspects of Professional Practice* (1993).

Dickson, D. T. *The Williamson Case: Effective Testimony in a Child Abuse Case* (Video) (1990a).

———. *The Williamson Case: Effective Testimony in a Termination of Parental Rights Case* (Video) (1990b).

———. *State v. Swan: Effective Testimony in a Criminal Child Sexual Abuse Trial* (Video) (1991).

Helfer, R., and Kempe, C. H. (Eds.) *The Battered Child* (4th ed., 1987).

Huber, P. W. *Galileo's Revenge: Junk Science in the Courtroom* (1991).

Kempe, C. H., Silverman, F. N., Steele, B. F., Droegmuller, W., and Silver, H., "The battered child syndrome", 181 *J. American Medical Association* 17 (1962).

Myers, J. E. B. *Evidence in Child Abuse and Neglect Cases* (2nd ed., 1992).

———. "Expert testimony describing psychological syndromes," 24 *Pacific L.R.* 1449 (1993).

———. "Expert testimony in child sexual abuse litigation," 68 *Nebraska L.R.* 1 (1989).

Nietzel, M. T., and Dillehay, R. C. *Psychological Consultation in the Courtroom* (1986).

Summit, R. C. "The child sexual abuse accommodation syndrome," 7 *Child Abuse and Neglect* 177 (1983).

NOTES

Chapter 1
Law in the Health and Human Services

1. One indication is the number of journals devoted to legal issues in the health and human services. See for example, *Law and Human Behavior, Law and Society, Law and Social Work, Law and Psychology Review, Law and Psychiatry, Law and the Behavioral Sciences, Law and Medicine, Law, Medicine and Health Care,* among others.
2. See, for example, the Hill-Burton Act, 42 U.S.C. §291 *et seq.*
3. Cardozo's elements are discussed in detail in E. A. Hoebel, *Law of Primitive Man,* 1954.
4. ". . . That branch or department of law which is concerned with the state in its political or sovereign capacity, including constitutional and administrative law, and with the definition, regulation, and enforcement of rights in cases where the state is regarded as the subject of the right or the object of the duty—including criminal law and criminal procedure, . . ." (Black's *Law Dictionary,* 1991).
5. "That portion of the law which defines, regulates, enforces, and administers relationships among individuals, associations and corporations. As used in contradistinction to public law, the term means all that part of law which is administered between citizen and citizen, or which is concerned with the definition, regulation, and enforcement of rights in cases where both the person in whom the rights inhere and the person upon whom the obligation is incident are private individuals" (Black's *Law Dictionary,* 1991).
6. Executive Order 12564 mandates a drug free workplace; Executive Order 12291 mandates care for newborn children with disabilities.
7. See generally the Administrative Procedures Act, 5 U.S.C. §552; see also K. C. Davis and R. J. Pierce, *Administrative Law Treatise,* Chapter 17 (1994).
8. Davis's broader point, which echoes the approach of Professor Karl Llewellyn years earlier, is that the individuals who exercise discretion are in a sense making the law, and the law they make is just as important as the law of the legislature and the judge. For individuals within the health and human services, where a wide range of administrative rules and reg-

ulations govern much of their life, this is particularly important. See Davis, *Discretionary Justice*, 1969; Llewellyn, *The Bramble Bush*, 1960.

9. See 38 U.S.C. Sec. 7332 (f), and the discussion in Chapter 13. In general, state laws are valid unless they interfere with a federal interest. In *Cobb v. Cobb*, 545 N.E.2d 1161 (1989), the Massachusetts court held that state domestic violence laws may apply on a military base where there is no federal law. Similarly, *In re Terry Y.*, 101 Cal. App.3d 178, 161 Cal. Rptr. 452 (1980), the California court upheld the enforcement of state child abuse statutes on a military reservation in the absence of federal law.

10. This discussion includes only so-called "constitutional" courts in the federal system, that is, established under the authority of Article III. In addition, there are a number of specialized "congressional" courts, created by Congress under the authority of Article I, including claims, customs, patent, and tax courts, and the military justice system. See, generally, Wright, 1976.

11. Federal appellate courts were known as circuit courts because early judges would "ride the circuit," holding court in a number of states and towns.

12. There are thirteen federal circuit courts covering the fifty states, District of Columbia, the federal government, and the various commonwealths and territories. For example, the Court of Appeals for the Third Circuit hears appeals from federal district courts in Delaware, New Jersey, Pennsylvania, and the Virgin Islands; the Ninth Circuit hears appeals from district courts in Alaska, Arizona, California, Hawaii, Idaho, Montana, Nevada, Oregon, Washington, and Guam. For laws pertaining to U.S. district courts see, generally, 28 U.S.C. §81 *et seq.*; for U.S. courts of appeals, 28 U.S. §41; for the U.S. Supreme Court, 28 U.S. §1251 *ff*. The number of judges for a court of appeals ranges from six in the First Circuit to twenty-eight in the Ninth Circuit. 28 U.S.C. §44. Generally one district court judge hears a case, three federal appeals court judges hear an appeal, and all nine U.S. Supreme Court judges hear a final appeal. The three court of appeals judges are called a panel. On occasion, an entire court of appeals will hear an appeal, in which case it is said to be sitting *en banc*.

13. ". . . It is the power of the court to decide a matter in controversy and presupposes the existence of a duly constituted court with control over the subject matter and the parties. Jurisdiction defines the powers of courts to inquire into facts, apply the law, make decisions, and declare judgement" (Black's *Law Dictionary*, 1991).

14. For federal statutory law, see 28 U.S.C. §1331 *ff*. for federal district court jurisdiction; 28 U.S.C. §1291 *ff*. for circuit court jurisdiction; and 28 U.S.C. §1251 *ff*. for U.S. Supreme Court jurisdiction. Also note that under 28 U.S.C. §2284 a three-judge district court may be convened under special

circumstances, and under 28 U.S.C. §1253 decisions of this court may be appealed directly to the U.S. Supreme Court.
15. In many instances, the Court only states that *certiorari* was denied. In the 1991–1992 term, the U.S. Supreme Court had 6,770 cases on its docket; 127 cases were argued before the court, resulting in 123 opinions, and four cases set down for re-argument. 120 L.Ed.2d c-2 (1992).

Chapter 2
Reading and Using Legal Materials

1. For a lively discussion of legal language, see D. Mellink, *The Language of Law* (1963).
2. " 'Party' is a technical word having a precise meaning in legal parlance; it refers to those by or against whom a legal suit is brought, whether in law or in equity, the party plaintiff or defendant, whether composed of one or more individuals and whether natural or legal persons; all others who may be affected by the suit, indirectly or consequently, are persons interested but not parties" (Black's *Law Dictionary*, 1991).
3. "The requirement of 'standing' is satisfied if it can be said that the plaintiff has a legally protectable and tangible interest at stake in the litigation" (Black's *Law Dictionary*, 1991).
4. "It is the power of the court to decide a matter in controversy and presupposes the existence of a duly constituted court with control over the subject matter and the parties" (Black's *Law Dictionary*, 1991).
5. See generally K. Llewellyn, *The Bramble Bush* (1950); K. Llewellyn, *The Common Law Tradition—Deciding Appeals* (1960).
6. See generally F. James and G. Hazard, *Civil Procedure*, 1985.
7. For a classic discussion of how courts reach decisions, see E. Levi, *Introduction to Legal Reasoning* (1974).
8. For example in *Coy v. Iowa*, 487 U.S. 1012 (1988), the Court invalidated the conviction of an alleged child sexual abuser as a violation of the Fifth Amendment right to confront one's accuser because the defendant was separated from the victim witness by an opaque screen. Justice O'Connor filed a concurring opinion, supporting the decision, but observing that there could be times when the general requirement of face-to-face confrontation might have to yield to the protection of the victim, particularly if there was a showing of probable harm by the confrontation. In *Maryland v. Craig*, 497 U.S. 836 (1990), Justice O'Connor wrote the majority opinion, upholding the use of closed circuit television in a child sexual abuse trial where the statute required that the judge first determine probable harm to the victim witness.
9. P. Kurland, *Landmark Briefs of the Supreme Court of the United States*, Vol. 57 (1975), p. 320.

10. Administrative Procedures Act, 5 U. S. C. §552.
11. "A title X project may not provide counseling concerning the use of abortion as a method of family planning or provide referral for abortion as a method of family planning." 42 C. F. R. §59.8 (a)(1).
12. Two good sources for further information are Statsky and Wernet, *Case Analysis* (1989) and *A Uniform System of Citation*, sometimes called the *Bluebook*, now in its 13th edition.
13. The geographic designations are rough at best. For example, Illinois and Ohio are found in the Northeast Reporter, Kansas in the Pacific Reporter.

Chapter 3
Constitutional Law, Due Process, and Equal Protection

1. Health and human services professionals should become familiar with relevant state constitutions, since these documents are a source of important legal principles and decisions.
2. Of the companion amendments, the Thirteenth prohibits slavery and involuntary servitude; the Fifteenth prohibits the denial of voting rights on the basis of race, color, or previous servitude.
3. Early cases include *Ex parte Virginia*, 100 U.S. 339 (1880), holding that state action includes actions of the legislative, executive, and judicial authorities and their agencies, officials, and agents; the *Civil Rights Cases*, 109 U.S. 3 (1883), upholding a variety of racially discriminatory actions because they were committed by private citizens, not state officials; and *Shelley v. Kramer*, 334 U.S. 1 (1948), holding judicially enforceable racially restrictive covenants on private property invalid as an unconstitutional use of state action. The lines remain unclear and debated. See generally Tribe, 1978: 1147 *ff.* "The Court itself has acknowledged the stubborn individuality of state action cases. '[F]ormulating an infallible test' of state action, the Court has said is 'an impossible task.' 'Only by sifting facts and weighing circumstances can the non obvious involvement of the State in private conduct be attributed its true significance.' " (Citing the Court in *Reitman v. Mulkey*, 387 U.S. 369 at 378 [1967], and *Burton v. Wilmington Parking Authority*, 365 U.S. 715 at 722 [1961].)
4. But see *Paul v. Davis*, 424 U.S. 693 (1976), which suggests that damage to a reputation alone is not a protected interest but that it must be tied to some other harm, such as loss of employment.
5. "Doctrine that due process clauses of the Fifth and Fourteenth Amendments to the United States Constitution require legislation to be fair and reasonable in content as well as application" (Black's *Law Dictionary*, 1991).
6. For example in *Lochner v. New York*, 198 U.S. 45 (1905), the Supreme Court struck down a New York statute limiting employment in bakeries to sixty

hours per week and ten hours per day, holding that the statute was an unconstitutional interference "with the liberty of person or the right of free contract. . . ." The Court said "Under such circumstances the freedom of master and employee to contract with each other in relation to their employment, and in defining the same, cannot be prohibited or interfered with, without violating the Federal Constitution."

7. Similarly, in *Pierce v. Society of Sisters*, 268 U.S. 510 (1925), the court held unconstitutional an Oregon statute forbidding children to attend parochial school, basing the decision on "The liberty of parents and guardians to direct the upbringing and education of children under their control."

8. In *Loving v. Virginia*, 388 U.S. 1 (1967), the Court struck down a state statute criminalizing interracial marriage. In *Skinner v. Oklahoma*, 316 U.S. 535 (1942), the court invalidated a state statute which provided for sterilization of those convicted of two or more felonies which involved "moral turpitude." In a series of decisions about contraception, the court invalidated prohibitions on the purchase and use of contraceptives by married couples (*Griswold v. Connecticut*), by unmarried individuals (*Eisenstadt v. Baird*, 405 U.S. 438 [1972]), and by those under age sixteen (*Carey v. Population Services*, 431 U.S. 678 [1976]). In *Roe v. Wade*, the Court invalidated a state criminal statute prohibiting performing or having abortions, as an unconstitutional infringement on a woman's right to make decisions about her body. More recently, in *Cruzan v. The Director*, 110 S.Ct. 2841 (1990), the Court acknowledged an individual's right to make advance directives about termination of life support systems, while supporting the state's requirement that such directives show clear and convincing intent on the part of the individual.

9. In *Griswold v. Connecticut*, 381 U.S. 479 (1965), the Court in holding a statute prohibiting the use of contraceptives to be unconstitutional stated that "the First Amendment has a penumbra where privacy is protected from governmental intrusion." 381 U.S. at 483. In *Roe v. Wade*, 410 U.S. 113 (1973), the court stated: "This right of privacy, whether it be founded in the Fourteenth Amendment's concept of personal liberty and restrictions upon state action, as we feel it is, or, as the district court determined, in the Ninth Amendment's reservation of rights to the people, is broad enough to encompass a woman's decision whether or not to terminate her pregnancy." 410 U.S. at 153.

10. "The Equal Protection Clause directs that 'all persons similarly circumstanced shall be treated alike.' But so too, '[t]he Constitution does not require things which are different in fact or opinion to be treated in law as though they were the same.' " *Plyler v. Doe*, 457 U.S. 202, 216 (1981). See also *Lindsley v. Natural Carbonic Gas Co.*, 220 U.S. 61 (1911): "If the classification has some reasonable basis, it does not offend the Constitution sim-

ply because the classification is not made with mathematical nicety or because in practice it results in some inequality"; and, generally, W. Murphy, J. Fleming, and W. Harris, *American Constitutional Interpretation*, 1986.

For a case upholding state-imposed limits on welfare allowances that functioned to provide less per capita to large than small families, see *Dandrige v. Williams*, 397 U.S. 471 (1970): "In the area of economics and social welfare, a State does not violate the Equal Protection Clause merely because the classifications made by its laws are imperfect."

For a case finding invidious discrimination in residency requirements for receipt of welfare benefits, see *Shapiro v. Thompson*, 394 U.S. 618 (1969): "Appellees' central contention is that the statutory prohibition of benefits to residents of less than a year creates a classification which constitutes an invidious discrimination denying them equal protection under the laws. We agree."

11. To complicate the picture, some judges and commentators reject this rigid approach. They argue the two- or three-tiered analysis is unnecessarily limiting and artificial, and that the analysis should vary with each situation. In *San Antonio School Board v. Rodriguez*, 411 U.S. 1 (1973), Justice Marshall argued: "A principled reading of what this Court has done reveals that it has applied a spectrum of standards in reviewing discrimination allegedly violative of the Equal Protection clause. This spectrum clearly comprehends variations in the degree of care with which the Court will scrutinize particular classifications, depending, I believe, on the constitutional and societal importance of the interest adversely affected and the recognized invidiousness of the basis upon which the particular classification is drawn." 411 U.S. at 31.

Chapter 4
Ethics and Law in the Health and Human Services

1. See, for example, the American Psychiatric Association, *Principles of Medical Ethics*, 1992, pp. 10–18.
2. See, for example, Rhodes, 1986; Reamer, 1990.
3. For example, violations of confidentiality in federally funded alcohol or drug abuse programs or violations of the Federal Privacy Act are criminal offenses.
4. See p. 93.
5. See p. 88.
6. The American Psychological Association's Ethical Standard 1.02 states, "If psychologists' ethical responsibilities conflict with law, psychologists make known their commitment to the Ethics Code and take steps to resolve the conflict in a responsible manner."

7. American Psychiatric Association, *Principles of Medical Ethics* 1992, Section 3.1:

"It would seem self-evident that a psychiatrist who is a law-breaker might be ethically unsuited to practice his/her profession. When such illegal activities bear directly upon his/her practice, this would obviously be the case. However, in other instances, illegal activities such as those concerning the right to protest social injustices might not bear on either the image of the psychiatrist or the ability of the specific psychiatrist to treat his/her patient ethically and well. While no committee or board could offer prior assurances that any illegal activity would not be considered unethical, it is conceivable that an individual could violate a law without being guilty of professionally unethical behavior."

8. See p. 87.

9. For example, Section G of the Code of Ethics for the National Association of Social Workers states: "The social worker should make every effort to foster maximum self-determination on the part of clients."

10. Reprinted from AAMFT Code of Ethics. Copyright 1991, American Association for Marriage and Family Therapy. Reprinted with permission. No additional copies may be made without obtaining permission from AAMFT.

11. "Psychologists obtain appropriate informed consent to therapy or related procedures, using language that is reasonably understandable to participants. The content of informed consent will vary depending on many circumstances; however, informed consent generally implies that the person (1) has the capacity to consent, (2) has been informed of significant information concerning the procedure, (3) has freely and without undue influence expressed consent, and (4) consent has been appropriately documented" (APA 4.02(a)).

12. "Psychologists take reasonable steps to avoid harming their patients or clients, research participants, students, and others with whom they work, and to minimize harm where it is foreseeable and avoidable" (APA 1.14).

13. "Psychologists do not engage in sexual relationships with students or supervisees in training over whom the psychologist has evaluative or direct authority, because such relationships are so likely to impair judgment or be exploitative" (APA 1.19). "Sexual involvement between a faculty member or supervisor and a trainee or student, in those situations in which an abuse of power can occur, often takes advantage of inequalities in the working relationship and may be unethical . . ." (AMA-APA 4-14). "Sexual intimacy with students or supervisees is prohibited" (AAMFT 4.1).

Chapter 5
Privacy, Personal Autonomy, and Records

1. In *Griswold v. Connecticut*, 381 U.S. 479 (1965), the Court in holding a statute prohibiting the use of contraceptives to be unconstitutional stated that "the First Amendment has a penumbra where privacy is protected from governmental intrusion." 381 U.S. at 483. In *Roe v. Wade*, 410 U.S. 113 (1973), the Court stated, "This right of privacy, whether it be founded in the Fourteenth Amendment's concept of personal liberty and restrictions upon state action, as we feel it is, or, as the District court determined, in the Ninth Amendment's reservation of rights to the people, is broad enough to encompass a woman's decision whether or not to terminate her pregnancy." 410 U.S. at 153.

2. In *Whalen v. Roe*, 429 U.S. 589 (1976), the Court said:

   "The cases sometimes characterized as protecting 'privacy' have in fact involved at least two different kinds of interests. One is the individual interest in avoiding disclosure of personal matters, and another is the interest in independence in making certain kinds of important decisions." 429 U.S. at 598.

   In a footnote in *Whalen*, the Court cites Professor Kurland's analysis: "The concept of a constitutional right of privacy still remains largely undefined. There are at least three facets that have been partially revealed, but their form and shape remain to be fully ascertained. The first is the right of the individual to be free in his private affairs from governmental surveillance and intrusion. The second is the right of an individual not to have his private affairs made public by the government. The third is the right of an individual to be free in action, thought, experience and belief from governmental compulsion." 429 U.S. at 599.

3. Personal notes or memoranda that are not part of the official record are probably excluded from coverage. See 40 Fed. Reg. 28,952 (1975).

4. As required under the Freedom of Information Act unless it is covered by the exemptions of that act, including national security, personal privacy and privileged information.

5. Under a(7) "routine use" means "with respect to the disclosure to a record, the use of such record for a purpose which is compatible with the purpose for which it was collected." Section (e)(4)(D) requires publication at least annually in the *Federal Register* "a notice of the existence and character of the system of records, which notice shall include . . . each routine use of the records contained in the system, including the categories of users and the purpose of such use."

Chapter 6
Confidential Communications: Principles and Limitations

1. For the detailed regulations, including definitions of federal assistance, informed consent, exceptions, and notice to patients, see 42 C.F.R. Part 2, Sec. 2.1 *ff.*
2. See generally Myers, 1992: 34–42 for a detailed discussion of *Ritchie* issues. Related is the expungement of child abuse records, since future employment in some areas may be conditioned on inspection of child abuse records, which may contain unsubstantiated information.
3. For example, in *In Re Roger B.*, 418 N.E. 2d 751 (1981), the Illinois Supreme Court upheld the constitutionality of a state statute protecting the confidentiality of adoption records, allowing them to be opened only with a court order based on good cause. In *Mills v. Atlantic City Dept. of Vital Statistics*, 148 N.J. Super. 302 (1977), a New Jersey court held that an adult adoptee's psychological need to know constituted good cause to access adoption records and outlined a series of steps to be followed. A number of states have enacted registry or search statutes, allowing biological parents and adult adoptees to locate each other through a state registry if the necessary parties have consented. See, for example, N.Y. Pub. Health §4138. See, generally, A. E. Crane, "Unsealing adoption records: The right to know versus the right to privacy," 1986 *Annual Survey of American Law* 645.
4. In *Doe v. Borough of Barrington* (see p. 110) the court held that the Doe family had a right of privacy such that the AIDS-infected condition of Jane Doe's husband could not be revealed to others without consent, and held that the police violated the family's constitutional right of privacy in releasing this information. Recall in that case the speed with which the information spread throughout the community. For a court decision holding a health care agency liable see *Behringer v. Princeton Medical Center* (p. 447).
5. For a thorough analysis of the history and rationales underlying privilege, see Note, "Developments in the Law—Privileged Communications," 98 *Harvard L. R.* 1450–1666 (1985).
6. "In the normal case, however, parents exercise privileges on behalf of their children. When a parent has a conflict of interest with his or her child, however, or is accused of harming the child, someone other than the parent should be responsible for the child's privileges. In criminal child abuse litigation, it is clear that the defendant may not assert a child's privilege to prevent admission of the child's statements to a professional." (Myers, 1992:29)
7. With greater or lesser specificity, the codes of ethics of physicians, psychologists, psychiatrists, social workers, family therapists, and coun-

selors, among others, call for providing the patient or client with information about confidentiality and its limits. See, generally, Chapter 4.

8. See *Boynton v. Burglass*, 590 So. 2d 446 (1991); Ohio Rev. Code Ann. §5122.34.

9. In *Schuster v. Altenberg*, 424 N.W.2d 159, the Wisconsin court said "The duty to warn or to institute commitment proceedings is not limited by a requirement that threats made be directed to an identifiable target." 424 N.W.2d at 165. In *Hamman v. County of Maricopa*, 775 P.2d 1122 (1989), the Arizona court extended the range of foreseeable victims of danger to all those "within the zone of danger . . . subject to probable risk of the patient's violent conduct." 775 P.2d at 1128.

10. These states include California (Cal. Civ. Code §43.92), Colorado (Colo. Rev. Stats. §13-21-117), Indiana (Ind. Stats. Ann. §34-4-12.4), Kentucky (Ky. Rev. Stats. §202A.400), Louisiana (La. Rev. Stats. §9:2800.2), Massachusetts (Mass. Gen. Laws, ch. 112 §129), Minnesota (Minn. Stats. §148.975-976), Montana (Mont. Code §27-1), New Hampshire (N.H. Rev. Stats., §329.31), Ohio (Ohio Rev. Code §5122.34), and Utah (Utah Code §78-14a-102). (Applebaum et al., 1989:827). Recently New Jersey (N.J. Stats. 2A:62A-16) and New York (N.Y. Mental Hyg. Law §3313[c][6]) have passed similar legislation.

11. See *Boynton v. Burglass*, 590 So.2d 446 (1991): "No person shall be liable for any harm that results to any other person as a result of failing to disclose any confidential information about a mental health client, or failing to otherwise attempt to protect such other person from harm by such client." See also, Ohio Rev. Code Ann. §5122.34.

12. The health and human services professional must also be aware of court decisions that may have bearing on how a statute is interpreted. For example, in *Commonwealth v. Collett*, 439 N.E. 2d 1223 (1982), the Massachusetts court said that the then existing exception to social worker privilege, which stated that the social worker "shall not be required to treat as confidential a communication that reveals the contemplation or commission of a crime or a harmful act" did not mean that the social worker could decide whether or not to treat the communication as confidential, but meant that the communication was not privileged and must be disclosed. In a later Massachusetts case, *Allen v. Holyoke Hospital*, 496 N.E. 1368 (1986), the court held that another section of the statute which read "No social worker . . . shall disclose any information he may have acquired from a person consulting him in his professional capacity . . ." did not extend to information in the agency files that did not come from direct communications but came from social workers' "personal observations in the client's home."

13. See, generally, J. E. B. Myers, "A Survey of Child Abuse and Neglect Reporting Statutes," 10 *J. of Juvenile Law* 1–72 (1986).

14. House Select Committee on Aging, 97th Cong., 1st Sess., *Elder Abuse: An Examination of a Hidden Problem*, 1981. See, generally, "Elder Abuse in California," 42 *Hastings L. J.* 859 (1991).

Chapter 7
Informed Consent

1. See, generally, Faden and Beauchamp, *A History and Theory of Informed Consent*, 1986, Chapter 1.
2. Faden and Beauchamp, Chapter 2. Also see, generally, Chapter 15 of this book, Malpractice and Administrative Liability.
3. Cited in Faden and Beauchamp, 1986: 117.
4. Katz points out the court in the *Salgo* case took opposite approaches, stating clearly at one point "[a] physician violates his duty to his patient and subjects himself to liability if he withholds any facts which are necessary to form the basis of an intelligent consent by the patient to the proposed treatment," and later: "[I]n discussing the element of risk a certain amount of discretion must be employed consistent with the full disclosure of facts necessary to an informed consent" (Katz, *The Silent World of Doctor and Patient*, 1984: 61).
5. Meisel and Roth have described the elements in the medical context as ". . . when *information* is disclosed by a physician to a *competent* person, that person will *understand* the information and *voluntarily* make a *decision* to accept or refuse the recommended medical procedure." (Cited in Merz and Trischoff, 1990: 322.)
6. "By recognizing this situation, the law allows (the professional) . . . to withhold such information or to phrase it in a manner that will not upset the patient. This therapeutic privilege may serve as a valid defense in negligent consent litigation" (Rozovsky, 1990: 114–115).
7. See for example *Holt v. Nelson*, 523 P.2d 211 (1974); Del. Code Ann. Tit. 18, §6852; N.Y. Pub Health Law §2805-d; Vt. Stat. Ann. Tit. 12, §1909.
8. See for example, *Luka v. Lowrie*, 136 N.W. 1106 (1912), where the Michigan court found no negligence in an emergency amputation of a fifteen-year-old boy's foot after he was run over by a train and the physician decided that immediate surgery was necessary to save the boy's life. For examples of state statutes permitting emergency treatment, see Ala. Code §22-8-1 (1971); Fla. Code §88-2905 (1971); Idaho Code §39-4303 (1975); Pa Stat. Ann. Tit. 35, §10104 (emergency treatment of minors).
9. See for example Ill. Ann. Stat. ch. 111, §4504 (1980), and Vt. Stat. Ann. tit. 18, §4226 (1975)—twelve years; Idaho Code §39-3801, Wash. Rev. Code Ann. §70-24-110—fourteen years.
10. "A document which governs the withholding or withdrawal of life-sustaining treatment from an individual in the event of an incurable or ir-

reversible condition that will cause death within a relatively short time and when such person is no longer able to make decisions regarding his or her medical treatment" (Black's *Law Dictionary*, 1991).

11. For a more detailed discussion of the role of the guardian in these situations and the decision-making criteria to be used, see generally Chapter 8.

12. The New Jersey Advanced Directive Act, N.J.S.A. 26:2H-64, is a recent, complex, detailed example. Missouri and a number of states require clear and convincing evidence and courts have read the statute narrowly. (See *Cruzan*, p. 201). New Jersey courts have decided a series of cases allowing the removal of life support systems under various circumstances. See, for example, *In re Quinlan* (p. 217), *Matter of Conroy* (p. 221). Compare *In re Westchester County Medical Center on behalf of O'Connor*, 531 N.E.2d 607 (1988), where the New York court refused to approve the request of a family not to insert a feeding tube into a seventy-seven-year-old incompetent woman because her intent not to be sustained on life support systems lacked specificity and therefore did not meet the clear and convincing standard.

13. The statute contains an exception where state law "allows for an objection on the basis of conscience for any health care provider or any agency of such provider which, as a matter of conscience, cannot implement an advance directive."

Chapter 8
Incompetence and Guardianship

1. One of the most complete current compilations of state laws is found in Brakel, *et al.*, 1985.

2. Faden and Beauchamp present a behavioral definition of competence, "the ability to perform a task," and argue that while this is basic, there will be a range of criteria of competence depending on the context and the specific task (Faden and Beauchamp, 1986: 288).

3. Drane (1985) has proposed a "sliding scale" model for medical decision-making, based on seriousness of the decision. Other commentators have suggested a variety of single or multiple standards. For a summary of other approaches see Drane, 1985.

4. Colorado is typical of the Uniform Probate Code: " 'Incapacitated person' means any person who is impaired by reason of mental illness, mental deficiency, physical illness, or disability, advanced age, chronic use of drugs, chronic intoxication or other cause (except minority) to the extent that he lacks sufficient understanding or capacity to make or communicate responsible decisions concerning his person." Colo. Rev. Stat. 15-14-101(1) (1989).

5. Similarly, New Jersey specifies: A mentally incompetent person means "a person who is impaired by reason of mental illness or mental deficiency to the extent that he lacks sufficient capacity to govern himself and manage his affairs." N.J. Stat. Ann. 3B: 1-2.

   Illinois defines a "disabled person" as one eighteen years or older who "(a) because of mental deterioration or physical incapacity is not fully able to manage his person or estate, or (b) is mentally ill or developmentally disabled and who because of his mental illness or developmental disability is not fully able to manage his person or estate, or (c) because of gambling, idleness, debauchery or excessive use of intoxicants or drugs, so spends or wastes his estate as to expose himself or his family to want or suffering." Ill. Ann. Stat. ch. 110 1/2, sec. 11a-2 (1989).

6. The 1988 ABA National Guardianship Symposium recommends "that notice be served personally on the proposed ward, and in addition, that notice by mail be made on the proposed ward's custodian, spouse, next of kin, the proposed guardian, and key service providers involved in the respondent's care. . . . Notice should be in plain language and large type. It should indicate the time and place of the hearing, the possible adverse consequences to the respondent of the proceedings and a list of rights to which the respondent is entitled. The notice should be accompanied by a copy of the petition, and service should occur at least 14 days before the hearing so that respondent's counsel has enough time to prepare" (Parry, 1988: 401).

7. "The key to understanding what the client wants is good communication between attorney and client. This is true for all clients, but especially for clients with special needs. Allegedly incompetent clients may have mental illnesses, developmental or cognitive problems or be suffering side effects from their medications. Unfortunately, most lawyers are not equipped to communicate well with a client severely impaired by one of these problems" (Parry, 1988: 403).

8. Parry notes: "The wisdom of this [medical] approach is highly questionable given the fact that diagnosis and evaluation of mental disorders has undergone dramatic changes over the years. It used to be generally true that doctors cared for every physical or mental disorder. More recently, doctors' roles have been changing and at least two treatment models are competing with the medical model for prominence. A therapeutic model is used by many psychologists, clinical social workers, and psychiatrists to treat mentally ill patients, and a developmental model is used by a number of professionals, in addition to the three groups just listed, to manage and care for mentally retarded and other developmentally disabled persons. At the same time, most general physicians have little training or experience handling psychiatric or developmental disorders" (Parry, in Brakel, 1985: 382).

9. For a reaction to this report and a series of recommendations, see Parry, 1988: 398.

Chapter 9
Families and Children I: Family Composition, Marriage, Divorce, Children, and the Law

1. The changes are all the more striking when the data are controlled for race. In 1991, almost 80 percent of white children lived with both parents, 18 percent lived only with their mothers. Thirty-nine percent of black children lived with both parents, 58 percent lived with their mothers. Sixty-six percent of those classified as Hispanic lived with both parents, 28 percent with their mothers (U.S. Census Bureau, 1993).
2. See also *Zablocki v. Redhail*, 434 U.S. 374 (1978), striking down a Wisconsin statute forbidding marriage by a noncustodial parent without proof of compliance with child support orders as an unconstitutional infringement on this right, and *Turner v. Safley*, 482 U.S. 78 (1987), invalidating Missouri restrictions on marriage by prison inmates.
3. However, Hawaii may be close to permitting such marriages. See *New York Times*, April 25, 1994.
4. The states are Alabama, Colorado, Georgia, Idaho, Iowa, Kansas, Montana, Ohio, Oklahoma, Pennsylvania, Rhode Island, South Carolina, and Texas (Areen, 1985).
5. For example, Texas requires that the couple agree to be married, after the agreement live together in the state as husband and wife, and represent to others that they are married. Tex. Fam. Code Ann. 1.91(a)(2). States vary as to the requirement for living together, ranging from weeks to years.
6. There is no constitutional right to appointed counsel for indigents in divorce cases. See, for example, *In re Smiley*, 330 N.E.2d 53 (N.Y. 1975). Legal Services or Legal Aid may provide counsel to those meeting income requirements, but this will depend on resources and availability. Under *Boddie v. Connecticut*, 401 U.S. 371 (1971), the Court struck down filing and process service fees as applied to indigents as a denial of due process: "Drawing upon the principles established by the cases just canvassed, we conclude that the State's refusal to admit these appellants to its courts, the sole means in Connecticut for obtaining a divorce, must be regarded as the equivalent of denying them an opportunity to be heard upon their claimed right to a dissolution of their marriages, and, in the absence of a sufficient countervailing justification for the State's action, a denial of due process." 401 U.S. at 380.
7. States with community property laws include Arizona, California, Idaho, Louisiana, Nevada, New Mexico, Texas, and Washington.

8. See Child Support Enforcement Amendments of 1984, P.L. 98-378, mandating that all states have guidelines available for use by their courts in determining child support. See also U.S. Dept. of Health and Human Services, Office of Child Support Enforcement, *Development of Guidelines for Child Support Orders*, 1987.

9. In *Ross v. Ross*, 400 A.2d 1233 (1979), a New Jersey court extended the child support obligation until the completion of law school. However, in *Sakovits v. Sakovits*, 429 A.2d 1091 (1981), another New Jersey court found no obligation for a college education where the child had been living independently and had been out of high school for four years.

10. A majority of the states now either permit or prefer joint custody. See Areen, 1985: 514 *ff.* California by statute permits joint custody at the discretion of the court, and if both parties agree, there is a presumption that joint custody is in the best interests of the child. Cal. Civ. Code §4600.5.

11. See generally, L. Teitelbaum, "Forward: The Meanings of the Rights of Children," 10 *N. Mex. L. Rev.* 235 (1980). Teitelbaum uses the terms "integrative" and "autonomous."

12. The term juvenile court is used here, but depending on the jurisdiction, the court may have other names such as family court or juvenile and domestic relations court.

13. In *Kent v. United States*, 383 U.S. 541 (1966), the Supreme Court required a waiver hearing with assistance of counsel before a valid waiver to adult criminal court can take place.

Chapter 10
Families and Children II: Child Abuse, Termination of Parental Rights, Foster Care, and Domestic Violence

1. For example, the New Jersey Division of Youth and Family Services reports substantiation rates of 35 percent, 36 percent, and 35 percent in the years 1990–1992. (N.J. Department of Human Services, Division of Youth and Family Services, *Child Abuse and Neglect in New Jersey 1992 Annual Report*, July 1993.)

2. For a thorough discussion of child abuse statutes and a state-by-state survey, see J. E. B. Myers, "A survey of child abuse and neglect reporting statutes," 10 *J. of Juvenile Law* 1–72 (1986).

3. In addition, amendments to the N.Y. Social Services Law extend the abuse and neglect provisions to residential care and to individuals between eighteen and twenty-one years who have a handicapping condition and are in residential care. N.Y. Social Services Law §412.

4. The issues are complex since the rights of the parent, particularly the mother, are involved as well as the rights of the unborn child, which raises the thorny legal issue whether and to what extent do the unborn

have rights. For a detailed discussion, see "Note: maternal rights and fetal wrongs: The case against the criminalization of 'fetal abuse'," 101 *Harvard L.R.* 994–1012 (1988).

5. For a complete list of state mandatory reporting requirements, see Myers, 1986: 1–72.

6. See *State v. Motherwell*, 788 P.2d 1066, which upheld the Washington statutory exception for clergy, but held that religious counselors were required to report and could be subject to the criminal misdemeanor penalty for failure to report. See also Oregon Rev. Stats. §418.750 (1987).

7. See, generally, Cole, 1987.

8. The two legal proceedings may occur either simultaneously or in sequence. Which would come first will depend upon each state's practice and protocols developed between the state's protective services and criminal justice agencies.

9. For example, the statute of limitations in New Jersey has been extended to age twenty-three. N.J.S.A. 2C:1–6.

10. See also: *Johnson v. Johnson*, 701 F.Supp. 1363 (1988), and *Evans v. Eckelman*, 265 Cal. Rptr. 605, 216 Cal. App. 3d 1609 (1990). In the latter case, three brothers aged twenty-eight to thirty-one sued for damages related to sexual abuse committed by their foster father twenty-one years before. The court held that the action could go forth since the brothers could allege an "unawareness of wrongful acts", and that they had "repressed into adulthood memory of the events themselves." Some states have extended this liability by statute. See Washington Statutes, §4.16.340(2), New Jersey Statutes 2A:61B-1. In New Jersey, the civil action must commence within two years of "reasonable discovery," and a prevailing plaintiff will be awarded a minimum of $10,000 damages plus attorney fees. The reliability of "false-memory" or "recovered memory" testimony is currently being hotly debated. Myers (1993) argues that expert testimony in this area should be subjected to more stringent standards of admissibility. Several recent books deal with the controversy. See L. Wright, *Remembering Satan* (1994) and M. Yapko, *Suggestions of Abuse: True and False Memories of Childhood Sexual Trauma* (1994).

11. See generally Besharov, 1985: 108–129.

12. S. Bennett, "Ending the continuous reign of terror: Sleeping husbands, battered wives, and the right to self defense," 24 *Wake Forest L.R.* 959–993 (1989). Like child abuse, domestic violence has long been condoned by courts and law enforcement officers. At common law, both children and wives were considered chattels, property of the male head of the family. Flowing from this was the common law "rule of thumb," limiting the thickness of the rod which could be used to beat the spouse. On its face this was a limitation on the power of the male head of household, but ar-

guably it had the reverse effect since it legitimated the use of force and the power of the head of the household over the other members.

13. Estimates are that two to four million women are subjected to domestic violence each year (Langan and Innes: 1986: 1).

14. As of 1990, twenty-four states and the District of Columbia provided protection to same sex couples, twenty-four other states and the Virgin Islands restricted coverage to opposite-sex couples (Lengyel, 1990: 64).

Chapter 11
Law and the Mentally Ill

1. See Brakel, *et al.*, 1985: 47; and E. F. Torrey, *Nowhere to Go* (1988).

2. For a listing by state, including requirements for treatment in the least restrictive setting, see Brakel *et al.*, 1985: Chapter 2.

3 See the Community Mental Health Centers Act, 2 U.S.C. §§200–207.

4. See Brakel, *et al.*, 1985: 56–72 and 189–190; Reed and Lewis (1990).

5. Brakel, *et al.*, 1985: Chapter 3. The data are striking. While voluntary admissions overall have leveled off or declined over the past few decades, there are major differences across states. According to Brakel, about two-thirds of the admissions in Illinois and Massachusetts in 1980 were voluntary, while three-quarters of the commitments to Connecticut were involuntary. Brakel also notes that 85 percent of the admissions to psychiatric wards of public general hospitals were voluntary (Brakel, *et al.*, 1985: 178–179).

6. For studies indicating many voluntary patients are legally incompetent to make an admission decision, see Applebaum, P. S., Mirkin, S. A., and Bateman, A. L., "Empirical assessment of competency to consent to psychiatric hospitalization," 138 *Am. J. Psychiatry* 1170 (1981), and Norko, Billick, McCarrick, and Schwartz, "A clinical study of competency to consent to voluntary psychiatric hospitalization," 11 *Am J. Forensic Psychiatry* 3 (1990). See generally, B. J. Winick, "Consent to voluntary hospitalization," 14 *International J. Law and Psychiatry* 169 (1991).

7. See *Drope v. Missouri*, 420 U.S. 162 at 171–175 (1975), and *Dusky v. U.S.* 362 U.S. 402 (1960). Also see *Lafferty v. Cook*, 949 F.2d 1546 (1991).

8. "We hold, consequently, that a person charged by a State with a criminal offense who is committed solely on account of his incapacity to proceed to trial cannot be held more than a reasonable period of time necessary to determine whether there is a substantial probability that he will attain that capacity in the foreseeable future. If it is determined that this is not the case, then the State must either institute the customary civil commitment proceeding that would be required to commit indefinitely any other citizen, or release the defendant." 406 U.S. at 758. Weiner notes that

many states still permit indefinite hospitalization without civil commitment proceedings in these cases (Brakel, *et al.*, 1985: 704).

9. A number of states have enacted registration laws, which require released sexual offenders to register with the local police. While in some states the registration is used solely for police investigations, in others such as Washington and Louisiana, the material is public and can be disseminated widely. The Violent Crime Control and Law Enforcement Act, signed into law in September 1994 contains provisions requiring states to enact sexual predator registration provisions within three years or face reductions in federal crime control funding. Under the Act, a state agency or law enforcement agency may be given the discretion to notify the public when a sexual predator is released.

10. A number of states have had sexual psychopath statutes for many years with mandatory treatment. See Brakel, 1985: 739–740.

11. For contrasting views of the Washington statute, compare "Note: Washington's sexually violent predator law: The need to bar unreliable psychiatric predictions of dangerousness from civil commitment proceedings," 39 *UCLA L.R.* 213 (1991), with A. Brooks, "The constitutionality and morality of civilly committing violent sexual predators," 15 *Univ. Puget Sound L.R.* 709–754 (1992).

12. Morton Birnbaum is generally credited with having first proposed a constitutional right to treatment. See M. Birnbaum, "The right to treatment," 46 *American Bar Association J.* 449 (1960).

13. For more information on this aspect of the case, see B. Bernstein and S. Armstrong, *The Brethren* (1979).

Chapter 12
Legal Issues for Individuals with Disabilities

1. The Architectural Barriers Act of 1968, 42 U.S.C. §4151 *et seq.*; the Rehabilitation Act of 1973, 29 U.S.C. §794; the Education for All Handicapped Children Act of 1975, 20 U.S.C. §1401 *et seq.*; the Developmentally Disabled Assistance and Bill of Rights Act of 1978, 42 U.S.C., §6000 *et seq.*; and the Americans with Disabilities Act of 1990, 42 U.S.C. §12101 *et seq.* In addition, important amendments were added in the Rehabilitation Comprehensive Services and Developmental Disabilities Amendments Act of 1978, 29 U.S.C. §701 *et seq.*

2. For guidelines and standards, see 36 C.F.R. §1190. Individual states have adopted their own barrier-free codes and enforcement systems. In *Rose v. U.S. Postal Service*, 566 F. Supp 367, the court held that barrier-free access requirements apply to buildings "designed, constructed, or altered," but not leased.

3. The term "individual with a disability" has been substituted for "handicapped individual" in §504 to be consistent with the A.D.A.
4. Also included are other service establishments, private schools, day care centers, senior citizen centers, homeless shelters, food banks, adoption agencies, and other social service centers. (§12167)
5. The Act specifies "reasonable accommodation" may include:
   "(A) making existing facilities used by employees readily accessible to and usable by individuals with disabilities; and
   (B) job restructuring, part-time or modified work schedules, reassignment to a vacant position, acquisition or modification of equipment or devices, appropriate adjustment or modifications of examinations, training materials or policies, the provision of qualified readers or interpreters, and other similar accommodations for individuals with disabilities." 42 U.S.C. §12111.
6. "(A) IN GENERAL—the term 'undue hardship' means an action requiring significant difficulty or expense, when considered in light of the factors set forth in subparagraph (b). . . .
   (b) FACTORS TO BE CONSIDERED—In determining whether an accommodation would impose an undue hardship on a covered entity, factors to be considered include—
   (i) the nature and cost of the accommodation needed under this Act;
   (ii) the overall financial resources of the facility or facilities involved in the provision of the reasonable accommodation; the number of persons employed at such facility; the effect of expenses and resources, or the impact otherwise of such accommodation upon the operation of the facility;
   (iii) the overall financial resources of the covered entity; the overall size of the business of a covered entity with respect to the number of its employees; the number, type, and location of its facilities; and
   (iv) the type of operation or operations of the covered entity, including compensation, structure, functions of the workforce of such entity; the geographic separateness, administrative, or fiscal relationship of the facility or facilities in question to the covered entity." 42 U.S.C. §12111.
7. See *Southeastern Community College v. Davis*, 442 US 397 (1979).
8. "It may be a defense to a charge of discrimination under this Act that an alleged application of qualification standards, tests, or selection criteria that screen out or tend to screen out or otherwise deny a job or benefit to an individual with a disability has been shown to be job-related and consistent with business necessity, and such performance cannot be accomplished by reasonable accommodation, as required under this title." 42 U.S.C. §12113.
9. See R. J. Henderson, "Addiction as a disability . . ." 44 *Vanderbilt L.R.* 713 (1991).

10. For two major early cases on the educational rights of handicapped children, see *Pennsylvania Assn. for Retarded Children v. Commonwealth*, 334 F.Supp. 1257 (1971) and 343 F. Supp. 279 (1972), and *Mills v. Board of Education of District of Columbia*, 348 F.Supp. 866 (1972).

11. "Children with specific learning disabilities" are "those children who have a disorder in one or more of the basic psychological processes involved in understanding or in using language, spoken or written, which disorder may manifest itself in imperfect ability to listen, think, speak, read, write, spell or do mathematical calculations. Such disorders include such conditions as perceptual disabilities, brain injury, minimal brain dysfunction, dyslexia, and developmental aphasia. Such term does not include children who have learning problems which are primarily the result of visual, hearing, or motor disabilities, of mental retardation, of emotional disturbance, or of environmental, cultural, or economic disadvantage." 20 U.S.C. §1401(a)(15).

Chapter 13
AIDS and the Law

1. CDC, *Morbidity and Mortality Weekly* and CDC *HIV/AIDS Surveillance Year End Report* 3 (March 1991). Note that the CDC has recently revised the definition of AIDS, which may result in an increase of cases. Along with the increase in prevalence and mortality, the costs are also staggering. In its legislative findings accompanying statutes on AIDS treatment, the California legislature found that the average cost of treating an AIDS patient was $150,000; that the total health costs of the first 10,000 AIDS cases exceeded $6 billion, and that by 1990, California alone would spend almost $5 billion in medical costs for care and treatment of 30,000 AIDS patients. Cal. Health and Safety Code §199.47.

2. By 1993, 85 percent of 330,000 reported cases in the United States involved homosexual males and / or i.v. drug users. Seven percent of the cases involved heterosexual contact. There were almost 5,000 cases of pediatric (under thirteen years) AIDS. Women, while comprising a small part of the total reported cases had one of the largest percentage increases (*HIV/AIDS Surveillance Report*, October 1993).

3. "In those early years, the federal government viewed AIDS as a budget problem, local public health officials saw it as a political problem, gay leaders considered AIDS as a public relations problem, and the news media regarded it as a homosexual problem that wouldn't interest anybody else. Consequently, few confronted AIDS for what it was, a profoundly threatening medical crisis." Shilts, 1987: xxiii.

4. For example, one major index of legal journals, *The Index of Legal Periodi-*

cals, began indexing legal articles about AIDS in 1987, and not until 1991 was AIDS classified as a separate topic.

5. Among recently litigated cases in these areas which will not be covered in the text are: testing of prisoners, see *Haywood Co. v. Hudson*, 740 S.W.2d 718 (Tenn. 1987), and *Glick v. Henderson*, 855 F.2d 536 (1988); and physician liability for failure to diagnose AIDS, see *Maynard v. N.J.*, 719 F.Supp. 292 (1989).

6. For example, the Massachusetts statute provides:

"No health care facility, as defined in section seventy E, and no physician or health care provider shall (1) test any person for the presence of the HTLV-III antibody or antigen without first obtaining his written informed consent; (2) disclose the results of such test to any person other than the subject thereof without first obtaining the subject's written informed consent; or (3) identify the subject of such tests to any person without first obtaining the subject's written informed consent.

No employer shall require HTLV-III antibody or antigen tests as a condition for employment.

Whoever violates the provisions of this section shall be deemed to have violated section two of chapter ninety-three A. . . ." Mass. Pub. Health ch. 111 §70F.

7. The California statute provides for civil penalties of $1,000, $5,000, and $10,000 for wrongful disclosure of the results of an HIV test, depending whether the disclosure was (a) negligent, (b) willful or (c) both willful and negligent, and the disclosure either "identifies or provides identifying characteristics" of the person tested. A person who negligently or willfully discloses the results is also liable for civil damages for economic, bodily, or psychological harm, and the statute further provides that negligent and willful disclosure resulting in economic, bodily, or psychological harm to the individual is also a misdemeanor and punishable up to one year in a county jail (Cal. Health and Safety Code §199.21). In the California statute, each wrongful disclosure made is a separate violation of the act.

8. For testing within the Federal Bureau of Prisons, see 28 C.F.R. §549.11, 28 C.F.R. §549.16a(1).

9. A direct threat is one which presents a significant risk to health or safety that cannot be eliminated by modifications of policies, practices or procedures or by the provision of auxiliary aids or services. See 28 C.F.R. §§36.208, 36.302, 36.303. See generally Note: "Access to medical care," 1992.

Chapter 14
Law in the Workplace: Sexual Harassment, Drug Testing,
and Employee Assistance Programs

1. See MacKinnon, 1979, for an early and detailed discussion of the topic.
2. A New York Times/CBS Newspoll indicates this pattern continues. Forty per cent of the women sampled said they had been sexually harassed at work. (*New York Times*, Jan. 23, 1991).
3. For a behind the scenes description of the politics involved in the passage of Title VII and the inclusion of sex discrimination within its coverage, see Davis, 1991; 38–45.
4. In *Corne v. Bausch and Lomb*, 390 F.Supp. 161 (1975), the court denied a sexual harassment claim by two female employees, stating that Title VII did not include sexual harassment.
5. In *Williams v. Saxbe*, 413 F.Supp. 654 (1976), the Court upheld a Title VII sexual harassment claim where a female employee was fired after she rejected her supervisor's sexual demands. The Court held that the practice of the supervisor could be viewed as the practice of the agency: "If this was a policy or practice of plaintiff's supervisor, then it was the agency's policy or practice, which is prohibited by Title VII." 413 F.Supp. at 663.
6. In *Bundy v. Jackson*, the court said "Bundy's claim . . . is essentially that 'conditions of employment' include the psychological and emotional work environment." 641 F. 2d at 944.
7. Only companies and agencies with fifteen or more employees are covered under the federal law. See also 29 CFR 1604.11(a) for EEOC guidelines as to what constitutes sexual harassment:

   "1. submission to such conduct is made either explicitly or implicitly a term or condition of an individual's employment;
   2. submission to or rejection of such conduct by an individual is used as the basis for employment decisions affecting such individual; and
   3. such conduct has the purpose or effect of unreasonably interfering with an individual's work performance or creating an intimidating, hostile or offensive working environment."
8. See *Barrett v. Omaha National Bank* (1983) and *Ferguson v. E.I. DuPont de Nemours* (1983).
9. For example, a federal court rejected the IRS's disciplining of a supervisor for his nonwork time and nonworkplace conduct, saying that the "IRS's job is to collect taxes and not to act as chaperon for its agents." (*Grubka v. Treasury Department*, CA FC, 10/11/88, 48 *FEP Cases* 48).
10. See, for example, Conn. Gen. Stat. Ann. §§31.51t–31.5bb; Fla. Stat. Ann. §440.09(6)(a); Minn. Stat. Ann. §181.950–59; Or. Rev. Stat. §659.225.
11. See generally Olsen, 1991.
12. See *Kelley v. Schlumberger Technology Corporation*, 849 F. 2d 41 (1st Cir.

1988), upholding an award of $125,000 for emotional distress and invasion of privacy stemming from testing that required a company representative to watch while plaintiff produced a urine sample; *Luck v. Southern Pacific Transportation Company,* 218 Cal. App. 3d 1, 267 Cal. Rptr. 618 (1990), upholding an award of almost $500,000 for wrongful discharge.

Chapter 15
Malpractice and Administrative Liability

1. Note that these data are for successful litigated claims, which is probably a fairly small proportion of all actions brought or settled prior to trial. In addition, publicity, changes in professional ethics, and the move toward criminalizing therapist-client sexual contact has probably reduced the number of sexual malpractice claims. Swenson (1993: 169) cites a more recent report of common suits brought against mental health professionals as including (1) failure to treat, (2) failure to diagnose or treat adequately, (3) breach of confidentiality, (4) sexual behavior with clients, (5) failure to warn about dangerous clients.

2. Pozgar offers a more detailed formulation: "Negligence is the omission or commission of an act that a reasonably prudent person would or would not do under given circumstances. It is a form of conduct caused by heedlessness or carelessness that constitutes a departure from the standard of care generally imposed on reasonable members of society. Negligence can occur where one has considered the consequences of an act and has exercised the best possible judgment, where one fails to guard against a risk that should be appreciated, or where one engages in certain behavior expected to involve unreasonable danger to others" (Pozgar, 1990: 16).

3. If the practitioner is not acting as a professional, but the client or patient assumes professional status, then the individual may still be held to a professional standard. Examples include where a license has lapsed, been revoked, or never existed but the individual claims to be a licensed professional.

4. In negligence actions—of which malpractice is a part—the elements are: "1. A duty, or obligation, recognized by the law, requiring the person to conform to a certain standard of conduct, for the protection of others against unreasonable risks. 2. A failure on the person's part to conform to the standard required: a breach of the duty. . . . 3. A reasonably close causal connection between the conduct and the resulting injury. This is what is commonly known as 'legal cause,' or 'proximate cause,' and which includes the notion of cause in fact. 4. Actual loss or damage resulting to the interests of another. Since the action for negligence devel-

oped chiefly out of the old form of action on the case, it retained the rule of that action, that proof of damage was an essential part of the plaintiff's case" (Keeton, *et al.*, 1984: 164–165).

5. Keeton distinguishes between "misfeasance" and "nonfeasance": "In early common law one who injured another by a positive, affirmative act, was held liable without any great regard even for his fault. But the courts were far too much occupied with the more flagrant forms of misbehavior to be greatly concerned with one who merely did nothing, even though another might suffer harm because of his omission to act. Hence there arose very early a difference, still deeply rooted in the law of negligence, between "misfeasance" and "nonfeasance.". . . During the last century, liability for "nonfeasance" has been extended still further to a limited group of relations, in which custom, public sentiment and views of social policy have led the courts to find a duty of affirmative action. In such relationships the plaintiff is typically in some respect particularly vulnerable and dependent upon the defendant who, correspondingly, holds considerable power over the plaintiff's welfare" (Keeton, *et al.*, 1984: 373–374).

6. "The standard of conduct imposed by the law is an external one, based upon what society demands generally of its members, rather than upon the actor's personal morality or individual sense of right and wrong. A failure to conform to the standard is negligence, therefore, even if it is due to clumsiness, stupidity, forgetfulness, and excitable temperament, or even sheer ignorance" (Keeton, *et al.*, 1985: 169).

7. "Professional persons in general, and those who undertake any work calling for special skill, are required not only to exercise reasonable care in what they do, but also to possess a standard minimum of special knowledge and ability . . ." (Keeton, *et al.*, 1984: 185).

8. Doctrines of *res ipsa loquitur* (the thing speaks for itself) and negligence *per se* sometimes may be used in place of expert witness testimony. In the former, "the negligence is felt to be so evident that any reasonable common man—in this case the judge and jury members—can see it;" in the latter, "a violation of statute, governmental guidelines . . . or a court order may be a basis for action when (1) the injured party is a member of the class for whose benefit the statute was enacted, (2) the resultant injury is of the type contemplated by the statute, and (3) the breach is the proximate cause of the injury" (Schutz, 1982: 4–5). For an example of the former, see *Hammer v. Rosen*, p. 549.

9. Punitive damages are generally not available but might be assessed for particularly outrageous conduct.

10. An alternate approach would be to examine various legal theories under which the injured party might sue, such as breach of contract, negligence, and violation of a fiduciary duty, which is used more frequently in the

legal literature. For the health and human services professional, the examination of particular types of malpractice is more useful.

11. The issues and cases are complex. See *Monroe v. Papp*, 365 U.S. 167 (1961); *Monell v. Department of Social Services*, 436 U.S. 658 (1978); *City of Canton v. Harris*, 489 U.S. 378 (1989); and *Harlow v. Fitzgerald*, 457 U.S. 800 (1981). See, generally, Blum, 1990.

12. "Discretionary acts: Those acts wherein there is no hard and fast rule as to course of conduct that one must or must not take. . . . One which requires exercise in judgement and choice . . ." (Black's *Law Dictionary*, 1991).

13. "That which involves obedience to instructions, but demands no special discretion, judgment or skill. An act is 'ministerial' when its performance is positively commanded and so plainly prescribed as to be free from doubt. Official's duty is 'ministerial' when it is absolute, certain and imperative, involving merely execution of a specific duty arising from fixed and designated facts" (Black's *Law Dictionary*, 1991).

Chapter 16
Courtroom Testimony: Fact and Expert Witnesses

1. The professional could also appear as a character witness or as a material witness, among other roles. See Barker and Branson, 1993: 13 *ff*.

2. "Experienced cross-examining lawyers have an arsenal of tactics that may be used to undermine the [witness's] credibility. They may ask leading questions, use intimidating countenances, and attempt to make the witness feel vulnerable to charges of wrongdoing or incompetence. Phrasing questions in such a way that the witness cannot give proper answers is another tactic. . . . Some lawyers favor attempts to intimidate the witness. This is frequently done by affecting a tone of hostility, sarcasm, ridicule. . . . But if the questions cause the witness to seem evasive, apologetic, or angry, the attempt to weaken the worker's credibility has worked" (Barker and Branson, 1993: 22–23.)

3. See generally Federal Rule of Evidence 803(2).

4. Another exception is "past recollection recorded" where "a memorandum or record concerning a matter about which a witness once had knowledge but now has insufficient recollection to enable him to testify fully and accurately, shown to have been made or adopted by the witness when the matter was fresh in his memory and to reflect that knowledge correctly, is not excluded by the hearsay rule, even though the declarant is available as a witness. . . . Under this doctrine, a written report or other document is properly admissible into evidence if witness has testified that on examination of the document he has no independent recollection of the matters contained therein." (Black's *Law Dictionary*, 1991).

Related rules are "present recollection revived": "The use by a witness of some writing or other object to refresh his recollection so that he may testify about past events from present recollection," and "present recollection recorded": "A witness may use any document which helps revive or 'jog' his memory of a past event and such document does not thereby become evidence though the opponent is entitled to see and examine the document and to impeach the credibility of the witness with it" (Black's *Law Dictionary*, 1991).

5. Nietzel and Dillehay identify the following as topics for expert testimony by psychologists: insanity defense/criminal responsibility, competence to stand trial, sentencing, eyewitness identification, trial procedure, civil commitment, psychological damages in civil cases, psychological autopsies, negligence and product liability, trademark litigation, class action suits, guardianship and conservatorship, child custody, adoption and termination of parental rights, professional malpractice, and social issues in litigation. (See Nietzel and Dillehay, 1986: 99 *ff.*).

6. "Another reason not to accept an offer to stipulate as to the witness' qualifications is that the recitation of those credentials puts the witness at ease and causes him to demonstrate increased self-confidence. It is almost as if he impresses himself with his own training, experience and achievements and becomes convinced that he is particularly qualified to educate the jury on the issue which is within his area of specialization" (Baldwin, 1994: 22–5).

7. Myers notes: "*Frye* raises several difficult questions. When is evidence scientific? What is the 'particular field' to which a scientific principle or application belongs? What is meant by 'general acceptance' within the relevant field? How does one prove general acceptance? Finally, when an expert's testimony is based on the novel application of a well-accepted scientific principle, must the proponent establish the reliability of the underlying principle as well as the novel application?" (Myers, 1992: 260).

8. In *Estelle v. McGuire*, 116 L.Ed.2d 394 (1991), the Supreme Court upheld the introduction of battered child syndrome evidence. "That syndrome exists when a child has sustained repeated and/or serious injuries by non-accidental means."

9. "The demonstration of battered child syndrome 'simply indicates that a child found with [serious, repeated injuries] has not suffered those injuries by accidental means.' Thus, evidence demonstrating battered child syndrome helps to prove that the child died at the hands of another and not by falling off a couch, for example; it also tends to establish that the 'other' whoever it may be, inflicted the injury intentionally." *Estelle v. McGuire*, 116 L.Ed.2d at 396 (1991).

10. "The term CSAAS was coined by psychiatrist Roland Summit to describe how children accommodate to ongoing sexual abuse. Children 'learn to

accept the situation and survive. There is no way out, no place to run. The healthy, normal, emotionally resilient child will learn to accommodate to the reality of continuing sexual abuse.' Summit described five aspects of the accommodation syndrome: (1) secrecy, (2) helplessness, (3) entrapment and accommodation, (4) delayed, conflicted and unconvincing disclosure and (5) retraction and recantation" (Myers, 1993: 1456, summarizing Summit, 1983).

INDEX OF CASES

Principal cases are in italics; other discussed or referenced cases are in roman.

Abille v. United States, 533
Addington v. Texas, 386
Allen v. Holyoke Hospital, 604
Allison D. v. Virginia M., 290
American Postal Workers Union v.
  Frank, 515
Application of Milton S. Hershey Med. Ctr.,
  462
Argersinger v. Hamlin, 27

Baker v. Nelson, 263
Baker v. United States, 526
Bakker v. Welsh, 195
Balistreri v. Pacifica Police Dep't., 373
Barefoot v. Estelle, 381
Baron v. Mayor of Baltimore, 22
Barrett v. Omaha National Bank, 616
Bartley v. Kremens, 391
Beck v. Beck, 293
Behringer Est. v. Princeton Medical Center,
  447, 466, 603
Bellah v. Greenson, 152
Bellotti v. Baird, 197
Ben-Shalom v. March, 71
Bethel Sch. Dist. No. 403 v. Fraser, 77,
  309
Betts v. Brady, 22, 26, 27
Board of Ed. v. Cooperman, 477
Boddie v. Connecticut, 608
Borough of Glassboro v. Vallorosi, 254
Bowen v. American Hospital
  Association, 231

Bowers v. Hardwick, 105
Boynton v. Burglass, 604
Brady v. Hopper, 146
Braschi v. Stahl Associates Company, 254
Broderick v. Ruder, 495
Brown v. Bd. of Education, 74, 301
Brown v. Bd. of Education (II), 74
Buck v. Bell, 227, 423
Buhrie v. Wyoming, 363
Bundy v. Jackson, 485, 616
Burton v. Wilmington Parking
  Authority, 49, 598

Canterbury v. Spence, 168, 190
Capau v. City of Plainfield, 507
Carey v. Population Services
  International, 98, 294
Chalk v. U.S. District Court, 414, 446, 467
City of Canton v. Harris, 619
City of Richmond v. J.A. Croson
  Company, 74
Civil Rights Cases, 598
Cleburne v. Cleburne Living Center, 61, 62
Cobb v. Cobb, 596
Cobbs v. Grant, 167
Comiskey v. State, 530
Commonwealth v. Barnhart, 326
Commonwealth v. Collett, 604
Commonwealth v. Lazarovich, 584
Conservatorship of Valerie N., 228
Corne v. Bausch and Lomb, 616
Cosgrove v. Lawrence, 556

Coy v. Iowa, 328, 597
Craig v. Boren, 70
Cruzan v. Director, Mo. Health Dep't., 201,
    599
Curran v. Bosze, 232
Cutter v. Brownbridge, 540

D.Y.F.S. v. A.W., 335
Dandridge v. Williams, 600
Daubert v. Merril Dow Pharmaceuticals,
    Inc., 580, 581
DeLorean v. DeLorean, 271
DeShaney v. Winnebago Co. Dep't. Soc.
    Serv., 372, 558
Destafano v. Grabrian, 548
District 27 Comm. Sch. Bd. v. Bd. of Ed.,
    477
Doe v. Borough of Barrington, 110, 447,
    558, 603
Doe v. Dolton Elementary Sch. Dist. No.
    148, 471
Doe v. Roe, 540
Donaldson v. O'Conner, 401
Dornhecker v. Malibu Grand Prix Corp.,
    502
Drope v. Missouri, 611
Drummond v. Fulton Co. Dept. of Fam. &
    Child Serv., 349
Dusky v. U.S., 611

Eady v. Alter, 532
829 Seventh Ave. v. Reider, 256
Eisel v. Bd. of Ed., 148
Eisenstadt v. Baird, 98
Ellison v. Brady, 496
Estelle v. Gamble, 565
Estelle v. McGuire, 620
Estelle v. Smith, 138
Evans v. Eckelman, 610
Ex parte Virginia, 598

Ferguson v. E.I. DuPont de Nemours,
    616
Florence Co. v. Carter, 443
Frank v. State, 570
Franklin v. Gwinnett Co. Pub. Sch.,
    506

Fronterio v. Richardson, 70
Frye v. U.S., 580, 581, 620
Furman v. Georgia, 50

Garcia by Garcia v. Miera, 306
Gideon v. Wainwright, 22, 23
Gillard v. Schmidt, 117
Ginsburg v. New York, 294
Glanz v. Vernick, 477
Glick v. Henderson, 615
Glover v. East Neb. Comm. Off.
    Retardation, 455
Goldberg v. Kelley, 51
Goss v. Lopez, 54, 302
Graham v. Richardson, 75
Griswold v. Connecticut, 96, 599, 602
Grubka v. Treasury Department,
    616
Guardianship of Philip B., 435
Gulf & Ship Island R.R. Co. v. Sullivan,
    195
Gutierrez v. Thorne, 553

H.L. v. Matheson, 198
Halderman v. Pennhurst State School,
    416, 417, 557
Hall v. Tawney, 306
Hamman v. Co. of Maricopa, 604
Hammer v. Rosen, 549
Harlow v. Fitzgerald, 368, 570, 619
Harris v. Forklift Systems, 488, 494
Harris v. McRae, 103, 104
Hart v. Brown, 237
Haywood Co. v. Hudson, 615
Hazelwood Sch. Dist. v. Kuhlmeier, 77,
    294, 310
Hendrick Hudson Dist. Bd. of Ed. v.
    Rowley, 442
Henson v. City of Dundee, 485
Hewitt v. Hewitt, 257
High Tech Gays v. Def. Ind. Sec. Clear.
    Off., 70, 71, 109
Hill v. State, 363
Hilscher v. State, 533
Hodgson v. Minnesota, 197
Holt v. Nelson, 605
Horak v. Biris, 544

Ibn-Tamas v. U.S., 362
In Interest of S.H.A., 342
In Re A.C., 237
In Re Gault, 295
In Re Grady, 227, 423
In Re Green, 325
In Re H. Children, 321
In Re Milton, 185
In Re Quinlan, 217, 606
In Re Robert Paul P., 263
In Re Roger B., 263, 603
In Re Roger S., 391
In Re Seiferth, 325
In Re Smiley, 608
In Re Snyder, 312
In Re Terry Y, 596
In Re Vulon Children, 318
In Re Westchester Co. Med. Ctr. on
    behalf of O'Connor, 221, 606
In Re Winship, 301
Ingraham v. Wright, 76, 302

Jablonski by Pahls v. U.S., 147
Jackson v. Indiana, 392
Jackson v. Metropolitan Edison Co., 50
Jarrett v. Jarrett, 273
Jhordan C. v. Mary K., 293
John R. v. Oakland Unified Sch. Dist.,
    557
Johnetta J. v. Municipal Court, 446
Johnson v. Johnson, 610
Johnson v. Zerbst, 22, 26

Karin T. v. Michael T., 262
Kelley v. Schlumberger Tech. Corp., 616
Kent v. U.S., 609
Kent v. Whitaker, 557
King v. Palmer, 489
Korematsu v. U.S., 75

L.L. v. Medical Protective Co., 548
Lafferty v. Cook, 611
Landeroos v. Flood, 326
Largey v. Rothman, 158
Lassiter v. Dept. of Soc. Serv., 22, 28, 33,
    335
Leckelt v. Bd. of Commissioners, 471

Lehr v. Robertson, 261
Lindsley v. Natural Carbonic Gas Co.,
    599
Lipari v. Sears Roebuck & Co., 147
Lochner v. New York, 598
Love v. Superior Court, 466
Loving v. Virginia, 73, 263, 599
Luck v. Southern Pacific Trans. Co., 617
Luka v. Lowrie, 605

M.A.B. v. R.B., 277
M'Naghten's Case, 392
MacDonald v. Clinger, 538
Maher v. Roe, 103
Mahoney v. Mahoney, 271
Marvin v. Marvin, 256, 267
Mary V. v. John D., 334
Maryland v. Craig, 328, 597
Massachusetts Bd. of Retirement v.
    Murgia, 67
Mathews v. Eldridge, 34
Matter of Baby M., 283, 353
Matter of Conroy, 221, 606
Matter of Farrell, 221
Matter of Hofbauer, 231, 322
Matter of Jobes, 221
Matter of Mary Moe, 198
Matter of Moe, 428
Matter of Peters by Johanning, 221
Matter of Romero, 429
Matter of Sampson, 325
Maynard v. New Jersey, 615
Mazza v. Huffaker, 541
McKee v. Rockwell, 372
McKeiver v. Pennsylvania, 301
McLaughlin v. Florida, 73
Menendez v. Superior Court, 134, 147
Meritor Savings v. Vinson, 489, 501, 504
Meyer v. Nebraska, 59, 96, 248
Michael H. v. Gerald D., 261
Milano v. McIntosh, 146
Mills v. Atlantic City Dept. of Vital
    Statistics, 603
Mills v. Bd. of Ed. of Dist. of Columbia,
    614
Mills v. Rogers, 406
Miranda v. Arizona, 138, 381

Mississippi Band of Choctaw Indians v.
   Holyfield, 353
Mississippi College for Women v. Hogan, 68
Monell v. Dep't. of Soc. Serv., 619
Monroe v. Papp, 619
Moore v. East Cleveland, 249

Nally v. Grace Comm. Church, 153
Nancy S. v. Michele G., 292
Natanson v. Kline, 157
National Bank of South Dakota v. Leir, 566
New Jersey v. T.L.O., 76, 306
Norwood Hospital v. Munoz, 180

O'Brien v. O'Brien, 267
O'Connor v. Donaldson, 398, 401, 557
Olmstead v. U.S., 60
Orr v. Bowen, 264

Palmore v. Sidoti, 71
Parham v. J.R., 228, 387, 422
Paroline v. UNISYS Corp., 504
Paul v. Davis, 598
Penn. Assn. for Retarded Children v.
   Commonwealth, 614
Pennhurst State School v. Halderman,
   417
Pennsylvania v. Ritchie, 125
People ex rel. Wallace v. Labrenz, 325
People in the Interest of O.E.P., 327
People v. Battaglia, 139
People v. Younghauz, 139
Pierce v. Society of Sisters, 96, 248, 599
Planned Parenthood of America v.
   Casey, 104, 193
Planned Parenthood of America v.
   Heckler, 39
Planned Parenthood of Mo. v. Danforth,
   103, 190, 191, 192, 195
Plyler v. Doe, 61, 71, 599
Poe v. Ullman, 59
Policemen's Benevolent Assn. of N.J. v.
   Washington Twp., 511
Powell v. Alabama, 22
Powell v. Texas, 76
Prince v. Massachusetts, 248, 326

R.A.V. v. St. Paul, 77
Rabidue v. Osceola Refining Co., 496
Reitman v. Mulkey, 598
Relf v. Weinberger, 174, 179
Rennie v. Klein, 402, 406
Rivers v. Katz, 406
Robinson v. California, 75
Roe v. Roe, 282
Roe v. Wade, 98, 103, 190, 195, 599
Rogers v. Commissioner Dep't Mental
   Health, 406
Rogers v. Okin, 406
Rose v. U.S. Postal Service, 612
Ross v. Ross, 609
Rouse v. Cameron, 401
Roy v. Hartogs, 548
Rust v. Sullivan, 41

Sakovits v. Sakovits, 609
Salgo v. Leland Stanford Jr. Bd. of
   Trustees, 157
San Antonio Indep. Sch. Dist. v.
   Rodriguez, 302, 600
Santosky v. Kramer, 335
Sard v. Hardy, 164
Schloendorff v. Society of New York
   Hospitals, 157
School Bd. of Nassau Co. v. Arline, 409, 466
Schramek v. Bohren, 356
Schuster v. Altenberg, 147, 604
Secy. of Pub. Welf. v. Institutionalized
   Juveniles, 391
Shapiro v. Thompson, 600
Shelley v. Kramer, 598
Shoemaker v. Handel, 511
Simmons v. United States, 550
Sinhogar v. Perry, 569
Skinner v. Oklahoma, 96, 599
Skinner v. Railway Labor Executives
   Assn., 515
Slater v. Baker and Stapleton, 157
Smith v. Org. of Foster Fam. For
   Equality and Reform, 348
Smith v. Seibly, 194
Smith v. State, 363
Sorentino v. Fam. & Child. Soc. of
   Elizabeth, 353

Sorichetti v. City of New York, 368
Southeastern Community College v.
    Davis, 613
Stanley v. Georgia, 105
Stanley v. Illinois, 257
State in the Interest of J.P.B., 135
State v. Crandall, 333
State v. J.O., 584
State v. Kelly, 353, 357
State v. Koss, 363
State v. Martin, 133
State v. Michaels, 333
State v. Miller, 129
State v. Mooney, 76
State v. Motherwell, 610
State v. Perricone, 325
State v. Stark, 455
Steele v. Offshore Shipbuilding Inc., 504
Stewart v. Stewart, 283
Strunk v. Strunk, 237
Sup't. of Belchertown v. Saikewicz, 221

Taig v. State of New York, 532
*Tarasoff v. Regents of University of
    California, 140,* 144–148, 523
Thomas v. Atascadero Unified School
    District, 477
Thompson v. County of Alameda, 146
Thurman v. City of Torrington, 372
*Tinker v. Des Moines Indep. Comm. Sch.
    Dist.,* 77, 294, 307
Treasury Employees v. Von Raab, 511
Turner v. Safley, 608

U.S. v. Boise, 583
U.S. v. University Hospital, 231
University of California Regents v.
    Bakke, 74

Village of Belle Terre v. Boraas, 253
Vinson v. Taylor, 495

Walker v. Superior Court, 326
Waltman v. International Paper Co., 504
Wangen v. Knudson, 518
Washington v. Davis, 74
Watkins v. U.S. Army, 71
Watson v. City of Kansas City, 363
Weber v. Stony Brook Hospital, 228
Whalen v. Roe, 602
Williams v. Saxbe, 489, 616
Wilson v. Corbin, 529
Wilson v. State, 531
Wisconsin v. Constantineau, 50
Wisconsin v. Yoder, 311
Wolff v. McDonnell, 50
Wood v. Strickland, 401
Wyatt v. Stickney, 394, 401
Wyatt v. Aderholt, 401

Youngberg v. Romeo, 406, 417
Younts v. St. Francis Hosp. & School of
    Nursing, 195

Zablocki v. Redhail, 608
Zinermon v. Burch, 169, 377
Zipkin v. Freeman, 548

GENERAL INDEX

Abortion, 96, 98–105
  abortion counseling, 41
  abortion funding, 103–104
  informed consent, 190–193
  minor's consent, 195–198
  minors' right to abortion, 104
  parental notification, 198
  pregnant woman's informed consent, 191
  privacy right, 98–105
  spousal consent, 103, 192–193
  "undue burden" standard, 105
Addiction, 75–76
  alcohol and drugs, 75–76
Administrative discretion, 10
Administrative law, 8, 9, 10
Administrative liability, 549–570
  charitable immunity, 570
  discretionary acts, 566–570
  governmental functions, 566–570
  ministerial acts, 566–570
  proprietary functions, 566–570
  respondeat superior, 549–550
  scope of employment, 549–557
  sexual harassment, 488, 501–506
  sovereign immunity, 565–570
Administrative Procedures Act, 595, 598
Adoption
  Native Americans, 353
  same-sex couples, 263
  same-sex parents, 292
  transracial, 353
Adoption records, confidentiality, 125
Advanced directives, 199–206

Adversary system, 15–16
Affirmative action, 74–75
Age-based classifications, 67
AIDS, 110–114, 444–479
  AIDS training, 113–114
  Americans with Disabilities Act, 477–478
  child custody, 283
  confidentiality, 126, 446–466
  disclosure by health care workers, 454, 462–466
  disclosure to patients or clients, 462–466
  disclosure to spouse or sexual partner, 460–462
  discrimination, 466–478
  discrimination in health care agencies, 477–478
  discrimination in schools, 471–477
  discrimination in workplace, 467–471
  liability for disclosure, 447–454
  mandatory blood testing, 455–460,
  privacy, 110–114
  transmission, 446
  Veterans Administration, 461–462
Alcohol addiction, 75–76
Alcohol and drugs, drug testing in workplace, 506–517
Alcohol treatment programs, confidentiality, 124
Aliens, 61, 71
Alimony, 266–267
  palimony, 267
  permanent, 266

Alimony (*cont.*)
  rehabilitation, 266
  reimbursement, 266
American Association for Marriage and
    Family Therapy (AAMFT), 83
  confidentiality, 86
  discrimination, 91
  exploitation, 93
  knowledge of law, 84
  professional competence, 92
  sexual harassment, 91
  sexual intimacies, 94
American Counseling Association
    (ACA), 83
  confidentiality, 86
  exploitation, 93
  limits to confidentiality, 87
  notification of limits, 88
  privacy, 85
  professional competence, 92
  sexual harassment, 91
  sexual intimacies, 93
American Jurisprudence, 45
American Law Reports, 45
American Medical Association
  AIDS treatment, 477
  ethics: *see* American Psychiatric
    Association
American Psychiatric Association
    (APA), 83
  confidentiality, 85, 87
  discrimination, 90
  exploitation, 93
  informed consent, 90
  knowledge of law, 84
  limits to confidentiality, 87
  notification of limits, 88
  predictions to dangerousness, 146,
    381–386
  professional competence, 92
  sexual intimacies, 93
American Psychological Association
    (APA), 83
  confidentiality, 85, 86
  discrimination, 90
  incompetence and guardianship, 90
  informed consent, 89

  knowledge of law, 84
  limits to confidentiality, 87
  notification of limits, 88
  privacy, 84
  professional competence, 92
  sexual harassment, 91
  sexual intimacies, 93–94
American School Counselor Association
    (ASCA), 83
  confidentiality, 86
  knowledge of law, 84
  limits to confidentiality, 88
  notification of limits, 88–89
Americans with Disabilities Act, 407,
    414–416
  AIDS, 477–478
  discrimination in public
    accommodations, 414
  discrimination in public services, 414
  employment discrimination, 414–416
Amicus curiae, 17
Annulment, 266
Architectural Barriers Act, 407
Artificial insemination, 247, 262, 290–293
  child custody and visitation, 290–293
Asterisks (***), 20

Barrier-free access, 407
Battered child syndrome, 583–584
  failure to diagnose, 326
Battered spouse syndrome, 357–363
  subjective or objective standard, 363
Best interests standard, 216
  child custody, 273–283
  guardian decision making, 216,
    217–220, 232–243
  sterilization, 423–434
Bill of Rights, 47–48
Buckley Amendment, 125
Burden of proof, 17

Case law, 8, 9
Charitable immunity, 570
Child abuse, 314–334
  alternative medical treatment,
    322–325

battered child syndrome, 583–584
blood transfusions, 325–326
child sexual abuse accommodation
    syndrome, 584–592
child witness, 328–334
civil hearings, 327
civil liability for commission of child
    abuse, 334
civil liability for failure to diagnose or
    report, 326
closed circuit testimony, 327–333
competence to testify, 333
confrontation, 328–333
criminal trials, 327–328
defining, 314–316
degree of certainty, 317–318
delayed discovery, 334
determining abuse, 317–326
elements, 318–326
exposure to drugs *in utero*, 316
faith healing, 325, 326
hearings, 327–333
hearsay, 327
Miranda warnings, 139
moral standards, 321
religious beliefs, 325–326
reporting, 154, 316–317
sexual abuse, 328–334
statute of limitations, 334
Child Abuse Prevention and Treatment
    Act, 11
Child custody and visitation, 71–73,
    272–293
    AIDS, 283
    best interest standard, 273–289
    de facto parent, 290–292
    gays and lesbians, 277–282, 290–293
    joint custody, 272, 293
    same-sex parents, 290–293
    surrogate mothers, 283–289
Child sexual abuse, 328–334
Child sexual abuse accommodation
    syndrome, 584–592
Child support, 271–272
    Child Support Enforcement
        Amendments, 272
    enforcement, 272

Federal Child Support Act, 272
    Uniform Reciprocal Enforcement of
        Support Act, 272
    Child Support Enforcement
        Amendments, 272
Children
    abuse: *see* Child abuse
    capacity to consent, 193
    child custody, 272–293
    child support, 271–272
    children and the law, 294–312
    civil commitment, 387–391
    competence to testify, 333
    consent to an abortion, 195–198
    consent to treatment for sexually
        transmitted diseases, 198
    disabled children
        making decisions for, 434–439
        education: *see* Individuals with
            Disabilities Education Act
    emancipated minors, 194
    health care decisions, 228–237
    mature minors, 195
    rights of children, 311–312
Citations, 42–44
Civil commitment
    involuntary commitment, 378–386
    mentally ill criminal offenders,
        393–394
    minors, 387–391
Civil law, 7
Civil law countries, 7
Civil Rights Act, 557–565; *see also* Title
    VII
CIvil Rights Act of 1964, 302
Class action, 16
Code of Federal Regulations, 44
Codes of ethics, 81–94
    codes of ethics and law, 82–84
    confidentiality and limitations, 85–89
    discrimination, 90–91
    exploitation, 92–93
    incompetence and guardianship, 90
    informed consent, 89–90
    knowledge of law, 84
    limitations to confidentiality, 87
    malpractice, 92–94

Codes of ethics (*cont.*)
    notice of limits of confidentiality,
        88–89
    privacy and records, 84–85
    professional competence, 92
    sexual harassment, 91
    sexual intimacies, 93
Cohabitation and domestic
        partnerships, 254–257
    domestic partnership ordinances, 256
Common law, 7
Common law countries, 7
Common law marriage, 264
    benefits to surviving spouse, 264
    social security benefits, 264
Computer Matching and Privacy
        Protection Act, 114, 116–117
Computerized retrieval systems, 45
Confidential communications, 122–155
Confidentiality, 122–126
    adoption records, 125
    AIDS, 126
    basic concepts, 122–123
    child abuse reports, 154
    child protective services records, 125
    codes of ethics, 85–89
    disclosing limits, 135–140
    duty to protect, 140–154
    educational records, 125
    elder abuse, 154
    employee assistance programs, 517
    federal drug and alcohol programs,
        124
    group settings, 139
    health, mental health, and
        developmental disabilities records,
        124–125
    juvenile court records, 125
    limitations, 135–140
    violations, 123–124
Constitutional amendments, 47
Constitutional law, 8, 9, 46–78
Contraceptives
    privacy right, 96–98
    sales to minors, 294
Corporal punishment in schools, 76,
    302–306

Corpus Juris Secundum, 45
Court decisions, 18
    briefing, 20–22
    citations, 43–44
Courtroom testimony, 573–593
    battered child syndrome, 583–584
    child sexual abuse accommodation
        syndrome, 584–592
    expert witness testimony, 575–579
    fact witness testimony, 573–574
    medical and psychological
        syndromes, 582–592
    qualifying as an expert, 576–577
    reliability of expert testimony, 579–592
    rules of evidence, 574–575
Criminal law, 7
Cruel and unusual punishment
    alcohol and drugs, 75–76
    public school discipline, 302–306
Current Law Index, 45

Damages
    compensatory damages, 19
    monetary damages, 19
    punitive damages, 19
Dangerousness, 381–386
Degree of proof: *see* Standard of proof
Developmental disability, defined, 408
Developmentally disabled, 407–443
    Americans with Disabilities Act, 407,
        414–416, 477–478
    Architectural Barriers Act, 407
    barrier-free access, 407
    definitions and rights, 408
    Developmentally Disabled Assistance
        and Bill of Rights Act, 407
    Education of Handicapped Children
        Act: *see* Individuals with
        Disabilities Education Act
    guardianship, 221–232, 423–439
    health care decisions for minors,
        228–232, 434–439
    Individuals with Disabilities
        Education Act (IDEA), 407, 439–443
    Rehabilitation Act, 407
    Rehabilitation Comprehensive
        Services and Developmental

Disabilities Act, 407
right to habilitation, 416–422
rights of the developmentally
disabled, 408
Section 504 of the Rehabilitation Act,
408–414, 466–477
sterilization decisions, 423–434
Developmentally Disabled Assistance
and Bill of Rights Act, 407, 408
Digests, 45
Discrimination
age, 67
AIDS, 466–478
alienage, 61, 71
codes of ethics, 90–91
disability, 408–414, 466–477
education, 73–74, 301–302
gender, 61–71
illegitimacy, 61
mentally retarded, 62–67
race, 71–75, 301–302
sex discrimination, 483–506
Diversity jurisdiction, 13
Divorce, 265–293
alimony, 266–267
annulment, 266
child custody and visitation, 272–293
child support, 271–272
divorce mediation, 265
no-fault and fault divorces, 265–266
palimony, 267
prenuptial contracts, 271
pro se divorces, 265
property division, 267–271
separation, 266
Domestic partnerships, 254–257,
264–265
Domestic violence, 353–373
arrests, 355
battered spouse syndrome, 357–363
definitions, 355
ex parte appearance, 356
liability for failure to enforce laws,
363–373
protective orders, 355
restraining order, 355
self-defense, 357–363

shelters, 356
statutes, 354–356
temporary restraining order, 355
Drug addiction, 75
Drug testing in the workplace, 506–517
Drug-Free Workplace Act, 516
private sector drug testing, 516–517
public sector drug testing, 507–516
Drug treatment programs, bound by
confidentiality laws, 124
Drug-Free Workplace Act, 515
Due process, 22–35, 48–60, 295–301
deprivation, 50
juvenile courts, 295–301
procedural, 50–58, 295–301
right to counsel, 22–34, 335
rudimentary, 51, 54–58
schools, 54–58
substantive, 49, 59–60
termination of parental rights, 335
unwed fathers, 257–261
welfare hearings, 51–54
Duty to protect, 140–154
children, 148–152
foreseeable danger, 146
identifiable victim, 146–147
immunity from liability, 153
self-harm, 148–153
steps to protect, 147–148
who must take steps to protect, 145

Education
AIDS children, 471–477
Buckley Amendment, 125
confidentiality of records, 125
corporal punishment, 76, 302–306
disabled children, 439–443
discrimination and funding, 301–302
duty to protect students, 148–152
free speech, 77, 306–310
privacy, 96, 117–120, 311–312
searches, 76, 306
separate but equal, 74
sexual harassment, 506
special admissions programs, 74
suicides, 148–152
suspensions, 54–59

Education (*cont.*)
  Title IX of the Educational
    Amendments, 506
Education of Handicapped Children
  Act: *see* Individuals with
    Disabilities Education Act
Elder abuse, reporting, 154
Emancipated minors, 194
Employee assistance programs (EAPs),
    517–519
  confidentiality and privacy, 517
  informed consent, 518
  liability issues, 518
Employer liability
  administrative liability, 549–570
  sexual harassment, 488, 501–506
Employment Retirement Income
    Security Act, 271
  Retirement Equity Act, 271
En banc, 596
Equal Employment Opportunity
    Commission, 485–494
  guidelines, 488
Equal protection, 48, 49, 60–75
  age-based, 67
  alienage and national origin, 61, 75
  aliens, 61, 71
  gender-based, 61, 67–71
  highly suspect, 61, 71–75
  intermediate or quasi-suspect, 61,
    67–71
  national origin, 61, 75
  race-based, 61, 71–75, 301
  rational basis, 62–67
Equal Rights Amendment, 48
Executive orders, 10
Expert witness, 575–592
Expert witness testimony
  battered child syndrome, 583–584
  child sexual abuse accommodation
    syndrome, 584–592
  medical and psychological
    syndromes, 582–592
  qualifying as an expert, 576–577
  reliability of expert testimony, 579–
    592
Exploitation, codes of ethics, 92–93

Fact witness testimony, 573–574
Fair hearings, 51–54
Families and children, 247–374
  child abuse, 314–334
  cohabitation and domestic
    partnerships, 254–257, 264–265
  composition, 247–248, 249–262
  definitions, 249
  divorce, 265–293
  domestic violence, 353–373
  extended family, 249–254
  foster care and adoption, 348–353
  marriage, 263–264
  parents, 257–262
  privacy, 248
  same-sex couples, 254–257
  same-sex parents, 290–293
  surrogate mothers, 283–289
  termination of parental rights,
    334–348
  unwed fathers, 257–262
Family planning, 35–41
Federal Child Support Act, 272
Federal court decisions, 43
Federal courts, 12–14
  congressional courts, 596
  constitutional courts, 596
Federal enclaves, 12
Federal jurisdiction, 13
Federal Mental Health Systems Act, 398
Federal Privacy Act, 114–117
  Computer Matching and Privacy
    Protection Act, 114
  disclosure, 115–117
  records, 114
  violations and penalties, 116
Federal Register, 44
Federal regulations, 35–41, 44
Federal Reporter, 43
Federal statutes, 42
  Session Laws, 42
  Statutes at Large, 42
  United States Code, 42
Federal Supplement, 43
Federal Tort Claims Act, 565
Federalism, 11–12
Finding legal materials, 41–45

Foster care, 348–353
  removal of foster children, 349–353
Fourteenth Amendment, 48–75
  equal protection, 60–75
  procedural due process, 50–58
  state action, 49
  substantive due process, 59–60
Free appropriate public education
  (FAPE), 440, 442–443
Free speech, 76, 306–310
  fighting words, 76
  hate speech, 76
  public schools, 306–310
Freedom of Information Act (FOIA),
  114

Gays and lesbians, 70–71, 105–109,
  254–257, 277–282, 290–293
  adoption, 263, 292
  child custody, 277–282
  domestic partnerships, 245–257
  right to privacy, 105–109
  visitation, 290–293
Guardians: *see* Incompetence and
  guardianship

Habeas corpus, 26
Habilitation, 416–422
Health care decisions
  for minors, 228–237
  for unborn, 237–243
  sterilization decisions for incompetent
    individuals, 227–228, 423–434
  treatment refusals and termination of
    life support systems, 217–227
Hearsay evidence, 575
High school suspensions, 54–59
Hill-Burton Act, 595
Holding, 18
Homeless, 76
Human subject experimentation,
    informed consent obtained for,
    89–90, 206–207
Hyde Amendment, 104

Illegitimacy, 61
In forma pauperis, 27

Incompetence and guardianship,
    208–244
  appointment, powers, and limitations,
    214–215
  best interests standard, 216, 217–220,
    232–237
  codes of ethics, 90
  definitions, 209–212
  determinations, 209–214
  guardian decision making, 214–243,
    423–439
  health care decisions, 217–243
  health care decisions for minors,
    228–237
  health care decisions for unborn,
    237–243
  incompetency proceedings, 212–214
  statutory definitions, 211–212
  sterilization decisions, 227–228,
    423–434
  substitute judgment standard, 216,
    221–227, 232–243
  treatment refusals and termination of
    life support systems, 217–221
Incompetence to stand trial, 392
Incompetency proceedings, 212–215
  legal representation, 213
  notice, 212
  personal presence, 213
  standard of proof, 213
Index of Legal Periodicals, 45
Indian Child Welfare Act, 335
Individualized education program
    (IEP), 441–443
Individuals with Disabilities Education
    Act (IDEA), 407, 434–439
  children with disabilities, 440
  free appropriate public education,
    440, 442–443
  individualized education program,
    441–443
  related services, 440
  special education, 440
  transition services, 440–441
Informed consent, 156–207
  abortion, 190–193, 195–198
  adequate disclosure, 158–169

Informed consent (*cont.*)
  advanced directives, living wills, and
    health care proxies, 199–206
  basic principles, 156
  capacity, 169–174
  codes of ethics, 89–90
  coercion, 174–179
  elements, 158
  emancipated minors, 194
  employee assistance programs, 518
  ethical and legal foundations, 156–158
  limits to disclosure, 168–169
  mature minors, 195
  medical emergencies, 190
  minors, 193–198
  minor's consent to an abortion,
    195–198
  minor's consent to treatment for
    sexually transmitted diseases,
    drugs, and alcohol, 198
  professional standard, 158–164
  reasonable patient standard, 158–164
  refusals, 180–190
  religious beliefs, 180–190
  research and human subject
    experimentation, 206–207
  state restrictions on the withdrawal of
    life support systems, 201–205
  termination of life support systems,
    198–206
  therapeutic privilege, 168–169
  voluntary choice, 174–179
  voluntary mental hospital admissions,
    376–378
  withdrawal of consent, 179–180
Injunctions, 19
Insanity defense, 392
Involuntary civil commitment, 378–386
  commitment hearings, 380–381
  commitment standards, 378–386
  dangerousness, 381–386
  standard of proof, 386

Joint custody, 293
Judgments, 18
Jurisdiction, 13, 18
  original jurisdiction, 14

personal jurisdiction, 18
  subject matter jurisdiction, 18
Juvenile court, 294–301
  jury trials, 301
  procedures, 295–301
  records, 125
  standard of proof, 301
Juvenile delinquency, 294–295

Law
  administrative law, 8, 9, 10
  case law, 8, 9
  civil law, 7
  classifications, 7
  common law, 7
  constitutional law, 8, 9, 46–78
  criminal law, 7
  definitions, 5
  enforcement, 6
  executive orders, 10
  Federal Register, 10
  normative order, 5
  precedent, 6
  private law, 8
  procedural law, 8
  public law, 8
  statutory law, 8, 9
  substantive law, 8
  types of law, 8
  who makes law, 10
Law reviews, 45
Legal citations, 42–44
Legal research, 41–45
Legal Resource Index, 45
Legal systems, 10–12
Liability
  administrative liability, 549–570
  AIDS, 113–114, 447–454
  child abuse, 334
  domestic violence, 363–373
  duty to protect, 140–154
  employee assistance programs, 518
  limits and immunities, 153, 557–570
  malpractice and liability, 520–572
  municipal government, 113–114,
    363–373
Liberty interest, 50, 59–60, 95–109

Living wills, 199–200
Loose-leaf services, 45

Malpractice and liability, 520–572
  administrative liability, 549–570
  basic concepts, 522–525
  breach of duty, 523
  codes of ethics, 92–94
  duty, 523
  duty to protect, 140–154
  harm or injury, 524
  inadequate diagnosis, 526–530
  inadequate supervision, 530–538
  legal context, 521–522
  limits to liability, 557–570
  monetary awards, 525
  negligence and malpractice, 521–522
  nontraditional therapy, 549
  preventing malpractice, 570–571
  proximate cause, 524
  self-inflicted harm, 525–538
  sexual relations, 541–549
  violation of civil or constitutional
    rights, 557–565
  violations of privacy and
    confidentiality, 538–540
Marriage and cohabitation, 254–257,
  263–265
  common law marriage, 264
  definitions, 263
  domestic partnerships, 254–257,
    264–265
  regulation of marriage, 263
  right to privacy, 263
  same-sex marriage, 263
Mature minors, 195
Mental illness, 375–406
  dangerousness, 381–386
  deinstitutionalization, 375
  involuntary civil commitment,
    378–386
  involuntary commitment hearings,
    380–381
  mentally ill criminal offender, 391–394
  patient's rights, 394–406
  right to liberty, 398–401
  right to refuse treatment, 402–406

  right to treatment, 394–398, 401
  voluntary admission, 169–174,
    376–378
Mental retardation: *see* Developmental
  disabilities
Mentally ill criminal offender, 391–394
  civil commitment, 393–394
  incompetence to stand trial, 392
  insanity defense, 392
  sexually violent predator statutes,
    393–394
Minors: *see* Children
Miranda warning, 135–139, 381

National Association of Social Workers
  (NASW), 83
  awareness of law, 84
  confidentiality, 85, 87
  discrimination, 90–91
  exploitation, 93
  incompetence and guardianship, 90
  informed consent, 90
  knowledge of law, 84
  limits to confidentiality, 87
  notification of limits, 88
  professional competence, 92
  sexual intimacies, 93
National Reporter System, 44
No-fault divorce, 265–266
Normative order, 5

Obscenity
  privacy, 105
  sale to minors, 294

Parents, 257–262
  de facto parents, 290–292
Parties, 16–17
Patient Self-Determination Act (PSDA),
  205–206
Precedent, 6, 18
Predictability, 6
Prenuptial contracts, 271
Preventing malpractice, 570–571
Privacy, 60, 95–121
  abortion, 98–105
  contraception, 96–98

Privacy (*cont.*)
  family privacy, 248
  Federal Privacy Act, 114–117
  obscene material, 105
  personal autonomy, 95–105
  protection from governmental
    disclosure, 110–114
  protection from governmental
    intrusion, 117–120
  sexual conduct, 105–109
Privacy and confidentiality
  AIDS, 110–114, 446–466
  codes of ethics, 84–85, 86, 87
  malpractice, 538–540
Private law, 8
Privilege, 122
Privileged communications, 122–123,
    127–134
  client's reasonable belief, 129–134
  duty to protect, 140–153
  holder of privilege, 128
  limitations, 135–153
  professionals with privilege, 128–129,
    134
  waiver, 134
  what is privileged, 128–129
  who can claim, 128–129
Privileges and immunities, 49
Procedural due process, 50–58
  models, 51–58, 295–301
Procedural law, 8
Property division, 267–271
  nonfinancial contributions, 267
Proximate cause, 524
Psychological bonding, 353
Public law, 8

Quasi-suspect classifications, 61, 67–
    71

Race
  affirmative action, 74–75
  child custody, 71–75
  foster care and adoption, 349–353
  race-based classifications, 61, 71–75
  racial discrimination in schools,
    301–302

racial segregation, 73–74
racially disproportionate impact, 74
Rational basis classification, 62–67
Records and record-keeping, 114–117,
    120–121
  adoption, 125
  child protective services agencies,
    125
  computerized retrieval systems, 45
  drug and alcohol treatment programs,
    124
  education, 125–126
  Federal Privacy Act, 114–117
  informed consent, 163, 169
  juvenile court, 125
  malpractice, 533–537
Regional reporters, 44
Rehabilitation Act of 1973, 407; *see also*
    Section 504
Rehabilitation Comprehensive Services
    and Developmental Disabilities Act,
    407
Res judicata, 18
Research and human subject
    experimentation, informed consent,
    89–90, 206–207
Respondeat superior, 549–550
Restraining orders, 19; *see also* Domestic
    violence
Right to counsel, 22–34, 335
  civil cases, 28–34
  criminal cases, 22–28
Right to habilitation, 416–422
Right to liberty, 398–401
Right to privacy. *see* Privacy
Right to refuse medication, 402–406
Right to refuse treatment, 402
Right to treatment, 394–398, 401
Rights of children, 311–312
Rights of the developmentally disabled,
    408
Rules of evidence, 574–575

Schools: *see* Education
Search and seizure, 76, 117–120, 306
Secondary legal materials, 44
Section (§), 35

Section 504 of the Rehabilitation Act, 408–414, 466–478
  handicapped person, 408
  otherwise qualified, 408
  persons with AIDS, 466–478
  physical impairment, 408
Section 1983 liability, 557–565
Segregation of public schools, 301–302
Separation, 266
Sex discrimination
  gender-based classifications, 61, 67–70
  sexual harassment, 483–506
  Title VII of the Civil Rights Act, 484
  Title IX of the Educational Amendments, 506
Sexual harassment, 483–506
  abusive work environment, 496–501
  codes of ethics, 91
  education, 506
  employer liability, 488, 500–505
  establishing, 488
  hostile environment, 485–488, 489–501
  indirect hostile environment, 495–496
  litigation, 484–485
  objective standard, 500–501
  quid pro quo, 485, 489
  reasonable person standard, 496–501
  subjective standard, 500–501
  unwelcome conduct, 494
Sexual intimacies, codes of ethics, 93
Sodomy, 105–109
Sovereign immunity, 565–570
Specific performance, 19
Standard of proof (degree of proof), 17
  beyond a reasonable doubt, 17
  clear and convincing, 17
  incompetence determinations, 213
  juvenile courts, 301
  mental hospital commitments, 386
  preponderance of evidence, 17
  termination of parental rights, 335
Standing, 17
Stare decisis, 6
State action, 49
State court decisions, 44
State regulations, 44
State statutes, 42–43

Statutory law, 8, 9
Sterilization
  developmentally disabled, 423–434
  incompetent individuals, 227–228, 423–434
  privacy right, 96
Substantive due process, 49, 59–60, 95, 109
Substantive law, 8
Substitute judgment standard, 216, 221–227, 232–243
Suicide, duty to protect from, 148–153
Summary judgment, 19
Supervisory liability, 549–570
Supremacy clause, 11
Supreme Court Reporter, 43
Supreme Court Reports, Lawyers Edition, 43
Surrogate contracts, 283–289
Surrogate mothers, 283–289
Syndromes, medical and psychological, 582–592

Termination of life-support systems, 198–206
  incompetence and guardianship, 217–221
  state restrictions on the withdrawal of life-support systems, 201–205
Termination of parental rights, 334–348
  emotional neglect, 335–342
  failure to thrive, 342–347
  mental retardation or mental illness, 342
  right to counsel, 335
  standard of proof, 335
  standards, 335–348
Title VII of the Civil Rights Act, 484
  Title VII liability, 504–505
Title IX of the Educational Amendments, 506

U.S. Constitution, 8, 9, 46–47
U.S. courts of appeal, 12–13
U.S. district courts, 12–13
U.S. Law Weekly, 43
U.S. Reports, 43

U.S. Supreme Court, 12–14
Uniform Reciprocal Enforcement of
    Support Act, 272
United States Code, 42
Unwed fathers, 257–261

Veterans Administration
    disclosure of AIDS, 461–462
    federal enclaves, 12
Vicarious liability: *see Respondeat superior*

Waiver of privilege, 134
Wards: *see* Guardians
Welfare, 51–54, 600
Welfare fair hearings, 51–54
Writ of *certiorari*, 14

Zoning
    extended families, 249–254
    housing for mentally retarded, 62–67

Printed in the United States
99798LV00003B/1-3/A

9 780743 267434